The bridge over the moat and the gate-house to Durants Arbour at Ponders End, the home of the Wroth Family who dominated Enfield for nearly four centuries.

A HISTORY OF ENFIELD

Volume One - Before 1837

A PARISH
NEAR LONDON

BY

David Pam

Enfield Preservation Society

1990

for Maisie

ISBN 0 907318 09 6

Published by Enfield Preservation Society Ltd., 107, Parsonage Lane, Enfield, Middlesex EN2 0AB.

Designed and produced by Moorland Publishing Co, Ltd., Ashbourne, Derbyshire.

Typeset by Input Typesetting Ltd., London, SW19 8DR

Printed in the UK by
Butler & Tanner Ltd
Frome
Somerset

Contents

Illustrations

Maps and Plans

Table of Abbreviations used in references

Sources in the Public Record Office (PRO)

C2	Chancery proceedings Eliz I-Chas I
C5-C8	Chancery proceedings James I–1714
C12	Chancery proceedings 1758–1800
C54	Chancery Close Rolls 1204–1903
C66	Chancery Patent Rolls
C93	Commissioners for Charitable Uses, Inquisitions and Decrees Eliz I-Geo III
Cal Inq	Calendar of Inquisitions Miscellaneous 7 vols Henry III-Henry V
DL1	Duchy of Lancaster Pleadings Henry VII–1835
DL3	Duchy of Lancaster Depositions and Examinations Ser. I Henry VII-Philip and Mary
DL4	Duchy of Lancaster Depositions and Examinations Ser. II 1558–1818
DL5	Duchy of Lancaster Entry Book of Decrees and Orders 1472–1872
DL9	Duchy of Lancaster Affidavits, Certificates, Orders, Petitions etc. 1560–1857
DL29	Duchy of Lancaster Ministers Accounts Edward I–1851
DL43	Duchy of Lancaster Rentals and Surveys Henry III-George III
DL44	Duchy of Lancaster Special Commissions and Returns 1558–1853
E40	Exchequer T. R. Ancient Deeds 1100–1603
E112	King's Remembrancer Bills and Answers Henry VIII–1841
E178	Special Commissions of Inquiry Elizabeth I-Victoria
E179	Subsidy Rolls etc Henry II-William and Mary
E301	Augmentation Office Chantry Certificates etc
E305	Deeds of Purchase and Exchange Henry VIII-Edward VI
E315	Augmentation Office Miscellanea 1100–1800
E351	Pipe Office Declared Accounts 1500–1817
E379	Sheriffs' Accounts of Seizures Henry VI–1660
HO	Home Office
JUST 1	Eyre and Assize Rolls etc 1201–1482

JUST 3	Gaol Delivery Rolls 1271–1476
KB9	Ancient Indictments Edward I–1675
LR12	Land Revenue Receivers Accounts Henry VIII–1832
MPC	Maps and Plans
PROB2	Prerogative Court of Canterbury Inventories Ser I 1417–1660
PROB3	Prerogative Court of Canterbury Inventories Ser II 1702–1782
PROB4	Prerogative Court of Canterbury Parchment Inventories 1660–1720
PROB5	Prerogative Court of Canterbury Paper Inventories 1661–1732
PROB11	Prerogative Court of Canterbury Registered Copy Wills 1384–1858
PROB18	Prerogative Court of Canterbury Allegations 1661–1858 (pleadings in testamentary litigation)
PROB24	Prerogative Court of Canterbury Depositions 1657–1809
PROB25	Prerogative Court of Canterbury Answers 1664–1854 (ie answers to allegations PROB18)
PROB31	Prerogative Court of Canterbury Exhibits 1722–1858 (documents brought into court as inventories, wills etc)
PROB32	Prerogative Court of Canterbury Filed Exhibits with Inventories (mainly London and Middlesex estates)
REQ2	Proceedings in the Court of Requests Henry VII-Charles I
SC2	Court Rolls 1200–1900
SC6	Ministers and Receivers Accounts Henry III–1691
SP12	State Papers Domestic Elizabeth I 1558–1603
SP14	State Papers Domestic James I 1603–1625
SP15	State Papers Domestic Addenda Edward VI-James I 1547–1625
SP16	State Papers Domestic Charles I 1625–1649
SP18	State Papers Domestic Interregnum 1649–1660
SP19	State Papers Domestic Committee for the Advance of Money 1642–1656
SP28	Commonwealth Exchequer Papers 1642–1660
SP38	Doquets 1549–1761 (abstracts of warrants for grants bound up into volumes)
STAC5	Star Chamber Proceedings Elizabeth I

Sources in the Guildhall Library

OBSP	Old Bailey Sessions Papers 1684–1913 248 vols
9171	London Commissary Court Registers of wills 1374–1857
9172	London Commissary Court Original wills 1523–1857
9174	London Commissary Court Inventories and declarations 1634–1741
9185	London Commissary Court Exhibita 1685–1826 including inventories 1685–1764
9537	London Diocese Episcopal visitations: Visitation books
9558	London Diocese Diocese book listing incumbents patrons curates

9580   London Diocese Register books for dissenters meeting
                             houses 1791–1852

Sources in the British Library (BL)
Lans   Lansdowne manuscripts
Add   Additional manuscripts

Sources in the Greater London Record Office (GLRO)
Acc 16   Court books, rentals, surveys, abstract of court rolls in the
                             manor of Worcesters
Acc 262   Stowe manuscripts
Acc 285   Deeds relating to premises in Enfield 1709–10 and 1772
Acc 407   Deeds acquired from Essex County Record Office
Acc 655   Documents relating to Enfield etc and New River
Acc 727   Documents relating to the property of James Pateshal
                             Jones in Enfield
Acc 801   Connop family estate papers
Acc 903   Enfield Parochial Charities Property deeds 1364-
Acc 1084   Burleigh House and estate: sale catalogues and
                             correspondence
DLC   Records of the Consistory Court of London
DRO4   Records of the parish of St Andrew, Enfield
MJ.OC   General orders of court books/county minute books
                             1716–1970
MJ.SBB   Sessions of peace and oyer and terminer books 1639–1889
MJ.SBR   Sessions of Peace registers 1608–1667
MR.PLT   Land Tax assessments 1767, 1780–1832
MR.LV   Licensed victuallers 1716–1829
MR.PP   Poll books 1749, 1768–69, 1806
MR.RO   Oath rolls 1673–1873
OB.SR   Gaol delivery rolls 1549–1755

Other Sources
Bodl.Rawl.   Rawlinson manuscripts in the Bodleian Library
Cal.Pat.   Calendar of Patent Rolls
CLRO   City of London Record Office
CSPD   Calendar of State Papers Domestic
DNB   Dictionary of National Biography
EGS   Deeds relating to the Enfield Grammar School, by kind
                             permission of Mr D Swailes (solicitor) River Front Enfield
Enfield   Enfield Public Libraries local history collection at the
                             Town Hall, Green Lanes N.13
HCJ   House of Commons Journals
Hatfield   CP The Cecil Papers at Hatfield House, by kind
                             permission of the Marquess of Salisbury
HMC   Historic Manuscripts Commission
                             Carew Calendar of the Carew Papers in the Lambeth
                             Library
                             Rutland Calendar of the Rutland manuscripts
                             Salisbury Calendar of the Cecil Papers at Hatfield House

L&P Henry VIII   Letters and Papers of Henry VIII
P.P   Parliamentary Papers
Parish register   Available on microfilm at GLRO
Tottenham manor rolls at Bruce Castle, Lordship Lane, Tottenham N17
VCH   Victoria County History, Middlesex vol 5
Vestry order book   (see list below)
WAM   Westminster Abbey manuscripts

Vestry order books
At Enfield
1671–1690
1797–1807
1807–1822
1823–1840
1840–1852
1852–1860
1860–1868
1868–1880
1880–1899
1900–1907
At St Andrews Church
1690–1744

Preface

The task of the parish historian differs somewhat from that of the national historians whose aim is often to reinterpret events which others before him have related and explained in ways of their own. The parish historian will seldom have predecessors to whom he can profitably turn. He must uncover the story for himself from primary sources, mainly documents, many of which will have lain unconsulted for centuries.

The parish historian is first of all a story-teller, since he must discover and relate what happened before he can offer any explanation of causes and effects. Because he has to gain and retain the interest of the local reader, he must write in such a way that those who never read history, perhaps scarcely read anything but a newspaper, will not lay down his book in despair. He must illustrate the condition of life in the community, not with a table or a graph, but with a story and in this he will have an advantage, for where the social historian, too often, can only find his examples out of literature, the parish historian can discover his in the parish chest, he can use the very words of witnesses in courts of law, quote the pronouncements of important vestrymen and search for sense or absurdity at the local board of health. He will soon discover that Mr Micawber was not unique and that the beadle was not always Mr Bumble. His late twentieth century reader must be induced by some magic to relate to the seventeenth or the eighteenth century parishioner or the nineteenth century factory worker, must be brought to understand the way he thought, see his problems and his pleasures, savour his misfortunes and his triumphs. This invocation of magic will make no inordinate demands upon his powers, for the magic is embodied in the documents, many of which tell their own stories and may be couched in the very words of those long dead in whose footprints we daily walk.

It particularly falls to the parish historian to portray the lives of ordinary men and women who have played an inconspicuous role in life. It is in pursuit of this purpose that he must pore over the dusty records at Chancery Lane, or in his county record office, wade through endless indexes, and turn over numerous documents in innumerable bundles. He is required to search a mass of obscure material which the national historian is forced, by the very nature of his task, to ignore. His sole objective must be to tell the story of one place, one community, seeking pure truth, using no romantic sweeteners and no adulterated evidence.

Parish history is the study of the past as it were through a microscope. The historian who chooses the parish as his field will have chosen the smallest community on which material has been gathered together over the centuries by the natural processes of accumulation. It is also the smallest unit on which material can readily be gathered together by the searcher. Smaller communities have existed, and still do exist, and have identities of their own, but smaller areas are seldom named in indexes or calendars, nor are they frequently mentioned in documents. The parish was the arena in which most of our ancestors lived. Village life revolved around the parish church: even after the advent of nonconformity the dissenters brought their grievances into the vestry and their dead into the parish churchyard. For centuries the villager was concerned little about his county or his country, those beyond the parish boundaries were known as strangers or foreigners. Hundreds of local conservation societies throughout England, many with a membership of a thousand or more, are the proof that local communities are neither dead nor moribund in the late twentieth century; if they were it might indeed be unprofitable to publish this book.

No community ever dwelt in isolation, least of all a parish near London. The local historian must take account of neighbouring, perhaps larger communities, what trade, what transactions were negotiated among them. He must appreciate the changes wrought by those who passed through his village and those who, seeing a possibility of earning a livelihood in the place, settled and made a home. He must take into consideration the effect on his parish of measures taken nationally or in the county.

The local historian working in the area of Greater London is blessed with many advantages. He has to hand the vast collections of the Public Record Office without which no comprehensive parish history could be written. He has the British Library on his doorstep with its unrivalled collection of manuscripts and official publications, the Guildhall Library, a treasure house of wills and inventories, a county record office both large and well organised and, in almost every London borough, a local history collection with a staff eager and able to help. He may also find material in half a dozen other repositories as I have at Hatfield House, Westminster Abbey, in the City of London Record Office, at the House of Lords, the Bodleian, Cambridge University Library and at Trinity College Cambridge.

All dates and spellings have been modernised except where the original spelling was thought to be essential to the understanding of any quotation. I have extended the area covered to include certain places like Grange Park, Bush Hill Park and Winchmore Hill, parts of which were within the ancient parish of Enfield, and whose residents often consider that they belong to Enfield.

Acknowledgments

My thanks are due to my brother Charles who has read the whole of this volume. He has offered many suggestions and has eradicated innumerable mistakes. Dr Stephen Doree has spent a great deal of time reading and making observations on Part One. Valerie Carter, Dr Nita Burnby, Andrew Combe and Christopher Simons have read the manuscript in whole or in part and I am grateful for the advice they have given. I have been fortunate in being able to discuss avenues of research with Bert Mason, a truly professional searcher. From time to time I have asked questions of Graham Dalling our local history officer; he has invariably responded immediately and in great detail. Brian Warren and Terence Goulding have drawn the maps which add so much to the understanding of the book. I owe a great debt of gratitude to all the librarians and archivists whose collections I have consulted, to the Marquess of Salisbury for permission to use the library at Hatfield and to Peter Morgan our vicar for allowing me to see the material in St Andrews Church. For the vast amount of typing and re-typing, my thanks to Kate Godfrey and my wife.

Many of the illustration have been borrowed from the London Borough of Enfield Libraries, thanks to the former librarian Paul Turner. Irene and Stanley Smith have helped greatly in finding and presenting other illustrations; the list of illustrations names many who have generously allowed me to use material belonging to them and I am grateful. My acknowledgment of the help given by many others may be found within the pages of this book.

PART ONE

Before 1660

Introduction

The ancient parish of Enfield which existed in 1086 contained 15,206 acres of which the woodland, enclosed as Enfield Chase about 1140, comprised 8,349 acres. The situation of the parish, ten miles north of London, was as important a factor in its fortunes in mediaeval, as in modern times. Along the old road through Ponders End passed travellers of all classes, and along it Enfield men took their produce to sell in the city.

Enfield was already an old village when William's officers made their survey in 1086. Its existence, as part of an estate associated with the office of staller, an officer holding responsibility for the defence of London, can be traced, albeit tentatively, through Saxon and on into Norman times. Much of the potential arable land was cultivated by 1086. The rich grasslands along the River Lea had been drained and converted to meadow. The vast area of woodland, which covered two-thirds of the parish, swarmed with pigs. This area, which was later enclosed as Enfield Chase, was to provide common rights which shielded the poor against natural disasters and human misfortune through all the centuries until those rights were at last extinguished in 1777.

The problem of poverty became very serious in the early fourteenth century. As in most parts of England, the population had grown through the thirteenth and early fourteenth centuries, and this had resulted in the land being divided among an increased number of peasants whose holdings were too small to feed themselves and their families. Some eighty-five per cent of holdings in Enfield, in 1340, were of less than ten acres. In these circumstances a series of bad harvests, such as occurred in 1315–18, was enough to reduce smallholders to a wretched existence, forcing them to steal to stay alive. In those four years, thirty-nine men from the parishes of Enfield and Edmonton were presented for theft, mostly of food, before the king's courts, twenty-five of them were hanged.

The devastating effect of the Black Death in 1349 is revealed by the considerable quantity of land which went out of cultivation, because there were no tenants to replace those who had died. The decline of arable farming is further indicated by the dereliction of the mill. There is strong evidence of soil exhaustion in parts of the parish, and also in the neighbouring parish of Edmonton. The crop on the Enfield demesne in 1322, a mixture, mainly rye with a little wheat, yielded not much more than six bushels to an acre, and the yield would obviously have been less on peasant land. Inquisitions in the second half of the century describe the soil as barren. A two year crop rotation had replaced the three year rotation in parts of the parish by 1362. Large areas of former demesne arable, throughout the 1360s, could be used only as rough sheep pasture, this moreover at a time when high grain prices should have made arable farming especially profitable in a parish so near to London.

Plague and poverty in the fourteenth century gave rise to a morbid concern with death and purgatory in the fifteenth. Almost every Enfield will written at this time asked forgiveness for tithes and offerings negligently withheld during lifetime, and sought intercession after death at one or more of the eight altars in the church. The souls of those too poor to make specific bequests in wills were cared for by a small contribution to the brotherhood of Our Lady. All these precautionary arrangements were swept away by the commissioners of the Court of Augmentations in 1547.

Enfield by the early sixteenth century had become prosperous. The great increase in urban as against rural wealth, which occurred between the taxations of 1334 and 1524 has been demonstrated by A. R. Bridbury.[1] The ratio of the 1334 tax contribution, to that of 1524, for most towns lies within the range of 1:1, denoting stagnation or decline, to 1:8 for very prosperous towns. The ratio in Enfield was 1:7. This parish therefore, it seems, had by 1524 become a wealthy town. It was now among the more thickly-settled parishes in the country with nearly thirty-two taxpayers per thousand acres (excluding the Chase).

Chapter two describes the sources of this new-found wealth and presents an image of Tudor Enfield, the church, the great house at Elsings, the village green and the settlements strung out along the edges of the Chase and along the Ware road from South Street to Waltham Cross. It also says a little of those who dwelt in the mansions, and in the houses and cottages that lined the village streets in the sixteenth century. It describes the land whereon they worked, their daily labour, controlled by an elaborate system of crop rotation imposed over some forty common fields by the cultivators of the soil who stubbornly, and often successfully, defended their common rights against all encroachment. The village grew in prosperity, not so much through its agriculture as by means of trade. Intelligent and ruthless men were able to exploit the insatiable demand of a rapidly expanding population in London, particularly for beer. They took full advantage both of the opportunity afforded by the situation of their parish on a busy road north out of the City, and the privilege granted to the manor of Enfield, as part of the Duchy of Lancaster, to be exempted from tolls of all kinds. For many years these men, calling themselves maltmen, controlled the markets in the Home Counties north of London and made the brewers in the City and in Southwark, dance to their tune. They were even able to challenge the City Corporation and, after a long struggle, emerged without defeat. At times they resisted the local magnates and, when defeated, resumed their challenge time and time again, sometimes at intervals of twenty or thirty years. At times they allied themselves with the great local landowners, particularly with the Wroths, to defy the Church and even to extract a compromise from the powerful Cecils at Theobalds. The strength of this yeoman or maltman class was maintained by the long continuance in the parish of certain substantial families. Hunsdon, Cordell, Curtis, Curle, Woodham and Wyberd were names which recurred from mediaeval to modern times. These families became inextricably interwoven.

Enfield continued to prosper during the reign of James I. A market was established, and the annual fair became an event of such importance that an imposing gateway was erected at the entrance to the close in which it was held. The school was improved and new inns and public houses were opened. Traders and tradesmen advanced their standing in the community and took control of the affairs of the parish by means of a select vestry. The larger farmers did well and their prosperity continued even when harvests were poor, because at such times they had a surplus over their own requirements which they could sell at prices inflated by the scarcity. The elaborate hierarchy of village society was displayed each Sunday in the parish church where the great had their pews in the front of the nave and each row behind to the very back of the gallery indicated a diminishing degree of standing and wealth.

Contemporary with this growth in prosperity came an increase in numbers of the poor. They set up their hovels on the roadside waste, often on the edge of the Chase, and augmented their meagre earnings by gathering and selling the wood and perhaps feeding a beast or two on the common. The worst poverty in the parish was mitigated, for those who belonged to the parish, by an elaborate system of relief through the distribution of materials to poor spinners and weavers, the whole scheme was financed by the local charities. The income from these charities had grown to be so substantial that the levy of a poor rate was not required before the end of the seventeenth century. Those of the poor who had no claim on the parish might die on the roadside and only a nameless entry in the parish register would mark their passing.

King James was succeeded in 1625 by his son Charles. Right from the start King Charles I was in financial difficulties, and the dubious legality of the means he used to get hold of money, created an unwarranted sense of grievance at all levels in this village society. So out of proportion was this sense of grievance to the sums which the King demanded, that it is probable that more fundamental reasons lay behind the protests and non-cooperation of the people, and that these concerned changes in religious worship. Disaffection towards the King led to a brief enthusiasm for the cause of Parliament but, as the very real financial burden of the civil war bore ever more heavily on people's resources, that enthusiasm rapidly declined. The Interregnum ended with bloodshed and the destruction of property in Enfield. Shouts for Charles Stuart echoed across Enfield Chase in the summer of 1659.

Notes to Introduction

1.   A. R. Bridbury *Economic Growth: England in the Late Middle Ages* Allen & Unwin 1962 pp 79–82.

Chapter One

The Mediaeval Village

1. The Village Green

The centre of Enfield in the thirteenth century was Enfield Green, occasionally called Church Green (now the Town). Its shape can still be recognised, in 1989, despite the encroachments and the accretions of the last seven hundred years. It was watered by a brook known later as Saddlers Mill stream, of which there now remains little trace. The village centre sat on the edge of a wide area of brickearth across which stretched the great common arable fields of the parish. The land to the west was London clay, too difficult to cultivate by the means then available. It remained forested until the end of the eighteenth century.

The village centre had probably existed on this site for many centuries, but its earlier shape may have been quite different from that of the thirteenth century. Its origins must remain, in the absence of archaeological evidence, a matter for speculation. The pattern of village houses, with the church and the manor house neatly arranged around a village green, was not the normal pattern of settlement before the year 1000. Investigations have been carried out on the sites of a large number of deserted villages and these have shown that the first appearance of many village greens was in the eleventh or the twelfth century. Before the year 1000, village centres like Enfield either did not exist, or they existed only as irregular conglomerations of dwellings, without streets or village greens. Most village greens came into existence within a hundred years on either side of the Norman Conquest.

The mediaeval Manor House, in the thirteenth century, stood on the south side of Enfield Green. It was a substantial building, so large that it could accommodate the Earl of Hereford and all his retinue when he came to see the fortification of the house in 1347.[1] He was in residence there from April, and departed at the end of November.[2] The Manor House was approached through a gatehouse which opened from the village green; in the grounds stood a thatched barn and a dovecot. A survey of Enfield made in 1572 notes what may have been the site of this earlier Manor House, describing it as 'Lockstones hill with a moat about it'. It then lay within the seven acre grounds of the later Manor House.[3] The deer park adjoining, in which there was a fish pond, had been enclosed out of the forest at some time before the Conquest. A pale fence divided it from the great park, or Enfield Chase, which had been emparked about 1140 and lay entirely within the manor and parish of Enfield. Thus the lords of the manor of Enfield had the opportunity of hunting, and a ready supply of game, fish and fowl, whenever their business induced them to visit their manor.

Enfield Green was known by that name at least as early as 1267. That is the

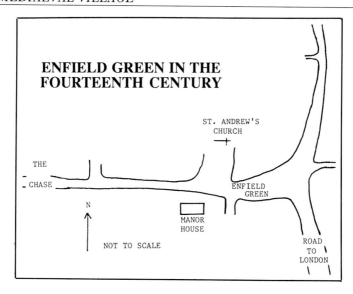

ENFIELD GREEN IN THE FOURTEENTH CENTURY

ST. ANDREW'S CHURCH

THE CHASE

ENFIELD GREEN

N

MANOR HOUSE

NOT TO SCALE

ROAD TO LONDON

date of a document in which are related the details of a murder committed on 25 April that year, at three o'clock in the afternoon. It occurred on the east side of Enfield Green (near the Silver Street, London Road end of what is now the Town); Andrew Aurifaber (Goldsmith) of London attacked and wounded Richard le Chamberleng who was carried to his house at Enfield where he died on the following day. Goldsmith was able to escape punishment on a technicality. The prosecution had been brought by Alice the victim's sister, and Goldsmith was upheld in his claim that a woman ought not to bring an action for murder, unless it had resulted in the death of her own husband. Alice was committed to gaol, though pardoned subsequently.[4]

The lord of the manor was granted a weekly market in Enfield in 1303, as well as two annual fairs, each of three days, beginning respectively on 15 August and on St Andrew's day, 30 November.[5] The period from 1100 to 1300 in England had seen a growth in population, increased food production and an expansion of trade. Many lords of manors, anxious to enhance their incomes, obtained market grants from the Crown. Often they paid substantial sums of money in the hope that they would retrieve their outlay through the fees paid by those who would come to sell their produce. Many markets were established but few succeeded, and hardly any were to survive economic depression in the fourteenth century. It required more than a grant to create a market, and there is no evidence of any market functioning in Enfield during the best part of three hundred years.[6] A survey of c. 1340[7] lists five shops set up on the green, next to the Manor House. Three were in the hands of Robert Rynge while the others were held by Margaret Mabbe and William Goddard; they paid sixpence a year rent for each. Another survey, some thirty years later, shows that an additional shop had been built, and some indication is given of its size, for the piece of land on which it stood measured no more than ten feet by ten and a half feet.[8] This would suggest that the shops on Enfield Green were little more than stalls. The annual accounts of the manor in 1419 record that there were shambles (stalls for butchers) before the gate of the Manor House,[9] and at least six shops existed on Enfield Green in 1470, as well as a bakehouse next to the church.[10]

The Church of St Andrew stood on the north side of the village green. Its appearance in the mid-fourteenth century can only be inferred from what little evidence remains in the building. The tower, which dates from the late fourteenth century, had not been built, though there may have been an earlier one, or perhaps a timber bell-turret. The arcades of the nave appeared much as they do today. The present clerestory is of the early sixteenth century, but the larger stones which can be seen below it suggest the existence of an earlier one. The aisles were more narrow and lower than their present counterparts. During the fourteenth century openings were cut through the walls of the thirteenth century chancel and chapels were added; to the north, the chapel of Our Lady, and to the south the chapel of St James. There would almost certainly have been a porch on the south side, but not the one shown in the print (p.43). Enfield was a valuable living, worth around £40 a year to the rector, who was the Abbot of Walden.[11] (i.e. Saffron Walden)

The vicarage lay to the east of the church. It had been granted to Bartholomew, the vicar of Enfield (1272–1289), during the reign of Edward I, by Godfrey de Beston. Richard Plessitis had added further land from his garden, which was described as lying between the churchyard and the King's highway called 'Ernyng-strate' (thus it is probably the present site of the vicarage in Silver Street).[12]

The life of the village community revolved around the church and the Manor House. One day can serve to illustrate because the various events which took place on 4 March 1338 in and around the church were recalled and set down fifteen years later. The purpose was to establish the date of the birth and baptism (apparently on the same day) of Maud Durant, and thus to prove her right to inherit the property of her dead father. The village elders were called forth to give evidence. Hugh de Braybrok, who was sixty years of age, remembered the day when Maud was born and baptised, he said, for he had met Alice de Dephams (from Edmonton) who was one of the godmothers, coming from the church, and she had told him that the child had been christened. John atte Bregge recalled that he too had been in the church, for on that day he had attended the burial of his sister Joan. Ellis le Fevere remembered that John Simon had sought sanctuary in the church on that very day. He had sheltered there for forty days to escape justice after he had robbed Richard Daddington on Enfield Chase. Richard atte Felde had brought his son John to be baptised on that same day. John de Mandeville too was in church, and saw Hervey, then the vicar, make a record of Maud's birth in a psalter which, he believed, still remained within the church. John Tebaud had that morning met Maud's father, Thomas Durant, who had invited him home at midday for a meal and he recalled that just as they approached Durants, Joan Ansels, one of the servants, had rushed out in order to be before anyone else in breaking the good news of the birth to her master.

William Pymme had been there to attend at the burial of his brother Edmund. William Saleman had a happier reason to remember the events of that 4 March, for it was the day on which his father had given him by charter, a messuage and ten acres in Enfield and, as he was on his way with others to the Manor House to receive seisin (delivery) of the property, he met Alice de Dephams with Maud atte Marsh, the two godmothers, coming from the church. Thomas Huchon told how Thomas Durant had laid on a feast for his neighbours to celebrate the birth and that he had been employed to catch fish from the stewponds. But the day had not been given over entirely to celebration. Thomas Durant had been one of the tax collectors for Enfield and John Bursser, the other collector, recalled that the two of them had sat down at Durants Arbour, and there had made up their accounts that very afternoon.[13]

2. The King's Justice in the Village

Trial by jury in criminal cases was an innovation in the early thirteenth century. Trial by ordeal died out following the withdrawal of Church sanction in 1215. Trial by battle could only be used when the case had been brought by a private prosecutor and a successful defence by this method was not now considered convincing. There is a curious local case from the year 1220, heard in the Court of Common Pleas, which shows this transition towards trial by jury. It arose from a complaint made in the manor court at Cheshunt, by Hamo de la Mare (Marsh) against Philip le King who, Hamo alleged, had stolen his mare from off the common pasture. Philip had since given the mare, as part of a marriage settlement, to one Edward, now his son-in-law. Indeed Hamo had found the horse, which he recognised by a split in its ear, working as a plough horse for this Edward.

While the case was pending, Edward secured as a witness on his behalf a certain Elias Piggin. Elias, who turned out to be a swordsman and a professional champion, asserted that it was he who had sold the mare to Edward. This was done with the intention that the dispute would no longer lie between Hamo and Edward but would now lie between Hamo and Elias who could demand trial by battle; such a contest would inevitably have ended in the death of Hamo. Hamo however avoided the trap by offering one mark (a mark was 13s 4d, now 66p) considerably more than the animal was worth, to have an inquest. Juries of eight men were drawn from each of the neighbouring parishes, Waltham Holy Cross, Cheshunt, Wormley and Enfield. Elias stated before the court that he had been given the horse in Wales (which was far enough away to make verification difficult) as a payment for lessons in the art of fencing, and that he had brought the animal to Waltham Holy Cross where he had sold it to Edward for 3s 1d. Hamo maintained that the horse was his. He had foaled it, he said, and still owned its dam.

The four juries, having heard the evidence, presented four separate reports. The Enfield jury was favourable to Hamo who probably came from Enfield. The Waltham Abbey jury declared that Philip had had the horse working in his plough for two years and put forward the unlikely proposition that Edward had taken the horse by mistake. The Cheshunt jury arrived at an even more unlikely conclusion, proclaiming that Elias Piggin had acted in this matter for God's sake. They went on to ask that all men should pray for him. The outcome was that Hamo and Edward were given licence to compromise, the champion Elias was condemned to the amputation of his foot, and the part taken by Philip le King who, in modern terms, was the principal guilty party, was ignored by the court.[14]

General eyres (ie judges' circuits) took place from time to time throughout the thirteenth century. The method was slow, and sometimes years elapsed before cases were dealt with. When the itinerant justices visited a county to hold an eyre court a complete investigation took place of all the judicial and administrative business which had arisen since the previous eyre. In advance of their coming the sheriff would call a full gathering of the county court. The bailiff of the hundred of Edmonton (John le Taylur in 1274[15]) selected four electors, who chose a further eight freemen to provide evidence or verdicts as required. Fourteen jurymen are

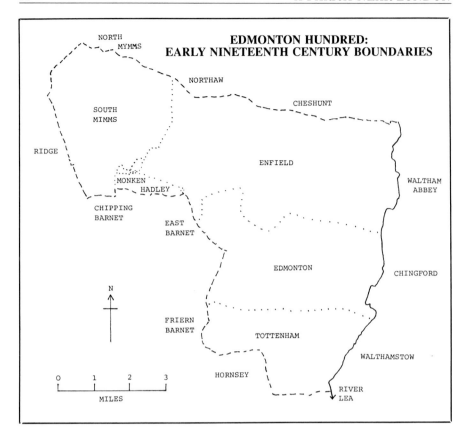

listed for the eyre of 1274 including, from Enfield, Sacrus son of Herbert, William Absolom and Robert le Newman.[16] They appear to have been small freeholders.

The Crown derived a growing income from the holding of eyre courts. In 1235,[17] for instance, £4 13s 4d was received from the hundred of Edmonton including 20s for 'murdrum' fines. These fines originated soon after the Conquest when so many Normans were found to have been murdered, and the culprits not found, that the authorities imposed a heavy fine on the community if the murderer was not brought to justice. The fine could only be avoided if it could be shown that the corpse was that of an Englishman.

At the time of the Barons' Revolt in the 1260s, when law and order threatened to break down, Richard le Messenger had been murdered. It was strongly suspected that Paternella la Lanende and Christiana Curteys were the guilty parties and that they had thrown the body into the River Lea, though it had never been found. The two women had fled. A 'murdrum' fine was imposed because the hundred was unable to prove that the victim was English.[18] The two races however came to be so merged by the fourteenth century that such fines were abolished.

In 1274 the Crown collected nearly £32 in the 'half hundred of Edmonton', as it was then described. The property of condemned criminals was confiscated, errors in legal procedures were punished with fines upon the whole parish (Enfield paid 60s) and those who failed to appear at court were fined according to their means.

The Abbot of Walden forfeited £5, and David le Pesteur, John Turpyn and Richard Godyng forty pence each.

Among the Crown cases heard before the 1235 eyre court is one which illustrates the operation of the law under Henry III. It involved Master Roger de Cantelupe, canonist, legist and diplomat, who served the King for over thirty years. The Cantelupes probably lived at the house later to be known as Durants Arbour at Ponders End.

A certain William de Horsete knocked one night at the door of the Cantelupe house and asked for lodging. The servant, William Godard (this surname recurs through many centuries of Enfield history), who answered the door, declared that if Horsete was an honest man he would be freely received and lodged, and thus he was admitted to stay the night. In the morning he had gone and had stolen a sack and a length of cloth.

Godard, with others, set out in pursuit and, after a search, found him hired as a ploughman nearby. They seized him and took him back to the house where he was secured in the stocks. By the following morning he had escaped and fled. Henry Hod the bailiff was enraged; he demanded that Horsete be recaptured and threatened Godard that if he failed to bring him back he would himself be set in the stocks. Godard therefore, in some trepidation, set out to seek the thief in London and eventually discovered him (graphic evidence of the size of the City) and, speaking fairly, persuaded him to come back to Enfield.

It was Henry Hod who ordered the brutal imprisonment that resulted in the death of William de Horsete. He commanded that two holes be made in the walls of the house through which the prisoner's feet were secured, so that his body lay within the building and his feet were outside. He was severely beaten and his hands were tied so tightly that the thongs cut through both skin and flesh, and the flesh was turned back and hung down as far as his fingers. He was refused all food and lay thus for fifteen days, and the dogs came and gnawed his feet. There the sheriff found him imprisoned and dead.

The jury acquitted Master Roger de Cantelupe, saying that he was not in the country when this was done, nor was his brother Robert, but that it was done by William Godard at the command of Henry Hod the bailiff. Godard was sent to gaol. Henry Hod fled and was sought from county to county and, because he did not appear, he was declared an outlaw.[19]

All male peasants over the age of twelve had to be members of a tithing or frankpledge, a group theoretically comprising ten, but in reality varying from four to thirty men, who were mutually responsible for the misdeeds of each and were headed by a tithing man. The view of frankpledge was a check made periodically to establish whether every peasant living in the manor had been included in a tithing. Many manorial lords claimed the right to hold their own view of frank-pledge and although such views were held regularly, usually twice a year, innumer-able cases in the King's courts show that many of the peasants remained outside any tithing; this was not usually revealed until they came before the courts accused of some crime.

There were a number of such cases before the itinerant justices in 1235. Gilbert, son of Matilda de Leg, was accused of theft. He lived in Barnet but was found not to be in any tithing. Pursued for his crimes, he fled and sought sanctuary in Enfield church where he confessed and chose to abjure the realm. The town of Chipping Barnet was fined 13s 4d. John, son of Agnes of Enfield, William son of Agnes of Enfield, William Cincht, William the son of Estiner, and Thomas the Colier were suspected of many robberies. They fled to avoid arrest and were outlawed; only one of the four was found to be within a tithing.[20]

Local juries were always reluctant to convict those who held property. The family of Thomas de la Forde had considerable holdings in Edmonton. An accusation was brought against him, and against Richard son of Benedict, by Margery, the daughter of Peter le Fevere of Enfield. She accused them of rape and, more seriously, of depriving her of her virginity. Richard was servant to the Earl of Hereford. The jury found both men guilty of rape but held that they were not guilty of the greater crime. Forde was gaoled but released upon payment of a fine, while Richard produced a pardon granted to cover his offence which had been obtained for him by the Earl, his master, from King Henry III.[21]

The theft of goods valued at twelvepence or less was not held to be sufficient to warrant death. Roger Bartha, taken for stealing a pig on Enfield Chase, worth eightpence, was given a short sentence in prison, but John Malyman, who stole two pigs from Godard Patryk in Edmonton, was hanged.[22] There were two ways by which those accused of crimes could shelter themselves from the severer punishments of the royal courts. The first of these was the opportunity given to those whose ability to read allowed them to plead benefit of clergy, and thus to subject themselves to the milder penalties of Church courts. The second was to take advantage of the provision of sanctuary when pursued by royal justice.

It was the duty of the coroner to deliver the fugitive from sanctuary and to provide him with a safe conduct to the nearest port from where he must take the first ship out to a foreign land. The coroner would sometimes leave the fugitive in sanctuary for weeks, perhaps until the village had offered him a sufficient inducement for his services. The villagers in these circumstances would be faced with the problem of preventing the escape of the prisoner, and with the expense of feeding him while he remained within their church. It is not surprising that frustration, on occasions, drove them to take the law into their own hands. Nicholas the bailiff, Geoffrey Belhoste, David Isabel, William le Prestre and Adam Bonhume, admitted that they had been present in 1228 when Reginald of Waleden had dragged out of the church Yungwinan, an Enfield man accused of theft. They were ordered to restore him to sanctuary and Enfield was amerced (ie fined) because he had been living in the parish outside a tithing.[23]

The thirteenth century was a time of great violence and quarrels often resulted in death. Among the Crown cases considered by the itinerant judges in 1294 there were ten murders within the parishes of Enfield and Edmonton. Travellers were particularly vulnerable as were those who offered lodgings. Geoffrey de Richmond, a merchant on his way through Enfield, was robbed and murdered by persons unknown.[24] Richard, groom to Richard de Mumpelers, was robbed of twenty marks and forty pence while travelling between Tottenham and Waltham Cross.[25] When a quarrel broke out between two Enfield men (John Dubell and Richard Dagon) on their way home together from Waltham Cross, John laid about Richard with his staff so viciously that his left arm was broken and he died of the injury seven days later.[26]

Drunkenness was often the cause of the violence. John Turpyn, with John his son and his wife Matilda, with her two sisters Hawis and Edith, were on their way home after drinking at a tavern until late at night. As they passed the house of Edmund David in Enfield, Hawis stopped, sat herself down and began hammering on the door with all her might, awakening the household. Edmund David sprang out of bed, seized an axe and rushed to the door. The drunken Hawis took to her heels, pursued by the enraged Edmund. In the struggle which ensued the younger John Turpyn killed Edmund with his own axe, whereupon the revellers fled. They were pursued and all except Hawis were taken and brought to Newgate. Placed on trial, they were acquitted of murder but, because they had fled, they were punished by the confiscation of their property. It proved scant punishment, for only old John had any goods, and these were worth but 5s 11d. Hawis was never taken and finally was outlawed.[27]

Another case heard in 1294 concerned Reginald de Suffolk and his son John. One servant from his household had already been hanged for murder by the judges at this eyre. John had broken into his father's house (probably at Ponders End) at night time and had stolen a bronze pot out of the kitchen; he then made off towards London. His father, with two servants, at once gave chase. What happened to the father is not revealed, but when the two servants, William Capprele and Adam de Sytewell, caught up with John he violently resisted their attempts to secure him until they knocked him senseless with a blow on the head. He never regained consciousness and the two men, fearing for themselves, left him lying in the High Road at Tottenham outside the house of Abraham Fabri. He was found and taken in by neighbours thereabouts, but he died three days later. Adam de Sytewell was arrested, William Capprele fled, but subsequently surrendered. Both were acquitted of a charge of murder, but were held guilty of having failed to raise the hue and cry.[28] William le Girdeler was arrested in 1324, accused by another malefactor, who had turned king's evidence. It was alleged that he had set fire to a brothel at Horsepoolstones (Enfield Wash) because he had been refused entry.[29]

The oppression of court officials weighed heavily upon the poor. John Mandeville was the sheriff's bailiff in Edmonton hundred in the mid-fourteenth century. His behaviour brought him before the king's court on several occasions. He was accused in 1346 of taking wood worth 2s, without just cause, from John atte Crouche who was listed in a contemporary survey as holding one acre of freehold land. Crouche had owed £5, but had repaid £4 16s 8d, he claimed. Nevertheless he was pursued relentlessly by Mandeville and by John de Wallyngford, the sheriff's bailiff errant for the county of Middlesex, and the following year they seized all his goods in Enfield. Mandeville came before the same court in 1352 for an assault on Richard Whyte who complained that Mandeville had dragged him by the beard and had threatened him in life and limb should he take action in the courts against him. He was further accused of extortion; it was alleged that he had demanded 60s from Matilda atte Hegge, an Enfield widow, 'by colour of his office'.[30]

3. Road and River

One great road to the north skirted the western boundary of the parish, another ran through Tottenham, Edmonton and eastern Enfield. This road seems to have had a hard surface even in the fourteenth century for it was sometimes referred to as the street called 'Stonistrate'[31]. Edmonton and Enfield were so close to London that a great deal of business was inevitably transacted in the City. In the thirteenth century, by far the biggest purchaser of land locally was the Augustinian Priory of the Holy Trinity at Aldgate, and in the fourteenth century many London merchants bought land in the neighbourhood.[32] Enfield farmers sold their produce in the London markets and streets. The thief who stole five pigs on Enfield Chase, sold them at Smithfield;[33] his more honest neighbours would undoubtedly have disposed of their stock in much the same way. Court cases tell a little of the traffic on the road; John Sone's haycart, drawn by a lame horse overturned while passing through Enfield,[34] and carts loaded with stockfish and bread were waylaid in Tottenham.[35]

Traffic became so heavy in the fourteenth century that special measures were required to maintain the highway between Shoreditch church and Edmonton church. A patent of 1365 empowered John Leviman, a carter, to charge one penny a week on every cart using the road, and one farthing a week on each packhorse, the money to be employed in maintaining the road. This system was continued at least until 1373. Despite such measures however, the road at this time was described as 'so deep and muddy and perilous that men, horses and carts can scarcely pass by it'.[36]

Parts of the Roman road, which the Saxons had known as Ermine Street, could still be seen traversing the great common fields in Edmonton where its line was used to define the eastern or western boundaries of innumerable plots of land. It was known to the peasants of the fourteenth century as 'Garsonsway'.[37]

The first documentary evidence of the use of the River Lea by boats is contained in the Anglo-Saxon Chronicle. It tells that in the winter of the year 894, the Danes rowed their ships up the Lea and, in the following year, built a fortress twenty miles above London. The English attacked, but were put to flight. During that autumn King Alfred set up a camp nearby to protect the corn harvest, after which he obstructed the river to prevent the Danes moving downstream. He then began the construction of two forts, one on each side of the River, at which the Danes abandoned their boats and retreated overland.

Alterations in the course of the River Lea at Waltham Abbey were made in 1190 when the Abbot of Waltham was granted a licence 'To turn the course of the water of Lin in the town of Waltham . . . for the convenience of navigation.'[38] A picture of the barge traffic on the Lea is revealed by evidence presented before the justices in eyre in 1294. Four men were bringing a barge loaded with hay down the river to London. John le Lung, reeve to the master of the Knights Templars at 'Byngelford', appears to have been in charge. He had with him William Roberts, Thomas atte Hulle and William son of John Mayheu. A quarrel broke out among them at Enfield, and William Mayheu was killed. His body was thrown into the river, but it was recovered and taken to the sheriff of Essex. The crew were arrested. John le Lung alone was found guilty and was hanged.[39]

Parliament and the City of London were concerned to keep the Lea open for navigation in the fifteenth century. The Act of 1424 gave the chancellor power to enquire into obstructions caused by millers and fishermen and, six years later, another Act empowered commissioners to borrow money to maintain the Lea. Repayment was to be made by means of a toll of fourpence to be levied for three years on every freighted boat. This is the first known instance of money borrowed for such public work, and for tolls to be charged for the repayment of the debt.[40] Fifty years later a Star Chamber jury laid down detailed directions in order to keep the river clear for the passage of boats.[41]

Fresh water fish was an important part of diet in the Middle Ages. Fish weirs, usually made of stakes with nets or basket work, were placed across the river. The Domesday survey records that Enfield's fisheries yielded an income of eight shillings a year. Two hundred eels, worth two shillings, were rendered as a rent in the manor of John Heyroun (a third part of the manor of Durants) in Enfield in 1326,[42] and a dish of fresh fish, worth one penny, was to be delivered each Friday as a rent in 1333.[43] Men like Walter Pappe (fischere) earned their livings taking fish from the River Lea. He comes to our notice only incidentally, when he was acquitted of stealing two swans belonging to the Abbot of Waltham out of the Lea at Tottenham.[44]

The Domesday survey of 1086 recorded one water-mill belonging to the manor of Enfield and another belonging to the manor of Edmonton, each stated to be worth ten shillings a year. Mills varied widely in value throughout Middlesex, and it would have to be considered a remarkable coincidence to find two mills each worth the same amount and situated in adjoining manors. (There were only three in the county, including these two, worth precisely ten shillings.) It therefore looks as though the two mills were managed as one unit which produced an annual profit of twenty shillings and, for accounting purposes, this was allocated equally to each manor.

Mills were a serious hindrance to navigation. It was necessary to make an artificial cut to bring the water to the water-wheel. In order to ensure that the mill had an adequate supply of water at all times, the miller usually built a weir across the river to hold back the stream, thus diverting the water, by a mill stream into a millpond. The centre of the weir would be made of planks held in place by beams. It was possible to remove these planks whenever a boat required to pass, but this would cause a fall in the level of the mill pond and every miller was reluctant to lose his precious water, particularly in times of drought. Weirs on some busy rivers had either a pair of swinging gates or a vertical gate, and these were known as flash locks, like Enfield lock. When the gates were opened, especially in the dry season, a 'flash' of water was released, which would carry the boat downstream over the shallows below the mill.

There were two mills on the mill stream off the River Lea in Enfield, in 1235.[45] Undoubtedly, this was the same stream which for centuries served the mill at Ponders End; it was later used as part of the Lee Navigation. A dispute arose in 1235 between the two mill owners. The mill held by Master Roger de Canteloupe lay above the one held by Robert son of Richard, who complained that Roger de Canteloupe had been obstructing the flow of water to his mill by raising the banks of the millpond, in some places by one foot and other places by two feet, so that when Canteloupe's mill was using the water for grinding, none was available at the lower mill. At both the head and foot of Canteloupe's millpond, sluices had been constructed which should never have been closed, except during hay-making so that the meadows would not be flooded, but Canteloupe's miller had been cutting off the flow of water to the lower mill at all times, and had brought his competitor to a standstill.

Roger de Canteloupe was not present when the case was heard. He may well have been abroad or elsewhere about the king's business, for he was a lawyer and diplomat in the royal service. The complaint had to be answered by his bailiff. With surprising impartiality the court found in favour of Robert son of Richard, and ordered that the hatches at the head of the millpond be kept open at all times; damages of one mark (66p) were awarded to Robert.[46]

Two corn-mills were recorded in Enfield in an inquisition* of 1289[47] and in every inquisition until 1362[48] when the mill which belonged to Garton's manor was described as being 'without stones and decayed'. The mill belonging to Humphrey

---

*An inquisition post mortem was an enquiry by the sheriff or escheator, following the death of a landowner, to discover what land he had held, its annual value, of whom held and by what services. It also enquired who was the heir and what was his/her age.

de Bohun remained in working order. There were also two fulling mills in Enfield
in 1289: one of them was not in use but even so it was valued at 13s 4d a year.
The other was held by Matthias le Felour at at 14s a year rent. One of these two
fulling mills remained operative and is shown in inquisitions in 1312,[49] 1333[50] and
in 1349,[51] indicating the persistence of a cloth industry in the area.

The fulling mill reproduced the action of trampling the cloth underfoot, which
was the ancient method of fulling. The mill consisted of two heavy wooden mallets
mechanically raised and allowed to fall on the cloth in a trough. After fulling and
scouring, the wet cloth was stretched on frames in the open air to dry. Woollen
cloth had to be fulled in order to felt and thicken the material; it caused the fibres
to adhere and it obliterated the gaps in the weave. The agents employed in the
process were various alkaline detergents like stale human urine, fullers earth and
the juices of certain plants. Some form of fulling was also applied to linen cloth in
order to separate the stiff groups of fibres into smaller softer ones.

4. The Manors, their Tenants and Officers

The land was divided into two parts, that held by the tenants of the manor and
that which was held by the lord; this was known as the demesne. There were only
three manors within the hundred of Edmonton at the time of the Domesday
survey of 1086. These were Tottenham which included the modern Wood Green,
Edmonton which included the present area of Southgate and had South Mimms
attached as a berewick, and Enfield which may have incorporated Hadley. Before
the Conquest, the manors of Enfield and Edmonton were owned by Ansgar, 'staller'
to Edward the Confessor. Ansgar is also thought to have been the sheriff of
Middlesex. The office of staller bore the responsibility for the defence of London.
Dr Stephen Doree, in his paper *Domesday Book and the Origins of Edmonton Hundred*,
tells how Ansgar, though wounded, took charge of the defence of London following
the Battle of Hastings. He tried to trick the future William I into accepting a bogus
surrender and died in prison. Many of the lands which passed from Ansgar to
Geoffrey de Mandeville were manors which belonged to the office of staller, among
them the estate which comprised the manors of Edmonton and Enfield. Stephen
Doree shows that this estate had a special function in the defence and provisioning
of the capital. He traces the ownership back to the Earl Tofi, Ansgar's grandfather,
and probably staller to King Canute in the early eleventh century. Stephen Doree
goes on to suggest that this estate may have existed, and may have served the
same purpose for as long as London had been a major urban centre, possibly even
into Roman times. These responsibilities, long associated with the ownership of
the manors of Edmonton and Enfield, certainly continued after the Conquest, and
Geoffrey de Mandeville, the new owner, became the first constable of the Tower
of London and sheriff of London and Middlesex.

The great antiquity of this estate is indicated by an examination of the northern
and western boundary, west of the point where Northaw meets Cheshunt, for here
the boundary coincides with the boundary of the diocese, which was probably
established in the sixth or seventh century. It is further suggested that this line
marks the original political frontier of the East Saxon Kingdom, surviving as the
boundary of the diocese and the hundred long after that kingdom had diminished
and had finally vanished in the late seventh or early eighth century. The dedication
of the church in Enfield (to St Andrew) was one usually associated with an early

phase of the Conversion to Christianity. The very large size of the parish of Enfield (over fifteen thousand acres) suggests that the church could have been a minster, created to serve the needs of a royal estate in the early days of the Conversion. Stephen Doree argues that Edmonton, Enfield, South Mimms and Monken Hadley constituted a royal estate under the East Saxon kings. This is suggested by the existence of the park in Enfield mentioned in 1086, for hunting rights were tradition-ally associated with royal courts. This park had probably existed before the division of the estate into parishes, for its boundaries cross the parish boundary between Edmonton and Enfield.

It is evident that Mandeville retained both Enfield and Edmonton in his own hands, because a yearly value is stated, not a rent. It was an extremely valuable property being equal, in 1086, to twelve per cent of the entire rental of the county of Middlesex which was among the richest counties in the country. The Domesday survey assesses the value of the manor before the Conquest, immediately following the Conquest, and twenty years later in 1086. Before the Conquest, the manor of Enfield was worth £50 a year; immediately afterwards its value had fallen to only £20, which suggests that some considerable devastation had occurred. The value rose over the ensuing twenty years to regain its pre-Conquest level by 1086.

The Domesday survey lists 114 households in Enfield, that is if the families of slaves are to be counted as households. The classification of these households was made under headings of which the definitions are now imprecisely known, and they were probably not very precisely known to King William's commissioners in 1086. Slaves were almost always employed on the demesne. In Somerset and Devon they worked two to a plough. Tottenham, with two ploughs on the demesne, had four slaves, but Enfield, with four ploughs, had no more than six slaves, while Edmonton, also with four ploughs, had only four slaves. Over the country as a whole nine per cent of those listed were slaves; in Edmonton hundred the percentage is 5.25. Slavery was declining at this time and the decline had gone further in this area than in parts of the country remote from London. It was in existence long before the Conquest, and the bordars, noted in the survey, may have been former slaves. Two hundred years later, when records again begin to throw light upon the workings of the manors, there were no longer any slaves living in Edmonton hundred.

Enfield had thirty cottars of whom eighteen were landless, five held seven acres between them, and the other seven farmed a total of twenty-three acres. The twenty Enfield bordars held an average of seven and a half acres each. Thus by 1086, the parish was home to fifty poor cottagers whose land holdings averaged only 3.6 acres each, and who would have been forced to seek employment as day labourers. There were fifty-seven villeins. The term 'villein', which originally meant nothing more than a villager, had by the time of the Conquest come to imply an unfree status. Villeins were obliged to perform works on the demesne and were subject to many restraints. They were the more substantial farmers in the community, though their holdings varied considerably in size. One of the villeins in Enfield held around a hundred and twelve acres, three others held about fifty-six acres each, seventeen held some twenty-eight acres, and thirty-six held around fourteen acres, a total of about twelve hundred acres.

The survey also states that in 1066, before the Conquest, there had been five sokemen in Enfield, and that they had held six hides (about six hundred and seventy acres) between them. Twenty years later this class of villager had disappeared, not only in Enfield, but throughout the whole of Middlesex. Sokemen under the Saxon kings had been free.

The survey noted that there was a priest in Enfield who held one virgate (about twenty-eight acres). No priest is mentioned in Edmonton but it does not follow that there was no church, merely that the priest held no land and was therefore dependent on his tithes.[52]

There had been many subdivisions, by the end of the thirteenth century, of the original manor of Enfield as recorded in 1086. All these new manors were held either from the Earl of Hereford or from the Abbot of Walden. Manors were estates, some large, some small, each owned by a lord who had a demesne (or home farm) which he might either farm himself or lease to others. In some manors there were dependent tenants who held their land partly by the payment of money rents and partly by work rents (that is they had to do certain clearly defined work on the lord's demesne), but these work rents were few and of small significance in this parish. Each of the manors had freeholders, who paid their rent in money and did no labour service (or very little) on the demesne. Many work rents were bought out with cash payments by the tenants over the two centuries 1200–1400.[53]

All justice had originally been the prerogative of the Crown, but lords of manors throughout the country had been granted, or had assumed over the years, certain jurisdictions and, of course, the fines which arose in administering them. It was to test the validity of the lords' claims that the king's justices, from time to time, sat to investigate by what right lords of manors held the power to administer the king's justice. Humphrey de Bohun, Earl of Hereford and Essex, who held the manor of Enfield, successfully claimed in 1294 the right of warren (the sole right to hunt all wild beasts other than deer), waifs (the right to seize abandoned property), the assize of bread and ale (i.e. the right to check the weight of a penny loaf and the strength of ale brewed) and a view of frankpledge,[54] (the right to check whether every male peasant, above the age of twelve, living within the manor, was included within a tithing.)

The manor of the rectory of Enfield belonged to the Abbot of Walden who also owned the rectories of the churches at Edmonton, South Mimms and Monken Hadley by a grant from Geoffrey de Mandeville Earl of Essex, in 1136 (according to the Chronicles). He claimed the right, before the king's justices, to hold the view of frankpledge in each of these rectory manors, as well as the assize of bread and ale. The jury of Edmonton hundred however, rejected his claim, declaring that he held such rights only in Enfield, and even there he had no right to a pillory or tumbrell. The jury insisted that the bailiff of the Earl of Hereford had always had the sole right, in Enfield, to try cases where blood had been shed,[55] though there is no evidence that he ever set up a gallows in his manor.

The division of men into freemen or villeins was universal but never simple; there was confusion concerning their respective rights among contemporaries. This is shown in a case brought by William Herward against Peter de la Berwe at the 1235 eyre for the county of Middlesex. He alleged that Berwe had unjustly turned him out of a freehold tenement and three and a half acres in Edmonton. Berwe defended his action by declaring that William Herward was a villein. Nevertheless the jury maintained that William had held the land freely; moreover they accepted his plea that he had been unjustly ejected. At the same time they agreed with Berwe that William was a villein who belonged to William de Say, lord of the manor of Edmonton. But they did not know, they admitted, whether such a bondman was legally entitled to hold freehold property. The jury therefore sidestepped the issue by declaring that, since Herward was a villein, he had no right to bring his action into that court, which was the king's court, and therefore open to freemen only.[56]

In the economy of the manors in Enfield, as well as of those in Edmonton, the part played by villein labour, by the beginning of the fourteenth century, was not of great importance. The accounts for 1322, and the inquisition of 1336, for the manor of Enfield,[57] show twenty-one acres of meadow mowed, and the hay gathered in, by seventeen customary tenants who held between them about 160 acres. There were in addition five cottagers who each mowed half an acre and did certain precaria (work on the demesne, in theory given freely) at harvest time, worth to the lord of the manor a total of 3s 4d. These five cottagers and thirteen molmen (who held small amounts of land in villeinage) were required to do eleven carrying services between them. At this time forty-eight acres of meadow were harvested by hired labour, but while the hired labour cost the lord 8½d an acre, bond labour cost him only 2½d an acre (the value of their food). The corn crop that year on 119 acres, was reaped entirely by hired labour, but at a cost of only 3½d an acre, obviously less labour was involved in reaping than in mowing.

The survey of c. 1340[58] lists ninety-three freeholders, eighteen molmen (three of whom also held freehold land and five of whom also held customary land), eighteen customary tenants (three of whom also held freehold) and five cottagers (two of whom also held land of molman tenure), 134 tenants in all, the terms under which each class of tenant held land are described below. Typical of the molmen were John le Souter and Robert Beryl who held a messuage and six acres, divided equally between them. Their duty was to find one man to hoe the lord's corn for one day, and on that day he was entitled to a breakfast of bread, cheese and ale at the lord's table. The fact that breakfast only was provided suggests that only a morning's work was required. The food was held to be worth three farthings. They were also required to send one man to reap the lord's corn for one day, (though in 1322 it was said to have been done entirely by hired labour). On this day the man was entitled to two meals at the lord's table. At nine o'clock he was given a breakfast of coarse or rye bread and meat stew; at mid-day he had a dish of either meat or fish, with rye bread and milk. The hoeing was worth three farthings to the lord, the reaping two pence. They were also liable to perform one carrying service yearly on foot. Two examples are cited; the carrying of letters to Plessy Walden (Pleshey near Chelmsford) and to Amondisham (Amersham): for this they would receive from the lord three farthings. Their money rent amounted to 3s a year.

Hugo atte Holme, another molman, held only a cottage and three quarters of an acre. He did the same works in the field as the other molmen, but no carrying service was required of him, and he paid 4d a year rent. William Couper held a messuage and eight acres for 2s a year. He did the full services as described above. The holdings of the molmen ranged from half an acre to nine acres.

Richard atte Forteys held a virgate of customary land, (perhaps thirty acres) but he also held freehold land and was frequently called upon to witness charters, and this could only be done by a free man. He paid 38s 4d, both as a rent and in lieu of labour services. His sole remaining obligation was to mow four acres of the lord's meadow, which should be worth 2s to the lord. Robert atte Holme, who held half a virgate, paid 19s 2d rent and mowed two acres.

The office of reeve was a burden which few would willingly undertake. The principal duties in 1340 were the collection of rents and the organisation of labour services. The reeve was chosen annually at the manor court from among those villeins holding half a virgate or less. The precise method of selection in Enfield is not known, but in Tottenham it was the custom that the homage (that is the jury at the court baron) elected two men each year from whom one was chosen by the lord. In Tottenham, in 1385, the homage elected Robert Reygate and Richard Brok, and Reygate was selected by the lord of the manor but he refused to serve. Although three times he was ordered to take the oath on pain of a fine of 6s 8d, he remained adamant and paid the fine. Whereupon Brok also refused to serve. This was too much; it was ordered in the manor court that his goods, lands and tenements be seized for his obstinacy and, faced with this threat, Richard Brok took the oath of office.[59]

The obligation to serve as hayward might fall upon villeins holding a quarter of a virgate, or upon cottagers. Adam Saleman held a cottage and five acres for which he paid 6s 10d a year. His labour services were similar to those of a molman with a holding of the same size, except that he had also to mow half an acre of the lord's meadow. When the cottager was appointed hayward for the year, he was free of all rent and services and was entitled to eat at the lord's table during harvest time. He was also to receive from the lord, one acre of rye (from unmanured land), and the grass around the edges of the lord's arable lands and around his meadow grounds. It was his duty to oversee the mowing until all the hay had been lifted from the meadows and stacked. It was his right to have the base of each haystack, to the value of half a penny, after the hay had been either sold or fed to the lord's stock. This he would use as fertiliser on his land. It was part of his office to collect for the lord, from among his tenants, on the feast of St Michael (29 September) 149 chickens worth one penny each, and at Easter to collect 252 eggs, to the value of twenty-one eggs for one penny.[60]

Certain light works on the demesne were still being done in 1419. Twenty day works were demanded of twenty-two customary tenants and molmen in hoeing the lord's corn. However nine of these customary tenements were, by this time, held by freemen, who paid 1¼d in lieu of each work.

The bailiff was a more important person than the reeve or hayward. John Kentyng, bailiff of Enfield manor in 1419, was paid 43s 9d for the collection of rents over a period of nine months, also a salary of 40s a year.[61] He could be held responsible by the lord of the manor for any dereliction of his duties and imprisoned, though he had the right to seek protection in the king's courts.

The last quarter of the fourteenth century was a period of high wages and low prices which made successful demesne farming difficult. By 1419[62] all the demesne arable of the manor of Enfield was offered for rent at twelve pence an acre. It was distributed in three common fields, 135 acres in Windmill field, 110 acres in Southbury field and 164 acres in Westbury field, a total of 419 acres. For half this land (210 acres) no tenants could be found. Whether this indicates a decline in the population due to the ravages of the Black Death, or whether a shilling an acre was more than the land was worth, is difficult to determine. That same year, on 29 September, Enfield became a Crown manor, as part of the Duchy of Lancaster, following the death of the previous owner, the Countess of Hereford. An account of 1438[63] shows that the demesne was let to a single tenant on a six year lease at £22 6s 8d a year rent. The Manor House went with the tenancy, except that the gatehouse was reserved for the use of the Duchy. The rent stood at £20 13s 4d in 1465,[64] thereafter the rent fell further and further behind the real value of the

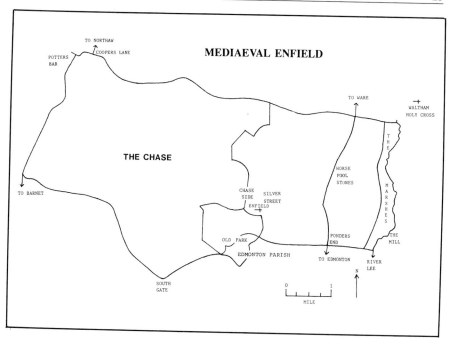

property until, in 1582, the rents received by Henry Middlemore from his tenants amounted to £132, while the rent paid by him to the Duchy was still only £26.[65]

5. The Land

The area of land which comprised the parish of Enfield was the shape of an oblong measuring some three to four miles south to north and eight miles east to west. It contained 15,206 acres. The shorter side in the east was the former course of the River Lea now obliterated beneath the reservoirs. The parish extended westward up the gently rising side of the valley for some three miles, then the ground rose more rapidly, from a hundred feet at Chase Side Enfield, to four hundred feet at Coopers Lane. Beside the river lay the marshes and, westward from these, a wide belt of brickearth stretched from the edge of the flood plain as far as the village green. The higher land in the western half of the parish is London clay and was forested in the eleventh century.

Within the boundaries of this parish were contained all the necessities for the survival of the community and the economic health of the estate. Meadows were created by draining the marsh land and the brickearth made excellent arable being easy to plough, though it required to be adequately manured. The forest in the west provided wood for fuel and timber for building and making tools; the foliage, and the crops from beech and oak trees, went to feed the animals; the glades within the woodland gave additional pasture.

Recent research has indicated that many mediaeval parishes are the direct descendents of the agricultural units into which the country was divided in Roman times and that these may well have been in existence during the late pre-historic period. They may even have been created to meet the population pressures and the expansion of agricultural land in the late Bronze Age. Territorial lords of multiple estates tended to convert existing land units into parishes. Tithes were often paid in kind from the produce of the land, and the Church thus came to have a vested interest in the maintenance of parish boundaries. Manor and parish were in many places synonymous, as they were (almost) in eleventh century Enfield, Edmonton and Tottenham.

Those who lived in any parish, particularly in a common field parish, had a vested interest in retaining the whole of their territory, for the village economy was finely balanced, and to lose any part of its resources might bring disaster, even starvation.[66]

At the time King William I made his great survey in 1086, some eighty per cent of the land suitable for arable in Enfield was under cultivation. The forest, on the heavy, difficult London clay, was to remain uncleared and unploughed into modern times; it covered more than half the parish. The cultivatable area was described by William's commissioners in the statement that Enfield had sufficient land to employ twenty-four plough teams. The area actually cultivated was indicated by the presence of twenty plough teams. The term 'plough team', in this part of England, meant eight oxen, and by tradition the land which such a team could plough is taken to be a hundred and twenty acres. This would mean that in 1086 there were some 2400 acres under the plough. This is of course a somewhat crude and dubious calculation, but its validity can be judged by a figure of just over 3,100 acres of arable, calculated from the 1572 survey of the whole parish.[67] The reader must bear in mind that there was no standard definition of the size of an acre.

In dealing with the pasture the commissioners merely stated that there was sufficient pasture for all the livestock. Most of the animals would have fed in the clearings within the woodlands, and on the stubble of the ploughed fields and meadows after the harvest had been collected, so that little land would have to be given over specifically for pasture. The meadows were then, as they remained until the present century, on the marshes along the River Lea which are now submerged beneath the waters of the reservoirs. The survey describes them as meadow for twenty-four plough teams and 25s in rent and profit.

The population of England grew throughout the twelfth and thirteenth centuries and the increasing number of mouths to feed meant that every possible acre of soil, even land of poor quality, had to be put under the plough. Rye was the main crop grown in the village in the late thirteenth century. Rye bread was the diet of the poor while those who could afford it ate wheaten bread. All grain had to be brought to the mill belonging to the manor and the lord took his proportion as payment. A number of smaller manors had come into existence by the thirteenth century. In Durants manor, lying in eastern Enfield in 1289,[68], the multure of the mill (this proportion forfeited to the lord) was five quarters of wheat at 3s 4d a quarter, and thirty quarters of rye at 2s 8d. At the water-mill belonging to the manor of Enfield in 1298, the miller, on behalf of lord of the manor, took five quarters of wheat, at 5s 4d a quarter, and forty quarters of rye at 2s.[69] Rye continued to be the main crop sown in the parish throughout the fourteenth and fifteenth centuries.

The expansion of population during the thirteenth century had brought about a growing scarcity of land, a rise in rents and a decline in wages; it had left many peasants with insufficient resources. It was for this reason that adverse climatic conditions, though in general the weather was probably no worse than it had been in earlier periods, had more sharply-felt effects. The years 1315 to 1320 saw a serious crisis in agriculture. The harvest of 1310 had been very poor, and between 1315 and 1317 there was widespread famine throughout the land, brought about by a series of harvest failures; the situation was worsened by the renewed heavy taxation which followed the English defeat at Bannockburn. The harvests of 1317 and 1318 were better, but the year 1319 brought plague among cattle and oxen. There were further bad harvests in 1320 and 1321. Hungry men were forced to steal in order to survive and there were many prosecutions in this area. A cart loaded with salt fish was attacked on its way through Tottenham in 1310.[70] John Godyn was hanged for the theft of three stooks of corn and two stooks of barley in 1315.[71] William Bene was acquitted of stealing hay to the value of 3s, John Bene was acquitted of stealing three stooks of corn and four stooks of oats, Geoffrey Bene was hanged for stealing butter. John Gosselyn was hanged for the theft of a cow in Edmonton.[72] Simon de Webbesnade and Simon de Konnebalton were hanged for the theft of bread in Enfield.[73] That same year Geoffrey atte Hache broke into Tottenham mill and forced open a chest to steal three bushels of mixil (a mixture of rye and wheat) worth fifteen pence. He was hanged and left no possessions. John Brokesle followed him to the gallows for breaking into a house and stealing an ink-pot and sixteen cheeses.[74] In the four years 1315–1318, thirty-nine crimes which had occurred in Edmonton and Enfield were dealt with at the Newgate gaol releases; twelve were acquitted, two of those who had been found guilty successfully pleaded benefit of clergy, and the remaining twenty-five were hanged. Of the twenty-seven thus adjudged guilty, eighteen were found to be utterly destitute, for they had no possessions at all, and six of the others were so poor that their combined wealth amounted to less than one pound.[75] The large number of prosecutions,many of which involved the theft of food, must indicate widespread and extreme poverty, especially when one bears in mind that harsh penalties failed to deter, and that it is probable that a much larger number of offenders were not brought to justice.

A picture of the working of the Enfield demesne is provided by a single manorial account which unexpectedly survives from the fourteenth century.[76] Humphrey de Bohun, the eighth lord of the manor of Enfield who held that same name, was killed at the Battle of Boroughbridge in 1322 while in rebellion against King Edward II. His manors and estates were taken into the King's hands, and thus this account found its way into the public records. It shows that the main crop was mixtil which sold that year, according to the quantity of wheat mixed with the rye, at 4s or 5s a quarter. It must have been mostly rye, for wheat was selling at 11s 3d a quarter. The bulk of the corn, still in sheaves, had been purchased in one lot, direct from the barns, for £20. This represented the produce from 117 acres of mixtil and two acres of wheat, and it works out to about six bushels to an acre. The average net yield (even after deduction of tithe and seed for sowing the following year) on the Winchester estates, 1209–1350, was in the order of eight bushels of mixed grain to an acre. (Titow, J.Z. *English rural society, 1200–1350.* p80–81). Thus the yield from the demesne of the manor of Enfield that year is by comparison low.

The multure of the mill was entirely of mixtil, which shows that the tenants also were growing this crop. The poorer peasants, having less stock to manure their land, would not have been able to reach even the low level of production (6 bushels to an acre) achieved by the lord. Just how close were the poor to starvation can be understood from the fact that two to two and a half bushels of seed would have to be kept for sowing.

The small margin of profit made by the lord of the manor was reduced further by his labour costs. Reaping, gathering and tying the sheaves was all done by hired labour and cost 3½d per acre. The bailiff was paid 1½d a day and the reeve 2d a day over a period of forty days throughout harvest time. To prevent the crop being stolen an extra man had to be employed to guard the corn and hay until it was disposed of, a matter of twelve weeks; he was paid 4s 4d.

The 1322 account shows that forty-eight acres of demesne meadow had been mown, lifted and stacked by hired labour; this had cost the lord 8½d an acre. A further twenty-one acres had been harvested by bondmen at only 2½d an acre, which shows why manorial lords were vigilant to maintain their rights over such tenants. The year had been a bad one for a great part of the hay had been lost and only enough remained to feed the lord's oxen; there was none to sell. There were thirty acres of pasture that year on part of which the lord's oxen were fed, and the remainder was let for 17s 4d. There was also separate pasture for the feeding of goats, which was let for 7s.

After the years of poor harvests, and the loss of cattle, the weather improved for a few years but, in the summers of 1325 and 1326, a great drought hit the south-east. There was a shortage of hay and many were driven to steal in order to save their cattle. The ownership of cattle indicated a status at least approaching that of a juryman and it is noticeable that the men who served on juries in Edmonton hundred proved very reluctant to send such people to the gallows. All the accused were of local families, including many whose names appear in charters. Alice atte Bregge and Amicia, wife of Richard Heward, were said to have stolen hay to the value of 3s from the meadows of the Abbot of Walden in Edmonton; they were acquitted.[77] Cecilia le Pottere, accused of stealing hay worth 4s from William de Causton in Edmonton, was also acquitted. Three cases occurred in Tottenham, at the same time, of the theft of hay worth 5s and 3s, and a quarter of mixtil and four bushels of beans worth 8s; again all the accused were acquitted. The jury also rejected accusations against John, son of Thomas Cok of Enfield, indicted for stealing hay to the value of 2s from Bartholomew de Honilane,[78] as also against John le Carter, who was said to have taken hay worth 5s from the meadows of the Abbot of Walden in Edmonton.[79]

From 1333 the English armies were involved in Scotland and the effect of this, and of the country's costly intervention in continental wars after 1336, imposed heavy burdens on the tax-paying population. The fall in agricultural prices from 1333, after three decades of high prices, added to the taxpayer's difficulties. Taxation from 1333 had been standardised at a high level and scarcely varied from year to year. The tax of a fifteenth on all moveable goods, for the year 1336, amounted for each parish in Edmonton hundred to:[80]

Parish	Tax £. s. d.			% of Edmonton hundred
Enfield	12	6	7¾	35.3
Edmonton	10	17	2	31.2
Tottenham	7	2	11	20.5
S. Mimms	4	11	8	13.1
TOTALS	34	18	5¾	100.0

making a total for Edmonton hundred of £34 18s 5¾d, out of £342 for the whole of Middlesex. Between 1336 and 1340 this tax was collected annually, but there were two taxes in the year 1336, which made a total for Enfield of £24 13s 4d. That same year the government imposed an embargo on the export of wool, which was the main cash crop in the parish. Wool producers were hit again the following year, by a duty of 40s on every sack of wool exported. A new tax was levied on wool in July 1338 which, in 1341 (the only year for which figures survive) amounted to £33 13s 6¼d. The scale of local wool production, at this time, can be worked out from these figures. Edmonton hundred contributed twenty-four sacks and three and a quarter pounds of wool, out of a total for the county of Middlesex of 236 sacks, 10 stone 11 lb. Indeed the contribution of Enfield (8 sacks 2 stone 7¼ lb) was among the highest in the county, and only exceeded in four other parishes.[81] Each of these sacks contained 364 lb of wool, the produce of some two hundred and sixty sheep.[82] The return would therefore represent some twenty-one hundred sheep kept in Enfield.

Until 1334 taxation caused little suffering to the poor, for there was a minimum level, usually set at the possession of goods worth ten shillings. After 1334 this rule was abandoned, and the smallholders suffered disproportionately, for the subsidy (tax) fell on moveable goods, and not on income, so that landlords, many of them wealthy Londoners, escaped lightly, while those who had to produce and sell in order to find the money for rents and taxes, suffered.[83]

A survey of the manor of Enfield, taken about 1340,[84] suggests that many of the tenants were living at below subsistence level. Arable holdings were as follows:

33 tenants held 1 acre or less
21 tenants held 1–3 acres
15 tenants held 3–5 acres
24 tenants held 5–10 acres

All these, eighty-five per cent of the total, held insufficient land to maintain themselves (Titow, J.Z. *English rural society, 1200–1350* p. 79, 89) and may have found it necessary to seek employment as labourers. Their smallholdings could only have been rendered viable by the existence of Enfield Chase. On this vast area of common waste, covering more than eight thousand acres, the poor were free to pasture a cow, perhaps some geese, to fatten their pig in autumn on the acorns and beechmast, and to gather wood for fuel and timber for the repair of their fences and cottages. Only seventeen tenants had holdings which may have been large enough to support them and their families:

8 tenants held 10–20 acres
5 tenants held around 30 acres
2 tenants held around 50 acres
John de Stanbourne held 128 acres
Jordan de Elsyng held 210 acres

It has been estimated that the Black Death cut the population of England by up to a half. It hit Tottenham in May 1348. Manor rolls indicate that so many had died in the village that month, that the lord of the manor of Aubeneys had ten holdings for which he could find no tenants. This was in marked contrast to the hunger for land which had existed in the neighbourhood in the earlier years.[85]

The year 1349 saw the onset of plague in Enfield. An inquisition taken in July that year, in the manor of Durants, shows that the plague had scarcely yet reached the area. Durants Arbour stood newly built and so impressed the jury that they saw fit to describe the house as 'optime edificata' (very well built). It is true that the value of the land was less than it once had been: arable was valued at 4d an acre, sown (nothing unsown) and meadow at only sixteen pence an acre.[86] By December, however, plague was rampant. Where only ten years earlier there had been great numbers of land-hungry tenants eager to take any plot that fell vacant, now sixty acres had come into the hands of the lord of the manor of Worcesters by the death of tenants and no new tenants could be found. The demesne arable (144 acres) was valued at little over 2d an acre,[87] perhaps because the condition of the soil had deteriorated from years of over-cropping and lack of manure. The neighbouring manor of Edmonton in 1359 had 400 acres of arable of which 160 acres were sown each year. This land was said to be worth only half a penny an acre, and no more, it was described as sandy (zabulos) and very much barren (valde steril).

A second pestilence hit Enfield in 1362. In the manor of Gartons (formerly part of the manor of Durants) the yields had fallen to such an extent that they were forced to introduce a two year rotation of crops instead of the former three year rotation, which meant that half the arable land was left idle every year. The forty acres which had been sown that year were valued at only one penny an acre. The remaining forty acres were being used as rough sheep pasture, presumably so that the sheep droppings might put some heart back into the land. The water-mill on the Lea lay derelict and without mill-stones, another indication that the production of grain had seriously diminished. The Gartons manor house too was worth nothing beyond the cost of its maintenance; even the dovecot was ruinous, and the roof had fallen in.[88]

Famine prices prevailed throughout the country in the years 1362, 1363 and 1364. An inquisition was taken on Enfield manor in 1363 which showed that the demesne arable had been entirely converted to pasture, and that it was valued still at only fourpence an acre, because it was sandy and stony. (Pasture in 1312 in Enfield had been worth a shilling an acre).[89] This conversion is all the more remarkable at a time when cereal prices were at their highest. The reason could have been that no labour could be found to plough and tend the land and, if so, it would indicate that the ravages of plague in 1362 were very severe indeed. It could also be accounted for by a very real exhaustion of the soil.

There was a further outbreak of plague in 1368; 1370 was a year of famine throughout the country, yet the demesne arable was still being used as rough pasture in 1373[90] and was again offered at only fourpence an acre.

No poll tax survives for Edmonton hundred, but the collector's account for the year 1377, enables an estimate to be made of the number paying. In that year £22 4s was collected which, at fourpence a head, represents 1,332 persons.[91] Accepting that the proportions of the population in each parish within the hundred bore a similar relationship, one to another, as did their contributions to the tax on moveables, it suggests that the numbers paying poll tax in each parish were:

Enfield	470
Edmonton	414
Tottenham	273
South Mimms	175
TOTAL	1332

Any attempt to calculate populations from these figures must allow for wide margins of error. It might be assumed that twenty-five per cent evaded payment, and that forty per cent of the population were exempt, being under fourteen. With these assumptions we have maximum population figures for 1377 as shown below in column A. To arrive at minimum figures I take the proportion of evasions to be only ten per cent, and thirty per cent to be under fourteen years old. This minimum estimate is shown in column B:

	A	B
Enfield	980	780
Edmonton	900	690
Tottenham	575	460
South Mimms	360	280

It was a good time for labourers. Wages rose throughout the country following the Black Death, and there were strenuous attempts to control them by legislation. There is evidence of resistance to this control. Two attacks were made on the king's justices in the summer of 1351; the first was on 25 June and in consequence John Yve, a tailor, and Thomas Yve his brother, John, son of Robert Tailor, Henry Squaddere and John Cok, all of Enfield, and William Blare of Edmonton, were arrested by John de Braye. They all escaped.[92] These same justices dealing with homicides, felonies and trespasses, as well as all things contrary to the Statute of Labourers were attacked again two weeks later in Tottenham, where they were driven from their sessions by a great multitude, and their prisoners freed.[93].

Throughout the 1370s wages in England continued to move steadily upward. At this same time prices began to fall, slowly at first, but accelerating in the late 1370s. They never recovered. Nothing is known of any repercussions in the parish of the Peasant's Revolt of 1381. There was serious trouble in neighbouring Barnet and at Waltham, just across the northern boundary, the Abbey was attacked. The list of those arrested in Middlesex includes no recognisable local names.[94]

6. Prayers for the Dead

Plague and famine in the fourteenth century gave rise to an overwhelming concern with death and purgatory in the fifteenth century. Life was lived in the shadow of the hereafter. A large painting of the resurrection looked down from the rood loft in St Andrews Church, to remind the congregation of the perils of purgatory and hell and the hope of salvation. The righteous were shown climbing ladders into heaven, while the damned were driven by demons into the mouth of hell. In the background stood a gibbet with its melancholy burden. (W. Robinson *History of Enfield* Vol. 2 p. 8)

The first concern of every man, as death approached and his mind dwelt upon the hereafter, was to propitiate his Maker. Having bequeathed his soul to Almighty God, to Our Blessed Lady, and to the holy company of saints, he turned to his parish church, seeking pardon for the tithes and other offerings he had failed to pay when in better health. I have found only one pre-Reformation will, among the many made by those who dwelt in Enfield and in the neighbouring villages, in which their parish church was not a beneficiary. Almost every will written in the fifteenth, and in the early sixteenth centuries begins with a gift to the high altar, 'for tithes and offerings forgotten, or negligently withholden'. Many made bequests

A large mediaeval painting on wood of the resurrection above the former rood loft in St Andrews Church

for candles to burn on the altar of their chosen saint, though it was at the altar of Our Lady that most sought intercession. There were no fewer than eight altars in the Church of St Andrews in Enfield.

Many vicars served more than one parish. One such was Edmund Causton, vicar from 1466 to 1491. His will suggests that he was far from poor. He supplemented his tithes by working a farm on which he kept some fifty sheep. He left 40s to Enfield church, towards the making of a silver chrismatory, 26s 8d for two silver candlesticks to set upon the high altar, 20s for an image of Our Lady, to be used in the chapel at Elsings, and eight sheets for distribution among the poor in Enfield. His second church was at Cressingham, Norfolk. He gave another pair of silver candlesticks for the high altar there, and 5s among the poor. He dressed sumptuously, for his will describes a black gown, and a russet gown, and two blue gowns, one lined, and the other furred at the hands, reminiscent of the monk in the *Canterbury Tales*

'I saw his sleeves y-purfiled at the hand
With gris*, and that the finest in the land'

Nevertheless he was humble enough to be buried in the churchyard 'beside the litell dore to St Jamys chapel on the south side'.[95]

Many voices were raised to supplicate for the soul of Thomas Thompson, Doctor of Divinity, vicar of the parish Church of Enfield, and parson of the parish Church of Welwyn. He died in 1540, and was buried in the chapel of St Johns College Cambridge. Masses and matins were sung at Michael House, and at Christs College, at Welwyn, and at Enfield, where £4 was bestowed among the priests and clerks, and to the poor, and 20s was granted to the churchwardens towards the maintenance of the church. His house at Enfield he left to a servant Thomas Betone whose wife was his kinswoman, together with £10, and a feather bed with its bolster and canopy. To Thomas Manners, Earl of Rutland, at Enfield House (Elsings),

*grey fur

he bequeathed a ring of gold with two rubies, and to 'my lady his wife', a ring of gold with a turquoise.[96]

The wealthy set up chantries in which a priest was employed to pray for the soul of the donor and for others named. The chantry of Baldwin de Radyngton was licensed in 1398 and endowed with lands to the value of £10 a year.[97] Another chantry was that of Agnes Myddleton who left an estate called Poynetts in Essex; the profits were to be used to pay a priest ten marks a year (£6 13s 4d) to pray daily at the altar of St Mary the Virgin, in the north chancel chapel, for the souls of Agnes and of her four husbands, all of whom she had outlived. She provided the instruments necessary, a broken salt-cellar and other silver to make a censer, a standing cup of silver for a chalice, and a gown of damask and beads of pearl for a cope, and to the priest John Dyer, a chalice of silver and gold.[98] The chantry, known as Blossoms chantry after the first of the four husbands, was established in 1471.

More common and less costly than chantries were obits or prayers to mark each anniversary of death. The money was usually provided by leaving property from which a fixed sum was paid each year out of the rents. John Hunsdon, maltman of Enfield, in 1473 left two acres one rood of meadow in Wildemarsh to his son John who was to find 6s 8d a year out of the profits to pay priests and clerks for singing, ringing the bells, and candles. Any remainder should be bestowed in bread and ale to refresh the neighbours and poor people coming to the service.[99] William Garrard left 3s 8d a year from a croft called Chalcroft, at Ponders End, for obits. The land was left to his wife for the term of her life, and after her death to his daughter. The money was to be paid: 2s 4d 'to be sung and rung for, 4d to the bead-roll for evermore, and 12d to twelve poor persons coming to the service'.[100]

Brotherhoods and fraternities sought the salvation, and sometimes the earthly welfare, of their members. The Brotherhood of Our Lady in Enfield received numerous gifts and employed a priest. The earliest mention of it which I have found is in the will of Walter Forde, a yeoman, written in 1464. By this he left a tenement to the Brotherhood 'with the intent to keep an obit for ever'; 13s 4d a year was received from this source.[101] John Alford (1500) left 'two wethers or else two shillings, his 'years mynde', (a prayer each year to intercede for his soul) to be maintained for seven years.[102] Occasionally the Brotherhood received gifts of land such as the half acre of arable in Longfield, from John Leper in 1494.[103] Robert Wroth of Durants, dying in 1535, gave twenty shillings.[104] Charles Nowell, serving in the household of Sir Thomas Lovell, that same year gave by his will a further 20s.[105] By about the year 1500, the brotherhood held lands and tenements from which was derived an annual income of £3 13s.[106]

A number of obits in Enfield failed to survive the ravages of time, the rapacity of new tenants, and changes in religious beliefs. Nevertheless the commissioners of the Court of Augmentations, in 1547, found that seven bequests for obits were still honoured, and 58s a year was still received for their maintenance. The major survival in the parish however, was the estate left to endow Agnes Myddleton's chantry. The income, in 1547, was £10 a year, and it was used to maintain the Brotherhood of Our Lady. John Bridgeman, the brotherhood priest, had for his salary £7 a year.[107] Subsequently it was stated before the Court of Augmentations that he earned his money by teaching the poor children of the parish.

Enfield parish church was much altered in the early sixteenth century. John Barley, in his will dated 1500, asked to be buried in the chapel of the Blessed Mary (the north chancel chapel) and left 20d towards the rebuilding.[108] This rebuilding was completed in 1531, for the date was shown on a stone formerly set in the east wall. Here can be seen the famous brass to Joyce Lady Tiptoft (d. 1446). It now lies under a painted stone canopy which was erected about 1530, probably in memory of Isabel Lady Lovell. A similar arch was ordered to be put up on the south side of the chancel by the will of Robert Wroth in 1535,[109] but it seems that it was never built. That further work was in progress at this time is apparent from gifts made by John Barley towards the 'new-making' of the chapel of St Jacob, the south chancel chapel. The clerestory was added, or more likely replaced, about 1520, at the expense of Sir Thomas Lovell, and his insignia, a falcon wing and a trefoil can be seen set on stones between the windows. The Roos window, so little of which now remains, was paid for by Eleanor, Countess of Rutland, in 1531. Made in London, it cost £3 18s 11d.

An inventory of church goods was drawn up in 1552.[110] Much of the plate remained, chalices and censers (the pans in which incense was burned), a pyx (a vessel to hold the host after consecration), and a pax, (a carved tablet kissed by the priest and people at Mass), weighing altogether 10lb 5ozs, and a cross of silver and gold which weighed 4lb. Many gorgeous, or gaudy, vestments survived; one of black velvet had a deacon and sub-deacon of black silk; it was to be worn with blue buckled garters. Another vestment was of blue damask with an offertory of red velvet. Some vestments had imagery work embroidered in silk and gold. There was a cope of blue satin of Bruges, decorated with flowers.

A satin cloth of green and red covered the high altar, there was another altar cloth of white damask with panes of tinsel, and another of red silk bearing a cross, with imagery work. Music was provided by a pair of organs. There were four bells to summon worshippers to church, and the sacring bell, (a small bell rung during the service of Mass) which was no longer used. The church clock tolled the hours, striking sonorously on the great bell which weighed twenty-two hundredweight. Even £7 in cash remained safe within the church.

Notes to Chapter One

1. *Cal. Inq. P.M.* V12, Cal. Pat. 22 Dec 1347
2. DL 29.42.825
3. DL 43.7.5
4. JUST 1.540.19
5. VCH Middx 5, 237
6. J.Z. Titow *English rural society, 1200–1360* p. 33 Allen + Unwin 1969
7. DL 43.7.1
8. DL 43.7.2
9. SC 6.915.26
10. DL 43.7.3
11. *Val. of Norw.*, ed. Lunt 359 *Tax Eccl* (Rec. Comm.) 17
12. Robinson. *Enfield* 1, 293
13. Cal. Inq. V10, 118
14. T. A. Plucknett, *Concise history of common law*, 5th ed. p. 118–121.
15. JUST 1.540.18
16. JUST 1.540
17. JUST 1.536
18. JUST 1.540.18
19. JUST 1.536
20. JUST 1.536.8

21. JUST 1.540.19
22. JUST 1.544.69v.
23. *Curia Regis Rolls* Vol.13, 986
24. JUST 1.544.61v.
25. JUST 3. 36.2.4
26. JUST 1.544.61
27. JUST 1.544.61v.
28. *ibid.*
29. JUST 3.42.2.32
30. KB 9.66.23
31. E40.2198
32. D. O. Pam. *The Hungry Years.* pp. 14–17 EHHS No 42
33. JUST 1.544.68v.
34. JUST 1.540.19
35. JUST 3.40.2.14, 15v.
36. Cal. Pat. 17 Nov. and 13 Dec. 1365, 13 Feb 1369, 8 Sep 1373
37. Hatfield 291.561, 478, 375, 294, 225, 100, 126, etc.
38. J. G. L. Burnby and M. Parker. *The Navigation of the River Lee 1190–1790,* p. 3
     EHHS No 36
39. JUST 1.544.62
40. Act 9 Henry VI c.5
41. Burnby and Parker. *Navigation of the River Lee.* p. 4
42. C 134.102.2
43. C 135.35.21
44. JUST 3.35.B.24
45. *Cal. Charter Rolls.* 1226–1257, 1337
46. JUST 1.536.1
47. C 133.54.3
48. C 135.170.63
49. C 134.36.7
50. C 135.35.21
51. C 135.170.63
52. Largely based on an unpublished paper by Dr David Avery
53. SC6.1146.20, C135.48.2, DL43.7.1
54. JUST 1.544.63
55. JUST 1.544.38v.
56. JUST 1.536.2r
57. SC6.1146.20, C135.48.2
58. DL43.7.1
59. Tottenham Manor Rolls MR 14 Mem. 6a.
60. DL 43.7.1
61. SC6.915.26
62. *ibid*
63. DL 29.42.825
64. DL 29.1010.23
65.   CP Genl 67.18
66. Christopher Taylor. *Village and Farmstead.* p 104–5.
67. DL 43.7.5, J.Z. Titow *English Rural Society* p.72
68. C 133.54.3
69. C 133.92.8.2
70. J. R. Maddicott *The English Peasantry and the Demands of the Crown 1294–1341* in
     Past and Present Suppt 1 1975, JUST 3.40.2.15v.
71. JUST 3.40.2.29.
72. JUST 3.40.2.33v.
73. JUST 3.40.2.38

74. JUST 3.40.2.12
75. JUST 3.41.1
76. SC6.1146.20
77. JUST 3.43.2.40
78. JUST 3.43.2
79. JUST 3.42.1.22
80. J. R. Maddicott *op cit* E 179.141.5
81. E 179.141.10
82. A. R. Bridbury. *Before the Black Death* in *Econ. Hist Rev.* XXX, 3, p. 398.
83. Maddicott *op cit* p. 51
84. DL 43.7.1
85. Tottenham Manor Rolls
86. C 135.104.4
87. C 135.95.14
88. C 135.170.23
89. C 135.177.8.3, C 134.26.7
90. C 135.225.9.19
91. E 179.141.21
92. *Cal. Pat. Rolls.* 25 June 1351
93. *ibid.* 6 July 1351
94. E. King *England 1175–1425* p. 61 *Rot. Parl.* V3.
95. PROB 11.9.12
96. PROB 11.28.23
97. W. Robinson. *History of Enfield* 1823 Vol.2 p. 161
98. Guildhall 9171.5.324
99. Guildhall 9171.6.145v
100. Guildhall 9171.9.64
101. G. H. Hodson and E. Ford *A History of Enfield* 1873 p 132
102. Guildhall 9171.8.229
103. Guildhall 9171.8.83v
104. PROB 11.25.36
105. PROB 11.21.28
106. Hodson & Ford. *Enfield.* pp. 133/4.
107. E 301.34.185
108. PROB 11.12.5
109. PROB 11.25.36
110. E 315.498.23 *Cal. Rutland MS* V.4 p. 265, 269

Chapter Two

Tudor Enfield

1. Yeomen and Tradesmen

Early death and quick remarriage in the sixteenth century often created families made up of the offspring of a number of unions each of which had ended by the death of one of the partners. When Thomas Brown married Alice Hunsdon in Enfield church, she brought with her the five children of her first marriage. He was accompanied by Margaret, the daughter of his previous marriage. Their wedded life was ended by his death in April 1503. He gave by his will,[1] written not long before he died, all his goods, after his debts had been paid, to Alice his wife. She should also have, for as long as she lived, all his lands and houses in Enfield but after her death his own daughter would inherit. It must have been a considerable property for Thomas Brown appears to have been a man of substance. Though humble enough to request burial in the churchyard, he left 13s 4d (one mark) to St Andrews Church, a goodly sum in 1503 and one which could have secured for him a place in the nave. He also left to Margaret 'A girdle of silk harnessed with silver and a chest which was sometime her mother's', a brass pot, a brass pan, 'a half garnish' of pewter vessel, a mattress, a bolster, a pair of blankets, a pair of sheets, a coverlet and canopy for a bed, with other household stuff, and 'a cow and a sow such as my wife and I be (agreed) upon'. He had provided something too for the five Hunsdon children, to John two horses with their halters and panniers (John was perhaps engaged in the malt trade), to William a bullock, and to both of them and the three girls such household goods as their mother might best spare.

Alice, a widow once more, married John Cacher but within four years he too was dead. He had obviously expected that she would find herself a fourth partner, for he left to his son John[2] 'The house that I wove in, after my wife be married', but as long as she remained a widow she could hold on to the property. The household, at the time of John Cacher's death in 1508, consisted of John's own two sons by a previous marriage, two of his wife's daughters Margaret and Isabel Hunsdon, and Margaret Brown the daughter of Alice's second husband. Yet not one of this assortment was neglected by the kindly John. He left 20s and a 'down bullock' to Margaret Hunsdon, a cow for Isabel Hunsdon, and 20s to Margaret Brown.

Alice was however, by now, in a position to decline any but the best offers. Seventeen years later she was still a widow,[3] and retained most of the property. Cacher's two sons were living together, probably unmarried, and assessed that year on goods to the value of only 40s. They had been under age at the time of their father's death and that, and their stepmother's longevity, had sadly diminished their prospects.

The local parish registers, which survive in Enfield from 1550, indicate that both men and women commonly remarried within months, even weeks following the death of a spouse. Men, when there were sons, usually provided for their widows only until the heir came of age, or until the widow remarried. An examination of fifty-three wills written by men who lived in the parishes of Tottenham, Edmonton and Enfield, between 1450 and 1500, shows that twenty-six had no sons or daughters living, and among the remaining twenty-seven only eleven had sons who were old enough to take over the property.

William Wilson, asked that he be buried in the Church of St Andrew 'as nighe unto my stool or seat as may be'. He took great care when making his will in 1542,[4] to secure the interests of all his sons. William, his eldest, lived at home, though he was married and had children. He had been working for his parents for more than sixteen years. He had been assessed in 1525 on a wage, not above average in the village, of 30s a year, though his father was one of the wealthiest men in the parish, and assessed on goods to the value of £20.[5] William by this will was given all his father's uncollected debts except 9s in the hands of a brewer (probably for malt). From his legacy he was to pay to his brothers Thomas, great John and 'lyttell' John, on the first anniversary of his father's death, 20s apiece, then at every quarter following a further 20s, until they had each received a total of £7. He was also to have half the house in which he now dwelt, agreeing with his mother which half she should have. The old man did not treat the grandchildren with a like impartiality. He left to each of them 6s 8d, but to Johanne Wilson he left 53s 4d, and it was a condition of the will that Thomas her father should give her a lamb each year, and keep and feed them (and any lambs born of them) for her until she married. Johanne was obviously grandfather's favourite.

Little John too was to receive further, 'the great table and the form that standeth by (it)', after the death of his mother, 'and my cow with a bell now, and when he doth marry, a feather-bed, two pairs of sheets, and one blanket'. The 1546 subsidy roll,[6] some four years later, shows that the widow was still living and holding the largest share of the property. She was then assessed at £20, Thomas was assessed at £15 and William, still living in the same house as his mother, at only £10. The two Johns were not assessed.

The wealthy widow was the most privileged among women whose claims in other circumstances were usually subordinated to those of their brothers. Thus Abraham Hunt, a tanner, who wrote his will in 1592,[7] divided his considerable property equally among his five daughters but made a proviso that if Barbara his wife should be with male child at the time of his death, the new-born boy would be the sole heir. The girls would then receive only £4 apiece when they reached the age of twenty-one, or earlier if they married.

Most Enfield tradesmen also farmed. John Hunsdon, the tanner, who died in 1476,[8] held only three or four acres in the common fields, yet he owned six oxen, two carts, a plough and horses, and was wealthy enough to possess ten silver spoons. Though he conformed to the beliefs of his time in leaving 3s to the various altars in Enfield church, he provided twice that amount (6s 8d) for the repair of the road between his house and the well. John Hunsdon's tan-house remained in his family and thirty years later it passed from another John Hunsdon to John Hunsdon his youngest son.[9] The choice of names within the family suggests that the Hunsdons were singularly unimaginative. This John Hunsdon, the son of John

Hunsdon, named his first born John, his second William and his third Edmund, but by this time he had exhausted his repertoire and his last born was another John. In fact no fewer than six John Hunsdons paid the 1525 subsidy in Enfield. This branch of the family lived at Church House, they also held the tan-house and another house called Bowtells.

William Garrard the fuller, who died in 1517,[10] farmed only on a small scale. He held three acres of meadow in the marsh, three acres of arable in the common fields, two closes at Sewardstone, and a croft at 'Trolls' bridge. His property consisted of the house in South Street, probably standing next to the fulling mill, another at Green Street, and a third on Enfield Green. All went to his widow to hold as long as she lived. She was to provide a dowry of 40s to each of their four daughters, and after her death the estate would be divided equally between them.

A detailed survey of the parish of Enfield was carried out in 1572 by Edmund Twynho, surveyor to the Duchy of Lancaster. He listed every house and cottage along the village streets, every strip of meadow in the common marsh. Every close of pasture and every orchard was measured and set down with its abutments. Though no map to accompany the survey has survived, it is sufficiently detailed to enable the local historian to follow the footsteps of the surveyor around the Elizabethan parish of Enfield.

2. Enfield Green

The 'old part of Enfield', as Edmund Alcock called it when he wrote his will in 1594,[11] lay around Enfield Green. There, stretching away to the west were the woodlands of Old Park and Enfield Chase. The line where the town ended and the Chase began is, even today, clearly delineated by the line of Gentlemans Row, Nunns Road, Chase Side Crescent, the front of St Michael's Hospital, and Batley Road. The park gate lay across what is now called Church Street at the junction with Gentlemans Row. A traveller in 1572,[12] coming from Barnet, would have passed the park gate and, looking about him, would have seen, on his right, five cottages. Three more lay on the left hand side of the road; these latter all belonged to Roger Grave the carpenter, and each had a small garden and an orchard. Beside them stood a substantial house where Robert Hill lived, with a close of one acre, and a garden and orchard.

Dolmans bridge carried the road over a little stream which widened here to form a pond (about where the post office now stands), and the traveller came upon the village green. The Manor House lay on the right; its grounds extended over seven acres in which were barns, stables, orchards and gardens, and a timber croft. The house, built on an 'E' shaped ground plan, faced south with its back turned towards the village green.[13] John Taylor lived there. In the year 1572 he was fifty-four years of age, and had held the manor for twenty-six years, since the death of his father. He had seen service as a young man in King Henry's wars in France, and in the navy. Since 1559 he had held the office of receiver of the Duchy of Lancaster revenues in the Home Counties but somehow, 'through ill-credit, many children, and great sickness', he had fallen into debt.[14] Things became so bad by 1582 that he was forced to sell the profitable lease of the manor to Henry Middlemore, with twenty-five years yet to run. A debt of £580 was owing to the Queen and this was taken over by Middlemore to be paid off yearly at a hundred marks (£66.66) a year. The whole transaction cost Middlemore £1,318 and this included £6 13s 4d paid for the goodwill of Mrs Taylor.

The estate consisted of the Manor House ('The Palace') and 442½ acres: 140 acres were leased to tenants whose leases had some eight or nine years yet to run, but whose rents were, by that time, well below the market rate. The whole of the Tudor period was one of steady inflation which bore very hard on the solvency of those landlords whose tenants held land and houses on long leases. These same long leases may have been a contributory factor to the financial downfall of the Taylors. There were eighty acres of pasture, ninety-two acres of meadow, and 270 acres of arable. Most of the arable lay in three common fields, eighty acres in Churchbury field, eighty acres in Southbury field, and sixty acres in Windmill field.

Henry Middlemore, having settled with old John Taylor, at once attempted to sell the property to Lord Burghley. 'Not that I dislike my bargain', he wrote, 'for no man else shall buy it of me for a great deal more money'. He offered it for £682, which was much less, he claimed, than he had paid. But he very much desired to cherish and retain Lord Burghley's good favour, and the estate, he thought, lying so close to Theobalds, might prove useful to his Lordship. Lord Burghley already owned a great deal of land, mostly coppice wood, in the area of Southgate and Winchmore Hill.

Middlemore begged an immediate answer, for he had recently sent down to some fairs to buy cattle to stock the farm. He apologised for not attending upon Lord Burghley in person, but he had recently been forced to wait so many hours to see his Lordship that he had taken an extreme cold; it was this that now prevented his attendance in person.[15] Lord Burghley apparently declined his offer, and Middlemore took up residence on Enfield Green. Henry Middlemore lived always on the verge of court life. He was cousin to Arthur Throgmorton and on many occasions acted as his aide and go-between. Local legend has so often associated the 'Palace' with Queen Elizabeth, that the author is relieved to be able to confirm, for those who delight in such matters, that she did visit the house, at least on one occasion. It was early August 1587, and she stayed with Henry Middlemore.[16]

Elizabeth, Henry's widow, was remarried to Sir Vincent Skynner (c.1595) and, by some arrangement, the Manor House and demesne were transferred to him. Robert Middlemore, Henry's son, was then a minor. Skynner magnanimously gave him and his sisters 'lodging and diet in his house', as he called it. Even after Robert married he continued to be a lodger in what had been his father's property, and this situation lasted the best part of twenty years. Skynner claimed that Henry's daughters had been left unprovided, and that he, with great bounty, had bestowed sums amounting to £1,000 on their preferment. He asserted that he had laid out money on repairs to the building and on replanting the orchard but, instead of showing due appreciation, Robert brought an action for debt in the Court of Kings Bench, whereupon the goods and the plate in the house were seized. Skynner computed that its value must amount to £2,000, but it was assessed in the inventory at only £190 19s 8d.

The lease of the property was returned to Robert and he was granted a new lease for sixty years in May 1611. Robert and Dorothy his wife, who died in 1610, are commemorated by a marble monument in the south chancel chapel in St Andrews Church. A reversion of this sixty year lease was subsequently acquired by the City of London who sold it, in February 1630, to Nicholas Rainton (later

The Manor House on Enfield Green, 1778.

Sir Nicholas) for £866, he paid £100 in cash and the remainder went to offset debts due to him from the City. The house and gardens in 1637 were occupied by Sir Thomas Trevor, one of the barons of the Exchequer. The freehold of the house seems to have been transferred to Nicholas Rainton (the great-nephew of Sir Nicholas) following the execution of King Charles in 1649.

Beyond the Manor House the traveller would have passed two cottages belonging to John White, with small gardens, or yards, at the rear. The next house was the 'George', an old inn even then. Before the Reformation it had belonged to St Leonards Church in Shoreditch. It was described in 1572, as having an upper storey and a cellar, and it was worth 40s a year.[17] The owner was William Budder, then a lad attending the Grammar School, 'to learn to write and read'; that at least was what had been required by his father's will. The father, William Budder, a yeoman, had died two years previously. His property had been substantial; he anticipated more than £30 from the sale of two of his houses, and left £100 for the boy in the hands of his godfather, as well as three silver goblets, twelve silver spoons, and a silver salt. All this was to be held for him until he came of age. His father's will provided that when the boy finished his schooling he was to be apprenticed to some trade. The widow Alice also received £100, and much silver. His cows were distributed among his many relatives and gifts of money among his numerous godchildren. He held land in Edmonton as well as in Enfield and gave to the poor in each parish 13s 4d. He left £10 to a maid servant, to be paid to her on the day of her marriage, but only on condition that she did not marry Christopher Muffet, formerly his servant. His sympathy encompassed a great-nephew, Thomas Budder, a lame boy, who should have a cow and, if his own son was to die, the cripple lad was to have his house at Little Woodside (ie. Chase Side).[18]

William Lowen, a keeper on the Chase, owned the adjoining cottage, which stood next to a cottage plot, garden, and an orchard, half an acre in all, belonging to Robert Hayes, a gentleman, who held various offices under the Duchy of Lancaster, and who had forty acres in Enfield, as well as a manor in Gloucestershire. In the last property on the south side of Enfield Green lived the wealthy Robert Deicrowe. This house, called Ansycles, stood in four acres of ground, with a garden, an orchard and a fish pond. It survived until its demolition in 1908, during a road widening to allow electric trams to turn the corner from London Road into the Town. Early twentieth century photographs show it crouched half concealed behind late nineteenth century shops.

On the east side of the green, after crossing the London way to Edmonton, stood three cottages separated by a pond from another cottage. Bury Lane (now Southbury Road) led eastward across the fields. On the north side of the green were two cottages and a number of garden plots where dwellings had formerly been. Two large houses occupied the remainder of the north side of Enfield Green. Nineteenth century photographs show them either to have been rebuilt or modernised by the addition of Georgian fronts. The first was owned by John Wilford, and the second by the same William Lowen who owned the cottage on the opposite side of the green. The frontage of what was later the market square was occupied by the house of Thomas Garlicke, a Londoner and a skinner by trade. It was called the Vyne, and behind it lay the earlier market place. Further west towards the Chase there was a house, a cottage and a barn, and a dwelling house which had formerly been an ox-house; and at Dolmans bridge, by the stream, stood the cottage called Dolmans, in half an acre of land.

St Andrews Church must have appeared in 1572 much as it is shown in the

Ansycles, half hidden behind Victorian shops at the junction of London Road and the Town.

Ansycles, demolition of shops and east gable.

The monument to Robert Deicrowe by whose will the twelve poorest people in the parish were to have a penny loaf each Sunday for ever.

print of 1793 (p 43) where it stands sunlit on the north side of the green. It was, as Professor Pevsner subsequently described it, 'a town church, not a village church'. Great changes were begun in the Church in this country in the late 1530s, coinciding with the rise to power of Thomas Cromwell. He was the driving force behind the publication of English versions of the Bible; Coverdale's in 1535, the Mathew Bible in 1537, and the Great Bible in 1539. Cromwell's injunction had gone out in 1536 ordering that the Bible in English should be displayed in the choir of every parish church. Such changes were resisted by many parish priests.

Dr Thomas Thompson, a master of St Johns College Cambridge, who had been appointed vicar of St Andrews in 1504, was getting old. He was adamantly opposed to such new-fangled reform, and persecuted the Bible readers in his parish. He called the reading of God's word 'a new learning', and 'a green learning that will fade away'. It was said that he had called the English Bible, 'the book of Arthur Cobler', and its readers he had labelled 'heretics'. He had sent the constable to John Hamon because he was reading the gospels aloud in English. The constable broke-up the reading. 'This must be left' he ordered, 'for I am sent by the honest men of this parish to warn you to leave your reading, for you cause others to hear you; it were better that they prayed on their beads than thus to come about you'.

When John Hamon came to church on Easter day 1539 the learned vicar, having heard his confession, revealed it to others, warning them to avoid Hamon. 'I have read all the heretics', he told them 'yet he passes them all; therefore leave his company'. Hamon went on to complain, in a petition to Thomas Cromwell in 1539, that he was hated because he had bidden the vicar to erase the Pope's name from all church books and had urged him to preach against the Pope's usurped

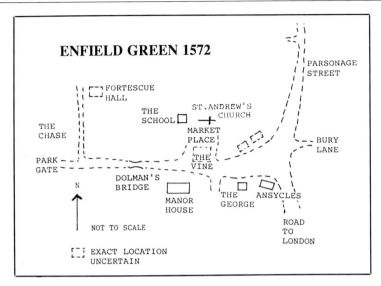

power. Dr Thompson, forced on the defensive by these attacks, had claimed that it was not part of his duty to preach against the Pope but of those that preached the quarter sermons. Hamon asked Cromwell to call Dr Thompson and the other parish priests before him to enquire into these matters.[19]

When Hamon appealed to Cromwell, he was fighting for a Lutheran orientated religious radicalism which already was a lost cause for the rest of Henry VIII's reign. In the following year Cromwell was executed and the conservative faction at court, led by Norfolk and Gardiner was basking in the King's favour. In 1543, Henry induced Parliament to pass the Act for the Advancement of True Religion which forbade the reading of the Bible by all except nobles, gentry, clergy, and substantial merchants.

In 1539 an Act of Parliament had completed the process of the dissolution of the monasteries. The churches of Edmonton and Enfield which had formerly belonged to Walden Abbey, were now granted to Thomas Lord Audley of Walden, but on his death in 1544 both churches reverted to the Crown. The King then presented Enfield church to Trinity College Cambridge. Thomas Thompson died in 1540; many prayers were offered for the salvation of his soul. He was followed at Enfield by Dr Henry Lockwood who, like his predecessor, was a master of St John's College Cambridge.[20]

The vicar in 1572 was Richard Clapham who had been appointed incumbent in 1557, during the reign of Queen Mary. He was by no means a poor man for, as well as his vicarage, he owned two cottages and a tenement in Parsonage Street (i.e. Silver Street). When he died in 1575, he left £20 for the poor in Enfield. No wife is mentioned in his will.[21] He lies buried in the chancel.

Leonard Chambers succeeded as vicar in 1579 and from the first, he came into conflict with his congregation. The conflict concerned the Sunday meat market, held at the church gate before divine service every Sunday morning. This was claimed to be 'an old and ancient usage'; it was one which may have been common in the district, for in Edmonton there had also been a Sunday meat market 'at the churchyard door', but that had ceased by 1560.[22] Chambers, from the very first, urged on by his belligerent minister, (probably a curate,) Leonard Thickpenny,

Two tenements on the north side of Enfield Green were noted in the 1572 survey. The Rummer (barrels outside) which separates them, originated in the seventeenth century. The large building beyond the Vestry House was formerly the Greyhound Inn.

engaged himself to abolish the Sunday meat market. He invited to Enfield on 13 October 1583, in support of his campaign, Dr Andrew Perne, master of Peterhouse, who threatened 'the laws of the realm against the market', and called upon Robert Wroth of Durants Arbour, the most powerful of the local magnates and a justice of peace, to see the law executed.

Wroth appears to have played a double game in this matter and, as Leonard Chambers bitterly related, 'gave out great speeches but nothing done'. Two years later, the struggle continuing, came Dr Roger Goad[23] of Kings College Cambridge, to plead and threaten for the cessation of the market, and once again Robert Wroth, 'did forbid the butchers with speeches to fear them', as did the churchwardens, with equal sincerity. Archbishop Whitgift himself intervened to condemn the 'profane market' and John Aylmer, Bishop of London, had sent Dr Stanley to Enfield in an endeavour to suppress the market. Sir Owen Hopton, a member of the High Commission, had prevented a butcher from Broxbourne coming to set up his stalls.

Robert Wroth, though he was a strongly protestant member in Parliament, strenuously supported the market. It would appear that his beliefs as a sabbatarian were outweighed by his dislike for the vicar and his friends. When an attempt was made to suppress the market on 11 December 1584, he was outspoken in his demand that it must continue. It was lawful by custom he asserted, and the parish had a profit thereby. Further it was lawful by God's word, and that he would defend against Chambers or any other divine. The vicar responded by citing both the commands of the Archbishop, and the commandments of the Almighty, yet the market continued.

At length Lord Burghley became involved, as he so often did in matters of apparent insignificance. At his summons the vicar hurried to Durants on 5 June 1585, there Wroth intercepted him in the outer courtyard as he entered demanding that he relent towards the market, but the vicar stood his ground calling upon Robert Wroth 'to continue that man he was at the sessions of the last Parliament'.[24]

The climax of the matter came a week later when, on Sunday morning early,

St Andrews Church 1793, looking much as it did in the reign of Queen Elizabeth I.

there came from Tottenham to the Enfield market a butcher, bringing an ox ready-dressed, and there laid out his victuals on the stall. Wroth and all the other magistrates saw him and took no action to prevent him. It was then that the minister Leonard Thickpenny, incited, in the opinion of the parishioners, by the vicar, 'in a very outrageous manner, very evil-beseeming a man of the Church and one of his calling, in a madding mood, most ruffian-like', violently pulled from the butcher most part of his meat and cast it upon the ground, 'most pitiful to behold'. Yet not contented with this outrage, and before the eyes of the butcher's shocked, hungry and disappointed customers, he threatened that he would kill the butcher if he were hanged for it within half an hour after he had done it.

The resentment of the parish was expressed in a long petition to Lord Burghley who was bailiff and steward of the manor. It was accompanied by a list of names of each of the heads of the 387 households in Enfield and it was sent into every quarter so that each man might indicate his approval (or his dissent) by making his usual mark or attempting a signature. All but nine parishoners gave their support. Turning the table on the vicar, they petitioned that their sabbaths should be respected. They complained that each Sunday they had 'quarrellings and brawl-ings', and that Leonard Chambers and Leonard Thickpenny were the cause of it all, so that every time they met together in church to serve their God they longed to be safe at home. It was their earnest desire that they might have ministers who were more quiet and discreet, 'whereby they might hear both divine service and preaching according to Her Majesty's injunctions'.[25]

The schoolhouse, in 1572, stood within an orchard of some two acres at the west end of the church. It was not the present building and was soon to be pulled down and rebuilt on the scale of which the parish could be proud. The school derived from a chantry established by the will of Agnes Myddleton, written on 2 May 1462. She left an estate called Poynetts in Hadleigh, Thundersley and South Benfleet, Essex, to set up this chantry in the north chancel chapel of St Andrews Church, then known as the chapel of Our Lady. Her executors were to appoint a priest to pray for the salvation of her soul, for the souls of her father and mother, and of her four husbands, Robert Blossom, John Hulfield, William Daubeney, and Charles Myddleton.[26]

Poynetts had originally belonged to Robert Blossom, the first of the four, and his name was adopted by the chantry when it came to be established. After Robert's death in 1427, the estate had been unsuccessfully claimed by his cousin John Blossom; thus the seed which flowered into the Enfield Grammar School, was all but lost before it germinated.[27] The widow, Agnes Blossom, married John Hulfield, an Enfield gentleman, who died in 1455.[28] Following his death she married William Daubeney, and finally, in 1457 Charles Myddleton.[29]

Her executors made over the estate in 1471 to the vicar of Enfield, Edmund Causton, and twelve trustees were appointed.[30] They were substantial tenants of the parish, men like John Hunsdon the elder, a wealthy maltman whose will was concerned as much with the welfare of his parish, as with the salvation of his soul. He left forty marks (£26 13s 4d) for the repair of the road between his house and the 'herse' (the frame used for drying skins) and £5 towards the repair and maintenance of Mill Marsh bridge.[31] Another of the trustees was Thomas Doo, a husbandman, whose interest in the welfare of the community was indicated by his gift of five marks to make a treasure house for the safe-keeping of the valuables in the parish church.[32] Then there was William Cordell, a maltman, and a man of standing in the village, having many godchildren.[33] Thus the chantry funds were, from the very first, controlled by independently minded laymen.

A further twenty-eight trustees were appointed in 1491.[34] They included four of Enfield's properous maltmen, with William Garrard a fuller, William Okburn a mercer, Walter West a weaver, and John Hunsdon a tanner. The families of many of these trustees had played, and were to play, leading roles in parish affairs over many generations. Thus descendants of the Cordells, Hunsdons and Kings, men named in the deed of 1491, were cousins to one William Garrett[35] who, a hundred years later, gave £50 towards the rebuilding of the school; and there were Cordells and Hunsdons among trustees appointed in 1598.[36] Other names too occur, active over centuries in the business of the parish. In many cases they recur from the fifteenth into the nineteenth century, names such as Wyberd, Curle, Curtis, Loft, Wodham, Aylward and, in every other parish document, the Cordells and the Hunsdons.

Further deeds appointing trustees were made on 16 December 1505 and on 12 February 1506; both bear the same fifty-five names.[37] A school was not mentioned in either of these deeds, yet it had certainly been established before the Chantries Act of 1547, and the income from the Poynetts estate was being used for its support. It seems likely that a school was set up soon after the deed of 1506. The earliest reference to it among Enfield wills which I have examined, is in that of John Cacher[38] in 1508. Under its terms he left fifty shillings to his brother Thomas to maintain John's son, Edward 'at the school'. John Cacher had been recently appointed a trustee.

A further possible reference to the school occurs in the will of William Potter, written in 1531[39] It records a debt of £10 which was owed to him by Richard Tattershall of St Albans. The money, when repaid, he said, should be bestowed upon his son Simon 'to keep him to school to his learning'. This same Simon Potter, later to rank as a gentleman, became the first named trustee when new appointments were made in 1558.

At the sale of the Poynetts estate in 1548, by the Court of Augmentations (under the Chantries Act of 1547), the churchwardens and others of the town of Enfield were prepared to swear upon oath, twice over, that the profits from this estate were used to find one priest, 'commonly called the chantry priest, who was given for his salary, for helping in the choir, and teaching the children, the sum of £6'. The yearly value of Poynetts was assessed at £10, and it was sold for £200,[40] but in the following year the money was returned to the purchasers, because it appeared to the chancellor of the Court of Augmentations that the Crown's claim was doubtful.[41] The Poynetts estate therefore was back in the hands of the parish within one year.

The chantry certificate states clearly that, although the estate had originally been given to support a chantry, it was in 1547 used to maintain the brotherhood priest of the Brotherhood of Our Lady at Enfield (see above p 29). John Bridgeman was the Brotherhood priest,[42] presumably therefore he was the schoolmaster. He had been employed by the Brotherhood at least since 1517, when he appeared as a witness to the will of John Hunsdon,[43] a role he was frequently called upon to fulfil, being present by the death bed both to administer extreme unction and, being literate, to write the will for the dying man. He was described consistently in such wills as 'my ghostly father' (ie father confessor). Bridgeman seems to have died about 1547.[44]

The parishioners of Enfield were lucky to get their endowment back for the school. The Act which brought about the dissolution of chantries stated that all schools which were legally part of chantry foundations were to be given continuation certificates and this legal existence was normally taken to mean that provision was made specifically for the school in the will that set the chantry up, which was not the case in the will of Agnes Myddleton.

The school was spoken of again in the will of the wealthy Enfield widow, Elizabeth Wood, in 1553[45]. She asked that her son Edward should keep Robert Parry's son at school 'until he can write and cast accounts and then to bind him apprentice to some good occupation'. She provided that if her son should refuse, then the duty was to fall upon her cousin Simon Potter who, as mentioned above, became the first named trustee appointed to govern the school in 1558.

The objectives of the trust were first set out following the appointment of new trustees in 1557.[46] After the maintenance of the buildings on the estate, the rents should be used on repairs to the school building in Enfield, and for the salary of a schoolmaster 'to teach grammar (ie Latin grammar) in the parish of Enfield to the children of the parishioners and inhabitants . . . for the better instruction and education of the children in the knowledge of good learning'.

In the following year, on 25 May 1558, six months before the end of Queen Mary's reign, at the time when Simon Potter, gentleman, was added to the list of trustees, a more detailed schedule of objectives was set forth.[47] The trustees were to employ a schoolmaster to 'teach, within the town of Enfield the children of the poor inhabitants of the parish, to know and read their alphabet letters, to read Latin and English, to understand grammar, and to write their Latins according to the use and trade of grammar schools'. The master was to be paid £6 13s 4d a year, and was to be a sufficient and able man of learning. The salary offered however, could hardly have been expected to attract a scholar. The subsequent

The school house, completed by 1597. Uvedale House was built onto the north end of the school in the early eighteenth century.

history of the school shows that the schoolmasters were forced to augment their salaries by taking private pupils, both as boarders and as day scholars. The more successful the master, the more the private school preponderated over the grammar school. Out of this situation conflict arose between trustees and schoolmasters through which the rich endowment was wasted away.

The schoolhouse was first mentioned in 1557 and was listed in the 1572 survey of Enfield. Moves to replace it with something more imposing were begun by William Garrett who, in 1586, left £50 'towards the building of a schoolhouse in Enfield, where I was born',[48] and soon afterwards work was begun. It stands today tall and substantial in red brick. Over £400 had been spent on its construction by 1593[49] and yet it remained unfinished. However a deed of 1598 speaks of the schoolhouse, 'now of late new-built',[50] thus it would seem to have been completed by that year.

Four sixteenth century schoolmasters were named in episcopal visitations; in 1580 John Hewes, 1589 John Young, 1592 Scott, and in 1598 John Preston.[51] The schoolmaster's house (probably that originally known as Prounces or Provinces) stood next to the school. The new trustees, appointed in 1598, planned to raise standards when they appointed John Preston both as schoolmaster and as second curate, in order that this might bring his salary to a more respectable level.[52] The powers of the trustees were extended to enable them to raise the master's pay (it remained still the same £6 13s 4d paid in 1471) at such times as the lease of Poynetts farm came to be renewed. But though John Preston received a further forty shillings a year in 1599, by the will of Roger Graves[53] who had been a trustee, the official remuneration remained absurdly low.

Fortescue Hall, in what is now Gentlemans Row. The house was demolished in 1816.

3. Chase Side to Whitewebbs

Facing westward across the Chase, along the line which we now call Gentleman's Row, there stood in 1572 four houses and one cottage. The first, probably the present Little Park, was owned by Master Fortescue. It had a garden and an orchard of one acre. The next was owned by Thomas Clarke and Richard Wright with two and a half acres attached. To the north stood a house belonging to Sir Thomas Wroth, and beyond was Fortescue Hall with a garden, orchard, and a close of three acres. This house was pulled down in 1816 (according to Robinson) and the materials sold. The print (above) shows the mansion after the casement windows had been replaced about 1780 by Captain Andrew Riddell. Robinson says that it had never been considered a good house, for the rooms, though numerous, had low ceilings.

There were a number of settlements spread out close to the eastern edge of Enfield Chase. Little Woodside lay along what is now Chase Side, north of the Parsonage Lane gate: it continued as far as the present Chase Side Crescent, and there were twelve dwellings. Further east Parsonage Street was the name of a group of dwellings on both sides of the present Silver Street and the southern end of Baker Street. The parsonage or Rectory House, at the corner of Parsonage Lane, was set in grounds of some six acres which stretched westward, almost to the edge of the Chase. This fine old mansion remained to grace the parish until it was destroyed in 1929. The rectory was held in 1572 by Trinity College Cambridge and was probably leased. Trinity College held land in Enfield as well as the entitlement to the greater tithe and the right to appoint the vicar who lived at the vicarage and was to receive the smaller tithe (see below p. 292). South of Parsonage Lane, in the present Silver Street, the vicar, Richard Clapham, had built a new cottage, one of three which he owned thereabouts, as well as the vicarage. Beyond

Enfield House (occasionally called Elsings) was a vast mansion which became a royal palace from the time of Henry VIII; it was abandoned by James I

the vicar's new cottage lay John Wilford's property, three cottages and a mansion house, then a tenement called Redlington (a house of that name still remains on the site). A few more cottages and gardens lay between Redlington and the vicarage, which survives, though it was much altered in the nineteenth century.

There were four cottages and two houses on the east side of Parsonage Street (Silver Street) between the village green and the Churchbury field gate (probably the present Churchbury Lane, Silver Street junction) then a cottage and the manor house of the manor of Worcesters. Beyond, to the north, were ten cottages, and a larger house called Coldharber which belonged to Robert Curtis.

Great Pipers and Little Pipers existed in 1572. A house called Little Pipers survives on the site in Clay Hill.

Joyce, Lady Tiptoft, from a brass in St Andrews Church.

Sir Thomas Lovell, who controlled the finances of the Crown under Henry VII and Henry VIII. Medallion by Torrigiani in Henry VII's chapel Westminster Abbey.

A little further on lay the hamlet of Baker Street, five tenements on the west side of the road, including a house called Forteys, held by Thomas Mayhewe, with two and a half acres, containing an orchard, garden and croft. There were nine tenements on the east side of the street, with a large house called Mortimers at the northern end.

A group of ten dwellings lay along the road leading down to Colebridge over Merryhills brook, near the present site of the Rose and Crown in Clay Hill; it was known as Bridge Street. On the north were Great Pipers and Little Pipers (a house of this name still exists there). On the other side of the road Cocker Lane led off to the south. This name persisted well into the present century when it was renamed Browning Road. West of the stream, the road became Clay Hill, and there were half a dozen cottages, including the tenement of Thomas Cordell, the brickmaker. At the beginning of the present Strayfield Road lay Moreshatch gate opening into Enfield Chase, with a further group of eleven tenements and cottages clustered around.

The hamlet of Whitewebbs, grouped around the present site of the King and Tinker, contained eight dwellings in all, excluding Whitewebbs House. This was not then where the present mansion stands, but lay to the north of Whitewebbs Lane.[54] Robert Huicke, physician to Henry VIII, Edward VI, and subsequently to Queen Elizabeth, had been granted the house by the Queen in 1570.

Romey Street was a group of eight dwellings along Whitewebbs Lane, near the junction with Bulls Cross. It included the Dairy House, which had originated as the dairy belonging to Sir Thomas Lovell's house at Elsings.

4. Elsings

The Queen's great house, Elsings (though it was usually called Enfield House after it had become the property of the Crown) lay above Maidens bridge (Forty Hill) on the south side of Maidens brook. It stood in 1572 somewhat neglected, though it had been maintained intermittently since the accession of Queen Elizabeth. Nevertheless, for much of the time, its ancient hall and splendid chambers were traversed only by servants. The house had once been filled with life and business. The sons of lords and gentlemen had received their education there in the household of Sir Thomas Lovell, many visitors came, and the vast expenditure brought prosperity to the townships in the neighbourhood.

The mansion had probably been rebuilt by John Tiptoft, the Earl of Worcester, whose father, Sir John Tiptoft, had acquired it with other Wroth property in Enfield and elsewhere in 1413, through his mother Agnes, daughter and heir of Sir John Wroth of Enfield. It came into the hands of Sir Thomas Lovell in 1508, through his wife Isabel. Lovell's likeness can be seen in Torrigiani's portrait medallion in Henry VII's chapel, Westminster Abbey, a hard-faced, formidable man of business. He dressed expensively, and almost exclusively in black. His gowns were of black velvet or satin, furred (lined) with martens' skins, or boge, and sometimes faced with black damask. His hats too were of black, and his tippets of black velvet. Lovell was a trusted servant of the crown, and both Henry VII, in 1497 and 1498, and Henry VIII stayed with him at Elsings. Henry VIII was there, for instance, in September 1509, and in January 1511. He left the Princess Mary in Lovell's care in 1518, when she was about two years old. On this occasion one of her servants was taken with a 'hot ague', and the King therefore ordered the child to be removed.[55]

The wealth of Sir Thomas was reflected in the size and grandeur of his establishment in Enfield. His chapel was served by six chaplains, and he had his own brewer and his own slaughterman. There were gardeners, a hunter, a warrener, a shepherd, a caterer, an usher, an organ player, and the schoolmaster John Smith, with nine or ten young gentlemen scholars in his charge. Among those serving in the household at the time of Sir Thomas's death in 1524 was one whose name, Lambert Simnel, will be familiar I believe to most of my readers. Many years earlier, in 1486–7, as a mere boy he had been used by the Yorkists as the figurehead for the first challenge they mounted against Henry VII. Their plan was to pass him off as the Earl of Warwick, son of the Duke of Clarence, although that young man was a prisoner in the Tower of London at that very time. In 1487 Lambert Simnel was crowned King Edward VI of England in the cathedral at Dublin with a diadem borrowed for the occasion from the head of a statue of the Virgin Mary. Supported by an army led by the Earl of Lincoln he was taken to England, but the Earl, his protector, was defeated at the battle of Stoke and the rebellion collapsed. Henry VII, with his usual sardonic humour mixed with shrewd calculation, instead of inflicting a barbarous traitor's death on the boy, employed him as a scullion in the royal kitchen from whence he eventually moved into the service of Sir Thomas Lovell. His name was not among the many who received gifts under the will of Sir Thomas, so perhaps he remained, even then, forgotten but not forgiven.

The profusion of Lovell's purchases brought prosperity to many in the village. Isabel Monk, widow, supplied a hundred and forty quarters of oats for £15 6s 8d and straw to the value of 36s. William Wodham, an Enfield wheelwright, for

Enfield Archaeological Society investigates the site of Enfield House, 1963–66.

making two pairs of wheels, six axle-trees and cart-ladders, was paid 30s 6d. John Bull, the blacksmith, received 40s 4d for the iron work on the carts. Seventy-two kyderkyns of ale were sent by Margery Penley of Cheshunt, the wife of an ale-brewer there. During the first seven months of the year 1524, her bill amounted to £5 8s. The local sawyer sawed 350 planks, and an Enfield tile-maker made and delivered 10,500 roof tiles, and 850 paving tiles. Timber was cut and carried to Elsings by Simon Lowen of Cuffley for 29s 11d. William Curtis, maltman, was paid £35 for 140 quarters of malt which he purchased at Westmill. William Bernerts, for charcoal, was paid £5. Andrew Wyston, another local smith, shod horses for Sir Thomas and repaired the water mill by Maidens bridge. John Watson the harness maker was paid 11s 8d, and the local cooper made good the great vats in the brewery. Maude Sewell of Enfield, a widow and poulterer, was paid £2 10s 9d for wild fowl. John Clare, another local poulterer, provided twenty capons 9s 9d, six dozen chickens 8s, and five hundred eggs for 5s. Thomas Smith delivered a hundred rabbits for 18s. Richard Marche, the yeoman of the wardrobe, was responsible for the clothing of the young gentlemen. John Smith the schoolmaster taught them to write and provided the penknives to sharpen their pens.

When necessary, purchases were brought from further afield, forty wethers in Smithfield, and eight from Westmill in Hertfordshire. Fresh fish and spices were bought in London, nails from Ryall in Lincolnshire, oxen from Warwickshire, and pikes from Cambridge.[56] Sir Thomas died at Elsings on 25 May 1524 at eight o'clock at night.

Elsings had two lodges, the old lodge, and the porters' lodge. The house was fortified, though not too seriously, one chamber on the top floor was described at 'next to the wards', another as 'in the round tower' and the place was surrounded by a moat. The entrance was over a wooden bridge and through a gatehouse, three storeys high. The hall was plainly furnished; it had five plank tables, and five old forms, a plain chair and a plain cupboard. There were two parlours, the great parlour and the dining parlour. The great parlour was probably used by the officers of the household. The tapestries were old, 140 sticks square (over a hundred square yards) 'broken sore' and there were carpets, tables, cupboards and forms, but the entire contents were valued at less than £4.

The dining parlour was more elaborately furnished. There were tapestries 200 sticks square (some 150 square yards) decorated with beasts and imagery. It had an English carpet, five yards long, curtains to the windows of green saye, five chairs and four cushions stuffed with feathers, two cupboards covered with carpets, a long table with three joined forms, an oyster board, and three joined stools. There was a fireplace, and another fireplace in the great chamber beyond. Here again the tapestries were decorated with wild beasts and the window curtains were of green saye embroidered with falcons wings. This was Lovell's emblem and you can see it displayed between the clerestory windows in Enfield parish church. There was also a large feather bed.

Sir Thomas seems to have spent as little as possible on furnishings. Almost every object in the house was described as 'old', 'sore worn', or 'broken'. Even in the king's lodging itself, the seven tapestries were described as 'sore worn', the bed curtains, of black and red panes, as 'old', the counterpane of red sarsnet as 'worn sore', a Flanders chair, stool and form as all 'old', and a cushion of red satin of Bruges, as 'worn'. Many of the important bedrooms contained altars, like the one in 'Mr Lovell's chamber' where there stood an altar board with hangings and curtains of red sarsnet, and an aumbry to store the vessels.

All the service rooms were on the ground floor; the counting house, with the 'auditor's' chamber, the kitchens and the 'clerk of the kitchens' chamber, the larder, and the chamber next, the armoury, the pantry, the buttery and the wardrobe, and several small bedrooms. Also on the ground floor were the hall, the great parlour and the dining parlour, the great chamber and 'my Lord of Oxford's' chamber. On the first floor were the chamber over the gate, the chamber of John Carleton (receiver to Sir Thomas) the chamber in the Round Tower, the inner chamber, the chamber over the armoury, the king's lodging with its closet, the king's 'paylet chamber', Mr Lovell's chamber, and 'my Lord of Oxford's closet'. The six chambers on the top floor were reached by a spiral staircase.

In the wardrobe were kept carpets, curtains, cushions, candlesticks, bedsteads, mattresses, 'pillows and pillowbeers', and counterpanes, a hundred pairs of sheets, holland or canvas, tablecloths and towels of cross diamonty, and other linen and cloth, 'chamber pots and chamber basons of latten', and water chafers of brass, and a miscellaneous collection of tables, chests, chairs and stools. The armoury contained ninety-nine suits of armour valued at £24 15s, but most of the arms were somewhat decayed; three old hand bills were worth but 6d each, forty old bows of ewe 8d each. In addition there were forty sheafs of arrows, but 'broken sore', and five old leather pots (helmets).

The chapel held vestments of red or white damask; of red, green or blue satin of Bruges; and of violet velvet, many embroidered with falcons' wings. Everywhere about the house this emblem could be seen; a cope of crimson velvet with falcon's wings embroidered, and another of crimson velvet with the same. There was a pair of organs and a reading desk, two great antiphoners, very old, written on parchment, a large 'grail' which was also inscribed on parchment, and three old 'grails' and a legend, and four old 'processioners' written on paper.

Thomas, Earl of Rutland, inherited the house and fifteen years later, in March 1539, King Henry VIII appropriated the property, giving Rutland in exchange various lands, rents and manors, including the late monasteries at Croxton in Leicestershire and Rievaulx in Yorkshire.[57] Extensive repairs at Elsings were immediately put in hand by James Nedeham, clerk of the king's works. The window of the king's great chamber, evidently an oriel, had to be supported by two great brick buttresses. The roofs of the hall and the kitchen were repaired 'where it rained in'. The great bridge at the main entrance was new planked, both the inner and outer courts were tidied up and, in December 1541, forms and trestles were set up in the hall for the Council, in readiness for Christmas.[58]

A further £53 was spent by Nedeham in preparation for a Christmas visit by Prince Edward, Princess Mary and Princess Elizabeth, in December 1542. Much of the material for this work was purchased locally, thirteen thousand plain tiles, five thousand bricks, and a hundred roof tiles were supplied by John Norton of Clay Hill. Alice Loft, widow, provided sixteen loads of sand for slaking the lime. John Curtis, for the digging and carriage of eight loads of loam, was paid 3s 6d. William Wood, a tanner of Waltham, supplied hair for the plasterers at 3d a bushel. Mother Barber of Waltham provided tile-pins, and candles and salt for the plumbers. Nails had to be bought in London, as also the rope for the scaffolding and planks to repair the stables, but this was all carted by John Curtis of Enfield. John Nowell, Thomas Green, William Bull, Thomas Nowell and Christopher Tomson, all Enfield men, and William Lowen of Cheshunt were employed in the carriage of timber from the Chase and the carting of bricks. All the glazing was done by John Hone the king's glazier.[59] Thomas Seymour, the brother of Henry's third wife, was appointed keeper of Elsings and of New Park in April 1545.[60] The Princess Elizabeth was then twelve years old. This same Lord Thomas Seymour was to be beheaded for treason three years later as a result of his overweening ambition. Among the accusations made against him was that he had indulged in horse play with the Princess while she was living with him and his wife, Catherine Parr, and that he had sought to marry her after Catherine's death.

Immediately following the accession of Edward VI in 1547, about £300 was spent on repairs to the house which was stated to have been 'of late in great ruin and decay'. Elsings was one of many properties, in Enfield and elsewhere, which, in 1550, were granted by the young King Edward to his sister, the Lady Elizabeth. The Enfield properties also included the manor of Enfield with the Manor House on Enfield Green, Old Park and Enfield Chase, the manor of Worcesters and New Park.[61] All these manors and houses reverted to the Crown when Elizabeth herself came to the throne in 1558. She then appointed John Astley keeper of Elsings.

The Queen made a number of short visits to her house at Enfield. It is known that she was there at the end of July 1564, in July 1568 and in July 1572. Repairs costing £169 were done in 1568. Six carpenters with two apprentices, two joiners, sixteen bricklayers and tilers, with seven apprentices, four plasterers with five labourers, three plumbers, four scourers to clean the sinks and privies, and thirty-five common labourers were employed over a period of about four weeks. The tradesmen were paid 1s a day, the apprentices 10d and and the labourers 8d. The carters, using their own carts, were paid 2s a day. Thomas Cordell supplied 38,000 plain house tiles at 9s a thousand, and 1,500 roof tiles at 8s a thousand. Widow Hewes sent in twenty pounds of small rope to hang canvas frames in front of the

Queen's windows, to keep out the sun. Armorial badges were inserted in the windows, six in the Queen's bed-chamber, and four in her receiving chamber. Work was carried out in all the principal rooms; the privy-chamber, the presence-chamber, the library, the gallery with the chamber adjoining, the great chamber, the lodgings of the Earl of Leicester, the Earl of Warwick, Lord Hunsdon, the Duke of Norfolk, the Marquis of Winchester, the Lord Chamberlain (Lord Howard of Effingham) and the Lord Steward (the Earl of Pembroke) as well as in Lord Burghley's chamber.[62] The hall and the chapel are mentioned in subsequent repair accounts for Elsings.[63]

Lord Burghley secured for himself the keepership of the house in 1576.[64] The office entitled him to sixty loads of wood a year out of Enfield Chase to keep the mansion warm and dry. Reparations, costing £31 15s, were carried out in September[65] that year, and £113 was spent in 1577;[66] then repairs were done annually until 1582.[67] Over the last twenty years of the Queen's reign, however, only minor repair work was carried out there by Lord Burghley. Theobalds close by, begun in 1564, was completed by 1585, and the Queen found that it cost less to stay there with the Cecils. She stayed with Henry Middlemore in August 1587 at the Manor House on Enfield Green. She was the guest of Robert Wroth at Durants Arbour in Ponders End in May 1591 and again in June 1594.[68] Such repairs as Burghley ordered at Elsings were paid for out of the revenues of the royal estates in Middlesex. Work to the value of £44 was done in 1589/90 when a pale fence was constructed between the court and the kitchen garden, and a bridge was built over Maidens brook into New Park. Stairs were installed in the Dairy House.[69] Repairs were made in 1593 to the keepers lodge, and to the old lodge, to the cheese house and to the barn. Gutters were repaired, as were the lead pipes which carried water into the house from the conduit. Forty-eight bushels of hair were purchased for the plasterers to mend the ceilings in the gatehouse and in the lodge. That year the work cost £87 16s.[70]

The house had fallen into a state of dilapidation by 1597. A letter to Sir Robert Cecil, who had taken over the office of keeper from his father, warned that it was in danger of falling down during the ensuing winter. The writer sought permission to cut down the willows and sallows which were growing about the ponds, walks and orchards, to use as fuel to dry and warm the place. He complained of Mr Manners's coachman, who had broken down the doors and carried away lead and glass, and of his housekeeper who had made 'all the spoil he can, and yet will not let a broom to sweep the house'. Manners himself had taken glass from the great house, to glaze his own lodging.[71] The allowance of sixty loads of wood, which should have been employed to maintain the Queen's house, was now diverted to Theobalds.

The hard winters during the 1590s gave rise to a shortage of fuel in the parish and neighbourhood. Enfield tenants no longer received their allowance of fuel at the customary price. The twigs and shreddings from the branches cut were no longer left to be picked up by the poor as had always been their right. Discontent in the parish broke out into open defiance in April 1602, when a large number of Enfield commoners felled and carried away twenty loads of wood apiece. This was no riot of the poor and must have originated in the vestry, or at the manor court, for those involved included many of the leading members of the community. The discontent of the poor was made apparent the following year in the middle of April 1603, at a most inopportune time, when Cecil was making elaborate preparations for the arrival of King James at Theobalds on his way down from Scotland. Cecil sent his servants into the Chase to collect the sixty loads of wood to which he was entitled as keeper of the King's house at Enfield, but his servants returned empty handed. They had been confronted and denied by a large gathering of Enfield women, covertly supported and urged on by Sir Robert Wroth, the greatest land-owner in the parish. The women remained respectful, yet resolute under question-ing. They were there, they said, to maintain that no Chase wood should be taken out of the 'town of Enfield', but that it should be used only at Elsings which now stood neglected and likely to fall into ruin for lack of firing. It became necessary to find a compromise with these stalwart women to ensure the comfort of the King. Forty loads of wood were now to be taken to Elsings and sixty to Theobalds, and it was declared, to all concerned, that all the brushwood was to be left on the ground for the poor people of Enfield and none henceforth should be sold.[72]

Some tidying up of the privy lodgings and kitchens occurred in 1605/6,[73] as if in preparation for a royal visit but, in 1607, the King acquired Theobalds, granting Cecil in return the old royal palace at Hatfield, with seventeen manors to finance the rebuilding there. The following year, in March, a royal warrant was issued to take down His Majesty's house in Enfield, and carefully to preserve the materials for use in new building at Theobalds.[74] Demolition was only partial and, in 1609/10, the remaining parts of the house were carefully restored at a cost of £1,388. Where the building had been taken down, the ground was levelled and a brick wall was erected to enclose it. Where it was restored, masons, carpenters, bricklayers, tilers, plasterers, plumbers, mat-layers, sawyers, gardeners, labourers, women and boys, were employed at daily rates ranging from 22d for the most skilled plasters, down to 6d or 4d for boys according to their ages. The total wages amounted to £570. Old posts, pales and rails were brought from Theobalds, the park there was being enlarged and the fence replaced by a brick wall. The material was used at Enfield to set up a new pale from the house down to the bridge, to confine the deer in New Park. Vast amounts of materials had to be purchased; 261,000 bricks, 18,000 tiles, over a hundred loads of lime, nearly nine hundred bushels of hair for the plasterers, 2,400 cwt of lead, 256 lb of solder, and 240 lb of red ochre and black.

It was necessary to build an enormous brick wall at the west end of the chapel to enclose that end of the house. This wall was three feet thick at the bottom, and sixty feet high from the foundation 'in the bottom of the ditch', presumably to the full height of the chapel. New floors had to be made in the great room over the dining chamber, and in the next room to it, 'in the third story over the gatehouse'.[75]

Philip Herbert, Earl of Montgomery now became keeper, presumably on the death of Robert Cecil in 1612. He occupied the house, and had his pew in Enfield church.[76] King James visited him at the house in September 1616 to attend the christening of his son.[77] The new year 1618 was celebrated with a masque at Elsings presented before the Marquis of Hamilton, the Lord Chamberlain, and the Earl of Montgomery. Sir George Goring took the part of a farmer's son, and various distinguished knights and gentlemen, playing as tillers of the soil, were there to dance at his wedding. There were 'many pleasant speeches and much mirth'. King James, who was then at Theobalds, heard of the festivities and desired the players to perform again before him and, when this was done, the King 'was much contented and very merry therewith'.[78]

Repairs in 1621/22 cost £107. Much of it was spent on the restoration of the four arbours in the garden. The joists and boarding of the roofs were replaced and covered with lead, and two small spouts were employed on each roof to carry off the water. New ceilings were then put up. In the great house itself, linen, canvas,

The magnificent stone fireplace and overmantel now in the Tudor Room at Little Park, Gentlemans Row probably originated at Enfield House.

rosin and tallow were used to bind up the water pipes. Mat-layers were paid 20d a day to lay new matting in nine lodgings. The Earl of Montgomery succeeded his brother as Lord Chamberlain in 1626, and issued several warrants for work to be done.[79]

The Earl purchased the house for £5,300, when King Charles I was desperate for money in April 1641. The sale included the land called the Warren and New Park (or Little Park), containing 375 acres.[80] The property had by then become part of the Duchy of Lancaster. The Manor of Worcesters, with which it had originally been held, was no longer Crown property since it had been sold to Robert Cecil in 1602. Elsings at the time had been excluded from the sale. Thus the house remained standing into the mid-seventeenth century. It was acquired by Nicholas Rainton following the death of Philip Herbert in 1650. When Rainton made an inventory of his property in 1656, to establish his claims before the commissioners for enclosure for Enfield Chase, he listed 'one very ancient house called Enfield House, with the courtyards, gardens, orchards, and the field adjoining called the Walks', and two ancient tenements adjoining the great house and occupied by Thomas Goodyear and Mr Thwaites (these presumably were the lodges). An ancient tenement at Bulls Cross 'sometime called the Deyry House', was occupied in 1656 by William Parnell.[81] More than a hundred years had passed since John Hill and Joan his wife tended the dairy there which had provided the milk, cheese and butter to provision the vast household of Sir Thomas Lovell.

The curtain comes down at last on Elsings and hides from us the final demolition. Nothing more appears to be recorded concerning the great house until the enterprising amateurs of the Enfield Archaeological Society investigated the site in 1963–6. Relics undoubtedly remain in the Tudor Room at Little Park, Gentlemans Row. The magnificent stone fireplace there bears the royal arms, the crowned Tudor rose, the crowned portcullis, and the initials E.R. There are also two plaster panels with the inscription *'ut ros super herbam est benevolentia regis'*; 'as dew upon the grass is the kindness of the king'. It would be pleasant if it could be established that these were installed at Elsings in 1550. It could then be interpreted as Elizabeth's way of saying thanks to her brother for his protection, and for the gift to her that year of the house and many other properties. These relics were installed by the Leggatt brothers in a specially designed room (the Tudor Room) at their house (now called Little Park) in Gentlemans Row, when the Manor House in Church Street (always known locally as the 'Palace') was destroyed in 1927 to make way for Pearson's shop. The 'Palace' appears never to have been in royal occupation, and these fittings may have been taken there when Elsings was finally demolished, or at the time of the partial demolition in 1609.

There were in 1572 another seven tenements along Bulls Cross Lane leading towards Maidens bridge, beyond lay a the settlement around Forty Green. Here were five tenements and a cottage to the north of Hoe Lane, and two more tenements between Hoe Lane and Carterhatch Lane. A further seven dwellings lay on the west side of Forty Green and Forty Hill.

5. Along the Old North Road

The old north road, by way of Bishopsgate, proceeded northward over Stamford Hill, through Tottenham and Edmonton. A traveller on his way from London towards Ware, who made the journey in 1572, would have seen the road crowded with pack-horses, carts, wagons and coaches: dust would fill his lungs in summer, and mud bespatter his clothes in winter. Some eight miles would have brought him to Enfield and, within a few hundred yards, he would come to South Street, a lane leading off the main road towards the east to the mill on the River Lea. Some twenty houses and three cottages, each with its garden and small orchard, and some with a croft to pasture a beast or two, lined both sides of the lane. These holdings were mostly small, ranging from one acre to half an acre, for the land on which the villagers worked lay elsewhere, in the great common fields of the parish.

The settlement along the main road north from South Street was known then, as it is now, as Ponders End. Between Bungie Lane (now Lincoln Road) and Bury Lane (now Southbury Road) the way was lined with cottages and farmsteads. There were twenty-one dwellings on the west side of the road, many of them cottages with a garden, often of only half a rood (about twenty yards by thirty). Colewells Lane (probably the present Queensway) led off westward into the fields. The land up to and beyond Bury Lane was occupied by Mr Colte who held 155 acres in Enfield. There stood his house called Suffolks, with a garden, an orchard and a grove of six acres. Much of his arable land lay nearby; Greater and Little Suffolks of forty acres, with a whole furlong in Southbury field of thirty-six acres, lying immediately to the south of the Suffolks, and thirty-one acres in Windmill field to the north of the Suffolks. On the other (eastern) side of the highway were eight tenements and three cottages.

Nicholas Clark had a house there called Sell Coblers with an orchard and a garden. He was by trade a harness-maker. When he died in 1578 he left the house to Katherine, the elder of his two daughters, married to John Doo, but he directed that Alice Frye, his second daughter, should be given the right to live there for twenty years, and further, that if she had children during this time she was to pay a rent of 6s 8d a year and the money was to be used for the repair of the house. Katherine was to have all her father's corn in the barn, forty sheep, and 'one garled (ie speckled) steer'. From the stock in his shop, she should have nine new collars (horse collars of course), eight new panniers, two new cart saddles and two new 'mantells'. She was to have his worst feather bed, one of the best blankets, a bolster and a pillow, and also two acres of land. Katherine's daughter Dennise was to be given twenty marks when she was eighteen but should she die before that time then the money should go to the next of Katherine's children, 'be it boy or wench'. Alice had as yet no children. Perhaps she was newly married, in which case she probably needed more in the way of household goods and furniture. He therefore gave her the best feather bed with a blanket, pillow and a pair of flaxen sheets, one platter, two pewter dishes, a candlestick, two saucers, a porringer*, one saltcellar, a pint pot, the painted hangings in the hall, a chest which was in the loft, a chest with a broken lid which stood in the chamber, and a counter. She inherited also three roods of land, and all her father's lamb's wool.[82]

Beyond Ponders End, for the next half a mile, the fields stretched out on both sides of the road with only the great moated manor house of Sir Thomas Wroth (Durants Arbour) some two hundred yards away to the east. The Wroth family dominated the parish throughout the sixteenth century. Robert, known as 'Robert the attorney', had succeeded to the family estates in 1518. His Enfield property included the manor of Durants; he also held considerable land in Somerset.[83] He was intimately connected with Sir Thomas Lovell, for whom he acted as attorney.[84]

*a small dish used for porridge

Wroth's two younger sons, William and John, were serving at Elsings when Sir Thomas died in 1524, and both received gifts by his will.[85] Wroth had been appointed a commissioner to collect the subsidy (tax) for the county of Middlesex in 1523[86] and was placed on the commission of peace for the county that same year.[87]

After the death of Lovell he served Thomas Cromwell, again in the capacity of attorney. A letter of 1531[88] shows him offering advice in a confident professional manner. He carefully cultivated his relationship with Cromwell. 'I hope you will not be displeased that I have not sent you any venison', he writes, and seeks Cromwell's help in obtaining favours for his dependents.[89] That same year he was appointed attorney to the Duchy of Lancaster, high steward of the Duchy lands in Middlesex and Hertfordshire, bailiff of the manor of Enfield, and steward of the manor of Savoy, and was granted the lordship of Finsbury.[90] When the manor of Edmonton came into the King's hands in 1535, he was appointed both steward and bailiff. That same year, through his connection with Cromwell, he was appointed to the Commission of First Fruits and Tenths for the counties of Middlesex and Hertfordshire,[91] set up to calculate the annual value of the property of monasteries in the area in preparation for their subsequent dissolution.

Robert wrote his will in 1535, 'seeing the sudden chance and mutability of the unstable and transitory world, and every day looking for the messenger of God . . .' He did not have long to wait; by the following September Robert Wroth was dead at the age of forty-one. He must have been impressed by the handsome four-centred arch which the Earl of Rutland had built on the north side of the chancel in Enfield church, for he asked that his executors should erect for him a like monument on the opposite side.[92] It seems never to have been built.

Thomas Wroth was seventeen when his father died. He had been educated at St Johns College Cambridge but, like most young men of his class, he had left without taking a degree, and had subsequently enrolled at Grays Inn to complete his education. The marriage (ie the wardship) of the young heir was granted by the King to Thomas Cromwell who sold it to Sir Richard Rich for £200, and Thomas married Mary, Rich's third daughter. Rich was portrayed most memorably in Robert Bolt's play *A Man for all Seasons* as the sixteenth century 'yuppy' who betrayed his benefactor Sir Thomas More. Like his father, Thomas found favour with those who held power. Even after the execution of Cromwell he continued to augment his holdings of offices, advowsons and other properties.

He was returned as member for Middlesex in the Parliaments of 1544 and 1546 and, through the influence of Cranmer, he was appointed gentleman usher to Prince Edward. Thus began the association with the Prince which was to prove so valuable to him. Henry VIII died in 1547 and a month later Wroth received his knighthood. During the Protectorate of Somerset he kept his place in the personal entourage of the young King, and offices and estates continued to be bestowed upon him. His influence on King Edward appeared to be growing and, in October 1549, he was appointed one of the four principal gentlemen of the privy chamber.[93] The fall of Somerset had occurred that summer and it must have suited Northumberland (at that time Earl of Warwick) to secure the support of one so close to King Edward. For his support Wroth was well rewarded. He was granted, on 24 December, the manors of Bardfield, Chigwell and Westhatch, all in Essex, and the reversion, after the death of the Duke of Northumberland, of all the offices connected with the manors of Elsings and Worcesters in Enfield and the manor of Edmonton. Further manors and other properties continued to fall into his lap.[94]

The end of the year 1551 was even more rewarding; during these few months he was granted property with an annual value of over £84. He became progressively more involved in government. His power and his property augmented week by week. Only two days before the death of the boy King, on 4 July 1553, Wroth was granted land in Sussex worth £87 a year which had belonged to the Duke of Norfolk, attainted for treason. Such good fortune could not last. Northumberland's plan to place the Lady Jane Grey upon the throne, collapsed like a pack of cards. London welcomed Queen Mary with bonfires in the street and bells ringing from church towers. Sir Thomas Wroth was committed to the Tower[95] where he remained from July until October. Soon after his release, he was implicated, probably unwillingly, in a plot against the Queen's Spanish marriage.[96] Wroth was fortunate in that he contrived to escape to the Continent and there, mostly in Strasbourg, he spent the following four years until the death of Queen Mary in November 1558.[97] It was at Strasbourg that the more moderate of the protestant refugees gathered, while the centre for the extremist Calvinists was Geneva.

His homecoming was something of a disappointment. Sir Thomas found his property largely intact, but Queen Elizabeth full of antipathy and distrust. Her grant to John Astley in 1560 of the various offices connected with the manors of Worcesters and Elsings, which Wroth had held in reversion after the death of the Duke of Northumberland, must have been a blow to his pride and prestige. Wroth lost other offices in Middlesex which the Queen granted to Francis Knolles.[98]

Sir Thomas was returned to Parliament as the member for Middlesex in 1559. No family in England can rival the record of the Wroths in the House of Commons. He had first sat for Middlesex in 1545, and between that date and 1604 there was only one Parliament, excluding the reign of Queen Mary, in which a Wroth did not represent the county. Sir Thomas consistently supported the efforts of the extreme protestants to secure the triumph of their cause through the House, but he never again achieved any position of power.[99] He was sent in 1562 as a special commissioner to Ireland where he laboured in vain for two years to produce order out of chaos. His only reward was the displeasure of the Queen.[100]

He died in October 1573. His funeral was puritan in its lack of ostentation. He asked for no monument, and made no charitable bequest despite his wealth. He left seven sons and seven daughters and his widow Mary. Provision for all these, except Robert his heir, had to be made in cash: it amounted to well over £5,000. To meet these commitments, and to pay his outstanding debts, two-thirds of the estate was to remain in the hands of executors for twenty-one years; Robert was to receive only one-third. A gold decorated bowl, once given to Sir Thomas by King Edward, must have revived memories of royal favour in former times, but the bulk of his plate had to be sold. He was buried in St Andrews Church on 15 October 1573.[101]

Thus Robert, at the age of thirty-three, found himself the owner of a large estate bearing many burdens. In addition to the two-thirds which were to remain in the hands of the executors, his mother was to hold the manor of Durants and many other valuable properties while she lived, and even then these were to pass to executors, as trustees, following her death unless the debts had previously been paid. Robert's education at St Johns College had been cut short when the family was forced to flee the country in 1554, and he was eighteen by the time they returned to England. He was elected to Parliament for the Borough of St Albans in 1563.[102]

Following his father's death he married Susan, daughter and heiress of John

Stonard, by whose will the couple inherited considerable property in Essex. Their combined estates stretched for three miles in the valley of the Roding.[103] Wroth seems to have purchased the lease of the manor of Loughton from Stonard for £11,000 in the year before his father-in-law's death, but the widow retained a life interest therein, and she lived on there until 1601. Robert's mother, the Lady Mary, did not die until 1590, so that a large proportion of his property remained in the hands of the two widows throughout much of his life. Robert Wroth received a knighthood in 1597.

Something of the character of the man can be seen in an incident which occurred during a protracted suit in Star Chamber against Thomas Colshill. Colshill held copyhold land within Wroth's manor of Chigwell, and had laid lead pipes across land which Wroth claimed belonged to him. Hearing of this encroachment, Wroth rode with three servants to investigate. There he found the pipes already in place and a number of Colshill's men standing guard. An argument ensued which ended in Wroth stating that it was his intention to dig up the pipes forthwith, and thereupon he sent his man, Toby Pylston, for a spade. Then, having made 'gentle speeches', as he called them, warning the other side against violence, he ordered Toby Pylston to dig up the conduit. Colshill's servants at once retired into their master's house, emerging in a few minutes armed with longbows and a pitchfork. That Robert Wroth survived the battle which followed can only be attributable to the very special grace in which he was held by the Almighty. He was standing with his back turned contemptuously upon the enemy when an arrow narrowly missed him (as he afterwards learned). Immediately another arrow was shot with great force and violence, he still standing quietly by facing the other way. The arrow pierced his hat in two places and would assuredly have killed him had it been but a quarter of an inch lower. Thereupon our hero, pulling off his hat and seeing two great holes in it, perceived that he was being shot at, he turned round to see Colshill's servants ready once again to shoot. Poor Toby was hit this time, but fortunately 'God's goodness' stretched even so far and the arrow, by 'the grace of the Almighty', alighted on the iron buckle of his girdle or it would have pierced his belly. Another arrow landed on Toby's gaskins (breeches) which would have done great harm had not the double lining and thickness protected him. A third arrow pierced the skirt of his doublet and went through, but again did no harm. Robert Wroth, seeing now the great danger in which he and his servants stood imperilled, drew his rapier and made towards his assailants cutting the bowstring of the foremost and forcing them to retreat to the main gate where they stood to defend their master's mansion. Here a further parley was taking place when suddenly one of Wroth's servants was hit by an arrow in the face 'from which he has since fallen into an extreme burning fever, and not yet cured.'[104] Concerning the survival or otherwise of Colshill's conduit, I have alas found no evidence.

Wroth played a leading role in the Parliament of 1593, being a member of no fewer than eighteen parliamentary committees. He employed his knowledge of precedents and procedures to maintain the rights of the Lower House, particularly the right to control taxation. The battle for the reform of religion through the House of Commons had been abandoned and in the Parliament of 1597–8, the puritans took up the problem of the poor. Sir Robert Wroth chaired the committee which considered no fewer than eleven bills on this matter, and from this committee came the two acts for which this Parliament is generally remembered, the Act for the Relief of the Poor which was to remain the basis of English poor law until the nineteenth century, and the Act for the Punishment of Rogues, Vagabonds and Sturdy Beggars.

In the Parliament of 1601, Robert Wroth was one of the leaders of the campaign for the abolition of monopolies. He was for many years a justice of the peace both in Middlesex and Essex.[105] He died in January 1606, his will being written only two days before his death. He provided for his three younger sons with three recently-acquired estates; they were also to receive £700 each within two years of his death, and were to share an annuity of £200 during the lifetime of Thomas, the youngest of the three. His heir, Sir Robert, was to have the remainder of his lands and property. He left instructions that Robert should not disturb any leases at their present rents. His servants should receive wages for a year, and meat, drink and lodging at the charge of his executor for a reasonable time while they sought other employment. He left £3 for the poor of Enfield, and so many poor men of Enfield as there had been years in his life were to have, each of them, a black gown and sixpence in money.[106]

Sir Robert, his son, was at that time living at Chigwell. He had married in September 1604 Mary Sidney, the eldest daughter of Lord Sidney of Penshurst, afterwards created Earl of Leicester. The marriage involved him in a new and extravagant life-style. Lady Mary, by virtue of her accomplishments, her birth and beauty, was an ornament of the Court, and a poet of some repute. They entertained King James at Loughton in 1606 and thereafter, according to Ben Jonson, the King was a frequent guest. They also entertained at Durants, for which he was praised by William Gamage, a versifier of no great reputation whose work was published in 1613.

'Thy durance keeps in Durants none I hear
Less be to partake of thy bounteous cheer'

And in case his readers might not be able to comprehend what he was talking about, he adds a footnote to explain that 'Sir Robert was a famous housekeeper'.

Robert purchased the freehold of the manor of Loughton Hall for £1224 in 1613. He made his will on 2 March 1614. On the following day his infant son was christened at Enfield. Eleven days later Sir Robert died. He was buried in the family chapel in St Andrews Church on 14 March. A contemporary letter tells that he left a young widow with a £1200 jointure, a son a month old, and his estate £23,000 in debt.[107]

It is probable that the life-style and expenditure of the couple had been out of proportion to their estate, considerable though it was. Six years after his death his executors were still being pursued by one Nicholas Polpill, who was owed £450 for 'lace, silk and such like commodities', and evidence speaks of debts amounting to £30,000. In his will he begged forgiveness of his wife for the inadequacy of the provision he had been able to make for her. 'Her sincere love, loyalty, virtuous conversation, and behaviour towards me, have deserved a far better recompense, if the care of satisfying my debts and supporting my house would have permitted.' Many of the creditors were not secured by bond or otherwise; these, he stipulated, 'shall be first paid because they most relied upon my word and credit'.

His baby son did not long survive. A coffin plate attached to the wall in the south chancel chapel in St Andrews Church (formerly the Wroth family chapel) records the death of James Wroth, 5 July 1616, aged two years five months. It is all that remains to commemorate the burial there of many of the Wroth family which, throughout Tudor times, played a leading role in national affairs, and whose influence and power within the parish could never be ignored.[108]

Leaving Durants Arbour behind, the traveller, in 1572, next came upon Green Street, a considerable settlement of twenty-seven dwellings on both sides of a road leading towards Enfield lock, with more houses along Cranes Lane (the present Alma Road). The area now called Enfield Highway was known then as Cocksmiths End. Most of the property there was owned by the Hunsdons; Henry Hunsdon, Thomas Hunsdon, Widow Hunsdon, William Hunsdon and John (Littleman) Hunsdon. There were thirteen dwellings in all. Each had its garden and orchard and, here and there, to east and west, ways led off into the common fields.

The last settlement along the old north road was Horsepoolstones, or Enfield Wash. Most of the dwellings were on the west side of the road because the Turkey brook ran along the other side all the way from Turkey Street past Bell Lane (then referred to simply as 'the lane'). North towards Waltham Cross lay only the fields on both sides of the road. A short way along Turkey Street was another small settlement, consisting of nineteen cottages and houses.

One traveller who frequented this road was Lord Burghley. He has left us a delightful account of the conduct of the Enfield watch, posted along the highway to apprehend those who had plotted to murder the Queen and to place the Roman Catholic Mary of Scots upon the throne of England in August 1586. In exasperation at their total lack of vigilance, he wrote complaining to Sir Francis Walsingham, his secretary of state;

'Sir, As I came from London homeward [to Theobalds] in my coach I saw, at every town's end, the number of ten or twelve standing with long staves; and, until I came to Enfield, I thought no other of them but that they had stayed for avoiding of the rain, or to drink at some ale-house. For so they did stand under pentices at ale-houses. But at Enfield, finding a dozen in a plump, when there was no rain, I bethought myself that they were appointed as watchmen for the apprehending of such as are missing. And thereupon I called some of them to me apart and asked them wherefore they stood there. And one of them answered, "To take three young men". And demanding how they should know the persons, one answered with these words; "Marry my Lord, by intelligence of their favour". "What mean you by that?" quoth I. "Marry" said they "One of the parties hath a hooked nose". "And have you" quoth I, "no other mark?". "No" said they. And then I asked who had appointed them, and they answered one Banks a head constable, whom I willed to be sent to me. Surely sir, whomsoever had the charge from you hath used the matter negligently, for these watchmen stand so openly in plumps that no suspected person will come near them, and if they be no better instructed but to find three persons by one of them having a hooked nose, they may miss thereof . . .'[109]

6. The Fields

Before I can describe the fields of Enfield prior to the coming of industry, it is essential to say something about the system of common field agriculture under which farming was organised in Enfield over the centuries, until the fields were enclosed by an Act of Parliament in 1803. A common field system required that the arable land be cultivated in strips, and that each farmer should hold a number of strips which lay scattered in the fields. After the reaping and gathering in of the corn, the fields were thrown open to the cattle and sheep of the community. The animals fed in the stubble and deposited manure upon the earth. A system of crop rotation was used, spring corn was sown one year, winter corn the following year, and in the third year the land rested and was thrown open to the livestock of all the village.

In order that this system should work effectively, there had to be common waste where the peasant could have pasture and the foliage of trees, which the cattle loved, at those times when crops were growing on the common fields. Waste land was needed where the peasant might find fuel to cook and keep warm, where he could take timber to build and repair his house, his barn and his fences, and where he could fatten his pig for the winter, on the acorns and beech mast.

Common field farming was a complex system which rendered the whole community, from the cottager to the lord of the manor, dependent one upon another. It was necessary therefore that it be efficiently regulated. This regulation was controlled by an assembly of those who worked the land; it usually met in the manor court of the principal manor within the parish.

Some readers will remember the three field system as expounded and drawn neatly on the board by some half-forgotten history teacher.

'These things have served their purpose let them be'[110]

The Enfield common field system, alas, is less easy to explain, for the parish contained some forty common fields in 1572 which ranged in size from Duck Lees of nine acres to Windmill field of 276 acres. Nevertheless a three-year crop rotation was rigorously enforced over them all.

The land was not evenly distributed among the 260 tenants, for more than half, 2,471 acres, was held by only ten people. At the same time there existed 156 tenants who each held five acres or less, some who held only a cottage and garden. There were moreover, many who held no land, nor even a cottage. This becomes apparent when comparing the muster roll of 1569,[111] with the 1572 survey.[112] There were 280 men named in the muster roll, but only fifty-three of them held land, cottages or houses in 1572, directly from the manors. Even allowing for the three years between these two documents, the figure suggests that many in the village were either sub-tenants or were landless, renting cottages from other tenants, or living with their families or employers. There were 322 dwellings listed in the survey of the parish made in 1572. Many were not occupied by their owners, for sixty-six landlords held around two hundred dwellings between them, one, John Wilford, owned fourteen.

An example of these landlords was Thomas Hawkins, a yeoman. He owned seventy-three acres, at the time of the 1572 survey, and a number of houses. His dwelling at Horsepoolstones may once have had owners of a higher class, for Hawkins's will in 1576 speaks of 'the great parlour there, and the dayze (dais) hall'. He left a wife, three sons, and a daughter. The household stuff listed in his will suggests that the family lived well. The bedstead had wood joints and turned pillars; there was a feather bed and bolster, two pillows, flaxen sheets, and a coverlet of carpet work, They had table cloths, towels, flaxen napkins, much brass, latten candlesticks, a great number of pewter platters, dishes, saucers, and porringers. The dais hall was furnished with a long table and a long form, a side table, a bench board and another form, a round table (made chair fashion) with a cupboard under it, two great turned chairs with whole backs, two great jointed stools, a great standing chest and a smaller one, a 'pair of bedsteads', and forty yards of painted cloth. All these goods were among the property which he left to his daughter who was, in addition, to have £20 when she attained the age of twenty.[113]

He also owned a house at Ponders End where John Cooke was living, a house in Baker Street let to John Thurgood, a house in 'Horse Pole Street', (Horsepoolstones) where John Ayre lived, the old Dairy House which had once been part of Sir Thomas Lovell's estate and which was rented in 1576 by Henry Hodge, and also a further house called Bowling Hill. Another of the landlords was William Curtis, a London pewterer. He owned about twenty acres in Enfield, two tenements and three cottages.[114]

A holding of ten acres is generally considered to have been the minimum required to support a family. Thirty-seven tenants held between five and ten acres each, while 156 held less than five acres so that there were 193 tenants who did not have sufficient land to adequately support their families. Twenty-eight tenants owned between twenty-one and fifty acres, and two owned between fifty and a hundred acres. Thus a great many in the parish may have had to work as labourers. This had long been the situation in Enfield. Some eighty-six of the 215 men assessed for King Henry VIII's subsidy in 1525, were assessed on wages. The pay in Enfield had then been much better than in the neighbouring parishes. In Tottenham for instance, only six in 1525 were considered to earn more than 20s a year, while the number in Enfield was thirty-eight; indeed twenty-eight Enfield men were paid 40s a year, and six received even more. In Edmonton only ten earned as much as 40s, none more.[115]

Farming must not be thought of in terms of a twentieth century farm for, though a farmer might have an acre or two for an orchard, garden or close, attached to his farmhouse, most of his land was dispersed in the nearby fields. John Cordell, who died in 1565, left twenty-eight acres, his ten and a half acres of arable being in seven pieces in five common fields. There were nine and a half acres of meadow in the marsh, four acres of pasture, and a further two acres of meadow. He owned three houses.

Most people lived near the land which they cultivated. A closer look at one field, Dungfield for instance, which lay between Bullsmoor Lane and Turkey Street, shows that it contained fifty-four acres in forty-seven pieces which belonged to twenty-three tenants. It is possible to establish from the 1572 survey, where fourteen of these tenants lived. Six lived in Turkey Street, six at Horsepoolstones (Enfield Wash) and two in Bulls Cross Lane (Bullsmoor Lane). Another three, Dr Huick, John Wilford and Humphrey Reynold were landlords, and the strips which they held would have been sub-let. Thus all those we can trace who farmed in Dungfield would have had less than half a mile to walk to reach the field.

A further check on these fourteen tenants who held land in Dungfield shows that their entire holdings lay within easy reach of their dwellings. Walter Deane held a total of twenty-six acres, fourteen and a half in Dungfield, six in Longfield (between Turkey Street and Hoe Lane), five in Southfield (bordering west on Dungfield), and half an acre in Northfield (north of Bullsmoor Lane). John Jersey, who held a total of fourteen acres, lived at Enfield Wash. He had five and a half acres in Longfield, three acres in Stronglands (north of what is now Ordnance Road), an acre in Mapulton field (bordering north on Hoe Lane), and an acre in Dungfield. And it was thus with all the seventeen tenants.[116]

The many who held less than ten acres in Enfield were enabled to survive

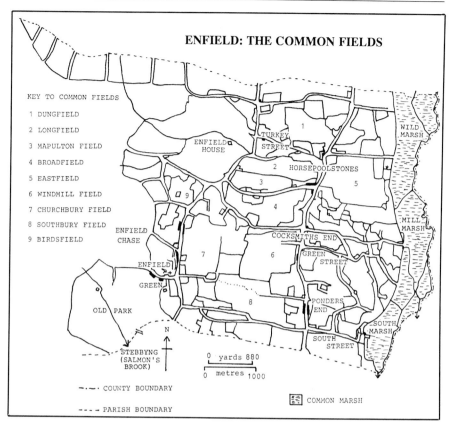

ENFIELD: THE COMMON FIELDS

KEY TO COMMON FIELDS

1 DUNGFIELD
2 LONGFIELD
3 MAPULTON FIELD
4 BROADFIELD
5 EASTFIELD
6 WINDMILL FIELD
7 CHURCHBURY FIELD
8 SOUTHBURY FIELD
9 BIRDSFIELD

ENFIELD CHASE

OLD PARK

STEBBYNG (SALMON'S BROOK)

0 yards 880
0 metres 1000

—·—· COUNTY BOUNDARY

— — — PARISH BOUNDARY

COMMON MARSH

because there were other means of making money in the village, and because they had rights of common on Enfield Chase. The Chase lay entirely within Enfield and its 8,349 acres occupied more than half the area of the parish. Its boundaries, roughly described in terms of 1989 roads, streets and footpaths, ran up Windmill Hill, down Slades Hill and by the footpath on the left to Worlds End Lane, thence southward to the gates of Highlands Hospital. The boundary then followed Green Dragon Lane to Hadley Way and by Hadley Way, Hounsden Road and Winchmore Hill Road to Southgate Circus, where the south gate of Enfield Chase then was. Turning north-west the boundary continued along Chase Side and Cockfosters Road to Games Road, thence by the footpath through Hadley Wood to the church at Monken Hadley, and thence north to Potters Bar. From Potters Bar the boundary turned east along Coopers Lane Road, Cattlegate Road and Whitewebbs Lane as far as the King and Tinker. From this point it followed Flash Lane to the Fallow Buck from where it continued south to Phipps Hatch Lane, then down Brigadier Hill and along Chase Side Enfield to the junction of Church Street and Windmill Hill.

The right to common might enable a man to prosper who owned but little land. John Aylward had only ten acres in 1572 which included a tenement with its garden and orchard in Turkey Street with a little pightle (a small enclosure) abutting on the main road, and five strips of land nearby in Dungfield. All his land was freehold. It was five years since his father had died and his mother Helen seems to have lived with him. She held not much more than an acre in 1572 and she had neither house nor cottage, but let me tell you of her will written in 1574. In it she gave her silver salt to Thomas her second son (who held five acres freehold), and to his daughter Sara she gave a red cow. Her best russet cassock she gave to her servant, Margaret Roodes, and to John she gave all her sheep and lambs, three bullocks, all her corn and peas that were growing, all her pigs, hens and geese, and much of her household goods.[117]

The principal livestock in Enfield was sheep. The price of wool remained high in the early sixteenth century; at that time Sir Thomas Lovell kept a flock of 500 at Elsings. Throughout the 1570s the Duchy constantly complained that the Chase was gravely overcharged with great numbers of sheep which belonged to wealthy yeomen and gentry. A flock of more than 800 was pastured there by Ralph Warter of Old Fold in Hadley. Others accused of overburdening the common with large flocks were Roger Graves, Henry Hunsdon, John Moddam and John Garrett, all of Enfield. Hunsdon and Garrett were considerable landowners, the former holding 124 acres, the latter forty-six. Graves however held only twelve acres, and Moddam a mere three and a half acres, yet they claimed an equal right to common pasture with Hunsdon and Garrett.[118]

Sheep are occasionally mentioned in Enfield wills where they are taken very seriously. Henry Hunsdon, who died in 1539, distributed his stock with great care. His sons, John and Reynold, were to have ten sheep each, 'five wether (castrated rams) and five mother sheep, neither the best, neither the worst, but one brother to choose one time the best until the number be fully chosen'. Their father suggested that they then might each take separate brands though, if they could agree, then they might keep the flock together, in which case Reynold should pay for the winter feeding and in recompense he should retain the lambs that were born. Presumably he had a ram.

The method of tenure for some 2440 acres is specified in the 1572 survey. Well over half (1472 acres) was freehold, 685 acres were held on leases, and there remained only 284 acres of copyhold or customary land. The survey retains a distinction between customary and copyhold though in fact the only difference between the two classes of tenure was that the claim of the copyholder could be upheld by his copy of court roll while that of the customary tenant was upheld only by the knowledge of a jury at the manor court. The type of tenure is not stated for the 622 acres in the common marsh, or for the land (934 acres) belonging to those manors not owned by the Crown, but evidence suggests that private landlords had long exerted pressure to convert copyhold to freehold. The manor of Honeylands and Pentriches (later Capels) was sold to Sir William Capel by Jane, the wife of Sir Thomas Lewknor in 1486 and it continued in private ownership until 1546 when Henry VIII acquired the property from Sir Giles Capel. The manor remained in the hands of the Crown until about 1565 when it was acquired by John Tamworth of London. Soon afterwards Tamworth summoned all his customary and copyhold tenants to a court where he persuaded many of them to surrender their lands and to purchase them freehold.[119]

The demesne of the manor of Enfield was described ten years after the survey, in 1582, at the time when it was sold to Henry Middlemore. It contained 442 acres which included 270 acres of arable, ninety-two acres of meadow and eighty acres of pasture. Much of the arable was dispersed in three common fields; eighty acres in Churchbury field, eighty acres in Southbury field and sixty acres in Windmill field. It was mostly held in small pieces which varied in size from two roods up to nine acres. The pasture lay in closes (small enclosures), the meadow in the common marsh.[120]

All the meadow and most of the arable was subject to the right of commoners to pasture their cattle at those times when the fields lay fallow. In the neighbouring parishes to the south the common had not survived so well. Almost all the common land in Tottenham was enclosed by the early seventeenth century. Some six hundred acres of common land had been lost to the Edmonton commoners in the fifteenth and early sixteenth centuries.[121]

Enfield had become part of the Duchy of Lancaster in 1419. The Duchy was not an improving landlord and the only pressure to enclose came from other landowners within the parish. This was successful at first, for it involved the most powerful landlords, but subsequently the resistance of the commoners became more organised. The struggle against the enclosers went on right through the sixteenth century.

John Wroth enclosed some thirty-three acres in 1490 and again in 1513 he enclosed forty-two acres.[122] Though he had been powerful enough to impose his will upon the parish, his alleged offence against the custom of the manor was not forgotten; the peasant believed that his common rights could never be diminished. Thus it was that thirty-six years later, when the land had come into the hands of Sir Thomas Wroth, the commoners broke into these enclosures which the Wroths had long converted to pasture, and drove their cattle in.[123] Sir Thomas was finally prevailed upon to reach an agreement with the commoners by which he paid 26s 8d each year to the churchwardens of the parish for distribution among the poor.[124]

Opposition to enclosure had become united and determined. In the 1520s John Taylor, a husbandman, (not John Taylor the farmer of the demesne) enclosed two and a half acres in Buryfield, Richard Marche, a yeoman, three acres in Cerlysfield, John Lee five acres in the same field, while John Ashely enclosed an acre in Fortyfield and John Mayhewe eight acres out of a common field called Resthecrofts. All these enclosures were broken open by their fellow tenants who drove cattle onto the growing corn. The enclosers sued in the Duchy Court for damages, whereupon the other commoners retaliated by bringing a suit seeking the restitution of their common rights. This caused the enclosers, as they complained, to attend at Westminster at the busy time of sowing, resulting in losses both of time and money.[125]

These enclosures were upheld, but the matter was again not forgotten. When action at law had failed to restore their common, the matter was brought before the commoners at the meeting of the manor court held on the Wednesday in Easter week 1528. At this court 'the common voice', as it was called, declared that the common fields which had been enclosed should be laid open 'and every man', it was said, 'was willing'. Thereupon, on Tuesday 14 May, there assembled a party of some sixty commoners which included all the parish constables, led by John Westbury, constable for the Ponders End quarter. In a peaceable manner, it was claimed, bearing only little staves or white rods in their hands, they proceeded together in a party to Thomas Butt's house where they claimed common in a close behind the house. John Westbury spoke to Thomas Butt and told him that they would break open the gaps in the close. Thomas Butt replied that they need not do that but that he himself would lay open the field, and he did so. From there the party made its way to Cerlysfield where Richard Marche had enclosed three, and John Lee five acres. They also cooperated, it was claimed, and assisted the commoners in laying open the enclosed land. At Fortyfield the commoners laid open John Asheley's enclosure. They put no cattle into any of these fields, they said, and offered no violence.[126]

The commoners soon faced a more formidable challenge arising from an enclosure made by John Taylor, (the father), the King's farmer of the demesne of the manor of Enfield. About 1530 he enclosed Oldbury declaring that it was his intention to sow eight acres of oats there. The commoners protested that this was the year that the land should lie fallow and open to the cattle of the commoners as it had always done every third year since before the memory of man. John Taylor ignored their protest and again reaffirmed his intention to sow oats and 'to abide the jeopardy thereof'.[127]

He offered an explanation of the animosity in which he was held by the commoners. Its real source, he said, lay in the fact that the land had for many years been broken up and let by the farmer of the demesne among a number of his tenants, and he now proposed to cultivate the land himself. Though his enclosure survived the protests of the commoners, it became yet another grievance to be passed on from this generation to the next. It surfaced again in 1572 when John Taylor, the son of the former John Taylor, was brought before his own manorial court to answer a plea by the commoners that he had enclosed fifty-two acres of demesne land, and Oldbury was included in the plea. The manor court ordered John Taylor to lay open all the fields for common or face a fine of £5 for every acre remaining enclosed. He refused to obey, and a fine of £262 was imposed.[128] He appealed to the Court of the Duchy of Lancaster where, as tenant of the Manor House and of the demesne of the manor of Enfield, as well as receiver of Duchy revenues in the Home Counties, he had considerable influence. The Duchy court found in his favour. Oldbury, as it looked in the time of Queen Elizabeth, was described as 'encompassed by great and huge ditches upon the banks of which stood great oaks and trees of two hundred years growth at least'.[129]

Twelve years later in 1584, after Henry Middlemore had purchased the demesne from John Taylor, the new owner was constrained to bring the dispute once more before the Duchy Court. The tenants still refused to accept the loss of their common rights. They had been excluded from them, they said, 'only by the countenance . . . and great threatening of the Taylors'. Immediately after Middlemore had moved in, the commoners opened up an enclosure of some forty acres called Longcroft and Fishersfield where, they claimed, the enclosure had blocked access to the only spring in the area at which they could water their cattle.

On the Whitsunday afternoon, 'at such time as all godly and well disposed persons had gone into the church to hear divine service', Edward Curtis and Robert Brown, with twenty or thirty others, met together at Longcroft where, it was alleged, they broke down the hedges and drove a hundred cattle onto the grass. They proclaimed that Longcroft and Fishersfield lay next to and open with the common field called Great Southbury field. They also declared that all those who occupied any ancient dwelling house within the parish had a right of common pasture in these two fields at those times when Great Southbury field lay unsown. For three months the commoners kept these fields open for their cattle.[130]

The persistence of the commoners was on occasion equalled by their ingenuity. A case of 1589 involved not only Robert Wroth, the son of Sir Thomas, but also Henry Middlemore. It concerned Johanne Potters field, a common field of ninety acres in what is now Lincoln Road, which had been enclosed by the tenants who held land there. Robert Wroth held more than fifty acres, Middlemore ten. Mistress Hayes, the widow of Robert Hayes who had held office under the Duchy of

Lancaster, held eight, there were four smaller holdings of two or three acres, while the high constable John Banks held five, and William Curle, a well-to-do maltman, held seven. Such a combination might have appeared unchallengeable. Not for the last time in Enfield it was the women who resisted this encroachment upon their rights. Twenty-nine women, mostly chosen because they were pregnant, appeared before the Middlesex sessions. Nine were the wives of labourers, four of maltmen; two were the wives of millers; there was the wife of a yeoman, a shoemaker, a tanner and a painter; the remainder were spinsters or widows. Those named were arrested when forty women armed, according to the indictment, with swords, knives, staves, daggers and cudgels, (though this appears to be a standard description in such indictments) assembled on 7 July at Johanne Potters field. They had torn down the fences recently put up by Alice Hayes, and now the women found themselves indicted before Wroth and Middlemore. Those behind the resistance drew up a petition to Lord Burghley in which they asked for the restoration of their common 'without which they were not able to maintain themselves, their wives and children . . . and that the women, being great with child and looking every hour to travail, may not go to prison'.[131]

The last document in which can be found the story of their protest is headed: 'The names of certain women of Enfield, indicted and sent to Newgate. These women was with child and brought to bed since'.[132] There follows a list of twenty-four women; to seven of them, it is noted, a child had been born. At the foot of the document has been written, so that the great Lord Treasurer might be made aware of all the circumstances, 'these seven children did suck'. Lord Burghley had at least been assured that the babies born in Newgate had survived.

7. Charity and the Poor

It had always been held that the impotent poor were the responsibility of the parish to which they belonged. They were relieved by the gifts made by their more wealthy neighbours in their wills. Thomas Morstede, citizen and surgeon of London, by his will written in 1450,[133] gave twenty shillings to be divided among sixty poor people in Enfield, John Sell, dying in 1455, left 6s 8d towards the repair of the highway near his house in Enfield and listed six poor persons among whom should be distributed twelve bushels of wheat.[134] Lawrence Cook, by his will of 1474, left 6s 8d for the relief of his destitute neighbours. Robert Forster, in 1483, left £10 6s 8d to the repair of the highway and of the church, and in alms to the poor.[135]

Before the Reformation men of sufficient means would often make chantry bequests in their wills which provided for prayers to be said after their deaths, to seek the salvation of their souls and those of their relatives. Some of the funds thus provided filtered through to provision for the poor, because the poor could more readily be enticed to pray at any service where money or victuals were being handed out. It was also, to be just, a means of dispensing charity. John Hunsdon died in 1473 and each year thereafter there was bestowed from his estate 6s 8d in bread, ale and alms to the refreshing of the neighbours and poor people attending a service to mark each anniversary of his death.[136] Another John Hunsdon who was buried in 1506, left a rent charge of 12d out of a meadow in Millmarsh to be distributed each year on the anniversary of his death among the poor that they might pray for his soul.[137] The will of William Garrard in 1517 ordered that 12d

The Roos window, a monument to Sir Thomas Lovell in St Andrews Church.

be distributed to twelve poor persons, that they might pray for him, each year, to mark the day of his death.[138]

A dirige (dirge or funeral chant) and Mass were to be sung, and £4 distributed among the priests, clerks and poor people who would pray in St Andrews Church to mark each anniversary of the death of Dr Thomas Thompson, the wealthy vicar of Enfield who died in 1541.[139] But chantries, anniversaries and all other funds for providing prayers for the dead were confiscated in 1548 by the government of Edward VI.

Sometimes the poor might be employed in the ritual of a rich man's funeral. The will of Robert Wheler, citizen and grocer of London, prescribed detailed instructions for his burial in Enfield in 1548. His former apprentice Robert Deicrowe was to provide twelve torches, at 5s apiece, to be borne about the corpse by twelve poor men of Enfield, and every of them to have for his labour, a black gown and a hood of black cotton (an expensive material at this time). About the hearse five tapers were to be carried by his five almsfolk, men and women, and everyone of them should have 'a gown of mantell fryse (of sixteen pence the yard) in remembrance of the five wounds of our Lord Jesus Christ'. Robert Deicrowe was to pay 4d a week in perpetuity to these almsfolk dwelling in Wheler's three almshouses. He was also charged to maintain for ten years an obit upon the anniversary of Wheler's death where he should distribute 10s among the poor of the parish.[140] The little monument which commemorates both Wheler and Deicrowe can be seen in the north chancel chapel of St Andrews Church. It was put up after the burial of Robert Deicrowe in 1586; originally it was in the chancel where the steps led down to the family vault, and where his wife had her pew near the north door. Deicrowe was a parish benefactor in his own right and provided a fixed charge of 53s 4d on property at Baynards Castle for a limited period of twenty-one years. The churchwardens were to use this money to purchase every Sunday

The Lovell monument in St Andrews Church, built over the famous Tiptoft brass.

twelve pennyworth of wheaten bread to be given to twelve of the poorest in the parish and, he goes on, 'the odd penny loose to be to him that sitteth and distributeth the bread'[141]

The burial of the rich and powerful might also provide colour and pageantry briefly to distract the poor from their endless round of unremitting labour. The funeral of Sir Thomas Lovell in 1525 was magnificently arranged. The body lay in his private chapel at Elsings for eleven days while masses and matins were sung. It was then removed in grand procession to Enfield church, led by the ministers of the church and his private chaplains. They were followed by many lords and knights, his banner of arms and his helm and crest carried aloft, then a chariot drawn by five horses draped in black, and the chariot covered by a black cloth bearing a white satin cross, and a hearse cloth over the coffin of black velvet, the pall embroidered with his arms. At each corner of the chariot were four gentlemen carrying four banners. The Lord Roos rode alone as chief mourner, followed by the officers, gentlemen and servants of the household bearing aloft forty staff torches. Lastly there came fifty poor men of the parish of Enfield carrying fifty staff torches; each was paid a shilling. At Enfield church matins were sung, and the mourners were fed on 'spiced bread and ipocras,'* and the following morning the procession reformed and set out for London, through Edmonton and Tottenham to the burial at Holywell Priory, and one penny was given to every poor person who stood at the road side.[142]

The debasement of the coinage in the 1540s, and the steadily increasing population, contributed to a rapid rise in prices which caused great suffering among the poor, particularly among those without land. As early as 1525 thirty-nine per cent of all those taxed in Enfield were dependent upon wages.[143] Harvest failures in the middle years of the century added to the distress. Famine swept the country in 1556. In times of such crises the parish was called upon to supplement whatever could be provided by charity. That year, nineteen poor families, having forty-seven children among them, were thrown upon parish relief, as well as widows and other indigent poor. Over and above these a further fifteen impoverished people, some with families, were licensed by the justices to beg from door to door throughout the parish.[144]

In normal times charity was expected to suffice and there continued to be a steady stream of gifts. Richard Clapham, vicar of Enfield, by his will written in 1575[145], provided £10 for the poor of his parish, to be distributed by four substantial parishioners, and a further £10 to be given to poor householders in the parish, at the discretion of his brother John. William Cole, a malt-carrier, after carefully allocating a few small sums of money, then his coat, doublet, cloak, hose, hat and cassock, among his friends and relatives, continued solemnly; 'If there be any more [property remaining] then I will it be sold to the uttermost and distributed to the poor of South Street'[146].

Here and there echoes of pre-Reformation practices lingered on into the reign of Queen Elizabeth. Richard Westbury a yeoman, in 1573[147] left twelve pence to the poor people of Enfield, 'to be prayed for', and Magdelene Tailor, a widow, in 1575[148] gave a quarter of corn to be ground and baked and given to the poor on the day of her burial. Thomas Hawkins[149], a yeoman, by his will of that same year allocated ten shillings to be distributed on the day of his burial 'amongst the poorest people of the parish of Enfield'.

*Hippocras; a wine flavoured with spices

A plate on the bread shelf marks the gift of Robert Ramston to the poor of Enfield.

William Curtis, citizen and pewterer of London with houses and land in Enfield, was quite definitely puritan in his will and ordered that eight sermons be preached within a year of his death in 1587, four at the Church of St Dionese Backchurch in Fenchurch Street and four in Enfield, and to each preacher he awarded five shillings. He left a further £10 to be divided, 6s 8d to every poor maid of the parish of Enfield that shall be married, while the money lasts, and 48s among twenty-four of the poorest persons dwelling in Baker Street and Parsonage Street (ie. Silver Street). Twenty-four poor children in the same areas were to have sixpence apiece[150].

Charity played a more and more important part in the provision of welfare in the latter part of the reign of Queen Elizabeth. Benefactors became increasingly concerned to ensure that their money was used effectively. Gifts were made in perpetuity. Robert Ramston, a gentleman of Chingford, provided forty shillings a year to be paid to the churchwardens of Enfield as a rent charge out of certain lands in Essex, to provide comfort and relief to the poor of Enfield. His gift is commemorated in the church on a brass plate attached to the Jacobean bread shelf in the north chancel chapel[151]. Likewise William Smith (1592), whose memorial brass is on the wall in the south chancel chapel, left £15 to the re-paving of the church. He also provided a rent charge of £4 a year, paid out of the rents of lands situated near Phipps Hatch gate, to be distributed among the poor inhabitants[152]. The gift of Thomas Wilson a London brewer, in 1590[153], was the first of a series of gifts by which freehold property was vested in the parish, with trustees appointed to ensure good administration. The rents from such properties would with judicious management rise with inflation.

A poor men's box was installed in the church into which donations were made both by the living and by the dead; no record however survives of the gifts made by the living. Robert Stockwell in 1549[154] left twenty pence to this poor men's box, and John Smytheson in 1552[155] contributed twelve pence. He also ordered that a colt be sold and the money distributed among the poor. Thomas Wodham (otherwise Wilkinson) left forty shillings to the poor men's box in 1562[156], John Cordell twenty shillings in 1565[157], John Goddard forty shillings in 1566[158], Helen Aylward a widow, left twelve pence in 1574[159], John Wyburd seven pence in 1571[160], and John Grubbe in 1576 left five shillings.[161]

The year 1596 was the third successive year in which the harvest failed throughout England. The rain, it seemed, would never cease, food prices rose and there was famine. The farm labourer and the smallholder, forced off the land by the conversion of arable to pasture, wandered away from village to village in search of work and when they found none they often resorted to begging, theft, and even violence. Rogues and vagabonds wandering alone or in gangs menaced small communities. They created a serious problem for the government, and Parliament sought to solve it by the legislation of 1598 and 1601. Such vagrants were to be arrested, whipped until bloody, and passed by the most direct route to the parish to which they belonged. There they were to be set to work. Persistent offenders should be committed to goal or to a house of correction, and the Act authorised justices of the peace to erect such houses in every county.

Quite different measures however were required to look after those too old, too ill, or too young to work, widows with small children and those who genuinely travelled in search of a job. These two acts also made every parish in England and Wales responsible for the relief of its own poor. The acts established compulsory rate-financed poor relief by which overseers of the poor were empowered to buy materials on which the poor could be set to work; they could also pay for the apprenticeship of poor children.

The poor rate however was still seen as a last resort, relief remaining principally a matter for charity. Further Elizabethan legislation was passed to encourage private benefactors to establish charitable trusts. Enfield became rich in such benefactions, and parish rents grew to be so substantial that for a time the parish was spared the necessity of imposing a poor rate. It has been estimated that in no year before 1660 was more than seven per cent of the money spent on poor relief derived from taxation.

8. Road and River

Enfield became a centre, in the sixteenth century, of a growing trade in malt. The parish was in a good position on the road to the north and the village was favoured, as a manor within the Duchy of Lancaster, in that the tenants were exempted from payment of tolls. These rights were asserted in 1524 by the maltman William Mellor 'that where he, and all other tenants and inhabitants within the town of Enfield, have continually, before this time, used to have free liberty to go toll free throughout England . . . one Richard Shorte of Newport, the 14 September last past, wrongfully there took away a horse and a quarter of malt . . . for toll'[162].

The village became a centre for the private trader who bought malt in the counties north of London for resale at profit to the brewers in the City. The trade played a major part in the prosperity of Enfield for well over a hundred years[163] and expanded as the population of London grew from about 60,000 in 1534 to 120,000 in 1582 and to 250,000 in 1605. A witness describing the activities of these maltmen gave evidence that Sir Thomas Wroth of Durants Arbour, who died in 1573, had counted 2,200 pack horses in one morning on the road between Shoreditch and Enfield.[164] Another witness, who claimed that Enfield traders had forced up the prices in London, refers to their having held back, he says, 'but four thousand horseload in one week'[165]. Four thousand horseloads comprised four thousand quarters*. The scale of these operations can be judged from the fact that, in the whole year 1579/80, the total of all shipments of grain received in the Port of London from provincial ports amounted to only 18,093 quarters[166].

Other evidence spoke of the rich badgers of Enfield who could lend the brewer grain worth £1,400 or £1,500[167], and of Enfield maltmen (a badger or maltman in Enfield was a trader in malt) who had a hundred hired horses each, carrying to London every day. The scale of the trade is confirmed by the evidence given in court cases. William Wyberd of Horsepoolstones had delivered to John Reynolds, citizen and skinner of London, in 1579, seven hundred and nine quarters of malt in somewhat less than three years[168]. Thomas Mansborowe of Enfield about the same time was indebted to John Chapman of Hitchin, a maltman, for the sum of £300. Thomas Wodham (otherwise Wilkinson) of Ponders End had a debt of £438 owed to him by Edward Mathew of London, brewer dwelling at the 'sign of the Bull in the Queen hyne'[169]. A witness in 1581, speaking of the effect on the Enfield malt traders of the re-opening of the River Lea for barge traffic, declared that the hay and provender of twelve hundred horses would thereby be saved[170].

The fifteenth century had seen a major change in the brewing industry. Ale, which was the native English drink, was brewed without hops and had to be consumed within a few days of brewing. The art of beer brewing had been introduced from the Low Countries and by 1440 it was well established in the City and in Southwark. Beer would keep and could therefore be brewed by common brewers to be sold in various inns and taverns about the town.

The Enfield trade was flourishing before the beginning of the sixteenth century. Some,who had made money, proudly proclaimed their trade in their wills. Maltmen's wills, unlike most others made in the fifteenth century, showed a greater concern with the well-being of their parish than with the welfare of their souls. Such a one was that of John Hunsdon who, although he left money for candles and gifts for the altars and £13 6s 8d to pay a priest for two years to pray for his soul, left twice that amount towards the repair of the highway, and in addition £5 for the repair of Millmarsh bridge[171], the only bridge in Enfield over the River Lea.

The Cordells were also maltmen. Robert who died in 1471, and his son William, styled themselves so, as did their cousin John Cordell. William owned three houses in the parish, his family dined on pewter, and to each of his three daughters he could leave four plates, four dishes and four saucers. 'Also I bequeath', he says, 'to Robert Bely my servant, Dobyn myne horse, and a blewe gown'[172].

Yet another substantial maltman was William Cacher. At his death in 1483, he left £4 to the repair of Our Lady Chapel in Enfield church and £30 to his son who was an apprentice in London. The money was owed to him by one William Clarke of London, a brewer. The malt trade is again mentioned in a deposition of 1512 in the court of the Duchy of Lancaster, where a certain John Brett of Standon, then sixty years of age, declared that the men of Standon always delivered their malt at Ware, and 'men of Enfield and other places' carried the malt to London[173].

Later in the sixteenth century Royston became a centre of exchange for malt from a wide area; it was delivered there for the Enfield traders. A little of this trade and something of the traders can be seen,in September 1535, from the will of Robert Curtis the elder. He had been for many years one of the most substantial men in the parish; in 1525 he had been assessed on goods to the value of £19[174],

---

* a quarter was a dry measure of 64 gallons or 8 bushels.

among the five highest assessments in the parish. He left a widow, three sons, and four unmarried daughters. His widow was to hold one of his houses in Parsonage Street (now Silver Street) for the term of her life, as also his freehold and copyhold land lying at Bridge Street (now Clay Hill), and after her death, the property was to go to his son Thomas. The family also farmed, for Thomas was to have a carthorse, carts, ploughs and harrows, provided that he would carry for his mother, her wood, hay and corn, and plough her land. Coldharber, their house in Baker Street, went to his son Robert who was to pay a rent of 6s 8d a year to the widow. His second house in Parsonage Street and the new barn there was for his son William, who was to have three horses and the hay and oats to feed them for the following six months, as well as ten quarters of malt to be delivered at Royston. He provided 40s for the marriage of his daughter Alice, also a cow and two ewes. Of his other daughters, Emery was to have two newly weaned cow calves and 3s 4d in money, Margaret two ewes and five quarters of malt delivered at Royston, and Annes, the fourth daughter, 20s[175].

Much of the trade was done by credit. In the case of Thomas Wodham of Ponders End, so completely was his capital involved that his bequests in 1562 were dependent on the recovery of a debt amounting to £438. The maltman had intended to leave £100 to each of his daughters, Katheren and Margaret, and £50 each to Elizabeth a third daughter, and Margaret his niece; all the money was to be paid when they reached the age of twenty, or on the day of marriage, should this be earlier. If the debt was not recoverable, the larger legacies would have to be reduced to £40 and the smaller to £20, and he seems almost to have despaired of getting the money back[176]. Apart from his dealings in malt, Thomas Wodham farmed on a considerable scale. He had taken a lease from Robert Deicrowe[177], for life or forty years, of a farmstead and eighty acres in Green Street. The annual rent was £8, together with six quarters of wheat and twelve bushels of malt. He also had to carry for his landlord five loads of wood, and two loads of hay.

The Enfield maltmen acquired something of an evil reputation. English people have always been conservative, and private trade, buying and selling outside the markets, being a new practice was regarded with suspicion. 'There be certain rich men dwelling at Enfield and places thereby', wrote a witness to Lord Burghley in 1583, and he went on to condemn them as middlemen who sought to push up prices for their own profit, a criminal offence at that time. He described their method of operating. They bought four or five hundred quarters of malt each at moderate prices, in advance of its production, and so arranged the deliveries that each country market was in turn stripped of its supplies. They then purchased whatever malt came into those markets in order to force up the price, and when this was sufficiently high, and the bakers and the brewers in London had become desperate for supplies, the Enfield traders would bring in their malt and corn which they would only sell direct, and not through the markets in the City. Many in London had been rendered bankrupt by these practices, some of the bakers and brewers owed so much money to the maltmen, this witness went on, that even £500 would not suffice to pay each man's debt[178].

The maltmen were a new kind of trader in that all their transactions were carried out privately, with none of the restrictions which had been imposed by the regulations of the market place. They disregarded such mediaeval notions as a 'just price'. To them, a man's credit was his ability to pay or to find others who could guarantee payment. The Curle family were among the leading maltmen of Enfield and typical of the private trader in that they were hard, exacting men.

They shared none of the feeling which still existed, even among City business men, that they owed some kind of duty one to another. The case of Henry Lever illustrates this. He had been in trade as an ale-brewer but things had gone badly for him and his debts for malt and other wares amounted to £1,000. He met his creditors in August 1595 to ask that he should be given twelve months to find the money to pay his debts and that, during that time, he should be permitted to move around in pursuance of his business, without fear of arrest. His creditors, pitying his ill-fortune, and having always found him an honest man, issued to him a letter of licence sealed by them all; all, that is, except Raphe Curle and two smaller creditors. Henry Lever, since that time, by means of a new credit had been able to resume his business. Raphe Curle however 'of a most wicked and unconscionable mind' was greedily seeking the recovery of his own debt at the expense of the other creditors. He lay in wait for Henry Lever, to arrest him and throw him into prison, and sought to attach (seize) his goods within the City of London[179]. No evidence has been forthcoming to tell how this conflict ended.

Credit was extended to the maltman by his suppliers, as well as by the maltman to the brewer. On occasions the money might be paid direct from brewer to supplier. About 1580 Thomas Mansborowe of Enfield, maltman, stood indebted to John Chapman of Hitchin for £300[180], but this was balanced by debts owed to Mansborowe in London, £255 by Henry Loftburye in East Smithfield, brewer, and other smaller debts. These, it had been agreed, should be set over to John Chapman. Payment however must have been too slow for Chapman's liking, and though it was claimed that the brewer had paid the greater part of the debt and had agreed with Chapman about the repayment of the remainder, he would not wait, and had seized four of Mansborowe's horses; yet he still detained the bonds and bills for which he had already been paid.

Credit was a matter of reputation; it could be secured by marriage, or through a recommendation by someone known to both parties. William Ligeart was given creditworthyness by his marriage to the daughter of Oliver Burr, a man of standing in the City[181]. Another of Burr's daughters had married John Hodge of Enfield. Having neither credit nor money for sufficient malt to carry on his brewing business, William Ligeart sought the assistance of his father-in-law who sent John Hodge into the country (lending him his gelding) to find some honest man to give credit for malt to the value of £200. 'And if he will not take my word', said Burr, 'I will give him my bond.' Saddling his father-in-law's gelding (this was stressed in the court as though the gelding itself had constituted a guarantee of payment) Hodge rode, as might be expected, to Enfield, and there he went to the house of William Curle, who was content with the word and did not demand the bond, and who duly delivered £200 worth of malt. But Ligeart fared badly and fell into debt, and Curle was obliged to come to an agreement with him to receive £10 a quarter. After five payments however the debtor died; much of his property fell into the hands of his father-in-law, including the brewhouse which Burr claimed as part payment for debts owed to himself. Curle asserted that the brewhouse was worth over £300 and began an action at common law against Burr, but in this he could not proceed without a bond, he therefore transferred the case to the Court of Requests[182].

A month later William Curle appeared again in the same court. This time he came to sue his former attorney. He complained bitterly that most part of his substance was in other men's hands. He was not only constrained to go to law to get his own money back, but to his further great expense, he had had the misfortune to retain Robert Themilthorpe as his attorney when the case had been presented in the Court of Common Pleas. Now, after consulting with some of his friends who had experience of the law, the maltman was suing his attorney for overcharging. His costs had amounted to twenty marks he said, which was far more than it ought to have been; and on top of this Themilthorpe was now demanding a further £10[183].

This expensive experience seems to have done nothing to deter the family from litigation. Four years later Henry his son was involved in the pursuit of a debt of £36, wherein he was well supported by his formidable father. This was another debt for malt for which Henry Hely, citizen and merchant tailor, had been arrested. Bail had been paid by three of his friends, 'honest citizens of London', and he had paid Curle £10 on account. Then he had sealed and delivered to Curle an agreement to pay the remaining £26. Despite this, Curle had refused to surrender his original bill saying that he had left it in the hands of a scrivener at Southwark, and now he pursued his action against the 'honest citizens' who had stood bail for Hely. One of these, Frances Johnson, a cook on Her Majesty's ship the 'Wasspight', had been arrested for the debt. He had escaped from the officer who had detained him; 'as lawful was for him so to do' asserted Hely. But a letter of attorney had been granted to William Curle the father, and so armed he did 'solicit, vex and trouble', both Frances Johnson and Henry Hely to their utter undoing'[184].

John Parke was another Enfield maltman whose credit appears to have been better than the credit of his customer. He died in 1580 owing £40 to Thomas Baker of Malandyne (Manuden) in Essex. He ordered the money to be paid so that Raphe Curle, who had stood surety for him, could be discharged. Yet he remained uncertain concerning some £66 which was owed to himself by James Heathe of the parish of St Olaves in Southwark. His daughters were to have £10 each on the day of their marriages, but only if it was found possible to recover this debt[185].

Efforts to improve the transport system throughout the country in the sixteenth and early seventeenth centuries concentrated on ports, harbours and inland waterways. Such improvements became essential with the dramatic growth of London both in population and in riches. During this period the River Thames was cleared for navigation above Oxford, and it was proposed to open the River Lea for boats and barges as far as Ware. The cost of water transport proved lower than the cost of carriage by road, especially for cheaper grains like barley which was widely grown in Hertfordshire. Even for the more expensive malt however, the difference was significant. The vital interests of many in Enfield were thought to be at stake, and the maltmen, with others who stood to lose money, gathered their forces to prevent change.

The project for using the River Lea to bring malt and grain from Hertfordshire to London was first considered in August 1560 when the Court of Aldermen of the City of London appointed four of its members to survey the River 'as far as Ware and upward to the head . . . some day next week'. The survey was made by two Dutchmen, Garrett Honrighe and Adrian Tymberman. They were paid £10, though this sum included their fee for 'making of a certain instrument whereby . . . water might be conveyed out of the Thames into diverse places of the City'[186]. The matter seems to have been put on one side for a time, and it was nearly seven years later when the Common Council asked Sir Thomas Lodge for a report 'to learn of him what he, and the two strangers born, that viewed the water of Lea, four or five years now past, thought therein'[187]. At the next meeting the following month (May 1567) the Council demanded that the business be pursued with urgency[188].

The result was the Act of 1571 which ordered that the River Lea be made navigable as far as Ware. This was a major undertaking which took ten years and cost £80,000. Opinions differ as to whether new cuts were constructed. Mr Corble, clerk to the Lee Conservancy Board in 1894, believed that the improvements were confined to cleaning the old river and containing it within embankments in certain parts of the marshes. On the other hand G. B. G. Bull(*Elizabethan Maps of the Lower Lea Valley* in *Geog. Jnl* pt. 3) seems to be of the opinion that a new cut was constructed. One great improvement and innovation was the construction of a pound lock at Waltham Abbey. It was among the earliest built in England, only preceded by those made on the Exeter Canal in 1564–7. Waltham Lock had been completed by about 1577. It had two sets of mitred gates, a design which was to be the pattern for the future. Recent archaeological excavation at Waltham Abbey shows that this new lock was to the south-west of a bend in the present Cornmill stream, which flowed past the former monastic buildings. The lock led into the Long Pool, a new cut, and so connected the Cornmill stream to what is now called the old River Lea. Such pound locks effected a great economy in the use of water compared with the old flash locks, and so were of great advantage to the millers; they were also far less dangerous for the boatmen[189].

The work on the Lea roused inexorable hostility. The methods by which it was financed gave justifiable cause for grievance since the costs seem to have been borne by those who owned land and other property along the river. Theirs too were the losses, for their osier beds had to be limited to a width of four feet; any outside this limit, the owners must pull up by the roots.It was ordered that the piles and stakes, which they had used to set nets to catch fish, must also be removed. All bridges had to be made higher by the owners of the surrounding land, on pain of a £10 fine. The boats and barges would take the water so precious to the millers. The rich water-meadows would be impoverished as a result of the flood control. These grievances, together with the anticipated effect of the river transport on the carrying trade by road, on the owners of packhorses, on the carriers who drove the teams, and above all on the maltmen themselves, gave rise to a sequence of events which disturbed the area and caused grave concern to the Privy Council from March 1580[190].

That year a bill of complaint was submitted from the loaders and carriers of grain to London. It was answered by Lord Burghley himself, who strongly supported the navigation. The complaints alleged that Enfield would be utterly ruined; but Burghley pointed out that the Enfield traders had long ruled the markets in London and in the country to their great advantage. Now, he said, with malt and grain brought in both by river and by road, prices would be forced down, and the Enfield traders would no longer be able to make great profits at the expense of the consumer[191].

The river seemed likely to prove a more efficient mode of transport than the road. A comparison of the costs can be seen in a statement by a baker who had, to by-pass the Enfield badgers, employed his own team of horses and traded direct with the farmers of Hertfordshire. 'The keeping of these ten horses', he said, 'cost me a hundred pounds a year at least'. Now, he claimed, he could have the same amount of malt delivered by boat for £30[192]. Another witness pointed out that it took sixty horses to carry sixty quarters of malt, and it took twelve men at least to drive them; but now the same amount of malt could be carried in one boat manned by only four or five men. Even the evidence from the carriers by road supports the case. Edward Cherie of Enfield admitted that he had made a breach in the river bank because he saw someone sell a quarter of malt, which had been carried by water, at sixpence less than he could sell his malt carried by packhorse[193]. Another important advantage of river transport was that the barges could be used on the return journey to carry coal and iron to places like Stanstead, Ware and Hertford, and from these places it could be made available to blacksmiths within a radius of a further eight or nine miles. The money earned on these return journeys, it was claimed, would at least bear the cost of replacing the barges. They were expensive to build. The largest, which carried up to forty-two quarters, cost £40; the small barges, carrying twenty-six quarters, cost forty marks (£26.66p). A cart, by contrast, could carry only eight quarters of malt (2 cwt) or five quarters of wheat. Barges could carry a quarter of malt from Ware to London for eightpence, and a quarter of wheat for twelvepence; the charge for a passenger was sixpence. Coal could be brought back for 6s 8d a chaldron (thirty-six bushels) and iron for 6s 8d a ton. The journey from Bow Bridge up to Ware took twelve hours, the journey downstream probably somewhat less. At Bow, where the Lea meets the Thames, the boatmen had to wait for a tide on which the barges could be rowed upstream to London in four hours. Wages of the boatmen varied from 8s to 10s a week[194].

Lord Burghley, having considered the arguments submitted by the parish of Enfield, concluded that in every way transport by river was more efficient than transport by road. Thereupon the landowners and traders around Enfield embarked on a campaign of sabotage to prove the contrary. It was to continue, initially, for over ten years. The first trouble occurred where the Lea passed through land belonging to Robert Wroth. The Wroths were the most powerful landowners in the area and were the owners of the mill at Ponders End. It was discovered in the summer of 1580 that 'a great flood of water' was running out of the river along the courses of two streams, Marditch and Lodersley, which had previously been dammed up[195]. Another ditch lying between Enfield and Edmonton, belonging to Mr Woodall, had also been opened to allow the water to escape. The aim of the saboteurs was to lower the water level in order to hold up the barges.

More serious interruptions of traffic came in August 1581 when there was an organised movement to cut the river banks, to sabotage the boats, and to set obstructions in the river. A contemporary account tells of a party of eight or nine men who gathered at 'Green Street Lane end'; every one of them carried a staff as they headed down Green Street towards the marsh. That night the river bank was cut next to Enfield lock. Many of those involved were subsequently named; Robert Spencer of Cocksmiths End (Enfield Highway) the son of William Spencer; William Cordell, a young man of twenty-four who had been employed by William Wyberd the maltman; Thomas Wilshere, servant to Raphe Curle the maltman; and John Lucke who had also threatened that he would 'go by water, and have an auger, to bore holes in the barges'. There was also John Mott, son of John Mott of Ponders End, Ezechial Burton, servant to William Gurnerd a smith, James Brown, and John, servant to John Doo, a maltman of Cocksmiths End. The enterprise seems to have been organised from Richard Wodham's house in Green Street. Wodham was a dealer in malt on a considerable scale. He was implicated first by John Hunsdon who gave evidence against his step-brother William Cordell who, he reported, was called out of his bed in the night time, between eight and ten o'clock, by somebody 'whom he knoweth not'. Cordell, asked in the morning when he did rise and where he had been, answered that he had been to Richard Wodham's house 'to eat a messe of cream with young fellows', and refused to say who had called him up.[196]

Richard Wodham was further implicated, for it was alleged that, finding several watermen busy repairing the river bank while their barge lay aground a little above, he bade them God's speed and declared, watching them at their labours, 'This is but folly, for within these three or four days, you shall have it cut deeper than ever it was, that you may bury a horse in the hole'[197]. This duly came to pass.

Early the following month came an attempt to set fire to Waltham lock carried out by William Shambroke, William Cocke and John Shelley, all of Cheshunt. The attempt was made at night time, using brimstone, rosin and straw which Shambroke had purchased in London for a groat (4d). The others had agreed to share the expense with him. Shambroke was a most indiscreet conspirator. A month before the event he had told Edward King of Turners Hill that he and Cocke intended to make an attempt on the lock. On the Sunday before the fire he had said the same thing to Edward's son Henry. Young Henry was intent on going to see the sport but he was wisely persuaded to stay at home by George Andrew at Cheshunt mill who pointed out to him that it could be a hanging matter. George himself already knew about the project (as probably did half the population of Cheshunt and Enfield), for all three of the accused had come to see him in May because they wanted to borrow his hand-saw. But George prudently demanded to know what they wanted to use it for, and when he learned that they proposed to saw the new lock, he had decided that it would be safer not to be involved. Two of the watermen told the court that Christopher Penyfather of Cheshunt also knew who had been responsible for the outrage. He had told them so, and had openly declared that he would be glad if there was a barrel of gunpowder at the bottom of the lock and another in the bottom of the barge, 'so as the men wert out of it'. Another accused, but apparently with a quite different motive, was Aron Yong of Waltham Abbey, a tailor. He had sold a chain which belonged to the lock, to a smith named Davie of Waltham Cross, for sixpence. he said he had found it lying in a ditch near the old lock.[198] The blame for all this sabotage was squarely placed upon men from Enfield, as Shambroke said he verily believed that neither the attempt on Waltham lock, nor any other damage to the river would have been done but by the procurement of Enfield men.[199]

Lord Burghley set up a commission of three important gentlemen to investigate the trouble under the chairmanship of Thomas Fanshaw of Ware Park, remembrancer of the Exchequer. The others were Sir Henry Cocke of Broxbourne, cofferer at the court of Elizabeth I, probably the highest working court official, and Henry Baeshe of Stanstead Abbots, one time surveyor general of the navy. But the sabotage blatantly continued even as their investigations proceeded. Further breaches occurred which allowed the water to flow out of the river into Master Wroth's mill stream. While Robert Wroth was instigating the trouble and encouraging the trouble-makers, the commission felt itself unable to act effectively unless Lord Burghley himself, or some other powerful figure, was present. They suggested that, if Lord Burghley was unwilling, then Lord Hunsdon[200] should join the commission, and that the investigations should be removed from Enfield to Westminster. A week or two later Lord Hunsdon was sent down to take charge. It is remarkable that three men of this importance should be appointed, and even more remarkable that Lord Hunsdon, first cousin to the Queen herself (and subsequently the occupier of the tallest tomb in Westminster Abbey) should be involved in what was merely a local dispute. Despite their presence the wrecking continued. Stakes were now driven into the bed of the river to prevent the passage of boats.

Tudor governments lived in a state of constant apprehension for they had no adequate force to suppress riot or rebellion. This accounts for the obvious anxiety of the commission, and Lord Hunsdon, although he had recently been occupied against a serious insurrection in the North, expressed deep concern in his first despatch to the Lord High Treasurer. In it he reported, 'lewd speech used, that if the river should not be overthrown, that then they would rise against the maintainers, and that it would cost many men's lives . . . The next way', he says, 'in my opinion, to stir rebellion'.[200]

The matter, at the suggestion of Lord Hunsdon, was handed over to the Commission of Sewers for the River Lea[201] under the chairmanship of William Fleetwood, recorder of the City of London. Robert Wroth himself was a member of the Commission but was not present when it met on 5 October. Despite a letter written to him personally by Lord Burghley, he had continued in the most outspoken opposition, declaring that 'the Lords of the Council had done them great wrong, and rather than [they] shall force us to make up the breaches again we will be hanged at our own gates'[202]. He offered encouragement to offenders brought before him, and had made a great stir at the swanemote.* All this had caused Fleetwood to write to Lord Burghley of him 'I fear the gentleman be overmuch puffed in pride with overmuch living and wealth'[203]. Another great local landowner, however, took care to be present at the meeting of the Commission of Sewers. This was Jasper Leake, a recusant (Roman Catholic) gentleman from the neighbouring parish of Edmonton. He was one likely to oppose the puritan Wroths at every possible opportunity. Many new breaches had been made and Lady Wroth, Robert's mother, it was suggested, ought to be examined (since the sabotage occurred on her land) to ascertain whether she had commanded, or assented to it[204].

In the end the culprits, 'who had bound themselves by promise not to betray the matter', at last broke down, or at least a few of them did, and confessed. The chief offenders were brought before the commissioners at Mr Sheriff Martin's house at Tottenham, on 21 October 1581. William Fleetwood wrote a graphic description of the protracted proceedings. The prisoners were closely examined throughout the morning and divulged nothing, but in the afternoon one poor man, under the threat that he would be sent to Newgate for perjury, broke down and confessed, and in his evidence implicated many of Wroth's men. One of these, his horse-keeper, was forced to confess, but another, his purveyor of wheat and malt, would admit nothing. Others refused to take the oath, or to be examined. John Goddard, the high constable of Edmonton hundred, defended them in this, and under oath not only concealed the truth, but entered into a fierce defence of all their actions, and made what was described as 'a clamorous speech tending towards rebellion.'

Goddard was committed to Newgate, and Fleetwood demanded that he be removed from the office of high constable, wherein he had been placed on the insistance of Robert Wroth, who had dismissed his predecessor Curle, an Edmonton man and had sent him to Newgate upon some trifling occasion. Goddard was related to the two important maltman families of Wyberd and Loft.

Despite all he had seen during his long service to the Crown, Fleetwood expressed himself with indignation when he wrote to Lord Burghley;

I assure your lordship, I never met with such stubborn varlets as those that appeared before us this day . . . I have persuaded my fellows to meet at London,

---

*an assembly to control the feeding of pigs, presumably this would have been in Epping Forest.

at the Sessions Hall of Newgate, which is a fitter school-house for such lewd people as these . . . [205]

A number of Enfield men were committed to Newgate, the Marshalsea, and the Gate House prisons. Included is the name of one Nicholas Dixe, servant to the miller at Enfield, a man of many words and little discretion. He had told certain watermen that he could have thirty, or forty, or (warming to his subject) a hundred men to resist the watermen, and that if the navigation continued it would cost many hundreds of lives and more. Such speeches he used many times to the watermen. His garrulous words landed him in the Marshalsea and left his wife pleading for him to the Lord High Treasurer, that her

> 'poor husband, for certain words he is accused to have uttered, which . . . he cannot altogether deny to have spoken, but not in such sort as is supposed, for which rash and inadvised speech, he most humbly craveth favour and pardon, being heartily sorry for his offence, and, unless your good Lordship, of your accustomed goodness and clemency, show your lawful favour in this his miserable and distressed estate . . .'with three small children depending only upon the labour of your petitioner's poor husband. In tender consideration whereof may it please your good Lordship to pity our poor and miserable estate, to grant that he may be released from his imprisonment . . . [206]

Now the troubles at last seemed to be over. Those banks, weirs and other defects which were listed in 1583, were probably caused by the long break in river traffic. The regular and renewed passing of boats would help to keep the waterway clear. Occasional incidents still occurred; a letter from Ware complained that former breaches had lately been broken open again, but relative peace lasted for ten years. There were many who exulted that the maltmen and badgers were now 'utterly prevented from their former practices'. The number of barges using the river had, by 1591, grown to thirty and, on average, a thousand quarters of corn were carried to London each week. So much had the traffic by road diminished that a commission was set up to examine the loss of toll on the bridges at Stanstead, Hertford and Ware. This they found had fallen by £16 a year, so that the toll could no longer be let, even for forty marks. The commissioners proposed the imposition of a toll on barges using the river.[207]

The trouble that broke out in 1592 was worse than it had been before. Accusations against inhabitants of Enfield, Waltham, Hoddesdon, Cheshunt, and even of Luton, alleged the existence of a vast plot. It was said that certain men now conspired to get the whole trade in malt and grain into their own hands, and to this end sought to close the Lea for transport. Many of the conspirators were named and they included some who had been involved in the troubles a decade earlier. There was John Harlowe, the miller at Mr Wroth's mill at Ponders End, Richard Wodham of Green Street, the Curles, the Curtises, the Lofts and the Wyberds; and the Shambrokes were again to the fore. John Goddard, the former high constable, was named.

On 31 May 1592 a large party, mostly coming from Enfield, armed with swords, bill staves, pitchforks, mattocks, spades and shovels, gathered at ten o'clock at night near the High Bridge at Waltham, where they were joined by some of the servants of Sir Edward Denny. Until four o'clock in the morning they worked to tear down the bridge, then they rebuilt it so low that barges could no longer pass underneath. Subsequently, in defence of their action, it was claimed that the new lock (that is the pound lock) was not on the River Lea, but stood on freehold land belonging to Sir Edward. The high bridge lay downstream from this lock. It had been heightened at the time the lock was built, some sixteen years earlier. Sir Edward was then a minor, and it been done without his consent. Since that time he had been persuaded that it would be advantageous 'to the Commonwealth of the City and shires' both to destroy the lock, and to reduce the height of the bridge to its former level. And thus the deed was done.

The bargemen retaliated in July when forty-six of them, sixteen of whom came from Ware, smashed the mill race at Sir Edward Denny's mill near Waltham Abbey and diverted the mill stream, seeking thereby to open a new route through an old lock known as Netherlock. Denny's servants were beaten when they attempted to intervene. In response to this a great party of men from Cheshunt and Enfield assembled on 19 July at the same place, determined to prevent the barges from using this new route. The boatmen were forced to run for their lives. Eighty people were said to have been involved. Stones, timber and earth were cast into the river so that the boats were once again held up, and detained so long 'that their sacks were rotten with long lying, and the corn issued out and was spoiled'.

A party of twenty-six rioters gathered again at the same place on 24 July. They were armed with long piked staves, bills, swords and daggers, and attacked the bargemen while they were towing the barges so that they were forced to run into the water to save their lives. Again and again they lay in ambush, so that the bargees no longer dared to pass down the river. One bargeman, on 28 July, was wounded in the shoulder with a piked staff. When the boatmen attempted to clear the river on 7 August, they were assaulted by twelve men, including several of Sir Edward Denny's servants armed with bows and arrows, so that they were forced to forsake their work. A number of Enfield men came with carts and brought great trees to lay across the stream on 20 November.

The situation deteriorated in December; on the 18th an attack was mounted by eighty armed men, accompanied by a surgeon who was present to attend the wounded. The rioters overran the boats, threw the crews into the water and in what they themselves called 'a lusty riot', they heaved the corn and malt into the river. The fight was renewed three days before Christmas and in this skirmish tackle, lines and masts were cut to pieces, and one barge was sunk; and 'so drowned a great quantity of corn'.

The barge owners and the bargees complained that none of these outrages had ever been punished, nor had enquiries even been begun. Certain justices were in league with the rioters, and fourteen of the bargees had been called before Robert Wroth at a sessions held at Waltham. There they were fined sums varying from 10s to £5, and were threatened with imprisonment in Colchester gaol if they failed to pay. The government was anxious to bring an end to the disturbances. Fanshawe and the City asked for a *subpoena* to be directed to Wroth and forty-nine others, but in the event only seven men including William Mayhew, Thomas Curtis, Robert Sparkes and John Harlowe, the miller from Ponders End, were called upon to present the case for the defence. They did not include any members of the families of Robert Wroth, Sir Edward Denny, or of any other gentry involved.

The Court of Star Chamber, in November 1594, declared that passage on the river had always been, and ought always to be, free. It was also asserted that, since 1577 or 1578, barges of six or seven tons had passed through the new lock. It was the opinion of the court that carriage by water was far cheaper, but that more men would be maintained in work by road transport. It was suggested that both methods ought to be employed. Finally it was ordered that a tow-path should be constructed, as was the case on all other great rivers[208].

Thirty-four barges now plied the Lea, their capacities ranging from twenty-six to forty-two quarters (10½ cwt). No barge drew more than sixteen inches of water. They are shown on a delightful colour-wash strip map of the river from Tottenham to Cheshunt which is in the library at Hatfield House. It measures six and a half feet in length, by five and three quarter inches wide[209]. At Tottenham the map shows the barges with their square sails hoisted, using stern end steering oars, while the two shown passing Enfield lock are each hauled by three bargees with the rope looped over one shoulder and under the other arm; one end is attached to the top of the mast. The larger barges were worked by a crew of four, the smaller by three men.

The struggle between the road and the river took a long time to subside. As late as 1604 a bill was presented in Parliament 'for the suppression of the inconvenience growing by barges on the River Lea'. It failed however even to get a first reading[210].

After the turmoil of the late sixteenth century the barge-masters were left to contend with the everyday difficulties of keeping the river open. Much of the trade still went by road. Large numbers of Enfield badgers trading in malt continued to be licenced at the Middlesex sessions each year in April and October. Far more of these badgers came from Enfield than from any other parish in the county. There were 118 licenced in 1608 of whom forty-two were Enfield men, and in the following year fifty-four Enfield men were licenced[211].

When a select vestry was set up in 1615, it consisted of the vicar and twelve leading parishioners. Three were gentlemen, and of the remaining nine, five were maltmen[212]. The market committee that same year comprised Sir Nicholas Salter, two gentlemen, and four others, three of whom were maltmen[213]. Though licensed as badgers, these men were always termed maltmen when they appeared elsewhere in the sessions records.

Many were trading in a big way, and their business methods do not seem to have become more civilised since the sixteenth century. John Horne, a brewer from Southwark complained in 1616[214] that he had for many years bought most of his malt from the brothers John and Robert Cooper of Enfield. Over the years he had purchased from them malt to the value of about £5,000, and had given bonds and bills each time that he had incurred debts. He claimed that he had paid his accounts but had unwisely left many bills and bonds in the hands of the Coopers. Now, he said, because of the credit he had granted to bad customers, because of the dishonest dealings of his own servants, and in consequence of his long sickness, he was bankrupt. Though his credit remained good, the Coopers, by means of the bonds they had unjustly retained which amounted to £150, threatened him with arrest and imprisonment. By these means they forced him to buy malt from them only, but they raised their prices and demanded 30s a quarter for the worst malt, which should have cost 20s. They sent short measure and he dared not complain. In consequence he fell further into debt and at Christmas could not find the £150 to pay the Coopers. They demanded fresh security, and when he failed to produce it they sued him in the Court of Common Pleas. There he was induced to admit a debt of £300 (the other £150, he said, was for malt not yet delivered). The court ordered him to pay £80 a year, but now the Coopers refused to send him any more malt. John Cooper then arranged a meeting with the brewer, pretending that he wished to reach a settlement, but when John Horne arrived at the place agreed upon, he was arrested for a debt of £400. Thus Horne was faced with prison; the only alternative offered to him was an arrangement whereby he made a deed of gift to the Coopers of his whole estate, including the brewhouse. By this arrangement they proposed to manage the business, promising to pay him half the profits; but they insisted it must be a matter of trust In this way all the brewer's property, which he claimed was worth £600, fell into the hands of the Coopers. But instead of managing it, they sold off the horses, drays and casks, and even seized the lease of his house. That was the brewer's story; unfortunately the Coopers' version has not survived.

Enfield maltmen continued to do well in the years before the Civil War, and continued to play a leading role in parish affairs. Eight out of sixteen of the jury appointed for a view of frankpledge in 1625, and five out of fifteen members of the homage in 1626, were maltmen. So were five out of the six appointed to make an assessment of the parish that same year, and twenty-one maltmen's names appeared in the list of seventy-eight who paid the tax[215].

Their wills maintain the impression of prosperity. Robert Spenser, who died in 1625, lived at Ponders End where he had added a new hall to the house. He left the property to his son Henry, yet was able to make provision for another of his sons by the payment of £40 in four instalments over two years. William, the eldest, seems to have been estranged from his father; he was to receive £5, if he came personally to demand it within twelve months. This William was also a maltman[216].

The trade continued; as late as 1638 there were twenty-three badgers licensed in Enfield, which was still more than in any other parish in Middlesex.

Notes to Chapter Two

1   PROB 11. 14. 9
2   PROB 11. 16. 5
3   E179. 238. 97
4   GLRO DLC 355. 17
5   E179. 238. 97
6   E179. 238. 101
7   Guildhall 9171. 18. 28
8   DL 43. 7. 5, Guildhall 9171. 6. 197
9   PROB 11. 15. 18
10 Guildhall 9171. 9. 64
11 Guildhall 9171. 18. 181
12 DL43. 7. 5
13 MPC 50A
14 SP15. 29. 68
15 CPGen. 67. 17, 18, T. Lewis and D. O. Pam *William and Robert Cecil as Landowners in Edmonton.* E. H. H. S No22, 1970
16 E. K. Chambers *Elizabeth Stage* V4, 1923 pp 79, 81, 84, 88, C2Jac I 38. 67, CLRO 114D, DL43. 7. 8
17 DL3. 7. 4 f5
18 Guildhall 9171. 16. 15
19 L+P Henry VIII V14 Pt 2 p 349
20 PROB 11. 28. 23
21 GLRO DLC 358. 1 219
22 PROB11. 43. 49 the will of John Sadler of Edmonton
23 Roger Goad DD 1538–1610 Provost of Kings College Cambridge 1570, Lady Margaret preacher 1572–77 and vice-chancellor of the University 1576

24 BL. Lans 47. 18
25 *ibid*
26 the will of Agnes Myddleton, 1462 Guildhall 9171. 5. 324
27 EGS 14
28 EGS 12
29 EGS 14
30 EGS 17, 18
31 Guildhall 9171. 6. 145
32 PROB 11. 6. 7
33 PROB 11. 8. 32
34 EGS 20
35 PROB 11. 69. 59
36 Guildhall 9537. 8
37 EGS 24, 25
38 PROB 11. 16. 5
39 PROB 11. 24. 2
40 E315. 68. 213
41 EGS 19A (eighteenth century copy)
42 E301. 34. 185
43 PROB 11. 18. 29
44 eg wills of John Godard PROB 11. 20. 6, Charles Nowell PROB 11. 21. 28 and
    Thomas Brewster Guildhall 9171. 10. 218
45 E301. 34. 185
46 EGS 26
47 EGS 30 B
48 PROB 11. 69. 59
49 WAM 9351
50 EGS 31
51 WAM 9351
52 Guildhall 9537. 8
53 Guildhall 9173A 3. 211
54 E178. 4166 dated 1606
55 PROB 2. 199 *L+P Henry VIII passim*
56 BL Add 12462, PROB 11. 23. 27
57 E305 A35
58 *History of the Kings Works* V4 HMSO 1982 p 86–89
59 BL Add 10109 f 115–122
60 *L+P Henry VIII*
61 *Cal Pat Rolls* 1549–1551 p 240
62 Bodl Rawl A 195c. f243–251
63 *Kings Works* V4 p 87
64 CP Gen 67. 10
65 E 351. 3211
66 E 351. 3212
67 *Kings Works* V4 p 86–89
68 E. K. Chambers *op cit* V4 p 79, 81, 84, 88
69 LR 12. 36. 1329
70 LR 12. 16. 469
71 *HMC Salisbury* V7 p 458
72 SP 14. 25 For a fuller account see D. O. Pam *The Story of Enfield Chase* Enfield
    Preservation Soc. 1984 p 48–50
73 E351. 3241
74 SP38. 9
75 E351. 3244
76 Enfield D 1105

77   SP 14. 88. 68
78   SP 14. 95. 14
79   E351. 3255
81   GLRO Acc 18. 8
82   Guildhall 9171. 16. 415
83   *L+P Henry VIII* ii (2) 4532
84   *Cal Rutland MS* iv 260
85   PROB 11. 23. 27
86   L + P Henry VIII iii (2) 3282, 3504
87   *ibid* iii (2) 3495 (18)
88   *ibid* v 1692
89   *ibid* v 1691
90   *ibid* viii 291 (10), ix 478 p 157
91   ibid viii 129
92   PROB 11. 25. 36
93   *DNB* Heirs under age became wards of the Crown, such wardships could be granted in return for services rendered, or could be sold.
94   *Cal Pat Edw VI* iii 68, 327, 329, iv 6
95   DNB, *Cal Alan Finch MS* i 3 (19 July 1553) Grey Friars Chron 80–81
96   *Chron Queen Jane* Camden Soc. Ser. 1. 53 (1852) p 182–3, *DNB*, SP 11. 3. 20
97   C. Garrett *Marian Exiles* CUP 1966 p 345
98   Cal Pat Eliz i 294, 351
99   Fuidge, Norah M. *The Personnel of the House of Commons 1563–7* London MA thesis 1950
100 *Cal Carew MS*, 1515–1574, 240, 241, *Cal S P. Ireland passim*
101 PROB 11. 57. 16
102 *DNB*
103 E. C. Waller *An Extinct County Family: Wroth of Loughton Hall* in Trans Essex Arch, Soc. N.S. V9
104 STAC 5 W6. 22 (1580)
105 Sir Simonds D'Ewes *Journals of the Parliaments of Elizabeth* 1682 *passim* D. O. Pam *Protestant Gentlemen, the Wroths of Durants Arbour Enfield* E. H. H. S No 25 1972 J. E. Neale *Elizabeth I and her Parliaments* V2 p 347
106 PROB 11. 107. 9
107 E112. 101. 1224, William Gamage *Linsi Woolsie . . .* 1613 quoted in W. C. Waller *op cit*, S P Dom James I 76. 49
108 E112. 101. 1224, Waller *op cit*
109 SP 12. 192. 22 printed in A. L. Rowse *The England of Elizabeth* (1951) p 357
110 T. S. Eliot *Little Gidding*
111 SP 12. 64. 2
112 DL 43. 7. 5
113 Guildhall 9171. 16. 261, 'latten' brass or similar alloy
114 DL43. 7. 5
115 E179. 141. 111, E179. 238. 97
116 D. O. Pam *Elizabethan Enfield* EHHS No 30 1975 p 3
117 Guildhall 9171. 16. 213
118 CP Gen 67. 14, BL Lans. 105. 11, DL1. 115A27 CP Legal 33. 4, 14 *etc.*
119 GLRO DLC 355. 1, *VCH Middlesex* V5 p 228, C8. 35. 441
120 CP Gen 17, 18, E112. 101. 1221, C8. 35. 441 *V. C. H Middlesex* V5 1976 p 225
121 D. O. Pam *The Fight for Common Rights in Enfield and Edmonton 1400–1600* EHHS No 27 1974
122 DL1. 19. 1E6
123 DL1. 27. W2
124 DL43. 7. 4 f5
125 DL3. 18. E2

126 DL1. 21. M3
127 DL3. 18. E2
128 DL1. 131. T8
129 DL44. 206
130 DL1. 131. T8
131 BL Lans 53. 30
132 BL Lans 59. 31
133 PROB 11. 1. 12
134 Guildhall 9171. 5. 151
135 PROB 11. 7. 22
136 Guildhall 9171. 6. 115
137 PROB 11. 15. 18
138 PROB 11. 7. 22
139 PROB 11. 28. 23
140 PROB 11. 32. 22
141 PROB 11. 69. 28
142 PROB 11. 23. 27 BL Add 12462
143 Subsidy roll E179. 141. 111, E179. 238. 97
144 Enfield D 208
145 GLRO DLC 358. 1. 219
146 Guildhall 9171. 16. 226
147 Guildhall 9171. 16. 163
148 Guildhall 9171. 16. 247
149 Guildhall 9171. 16. 261
150 PROB 11. 72. 35
151 W. Robinson *History of Enfield* 1823 V2 p 36
152 PROB 11. 79. 77
153 PROB 11. 76. 84
154 PROB 11. 32. 41
155 GLRO DLC 356. 126
156 PROB 11. 45. 25
157 GLRO DLC 358. 1. 78
158 PROB 11. 48. 4
159 Guildhall 9171. 16. 213
160 Guildhall 9171. 16. 81
161 Guildhall 9171. 16. 246
162 DL1. 3
163 E179. 141. 111
164 BL Lans 38. 35 Letter from Thomas Hudder
165 BL Lans 32. 106
166 P. V. McGrath *The Marketing of Food, Fodder and Livestock in the London Area in the Seventeenth Century.* London MA thesis 1948 p 118
167 BL Lans 32. 104
168 REQ 2. 291. 52
169 Guildhall 9171. 18. 441v. 1597
170 BL Lans 32. 108
171 Guildhall 9171. 6. 145
172 PROB 11. 8. 32
173 DL 3. 7. 48
174 E179. 238. 97
175 PROB 11. 25. 28
176 PROB 11. 45. 25
177 REQ 2. 162. 131
178 BL Lans 38. 89
179 REQ 2. 75. 21

180 REQ 2. 243. 13
181 D. O. Pam *Tudor Enfield: the Maltmen and the River Lea* EHHS No 18 1969 p 5
182 REQ 2. 189. 64
183 REQ 2. 88. 73
184 REQ 2. 223. 47
185 PROB 11. 63. 2
186 REP 14 f 382
187 REP 16 f 186
188 REP 16 f 205
189 J. G. L Burnby and M. Parker *The Navigation of the River Lee* EHHS No 36 1978
     p 5
190 D. O. Pam *Tudor Enfield* . . . p 8
191 J. G. L. Burnby *River Lee* p 5
192 BL Lans 32. 97
193 BL Lans 32. 105
194 CP 166. 47
195 BL Lans 32. 93
196 BL Lans 32. 98
197 *ibid*
198 BL Lans 32. 111
199 BL Lans 60. 37
200 BL Lans 32. 91
201 BL Lans 38. 100
202 BL Lans 32. 111. 2, 3
203 BL Lans 32. 102
204 BL Lans 32. 111
205 BL Lans 32. 102
206 BL Lans 60. 36, 32. 111. 2, 3
207 BL Lans 38. 89, DL44. 478 my thanks to Bert Mason for this reference
208 CLRO Court of Star Chamber 1594. Shelf 36c. I am grateful to Dr J G L
     Burnby for a transcript of this document
209 CP 166. 47
210 *J. House of Commons* 1604–5, pp 208, 237, 262, 283, 288, 290
211 *Cal Middlesex Sessions Rolls* 1608 and 1609 *passim*
212 GLRO DLC 340 f184.5, GLRO MJ, SBR 2
213 C 66. 2179. 10
214 REQ 2. 396. 37
215 SC 2. 188. 56, E179. 143. 327
216 Guildhall 9171. 25. 7

Chapter Three

Enfield 1603–1660

1. Plague and Population

Few within the parish of Enfield could have been unaware of the arrival at Theobalds of the new king from Scotland on 3 May 1603. The elaborate preparations made by Sir Robert Cecil had not passed unnoticed, nor the vast throng of people who pressed northward through Ponders End and Horsepoolstones, eager to pay him homage. From sunrise to sunset they passed in their hundreds, on horseback or on foot, crowding the highway and filling the air with clouds of dust.[1]

The year of James' accession, 1603, had begun well, for the previous harvest throughout the country had been good. There were seven burials in Enfield parish churchyard in January, nine in February, four in March, seven in April, only one during May, four in June, and an ominous ten in July. The summer was fine, but warm weather brought the risk of contagion. It is perhaps possible, but only with hindsight, to detect the beginning of an epidemic with the death at Whitewebbs in April of Thomas Hammond's wife, followed by those of John Hammond and his wife Elizabeth in July, for it was in this remote hamlet that the plague struck in August.

Alice Phillips died on the first day of that month. Thereafter. the clerk who recorded the burials in the parish register carefully distinguished the entries of those who had died of plague. On the sixth it was a maid from John Hammond's house. Two days later, the son of Thomas Hammond, followed by the widow Katherine Dods, and Anthony Vinson and John Hakins, then another son of Thomas Hammond, followed by his daughter Elizabeth. Within two weeks of the outbreak, six households were stricken in this tiny hamlet. Thereafter the disease, intermixed with a few cases of smallpox, spread quickly – first to Bulls Cross, then to the cottages around Moreshatch (by the Fallow Buck); and so it seeped into every corner of the parish. Twenty-five perished of plague during that August.

The epidemic became worse in September when forty-four died of the plague and in addition, two died of suspected plague. There were forty-one plague deaths in October, and the scourge continued through the first nine days of November during which time there were twenty-three plague deaths. From the tenth day of that month a new clerk recorded the burials. His entries were written without the care shown by his predecessor, and are not so precise; moreover he provides posterity with no cause of death. Forty-seven burials were recorded in November, twenty after the new clerk had taken over; it is likely therefore that a proportion of these too died of the plague since there had been only five burials in the previous November. Even in December there were twenty-five burials compared with only eight in the previous December. Three were from the Chamberlain household and two were Wroths from Durants Arbour, both families from the top end of the social ladder, while from the bottom end, three Godfreys died, from the family of a suspected witch.

Seventy households are known to have suffered deaths from the plague (about one dwelling in six). Many other houses must have been stricken, but are not recorded because their occupants recovered. A considerable immunity may have developed, for in thirty-nine households there was only a single fatality. Where more than one death did occur, the victims usually succumbed one after another within a week or two. Alice Holden at John Bosome's house in Ponders End died on 17 September, Bosome's son William on the 18th, and John himself on the 28th. The son and the daughter of Thomas Butterfield died, one on the 8th, and one on 9 November. Thomas and Richard, the two sons of Thomas Cordell, died on 2nd and 3 October. Francis Green's wife died on 21 August, and his step-daughter on the 27th. At Thomas Hammond's place at Whitewebbs, one son died on 8 August, another on the 13th, and a daughter the following day. Thomas Hunsdon's son and daughter died within three days in November.

Children proved to be the most vulnerable members of the community; seventy-nine (possibly eighty-three, for four were described as maids) of the 134 marked as having died of plague, were children.[2]

This was probably the worst outbreak in Enfield since deaths were first recorded in the parish register in 1550 and the scourge was felt among all classes in the community. People must have become accustomed to these visitations, for plague was endemic. There had been twenty-eight plague deaths in Enfield in 1563; fifteen years later in 1578, forty-nine parishioners had died of plague; in 1593 there were fifty-three deaths; and in 1603 the plague had returned more rapacious than ever. Thereafter visitations became less catastrophic. It took a nurse child from Thomas Hammond's house in 1607, but it spread no further. Perhaps that household, which had suffered so badly in 1603, had acquired immunity. Plague returned in 1609, unseasonably in January, when one man and his son died. It claimed a further victim in March, and there was a minor outbreak in the summer when nine died, including four children; there were three more deaths in July 1610.[3]

There was a further severe outbreak of bubonic plague in 1625. The register records sixty-five plague deaths that year. This epidemic began slowly, with one death in June, two in July, eighteen in August, twenty-five in September; thereafter the numbers diminished through October and November. There may well have been some whose deaths went unrecorded, for the outbreak was considered so severe by the Middlesex justices of peace that they ordered the levy of a special county rate for the relief of 'the poor and visited people of Enfield'[4] The money seems to have been used by the parish to build a pest house of three rooms on the edge of the Chase, on what we now call Chase Green. This building belonged to a Mr Pope early in the twentieth century and was still known as the Pest House when it was demolished in 1910. At that time a maypole was erected there every year on May Day.[5]

Plague returned in 1637 and again in 1641. Attempts were made to contain the disease by sealing up stricken houses and by limiting the numbers attending the funerals of plague victims. This may have prevented the spread of an epidemic in Enfield in 1637 when deaths were restricted to only three households; of the eleven that died, six came from the house of John Helme, and four belonged to the house of the widow Sara Clay. Plague was usually difficult to contain, for the people would seldom obey the orders of the justices. Many secretly escaped out of infected houses before the disease had been identified by the authorities, and great numbers would accompany the dead to burial by night.

A reasonably credible calculation can be made of the size of the early Stuart population of the parish and its distribution, for the names of all males of eighteen and over who subscribed to the Oath of Protestation in 1641 (swearing loyalty to Parliament) are listed. Only one man, John Wharley, a servant living in the Bulls Cross quarter and a Roman Catholic, refused to take the oath. The numbers who subscribed in each quarter are given below. I have calculated the population, assuming in the first place that the number of females was approximately equal to the number of males and, in the second, that forty per cent of the population was under the age of eighteen. I suspect that the figures arrived at are somewhat too low.

	Subscribed	Estimated Population
Enfield Green	180	600
Parsonage	43	143
Bulls Cross	113	377
Ponders End	61	203
Horsepoolstones	97	324
TOTAL	494	1647

Parsonage would probably have comprised the Baker Street and Chase Side areas, Bulls Cross covered the whole of the northern part of the parish from Whitewebbs to Freezywater, Horsepoolstones was Enfield Wash.[6]

The last outbreak of plague swept through Enfield in the year 1665, the year which has always retained its place in popular memory as the year of the Great Plague. The risk of contagion was so great that not all those who died were brought to the parish churchyard. The parish clerk, in his register, solemnly recorded the matter in these words:

Many of these hereafter mentioned, in the year 1665 . . . who were supposed to die, some of them of the sickness and tokens, were buried, some of them in the churchyard, and some of them in other places in the parish.

The old Lock hospital on the parish boundary at Waltham Cross was used to shelter the stricken, and many died there. Among the sick buried from the hospital were James and Anne Whittaker and Francis Pixley, Anne Humphrey and Elizabeth Stevens two of the nurses there also died, and Daniel Jarvis one of the bearers employed to carry the dead, also the widow Elizabeth Smith who had been engaged as a searcher to seek out and mark stricken houses.

That same year the plague struck the house of Francis Rosse who was landlord at the George on Enfield Green. In quick succession there died Richard Mead the man-servant, Mary the landlord's daughter, a maidservant, Jane another of the daughters, and the baby (both upon the same day), then Mary the landlord's wife. Finally, a week later, the bodies of two more maidservants were borne to the graveyard.

These recurring crises created in some a spirit of fatalism expressed with perfection in the poem by Thomas Nashe:

'The plague full swift goes by,
I am sick, I must die

Lord have mercy on us'[7]

There were some who sought to find the origins of such disasters in the malevolent powers of witchcraft.

2. Witchcraft

The cult of witchcraft, promoted and propagated by the churches, spread from Europe into Scotland and England in the second half of the sixteenth century. Witchcraft could provide an explanation of every unexplained misfortune in a village. Accusations of witchcraft often arose from bitter quarrels among neighbours. Oddity or deformity could give rise to the charge which, once made, was fed by malicious gossip which recalled with relish every mishap that had never been accounted for, and added such detail as was necessary to throw suspicion, even conviction, upon the chosen victim.

Accusations of witchcraft were made against Agnes Godfrey, the wife of John Godfrey, a yeoman on Enfield Green, on 30 November 1609. They arose from three unexplained happenings that year which had set the villagers whispering together whenever they met. Jasper Tappes had died suddenly on 7 June and no one could fathom the cause. Then in November a steer, a pig, a little pig and a mare died, and they all belonged to Mr William Durant. About that same time, one Francis Baker fell ill and began mysteriously to waste away.

It was widely held that Agnes Godfrey was responsible for these misfortunes, and the village gossips related, one to another, all the strange and unexplained events they could remember, and concluded that she must have been the cause. Eleven years ago, one recalled, William Harvey, a one-year-old baby had died, though he had been in good health until that time. A year before that, whispered another, Thomas Phillips (he was about the same age) had suddenly gone and no one knew a reason for his death. These rumours grew into suspicions, the suspicions into accusations, and at last they were brought to the attention of those in authority, and were included in an indictment against Agnes Godfrey at the Old Bailey on 16 February 1610. The court found her guilty of killing Mr Durant's livestock, also of causing the death by witchcraft of the infant Thomas Phillips. Nevertheless, somehow she not only avoided the gallows, but seems to have escaped punishment altogether.

The belief that she was a witch persisted in the parish. Twelve years later, in May 1621, William Durant, now wasting away and losing flesh, attributed his suffering to her evil sorceries. Again the gossips whispered together of old and unexplained misfortunes in the village. Robert Coxe, in July 1613, had died in the most mysterious circumstances; then there was Henry Butterfield whose death in March 1619 had no apparent cause. These further charges were laid at the door of Agnes Godfrey, and were included to add weight to a new indictment against her at the Old Bailey, but on this occasion she was acquitted on all counts.[8]

When these charges of witchcraft had first been brought against her, she was forty-six years old, though probably prematurely aged by poverty and incessant child-bearing. She had been born in January 1564, Agneta Mallis (or Marris). Married when she was not much more than sixteen, she gave birth to her first child, Thomasine, before her seventeenth birthday. Thereafter she brought a child into the world every two or three years for the next twenty years or so. The baptisms of six of her children are recorded in the register; the burial register gives two more names. The family was poverty-stricken and inept. The parish register notes contemptuously the burial of a 'half starved bastard' from John Godfrey's at the end of the year 1603. The child must have belonged to Thomasine. She herself did not long survive, for both she and her brother Thomas were buried on Christmas eve that year. Another of the family, Henry, had been taken by the plague at the end of October 1603. John Godfrey, the husband, survived until 1630; Agnes was carried to the churchyard two years later, at the age of sixty-eight. This was more than ten years after her second trial for witchcraft.[9]

The widow Agnes Berry, another alleged Enfield witch, was less fortunate. Indicted for causing Grace Halsey to become lame by means of witchcraft, she admitted guilt and was condemned to be hanged in August 1615.[10] We of the late twentieth century have not the right to judge too critically the spirit of persecution which sprouted amidst the poverty, the misery of cold, damp, dark cottages, the close and constant proximity of dirty, smelly, perhaps noisy neighbours, which helped to create a village atmosphere so heavy with hatred that it could on occasion give rise to charges such as these, and that made against Sarah Croxon in July 1626. Her neighbours denounced her as a common scold, as a disturber of the peace, a slanderer, and a stirrer-up of strife. The bench of magistrates, upon hearing the complaint, ordered the constable to seize Sarah Croxon, to place her in a cucking stool, and to duck her in water within the parish of Enfield.[11]

3. Whitewebbs

Just before Parliament met in the autumn of 1605, an abominable plot was revealed to the nation. A number of Roman Catholic conspirators planned to blow up King James and both Houses of Parliament, by means of barrels of gunpowder stored in a cellar at Westminster. The plot, directed by Robert Catesby, was discovered and Guido Fawkes, who would have applied the torch to the gunpowder, was arrested. So runs the official version of the story.

The old house called Whitewebbs, not far from the Cecils' great mansion at Theobalds, was one of the principal meeting places of the alleged conspirators. It lay in a secluded spot to the north of Enfield Chase, almost on the county boundary between Hertford and Middlesex. It was a situation well chosen to allow the many Roman Catholic gentlemen and priests to visit the Jesuit, Henry Garnet, in relative safety. The house was large enough to accommodate up to fourteen guests. Anne Vaux had rented the place under the name of Parkin. She lived there with her sister Eleanor Brooksby and shared the charges of housekeeping with Garnet. James Johnson, a faithful servant, acted as caretaker. He had moved in around February 1600, Eleanor and Anne three months later.

Thomas Wilson and Israel Amyss, Robert Cecil's surveyor, were sent to the house following the failure of the plot in November 1605. They were required to take note of the contents and to question the servants. Anne Vaux was by that time a prisoner in the Tower. The two investigators would have entered by the door into the hall, which was unfurnished and used as a vestibule. At one end was the little parlour, probably the main living room, for it held a square table covered with a green cloth carpet, two leather chairs and three stools upholstered in green cloth. There were screens to ward off the draughts, bellows to encourage the fire, and three green cloth cushions stuffed with flock. A pair of playing tables was

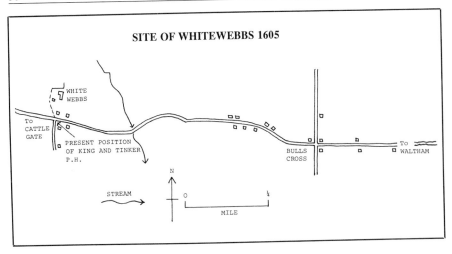

SITE OF WHITEWEBBS 1605

WHITE WEBBS

TO CATTLE GATE

PRESENT POSITION OF KING AND TINKER P.H.

BULLS CROSS

TO WALTHAM

N

STREAM

0   ½

MILE

available for the amusement of guests. The great parlour was now used for sleeping accommodation, as was the little chamber next to it, wherein stood a Spanish bedstead.

The kitchen must surely have gleamed with its brass pots, kettles and posnets (small cooking pots on three feet); its spit was turned by a jack, and there was a dripping pan. The pewter included five chamber pots, twelve porringers, nine platters, eight fruit dishes, and two butter dishes. Light was provided by candles; there were ten candlesticks, great and small. For warmth they burned wood; nine loads of talwood (logs of four foot length) lay in store, with three hundred faggots, also a little coal (probably charcoal).

Upstairs was a gallery where guests could take their leisure, walk in winter weather or hear music played upon the virginal. On one occasion Charles de Ligney, a French gentleman, described having met Garnet there in company with several Jesuits and other gentlemen who were playing music; among them was William Byrd. The gallery had a fireplace to make things comfortable, and a little brass clock to remind the guests that time was passing. The house had eight bedrooms, and beds to sleep eighteen. Above the gallery was the garret.

Only the servants James Johnson, Elizabeth Shepherd and Jane Robinson were in occupation when Cecil's investigators entered. They searched assiduously, hoping to please Cecil with the discovery of incriminating evidence, but the only arms they found were a case of pistols and two fowling pieces for which there was no ammunition. But they did discover in a trunk a number of popish books and relics. They declared Johnson to be a very obstinate papist, so too were the women, and they were examined closely. Since Johnson appeared 'so very perverse' the investigators felt it was their duty to commit him into custody; in their 'poor opinions' they took him to be 'a very dangerous person'. The house, they said, 'was contrived into many lodgings and rooms, with many doors and trap doors out, on all sides', but they found no secret ways in and out. Either these were very carefully hidden or, more probably, did not exist. Their work completed, the investigators left the house, having placed the two popish women servants under strict guard. Henry Garnet died on the scaffold in 1606. Anne Vaux survived and for many years maintained a school for Roman Catholic children near Derby.

Whitewebbs House stood in a field almost opposite the King and Tinker. It was sold as part of the Breton estates in 1787. The purchaser was Michel Garnault, who pulled the house down in 1790. The present house called Whitewebbs was built by Dr Wilkinson in 1791.[12]

4. Nurse Children

Many of the women of Enfield augmented the meagre earnings of their husbands by wet-nursing children sent out from London. There is no way to discover how many babies were thus brought into the parish, but the scale of the trade can be seen from the fact that 125 of these infants died here, and were buried in the churchyard during the ten years January 1604 to December 1613. About sixty entries in the register name the households in which children had been nursed and, from the occasional address given, it can be seen that the trade was carried on in every quarter of the parish; in Ponders End, South Street, Green Street, Turkey Street, Chase Side (the Woodside), Baker Street and Clay Hill. Only three of the families named buried more than one of these nurse children.

During the time of plague, in the summer of 1636, King Charles became gravely alarmed at the great numbers of these children, both nurse children and children at school in Enfield, who were housed so dangerously near to his house at Theobalds. The parents or their servants were constantly passing back and forth, whereby they might carry infection into the neighbourhood. Star Chamber ordered the immediate removal of these children in June, but in September, finding that the order had not been obeyed, it was reiterated in stronger terms, and local magistrates were told that they must inform themselves what houses within six miles of Theobalds had received such inmates. Londoners, many of whom had dwellings in the neighbourhood, were forbidden during the time of infection to travel to and from London on pain of being removed and having their houses shut.[13]

5. Beggars and Travellers

Innumerable bedraggled beggars pestered the town; some passed through, some attempted to glean a livelihood from what little was left over in the village. They had to survive without even the shelter and security given by a poor labourer's cottage. In the winter their hardships often became unbearable. A severe frost set in on 5 December 1607 and lasted until the middle of February: it was so cold that bonfires were burned on the ice covering the Thames. That December a strange woman was found dead in the fields by Bulls Cross. In January there died two infants born of a beggar-woman at Ponders End, and the body of a baby was found in Turkey Street. In February a beggar's child was brought to the churchyard from Doe's house in Turkey Street and, a few days later, the body of another beggar's child was brought in from Forty Hill.[14]

The plight of such children was sad indeed. Elizabeth Turner, a child, was found wandering in 1641 in a sluttish condition, and lame in both feet. She told her story. Her mother, who had lived at Whitefriars, had paid £5 to Giles Andrews to take her as his apprentice, but he had transferred the girl to one Adam Harker paying him only £3 of the £5. Harker was a cobbler, described as 'a very poor man' and because he had been paid only £3, he sent the child back. That was inconvenient, for the mother had just made the acquaintance of a 'young fellow'. She therefore sent her daughter to relatives in Enfield, and at once married and departed to a place unknown. There being no further money forthcoming from the mother, the child was turned loose to fend for herself, with little success. Harker being now dead, the officers of Enfield sent her to be cared for to the overseers in the parish of St Giles.[15]

There were many travelling into or away from London who died by the wayside. A 'poor woman from the highway' in January 1608, Thomas Flood, a tinker's child, in May 1609, a child abandoned at Ponders End in September that year, a stranger who died at the Three Tuns in October. A traveller was found dead by the highway in 1611, and two strangers died at Prentices, an inn or hostelry, in 1612. The following summer, another poor man travelling the road died at Ponders End, and in the autumn a cripple was found dead at the roadside at Cocksmiths end. A week or two later a poor woman was found dead, and in January another poor traveller. A traveller's child died at Bulls Cross in October 1614 and, in August the following year, 'a stranger that came by the way'. In October that year died young John Greene, the son of a bagpipe player; also died 'Thomas a stranger'.

Behind the brief entries in the parish register of those whose deaths were far from home, must lie many sad stories. Occasionally it was a soldier; Thomas Butcher, a Cambridgeshire man, dead in Turkey Street at George Burrell's house, and John Reed, a soldier, on his way to friends at Southampton. Another poor traveller was taken ill to the constable's house in Turkey Street, and died there. Another died at Bulls Cross, another at Green Street, and the body of poor little Mary Rawlins, 'a child being a stranger', was brought to the churchyard. In November 1623 Thomas Bond, a baby born at Little Chesterton in Essex, died in the barn at Durants in Ponders End. That same month Robert Barnfather died in Enfield, on his way with a pass to Newcastle where he had formerly lived, and in December died William Cockman, a beggar's child. In September 1630 a 'Welsh wench' was buried from John Harvey's of Marsh Lane, October saw the death of an Irishman's child, and in July 1631, a blackamore was buried from Mr Jackson's.[16]

6. The Grammar School

Richard Ward, the parish schoolmaster, was in 1611 still paid the same salary, ten marks (£6 13s 4d) which had been the standard payment for chantry priests in parish churches 150 years earlier. That year he demanded an increase and in consequence found himself threatened with dismissal. He therefore submitted his grievance to the court of the Bishop of London who decreed that his pay must be doubled from the following Christmas, and that the trustees must not dispossess him of his place so long as he behaved himself in a decent and orderly manner. The Enfield vestry complied with the court's decision on 28 October 1614.[17]

The salary of Richard Ward had been increased again by 1621 to £20 a year. He was to teach the children the 'cross-row or alphabet letters', and Latin grammar and arithmetic. The management of the school was to remain in the hands of trustees, assisted by a vestry of at least ten parishioners. The chamber and garret over the school were reserved for the use of the trustees and the vestry. A further small addition was made to the schoolmaster's income when, in 1621, he received a 10s addition to his quarter's salary for keeping the accounts of the Poynetts

The New River through Enfield.

Sir Hugh Myddelton.

estate; this became a regular source of income to him. Richard Ward was succeeded as schoolmaster in 1647 by William Holmes who remained in office until his death in 1664.[18] As historians of this period would, in general, agree there was a fivefold increase in prices in the period 1500–1630, Ward's threefold increase in salary therefore still left him a victim of rising prices, a fate not unknown to schoolmasters in other ages.

7. The New River

The appearance of the village centre was much changed, and the villagers considerably disturbed in 1612 by the building of the New River. The beauty of Enfield Town today is greatly enhanced by its meanderings around Enfield Park, across Chase Green and along Silver Street, where it adds elegance even to the Civic Centre. The scheme to construct a conduit to bring water to the City of London from springs in Hertfordshire was first devised by Edmund Colthurst in about 1600, and presented as a bill before Parliament in 1606. But it was not Colthurst who was appointed by the Common Council to carry out the undertaking for the City of London, but Hugh Myddelton, a citizen and a goldsmith. Unlike Colthurst, Myddelton had the capital to carry out the work.

The first record of expenditure on the construction of the New River was on 16 March 1609. It was a payment for horse hire at Waltham for the first survey, carried out by Edward Wright, a mathematician of some repute. By the end of September over 130 labourers were employed, and digging had progressed as far as Wormley by January 1610. But at this point all work was halted for twenty-two months, until November 1611. It was at Wormley that the first of the great

The aqueduct at Bush Hill.

The Clarendon Arch 1682.

loops had to be constructed. It was not engineering difficulties however which prevented progress, but the obstruction of landowners who wanted to secure the maximum compensation.

The City came to Myddelton's assistance and appealed to the Privy Council. The local landowners retaliated by an appeal to the House of Commons, where those obstructing the building of the New River presented a bill to repeal the two acts by which Myddelton was empowered to purchase land and to carry out the work. There were complaints that the New River would lower the level of the River Lea and hinder navigation, and that it would reduce the power of the watermills. The future of the enterprise appeared to be in jeopardy, but in February King James dissolved Parliament. This however did not solve Myddelton's problems for his opponents were still free to continue their obstruction. In 1611 he was forced into negotiations with Robert Cecil, acting on behalf of King James I, who was constantly searching for new sources of income and, with this in mind, he agreed to become a partner. He was to meet half the expenditure and to receive half the profit. This arrangement, forced upon Myddelton by the weakness of his position, nevertheless gave him the power to overcome the obstruction of the landowners.

The work reached Theobalds and Northfield by 11 April 1612, Churchbury field in Enfield by 16 May, Buttes Farm in Southgate by 13 June, and Mynceing Wood in Southgate by 11 July. It was planned to follow approximately the hundred foot contour line, with a very slow fall. The valleys of the various streams flowing east had to be circumvented by long detours to the west to points where the New River could be carried over the streams in wooden troughs. Occasionally the stream was carried over the New River in what was called a flash. It was possible by this arrangement to tap the stream. There were flashes at Wormley, and in the Chase at Enfield.

A major aqueduct over Salmons brook was built at Bush Hill, where the valley was narrow and the detour would have been especially long. The work was carried out by a man named Parnell for a lump sum payment and therefore no details of the construction have survived. Repairs however were required within a few years and the accounts for these reveal some facts about the original construction. Four hundred boards were used to repair the bottom of the frame in January 1614; three barrels of tar were purchased at 20s a barrel, also rosin, pitch and oakum, and a hundred pounds of hard tallow to mix with the pitch, tar and rosin. Alice Crew was paid £5 3s for nails. Shipwrights were employed to caulk the frame. No lead is mentioned, and no plumbers were employed. Later in the century this aqueduct was lined with lead. The frame was originally supported along part of its length by timber arches.

This aqueduct at Bush Hill was known as 'the boarded river'. It is shown in an engraving of 1784 (p. 103). The buildings in the foreground were the huts for the workmen engaged on constructing an embankment to replace the wooden arches. On the further side of the trough is a house in which lived Abraham Cressey, 'many years an industrious and faithful servant of the Company', who seems to have been employed as the 'overlooker' to supervise the twelve walksmen who took care of the sector through Enfield and Edmonton. A house for Mr Ellis, clerk of the works, was subsequently built on the site. The building on the extreme right is the Green Dragon at Winchmore Hill. Salmons brook now crosses beneath a brick arch at Bush Hill, the keystone of which bears the arms of the Earl of Clarendon with the words: 'This arch was rebuilt in the year 1682 by Henry Earl of Clarendon'. Above the keystone is another stone with the inscription 'The frame and lead was raised one foot higher AD1725'.

The digging of the New River had been begun using what was called the 'ingen'. It appears to have been an enormous plough drawn by seventeen horses, but apparently it was not a success. During the hold-up in 1610, it was taken back to Mr Thorogood at Hoddesdon and was never used again. More than 200 labourers were employed: they were paid 10d a day, though when they had to work in water they might earn an extra 2d. The excavators were paid at so much a pole (5½ feet) depending on the depth and the type of soil. Payment ranged from 6d at a depth of six inches, to 12s at a depth of thirteen feet. Many carpenters were employed, wharfing the banks and erecting bridges: they were paid 1s 4d a day. Mole-catchers had been engaged to protect the work from damage.

King Charles disposed of the Crown's interest in the undertaking in 1631 for an annual payment of £500. The New River Company never achieved a profit during the lifetime of Sir Hugh, but the destruction of many conduits in the Great Fire of London in 1666 increased the demand for water. According to John Aubrey, demand had become so great by 1682 that the supply of water to private houses in London had to be restricted to two days a week. To improve the supply a new reservoir was built at a higher level in what is now Claremont Square, Finsbury.

Henry Mill was appointed surveyor in 1720, and made a survey in 1723. His assistant was Robert Mylne who succeeded him as surveyor in 1771. Among Mylne's many improvements was the construction of the embankment at Bush Hill. His son, William Chadwell Mylne, shortened the river from 38.8 miles to twenty-seven. The increased demand for water during the nineteenth century was met by the expedient of sinking wells alongside the New River. In the Enfield area were Whitewebbs well, Hoe Lane well and pumping station, Bush Hill reservoir, Southgate reservoir (in Reservoir Road), Highfield well and pumping station,

Bourne Hill reservoir (which is still there) and Betstile well and pumping station (at Grove Road). The New River was taken over by the Metropolitan Water Board in 1903.[19]

8. The Select Vestry

In the early years of the seventeenth century the affairs of the parish were governed by an open vestry, but the untidiness of such uncontrolled democracy was offensive to the vicar, the churchwardens, and the more substantial members of the village community. They complained of the great confusion and disorder at their parish meetings, brought about, they claimed, by the ignorance of some of the poorer parishioners who attended there in great numbers and prevented the smooth running of parish business, and who were ever ready to thwart the aims and the plans of their betters. The vicar and his supporters therefore petitioned the Bishop of London to establish a select vestry in Enfield.

It was to consist of the vicar and the four churchwardens, with twelve substantial parishioners who were named in the petition. The sort of men selected were such as might be called upon to hold parish office as churchwardens or overseers. They were to be vestry members for life unless they should grow too old and decrepit, or should move out of the parish, or should become scandalous by drunkenness, whoredom or other gross misdemeanour. The vestry was a self-perpetuating body; any vacancies were to be filled by the votes of at least nine existing members, and the vicar's vote was to count double. The bishop, considering that such an arrangement would tend to the peace, quiet and good of the parish and church, readily granted, on 2 November 1615, the petitioners' request.[20]

Just how long the select vestry lasted is difficult to determine, but a description of a vestry in 1648 speaks of many copyholders, freeholders and inhabitants being present,[21] so that it would appear that with or without the bishop's permission, a full vestry had by then been restored. Certainly there was a motion in vestry in November 1673 supported by the vicar, by Nicholas Rainton, Edward Dobson, William Avery and other eminent parishioners, again proposing a select vestry, but apparently it had no result. A further application was made in February 1699 to the Bishop of London, and a select vestry was this time reimposed.[22]

9. The Market

In the year 1616 the parish was granted a market which was to be held all day every Saturday. There was to be a market court (a court of pie powder) to ensure fair trading. A market house was to be erected, and stalls for the use of market traders. The old market place at the church gate existed already, in the same place as it had been in the time of Leonard Chambers. It lay behind (ie. to the north of) a tenement on Enfield Green known as the Vine, which fronted the present site of the Market Place. The parish purchased this house in 1632, though without any immediate intention to demolish. Indeed, at the time it was stipulated that no lease of the premises could be made for less than twenty-one years. The income derived from the market was to be employed for the relief of the poor. Many of those named in the charter as market trustees, were already members of the select vestry.[23]

The market and the annual fair were flourishing by 1648. The Vine had been demolished, and the site had been used to extend the Market Place, around which had been put a rail with gates. Fourteen tiled stalls had been built and seven boarded stalls, and ninety tiled trestles were ready for use. There was a market cross, a market house and a building wherein were kept 'just and even scales and lawfully sealed weights', against which those of the traders could be tested. A pump had been set up with a sink to carry off the water into Whitlocks lane on the western side of the Market Place.

The King's Head had been built, perhaps to replace the Vine. It stood on parish land and the first floor extended from its foundations out over the Market Place. It was sited to take advantage of the increased trade of the market and the fair. The fair was held each year in November, on St Andrews day, in St Andrews close which extended eastward as far as the Kings Head. To impress all those who came to Enfield with the importance of the fair, an elaborate gate-house had been set up at the western end of the close. It had a staircase on either side leading up to a chamber over the gateway. An indication of its size, and presumably of its dignity, can be deduced from an inventory of 1730. The chamber may by that time have been used to house guests from the Kings Head when the inn was full. It contained a fireplace, a bedstead with green furniture, a table and seven chairs, a couch, a press bedstead and a bell.

The market, with all its shops and stalls, the Kings Head, the fair, with St Andrews close, (except the school and the schoolmaster's house) were leased in 1648 to Robert Prentice for a term of twenty-one years. He was to pay an initial sum of £20 and an annual rent of £12. More shops and stalls were put up in the Market Place in 1656 by the order of the vestry, and Robert Curtis was paid £20 for the work. For a time he was to receive the rents, but subsequently the properties were transferred to the parish, 'the profits to be used to the benefit of the poor'. Another shop, built by Mary Piggott and occupied by her son Thomas, was also bought back by the parish for £3.[24]

10. The Church

The church remained the centre of village life. It was the one building wherein the parish regularly assembled, and here they ranged themselves in their pews according to a rigid social hierarchy which extended from the front of the nave to the back of the gallery. The front pew was reserved for Philip Herbert, Earl of Montgomery, the next for Sir Nicholas Salter who held the lease of the Manor House on the other side of the green. The third was for John Wroth of Durants Arbour, the fourth for Mr Nicholas Rainton, who had not yet built his fine house at Forty Hill.

Behind these sat the lesser gentry; Mr John Deicrowe, who lived in a house west of the Market Place later known as Burleigh House. Mr John Banks, the bailiff, who lived at the Woodside or Chase Side as we now call it, Mr Hugh Mascall and Mr Thomas Curtis. Then came the important yeomen, Henry Loft, Henry Hunsdon the younger, Elizeus Wiberd, Henry Hunsdon the elder of Horsepool-stones (Enfield Wash). Beyond the gentry and wealthy yeomen came the rows of lesser mortals, to the very back of the gallery where, in their twopenny pews (2d a year that is) sat Thomas Argent, Edward Matthews, Matthew Budden, Jude Hammond, John Tybballs, William Fall and others of the poorer sort. The men sat on the south side of the church, and in the gallery, the women on the north side, in the chancel, (presumably reserved for the more wealthy) and in other 'out places'.[25]

A similar hierarchy was maintained after death. The cheapest burial was without a coffin: 2d for the grave, 9d to the vicar, and 10d to the clerk. Strangers were always charged double. Graves were to be made five feet deep. Burial charges when a coffin was used were doubled. Burial in church, with the great bell tolled for one hour, cost 17s 2d; burial in the chancel cost 32s 4d.[26]

Robert Loft, by his will of 1631 provided £4 a year to pay a lecturer to preach on Sunday afternoons in Enfield church.[27]

11. The Relief of Poverty

The 1620s were years of great hardship and the select vestry ran an elaborate system for the relief of poverty by the provision of work to the poor. The evidence is provided by an account book which covers the years November 1623 to April 1628.* In this book the left-hand page of each opening bears a record of the distribution of materials to poor spinners and weavers, the facing page shows payment made to them for the work done. The book also contains a record of cloth and yarn delivered for sale from February 1624 to March 1 1626.

During the year 1624, £97 10s was paid out to poor spinners and weavers. The monthly payments were at their highest in January when £17 5s 8d was dispensed. They declined thereafter through the year, to only 9s 5d in August. The work seems to have been distributed according to need; Robert Antonie's wife, for instance, earned 4s 9d in January, 5s 9d in February, 2s 4d in March, and 3s 9d in April, while Matthew Brook's wife received no work from January to March, but work for which she was paid 14½d in April and 6d in May. It is probable that a shilling a week, at this time, would have been sufficient to provide subsistence for a rural family. Large numbers in the township were thus relieved from time to time. In November 1623, for instance, 120 pounds of hemp, 353 pounds of tow (flax mixed with jute or hemp) 27 pounds of wool and 238 pounds of flax were distributed to ninety-four people including thirty-six widows. Widow Bassyll and Thomas Steavens had four pounds of woollen yarn wherewith to knit stockings. Six weavers were employed during that same month, and received between them a total of £19. Most of the selling was done in London, by the weaver George Acres. Some was sold as yarn, much more as cloth woven into various widths. Many napkins were made and sold, a few pairs of stockings, and a few sacks. Receipts from these sales in the year 1624 amounted to £174, this left a margin over the wages paid that year of £76 which could be used towards the cost of new materials. The scheme, which must have required considerable ability to organise, was under the management of Robert Curtis, deputy collector of the queen's rents, who was also a member of the select vestry. Although the Acts of 1598 and 1601 gave the overseers power to tax those with sufficient means in order to raise a supply of materials, the money which financed this scheme probably came from the various properties owned by the parish. Inside the back cover of this same account book (which is damaged) there is a list of the annual income which was

---

*My thanks to Dr Ford of Cambridge University who first drew my attention to this volume.

at the disposal of the vestry; it amounted to £73. Further funds were listed, amounting to £27 7s 6d a year and described as 'tied to the poor'.[28]

The efforts of the vestry were, from time to time, augmented by those who made gifts in their wills. In 1627, John Deicrowe left his copyhold land in Enfield to his friend Thomas Sone, citizen and grocer of London, laying upon him the obligation to pay £4 a year from the profits to two poor persons selected by the overseers. A further 40s was to be spent, within eight days, on bread for distribution among the poor. His freehold house on Enfield Green was left in the hands of his half brother Benjamin Deicrowe.[29]

12. Forty Hall

The Crown had disposed of much of its property in Enfield in 1602, when Queen Elizabeth granted the manor of Worcesters to Robert Cecil. The Cecils at this time had their great mansion Theobalds, just north of the parish boundary in Cheshunt. They also held some 830 acres, including many coppices, in Edmonton, south of the Enfield boundary. Theobalds was granted to King James in 1607. He gave Cecil the old palace at Hatfield in exchange with some seventeen manors to finance the rebuilding there. The manor of Worcesters remained in the hands of the Cecils until 1616, when they sold it to Nicholas Rainton. At about the same time, the Cecils disposed of their land in Edmonton for somewhat over £7,000.

Sir Nicholas Salter held the lease of the manor of Enfield in 1626; Nicholas Rainton held the manor of Worcesters; John Wroth held the manors of Durants, Suffolks, Pentridges and Honylands, and also rented the Rectory manor from Trinity College Cambridge. The little manor of Elsings was divided between William Wilford and Henry Hunsdon.[30]

Nicholas Rainton, in 1629, began building his fine new house at Forty Hill to replace an 'ancient house' on the site. Much of his early seventeenth century interior has survived. The visitor entering Forty Hall by the north door finds himself in an entrance hall, beautifully if somewhat too elaborately decorated in plasterwork of the late eighteenth century. This area would originally have been given over to the screens passage and pantry. It is possible that the arches on the south wall (opposite the door) are remnants of original decoration in the Jacobean manner, and that the eastern-most arch was the entrance to the kitchen.

The dining room on the left, formerly the hall, retains all its original features; screen, chimney piece, wall panelling, and a geometrical plaster ceiling. The screen is a good example of expensive, not too modern work of c.1630. It is in three bays, the middle bay having a segmental arch, but this was filled in with a door in the eighteenth century. There are cherub heads in the spandrels. The chimney-piece, a fine bold structure in wood with a marble inner surround, rises to the full height of the room.

The present staircase is of 1895 and we have no idea what the original staircase looked like. The drawing room remains unaltered. The huge chimney-piece is bolder and less refined than the one in the hall. The Rainton room assumed its present form in the late eighteenth century, when the room was extended to take in the screens passage and the open screen at the east end was put in. Over the fireplace is a portrait of Sir Nicholas by Dobson dated 1643.

The first floor room over the hall has its original plaster ceiling, with eighteenth century panelling on the walls. The ceiling of the room above the drawing room

Forty Hall from the north.

is dated 1629, and here too the panelling is of the eighteenth century. The middle room facing west has its original wainscoting and its fireplace.

A magnificent courtyard lies to the north-west of the house. It has early seventeenth century buildings on the south and west. On the north it has an embattled wall in warm red brick, and a fine arched gateway with small lodges on either side.[31]

Nicholas Rainton was the only senior alderman to show sympathy for the parliamentary puritans before 1642. He was by trade a mercer, importing satin and taffeta from Florence and velvet from Genoa. His estate in 1643 was assessed at £20,000. He became an alderman in 1621, was appointed sheriff in 1621–2, and was twice master of the Haberdashers Company. Forty Hall was completed and ready in 1632–3, the year in which he was elected Lord Mayor. He was knighted in the following May.

Sir Nicholas was one of the aldermen who refused to lend money to Charles I in 1639, and in May 1640 he was briefly imprisoned for his refusal to provide a list of the wealthiest men in his ward, required by the King that he might extract money from them in the form of a forced loan. Rainton, in January 1642, was the only senior alderman to be elected to the Committee of Safety, but he was getting old and he begged to be excused, pleading 'many other employments'.[32]

He died in 1646; his wife Rebecca had died in 1640. The splendid monument in St Andrews Church portrays Sir Nicholas on the top shelf, propped up on one elbow, his head resting on his right hand. He is shown in armour, over which he wears his robes as Lord Mayor, with the collar and badge. On the second shelf is Rebecca, reclining in a similar attitude, and reading the ten commandments. The posture in which this stern-faced old couple are depicted was one which had been fashionable for about eighty years but by this time was becoming old-fashioned. It represents their eternal contemplation of Elysian fields

'But propped on beds of amaranth and moly,
How sweet, while warm airs lull us blowing lowly'

Below, his son (also Nicholas) who died in September 1642, and his daughter-in-law who died in August 1641 (also named Rebecca) kneel, one at each side of a prayer desk. Behind the father, on their knees, their two sons, behind the mother their three daughters and, at the foot of the desk, an infant lies in a cradle, wrapped in swaddling clothes (probably Thomas who died in 1636). By the time Sir Nicholas died in 1646, all his grandchildren had followed their parents to the grave. Forty Hall and the manor of Worcesters were left in the hands of trustees, for his nephew, another Nicholas Rainton.[33]

Not only the great landowners, but minor gentlemen and wealthy tradesmen now paid more attention to the furnishing, appearance and comfort of their homes. Thomas Lambert the elder, sometimes called Mr Thomas Lambert, was well placed in the hierarchy of the parish: in church he had the second pew on the south side of the south aisle. His parlour, in 1622, was furnished with a court cupboard, a wainscot cupboard with a press, and four stools, 'all of one fashion'. There was a wainscot chair for the master and, in the hearth, a pair of 'creeps' (creepers*), a pair of tongs and a fire shovel.[34]

William Randell was a licensed victualler, who styled himself a yeoman, and described his house as a mansion. His hall was hung with painted cloths, and

*small andirons

Forty Hall, the screen.

Forty Hall, fireplace in dining room.

Forty Hall, fireplace in drawing room.

Sir Nicholas Rainton,
portrait by William
Dobson.

contained a settle (a long high-backed bench), a long framed table, a little table, and a cupboard with a press. He allocated to his widow, while she remained single, three good and convenient rooms in the house, and she was to share with his son the use of the hall, and of the chimneys and oven in the hall and the kitchen.[35]

13. The Farmers

The year 1630 was particularly hard; there was near famine in some places, which lasted for three years. The Lord Mayor of London, in a letter to the Privy Council on 26 May, told how in 1629 'spring fell out so unseasonable that grass grew very short'. There was insufficient hay, straw and fodder for feeding the cattle through the winter and, in consequence, a great slaughter of livestock in the autumn of 1629 and during the winter that followed. In the spring, instead of the usual seventeen or eighteen hundred veals brought to Cheapside market on a Saturday, only two or three hundred were offered for sale. The harvest in 1630 was disastrous. There was a failure in all the main crops grown in Enfield; wheat, oats and barley. Prices rose to a height never previously equalled, and not to be reached again until the late 1640s.[36]

A special committee of the Privy Council was constituted in June 1630 as a commission for the poor. It was charged to ensure the enforcement of the Elizabethan poor laws, and to establish local commissions in areas where distress was particularly acute. The local justices were required to nominate a jury in Enfield which was to report on the resources and prospects of a number of farmers and tradesmen within the parish.[37] The report was submitted on 23 October 1630. It showed that those who held most land had a surplus of produce to sell which, with prices at a higher level than ever before, must have given them a substantial profit. The survival of many farmers holding less than sixty acres depended very much

Forty Hall, gateway to the courtyard.

Sir Nicholas Rainton who died in 1646, Rebecca his wife died in 1640. Below, his son and his wife kneel at a prayer desk with their two sons and three daughters. Thomas, wrapped in swaddling clothes, died an infant in 1636.

on the number of mouths to be fed, for each person consumed on average six bushels of bread corn a year (there are eight bushels in one quarter). Those that farmed less than about thirty acres might face starvation. Many Enfield farmers however had other sources of income to protect them from ruin. The main winter crop in Enfield was wheat and rye, often sown together in September and called maslin. Bread made from this mixture was held to be more moist than wheaten bread. Oats were sown in March, and usually used here for feeding stock. Small areas of peas and barley were also sown at the same time.

Robert Baldwyn was one of the more prosperous farmers, holding about seventy acres. He had, in the autumn of 1630, sown fifteen acres of wheat and rye, and was preparing the soil to sow in the new year thirty-three acres of oats, peas and barley. He had laid safely into his barns and house, the harvest of eighteen and a half acres of wheat, one and a half acres of rye, twenty-five acres of oats, three and a half acres of peas, and three acres of barley. There remained of this, sixty quarters of oats, peas and barley, and twenty quarters of wheat. His household consisted of himself, his wife, son, and four servants.

Robert Curtis cultivated about fifty-five acres of arable, but there were ten mouths to feed, for he had a wife, six children and two servants. He received however additional remuneration as the local collector of Queen Henrietta's rents.[38] (The manor of Edmonton was part of the Queen's jointure from 1629 until 1650, and from 1660 until her death in 1669). Curtis had sown, in the autumn of 1630, twenty acres of wheat, and was preparing to sow seventeen acres of oats, peas and barley. He had reaped, at harvest, fourteen acres of wheat and rye, three acres of barley, three acres of peas, and eighteen acres of oats. In his barn the commissioners were shown twenty quarters of oats, peas and barley, and five quarters of wheat and rye.

Christopher Hill farmed forty-five acres of arable. He lived with his wife, child, his mother and five servants. He had sown, in the autumn, fifteen acres of wheat, and was ready to sow fifteen acres with oats. He had reaped at harvest fifteen acres of wheat and rye, and had ten quarters of wheat and rye remaining in his barn. But he was a brewer in addition, with a good business, using four and a half quarters of malt every week, from which he produced something like four hundred gallons of beer. Some of his servants were undoubtedly employed in the brewery.

Robert Piggott farmed thirty-three acres, he was also licenced as a badger and dealt in malt, though in times of shortage severe restrictions were imposed, or were supposed to be imposed, on the production of malt from barley. He lived with his wife and four children and had two servants. He had sown twelve acres of wheat and rye, and had ten acres ready to be sown with oats. At harvest he had gathered in ten acres of wheat and rye and twelve acres of oats, yet he had only two quarters of wheat and rye remaining in the barn, and no oats. His position should therefore have been precarious.

Thomas Sterne was a butcher at Ponders End. There were eight in his household, his wife, three children and three servants, though he farmed little over twenty acres of arable, and a holding of less than thirty acres was generally considered too small to require hired workers. He had sown in the autumn five acres of wheat, and had prepared the ground for eight acres of oats. He had, it was reported, hardly sufficient wheat and rye to feed his household through the winter, but he had twenty-four quarters of oats unspent.

The house of Francis Bettes stood in Cocker Lane (now Browning Road by Hilly Fields Park). There was a small orchard and an acre of pasture attached, and he held five acres of valuable meadow in the marsh. That autumn he had sown seven acres of wheat, and would sow six acres of oats. He had reaped six acres of wheat, six acres of oats, and one and a half acres of barley at harvest time, but there was not sufficient left in the barn to support the family through the winter.

John Collins, who farmed only seven or eight acres, had a wife and five children to support. He was licensed to trade as a kidder*, by which he may have earned a little extra.[39] He had been unable to sow any wheat in the autumn, perhaps because the family had been forced to consume what should have been sown as seed. He had harvested one and a half acres of wheat, half an acre of rye and three acres of oats, but this had already been eaten, except three bushels of wheat threshed out in a tub. It required two and a half bushels of wheat or four bushels of oats to sow one acre.

John Loft's holding was even smaller. He had a wife, two children and one servant. He too had been unable to sow any corn that year. He had reaped five roods of wheat, and one and a half acres of oats, certainly insufficient to feed the family. But he was licensed to trade as a kidder;[40] he was also a shoemaker, and by some means he managed to survive. The parish registers report no burials from any of these families during the ensuing twelve months.

Even in this year of hardship, tithe had to be paid. The rectory, held by Trinity College Cambridge, was leased in two equal parts to Thomas Darker and John Wroth. Each had taken his due, thirty quarters of wheat and rye, and forty quarters of oats, peas and barley.

14. Bread and Beer

There were four bakers in the parish. John Colwyn, who had been a baker for about twenty years, baked between eight and ten bushels a week. Richard Rolfe was a brown baker (he baked brown bread from maslin flour). He had been apprenticed to the trade and had worked in it for thirty years. Widow Taylor baked 'household' bread (bread of second quality). She was also licensed as a badger, buying and selling meal. The fourth baker, William Pricklove, also baked household bread. He had formerly been a wheelwright but was now too old to work at his trade.

There were three common brewers. Christopher Hill had been brought up to the trade, but had had his own business for only two years. He brewed four and a half quarters of malt a week. His principal competitor was Edward Heath who had been apprenticed to the trade and now held the George Inn on Enfield Green,[41] where he brewed four quarters of malt each week. His household was a large one, for he had a wife, three sons, three men servants and two maids. He also farmed thirty-six acres of arable. In 1643 he came to an agreement with Henry Wroth to supply beer for the household at Durants for some twenty to thirty persons. Over the following four years before he died, he sent two hundred barrels at 6s a barrel, and twenty barrels of strong beer. When Wroth had run into debt, he sold Heath a parcel of wood, standing, to the value of £36 to offset the debt. Nevertheless his widow had to sue Wroth for £27 14s.[42] The third brewer was Edward Moss, in a much smaller way of business.

There were no fewer than thirty-nine licensed and unlicensed public houses in

*a minor trader engaged in buying and selling grain; they did not handle malt.

the parish, about one dwelling in ten.[43] Seven of the licensees were women. Robert Rash was at the White Hart in Ponders End in 1630. He brewed his own beer and farmed twenty acres. He was married with two children and employed four servants. John Garman was another publican who brewed his own beer. The rest of the houses would have been supplied either by Edward Heath, who served the pubs around Enfield Green, Chase Side and Baker Street, or Christopher Hill supplying the houses along the road from Ponders End to Horsepoolstones. For most of the publicans, the keeping of a public house was a full-time occupation, though a few engaged in other trades. William Stanborough was a kidder, trading in meal; Michael Kirby, who was a glazier, kept a house on Enfield Green jointly with his mother who had a licence to sell wine. William Barnes was both publican and sexton. William Heydon and William Coverley combined ale-house keeping with brick-making, Andrew Haydon was also a gardener, Jeffrey Bisseter a joiner, and three of the victuallers worked as tailors.

15. Domestic Servants

The life of the servant or apprentice who lived within the household of his master was generally more comfortable than it would have been with his own family, the food more adequate, and the bed dry. Yet servants often had to endure an authoritarian discipline, occasionally amounting to tyranny. It was possible to appeal against grave neglect or inhuman treatment to a justice of the peace. Ann Church complained to Edward Nowell, the Edmonton justice, that her master, Edward Coaker, described sometimes as a gentleman, sometimes as a grocer, had turned her out of his house, had refused to pay the wages due to her, and would not even allow her to take away her clothes.

The dispute which had arisen between them concerned the date of the end of her contract. She claimed that it terminated three weeks before Whitsun 1629, while he insisted that her time did not run out until mid-summer. Mr Justice Nowell endeavoured patiently to reconcile their differences, and attempted to persuade Coaker that, in the meantime, he should take the young woman back into his service. His efforts towards conciliation only infuriated Coaker. He refused to take her back into his service; he refused to pay her wages; he even refused to allow her to collect her own clothes, and ended by declaring, to Mr Nowell's face, that that important gentleman was no competent judge. He insisted that he must have a more unbiassed judgement and at last, becoming more and more infuriated, he declared that neither Mr Nowell nor any other justice had the right to interfere between a master and his servant. It was his right, he proclaimed, that he should order and govern himself.

Mr Nowell then informed him, still trying to be reasonable, that if he could not accept his judgement, he would have to refer the matter to quarter sessions. To this Coaker responded in a rage that quarter sessions should have nothing to do with his business, a more judicial hearing is what he would have; and upon Mr Nowell insisting and requiring of him sureties for his appearance at quarter sessions he stalked out, declaring that he was a free man, and would not be bound. And when Mr Nowell, himself at last becoming annoyed, commanded his man to make a mittimus (a warrant) to send Coaker to gaol, Coaker sneered and said with heavy sarcasm that the lord keeper must be a wise man to make such wise justices. The bench, being told of this, was overwhelmed with exasperation and offended dignity, and committed Edward Coaker to Newgate, until he did find sureties. They ordered that he must pay Ann Church her wages, return her clothes, and give her a discharge from his service before he could be released.[44]

The harsh cruelty with which a servant could be treated is displayed in the case of Sibbell Clarke (in June 1608). She was servant to Thomas Kenton, a yeoman of Monken Hadley. He had hung a horse lock on the girl's leg, and to free herself, she was forced to bear it all the way to the sessions at Clerkenwell. The court was shocked, and discharged her from Kenton's service, ordering him to pay her the ten weeks wages due to her.[45]

The full extent, however, to which a servant could suffer at the hands of a cruel and tyrannical master is shown in the case (in 1638) of Joan Nicolls, servant to Thomas Wheeler, a gentleman (so called) of Tottenham. Her complaint was referred to Mr Nowell and Mr Huxley, justices of peace, but by that time, her master had so cruelly beaten and misused her that she had become very lame and helpless and unfit for future service. In this condition he had thrown her out of the house, though the term of her contract was not yet complete. The justices ordered Mr Wheeler to take his servant back. This he refused to do, nor would he provide for her, nor relieve her in any way. In her helpless state she seemed destined to become a vagrant. But the magistrate ordered the churchwardens and overseers of Tottenham to provide for Joan Nicolls, and insisted that they should charge Thomas Wheeler the full expense of her maintenance.[46]

Many servants of course were treated with consideration, like Elizabeth Wells, servant to Benjamin Deicrowe. He left her a tenement and a croft on Enfield Green with a piece of waste land adjoining, that is if she was still unmarried at the time of his death.[47]

16. Cottagers

The poor were increasing. Forty-six new cottages were erected in the parish in the twenty years 1615 to 1635, including ten on Enfield Green and eleven on the Chase. Twenty-five of the cottages were lived in by those who had built them, or by their widows or children. The remainder were built (if that word does not suggest too elaborate a construction) for rent. The area of Enfield Green must have been somewhat diminished by the land taken for these cottages. Jude Hammond built two there and, at his death, left his widow in one and his son in the other. Michael Kirby, a glazier, just tacked an outhouse on the end of his ale-house and let it to the shoemaker John Boulton. Two poor women, destitute of shelter, were housed by the parish in two of the cottages. Another two cottages on the green were erected by the wealthy Benjamin Deicrowe, while another which had formerly been a shop, was converted to a cottage by the parish clerk. There were a number of cottages newly built on the Chase. William Pavey, who had once gained a livelihood by begging in a hole by Hadley windmill, built himself a cottage over the hole and he now sold ale there without a licence. One of the cottagers was a brickmaker, another a shoemaker. The cottage built by Richard Hawton was now lived in by John Hitchen who had married his widow. William Abraham, a husbandman, owned two cottages, one of which, in South Street, he let to another husbandman William Keame.[48] The pest-house which had been put up in the parish during the great plague of 1625, being of three rooms, now housed three families who might have to move out in the event of another serious outbreak.[49]

The cottages were presented at the Duchy Court as being illegally erected, and King Charles's pleasure was signified by the steward of the manor, that the cottagers should have 'a convenient time to remove themselves, and to dispose themselves otherwhere, and that their cottages should be pulled down and razed level with the ground'. Two years later it was found that the injunction had not been obeyed. Thereupon an order was issued that the occupants should have until the end of September 1637 (about seven months) to pull down their own cottages but, as a concession, they should be allowed to sell the building materials. Their cottages would be demolished if they failed to comply and those that put them up would have to pay a fine of £10. The cottagers themselves would suffer such penalties as the law required.[50]

Despite such peremptory orders with penalties ordained, it is unlikely that many cottages were demolished. At least a number of those presented in 1635 as living in unlicenced cottages around Enfield Green were still living in the same neighbourhood when the oath of protestation was taken in 1641.[51] Nevertheless such decrees enabled the Crown to extract money from the cottagers. The commissioners for newly erected cottages visited the area in 1638, sitting at the Bull in Tottenham. From there they summoned the Enfield cottagers; it was a journey of five or six mile each way. Thomas Mousdale was a labourer living on what we now call Chase Green, by the New River. He had built the cottage for himself twelve years earlier; it was in a poor state, he said, ready to fall down at any time. The commissioners informed him that if he paid them 3s 6d, this would give him the right to rebuild. Mousdale and eight other cottagers each handed over 3s 6d. The commissioners then declared that they had only compounded for their past offences, whereupon Mousdale, disgruntled, told them that he was sorry he had paid them anything.[52] Such shabby devices to raise money did not enhance the popularity of King Charles among his poorer subjects.

It is difficult to make a clear distinction between cottages and houses, for not all labourers lived in one-roomed hovels. Officially a cottage was any dwelling not having the statutory four acres of land, either enclosed with it or in the common fields. Robert Cooke, who described himself as a labourer, lay in his cottage near to death in April 1623. Looking about him he listed his treasured possessions. There were the two beds in the room where he lay, with two pairs of sheets, and two chests. There was the table in the kitchen, and in the hall stood a table, form and three joint stools. The parlour contained a bed. His furniture like that of most of the poorer sort, seems to have been somewhat limited, beds to sleep on, tables to eat off, benches and stools to sit upon, and chests in which to store everything.[53] Agnes Saunders, another cottager and a widow, had carefully sorted all her possessions into chests and boxes before her last illness. Everything intended for her son Richard she put into her long joint chest; whatever was for her son John into the little joint chest and also into the little box. Her clothes and the contents of the linen chest, she allocated for her daughter Jane and her children. With things thus carefully arranged, she could die in peace.[54]

17. Ship Money and Other Grievances

Ship money was the most famous of Charles I's fiscal devices. He had some justification for raising such a tax; the fleet was in disrepair, foreign warships and Barbary corsairs invaded our territorial waters with impunity. The tax was accepted at first but mistrust grew. The King appeared too willing to use his refurbished fleet to help Spain, and his army to impose a Laudian prayer book on Scotland. In Enfield, the Crown precipitated a crisis in 1637 by lowering the assessments of City merchants and government officers recently settled in the parish, while raising those of the long established yeomanry. A petition to protest against these alterations was presented to the Privy Council from 'the yeomen and ancient inhabitants of Enfield'. The ten assessments which the sheriff had raised were, with the exception of Captain Wroth, those of minor gentlemen and yeomen.[55] Henry Hunsdon, it was said, held £30 a year in lands; his payment had been raised from 16s to 20s. The injustice against which he protested can perhaps be placed in perspective by noting that in 1643 he handed over to the county committee raising money for the parliamentary army a horse valued (not by himself) at £9, plate to the value of £15, and £5 cash.[56] There had been Hunsdons in the parish, many of them substantial tradesmen, at least since the early fifteenth century. Mr John Wilford, having in the parish lands of inheritance valued at £100, was raised from 26s 8d to £2. His was another long established Enfield family. Robert Curtis, despite being 'a poor man' and having ten children, had his assessment raised from 10s to 12s. There had been Curtises in the parish since the time of Henry VII.

In contrast the sheriff lowered the assessments made on Sir Thomas Trevor, one of the barons of the Exchequer, Sir Nicholas Rainton, former Lord Mayor, Doctor Roberts, the wealthy vicar, Sir Thomas Sone, citizen and grocer of London, Mr Charles Crosby who held two keepers' places one at Old Park and one in the Chase, Mr Dighton, another keeper, Mr Daniel Brangwyn, chandler of London, and Richard Brownlow an official of the Court of Common Pleas.[57]

Ship money that year had been particularly difficult to collect in Middlesex. On 16 September 1638 warrants were issued to call the collectors before the Privy Council; the collectors failed to appear. The following January, £1152 out of a total of £5000 still remained unpaid.[58] It is possible that the sheriffs were, with intent, stirring up dissatisfaction by tampering with the assessments. As the collectors complained, even poor cottagers with nothing to live on but their labour had been assessed. The collectors considered that this might admit of no better construction than that it had been done in order to stir up strife among the poor.[59]

The smaller farmers had another grievance in 1638, not only against the Crown but also against their more wealthy neighbours. The close proximity of the King's house at Theobalds imposed a heavy burden of carrying services on the parish, and the greatest weight fell upon the poor. Many wealthy men, particularly Londoners, had houses and lands in Enfield where they maintained coaches and fine horses, but because they kept no carts they were able to avoid contributing help towards the constant carriage of provisions demanded by the King. Moreover there were rich yeomen, some who held 200 acres worth £40 to £80 a year, who had excellent teams of horses for their ploughs, yet they would do no more carrying services than their poor neighbours whose broken down hacks had to be harnessed four to a cart, and who were forced to leave their work undone, often at harvest time when failure to bring in the grain might mean starvation.[60]

In November 1637 the parish received the account from the carpenter who carried out the work of railing in the communion table; £3 7s 6d for materials, work in the arch £3 6s 8d, making ready the pillars 8s, and work on the screen £3.[61] Thus it cost the parish over £10, and by no means everyone approved of Laud's changes. When they told William Billings, one of the churchwardens, that he must now bow low at the name of Jesus, he expressed his serious concern, declaring 'that may be that is near to Rome'.[62]

18. Coat and Conduct Money

The reader will hardly need to be reminded of the events which led to the Civil War in England in the mid-seventeenth century. The attempt by King Charles to impose on Scotland the English book of Common Prayer in 1637, and the riots against it which culminated in a National Covenant, with the raising of an army under Alexander Leslie, are well-known and oft-related events of national history. In June 1639 came King Charles' inept attempt to suppress the rebellion in Scotland by military force and his ignominious defeat. Yet he remained stubbornly faithful to his bankrupt policy and was determined to raise a new army. Money was short, disaffection widespread. Two hundred men who had been pressed to serve in London and Middlesex mutinied on 10 April 1640 aboard ship, and sixty of them deserted.[63]

On 13 April 1640 the Short Parliament opened, and on 4 May its members demanded the abolition of coat and conduct money, by means of which the King hoped to raise a new army. He was forced to dissolve Parliament almost at once, and orders were sent out to the deputy lieutenants to insist that coat and conduct money be collected. Some Middlesex parishes; Fulham, Hammersmith, Chiswick and Shoreditch, met their obligations almost in full. Others; Pinner, Harrow, Acton, Willesdon, Stoke Newington and Enfield, paid only a small proportion of the money demanded. The task of the collector Sir John Franklyn, was an unenviable one. Pressed by the Privy Council, he offered to send in the names of those he considered able to pay. As for the poorer sort, he thought it wiser not to press them, they being in the middle of harvesting and 'labouring to get money to put bread into their mouths [they] would be very clamorous if they should be hindered'. Pleading ill-health, he asked to be discharged.[64]

Only £14 8s out of a total of £44 had been collected in Enfield, yet the amounts demanded were comparatively small. The assertion made by many of the taxpayers that they had no money, cannot be believed. Robert Baldwyn was asked to pay only 8s and could not, yet in 1643 an assessment declared him to be worth £2,000 and he paid £26 to the county treasurer. Robert Franklyn, from whom 8s was demanded, also claimed that he had no money, yet he was assessed in 1643 to be worth £1500, and paid the treasurer £25. Both these men had protested over their ship money assessment. John Loft, who was unable to find 4s to help the King to suppress rebellion in Scotland, voluntarily found that amount two years later for the 'poor distressed protestants in Ireland' and also paid £4 to the county treasurer that same year.[65]

Others made their excuses in more legalistic language. Mr John Wilford sent word by the headborough that he 'doth not deny payment (15s) so it may appear lawful'. It was not proved lawful to his satisfaction and he did not pay, and twenty-nine others repeated his words to the collector. And they also did not pay. The holders of offices under the Crown, Charles Crosby keeper of Old Park, John Smith keeper of Little Park, Dighton and Potter, keepers on the Chase, the King's woodward, and Robert Curtis, the deputy collector of the Queen's rents, all denied payment on the grounds that they were exempted by their offices. In his adversity the King found few friends and little gratitude for former favours.

The figures for the collection of coat and conduct money in Enfield and in the two neighbouring parishes in Edmonton hundred, even including money remaining in the hands of parish constables, which may or may not eventually have been paid in, are given below:

	Money demanded £	paid in £	percentage
Edmonton	44	40	91
Tottenham	33	22 10s	68
Enfield	44	17	38.5[66]

The Long Parliament met in November 1640. That month came the Irish rebellion and tales of atrocities spread shock and dismay into remote villages across England. A nationwide collection was launched for 'the poor protestants in Ireland', yet still the taxpayers of Enfield kept a tight hold on their money. In Tottenham £51 was collected, in Edmonton £47, but money was subscribed in only two of the four quarters of the parish of Enfield. Enfield Green gave £16 12s 2d and Horsepoolstones £6 11s 6d, making a meagre total of £23 3s 8d, 'whereof two pieces of gold were light'. It is not that the lists are missing for the remainder of the parish, for the above sum is the total that was paid in by Orledge Cordell, the high constable.[67]

19. The Demands of Parliament

A declaration was made in both Houses of Parliament in July 1642 that the king had begun the Civil War. Parliament, in anticipation, had issued an ordinance in June for the collection of money, plate and horses on a voluntary basis. Twentyeight of the more substantial inhabitants of Enfield subscribed £1155, but when in the following year, Parliament made an assessment on all parishes within twenty miles of London, the amount already subscribed under the voluntary ordinance was allowed for from the tax demanded. Under these two collections £1895 14s 11d was paid by ninety-two taxpayers in Enfield. Thus payment towards Parliament's preparation for war hit the gentlemen and yeomen of Enfield very hard. Many of the assessments were so high as to be unrealistic, and in a number of cases more was demanded than was finally paid. Sir Thomas Trevor, who had a lease of the Manor House, was required to pay £200; he had contributed plate to the value of £50 on 15 June, and in July he paid £70 in cash. The Committee for Advance of Money then ordered his discharge. The vicar, Dr William Roberts, paid £50 of the £100 demanded of him and he was discharged. John Wroth of Durants had handed over plate to the value of £45 on 2 September 1642 and paid £12 in the following June. Captain Henry Wroth paid £100. William Billings paid £30 against the £50 required of him; he was the churchwarden who in 1636 had shown his antipathy to the new Laudian ritual. John Evington exceeded the £50 demanded of him, providing £40 in plate and a gelding with its harness to the value of £20. Christopher Hill the brewer sent in to the Committee on 11 November 1642 a mare, a gelding, a great draught gelding, and a draught horse, a bay mare, and a bay horse with its furniture, to the total value of £52 though only £50 had been required of him.

Henry Hunsdon having, it had been said in 1637 only £30 in lands of inheritance, for which reason he objected to the raising of his ship money from 16s to 20s, sent a horse valued at £9, £15 in plate and £5 in money to meet his obligation in full. Thomas Darker who held a lease of one half of the rectory, giving him the right to collect half the tithe (upon a rack rent), had resisted in 1637 the raising of his ship money from 20s to 30s. In November 1642 he contributed £3 2s in plate and a grey horse valued at £15, though he had been required to pay only £15.[68]

Parliament was thrown into consternation by the advance of the king's army as far as Brentford in November 1642. In all the churches around Enfield a message was read from the pulpits telling of the sufferings of the Brentford people at the hands of the king's soldiers, so that compassion might be aroused and a generous collection made.[69] Parliamentary troops under Colonel Browne were stationed at Edmonton and at Tottenham early in 1643.[70] The first billeting accounts which survive for Enfield cover the beginning of the year 1644 when Sir William Brereton's troop of horse was billeted on the yeomen and minor gentlemen of the parish (those that had stables) from 17 February until 6 April. Peter Bannester, the cornet, and John Chadwick, the doctor, were lodged with Robert Curtis for forty-nine days. He provided food for the men at 8d a day each and five bushels of oats at 16d the bushel. Edward Hunsdon quartered two troopers, as did Robert Franklyn, Robert Baldwyn, Edward Harrison and John Loft, also Edward Heath at the George and Robert Rashe at the White Hart in Ponders End. Others with less accommodation quartered one, like Daniel Brangwyn, in whose house lodged Ralph the trumpeter. Some were able to provide oats, some supplied hay at 8d the truss. Captain Sankey was billeted at Fortescue Hall with Mr John Evington. Someone named Cornelius stayed with Mrs Ann Randall, and a Dutchman was also billeted there. Mr Henry Wroth quartered John Mattershed and his servant. The quartermaster paid out nearly £120 in the village to cover this forty-nine day sojourn.[71]

The weekly (later monthly) assessments, which were to continue until the Restoration, began in 1643. The account books are missing, and only the monthly totals for one year from 25 October 1644 survive. Except Enfield, all the parishes in the hundred paid well, finding the very considerable sums demanded of them almost in full. In the first month Edmonton paid £93, Tottenham £72, even South Mimms paid £72 and Monken Hadley £22; Enfield paid £92, but this was nearly £8 short. In the second and third months all the parishes except Enfield met their obligations. Also in the sixth and seventh months, all paid well except Enfield, where £50 was demanded and less than £20 paid. Over the next two monthly periods, Edmonton and Tottenham fell into the ways of Enfield. Only the two outlying parishes in the hundred, South Mimms and Monken Hadley, met their obligations, though Enfield did better on this occasion, paying £46 of the £50 asked for. In the tenth and eleventh months Edmonton paid only £14 of the £47 demanded, Tottenham £21 out of £36. No payment is listed against the £50 required of Enfield, and this time no payment is listed in Hadley. South Mimms again paid almost in full.[72]

The recalcitrance of the taxpayers was not without its consequences; in January 1645 Major General Richard Browne, encamped outside the royalist stronghold of Oxford, wrote to the committee for Middlesex to complain. The committee had sent him forty horse and, though they had paid them for some weeks, now the payments had stopped, so that 'these, as well as the rest begin to run away ... Our men, for want of pay, desert us daily, their duty is hard, their quarters very straight, victuals scant, and no money sent to us'.[73]

20. The Church in the Interregnum

Dr William Roberts, who had been vicar since 1616, is said to have been ejected from his benefice in 1642 though his successor, Mr Walter Bridges, was not presented by Trinity College Cambridge until after Dr Roberts's death in 1646. The first of Bridges's children to be baptized in Enfield was Abigail in August 1647. Bridges was described in 1650 as an 'able and painful (ie painstaking) preacher'. His vicarage still stands in Silver Street. It then had two orchards and a close of pasture enclosed with the house. The vicar also had two acres in the common fields; his land was said to be worth £8 a year. The petty tithes and the income he received for his services at burials, marriages and the baptisms of strangers brought him an income of about £50 a year, which was a better living that those of the vicars of neighbouring parishes. In Edmonton the vicarage was ruinous, the glebe was worth about £6 a year, and other profits were described as uncertain. The incumbent at South Mimms, George Pierce, had been sequestered, (ie his living had been taken away from him) yet he had persisted in serving the church without the consent of the 'well affected' (ie the puritans) in the parish. The congregation there, it was said, had suffered by reason of the 'smallness of means' and had long been destitute of a 'pious preacher'. At Monken Hadley too, the vicar had been sequestered. His former income remained in the hands of the parishioners who had used the money, they claimed, to hire preachers, although a fifth part had been reserved for the support of the two daughters of the former vicar. A church rate, demanded in 1658, met with a contemptuous refusal to pay. The Restoration found Hadley church ruinous and the churchyard open to pigs and cattle.

Enfield rectory was leased by Trinity College Cambridge to Sir William Langley for twenty-one years, at a rent of £18 13s 8d in money, fourteen quarters of wheat, and eighteen and a half bushels of malt. Sir William received the tithe of corn and hay which was valued at £230 a year. He also held the Rectory House with its great barn. This mansion stood north-west of the junction of Parsonage Lane with Baker Street. The grounds contained a fish pond, two small orchards, and four closes of pasture, about eight acres in all, which stretched westward almost to the edge of the Chase. Also included with the rectory were twenty-four acres of arable in the common fields and five acres of meadow in the marsh.[74]

During the Interregnum there was considerable opposition throughout the country to the payment of tithes. Petitions were submitted to Parliament (the Rump) in June 1659 and in a vote on abolition the House divided equally. The closeness of the vote encouraged enemies of the established church to push the abolition of tithes through Parliament. Particularly active in the campaign were the Quakers, but they were widely suspected of being dangerous extremists and a reaction against them in Parliament resulted in a motion which insisted that tithes must be collected in order to encourage godly preaching.

Walter Bridges in Enfield however was having some difficulty in collecting his petty tithes*. After he had quitted the vicarage in April 1658, he submitted a complaint against John Swallow, John Mansborough (otherwise Sayer) Margaret Taylor, Bennett Wigge, Richard Fulham, George Richardson, Robert Wood and Widow Cullum: all had refused to pay their tithes for more than eleven years. The vicar claimed that John Swallow kept a hundred sheep, and calculated that they

---

*an account of what constituted the petty as against the greater tithe is given below p. 292.

bore for him fifty lambs every year worth 5s each, and a hundred fleeces worth 2s each. He had sixteen cows which, the vicar alleged, provided him with fifteen calves yearly worth 20s each. He had from his three mares three colts each year worth 20s each, and he had gathered great quantities of apples, pears and other fruit. All this, the vicar worked out, should have rendered him liable to pay upwards of 30s a year in tithe. John Mansborough on Enfield Green should have paid at least 18s a year, Margaret Taylor 20s, Bennett Wigge of Ponders End also 20s, George Richardson of Bulls Cross 50s, Robert Wood of Enfield Green also 50s, and Widow Cullum 30s.[75]

Walter Bridges left the parish at the beginning of April 1658. For some time only strangers preached from the pulpit, and the registers were neglected.[76] Mr Daniel Manning was appointed in March 1659, and he also found difficulty in collecting his tithe. Fourteen of his parishioners produced reasons for refusing to pay; in this they were led by William Covell, a former army captain of whom I shall be writing later, and William Hodge. The vicar claimed that Hodge fed 300 sheep in Enfield, of which he had yearly the fleeces and 250 lambs. He pastured twelve cows which provided him with twelve calves, and four mares which gave him four colts. From his orchard he gathered twenty bushels of apples and a great quantity of cherries and plums, the tithe whereof was worth 20s a year. His ten pigs, according to the vicar, provided ten piglets each year. He had six hives which gave him honey and wax. There were many hens, geese, chickens and ducks, which supplied eggs, and all these should have been liable to small tithes payable to the vicar.[77] Though Daniel Manning was deprived of his living following the Restoration of Charles II in 1660 he remained in Enfield, where he died and was buried in the churchyard in March 1665.[78]

21. William Covell's Utopia

The Interregnum, the period between the execution of Charles I in 1649 and the Restoration in 1660 of the monarchy, was more fertile than any previous period in radical ideas in religion and social organisation. Among the many groups which appeared was the Digger movement, landless men who felt they had a right to occupy and cultivate the commons. Their most famous exploit occurred in 1649–50 when they occupied and cultivated common land at St Georges, Weybridge, until expelled by an indignant local population. Evidence that the Diggers had extended their operations into Enfield is provided by a marginal note added to a broadside issued in May 1650 by poor squatters on the commons at Iver in Buckinghamshire. It tells that the Diggers had begun their communal cultivation of the waste in Barnet and in Enfield, and that they had threatened that they would leave their children to be supported by these parishes if the vestries took measures to evict them.[79]

During the Civil War and Interregnum, two or three hundred poor families had drifted into Enfield where they built themselves cottages on the Chase and in other corners and waste places in the parish.[80] There they scraped a living by cutting and selling wood, perhaps kept a cow, a pig, or a few geese or hens on the common. Thus the years following the death of Oliver Cromwell saw the parish burdened with the poor. The enclosures on the Chase cut them off from their principle source of livelihood. A calamitous fire at Ponders End in September 1657 had destroyed many homes, carts and tools, and stored crops. Damage was estimated to have amounted to £1182.[81] The sufferings of the poor inspired William Covell to promote a scheme for a new Utopia in Enfield. Covell lived in a substantial house at Bulls Cross, on the edge of Enfield Chase, on land which had formerly been part of the Chase but which had been taken into Theobalds Park by James I. The area was known as the Old Chase. In that quarter, forty-nine per cent of households were too poor to pay hearth tax in 1665.[82] Covell described himself as a preacher, but he had been a captain in the army until 1650 and had served under Cromwell in Scotland. There had been complaints about his radical and antinomian views (that Christians are emancipated by the Gospels from an obligation to keep moral laws). He was called before his general, where he fearlessly defended his beliefs, and Cromwell allowed him to return to his troop. After further complaints however he was dismissed. Despite this, at the next rendezvous he appeared at the head of his troop. He was ordered by Cromwell to leave and was subsequently cashiered at a court martial.[83]

His ideas for social reform were embodied in a pamphlet called *A Declaration unto Parliament* 1659.[84] It was printed and addressed to the Council of State, the army, and to Parliament. He blamed the poverty, so evident in his own parish, on the buying and selling of goods and labour. The ruling classes, he held, combined to maintain oppression. Covell did not then conclude, as the Marxists were later to do, that the poor should themselves unite to overthrow the system; he advocated a commonwealth imposed from above by the army and Parliament. There would be religious toleration and equality before the law. There would be no state religion, and tithes would be employed for the care of the poor and the defence of the country. His later refusal to pay tithe, in which he was followed by many others in the parish, shows perhaps an attempt to put his beliefs into practice. He demanded the abolition of privileges and monopolies, and freedom for the poor to cultivate the waste land, as had been advocated by the leader of the Weybridge Diggers, Gerrard Winstanley. Private property would be allowed, but all trade would be by barter. He proposed to initiate his scheme for the transformation of England in Enfield, where 500 acres of the 1500 which had recently been granted to the commoners following the division and sale of the Chase, would be employed for the foundation of his first model co-operative.

Not that Covell in any way maintained very high principles in real life, for he did very well, and was none too scrupulous, in buying and selling Crown property. He sold sixty-two acres of land and six acres of wood in Theobalds Park in 1652 for £962. Following this he entered into an arrangement with Nathaniel Ludlow and Richard Hill to purchase further Crown land in Theobalds Park offered for sale at Worcester House. The three purchasers were to share the profit. Covell made, it was said, £300 by the sale to Gowen Lowry, but then he refused to share it and when pressed offered his collaborators £70 between them. Nevertheless he gave them only a note to require Lowry to pay them £40.[85]

Covell's proposals, however unrealistic, were offered as a solution to a very real problem. Immediately after the Restoration a scheme was put forward by Nicholas Rainton and other hard-headed 'tenants and inhabitants' of Enfield.[80] Their petition to Parliament asked for permission to enclose the common fields of the parish which, it was claimed, would greatly improve the petitioners' holdings. They would be prepared to raise a tax of 20s on every acre enclosed to pay for stock, to put the poor to work, and to create a fund to finance the emigration of those who were willing to go to Ireland or to any other overseas colony.[86]

Covell was not to be silenced by the Restoration. Within a short time he was addressing Charles II with unusual familiarity: 'King, thou hast taken upon thee to rule part of the King of King's great household'. He went on to plead for 'the poor oppressed people of God', enjoined the monarch to open the prison doors for debtors, warned him, 'Take heed of all thy officers, for if that they, through corruptions, shall anyway abuse the people, it will reflect on thee, and make thee little'.[87]

22. The Enclosure of the Chase

Following the execution of Charles I in January 1649, Parliament legislated to sell all royal parks and estates, with the intention that the money should be used to meet arrears of pay in the army. Among these properties was the manor and Chase of Enfield which were surveyed in August 1650. Any sale of Enfield Chase would inevitably involve a very serious loss of common rights in the parishes of South Mimms, Monken Hadley, Edmonton and Enfield. The probability of trouble among the commoners induced the government to postpone the sale. Nevertheless the three lodges, East Lodge, South Lodge and West Lodge, as well as Old Park and Theobalds Park, were sold.

One of those who secured a considerable estate in Theobalds Park was Edward Fynnis, a captain of a troop of horse. He purchased the property with his arrears of pay in 1650 and died the following year. His property was left in trust for his children in various hands. Two of the trustees were army officers, John Gladman and Anthony Spinage, who used the premises to maintain and pay nineteen troopers for the war in Scotland. They subsequently claimed that this, with the cost of surveying, enclosing and fencing, had seriously diminished the profits on the land.[88]

The difficulty of finding money to pay the troops continued and forced the government to take up again the sale of Enfield Chase on 30 August 1654. An order in council was issued declaring that the Chase should be surveyed and a third part of the land and the wood should be sold. Nevertheless it was two years before commissioners were appointed to determine who had rights, and what compensation it would be necessary to grant. Local opposition to any enclosure persisted and army protection had to be afforded to the commission. Pressure was now exerted on the commoners in an attempt to expedite the proceedings. The commoners accused the authorities of using violence against those who openly voiced dissent. They also accused the promoters of deforestation of deceiving Parliament by an assertion in the House that the Enfield commoners had consented to their proposals. It was in this false belief, they said, that orders had been agreed in Parliament, in September 1656, that Enfield Chase should be included among a number of other woods and parks formerly belonging to the king, which were to be surveyed and sold immediately.

The new survey of the Chase, begun in 1656, was not completed until November 1658 and by that time the situation had fundamentally changed, for Oliver Cromwell was dead. The survey calculated the area to be 7900 acres, excluding land attached to the lodges and already sold, and nine acres made up of small encroachments around the boundaries. The parishes were allotted small commons to compensate for their loss of common rights. The areas were:

to Enfield and Old Park	1,329 acres
to Edmonton	917 acres
to Hadley	240 acres
to South Mimms and Old Fold	913 acres

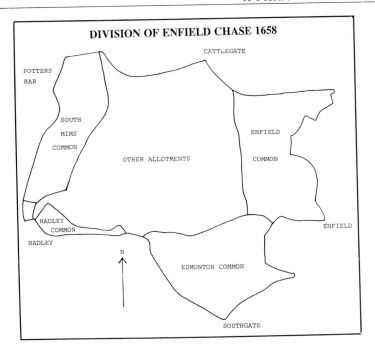

The state would acquire 4500 acres.

The boundaries of these parish allotments were drawn on a map and marked out on the ground. All the timber and wood growing upon them was to become the property of the state. They were so small, the commoners complained, that they would not maintain a tenth part of the cattle which formerly had been fed on the Chase. A deep sense of grievance was felt in the parishes, most especially in Enfield.

One third of the land which had been assigned to the state, it amounted to 1500 acres, came immediately on to the market and was quickly sold. A vast operation was launched to cut and sell a third of all the wood and timber, this glutted the markets and pushed down the prices. The new proprietors on Enfield Chase received no friendly welcome. They were mostly senior army officers who had purchased the land using debentures, which were promissary notes given to troops in lieu of pay. It was said that these great officers had bought them for as little as 1s 6d or 2s 6d in the pound, at times when their men had been in need of ready money for themselves and their families.

All this increased the hostility of the commoners. Around midsummer 1659, when the first crop was ripening on the new enclosures, there was an organised incursion on to the Chase. The hedges and ditches so recently constructed were destroyed and cattle put to feed upon the growing corn. The new proprietors, in desperation, sent for troops to protect their property.

These troops, it was alleged, viciously assaulted innocent by-standers and even attacked a party of labourers returning home from work. The military initiated many prosecutions in the neighbourhood, but onslaughts against their property continued. The president of the Council of State wrote on 1 June to three local justices of peace, Justinian Pagitt, John Huxley and Edwin Rich, telling them of the concern of the Council on learning that 'a rude multitude' from Enfield had broken open the enclosures and were now threatening to destroy the houses of the new proprietors. The Council had stationed two troops of horse in the neighbourhood and the justices were ordered to employ them for the protection of property belonging to the new owners. The justices however took no such action and within a week the president was forced to write again.

The situation was deteriorating all over the country. Wild assertions were being made in Enfield that they 'could call upon ten thousand out of Essex, and ten thousand out of Hertfordshire' to rise to their aid. The rage of the commoners was matched by the frustration of the owners. Lt Colonel Allen hired more foot soldiers who came without warrant from their commanders and shot and killed sheep and cattle belonging to the commoners. On one occasion the troops came right among the houses around Enfield Green where they rampaged around, inviting the villagers to come out and fight, calling them rogues and cowards, and threatening to burn their houses over their heads.

Matters reached a crisis on 10 July when redcoats and greycoats were called from Barnet, hired, it was said, at sixpence a day more than their ordinary pay. They were billeted overnight at Colonel Allen's house and the following morning they marched out to take control of the situation. They were met by a number of Enfield men (and women) estimated by those of the parish at twenty-five and at 250 by the army whose spokesman described the commoners as fighting with inveterate fury, pitching long poles into the ground with colours flying from the tops and 'making great shouts and declaring for Charles Stewart'.

The battle resulted in three dead, two Enfield men and one woman, and the capture of ten wounded troopers and the sergeant, 'run through the thigh with a half-pike and wounded in the head'. The captured soldiers were treated, it was said, with more barbarity than the Irish rebels ever treated an English settler. They were brought before a local magistrate and were consigned to Newgate Prison with their wounds still bleeding and no surgeon to attend them. Both sides proceeded to petition Parliament and both petitions were referred discreetly to a committee concerned with the Forest of Dean. The soldiers were eventually released but the troubles continued. The matter was settled by events outside the parish; troops under General Lambert blockaded the House of Commons in October and dissolved the Rump. The country was thrown into chaos out of which order was eventually restored by an army under General George Monck who marched down from Scotland and placed Charles II on the throne. The king entered London in May 1660 and the Chase became a royal deer park once again.[89]

Notes to Chapter Three

1   G. P. V. Akrigg *Jacobean Pageant* 1962 p. 19, Enfield parish register, J. M. Stratton and J. H. Brown *Agricultural Records AD220–1977.* 1978 p 44
2   Enfield parish register, there were 387 households in 1585
3   T. Lewis *People and Parish Registers* EHHS No 39 1979 pp 11–12
4   GLRO MJ SBR4. 307, parish register
5   DL43. 7. 8, *Recollections of Old Enfield,* 1910 reprinted EHHS 1983
6   *CSPD* 20 Oct. 1641, Protestation oath (copy in the House of Lords library)
7   Enfield parish register, Thomas Nashe *In Time of Pestilence* 1593
8   H. R. Trevor Roper *The European Witch Craze* in his *Reformation and Social Change* Macmillan 1967 J. C. Jeaffreson Middlesex County Records V2. li, lii, 57, 59
9   parish register

10   Jeaffreson *op cit* V2. liii, 116, 219
11   GLRO MJ. SBR 4. 417
12   Cal. Salisbury MS 17. 511, 523, 18. 60–61, 85. 100–101, 454–455, SP14. 216.
      193, Gunpowder box 7. 1, E178. 4166, P. Caraman *Henry Garnet* 1964 pp 264,
      317
13   SP16. 325. 7, SP16. 332. 23
14   parish register, J. M. Stratton *op cit* p 45
15   GLRO Middlesex session book 23. 31 Au 1641
16   parish register *passim*
17   GLRO DLC 340 f135
18   L. Birkett Marshall *A Brief History of Enfield Grammar School* 1958
19   G. C. Berry Sir Hugh Myddelton and the New River in *Trans. of the Hon. Soc. of
      Cymmrodorian* 1956
20   GLRO DLC 340 f. 184–5
21   GLRO Acc 903. 86
22   Enfield vestry order books
23   C66. 2179. 10
24   GLRO Acc 903. 29, 30, 86
25   Enfield D 1105
26   Enfield D 998. 1620
27   Peter Hardy *The Charities of Enfield* 1834 p 26
28   Enfield D 1105
29   Guildhall 9171. 25. 194
30   VCH Middlesex V5 p 226, CP62. 6, E178. 5478
31   GLRO Acc 16. 8, Nigel Hirshman *A History of Enfield* Pt1 *Domestic Buildings* ms
      copy Enfield
32   V. Pearl *London and the Outbreak of the Puritan Revolution* 1961
33   parish register
34   Guildhall 9171. 24. 173
35   Guildhall 9171. 26. 393
36   Joan Thirsk ed. *Agrarian History of England and Wales* V.4 1500–1640 CUP 1967
      p 624 and C.9 *Agricultural prices*
37   SP16. 531. 73 pp 114–9 are from this source, it contains a list of badgers, kidders,
      bakers, brewers and licensed victuallers
38   SP16. 461. 103
39   GLRO MJ SBR 6
40   ibid
41   DL43. 7. 8
42   C8. 75. 83
43   calculated from the hearth tax of 1664 at GLRO
44   GLRO MJ. SBR 5. 46
45   Jeaffreson *op cit* 2. 39
46   GLRO MJ. SBR 12. 25
47   Guildhall 9171. 25. 194
48   Guildhall 9171. 26. 520
49   DL43. 7. 8
50   DL5. 32. 273b
51   House of Lords Protestation oath Enfield
52   SP16. 392. 3
53   Guildhall 9171. 24. 226
54   Guildhall 9171. 24. 133
55   SP16. 407. 43, SP16. 376. 101 (ship money petitioners)
56   SP19A39
57   SP16. 376. 101
58   SP16. 409. 4

59 SP16. 401. 48
60 GLRO MJ SBR 6. 544
61 GLRO DRO4. 1a
62 Guildhall 9537. 15
63 *CSPD* 10 Ap 1640
64 SP16. 461. 103 f 222
65 SP19 A43, SP19 A39, SP19 A61, SP28. 193
66 SP16. 461. 103 f 251–256
67 SP28. 193
68 SP19 A61, 63, 65, 69, 71, 73, 39, 42
69 *CSPD* 20D 1642
70 SP28. 237
71 SP28. 198. 1
72 SP28. 166
73 *CSPD* 11 Jan 1645 p 247
74 *Survey of Church Livings in Middlesex* in *Home Counties Mag.* 6 p 316–8, Middlesex
    sessions books 1658
75 E112. 321. 420
76 parish register
77 E112. 321. 471
78 parish register
79 broadside printed in *Past and Present* 1949 pp 42, 64–5 C7. 128. 4
80 SP29. 22. 153
81 SP18. 180. 27
82 GLRO Enfield hearth tax 1664
83 *Mercurius Politicus* 20 Oct 1650, 1N 1650
84 Copy in the Goldsmiths Library Un. of London
85 C10. 57. 35, C8. 134. 18, SP29. 22. 153
86 SP29. 22. 153
87 W. Covell *A True Copy of a Letter Sent to the Kings Most Excellent Majesty* (copy B.
    L.)
88 E121. 3. 4. 9 (Old Park), E121. 5. 7. 14 (Theobalds), E121. 3. 4. 87, E320 L42
    (West Lodge), E121. 3. 4. 71, E317 Middx 20, E320 L32 (South Lodge) E121.
    3. 4. 70, E320 L 29 (East Lodge)
89 David Pam *The Story of Enfield Chase* EPS 1984 ch. 5

PART TWO

1660–1837

Introduction

Much of the property in this area formerly held by Charles I was not returned to the Crown in 1660. The magnificent palace at Theobalds had been destroyed, its park remained divided and cultivated by tenants. Old Park too had been broken up and was now used for agriculture. Parts of Enfield Chase had been enclosed and sold off in 1658, but there the recently created farms were taken back and re-absorbed into the park land which was restocked with deer. Common rights were re-established over the whole Chase, which was to survive for more than a hundred years.

Landowners in Enfield were more eager than ever to maximise profits from their estates by enclosure, both in order to improve the farms, and because the continued existence of common rights over the land prevented its potential use for building houses for wealthy Londoners. Enclosure still met fierce local resistance. Landlords also sought to convert their demesnes, or home farms, into pasture, both their common field plots and their enclosed land. They took every opportunity to change the copyhold tenures of their tenants into leaseholds. Copyhold land was land held by copy of court roll, at a rent controlled by the custom of the manor. As is shown below, by the late seventeenth century copyhold produced a meagre return to the landlord. The rents on leasehold land could be increased whenever the lease fell due, the shorter the lease the more rent could be kept in line with inflation.

The gap between the rich and the poor widened following the Restoration. The greater houses were furnished with elegance and good taste, paintings and prints adorned the walls, there were books in abundance and musical instruments, Turkey work carpets and upholstery, there was plate and jewelry in plenty. Many gentlemen held South Sea stock and Bank of England annuities and money was brought home from India. Local gentlemen engaged in trade both in this country and beyond the seas. Their wine cellars were well filled and their conservatories grew exotic fruits and flowers. Gentlemen and their wives dressed expensively and ran into debt.

Farmers and tradesmen comprised the social level below the gentry but most Enfield tradesmen were also farmers. Inventories show their houses stocked with vast quantities of good quality linen, walnut and mahogany furniture, pewter, copper and brass in their kitchens and mirrors on their walls. The value of the debts owed to them when they died, in most cases, far exceeded the value of their goods and money in hand. They lived in comfort with their coffee pots, chocolate pots and tea boards, plate warmers and warming pans for their beds.

The tanners were the most prosperous group in the parish, though the very high valuation shown in many of their inventories has something to do with the long time taken to process the hides; the stock in the tan pits often comprised three quarters of the value of their property. Many tanners invested their profits in real estate. Most of the leather produced was sold in London, but there were prosperous shoemakers and horse collar makers in Enfield.

The cloth industry in the parish, though it employed many people, does not appear to have made anyone rich. Indeed the trade remained tied ignominiously to the relief of the poor. Spinning was the principal occupation of the women in the workhouse and, although the parish register between 1702 and 1706 names seven weavers, only one will made by an Enfield weaver has survived. As one might expect from the large number of affluent people in Enfield, local tailors did well. Gentlefolk spent lavishly on dress and many inventories of tradesmen list clothes of high quality, plentiful but plain.

The Enfield market and the Enfield fair flourished in the years after the Restoration and that prosperity lasted for more than a hundred years. The late eighteenth century saw the market decline as communications with London improved.

There were large areas of brick earth in the parish, also in Edmonton, and there were many brickmakers. Mostly the bricks were used locally, for the poor state of the roads rendered carriage costly. Builders became wealthy, and inventories show their yards and premises stacked high with timber, bricks and tiles, and old materials to be re-used. Always the debts due to them at death far exceeded their assets in hand. It was a general rule that the more elevated the customer the more he was likely to owe.

The high standard of living thus demonstrated gave rise, in the post-Restoration period, to the provision of shops capable of meeting the demand for consumer goods. Almost all everyday requirements could be purchased in the town centre, from candles to curtain rings, from French barley to bedcords. The town centre could also provide facilities for borrowing money, either on goods pledged or by a mortgage on property. Interest rates had fallen through the seventeenth century and mortgages had become safer.

The most ancient industrial site in the parish, the mill at Ponders End, now comprised a leather mill and a corn mill. More than two thousand acres of common field land survived and most farms were a mixture of arable and livestock. There were flocks of between three and four hundred sheep, but cattle were kept in smaller numbers and many of those who claimed common on the Chase had only one or two beasts. The buying and selling of livestock in the late seventeenth century was often carried out in pubs, but later the business was done at Smithfield and the stock was taken there by a cattle drover.

The homes of the poor might be dark, cold, damp and full of children, but light, warmth, company, with games like skittles, shove ha'penny, even billiards, awaited the labourer in the public house. There a man could drink and forget his woes. Spirits were cheap, especially gin; small beer could be had at not much more than 2d a gallon, a gallon of best beer cost only 1s 8d. The best class of people frequented the King's Head and drank 'old red port'. The King's Head had its assembly rooms, members only and guests, for dancing and cards. The rooms were brightly lit and warm with curtains over the windows and doors to keep out the draughts.

'Lords and nobles' rubbed shoulders with country folk, pickpockets and other criminals at the Enfield races. Vast numbers out from London joined the locals; everybody came, journeymen, undertakers, tailors, barbers and snobs, all eager to win a fortune on the horses. Gambling had become a national addiction. Rich and poor could also intermingle on Chase Green where cricket was taken seriously from the beginning of the nineteenth century. The grass was mowed and the pitch was rolled under the direction of the formidable beadle. Matches were played both home and away for considerable wagers. Bets were laid, not only on results, but on individual performances. Some of the beadle's bets have survived among the vestry papers. Scorebooks were kept in which the 'notches' (runs) were recorded.

One little community, living around Enfield Wash, became the centre of a nation-wide controversy around Christmas 1754. Intimate details of their daily lives were revealed in the glare of public interest surrounding a case at the Old Bailey; what they bought in their little shops, how they were employed from day to day, the muddled ignorance of some, the astute book-keeping of others (albeit illiterate), all this was revealed before the world. Then the world lost interest and Enfield Wash receded into obscurity, life went on as before, the people continued to work at whatever jobs turned up, whether it was their own trade or not, and for whoever would pay them; by these means they kept the poor law at bay.

Law enforcement in the parish was maintained by the petty constable and its efficiency varied according to the character of the man appointed. The office itself carried little prestige and was regarded with contempt and derision by the better class of parishioners in vestry. Nevertheless some who held the office pursued their duties with considerable determination and enthusiasm. Towards the end of the century the beadle assumed the principle role in enforcing the law; beadles could be very different from Mr Bumble.

Hostility in the parish between those who had taken power during the Interregnum, and those who might be considered the natural governors of local affairs, persisted for more than ten years after the Restoration. The parish inherited a well funded grammar school and a fine building, but the low salary offered to the schoolmaster circumscribed its development. Every successful master was driven to concentrate his efforts on paying pupils so that the private school expanded at the expense of the public. The vestry encouraged the tendency for the sake of economy but on each occasion when the master achieved success they accused him of neglecting the parish boys and sought to eject him from office. Inevitably the master sought protection in the courts of law and the resulting legal costs consumed the school's rich endowments.

Many private boarding schools were set up in large houses in the parish through the eighteenth century; they provided education of a high standard but they were mostly attended by children from outside the parish. The Grammar School continued to educate boys from the poorer classes. It was assumed in 1825 that this was sufficient reason to lower the standards and Latin was eliminated. Interest in the education of the poor increased in the nineteenth century; charity schools were set up for girls both by the established church and by the nonconformists and there were dame schools, but by their very nature these leave little trace.

The vicar of Enfield was among some two thousand ministers ejected from their livings in 1662. A number of these ejected ministers settled in the area and gathered around them congregations of Presbyterians or Baptists while the Quakers established meeting houses. All were liable from time to time to punishment by the law, but the most assiduous persecution fell upon the Quakers, especially during the years 1682 to 1686. Republicanism lingered on in the neighbourhood after the Restoration, centred around a radical Baptist chapel at Theobalds. Plots real or imaginary kept informers busy, the most important of these locally being the Rye House plot which involved certain local gentlemen in some danger.

Fervour had become unfashionable by the eighteenth century. The burden of the tithe was widely resented, especially by the nonconformists. Yet attendance at some form of worship continued to be normal among the middle and upper classes. Galleries had to be erected on three sides of the parish church by 1830 and Congregational, Baptist and Methodist chapels had been built.

The growth of London, with the expansion of inland trade in the late seventeenth century, increased the volume of traffic along the Old North Road, those parishes through which it passed now found the burden of maintenance insupportable. The Stamford Hill Turnpike Trust for this reason was set up in 1713 to collect tolls and to maintain the road. The Trust met at the Angel Edmonton and most of the trustees were local gentlemen. They set up no gates north of Stamford Hill and Turnpike Lane, and local traffic continued to use the road without paying; it was the through traffic which paid.

After fifty years' existence the turnpike road remained primitive; no attempt was made to drain it and, until the 1760s, no cart bridges had been constructed over the many little streams flowing eastward toward the River Lea. Hundreds of loads of gravel were laid yearly, all the gravel cartage being done by statute labour and so costing nothing. Narrow wheeled traffic cut great ruts into the soft road surface and the Trust charged lower tolls for broad wheeled vehicles because these caused little damage.

Traffic moved by day and night. Certain public houses along the road were designated as night houses. Evidence shows them crowded in the early hours with travellers, drivers, guards and thieves. Ostlers were waiting to feed and water the horses; bread, meat and ale could be purchased. Road use increased even more rapidly in the second half of the eighteenth century and travel by stage-coach became common.

All the turnpike roads north of the Thames were consolidated in 1826, though the toll gates were not finally removed until 1872. At that time the main roads were handed over to the jurisdiction of local boards of health (with county grants). The parishes throughout the eighteenth century tried to make the road user pay for the parish roads by the imposition of statute labour on those who owned carts and carriages. A salaried road surveyor was first appointed in Enfield in 1824 and a highways board was set up in 1830.

Water transport on the River Lea remained in a state of mediaeval inefficiency; there was no towpath and the barges were still hauled by men. Conflict persisted between the interests of water transport and the millers and other users of the water. The difficulties of navigation were increased by the New River Company which took as much as one third of the water. Transport by water became so slow and expensive that by 1760 malt was again being carried by road. The river was surveyed by John Smeaton in 1766 and under his direction the Lee Navigation was constructed. Income from tolls rose rapidly over the last thirty years of the eighteenth century.

The series of acts on settlement and removal which followed the Restoration of Charles II threatened the vast majority of the population with instant and humiliating expulsion from any place where they were living, unless it happened to be the place where they could legitimately claim settlement; those at risk included people who had never asked for relief. Yet men had to move to find work, and mobility of labour was as important then as it is now. Thus a conflict was created between the need of the farmer for cheap labour and his yearning for low rates. A way round the oppressive settlement laws, throughout the seventeenth and eighteenth centuries, was provided by the settlement certificate. Many who were threatened with removal demanded and were given certificates from their own parishes which guaranteed to maintain them and their families wherever they might be forced to seek parish relief. Such certificates were recognised in the most unpropitious circumstances. From 1795 the law was changed and from that date nobody could be removed unless he had asked for relief.

Vagrancy was supposed to be a separate problem. Enfield was one of the parishes through which hundreds of vagrants arrested in London were carried north out of Middlesex. Sturdy beggars by law should have been whipped before being returned to their parishes of settlement but the punishment aroused so much hostility among the common people that it usually had to be omitted. Examinations of vagrants reveal their wanderings about the country; no amount of harassment by beadles and constables could confine them in the local workhouse.

Winter and summer, the Old North Road carried a stream of travellers towards London, the wealthy in their private coaches and the well-to-do by stage-coach. Those who could not afford to travel elegantly clambered aboard the great lumbering wagons which rolled slowly on by day and night. There were also people who could not pay even for this kind of conveyance, trudging hungry and ragged and sleeping rough. It is not surprising that some of the poor, particularly during the time of Civil War and Commonwealth, sought and found, around the edges of the Chase, house room and the means of survival and thankful for small mercies, stayed on in Enfield.

Thus poverty became a problem in the parish. It was a fortunate circumstance for those liable to support the poor that the income from the judicious and well designed benefactions of the sixteenth and early seventeenth centuries enabled the vestry to provide relief for many years without levying a rate. Charity funds were augmented from time to time by money paid for the privilege of a pew in church and by fines levied on those refusing to undertake parish offices. The more rapid growth of population in the eighteenth century however, so aggravated the problem that the burden of poverty had at last to be met by the poor rates.

The Enfield parish poor, until the last quarter of the eighteenth century, were tended from conception to the grave with some kindness. The parish child might be brought into this world, nursed, reared and apprenticed, tended when sick, cared for in old age and buried when dead. Chapter five shows how the parish welfare service paid midwives and wet nurses, it employed surgeons, physicians and apothecaries, even supplied trusses and on one occasion a wooden leg, and made arrangements with various London hospitals to take up the chronically sick and lunatics. A workhouse was set up in 1719.

The years 1730 to 1740 saw a rise in the cost of out-door relief which so alarmed the ratepayers that economy was urgently demanded. It is curious that throughout the rest of the eighteenth and early nineteenth centuries this same crisis recurred time and time again and was met by the same ineffective remedies, which failed each time for the same reasons. One popular solution with the ratepayers was to consign all applicants for out-door relief to the workhouse, but the workhouse was never large enough and, until the last years of the century, the vestry was seldom harsh enough. Relief by the provision of clothing, it was thought, would ensure that money was wisely spent, but the consistent application required to run such a scheme could never be forthcoming for long from unpaid officers whose tour of duty lasted only one year. Farming the poor, that is paying a contractor to look after them, was an experiment in which much faith was misplaced; it failed time and time again. Humiliation was tried and the paupers were forced to wear uniforms and badges of disgrace, but none of these remedies worked and the system inevitably reverted to its same old ways and problems. Through all this time there existed an element of unplanned kindness which may even have lifted, occasionally, the cloud of depression hanging over the dismal old workhouse.

The last quarter of the eighteenth century saw the cost of relief rise more rapidly than ever before. Hostility towards the able-bodied pauper increased. The poor were badly hit by the harvest failures of the 1790s. Later generations would be helped to meet such crises by employment in local factories, while earlier generations had found protection in their rights of common. These were lost to them through the enclosure of Enfield Chase in 1777 and of the common fields and marshes in 1803, and from that time onward they found themselves with no protection from poverty but that offered by charity and the poor law.

The measures taken by the magistrates at Speenhamland to supplement wages through the poor rate were not imitated in Enfield; instead the wealthy in the parish contributed to a fund to buy bread for resale cheap to the poor. The poor rate continued to rise; it amounted in the year 1800–1801 to £3980 and, although the population was 5881, there were only 460 ratepayers. It was becoming ever more difficult to collect the rates. A movement was set afoot in the parish to secure greater efficiency and economy. Measures were taken to eliminate graft and to reduce expenditure on entertaining the vestrymen. Any surviving sympathy towards the able-bodied pauper evaporated. Pauper children were packed off to the silk mills. Only the aged and infirm continued to be treated with consideration. The diet in the workhouse was critically compared with that of a working labourer and his family. The workhouse food was drastically reduced.

The resultant savings were considerable and expenditure was cut by nearly one half. Measures were proposed which might have done something for the industrious poor, but the parish, having saved itself a thousand pounds a year, was of the opinion that it had done enough.

Perhaps we ought to assume that widespread disaffection prevailed among the poor; we can certainly perceive the very visible measures taken by owners of property in Enfield to counteract possible insurrection. The condition of the poor very obviously deteriorated from the 1790. The Enfield Association, set up in 1794, was certainly more concerned with the protection of property than with the defence of the realm; this never seemed to have had a high priority in the vestry. The natural rulers of the parish did enter with some degree of enthusiasm in 1803 on a campaign to furnish volunteers for the forces, but their quota was never forthcoming and any patriotic fervour in the vestry quickly faded. Throughout the war the parish remained more than reluctant to pay what was due to the militia account. The vestry greeted the setting-up of the Royal Small Arms Factory in 1812 with apprehension, not enthusiasm, lest it should result in the burdening of the parish with higher rates. Many Enfield men, driven by poverty, joined the militia as substitutes for those who had been selected by ballot. Some joined the army for the same reason, others enlisted to avoid punishment for their crimes and made themselves a nuisance wherever they were billeted.

The period of depression following the end of the Napoleonic War saw the numbers of the poor again increase. Opinion hardened even further against them, and a climate was created for the institution of a new and much more impersonal poor law.

Chapter Four

Landlords and Gentlemen

1. The King's Parks

The return of Charles II in 1660 had brought about the restoration of Enfield Chase as a royal hunting ground and the re-establishment of common rights shared by the commoners in Enfield, Edmonton, South Mimms and Monken Hadley. The farms set up there during the Interregnum were taken back into the Chase. Such an abrupt change left problems unresolved. Transactions in progress for the purchase of Chase land were suddenly suspended. The would-be purchasers were forced, incongruously, to cite laws which had been annulled, so that they could claim back money in the king's court, which they had paid for the king's land, now restored to the king's Chase. Henry Dansey, Thomas Kidder and George Joyce had entered into a contract early in March 1659 to buy land on the Chase for which they had agreed to pay £13,920 14s 6d. One third was to have been paid in cash and two thirds in debentures. In addition they were to have paid 8d in the pound to meet the expenses of the contractors. A first payment having been due within eight weeks, the three would-be purchasers had paid over £464 (the 8d in the pound) only to find that they were unable to secure a conveyance because of the untimely deaths of two of the treasurers. Before new appointments could be made came the Restoration of 'His Sacred Majesty' and the likelihood of the purchase taking effect became remote. The would-be purchasers now hopefully claimed a refund of the money they had paid. The contractors, like so many others at this time, urged that they ought to be indemnified under the Act of Free Pardon, Indemnity and Oblivion.

As late as March 1660 Edward Randall was negotiating to sell trees off the Chase and still found those anxious to purchase. Robert Huddleston of Enfield, gentleman, was one who took the bait. Because the trees could not be felled immediately and because of the uncertainty of the times, Randall required that Huddleston enter into an obligation to pay £20 if the transaction was not completed. Some trees were felled but then the King's commissioners intervened and forbade the felling of any more or the removal of those already felled. Randall now sued Huddleston in the Court of King's Bench for payment of the £20 and caused him to be arrested.

Neither Theobalds Park nor Old Park were re-established in 1660; the land was now used for agriculture. Theobalds Park was granted to George Monck, Duke of Albermarle at the Restoration. He leased it to existing tenants; such a one was widow Malyn of Enfield who held two tenements and 197 acres for twenty-one years and paid the Duke £105 per year, not much over 10s an acre. Such low returns might have encouraged sub-letting at considerable profit but she leased

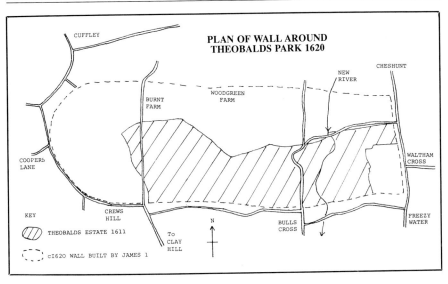

seventy acres of her holding to William Cox of Hertford for ten and a half years at an equally low annual rent of £32 (about 9s an acre). When she assigned the lease to her daughter on her marriage however, her son-in-law refused to accept Cox's rent and began proceedings to eject him. Following the death in 1689 of Christopher the second Duke who had held as tenant for life, King William bestowed Theobalds estate on his Dutch favourite, William, Earl of Portland. It was valued at this time at only £230 a year and comprised the former palace with its barns, stables, gardens and orchards, covering thirty acres, and the park, 2508 acres, with all the houses erected on it. The Earl found the palace and park occupied by fifty-three tenants all holding leases for twenty-one years or three lives and at low rents. He sought immediately to replace these tenancies with more economic arrangements. The tenants, knowing it would take time before he could eject them, retaliating by cutting and selling timber trees, grubbing up the hedges and ploughing the parkland to convert it from meadow and pasture into arable.

The Earl proceeded against his tenants in a ruthless manner. Philip Mitchell held the farm called the Queen's Lodgings of an annual value of £120, the corner house called Whatleys, worth £22 a year, and a tenement and meeting house called Prickmans House valued at £14 a year. He had, he said, been esteemed by the late Duke to be a good tenant and when his lease had expired in 1682, at the end of twenty-one years, he had been granted a further term of three lives (two of whom were still living) at a total rent of £152 a year. This he claimed was a rack rent, that is it represented the full value of the land.

The Duke had allowed him £200 to install six-inch pipes to bring water from the New River to his land; the work had cost Mitchell £300, and for this concession he had paid his landlord £12 a year. But two years before the Duke died the New River Company had taken up the pipes and had replaced them with one-inch pipes which were inadequate. He had therefore ceased to pay the £12. Portland now sued for the arrears and used this as a pretext to serve him with an order of ejectment. The court ordered him to deliver up the premises; he was allowed only the liberty to carry off his crop and the use of the barns until Christmas.[1]

New tenants were soon found, for the land provided adequate returns. Robert

Old Park. The house is now the club house of the Bush Hill Park Golf Club.

Bridgeman farmed seventy-four acres there. He cropped, in the year 1706, thirteen acres of wheat, thirteen acres of oats and fourteen acres of hay, all of which he had sold for £63. He must in addition have benefited from thirty-four acres for pasture, probably used to feed sheep; but these would not have been mentioned in the case from which this evidence comes since it was brought by the rector, and the tithe on fleeces and lambs were due to the vicar. The same case shows that Edward Pennyfather farmed fifty-eight acres in Theobalds Park, eight acres of wheat which sold for £24, twelve acres of barley which he sold for £30, twelve acres of oats which brought him £18, and nineteen acres of meadow[2] from which he sold fifteen loads of hay for £19, a total return of £91.

Old Park was another Crown property which had not been returned to its former use at the Restoration. This also was granted to George Monck. In 1650 it had been divided up and sold as farmland. Little changed with the new ownership. Richard Ashby, who had purchased forty acres there during the Interregnum, had leased it to Richard Mills, an Enfield carpenter, at £18 a year. Ashby's title was annulled, Mills's lease was now from the Duke, but he still paid only £18 which he claimed was the true value of the property. The Park was held, in 1685, by the second Duke of Albermarle, and following his death in 1688 it came into the possession of the Earl of Rutland.[3] Some of it was rented in 1707 by Robert Rickards, an Edmonton yeoman whose land lay across the boundary between his own parish and Enfield. He was forced to reveal the acreages of his crops because Edward Sheller, who had recently purchased the lease from Trinity College Cambridge of the right to collect the tithes for Enfield rectory, was making a strenuous

effort to extract a profit from his contract. Rickards claimed that he was not liable
to pay tithe, though he had to admit that he had always paid them to the Edmonton
rectory. He grew thirty-five acres of wheat at Old Park in 1706, ninety-two acres
of oats and thirty acres of hay, making a total of 157 acres. Pasture was not
accounted for, nor livestock, because these would have been subject to the lesser
tithe, payable to the vicar.[4]

2. The Raintons and their Successors at Forty Hall

The Raintons at Forty Hall had long been aware that their manor of Worcesters,
only eight or nine miles from London, could be better exploited in order to enhance
its value, but such improvement could only be achieved by the enclosure of the
common fields. Nicholas Rainton was also aware that land in Enfield was sought
to house Londoners wealthy enough to pay for a second home in the country where
they could escape the disease ridden, smell-laden air of the City. Inviolable common
fields circumscribed such development.

Despite the absence of government opposition to the enclosure of common land
in the late seventeenth century, encroachments on the common fields or the
common waste in Enfield still met with stubborn resistance from the commoners.
There remained some twenty-seven common arable fields in the parish containing
more than two thousand acres.[5] Sir Nicholas Rainton had long ago enclosed a
considerable area of common field land, that was in 1636. He was challenged at
the time in the Court of the Duchy of Lancaster, but the court maintained that
the land had been 'anciently enclosed'. This verdict was again challenged in
court in 1639 by William Billings and other tenants, but with no greater success.
Nevertheless the commoners were in no way prepared to concede victory to the
landlord. That November, while two of Sir Nicholas's servants were mending the
hedge in Highfield, along came Thomas Goodyer with his staff hook and threw
out a thorn bush newly planted, declaring defiantly that Sir Nicholas Rainton
might make up the hedge but it would be pulled down again and, 'if he had ability
of body to do it, he would do it himself' and that, despite all that Sir Nicholas
might do, they would put their cattle into the field. Notwithstanding these threats
the enclosures were maintained until the death of Sir Nicholas in August 1646.
Taking advantage of the conditions created by the Civil War and of the opportunity
afforded by the death of his over-powerful neighbour, that year this same William
Billings and his friends tore down the fences and claimed again that the land was
common. But application was made to the Duchy Court where an injunction was
issued to restrain them.[6]

After the death of Sir Nicholas, the manor of Worcesters came into the hands
of Nicholas Rainton his great-nephew, a minor. The most profitable part of this
manor in 1654 was the demesne. Nicholas farmed seventy acres himself and lived
at Forty Hall. Below, by Maidens brook, lay Enfield House formerly a royal
residence but now neglected and falling into ruin, its paths and gardens overgrown
with weeds. The remainder of the demesne, about 130 acres, was let either by lease
or to tenants at will. Richard Bincks held by lease a house in Chase Side with
which were enclosed a small field and an orchard, two roods in all, for which he
paid 36s 8d a year rent. William Parnell held by lease the Dairy House at Bulls
Cross with its garden, orchard and a close of four acres, as well as forty-one acres
of arable in the common fields and one and a half acres of meadow in the marsh.

He paid Rainton an annual rent of £35. Daniel Parnell, who held a tenement in Turkey Street and eleven acres of common field arable, paid £6 13s 4d rent. Widow Thredder, as a tenant at will, held a house at Bulls Cross with a close of one and a half acres attached. She also had nine acres in the common fields and three and a half acres of meadow in the marsh for which she paid £4 6s 8d a year.[7]

Some land in the manor outside the demesne was occupied by freeholders, it added little to Rainton's income. This same Richard Bincks held another house in Chase Side, freehold, with a croft of two acres, a piece of pasture at Cocker Lane and an acre of arable in Ferney field; for all this he paid Rainton only 7d a year. Rainton's copyhold was scarcely more profitable. The widow, Elizabeth Soane, paid only 6d a year for an acre of pasture and 1s 4d for two acres of common arable; Grave Glover, for five acres of pasture and two acres of arable in Southbury field, paid 6s 8d. Richard Pole gent, for nine acres of common arable, one and a half acres of meadow and three acres of pasture paid only 13s 4d a year.[8]

Following the Restoration, Nicholas Rainton looked about for ways to increase the value of his property both by enclosure, as his uncle had done, and also by the conversion of copyhold to leasehold. It was only upon enclosed land that new crops like clover could be sown. He promoted a bill in Parliament in 1660 to enclose all the common fields in the parish of Enfield. The sponsor of the bill and his supporters in the parish offered to pay 20s for each acre enclosed. They proposed to use the funds so raised to relieve the parish of the burden of its poor.[9] The bill failed to become law but the campaign continued; in 1665 Rainton made the claim that there existed a custom in Enfield by which each man was free to enclose his own lands within the common fields. He went on to assert that many hundreds of tenants, time out of mind, had made use of this custom.[10] Fortified by his self-justification he enclosed more of his demesne.

This assertion by Rainton that common field land had been enclosed piece-meal from time to time over the previous sixty years was borne out by many witnesses. Thirty instances were recalled in evidence which told of the enclosure of about 160 acres. It was asserted also that common field arable in Dungfield, Eastfield, and also in Stockings, Buttes and Hammonds Lees, had not been sown for many years, and all this time the land had been used for pasture or meadow.[11] The process of conversion from arable to meadow, though of enclosed land, is described in a case brought against Sir Basil Firebrace for his refusal to pay tithe on his enclosure at West Lodge. Fourteen acres of oats and grass seed were sown together in 1695 in order to lay the area to grass after the oats were cut. Six acres of oats and grass were sown together the following year.[12]

Many of Rainton's enclosures were opened up by the commoners, Thomas Saltmarsh the elder, Thomas Saltmarsh the younger, John Lofte yeoman and others in 1672. They drove large numbers of sheep to feed upon the corn and grass. Ten acres of very good wheat and oats and ten acres of clover grass were totally destroyed. There was considerable bitterness against Rainton. Joseph Collett, an Enfield commoner, who was also a sword cutler within the parish of St Martins in the Fields, claimed that Rainton had used threats against his wife to induce him to abandon his opposition. He had encountered Mr Rainton, he said, accompanied by his solicitor Mr South in Chancery Lane. There had been a heated altercation in the street, and Rainton had called him a knave, a rogue, a rascal, 'with a great deal more opprobrious language'. Rainton in turn claimed that Collett had abused him, 'with scurrilous words' and had declared that he would open up the enclosures notwithstanding 'all Mr Rainton's injunctions and all his perjured witnesses'. Mr

Rainton, he alleged, 'had made a rod township his own arse', and he would tell the court so much. He ended by asserting that he was a better gentleman than Mr Rainton.

Rainton's claims were opposed more soberly in court by Thomas Saltmarsh the elder and younger, Jeremiah Saltmarsh, Nicholas Saltmarsh, Edward Croxon, John Dashwood and Robert Jason Esq. Rainton, by this time, had aroused powerful opposition to his enclosures in the persons of the Duke of Albermarle, Sir Henry Wroth, Edward Wilford gent., Matthew Skinner gent., and many other gentlemen who owned land in the parish. The case however had been abandoned by 1673 leaving Rainton still in possession of his enclosures.[13]

Those who saw the possibility of using common field land for house building were encouraged by their landlord's success. John Tapper, Thomas Garret, John Tibbett and others enclosed five acres in Serles field which they had acquired from Rainton in exchange for an orchard of four acres, part of Stonecroft field planted with fruit trees which lay behind Tapper's house in Baker Street. Tapper at once proceeded to put up houses, barns and stables on his new enclosure, and converted the remainder into orchards and gardens. It was alleged that he raided the Chase for 'hundreds of cartloads of boughs, bushes and stakes to enclose the new property, and took 'many thousands of cartloads of sand' to the value of £500 some of which he used for the building and some of which he sold.[14]

Rainton also conveyed four acres in Brickhill field to Edward Helder; the land included the present site of Enfield Town railway station. Helder was an accomplished master bricklayer who had worked with Christopher Wren. On his new enclosure he built the magnificent house which later became the Cowden Clarke school-house. Helder thus became involved in the bitter fight against Rainton. His men were at work on the house in February 1675 when Mr Edward Dobson, bailiff of the manor of Enfield and keeper of East Bailey walk, came by with Henry Billings. Dobson threatened Helder with legal action, warning him to proceed no further with the building for he would pull down to the ground what had then been built.[15]

The house survived. John Keats received his schooling there under John Cowden Clarke. Charles, the schoolmaster's son, wrote describing Helder's work many years later:

> 'The structure was of rich red brick moulded into designs decorating the front with garlands of flowers and pomegranates, together with the heads of cherubim over two niches in the centre of the building'

The house served its last years as a railway station and, when it was demolished in 1872, it was taken down 'brick by brick, with the greatest care, each being numbered and packed in boxes of sawdust for carriage. Nothing could exceed the beauty of the workmanship, the bricks having been ground down to a perfect face and joined with beeswax and resin, no mortar or lime being used. In this manner the whole front was built in a solid block, the circular niches with their carved cherubs being afterwards cut out with a chisel'. The facade of the house can be seen in the Victoria and Albert Museum.

Edward Helder wrote his will on 14 June 1683 and soon afterwards he died. He left his widow Martha with ten children, all under the age of twenty-one. His property at death consisted of the lovely house in Brickhill field which was let to William Knot gentleman at £40 a year, six acres of arable let at 40s, and a tenement with fifteen acres of meadow which had an annual value of £27. Much of the estate

The Cowden Clarke schoolhouse, on the site now occupied by Enfield Town railway station, was built by Edward Helder in the late seventeenth century. The facade is in the Victoria and Albert museum.

was left in the hands of trustees for the benefit of his children, though the widow Martha was given the use of the freehold property and a third part of his leasehold property while she lived. Within ten years four of the children were dead, Thomas, the eldest, at the age of twenty-four, and three of the girls. Three of the younger children were apprenticed, Sarah to a child's-coat-maker, Robert to a shoemaker, and Susanah to a sempstress. Joshua, now the eldest, was a mariner. The money remained in the hands of the trustees. This unfortunately provoked Joshua, eager to lay hands on his share, to bring a suit against his mother in the Court of Chancery.[16] The result of the suit is obscure, but the costs ruined the family.

It came to be the practice by the end of the seventeenth century that those who wished to enclose their common land should be permitted to do so, but that they should pay for the privilege. Thus in 1691 Sir John Brattle paid £60 to the vestry after it had sanctioned his enclosure of twenty-two acres of common arable. Despite this, in June 1703, his enclosures were broken open and he was forced to appeal to the vestry in order to restore them.[17]

The Forty Hall estate was at this time the largest in Enfield. Nicholas Rainton's daughter Mary, in 1675, married Sir John Wolstenholme who lived at Minchenden on Southgate Green[34] and after the death of Nicholas Rainton in 1696 the estate came to Sir John and Mary. Two years later a marriage was arranged between their son Nicholas (later Sir Nicholas Wolstenholme) and Grace, the daughter of Sir Edward Waldoe, and the Forty Hall estate was settled on the young couple. Sir John was to receive £8000 from Sir Edward and a further £2000 when a child of the marriage attained the age of six months. The property settled included the manor of Worcesters, New Park (or Little Park) of 375 acres, the site of the late mansion house called Enfield House (Elsyngs), Forty Hall and a messuage in the tenure of Dr Robert Uvedale (the house known later in Enfield as the 'Palace').

From the £8000 paid to Sir John he gave Nicholas only £1000, little enough the young man thought, to furnish Forty Hall and to set up an equipage suitable for the daughter of Sir Edward Waldoe. He very soon ran into debt and thereafter he was constantly in difficulties and was forced continually to press his tenants for arrears of rents. His financial position became so bad that by the end of the year 1707, all the estate had to be put into the hands of trustees and, when Sir Nicholas died in February 1716, it was left in the trustees' hands with the instructions that they should sell his property in Northamptonshire and Yorkshire in order to pay his debts and to meet his obligations. Funeral expenses had to be paid and his sisters, Mary and Katherine, were to receive £3000 each. Any money left over from the sale was to be used, if sufficient, to purchase for each of his sisters an annuity of £200. With so many commitments the trustees strove to gather in all the outstanding rents. Daniel Babb, who had been employed by Sir Nicholas as his receiver of the rents, was sued for £356 owed by the tenants. Babb also acted as farmer of the rectory in Enfield and in this capacity he counter-claimed alleging that Sir Nicholas had not paid his tithe which stood at 5s for every acre of hard corn and 2s for every acre of other corn. He further claimed that he was owed £442 for money he had spent on repairs about the estate.[18]

Grace, now a widow, married William Ferdinand Carey, Lord Hunsdon, and the estate remained in their hands until her death in 1729. The property then came into the possession of Elizabeth and Mary, the nieces of Sir Nicholas, who came to live at Forty Hall. In 1740 Elizabeth married Eliab Breton and, after the death of Mary, he held the whole estate by right of his wife. A terrier,* undated but apparently drawn up early in the second half of the century, shows that the property was worth £2800 a year. Forty Hall with its grounds of twelve acres, was valued at £150 a year. The home farm of 152 acres, mostly meadow, was worth £300 a year. Fifty-seven tenants paid rent on the estate. Many held only houses, shops or barns; £7 was paid for two houses in Enfield Town, £3 10s was paid for one in Goat Lane. Sparrow Hall, lately rebuilt with a garden, barn, stable and three acres of meadow adjoining was stated to be worth £25 a year, but as yet no tenant had been found. The farms were small, four of them comprised between 100 and 110 acres with their rents averaging about £1 a acre; none were larger. Common marsh could be let for up to 25s an acre, gardens and enclosed meadows for as much as £2 an acre.

The land belonging to the estate was distributed throughout the parish, 128 acres at Whitewebbs, thirty at Clay Hill, and over four hundred acres belonged to farms at Green Street. Much of the common field arable was laid down as grass for feeding stock, described as 'arable or leys'. Quit rents, small rents paid on freehold or copyhold tenures in lieu of an original service, brought a negligible income, only £8 14s a year.[19] By this time, quit rents had become totally uneconomic. On the Duke of Chandos's manor of Enfield, which he held of the Duchy of Lancaster, in the three years from January 1775, quit rents earned £36 10s 5d, the fines arising in the manor court added £6 18s 2d. Out of this court dinners were provided annually which cost £26 13s 1d, so that the profit for these three years on freehold and copyhold amounted to £6 15s 6d.[20]

The price of land rose in the late eighteenth century with the increased profitability of agriculture to something like thirty times its annual value, though in the countryside around London good land could be sold at an even higher rate. Breton when selling land set his reserve price for the auctioneer at somewhat more than thirty times the annual rent and he seldom accepted less than he had stipulated. He began selling his estate in Enfield in 1771 with the sale by auction, at the King's Head in the Market Place, of the Old Fighting Cocks in Baker Street which

*A list of properties forming a landed estate.

sold for £132. Forty Hall, Bulls Cross Farm and Whitewebbs Farm were offered for sale in August 1773 but much of this property failed to reach the reserve price and was not sold. 'Forty Hall', wrote the auctioneer with inspired lyricism but with total disregard for the evidence, was 'built by Inigo Jones, it is an assemblage of Strength, Elegance and Convenience . . . the grand outline of that great Artist is judiciously joined with recent improvements and tasteful embellishments'. The attics, he claimed, would provide accommodation for numerous servants. The first floor contained ten bedchambers and dressing rooms; on the ground floor was a drawing room, dining room, parlour and a study. The staircase was in the same position as the present one (of c1895) the hall (presumably the entrance hall through the door on the east facing front) had a mosaic pavement. The cellars were paved with Purbeck stone. Around the inner courtyard were built coach houses, stables, a granary, barn, brewhouse, mill house and a laundry. (These buildings have now been converted to an exhibition gallery and a reception suite.) The outer courtyard was used for the farm, with cow houses, cart houses, barns, a pig-sty and a slaughter-house; a complete dog kennel and a rick yard adjoined. The highest bid was £12,800 but this was not accepted, being less than the reserve price. Bulls Cross farm and Whitewebbs Farm both failed to reach the reserve price, but 116 acres, mostly enclosed meadow, were sold for £6825, that is nearly £60 an acre. No common field land was offered at this time; apparently the possibility of a general act of inclosure had given landlords the hope that the land might at any time be much increased in value by the abolition of common rights.

A number of houses and gardens were also sold at a reasonable price, being mostly let to tenants at will. Thomas Liberty's house and collar-makers shop, let at £10 a year, sold for £130; Mrs Field's house and shop, let for £10 sold for £140; three acres of meadow let to Mr Fielding a butcher at £7, sold for £210. The Ship public house, where Mr Jones the landlord paid £14 a year, sold for £235. Nine and a half acres of orchard and meadow, containing 300 fruit trees of various kinds, let to tenants at will, sold for £500.

Other Breton properties, being held on long leases, failed to realise a price which reflected the value, for example the house which we now call Dower House, had sixty-four years still unexpired of its two hundred years lease granted in the early seventeenth century. There was another house held by a lease of which sixty-nine years remained, and there was a barn and two acres at Forty Hill with eleven years unexpired. All these were sold for only £740.

Eliab Breton in 1775 offered for sale a further 285 acres of freehold land; it comprised common marsh, common arable and closes, all lying at Ponders End. Some 150 acres reached the reserve price and were sold for £3895, about £26 an acre. Enclosed land was by far the most valuable; for example twelve acres of common marsh and seventeen acres of common arable sold for £23 an acre, but only nine and a half acres of enclosed meadow, with twenty-one acres of common arable, sold for £33 an acre.

Eliab Breton died on 19 December 1785. He had owned freehold estates in the Isle of Thanet which he left to Elizabeth his widow with directions to purchase annuities for his younger sons, William and Eliab. Much of the land which Eliab had purchased during his lifetime was sold in obedience to the terms of his will in the following May; it comprised 116 acres mostly common marsh and common arable, and £3350 was raised at the auction. None of the land was purchased by the tenants. The fruit trees in his conservatory were sold in the following September, and the 1786 harvest from the home farm from which clover, rye grass and hay was sold by auction in the February at about £2 a load.

All that remained of the Forty Hall estate, the mansion house in its park of 400 acres with 1800 acres of agricultural land, the whole having an annual value of £2600, was offered for sale by order of Eliab's executors at an auction held Thursday 24 and Friday 25 May 1787. The house itself and 160 acres again failed to reach the reserve price. It was bought subsequently by Captain Edmund Armstrong, an army agent, for £8800, and later, in November 1799, it was sold by him to Mr Meyer for £11,940.

Bulls Cross Farm was let to John Burgess on a lease which had sixteen years yet unexpired, at a rent of £120 a year. The farmhouse was the building later called Manor farm, and it had with it 104 acres, comprising twelve acres of meadow, fifteen acres of common field arable, thirty-one acres of enclosed arable and twenty-seven acres of pasture. Twelve acres were given over to growing seeds and there were four acres of orchards. It was purchased by Mr Mellish for £2900.

All of Whitewebbs Farm (127 acres), except the farmhouse, lay within the former Chase, (enclosed 1777) none of the land therefore was subject to common rights. It comprised seventy-seven acres of arable, the remainder being mostly meadow. It was let on a twenty-one year lease of which seventeen years yet remained. It was purchased for 4700 guineas, about £40 an acre.[21]

3. The Averys at Capel Manor

Enclosure was not the only means employed by lords of manors to enhance the value of their estates. They sought every possible opportunity to take copyhold property back into their own hands. It could then be offered leasehold as part of the demesne. William Avery held the manor of Capels (formerly Honeylands and Pentriches) lying in the parishes of Enfield and Cheshunt.

Samuel Bevyn was a copyhold tenant of the manor, living in a large house with fourteen hearths in Turkey Street. It had barns, stables and an orchard, with a close of pasture of one acre adjoining the orchard, and two acres of arable in Southfield divided into two halves by the New River, also two acres in Dungfield and three acres in Rammey marsh.

The property had been mortgaged in 1659 to Francis Patrick, citizen and saddler of London, for £250 and Bevyn had been unable to repay. The property was further encumbered when Bevyn had to borrow £60 from Charles Rich and this money all remained unpaid when he died in April 1669. Meanwhile, in 1666, John Green of Enfield had taken a lease from Bevyn of the mansion house and of the major part of the copyhold property. He had paid £100 down and had agreed a rent of £16 2s a year. Bevyn's only known heirs were second cousins living in Cardiff. John Green immediately sought an accommodation with them, negotiated through a Welsh draper who lived in London. Since the estate was encumbered with a debt of £400, it was now, according to Green, worth no more than £15 a year. He offered the Welsh cousins £50 for the purchase and this was accepted.

Green's pleasure in his bargain however was short lived. The homage (ie jury) at the following manor court which met in September, declared that since it was not known who was the heir to the copyhold, the property must revert to the lord of the manor, William Avery. At the three following manor courts a proclamation was made calling upon the heirs to present themselves but no-one appeared. The cousins in Cardiff, having pocketed the £50, had arranged with Avery, undoubtedly for some further small recompense, to 'abscond themselves'.[22]

A similar case occurred in the same manor in the last years of the century. Norton Avery was then lord of the manor. Thomas Gardners, a copyhold tenant at Bulls Cross, died without making a will. His son John could not appear at the manor court, he being for many years beyond the seas. Norton Avery, taking advantage of this circumstance, seized the property and promptly leased it to Michael Leonard. On his return John applied to be admitted copyhold tenant and offered the customary fine and rent. Norton Avery however declined to accept this, though such refusal was contrary to the law.

Landlords also wished to rid themselves of long and uneconomic leases. Francis Bettes, in 1663, held from William Avery the lease of the manor house of the manor of Capels (or Capels Farm) with various pieces of land in Enfield and Cheshunt. Avery had originally granted this lease, in February 1653, to John Butcher for twenty-one years at a yearly rent of £88 and the lease had been assigned by Butcher to Bettes. Avery now negotiated to purchase back the lease for £300, the price to include the corn, hay and grass then growing in the fields. A record of the transaction survives in Chancery because Bettes subsequently claimed that a small area of the land, known as Crooked Cossells, was not included in the lease but belonged to his wife. The proof of this he said was in a paper entitled 'a noate of what lands Thomas Woodham dyed seised of'. He had left it in the manor house and it had since been found by Avery.[23] Woodham was, we must presume, Bettes's wife's father. I have not discovered how the case concluded.

4. The Rich Family at Dower House

The years which followed the Restoration saw the gap widen between the rich and the poor. The wealthy lived in surroundings which denote opulence and a high level of taste. They purchased tapestries and damasks, Dutch and French furniture embellished with marquetry work, marbles and mirrors, paintings and prints, and chair upholstery and rugs of Turkey work.

Sir Edwyn Rich who died in April 1675 was extremely wealthy. He held property in Norfolk, Suffolk and around Fleet Street in London from which he derived an income of around £1500 a year. His money in bonds, bills, leases and mortgages exceeded £30,000. He was a bachelor, and the estate passed to his brothers, Richard and Charles, but all three were dead within a year or two. When Sir Richard died in July 1677, at the age of fifty-nine, an inventory was taken. The house adjoined the grounds of Forty Hall; (it is now called the Dower House). The furnishings were luxurious. The two tables in the parlour were covered with Turkey work carpets, there were seven Turkey work chairs and six leather chairs with cloth covered cushions, and a clock with weights. There were two paintings in that room, a pair of virginals, and a chess board with its men. The two tables in the inner parlour were also covered with Turkey work carpets; there were even carpets on the floor, and seventeen Turkey work chairs. Fourteen paintings adorned the walls of the inner parlour. The clothes, books and arms of the deceased were stored in a closet adjoining his bedroom; they were valued at £50. The chamber of Sir Richard Rich and the 'old lady's chamber' were hung with tapestries, five pieces in each room, measuring nine feet from ceiling to floor. The canopy and curtains to the old lady's bed were of paragon, lined with green print; there were window

The Dower House, formerly the Gables, at Forty Hill.

curtains of white. She had an old couch covered with cloth of silver, an old wrought velvet chair with an Irish stitch cushion, and an old foot carpet. There were two mirrors, and the linen in the room was worth £17.

The house was a modest one with ten hearths. The kitchen, buttery, parlour and inner parlour occupied the ground floor and four elegant chambers with two closets occupied the first floor. On the top floor were the maids' chambers, the men's garret and a closet. There appear to have been two maids (though perhaps more if they had to share the beds) for there were two feather beds. They had a table, three stools and a looking-glass, and an old cupboard and a chest in which to keep their belongings. In the out-buildings over the wash-house was a little chamber and room called the drugget room, being draped in that coarse woollen fabric. A map was displayed in the passage linking the two rooms.

Plate and jewelry in the house was valued at £132, and there was £140 in cash. Sir Charles had been engaged in business; his stock, stored in premises in the Strand and elsewhere, comprised stockings, hose, and gloves for men and women, mostly of silk, caps, satin and quilted, tapestry and other goods, all to the value of well over £200. Debts, bonds, bills and book debts owing to Sir Charles amounted to more than £6000, which was a large proportion of an estate valued at somewhat over £8,000. He left £10 to the poor at Enfield.

Sir Edwyn held the house in Enfield, with about six acres of land, on a 200 year lease at the very modest annual rent of £18. Edwyn Rich had surrendered his former lease and this very favourable one had been granted to him by Sir Nicholas Rainton in 1637. This was in consideration of the great sum of money Edwyn had spent on repairs to the building. There had then been a second dwelling on the site, very old and much decayed, and Edwyn had been given leave to demolish it. The property was still held on the same very favourable terms in 1770 though the landlord, by then Eliab Breton, claimed that it was worth £50 or £60 a year. The Reverend Andrew Kinross purchased the lease from Mary Cromwell in November 1766 for £500 and kept a high class academy there. By the time it was sold in May 1787 the house was occupied by the Reverend Mr Shaw and the lease, issued by Sir Nicholas Rainton in the time of Charles I, still had fifty-one years remaining. The property was purchased for £445.[24]

Those who have visited St Andrews Church may have noticed the monument to John Watt, a merchant of London, 'who gave a great and bountiful legacy to the hospital of St Bartholomew of which he was a governor'. He also gave £20 to the poor of Enfield. He died in October 1701 at the age of sixty-two. Among his other beneficiaries were Dr Uvedale and one of his daughters; Dr Gascgoigne the vicar was also remembered, and Mr Charles Bernard the well known surgeon who had attended him during his last illness. Like Uvedale, John Watt was an enthusiastic gardener. He left directions that his executors should sell his 'new brick messuage in Enfield, with stables coach-house, gardens . . . trees, plants, greens and other things therein', and desired that his garden should be kept in good order after his death until the property could be sold.[25]

5. The Wroths of Durants Arbour

John Wroth, who took over the Wroth estates in 1613 at the age of thirty-eight, was uncle to the late Robert Wroth. John died in 1642 and was buried at Enfield. An inquisition taken two years after his death shows that he had held the manor of Durants, half the manor of Cranes Farm, the manor of Suffolks, the Rectory manor and the manor of Capels, all in Enfield, and a half share of the mills there. He also held the manor of Loughton and the reversion, after the death of Robert's widow the Lady Mary Wroth, of the manor of Luxborough with 140 acres, and other property in Essex. He seems to have been living at Durants in 1637 with his brother Captain Henry Wroth who became heir to the family estates on the death of John in 1642. When Henry died, about 1655, the property was divided between his two sons, John who took Loughton and Luxborough and the mills at Enfield (by a marriage settlement of 1640) and Sir Henry who took the manors of Durants and Chigwell and who lived at Durants Arbour.

John married Anne, the widow of Joshua Galliard (sometimes spelt Gallard). She brought him the property in Edmonton known as Edmonton Berry or Bury Hall. Two sons of her first marriage, Joshua and John Galliard survived at the time of Anne's death in 1676, and a daughter, Judith. Her second marriage had produced two children, John and Anne Wroth. Anne Wroth was married twice, firstly to James Cowper, who for a time came into possession of Enfield mills, and the second time to James Howard who later became the Earl of Suffolk.

Sir Henry had been a royalist during the civil war and had received a knighthood from the King at Oxford in 1645. The following year he had been fined £60 for his delinquency in adhering to the royalist cause. On his return to Enfield he was plagued by debt and in 1657 he was obliged to mortgage Chigwell Hall together with more than 250 acres of meadow and pasture for £3,000.

The long hegemony of the Wroths in Enfield, which had lasted since the fourteenth century, came to an end with his death in 1671. His personal estate consisted of plate, jewelry and money owed to him, estimated at over £10,000, but his property remained burdened with debt. The manor house known as Durants

The great barn at Durants Arbour.

Arbour at Ponders End, has long disappeared. Richard Gough's description of the house in 1771 spoke of the long gallery with family pictures, 'among which were two or three of Judge Jeffreys'. He described the chapel at the south end of the house, 'built of pebbles, flint and clunch'. In the east wall was a 'round arch with Saxon capitals', stopped up. The room over was used in 1771 as a pigeon loft. The chapel was demolished in 1775. Respectable terraced houses now cover the site. Fred Thacker, an amiable antiquarian, paid a visit there on one of his perambulations in the early 1920s and walked along the bed of the moat, then recently run dry because the water had been diverted to an adjacent waterworks. The house there at that time was the one built by the Naylors about 1845 but there were many remains of the original mansion. Along the north side, by the road now called the Ride, stood a brick wall twelve feet high, pierced with slits, and there was a gate-house. The drawbridge had but recently gone, only the brick bridge remained. Fred Thacker, ever eager to acquire information, spoke to one of the locals harvesting apples close by, a thick-set ruddy man in engineer's overalls 'with a black moustache and a slightly beery nose, a jovial and breezy man' who won the antiquarian's heart by deploring all the old barns and pig-sties that had been pulled down. 'Not a nail in them' he said, 'all pegged with wood'.[26]

But to go back to the seventeenth century: on the death of Sir Henry, Durants at Ponders End was left in the hands of William Lord Maynard, his father-in-law, to be sold so that the money could be used to pay Sir Henry's debts and to fulfil his legacies. It was purchased by Sir Thomas Stringer of Grays Inn for £8,900.[27] The Wroth family chapel, which was the south chancel chapel in St Andrews Church, retains scarcely a trace of this family which once dominated the parish. It contains a fine monument, however, to Thomas Stringer, the second son of Sir Thomas. He was a colonel in the army of William III and died at Bruges in Flanders in 1706.

6. The Jasons of Green Street

Sir Robert Jason, who lived in a modest house called Wheelers in Green Street, was not poor. He had property throughout the country from which he could expect an income of £5,000 a year; he had also a personal estate said to be worth £10,000. Yet the Jason family seemed always to allow their financial difficulties to develop into crises. Their property in Enfield in 1652 consisted of eight farmhouses, twelve cottages, seventeen closes of pasture containing fifty-three acres, eleven acres of enclosed meadow and eighteen acres of common meadow in the marshes, and fifty-two acres of arable in the common fields. From all these he derived rents of £152 a year. He had been sued for debt in 1649 and because he had refused to pay he was declared an outlaw, and the court had ordered the confiscation of his property to the value of £210 a year. It was subsequently returned to him. He had two sons, Robert and Henry. Robert, the eldest, caused his father such grave displeasure that he constantly threatened to disinherit him and to leave everything to Henry. Henry, preferring an each way bet, came to an arrangement with his brother in order to secure for himself a one-third interest whichever way the wind blew. In this he was lucky for in 1673 Sir Robert died without carrying out his oft repeated threat.

Robert (the son) in 1671 had allegedly reached an age of discretion; he was thirty years old and at an Inn of Court. He had never been able to keep his expenditure within the bounds of his allowance and lived largely at the expense of his future prospects. Always short of cash, he was forced to seek the assistance of those who would supply him without any immediate prospect of payment. Such tradesmen were by no means altruistic. One was Robert Morley who provided him with money, clothes, jewels and horses, until he became enmeshed in debts and obligations. Robert came to an arrangement with Morley whereby he agreed, in return for £500 immediate cash, to pay Morley £100 per year after his father's death. He used his father's property in Enfield, valued at £1000 a year, as security for the loan. The following year his father died. Robert became Sir Robert yet still managed to avoid his obligations. Nine years later Robert Morley's widow, with five small children, complained that she had never received her £100 a year and did not know where the record of the transaction was enrolled, nor had she any account of what watches, diamond rings, gems, jewels, horses and other things, her late husband had supplied to Robert Jason.

He had incurred other debts too; Thomas Church claimed a debt of £500 for which the sheriff of Middlesex eventually seized much of the property which the new Sir Robert had inherited, including, in Enfield, the messuage called Wheelers and thirteen other tenements and four cottages, fifty-four acres of arable, fifteen acres of pasture and twelve acres of meadow, as well as various properties in Whitechapel.[28]

7. The Lesser Gentry

The possessions of John Cardrow of Enfield indicate a high level of sophistication – eight pictures in the parlour, earthenware in the cupboard, drinking glasses, a spice box, a comb box and two powder boxes, a close stool with a pewter pan, knives and forks, an escritoire and a draught board. There was a considerable amount of money in the house, in silver £11 2s and in gold twenty-five guineas and ten broad pieces worth over £40, also some copper farthings to the value of 2s. He had both wood and coal for fuel, books to the value of £3, two dimity cotton mantles and, among the children's clothes, a red damask flowered mantle, also two sweet bags and three pin cushions. He had property in Old Bailey and at Southwark from which he received £50 a year in rents.[29]

A gentleman could be recognised from his possessions, his clothes and his activities, not necessarily from his wealth. Charles Prior of Enfield who died in 1701, had been the owner of some thirty books; he had thirteen pictures and two pairs of pistols. His apparel comprised two wigs, a blue cloak, a morning gown, five coats, seven waistcoats, eight pairs of stockings and a diamond ring, although this was in pawn for £11. He had other rings too, and a silver hilted sword, but Mr Calvert at the Bell in Edmonton retained possession of these as an insurance against debts which Charles Prior had incurred. There was also a watch and some other things, but these were detained by George Pettis, formerly his servant, against payment of his wages. Mr Prior, it was said, had received many trophies as a commander in the militia, but these could no longer be found. Nevertheless there is no doubt that Charles Prior was a gentleman.[30]

Colonel John Culliford's house in 1719 was very tastefully furnished. The bed chambers each had its own colour scheme. In the ash-coloured room the bedstead was hung with serge lined with printed linen. The bedstead in the red room had red cheyney hangings lined with a striped material; the best chamber was in blue. The walls of the staircase and entry were hung with paintings, prints and maps. In the parlour there was a picture over the chimneypiece. He had a leaden pot to hold his tobacco. An escritoire stood in the closet of his bed chamber in which he kept his cash, twelve guineas and £1 12s 6d in silver. He held £3180 in South Sea Stock and £685 in Bank of England annuities, and twelve tickets in the lottery for the current year. In the cellar were nine and a half flasks of Florence, four quart bottles of French wine, ten quart bottles of port and six quart bottles of brandy, strong beer and small, and three dozen bottles of musty cider, (since thrown away).[31]

Though the house of William Andrews (1719) was of modest size, hall, parlour and kitchen on the ground floor, four chambers above and a garret, the owner was certainly a gentleman, for he displayed two coats of arms and four family portraits in the parlour. He had plate to the value of nearly £40 and £60 in cash about the house. He held £430 in investments. Seventy-two books were counted in the garret and in the front bedroom, also a quarto Bible. He kept a cheese toaster in the kitchen and an iron to warm his drinks. There were two cows in the yard to provide milk, and there he kept a chaise and two horses.[32]

Greenhouses were popular in the mansions about Enfield. Mr Gore of Bush Hill Park grew oranges. His conservatory was forty yards from the house and he employed Joseph More as a watchman to sleep there. On the night of January 4th 1745 Joseph awoke to find Mary Hurst struggling to get out through a hole twenty inches by fourteen, where she had removed a pane of glass. It was not that she was fat, but that she was encumbered with ten orange branches and ten branches of myrtle worth altogether a shilling. The jury found her guilty, but to the value of sixpence only, and she escaped with a whipping.[33]

At Forty Hall Eliab Breton grew orange, lemon and citron trees in tubs and pots. They ranged from four feet six to ten feet high; they were sold, loaded with fruit, in the September following his death in 1785.[34]

Household servants had certain advantages over others of their class; they lived in close proximity to their masters and thus they had to be kept in good health, clean, well dressed and with wigs and bodices supplied. It was common however for servants to be paid irregularly (or not at all) and often no proper record was kept. Bridget had served Mr James Pollard from August 1693 to July 1704; that was before she married Thomas Rayner, a bargeman from Ware. Her wages had been £4 15s a year. When Pollard died in June 1705 she alleged arrears amounting to £50, but his widow contested this, claiming that her former husband had paid Bridget several sums of money as part of her wages and that, in consequence, she owed her former servant only £25 9s.[35]

The land tax in the late seventeenth and early eighteenth centuries was a heavier burden on property owners in the south-east of England than in other parts of the country where assessments were much lighter. Many landlords in Enfield, however, were able to arrange that their tenants paid; the responsibility was therefore spread widely. The land tax for the year 1767 at 3s in the pound, was paid by 300 persons

Gough Park, at the junction of Clay Hill and Forty Hill; only the gate now survives.

of whom 102 were tenants. Eliab Breton of Forty Hall was at that time by far the greatest landowner in the parish, assessed at £979 on which he paid £139 10s.[36] His true rental however, with the value of that part of his estate in his own hands, was £2800.[37] Only five other landlords owned property with a rental assessed at more than £100. These were Samuel Clayton at Old Park, Israel Jalabert at West Lodge, Lord Lisburne at the Rectory, Pierce Galliard of Bury Hall in Edmonton, who held land in Enfield but passed the burden to his tenants, and George Berners who held the lease of the mills at Ponders End. On a total assessed rental of £6606, the taxpayers in Enfield paid £990 18s.

8. The 'Palace' on Enfield Green

The 1787 sale catalogue of the Breton estates contains in Lot 22, 'Queen Elizabeth's Palace' (the Manor House). It was at that time divided into two parts, one let to Mrs Percy at £14 a year, the other to Richard Elland for £15 a year. The premises extended 450 feet along that we now call Church Street and, according to the catalogue, it commanded one of the best situations in Enfield for building. The 'Old Palace', it was suggested, would furnish great quantities of material for this purpose[38]. A considerable part of the house was pulled down ten years later and separate dwellings were built with the materials on the site[39]. The remainder survived until 1928.

I ought to offer some explanation how this house, which was never a royal residence, came to be called a 'palace'. The idea seems to have caught on in the late eighteenth century which saw the beginnings of the Romantic Revival, bringing with it a new but fanciful interest in the past. Enfield had three local versifiers at this time, steeped in ancient lore and under the spell of the first and eldest of the

Richard Gough the antiquarian.

three, the eminent antiquarian, Richard Gough. It was almost inevitable that the mundane Manor House, because it contained a splendid fireplace and overmantle bearing the royal coat of arms and the initials E. R., should be transmuted by their romanticism into 'Queen Elizabeth's Palace'. I must quote a couple of verses from a 'poem' called the *'Royal Cedar'* written with tongue in cheek by John Sherwen, the second of the versifiers. 'This ancient song', he says, 'has escaped the observation of the elegant editor of the *'Reliques of English Poetry'*, (Thomas Percy 1765).

Whan gud Queene Besse dyd rule thyss Lande
Shee ruld ytt lyke a Queene
Shee conqwerr'd herr Foes onn ev'ry Hande
And she lived on Enfielde Green.

Her stately Palace there still doth stande
And a gudlie Gardenne gre
All ynn the same wyth her Lyllye white hand
She planted a Seeder Tre.

It's awful, but it wasn't meant to be taken seriously, neither the verse nor the history.[40]

The third of this triumvirate of poetasters was Isaac D'Israeli father of the famous Benjamin; he was twenty-seven years younger than his friend Sherwen. Isaac was born in Enfield and was sent to a school kept by a Scotsman named Morison (probably at Lincoln House Ponders End). He took an early resolution

Isaac D'sraeli.

to become a poet and a man of letters. He was never to be a poet but a number of his works are still remembered; *'Curiosities of literature'*, *'Quarrels of authors'* and above all, his *'Commentaries on the life and reign of Charles I'*

John Sherwen was a surgeon who had been employed as a young man by the East India Company in India and the Far East. He set up practice in Enfield in 1771 in a house called Silverton in Silver Street (where the Civic Centre now stands). He was the first to cultivate rhubarb in this country and he published many papers on medical subjects. He was a frequent contributor to the *Gentleman's Magazine*, mainly in an endeavour to prove the authenticity of the 'Rowley' poems whereof the subsequent exposure led to the tragic suicide of young Chatterton. Sherwen himself could write excellent verse. He died in Enfield in 1826[41].

Richard Gough was fourteen years older than Sherwen. He is best known for his edition of *'Camden's Britannia'*, his *'Sepulchral monuments'* and his *'British topography'* and he spent twenty years in visiting all the places described in these works. He took possession of Gough Park in Enfield in 1774 following the death of his mother. The house, and particularly the antiquarian's study, are described in a long poem

Gough Park and the bridge over the New River.

containing some of Sherwen's best verse, written a little after the style of Milton's
'*Il Penseroso*'.

With painted glass the windows dight,
Antiquity obscures the light
And round the learning lumbered room
Displays a scientific gloom,
Rich stores of antiquarian pelf
Are lodged upon the mantle shelf.

Old rusty tripods – glass
And fragments of Corinthian brass
All things that ancient times produce
So old that none can tell their use
Behold the shelves all loaded well
With books, black lettered books that tell
What e'er was done in days of yore
And often times a great deal more
Rare manuscripts they also keep
Both old and new a copious heap . . . [42]

After Gough's death his topographical works were given to the Bodleian Library
at Oxford. The remainder of his books were sold for £3,552, and his prints and
drawings for £517, in 1810. Gough Park was bought in 1807 by Thomas Jones, a
lavender planter. Lysons says that part of the house had been rebuilt and divided
into tenements.

9. Sir Robert at the Rectory

Sir Robert Nightingale, a bachelor, occupied the Rectory. The house stood north
of Parsonage Lane, its grounds stretching westward from Baker Street almost to
Chase Side. It was a good sized mansion with a hall, three large parlours, a kitchen
and two other rooms on the ground floor, five bed chambers above, and garrets
for the servants. In the yard were two coach houses and stables for twelve horses.
There were fruit trees planted against the walls in the garden, and three fish ponds
fed with water from the New River. Sir Robert, son of Sir Robert, had been
educated in Enfield at Dr Uvedale's school. His cousins were the Gascoigns who
will enter the story later. He had spent much of his life in India where he had
been president at the Bay of Bengal for the New East India Company. He returned
home in 1708 and was appointed a director of the Company. At that time he was
said to be worth some £60,000 and it was claimed that he had made £40 or £50
on each £100 in remitting the money to England. He must have been in his forties
when he died; his life-style had not been such as would lead to longevity. He drank
too much, especially at dinner, and when drunk he would fall easily into passions
of unreasonable but short-lived rage, especially if asked for money. In this state it
was said (but by those who wished to prove him *non compos mentis*) that almost
daily and nightly he befouled his bed and his breeches with his own excrement
and refused to allow himself to be cleaned.
    Those whose object it was to prove that his behaviour had been normal and
rational at the time when he had changed his will, recalled that, in the weeks

The ancient Rectory stood at the junction of Parsonage Lane with Baker Street.

before his death, he had received holy communion in the church and had placed a guinea in the basin as had always been his custom. The cousins Gascoign were to be the beneficiaries of this new will and they were to assume the name of Nightingale.

Seven or eight months before he died Sir Robert purchased several old houses in Chase Side at the end of his garden. These he had demolished in order to build six almshouses on the site. In preparation for this he sent Charles Welshman, his bricklayer, to Tooting to look at Sir James Bateman's almshouses there. He also employed John Bridges, a carpenter, with other Enfield tradesmen. The work was begun in the February before Sir Robert's death and when he died the almshouses were all but finished at a cost of £1500. Since no later source mentions these almshouses, it may be that they were demolished immediately after his death. Indeed they might have been finished but Sir Robert had interrupted the work in order to build a wall next to the road (probably the one shown in the photograph). They had to dam up the water feeding the ponds and canals in the yard, which were stocked with fish, before they could build the wall, and then had to construct an arch to allow the water through from the New River. The workmen declared that Sir Robert was of a 'very saving nature' and they avoided asking him for money when he was in a passion.

The lease of the Rectory from Trinity College Cambridge, of course included the greater tithe which he in turn leased to Aaron Ward who styled himself a labourer. That March, Aaron had paid Sir Robert the balance of his account for £300 in notes and cash. There were moidores, broad pieces, (a 20s piece of the early seventeenth century), guineas and silver. It was more than Aaron normally paid in at one time but Sir Robert, he said, figured the notes and cash and cast them up accurately and gave him a receipt. Aaron carried out various transactions for Sir Robert. At the beginning of June he was sent for and found Sir Robert sitting on a bench in the yard. Sir Robert demanded to know the price of hay and when Aaron told him he asked him to get enough to fill the Dutch barn, but he

The garden front at the Rectory.

The wall next to Parsonage Lane, built for Sir Robert Nightingale not long before his death in 1722.

must have nothing but the best. Aaron purchased thirty-five loads and a couple of weeks before he died Sir Robert paid him twelve guineas on account, promising to bring more money down from London, and asked Aaron to bring him twenty-four pounds of cherries which he had growing on his ground. A day or two later he sent a servant to Aaron's house with orders to come and see him. The hay had not been delivered. 'What Aaron,' he cried, 'won't you trust me for the hay?' But Aaron had already bought almost enough to fill the barn.

Sir Robert handsomely entertained the gentlemen of the neighbourhood at the Rectory where they played whist and picquet. Every Tuesday morning he would carefully examine his household accounts sitting in the kitchen. He was trading up to the time of his death. His ventures included a fourth part of the cargo of the galley the 'Nightingale', an eighth part of the ship the 'Grantham', a sixteenth part of the 'Macclesfield', a sixteenth part of the 'London', a sixteenth part of the 'Addison', a sixteenth part of the 'Devonshire', also some parts of the 'Dartmouth', the 'Marlborough', and the 'Hanover'. The 'Nightingale' had been insured for three or four thousand pounds; it was obviously named after its owner. He had also taken out insurance on the 'Enfield' (Commander Captain Rigby), for £8000, with the London Insurance Office. The 'Nightingale' had been taken by the French during the late war and had been retaken by the Dutch (our ally) and conveyed to Holland. Sir Robert had had a long struggle to secure the return of the vessel in which Lord Townshend had been involved, but that was now in the past.

James Colebrook who was building a fine new house at Southgate (Arnos Grove), was Sir Robert's banker and transacted all his monetary affairs. Some eight years earlier, when Sir Robert was negotiating a marriage, he had told Colebrook that he was worth £54,000. Colebrook claimed that Sir Robert had done well in placing his money with him, because Colebrook exacted various sums of money as premiums over and above the lawful rate of interest which stood at six per cent. Colebrook had been accused and threatened for taking more than the legal rate and fearing that the penalty, under the Statute Against Usury, would ruin him, he had 'applied to some great persons near His Majesty' and obtained 'His Majesty's most generous pardon'. The fruits of Mr Colebrook's ingenuity can be seen in the elegant house on Cannon Hill.[43]

10. The Downfall of the Deicrowes

Lawsuits tell of many estates encumbered with debt. Benjamin Deicrowe, citizen and pewterer, had inherited considerable property, twelve tenements at Puddle Dock in London and a number of properties in Enfield, including a large house on the north side of Church Street west of the Market Place. His debts were the result of a family dispute taken for settlement before the Court of Chancery. Benjamin, his father, had made his will in February 1627. He was then in very good health but in 1630 he had a severe stroke which left him paralysed and without memory or understanding. He lingered on in this sad condition for nine years. During this time Margaret his wife, despite the fact that she was unable to read, managed the business. Valentine, the eldest son, died during his father's illness and Benjamin became heir. On his father's death he contrived an agreement with his mother to pay her an annuity in lieu of her dowry. Benjamin bore the expense of his father's funeral, blacks, sweetmeats and everything, which amounted to £180. His mother however broke the agreement and obtained letters of administration for her husband's estate and the matter was taken to law as a result of which the family was burdened both with legal costs and by the extent of the legacies to be paid out.[44]

It is not surprising therefore that by February 1642 Benjamin found himself in want of money and borrowed £1,120 by mortgaging his property to William Toppesfield Esq. He was unable to repay the loan when it became due and by a civilised agreement the mortgage was transferred in October 1643 to Ralph Hartley, a London apothecary, with a proviso for redemption upon repayment of the £1,120 plus interest.

Benjamin's fortunes however did not improve; he was prosecuted by the apothecary and was forced to borrow £1,280 from an unscrupulous attorney James Mayoe to whom the mortgage on the Deicrowe property was now transferred. The attorney drew up a conveyance in March 1647 omitting any power to the mortgagor to redeem the property. Deicrowe for a time refused to execute the deed but, because Mayoe pleaded that any alteration would take much time and trouble and promised at some later date to execute a deed which would declare the true intent of their agreement, Benjamin was at last induced to give way and sealed the indenture. Subsequent requests to the attorney to fulfil his promise to execute a new deed were met with prevarication. He was told, quite falsely, that he could have no cause to doubt the honesty of the attorney who abhorred forfeitures; he was even persuaded to defeat the entail (which would have prevented Deicrowe from disposing of his property) by means of a common recovery.* Thus Benjamin was caught in the net woven by the wily lawyer so that when at last he became desperate and sought to escape by selling some of the mortgaged property to clear

---

*a type of collusive court action designed for this purpose.

Burleigh House, erected by an unscrupulous attorney James Mayoe. It was sold at a public auction in 1913.

the debt, Mayoe refused to listen, declaring that the property was his, and the deal fell through. The attorney was still in possession of the Deicrowe estate in 1648 when Benjamin, hearing that Mr Baron Atkins, an influential justice in the Court of Common Pleas, was seeking property to purchase, contracted with him to sell to him the greater part of the mortgaged property for £1,800. But again the conveyance was thwarted by the lawyer.

Benjamin had been ejected from his house which the attorney had demolished and had erected a smaller, more modern house on the site. This elegant mansion was later named Burleigh House by Mr Withers who came to live there as a tenant in 1865. It was demolished in 1913 and the site was occupied by the Rialto Cinema which is now a bingo hall: such is progress. When the contents and fittings from Burleigh House were sold at a public auction in February 1913, one item offered for sale was a carved stone chimney-piece decorated with figures of cranes and conventional fruit; it had a raised shield in the centre lettered B D M, Benjamin and Margaret Deicrowe. Amidst the ruin of his fortunes Benjamin died. Helen his widow moved into a much smaller house nearby. On behalf of her son, she appealed in the House of Lords and a recommendation was made to the Lord Chancellor to appoint a re-hearing.[45] Alas it was not successful; the hearth tax of 1665 records James Mayoe, 'the owner of an empty house (with nine hearths) on Enfield Green[46], and records Helen among those exempt, because of her poverty, from payment of the tax. When Helen died in 1667, her possessions were worth only £33. Mayoe was still holding the Deicrowe home in 1671 and ten years later the case remained enmeshed in the Court of Chancery. The property subsequently passed to Clement Mayoe and when he died, to his 'dear friend Robert Fish' who was the owner in 1697.[47]

The fortunes of Sir Basil Firebrace had risen with the velocity of a rocket, had shone briefly with all the splendour of a firework and had now declined and fallen to earth. He had mortgaged, by 1702, all his offices on Enfield Chase, his steward-ship of the manor of Edmonton, his manor of Swallow and Cabourne in Lincolnshire and 'The Three Tuns' in Cambridge, in order to secure a loan of £6000. He further borrowed, in March 1702, £2000 from Edward Stracey to repay a debt to George Finch, secured by a bond for £4000. Stracey managed to get £1000 back in June 1706 but £1120 remained and Sir Basil was forced to enter into a bond to pay by September on penalty of £2300.

He gave Stracey authority to find a buyer for the Lincolnshire property and in the following December, Stracey, hoping for repayment, prevailed upon the Duke of Newcastle to purchase it for £3642. Firebrace however used the money towards the repayment of the mortgage and Stracey received nothing. The following May, hearing that Sir Basil had attempted to commit suicide at his house in Fenchurch Street, Stracey, fearing that he might die without paying, hurried there to demand his money. Sir Basil did not die, nor did he pay.

Dr Henry Firebrace, Sir Basil's brother, who had stood surety for the debt, sold further property in November for more than £3,000 (Sir Basil at that time being held for debt in the prison of Queen's Bench). Stracey's hopes again revived and he hurried to demand payment in full. But Sir Basil sent word that if Stracey would not accept what he had been offered he would be pleased to live and die in prison.[48]

Burleigh House, the entrance hall.

Notes for Chapter 4

1   E112, 582. 22, E112. 582. 36
2   E112, 842. 1110
3   C10. 154. 87, Wm. Robinson *Enfield* 1 p. 122
4   E112. 842. 1111
5   DL4. 114. 20
6   DL5. 38. 347, DL9. 10
7   GLRO Acc 16. 8
8   GLRO Acc 16. 4
9   SP29. 22. 153
10 DL5. 38. 347
11 DL4. 114. 20
12 E112. 708. 1809
13 DL9. 14
14 DL1. 428
15 DL9. 14, DL5. 39. 156–7, vestry order book Au 1689
16 *St James Holiday Annual* 1875, C8. 425. 19
17 Vestry order book Au 1691, C10. 227. 21
18 E112. 984. 536, E112. 960. 46.
19 GLRO Acc 801. 38, Acc261. 1. 36b
20 GLRO Acc 262. 1. 34
21 Enfield. Sale catalogue Breton estate 1787
22 C5. 491. 27, C5. 441. 36, C10. 133. 57
23 C5. 607. 27, C8. 151. 26, C8. 242. 4
24 PROB 32. 14. 113, C12. 2077. 17, C12. 2068. 17
25 PROB 11. 466. f142
26 C6. 180. 30, Cal. Comm. for Compounding p 1567 F. S. Thacker River Lee ms in Herts Co Record Office
27 C5. 497. 84
28 E379. 89, C6. 72. 8, C10. 138. 83, C10. 178. 42
29 PROB 32. 38. 66
30 Guildhall 9174. 28
31 PROB 5. 2419
32 PROB 3. 18. 205
33 Guildhall OBSP 16–18 Ja 1745
34 Enfield Sale catalogue Breton estate 1787
35 E112. 810 134
36 GLRO MR. PLT 68
37 GLRO ACC 262. 1. 36b
38 Enfield Sale Catalogue Breton estate 1787
39 Wm Robinson *Enfield* 1 p 119
40 in Enfield local collection
41 DNB
42 in Enfield local collection
43 PROB 24. 60. 167–179,253, PROB 18. 37. 73, PROB 25. 11. 107, BL Add. 31169 f369
44 C8. 53. 4
45 C5. 420. 35
46 GLRO Hearth tax 1665
47 Guildhall 9171. 21. 97, Acc 1084. 1, for much of this I am grateful to Audrey Robinson and Dr Nita Burnby.
48 C8. 136. 77, C10. 454. 55, C6. 46. 153, for a fuller account see D. O. Pam *The Story of Enfield Chase*

Chapter Five
The Poor

1. Charity and the Poor

The hearth tax of 1665 shows that there were 560 houses in the parish. There had been only 322 houses in 1572. Thus these ninety-three years had seen an increase in the number of dwellings of seventy-four per cent. Great numbers of poor people had drifted into the parish during the Interregnum. Many of them had settled on the edge of the Chase where they gleaned a precarious living by pasturing a few animals and by stealing and selling wood. An Enfield petition of 1660 complained that two or three hundred families of poor people 'had removed themselves from several parts of the kingdom and settled them in new erected cottages built upon the Chase and in other corners and waste places of the parish'. Poverty was at its worst in the northern part of Enfield, the remote Bulls Cross quarter which extended eastward to include the areas of Enfield Wash and Freezywater. In this part of the parish, where most of the immigrants had settled, forty-nine per cent of households were too poor to pay the hearth tax.[1]

These vast movements of men and women in search of a livelihood emphasised a problem left unsolved by the Elizabethan legislation; it was one which urgently demanded resolution. In case after case it had to be decided which parish should be held responsible for those likely to become a burden on the rates. Each parish feared an influx of the poor but those, like Enfield, on the teeming roads leading into London, were particularly vulnerable. An immediate solution, and one which appealed to most overseers, was to expel immediately from parish territory any newcomer who might possibly become a liability on the community. At the same time, however, the farmers and tradesmen of the parish, from which class the overseers were selected, might urgently require labour. Therein lay a dilemma which various acts of the late seventeenth century strove to remedy.

The Act of 1662 legalised the removal of anyone newly arrived in a parish and thought likely to become chargeable, but such people had to be expelled within forty days of their arrival. Exempted were first the very small number able to rent property to the value of £10 a year, secondly those with sufficient means to indemnify the parish against the possibility of falling destitute and thirdly, the much larger number who were able to secure a certificate by which their own parish accepted responsibility for them whenever they should fall upon hard times.

The Act in a way gave an advantage to the poor immigrant for he had only to lie low for forty days and thereafter he could no longer be removed. This loophole was closed however by the Acts of 1685 and 1691 which laid down that the newcomer must give notice of his arrival to an overseer who must have the notice proclaimed in church, his forty days were then to run from the date of such notice.

The 1691 Act made it possible to acquire a settlement by paying rates and taxes, also by virtue of being bound apprentice to a master in the parish and, by an Act of 1697, this was extended to include unmarried persons hired to serve a year as servants in the parish.

Though a poor rate was levied in 1690 at 4d in the pound, for a long time the poor in Enfield were largely sustained by means of the parish rents. The income from these funds was substantial. During the 1690s there were no fewer than seventeen charities operating in the parish for the relief of the poor and to meet parish expenses. 'No parish in England has had so fine an estate', wrote Peter Hardy, looking back regretfully in 1809 over long years of mismanagement and the waste of rich resources[2]. His forbears in the late seventeenth century, however, found the income adequate. In the years 1698 to 1702 for instance the charities had provided, on average, an income of £177 7s 4d a year. The average expenditure in these five years was as follows:

	£	s	d
Pensions and casual relief	66	5	0
Apprenticeship of poor children	32	16	0
Medical and nursing for the poor	15	13	0
Repairs to the schoolhouse, roads and bridges	15	4	0
Expenses of parish officers	12	12	0
For reading prayers in the parish church	10	0	0
The schoolmaster's salary	20	0	0
	172	10	0

The remainder of the money was spent in repairs to the various properties from which the income was derived and in taxes on those properties.

The most important of these charities was the Benfleet Farm (Poynetts). The land had been given in 1473 to support a chantry for the benefit of the souls of Agnes Myddleton and of her four husbands. Early in the sixteenth century the funds had been converted to the support of a school and it had fortunately survived the Reformation. By the 1690s the income was £55 a year which maintained the free Grammar School and paid the salary of the schoolmaster, £20 and the usher, when there was one, £12.

Parish rents in the 1690s

Charity	Annual Income	Date of Foundation	
Benfleet Farm	£55	1473	
John David	£10	1620	
William Smith	£4	1592	F
Sir Nicholas Rainton	£6 10s	1646 Haberdashers Co.	F
Ann Osborne	£6 15s	1666	
William Billings	£1	1659	F
Henry Loft	£16	1631	F
John Deicrowe	£4	1627	F
North Mimms rent	£9	1623	
George Cock	£2 13s	1635	
Thomas Wilson	£24	1590	
Robert Rampston	£2	1585	F
Bull & Bell	£2 12s	1614	

Stonards field	£1	7s	1547		F
Prounces	£25		1516		
Market			1619		
Henry Dixon	£7		1693 Drapers Co.		F
Thomas Piggott		10s	1681		F
Jasper Nicholls					
Total income	£177	7s			

F indicates a fixed income from the property

Prounces had been given to the parish in 1516 by William May and Thomas Merywether. It included the school and the schoolmaster's house, the Old Coffee House, originally the home of John Prouns, and St Andrews croft, a close of pasture of two acres adjoining the King's Head.

The property which financed David's charity had been left to the parish by John David, a tailor, in 1620. It consisted of the Greyhound inn on the east side of the Market Place, with the three houses behind it. The rent, £10 a year, supported four poor widows in the 1690s but, by 1717, the annual value of the property had multiplied fourfold and the 'poor widows' received £11 each. The generosity of this provision can be appreciated by comparing it to the salary of the schoolmaster at £20 per annum.

The vestry became so concerned by its own unintended extravagance that, in 1718, the matter was laid before the Lord Chancellor to seek permission to amend the conditions laid down by John David a hundred years earlier, nevertheless the money continued to be distributed among only four pensioners. The rent of the market was also employed towards the relief of the poor. It was leased with Prounces, in 1669, to Robert Prentice, landlord of the King's Head, at a yearly rent of £25. A market house stood in the Market Place, probably the building shown in the print, with open sides and an octagonal roof mounted on wooden posts. There was also 'a small building called the market cross', (removed about 1810) and 'a little house called the weighing house' wherein were kept the scales and the weights by means of which disputes between customer and vendor might be settled. Six shops lined the west side of the square (where the Bradford and Bingley now stands). There was a shop belonging to Habucuck Kerby, the glazier, which adjoined the market house, also four other shops in the middle of the square. One of these belonged to Abraham Burnby, the shoemaker. There were twenty-four stalls for butchers.[3] The leasing of the market with Prounces probably followed the building of the King's Head on Prounces land. The parish derived an income from these two sources in 1690 which amounted to £35 a year. A new lease however was made three years later to Richard Ridde for twenty-one years. He paid £100 down and convenanted to spend £60 on repairs during his first year, because of which his rent was set at only £25 a year.[4]

Thomas Wilson left three tenements at Whitechapel to the parish of Enfield in 1590. A hundred years later the vestry received £24 a year profit from the rents. The property was then held on a lease for fifty-one years, this long term having been granted because the lessor had convenanted to rebuild two of the houses. The profit was employed for the relief of six poor men. The income from this source continued to grow, in the 1834 these privileged pensioners were getting £34 a year each.[5] The rent of the parish property at North Mimms provided a further £18 a year. It had been purchased with the money given by James I to compensate for common rights lost to the parish when land was taken out of Enfield Chase to

The Market Place, 1805.

The Bell, Enfield Highway, formerly the Bull and Bell.

extend his park at Theobalds. Another parish property was a little tenement and barn at Clay Hill which the vestry had bought by adding £20 to the £30 left to the parish by George Cock a brewer of Clerkenwell. The rent, £2 13s 4d a year in the 1690s, was used to buy bread which was distributed to the poor in the church on Sundays.

Ann Osborne, a widow of Southwark, left £100 in 1666 for the purchase of land, the rents to be used for the relief of poor widows, and for setting poor children to school that are fatherless and motherless. The parish had added a further £20 (in 1672) and had purchased another property at Clay Hill, one from which they were already receiving a rent charge of 20s, by the gift of John Billings, he had originally provided the money to clothe poor children. It was occupied by three tenants in the 1690s and their combined rents amounted to £6 15s a year which, after repairs, was divided between five widows. Jasper Nichols left £50 to the parish in 1614 with instructions that the interest on the money should be used to buy bread for distribution to the poor. But the parish used the money to buy the Bull and Bell (now the Bell) at Enfield Highway. It was subject at that time to a long lease which was also purchased; the rents were then used for the original purpose of the donor.

In all the above gifts property had been left to the parish, or money which had been left had been used to purchase property. Because of this the income grew and kept pace with inflation. Many other gifts however were a fixed charge on property: for example, Henry Loft, in 1631, left land and tenements in Enfield and Chigwell to his cousin Anthony Curtis on condition that the beneficiary and his heirs should pay, in perpuity, £12 a year for the support of six poor widows, £4 a year towards the clothing of the poor and £4 to provide a lecture in the church. Such gifts, though substantial in this case, were not proof against inflation and these same amounts were still received in 1691.

It was considered just that the money paid to secure the prestige of a well placed pew in the church and a vault beneath should be used to relieve the poor. John Greene of Turkey Street paid £50 for such a place, seven feet by six feet, to accommodate two pews (box pews of course) adjoining the north wall in St Andrews Church. This money was used to purchase property and the rents derived were expended on the poor. Greene's pew rent too, at £3 a year, was given over to the same purpose. In 1675, for example, half of it was used to meet the charges of Elizabeth Hatley, 'a poor lame woman lately carried from the parish to St Thomas Hospital in Southwark' The other half was given to John Browne and his family, 'being at present in a very sad state and lamentable condition he being swelled and lame in his limbs'.[6] Sir Basil Firebrace paid £8 for his pew which provided apprenticeships for two boys at £3 each and a girl at £2.

Likewise good use could be made of money paid by those who wished to be excused parish offices. The £10 paid by Mr Hibberd to avoid the position of surveyor was employed for the relief of the poor and to repay parish debts. Indeed the parish had been so reluctant to pay its debts that, in 1679, Robert Young, who had formerly been the overseer in the Green Street quarter, was forced to appeal twice to the justices in petty sessions at the Bell in Edmonton for £13 which the churchwardens owed to him. On the second occasion when the justices ordered the money to be paid, they threatened that they would instruct the constable to arrest the churchwardens 'and lodge them in the common gaol'.[7] A fine of £10 15s imposed on Mr Speed for stealing deer off the Chase bought an apprenticeship for Sarah Dodson, for Francis Deane, for Thomas Dodson and for Thomas Eedes.

It was the privilege of the vicar to distribute the money collected at the sacrament to the poor; in the 1720s it amounted to about £6 a year. The vicar distributed it as casual relief in amounts ranging from one shilling to five shillings; thus it went 'to a poor woman', 'to a poor stranger', 'to a poor woman whose husband lay ill at Forty Hill'. The biggest collection was that made on Easter Sunday which averaged around 21s in the 1720s. Money given at communion was also put into the poor's box as decreed by ancient custom. Substantial gifts were received occasionally such as £20 by the will of Sir Thomas Trevor who held considerable property at Ponders End; this property descended after his death in 1679 to his cousin Sir John Trevor. One of his Majesty's secretaries of state, Mr Secretary Coventry, in 1687 gave £10 which was immediately distributed to people in need. The vestry order book makes no further mention of a poor rate before 1699 (there had been a fourpenny rate in 1690) but by the end of the century the parish was nearly £32 in debt.[8]

2. Enfield Vestry and the Poor

The poor were cared for by their parishes; therein lay both the strength and the weakness of the old poor law. The poor were the parish poor, they were not the impersonal paupers of a union workhouse. It was 'old John Bassil's rent' that had to be paid, or 'poor lame Richard Duncarfe's; it was Widow Elsey's house that must be thatched, Widow Coombe who ought to have a new shift, Nat Fisher who required £1 13s 8d to keep him out of prison, or Widow Stephens whose burial had to be solemnized with beer paid for by the parish. The parish played the role which is now played by the state but it was insular in its outlook. The poor who belonged to the parish might be brought into the world by the parish midwife or surgeon, nursed and suckled by a parish nurse, apprenticed when old enough, cared for and maintained when sick, clothed, fed and housed when destitute, looked after in old age and buried with solemnity when dead.[9] All others of the poor who trespassed within the parish boundaries could be removed to whatever community was held to be responsible for them.

Whatever resources Enfield vestry had left over from these duties seem to have been spent in an attempt to exterminate any wildlife which had strayed into its territory. Seven foxes were killed in 1777; hedgehogs, which seem to the late twentieth century to be harmless enough, were slaughtered in great numbers at fourpence a head, and polecats at sixpence.[10]

The parish employed a clerk to look after its affairs, usually an attorney, capable of handling disputes with other parishes. He was paid £20 a year in the late eighteenth century. This office seems to have originated in Enfield after the Restoration of Charles II, John Butler in 1672 was paid £2 5s in part due to him for keeping the parish accounts and other writing for the parish.[11] The vestry was also responsible for the roads, except those which were taken into the control of the turnpike trust. In the late eighteenth century the parish kept a fire engine and paid John Bristowe £3 a year to oil and look after it. The vestry in 1815 applied to several insurance offices asking them to contribute to the cost of making a carriage for the fire engine. It was intended to find the remainder of the money required by a voluntary subscription. The vestry also maintained the church (except the chancel) and the churchyard, and controlled all the parish charities. The vestrymen celebrated each year with a dinner, but a very modest one for it cost the parish only 10s.[12]

Three overseers were appointed annually by the vestry, one each for Enfield Green and Bulls Cross (which included Enfield Wash and Freezywater) and one who served both the Green Street and the Ponders End quarters. No man was asked to serve more than one year though some, having had experience of the job, were employed as deputies. Thus James Jarvis was overseer in Enfield Green quarter in 1735 and acted as deputy for Mr Nightingale in 1739; Richard Glenn was overseer in 1743 and acted for Henry Cocker in 1744.[13] Three churchwardens were also appointed annually.

The sum of £10 in 1675 could secure exemption for life from all offices, that is the offices of headborough, ale-taster, constable, surveyor, overseer and churchwarden. By 1731 the charge had been increased to £21.[14] Mr Leeson, Mr Rious and William Pettyward Esq., in the year 1731, all paid the twenty guineas for total exemption. Mr Paling was charged only ten guineas, since he had already served the offices of surveyor and constable. Two others sought exemption from the office of overseer only, which cost them ten guineas. Though annual figures are not available the parish seems to have derived a regular and substantial income in this way. In the year 1741, for instance, six people selected as overseers all paid rather than serve. This exasperated the vestry and in April 1742 the price for avoidance of this one office alone was increased to £21.[15] The overseer was particularly responsible for the poor. Some who were appointed enjoyed their new found power and importance, but many resented the inevitable interference with business or pleasure and the time spent in attendance at the vestry. Such a one was Adam Hamilton, landlord at the Rose and Crown Enfield Highway and overseer in the Ponders End quarter. He wrote in July 1781 to apologise for his non-attendance at the parish meeting:

'Sir, It is impossible for me to attend vestry this day, my wife being ill, many
gentlemen wanting chaises and refreshment, and in the midst of hay. Therefore
I have sent you by bearer the account of the uncollected money.[16]

Even Londoners having what might be called a country house in Enfield could
find themselves saddled with this onerous office. Mr James Mills arrived at his
house at Scotland Green in Ponders End late one evening in April 1812 to be
presented with two papers which informed him that he had been appointed by two
magistrates to be an overseer of the poor for the current year. He had already
served that office twice in his City parish, he said, where, despite all the care, time
and attention he had given to the work, he had still found that he had been 'but
a novice to the tricks, manoeuvres, chicanery and impositions of the paupers'. The
calls of business allowed him to spend but little time in Enfield, how then would
the parish of Enfield be served? Moreover he was the father of eight children,
providing for whom with decency took every moment of his time and every part
of his 'small abilities'. These things he related to the gentlemen of the vestry in
the hope that they might amend their choice and appoint someone with more time
and attention to devote, but if they persisted in appointing him, he threatened, he
would let his son, a youth of sixteen, carry out the duties to the best of his
abilities. Having thus presented an ultimatum, a further matter occurred to him. He
understood, he wrote, that overseers begin to pay the poor before they receive
anything from the parish. This would be totally impossible in the present state of
mercantile and commercial affairs, especially with the very small capital available
to him. He had to admit this to prevent 'the disappointment of the poor. Whatever
money I receive from the parish', he adds, 'I certainly shall disburse under your
instructions to the utmost halfpenny, but beyond that I cannot go'.[17]

3. Nurse Children

The early death of the children of the poor was expected. There were many destitute
women like Sarah Ames. Examined in Enfield in January 1747, she told the
magistrates that she had been born in Uttoxeter (Staffordshire) and had married
David Reader, an Enfield labourer in 1736. She had borne him six children in
little over six years; all had died except Dinah, the last, now five, who had been
born a few weeks after the death of her father. Within one year of her widowhood
Sarah had married William Ames, a cutler. Her present distress (the reason for
her examination) arose from the fact that Ames had deserted her.[18]

Yet the parish made some effort to assist in the bearing and rearing of those
infants for whom it accepted responsibility. The midwife Sarah Fish brought many
new parishioners into Enfield and for those whose parents could not afford her
services, the parish paid. She brought to bed, in the year 1699, for instance, 'several
poor women', and the vestry gave her £1 3s 6d. In cases, not infrequent, where
the mother died, the child was put out to nurse, and again, where the father was
poor, the parish paid.

The vestry order book shows many payments made for nursing parish children
in the 1670s. Some women acted regularly like Judith Manning who, in February
1679, received £5, in part for keeping poor parish children[19]. The parish was
sometimes slow to pay the nurses and these payments were often in arrears. The
whole of the £9 rent from the North Mimms property in February 1681 went to

nurses of poor parish children whose payment was two years behind. R$_\epsilon$
of Waltham was given money in 1680 which had been due to his sis
recently dead, for keeping parish children.[20]

In 1681 three poor women were forced to petition quarter sessions decla
they had nursed various children and 'an ancient woman' for the parish o
and the churchwardens had withheld payment. Despite this, money was st
to them two years later when a certain William Clerke paid £5 to avoid a
office. At last the churchwardens were able to meet (in part) this long st$_\epsilon$
debt. Widow Carlton was given £1 17s for nursing two children of 'poor W
Lowen' in 1679.[21]

Many Enfield women continued to be employed in nursing babies sent out ι
London. Most came from families sufficiently well off that they could afford to .
a woman in a village where the child would be less prone to infection than in
City. Probably the nurse's own child would have had to be weaned early and ɼ
on paps and gruels, or perhaps weaned at nine months to allow the mother to ɡ
on for a further nine months feeding her employer's child. This would have ha
the potential advantage of increasing the intervals between her pregnancies. Th$_\epsilon$
nurse children came from all classes in society. It is recorded in the parish register
for the year 1669 that Henry, a nurse child, the son of Mr Richard Tillsley, was
buried within the church, and that Peter the nurse child of Mr Peter White was
buried in the chancel. Both families must have been prosperous to afford such a
privilege; both were from London. There were infant paupers sent by London
parishes, some without even a surname to their credit; Susanah, a poor parish
child, nursed with Samuel Billingham, and Robert a poor nurse child with John
Snows. In the four years following 1667, as an example, twenty-four nurse children
were buried in St Andrews churchyard or in the church.

4. Bastards

Bastards of the poor were not wanted in eighteenth century society and many
failed to survive the first months of life. Overt infanticide was nevertheless rare.
The coroner was called in November 1766 to view the bodies of Sarah Foster and
her new born female child; Sarah, he pronounced, had died in childbirth, the baby,
by persons unknown, not having the fear of God, had been cast into a tub of water
and drowned.[22]

Those who burdened the parish with bastards could expect no kindness from
the ratepayers in vestry and every effort was made to coerce the putative fathers
into supporting their illegitimate offspring. It was not bastardy that was an offence,
it was bastardy at the expense of the ratepayers. A man sworn by an indigent,
unmarried and pregnant woman to be the father of her child was liable to arrest
and he could be forced to give security to ensure that the child should not become
a burden on the rates. Such illegitimate children became the responsibility of the
parish in which they were born. Parish officers therefore used both vigilance,
cunning and cruelty to see that they were delivered in some other parish. Thus
when Elizabeth Roberts, a single woman, was found to be in labour in the parish
of Cheshunt, she was hurried across the boundary into Enfield. It was done, the
Enfield parish clerk objected, by indirect practices and contrary to the law.[23]

Where the reputed father was a man of sufficient substance he could be required
to deposit a bond by which he was obliged to pay a certain sum of money should

181

bert Ward
er Mary,

ing that
Enfield
l owed
parish
nding
lliam

om
ire
he
ut
o

ridgeman in the year 1705 was accused by
child and it was demanded of him that he
ond for £100. Very often the accused man had
fer such security, in which case he might be able
d to commit himself on his behalf. Thus Abraham
Essex, produced a bond for £100 signed by John
mas Howard a butcher of Pleshey in Essex. James
, the alleged father of Sarah Townshend's child, prod-
by his fellow gardener, Robert Archer. Such generosity
.[24] Mr Samuel Pritchett and Mr Samuel Osborne, had
be used to guarantee that Mr Samuel Ray would pay to
maintenance for his bastard child born to Pheobe Wilkes.
uently sought relief for the child and eight weeks maintenance
d from the guarantors.[25]

ously retained such bonds to be put into force if ever the child
. A bastard child, attributed to Mr John Blane, had been born in
71. She fell destitute in Enfield fifteen years later and Blane was
sist her under the threat that Enfield parish would provide the help
en enforce repayment from him.[26] The parish undoubtedly had the
ll honest men in instituting proceedings against John Towrey Reynolds
m Cross, he being an excise man and charged to be the father of a
child begotten upon Sarah Hodgkins.[27]

ctice grew up of taking immediate cash from the putative father, ostensibly
emnify the parish. Susan Clay in the Enfield workhouse had given birth to
ld fathered by W. Blackborow Esq of Clerkenwell Close. He had with some
iculty been found and secured in Clerkenwell Bridewell. From there he wrote
the Enfield vestry to enquire what sum they would require to exonerate him.
The business had cost the parish much money, £4 17s to trace the gentleman, and
there was the expense of the laying-in, birth and subsequent maintenance. Moreover, as the vestry clerk added with some indignation, 'it can never be imagined
but that the child must be wholly maintained by this parish'. He declined to accept
anything less than £20 plus expenses.[28] Peter Hardy writing in 1809, strongly
disapproved of this procedure. 'If a man pay £20 or any other sum . . . [this]
cannot discharge the father from his obligation to maintain the child, for the parish
is not bound by any illegal transaction and it is clear that £20, coming in aid of
the rates one year, would burden those who had to maintain the child many years
afterwards.'[29] Moreover the money had occasionally to be returned. In July 1800
Charles Baker applied to the vestry for the return of his twelve guineas on the
grounds that he had now married the young woman.[30]

Even when dealing with a gentleman the parish could not allow him to evade
the consequences of paternity. Between equals however the negotiations could be
carried on with politeness and with an appreciation of the amusing side of the
situation, though this aspect of the matter may not have been uppermost in the
mind of the young woman about to give birth to a pauper in the workhouse. John
Lucas Smart, the Enfield parish clerk, wrote in 1783 to a fellow attorney at
Towcester, Northants.

'Sir, I am obliged to apply to you on a disagreeable occasion. A pauper belonging
to the parish of Enfield, Johanna Harris, was, on 26 April, delivered in the
workhouse of a female bastard child and has sworn you to be the father. I should

be obliged to you for an answer, what security you wish to give this parish. If you will name any friend in London our overseer will call on him and, I make no doubt, settle the business.'

Wrote the provincial attorney in reply:

'Your very obliging letter came into my hands and though the contents are not very pleasing to me, yet for your civility, I confess I ought to have returned you a more speedy answer. The reason of my having any knowledge of the person you mention was that she and her children had a small property in my neighbourhood and came to me for advice. That I am the real father of the child I have not the least reason to believe yet, if the woman hath absolutely sworn it to me, I may perhaps be at a loss to find means to avoid being reputedly so. However, for your civility, I don't wish to give your parish any unnecessary trouble. All I wish of you is to favour me with an answer whether or not she has sworn to a time and place. This I think every woman in that situation ought to do because the man in the case has no other means of avoidance or remedy against the oath of a woman, and more especially as the intercourse was not frequent but very seldom and for the most part at a great distance from each other.' (distance in time obviously)

John Lucas Smart had a nice sense of humour. After the usual polite exchanges he replied to the above letter pointing out that Johanna Harris had informed him

'that she was with you only about a fortnight before she was delivered and acquainted you with her situation. If so', he went on, 'you must surely be apprised of what time and place – You then said that you would take care of her and the child, you wrote her a letter swearing to come to Enfield which she received after she was delivered. Your connections with her were at the 'Two Sailors' in Towcestre where one bed held you both when market business was over. I should be obliged to you for your immediate answer but doubt not you will consider it as a sporting cause, and suffer a non-suit – a verdict of imprudence – at least.'[31]

Since there were no blood tests it was difficult for a man to deny a woman's sworn testimony. It was a means sometimes used to extort money. Such accusations may even have been made for a laugh. Only this can explain Joseph Butler's plaintive letter to the parish clerk in 1786.[32]

'Sir, I heard that Suey the aunt (eighteenth century slang for a prostitute) at Enfield was with child and, at my great surprise, I understand that she has wickedly sworn me to be the father. There is nothing in the world so false, be sure of it. In short it is as true as it was with Sally Adams who swore the same against me, although she was not [even pregnant]. I think that if every woman was [with child] in the house (obviously a brothel) so they would lay it upon me. It would be a pity that the indiscretion of such a wretch should be believed. I leave your own feelings Sir to judge if you think I am really guilty . . . I cannot imagine you would entertain such an opinion of me.'

The work of the parish clerk thus had its lighter moments.

Where the father had no money the best course of action open to the parish was forcibly to join the happy couple in holy wedlock. Sarah Hodges was examined by Enfield magistrates on 4 January 1732 to swear to her great belly. Two days later a warrant was taken up for the arrest of John Horsman the reputed father. He was seized and examined on 10 January to establish from which parish he came. In the meantime the couple were joined in wedlock under the watchful eyes of the parish officers. An order was issued on 5 February and John, with Sarah now his wife, were carried to the parish of St Clements Dane. Poor Sarah returned to Enfield alone and deserted on 1 May.[33]

Another couple were brought to church by the parish beadle, John Scott and there joined in holy wedlock. He had taken Frances Porter into custody on 11 October 1810 and had carried her to Tottenham to swear before a magistrate that James Ansell was the father of her bastard child. The beadle's journey was in vain for there were no magistrates at home. Two days later he tried again, and this time he was successful. The following day he hired horse and cart and drove to East Barnet where he apprehended James Ansell. Having thus secured the couple, he locked them up in the watch-house and, appointing someone to guard them lest they should attempt to depart before he got back, he again procured a horse and cart and drove to Doctors Commons for a marriage licence. Although it cost the parish three guineas he knew that the vestry would consider their money well spent. Thus armed, he carried the bride and groom to church where he paid the marriage fees, again on behalf of the parish, and thus, after four days close confinement, James and Frances Ansell emerged as man and wife.[34]

Difficulties sometimes arose where the father of an illegitimate child lived in another parish. Abraham Tennant, a labourer of Shenley (Herts.), was ordered by the justices to pay £2 2s towards the lying-in of Mary Dollimore, and 3s a week thereafter as long as the child had to be supported by the parish. He had failed to pay.[35] A contribution of sixpence a week was usually required of the mother if she was unable to nurse and care for the child herself.

There were nineteen illegitimate children supported by parish pensions in 1805. Many of them were in the care of women like Sarah Richardson a thirty-one year old widow of Chase Side. She had four children of her own and for them she was allowed 7s a week, plus a shilling towards the rent. She also received 3s a week to support Sarah Phillips, a ten-year-old born out of wedlock.[36] Another who looked after parish children was Sarah Scales, married and aged forty-nine. Her husband was ten years older and they had four girls between seven and thirteen years of age. They were receiving 4s a week from the parish and one quartern-loaf. She was looking after the Claxton boys, William and John, aged six and four, whose father had gone to sea. For this she was paid 5s a week.

Many unmarried mothers nursed their children themselves; their lives were difficult and in the end they might be driven to enter the workhouse. A sad little letter written by Ann Brinkley from Hertford to her parents at Ponders End expresses her isolation and despair.

'Dear mother and farther', she writes, 'I took the hoptunety of riten to you. I ham wery hun hapy to think that I have not had a nanser from you since I sor larst. I shall Be Doun my Self. I shold have Ben doun my Self had I bin well,
    if they Dont ples to a loo me a mentanince for my childe I will bring hur doun and lev hur in the Hous for I carnt mantan hur my Self. Soo nomor from me at present.'[37]

Many parents callously abandoned their responsibilities. Mary Basdill bore two children by George Pope, both born in Enfield. When Sarah was eight and George was seven their parents got married and abandoned the children in Kensington. They were conveyed to Enfield and delivered in at the workhouse.

Illegitimate children were born into difficulties. John Collis (otherwise Leet) the child of Sarah Collis spinster, born at Enfield, had become a burden on the rates in the village of Orwell in Cambridgshire. The magistrates ordered the child to be removed to Enfield but he failed to arrive. The reason is stated briefly on the back of the returned order; 'the pauper is now dead'.[38] Elizabeth Pearcey was a single woman whose bastard child born in Islington was still at her breast; nevertheless an order was made that she be returned with the child to Enfield. There the churchwarden receiving her scrawled a brief instruction on the back of the order; 'to the master of the workhouse, "Please take into the House".' Such unfortunate women were allowed to settle nowhere but in their own parishes. The officers of the parish of St Mary Newington had discovered Honor Ely living there with her two-month-old baby daughter. They were removed at once and consigned to the Enfield workhouse.[39]

For many an unmarried mother the prospect of the years of ostracism and penury which she would have to face must have been too much to bear. Perhaps this may account for the child, 'newly born but at its full time', found floating in a basket down the River Lea at Eddy Reach two days before Christmas 1785. He was packed around with straw and sewn up with packthread in an endeavour to keep him dry and warm. But alas no miracle occurred to save this latter day Moses. When the bargeman opened the basket, the baby was dead.[40]

With the growing financial pressure on the parish in the early nineteenth century the attitude towards illegitimacy among the poor continued to harden. Mary Ann Jones, pregnant in 1812 with a second bastard, was threatened that if she laid-in in Enfield she would be arrested at the end of her month and punished. A motion was solemnly resolved in vestry the following year that no bastard child be put on the books of the parish until the mother had been punished.[41]

5. The Parish Apprentice

In the early part of the seventeenth century, up to 1640, as many girls as boys were apprenticed at the parish expense. Later in the century it was mainly boys, then from 1690 onward the proportions became equal again.

Apprentices	−1639	1640–59	1660–89	1690–1714
Boys	24	17	41	44
Girls	24	5	18	43

Every tradesman who took a parish child was obliged to give a bond rendering Enfield parish free from liability for maintenance of the child during the term of indenture. Before 1662 the majority of poor children were articled within the parish. After the Act of Settlement in 1662 more went to other parishes.[42]

Apprentices	1616–62	1662–1714
Enfield	46	59
Elsewhere	28	74

The dual purpose of these apprenticeships was to teach the child a trade, and to relieve the parish of the burden of his maintenance. In some cases the parish paid the fee out of the estate of the dead father. Norman Lacely, who died in 1625, left two sons and two daughters. An apprenticeship fee of £5 for his son James was paid from his estate with the stipulation that the money should be returned for the use of all the children in the event of James's death.[43] On occasions money was given to a widow to assist her to apprentice a son. Thus Sara Jarvis was given 40s in 1672[44] to be used for this purpose. Sometimes whole families were apprenticed on the death of the father. Only a few relatively lucky ones were kept together like William and Sara Card. Both parents being dead, they were sent to James Legg a cordwainer of Cheshunt. Mary and Jane Helder also stayed together with Alice Sherman, a button-maker.

On the death of William Calendar, a labourer, his daughter Susanna was sent for nine years into the household of Henry Thornborough, citizen and card-maker; her brother John to James Sones, citizen and turner, for eight years; and the little sister Margaret to Ann Beverley of London, a widow. Perhaps they met occasionally to give each other some re-assurance on the crowded streets of the great city. The three Chamberlain children were even less fortunate; Richard was sent to Stepney to learn to be a weaver, William to Friern Barnet (which seems an unlikely place) to learn to be a mariner, and Elizabeth to a framework knitter at Bethnal Green where she would learn to become a market woman.

The five Graham daughters were left to the care of the parish in 1704. That year, Catherine was sent to John Bannister, a victualler of Enfield, for seven years. Martha was sent to another Enfield victualler, Marmaduke Pybus, but three years later was moved to the household of William Huggins of Enfield and then, in 1709, to Richard Halsey of Enfield (possibly the child was difficult). Lucy went overseas to Daniel Groome in Maryland for five years, Elizabeth was taken by Mary Jefferson, an Enfield widow, and Mary went to a Shoreditch gardener for seven years.[45]

Some poor boys apprenticed to members of London companies could expect eventually to receive the freedom of the City like Edward Whitaker, bound to James Cooke of Enfield who was also a citizen and cloth worker of London, or Ben Meade bound to Thomas Smith silk weaver of Waltham Abbey who should 'cause Benjamin to be bound in London'.

The trades to which these children were bound varied widely from surgeon to shoemaker and included labourers and husbondmen but included none of the wealthy local tanners, probably because they had a strong voice in the vestry and preferred to apprentice their own children. The cost to the parish in apprenticeship fees averaged around £3. Thirty-nine children were apprenticed in the ten years following 1690 and all the costs were met from parish rents (ie the charities).

Another sort of arrangement might be made as when, on the death of Goody Snow in 1685, esquire Green took her two daughters into service. He was paid 4s a week. The parish sold all her belongings and paid her debts; what was left was spent on clothes for the eldest girl.[46]

Towards the end of the eighteenth century a number of boys from the workhouse were bound out through the Marine Society for service at sea. Others were sent out as apprentices to chimney-sweeps. This was a dangerous trade, very liable to cause cancer of the scrotum. Jonas Hanway, in 1767 and 1768, had promoted laws to insist that the premiums for parish boys to chimney-sweeps should be paid in two instalments as an encouragement to their masters to keep them alive at least for a year or two. Richard Whiffin from Stroud in Kent was supplied from time to time with young lads up to eleven years of age on mutual approval, though the approval on behalf of both parties was inevitably expressed by the master. Whiffin and his brother had been apprenticed out of the Enfield workhouse in 1767 as chimney-sweeps until they were twenty-one. They had survived the ordeal and both were now masters. Mr Whiffin was to find these boys meat, drink, clothing, linen, washing and lodging, and the parish was to bear the expense of the indentures and binding. In 1784 he received John Ravenhill and Joseph Hains and the parish paid him £2 for each, and the cost of the indentures, 6s.[47]

He wrote, on 21 December 1788 to acknowledge the receipt of yet another child:

'Gentlemen, This comes to let you know that I have received yours and the Boy and I intend to come up to meet you on Monday 5 January so if you will please to let me know wether it will sute you or not, for me to come up, upon expenses and not meet you. And, as for the office you menshon, I do not know (it) so if you please to let me know wot ale-house you will meet me at, I will be shore to come there, pray don't faile'.[48]

His brother Gascoyne Whiffin,[49] in the same trade as Sheerness, was also supplied with boys from Enfield. Little William Giles had been sent there by the parish, but his mother, much concerned about the welfare of her child, went all the way to Sheerness to ask for her boy back. Gascoyne Whiffin refused. Brother Richard explained the circumstances in a letter to Scott the beadle. He felt that his brother had a duty to the ratepayers to keep the boy until he had an answer from Enfield whether or not William Giles had been sent for by order of the beadle. 'The boy', he wrote, 'seems very fond of his master and likes very well to stay with him'. Unfortunately no record survives to tell us whether the mother was successful in rescuing her son.[50] William's fellow apprentice at that time was another Enfield boy named William Child aged eleven.

The Whiffins were survivors. Despite a workhouse upbringing and years of heat and soot climbing chimneys, Richard was still running a prosperous business in 1806. He must have been about fifty then. He was still getting his supply of boys from the Enfield workhouse and, adopting his most deferential tone, he wrote to the vestry to request;

'the favour to know if you have any boys fitting to be put out apprentice; as being in occupation a brazier and chimney-sweeper. A small age will be suitable. If it meets with your approbation . . . I can bring a testimony of character for thirty-five years past.'[51]

And he was still looking for boys to sweep his chimneys in 1820 by which time he had distinguished himself by becoming 'chimney-sweeper to His Majesty's Dock-yard and Board of Ordnance'.

'Gentlemen', he then wrote, 'I have taken the liberty of writing to you concerning an apprentis. If you have a boy of the age of eight years old that you woold like to let me have, i shall esteem it a favour gentlemen, if it meets with your approbation. And if you will write to the minnister and parrish officers of our parish, you will know my Carrecter, i hope to your sattisfaction. If you have two to spare, i shall have no objection. Being myself out of the same House' he reminded the select vestry, 'caused me to apply to you gentlemen.'[52]

Occasionally an apprentice would complain of his treatment, though seldom before he had attained an age of maturity. Such a complaint might be dealt with by one of the more civilised of the vestrymen like Richard Gough the famous antiquarian. Baker Brown complained to Richard Gough who then sent a letter explaining the circumstances to Mr Hunt the overseer. Brown had been placed as an apprentice, partly at the expense of the parish, and partly at the expense of his mother who was now dead. He complained that he had never been taught his trade (carpenter) and had been kept the whole time on making boxes.[54]

It was more often masters who complained against apprentices, especially during times of high food prices. John Lawford, a boy from the Enfield workhouse, was bound to Richard Chapman in Hoxton.

'I am exceedingly sorry to inform you,' wrote Chapman to the master of the workhouse in January 1800, 'that John Lawford, whom I received from you, proves to be a very different lad from what I had thought him to be. I have detected him in several bad actions and petty thefts, far worse than I could conceive from his years. Therefore I should be glad if you would let me have the indentures for if he does not mend I must be compelled to take severer measures.

Sir, with respect, your humble servant
Richard Chapman

and as an afterthought he added

'Sir, If it should meet with your approbation to exchange him for another, I should be exceedingly happy, as I am fearful of his growing worse.'

John was returned and sent on approval to Harlington, Bedfordshire. He was obviously a young man well able to manipulate the system for soon afterwards he managed to extract an allowance of 6s a week from the Enfield vestry to be paid to him in Harlington.[55]

6. The Parish Health Service

A surprisingly large amount of money was spent on a parish health service to care for the poor. Several medical men were involved in cures but in the period 1690 to 1710 the parish usually employed two, Mr Robert Murrell as surgeon, and Mr Thomas Wilford as physician. Murrell also owned the Greyhound on Enfield Green. He seems to have been particularly well paid by the parish over the years. Among the many payments recorded were £2 8s in February 1692, £4 for curing the wife of John Montague, a husbondman of Green Street whose leg was dangerously broken, and 'cures done on Edward Cuffley and Widow Stevens £11' in 1701. The following year, cures done on Margaret Lincoln brought him £3, and in the ensuing year his attention to Mary Duckit earned him £2 5s 4d. In 1709 he was paid £15 for cures done on a man's head and arm 'wounded by the mill'. He then proceeded to cure Grace Saxeby's leg, Widow Ingle's arm, and John Smedley's leg. In 1687 the parish paid Murrell £3 for 'setting and curing the arm of Thomas Adams'. Adams appears to have been singularly vulnerable for in the following March he broke his leg 'and not being able to sustain the chirugeon' the parish again paid, £3 this time, to a Mr Bennett, to set the broken limb.

Thomas Wilford acted as physician and there are many recorded payments to him. In 1709 he asserted that 'for performing a cure on Goody Roberts leg which had been very bad for above a year, by poultesses, fermentations, ointments, plasters and several bottles of diet drink, he deserved no less than 40s.'[56]

There were others occasionally called upon to provide medical attention to the poor. Thomas Jones may have been a surgeon. On one occasion he was employed in curing Widow Eede's son of a rupture for which he was paid 30s. Robert Piggott appears even less frequently in the records. He was given £2 for a cure on Mary Duckit in 1701: the poor woman had to be cured again by Robert Murrell two years later. Occasional evidence can be seen of the vestry's lack of faith in its medical men; Mr John Gaine was given only half of his payment of £5, for the cure of two children in 1685, 'but if he doth not perfectly cure he is not to have the other 50s'. Women like Margaret Crisp did treatments of a more rudimentary nature as: 'curing four children that are troubled with scald heads', for which she was paid 26s. Necessitous widows were employed to nurse the sick; thus Jane Helder 'in great necessity, and to looking to old John Boulton and his family in their sickness'.

The parish was paying by 1729 large sums of money for powders, purges, glysters, blisters, ointments and pills, bleedings and vomits, all of which may have done much to kill off the paupers in the workhouse. In an endeavour to control this expenditure Joseph Wilson was appointed to provide medicine and care for the poor as surgeon and apothecary at £21 a year, to commence at Christmas 1729. The workhouse infirmary was already used as a hospital for the poor. Early in 1740 an order was issued that no-one should be admitted without a certificate from Dr Wilson, signed by a magistrate.[57] Mr Wyburd in the 1760s was paid £2 per year for supplying medicines to the poor[63]. The position of parish apothecary remained remunerative. Messrs Pritchard and Sherwen, parish doctors, were paid £21 a year in 1755. James Field's bill for medicines and his salary (thirty guineas) for the year 1805/6, amounted to £74[64]. His salary was raised in February 1808 to forty guineas and when he resigned in April 1811 the status of the appointment was enhanced to surgeon and apothecary at £50 a year. Robert Rolphe, surgeon, was appointed[58].

The kind of work carried out by Rolphe in 1811 can be seen in his submission to the vestry[59].

Two journeys to Potters Bar and medicines for Martha Neale
Attendance on a boy at Mr Chains, Bulls Cross
Attendances on William Aimes at Whitewebbs from 9 May to 12 June
– madness – died.
Attendance on William Beedle, Ponders End 8 May to 7 July
– consumption – died.
Attendance on Hugh McCall, Hadley till 9 May
Attended in labour Elizabeth Storain 4 May
     Sarah Nevil 12 May
     Mary Curran 15 May
Attended Joseph Wilson bleeding of leg
To inoculating and attending in smallpox fifty-seven, one male
 infant died
To inoculating with cowpox eighteen
Extra attendance on paupers not belonging to the parish of Enfield Easter to
May 1811.
     Robert Rolphe surgeon

Subsequently the parish was divided into two and medical officers were appointed for the Highway and Bulls Cross on the one hand and the Town and Chase on the other. This arrangement lasted until September 1824 when Mr Asbury was appointed for the whole parish.

Many people stuck to ancient and well-tried recipes to cure their ills. These were probably much safer than professional medical advice, let alone treatment. I have found a couple among the Enfield vestry clerk's papers; they have been there since 1762. I offer them without recommendation;

> ¾lb of honey, 1lb of treacle, 2d worth of mithridate, 3d worth of sweet oil, pint of vinegar. One spoonful night and morning or offener for a cough.
>
> 2oz of curind (curry?), 2oz of whole ginger, a head of garlick, a stick of horse-radish steeped in one quart of gin. A cupfull every morning-fasting.[60]

Heavy manual labour was the cause of innumerable ruptures and trusses were supplied by the apothecary and paid for by the parish at £1 11s 6d each[61].

For those who could afford it there was private medicine. The medical profession advertised openly in the press, a typical example is this declaration:

> I, William Poole . . . having been afflicted with a rupture upwards of two years, with great pains and torture, by which I was rendered incapable of following my labour but by reading in the newspapers of the great cures done by Mr Woodward surgeon at the Kings Arms near Half-moon Street, Piccadilly I was thereby encouraged to apply to him and to my great comfort, by wearing his new invented bandage and taking the powders with drops I am now perfectly cured, gratis, though at the age of fifty-one, for which I return him my humble and hearty thanks . . .
>
> Winchmore Hill November 27 1753.[62]

Even an artificial leg was provided on the rates. It was purchased from John Payne in Bell Lane, Spitalfields. He wrote to the overseer in 1790:

> 'Sir, agreeable to your request, I send this to inform you i have a compleat leg that as been wore by a gentlman as good as I can make, which fits the man completely and will be 7s6d cheaper than one made on purpose for him which would be £1 11s 6d, the best like this. I can make at £1 or 15s but the best is cheapest, stronnger and made Easeyer. He as tryed this one and as no com-plaints. Therefore, if approved by you, it may be called for any day after Monday. The price is £1 4s with belts.
>
> N.B. The leg as been wore but little and better than new, the leather being well seasoned. It cost £1 11s 6d'.[63]

The parish in the 1780s made arrangements with various London hospitals which accepted the sick poor from Enfield and sent the account to the vestry for payment. Thus following the discharge of Catherine Bassett from Guys in Southwark, the parish received a bill for eighty-four days subsistence at fourpence a day 28s, twelve weeks washing her body linen 3s, and the fee for admission 2s 6d. Hannah Wright was a more difficult patient; she was unable to feed herself and her board cost the parish ten shillings a week. She had to be provided with two shifts, two caps, two aprons, two handkerchiefs and a pair of stockings. She was subsequently transferred to St Lukes. Honor Ely was in St Thomas Hospital in Southwark for thirty days and was brought home in a cart by the beadle. Honor was a parish problem, repeatedly found homeless in various London parishes and returned to Enfield with her illegitimate daughter.[64]

Occasionally the hospital was forced to ask for the money but payment was usually prompt. 'Gentlemen', wrote the clerk of the London Hospital at Whitechapel (1790), 'I take the liberty of reminding you that one of your poors of Enfield is still in this hospital, his name is Edward Ives recommended as an in-patient by Richard Gough Esq. It is usual for every parish to deposit a guinea . . .'.[65] The money was sent within a few days.

The uncontrollably insane were confined in Bedlam (Moorgate) or in St Lukes in Old Street. John Hockley the bailiff had a son 'in a sad condition in Bedlam'. The parish allowed him 2s a week towards the maintenance of his son there. Lunatics like James Gordon and Mary Jackson were put into St Lukes.[66] The less uncontrollable were secured in the madhouse at the parish workhouse. Attitudes towards lunacy became slowly more humane. Mrs Crouchley, an Enfield woman living at Hadley,[67] had several times been taken to the Enfield workhouse and secured until she was sufficiently recovered to be returned home. However she became highly deranged by September 1812, often threatening to kill her children and those of her neighbours. She would run into the street naked and into people's houses using obscene language. She had destroyed her furniture. Many of her neighbours were prepared to swear the peace against her. The parish officers at Barnet declared that they were afraid she would commit some awful act of violence. They threatened to commit her to St Albans but, said the Barnet parish clerk, 'I think it is a hard thing to send a lunatic to gaol when she ought to be taken care of by her parish'. She was received again into the Enfield workhouse and forms were prepared for her admission into St Lukes.

Some devoted souls, as in all ages, committed themselves to the lifelong care of the insane. John and Mary Benton had for years looked after their mad daughter, Mary. When her father died he left £100 for her care. She had reached the age of forty when her mother too passed away. Her will provided that the interest on £60 and the rents of two houses in Baker Street should be given to her other daughter Sarah Ruskin with the request that she care for poor Mary, 'as much as in her lies, that she do not at any time want for convenient and wholesome necessaries of life'.[68]

The greatest concern at the turn of the century in the sphere of public health was evoked by smallpox. The vestry in December 1801, anxious to isolate sufferers, ordered that the pest-house belonging to the workhouse should be put into a state of repair. At the turn of the century a considerable controversy raged between proponents of inoculation and of vaccination as to which was the better method of giving the population immunity against smallpox. Inoculation, the older method, entailed giving the patient a weak injection of smallpox; but in 1796 Dr Edward Jenner had performed his first vaccinations in which cowpox germs were introduced into the patient's body. The supporters of the new treatment claimed that it was far less dangerous to the patient than inoculation. The vestry was hostile to the idea of inoculation; even a request by the parish apothecary in 1811 to be allowed to inoculate the poor was rejected in a most high-handed manner. 'The parish officers', said a vestry resolution, 'are not authorised to propagate contagious diseases among the poor at the expense of the parish'. There were those that never sought any authorisation like Martin, a labourer, who continued to make a little on the side by inoculating against the smallpox and administering medicines. The vestry held this to be a great danger to the lives of many of the inhabitants.[69]

The promotion of vaccination was urged in June 1822 at a public meeting convened on the initiative of the London Smallpox Hospital. The aim was to secure general vaccination and the discontinuance of inoculation. The chair was taken by

James Meyer of Forty Hall and local medical practitioners were asked to endorse the plan. Public notices were stuck up threatening prosecution against those who 'exposed patients on the highways'. The select vestry was appointed to be a general committee to promote vaccination; it was to set up district committees in various parts of the parish.[70]

There was a rabies scare in August 1824 when it was reported in vestry that several dogs had been bitten by a mad dog. The vestry issued a strong recommendation to the magistrates, requesting them to ensure that all stray dogs be rounded up.[71] It was a cause of persistent concern at the time (it still is), but it gave rise to one of Charles Lamb's more jovial letters in 1827;

> 'All the dogs here are going mad, if you believe the overseers; but I protest they seem to me very rational and collected. But nothing is so deceitful as mad people, to those who are not used to them. Try him (Dash, Leigh Hunt's unruly hound) with hot water. If he won't lick it up, it is a sign he does not like it. Does he wag his tail horizontally or perpendicularly? that has decided the fate of many dogs in Enfield . . . [72]

7. The Parish Workhouse and the Casual Poor

The first to advocate a workhouse in Enfield was William Covell in 1660. His plans were grandiose and Utopian. He proposed almshouses for the aged and a workhouse where the people could be set to work. Education was to play a major role, for Hebrew, Greek, Latin and handicrafts would be taught. The workhouse which the parish finally set up in 1719 was less ambitious. A building was rented in Chase Side on the edge of the Chase: its site is now (1989) occupied by St Michael's Hospital. At first it was rented for seven years at £15 a year from Mrs Mary and Mrs Elizabeth Snagg who gave the parish an option to extend the lease to eleven or twenty-one years. Work had to be done to prepare the house for its new use; this cost £42. It was to be directed by thirteen governors or visitors who were to be chosen annually at the vestry in Easter week. The building was finally purchased by the parish in 1740.

There was much poverty in the parish in the 1730s. Forty-five paupers were buried in the churchyard in the year ended March 1731; the number included eighteen children, one man and three poor travelling women who had died on the road, and six inmates of the workhouse. The vicar received for burial 1s 6d for each adult and 1s 2d for each pauper child.[73] Thomas Mico was the workhouse master in the 1730s; he employed the children in spinning for which the parish derived an income of about 50s a month.[74] The year 1739 saw the first experiment in farming the poor. The parish entered into an agreement with Thomas Mico whereby he was to provide the poor in the house with meat, drink, soap, firing and candles, and was to mend their clothing; for this he was to receive 2s a head. He was to be allowed whatever profit he could derive from the work done in the house. It was firmly set down that the paupers must treat their master with respect, must never 'fall out and abuse him in a gross manner', nor must they ever leave the workhouse without informing the master, who was given power to bring recalcitrant paupers before a justice of peace.[75]

Throughout the first quarter of the eighteenth century expenditure on the poor was still met to a considerable extent out of the parish rents. It had not yet become an unbearable burden on the ratepayers, but by the 1730s half-yearly poor rates of 9d in the pound (occasionally 6d) were regularly levied, and by 1740 the parish was beginning to feel the painful burden of the poor. Thereafter rates were levied quarterly at 6d or 9d. The principle drain on parish resources was the never ending stream of paupers demanding outdoor relief. The cost of casual relief handed out by the overseers increased rapidly from £291 in the year 1731-2, to £734 in the year 1741-2. The attitude of the poor is perhaps reflected in the words of a long lost seventeenth century ballad; 'Hang care, the parish is bound to save us'. The parish however was reluctant. To restrict further demand the vestry ordered that from 25 March 1743 all applicants for relief must be sent into the workhouse. It was a policy advocated but never successfully executed at intervals throughout the eighteenth century and into the nineteenth, and it foreshadowed the terms of the Poor Law Reformation Act which would be enacted by Parliament almost a century later. Members perhaps sensed the impracticability of the resolution for they went on to suggest that there might be exceptions and these would have to be considered in vestry. Nevertheless, the cost to the parish did fall for a few years, to £417 in the year 1747-8, but thereafter it rose once more.[76]

The vestry continued to seek economies. In an attempt to make the best use of the money spent, casual relief was, where possible, provided in the form of clothing rather than cash which an improvident pauper could all too easily fritter away in an ale-house. Shoes were distributed, mostly to children, twenty-one pairs in June 1747, eight in July and fourteen in August, but this included shoes for a number of widows. Nine children including the seven offspring of the Thornton family were fitted out in February 1748. Relief in cash however continued to be doled out at the workhouse on almost a daily basis to a multitude of the lame, the sick, the pregnant, the unfortunate, the unemployed, the starving and the scrounger. Many applied with regularity for months, even for years. Robert Inever for instance received 1s 6d on 26 March 1748, on 30 March and on 5 April, and 1s on 9, 12, 15, 19 and 21 April. He then died and 1s was bestowed on the woman who laid out his body, 1s purchased the shroud, the coffin cost the parish 8s, and 6s was given to those who carried his body to the churchyard. Immediately after the burial the widow Katherine Inever called at the workhouse for her shilling allowance and continued to do so regularly for some years. John Cantrel the overseer in the Ponders and Horsepoolstones quarter, (also the publican at the Sun and Woolpack, Enfield Wash) handed out from time to time similar small sums, to Sarah Hartley (1s 6d), to Elizabeth Hodge (2s), to Martha Dean (1s 6d) and to many others.[77]

The difficulty in controlling casual relief, and the rising costs of the workhouse, again induced the vestry to experiment in farming the poor. This was an arrangement with a contractor who for a fixed sum annually agreed to undertake the care of all the poor belonging to the parish. By this means the vestry sought, hopefully, to limit its commitments, but the system never seemed to work. Apart from the brief experiment with Mr Mico, the first such contract was in 1751 when the parish appointed John Pollard, a frame-work knitter, as master of the workhouse. He was to receive £400 a year paid monthly, with a proviso, according to Pollard, that if this sum proved inadequate the parish would make good the deficiency. At the end of the year he claimed that he had expended the £400 but that debts of over £60 were yet unpaid to tradesmen for provisions which he had purchased for the workhouse. At a vestry at Easter 1753 the parish undertook to discharge these debts, but despite this, Pollard became involved in litigation, being sued by one of the tradesmen in the Court of King's Bench.[78] Thus this scheme to farm the poor ended ignominiously and was abandoned.

Forgetful of this failure, in 1765 the parish proposed to try again. An advertisement was placed in the *Daily Advertiser* for a workhouse-man and his wife. The applicants were to submit tenders for the provision of the food, drink, clothing, firing and laundry in the workhouse; they were also to supply the implements and materials to set the inmates to work. The parish was to provide all the household goods and bedding and was to pay a doctor and an apothecary who were to care for sick paupers and to take charge in those cases of childbirth too difficult for the midwife. The parish was also to recompense the minister for his services at pauper burials.

John Curtis of Enfield, whose tender was finally accepted by the vestry, offered to undertake the care of the poor at 2s 6d a head of all those in the workhouse. In arriving at this figure he argued that the high price of provisions made it impossible that he should do it for less. He calculated that, after allowing for the cost of soap, firing and candles, there would remain less than four pence a day for food and drink. The numbers in the workhouse ranged from fifty up to seventy. Though seventy paupers at 2s 6d a week, he pointed out, would bring him in a reasonable income of £455 a year, yet if that number was to decrease to an average of fifty his remuneration would be only £325. Out of this he would also have to find clothes which he claimed could hardly be provided for less than 40s per pauper per year. Thus for fifty persons clothing would cost him £100. On top of this, he would have to make payments to the casual poor and provide coffins for pauper burials. The contract finally agreed by John Curtis gave him £450 a year, to be paid weekly, and it was to run for one year.

There had been no shortage of applicants for the post; indeed, proposals from fifteen persons have survived in the parish records. Some of them planned to take advantage of the free labour of the paupers in their own businesses; such were John Phillips an Enfield stocking-maker, or Richard Scott a rope-maker from Stepney. Some were semi-literate like Tom Binns; others were from the professions, an attorney from Southwark, and a barber-surgeon dwelling at Little Old Bailey who was most anxious to impress the vestry with his interest in education and wrote to

'recommend a few spelyng books to be bought. And when thear work was don, the might be att Libertey of a Littel Lerning eche on according to thear Cappisety'.

Some had experience in farming the poor, others had less, like the sailor from Soho[79] who applied.

The experiment in contracting however was again short-lived and at the end of the year the vestry set up a committee to take over the work. Its first business was to formulate rules for the management of the poor. All those, both in the workhouse and outside, who received clothing from the parish, had now to be clothed in uniform dress and must wear a brass badge on the outside right hand sleeve of their coat or gown.[80] They were at no time to be relieved unless they were wearing this badge. If they lost it, or if they destroyed it, they should receive no further relief. The clothes provided were adequate, though not elegant. The men and boys were given a coat, a waistcoat, a pair of leather breeches, two shirts, a pair of shoes, two pairs of stockings and a felt hat.[81] The women and girls had a hat, two caps, a gown, a pair of stays, two petticoats, two shifts, a pair of shoes, two pairs of stockings, two neck handkerchiefs and two aprons. These were to be provided (for those above the age of twelve) at a cost (in 1784) of 30s, and for children between five and twelve, 13s 6d. For those under five, clothing should cost 7s 6d. All which was somewhat less than Mr Curtis had arrived at in his calculations.

The rules further stipulated that the children in the workhouse should be taught for two hours each day to read and write and to say their prayers and their catechism. One room was set aside as a schoolroom though its contents; a table-bedstead with a new flock bed, a bolster and bed-clothes, together with a chamber pot, had little to do with education except in the broadest sense. It did contain however a table, a form and two stools and in 1782 the parish purchased two spelling books and a Testament for the use of the children at a cost of 3s.[82]

During the time not given over to formal education the children were to be taught and employed in spinning, knitting and serving, and such other useful housewifery and manufactures as best would qualify them to be good servants. Their instructors were appointed from among the older inmates who were paid for this duty at 3d a week. The boys might also be taught to weave. According to Eden (writing of Ealing in 1797) a boy of ten or eleven could learn to weave tolerably well in a month. He would then be able to make a sack, worth 2s 6d, in about two days; but many of the boys, Eden added dispassionately, 'run away'.[83]

The day-to-day routine of running the workhouse was left in the hands of Elizabeth Enever. Details of her administration are revealed by her petty-cash book which had to be written up for her, she being unable to write. Many of the paupers were paid a few coppers a week for various tasks about the house; a comber was paid 2d a week and a reeler of yarn 3d. One man was employed as a gate-keeper and another as a gardener at 3d a week. The three women who did the washing were each paid 2d. There was a cook paid 2d, though the occasional dinner which had to be roasted was sent out to a bakehouse.[84] It was ordered that the whole house, above stairs and below, should be swept out every day and washed every week. Pigs were kept and occasionally slaughtered in the house. The comfort of the old was sought by the weekly distribution of 3½d worth of snuff among them. At the time when there was a fair in Enfield, the children were given a day off with 1s 6d to spend between them. And who would have thought of the vestry providing a go-cart for the kids, but there it is among the carpenters' accounts, just before Christmas 1790 'a new go-cart for the children to go in, 4s 7d'.[85] Real concern was shown in the attention given to the sick and bed-ridden. It was ordered in 1766 that they should be given a special diet suitable to their condition as directed by the doctor, and that nurses be appointed to care for them, if possible from among the inmates of the house, otherwise from outside. 'But if any idle people, old or young, shall pretend themselves to be sick, lame or blind, on purpose that they may not work, the surgeon shall inspect their ailments and if it appears that those people make false excuses they shall be severely punished.'[86] There is evidence too of kindness in the care of the dying. Old Robert Tanner had occasionally been paid 6d for reading the prayers, but he fell ill at the beginning of the year 1767.

10 February 1767 – a lemon for Robert Tanner	2d
11 February – half a pint of wine for Robert Tanner	6d
16 February – three half-pints of wine for Robert Tanner	1s 6d
and four lemons	6d

19 February – two women sitting up with Robert Tanner	6d
20 February – for laying-out Robert Tanner	6d
21 February – beer for burying Robert Tanner	1s 6d

Nevertheless death occurred so frequently in the workhouse that it must have become a matter of routine. On 16 September 1766 two of the women were occupied in laying-out Mary Ford; on the 30th they were at work on the bodies of Margaret Aub and William Heath (two burials could be provided more economically than one). John Richards was carried to the churchyard on 24 November, on 6 December Sophia Savage, on the 16 John Dyer, on the 30th Ann Tatham, and on the following day Mrs Harold. Mary Burr was buried on 10 January and on 21 February it was our friend Robert Tanner. These somewhat unceremonious pauper burials (despite 1s 6d beer money for bearers and grave-diggers on each occasion) must have rendered the dismal old place more depressing than ever.[87]

The parish had adapted a large old house in which to shelter the poor. The great parlour was turned into a committee room in which the select vestry or workhouse committee met; the little parlour served as a sitting-room for the master and mistress; the former hall became the dining room. Other rooms on the ground floor were used as a kitchen, a bakehouse, a school-room and a wash-house. The chambers above became small wards, some for men and some for women, each with four or five beds. Another served as the mad-house. It contained two wooden cradle bedsteads and the door could be adequately secured with two locks and four bolts. A pair of leather pinions was provided further to restrain the madman in his frenzy. With the passing of time, the workhouse accommodation became more and more inadequate and an old premises, 'over the way' was acquired where the front chamber, back chamber and garrets were used as dormitories for the men. Below stairs were stored three old chests without lids and two chamber pots, and there was a deal shelf to accommodate the dead.[88]

Following the administration of Elizabeth Enever, Zacharia Nichols was appointed workhouse-man but on what terms is unclear, and in May 1772 he was given notice to quit. No reason is provided but it is perhaps indicated in the proposals for the new appointment wherein it is stipulated that whoever was to be appointed must take no lodgers or boarders into the house.[89]

The vestry met irregularly, about twice a month, at one or other of the public houses at Enfield Town; at the George, the Rising Sun, the King's Head, or the Greyhound.[90] They were kept busy providing for the poor. In answer to government enquiries in 1776 Enfield reported that the numbers receiving regular pensions from the parish were 117 in the Town quarter, forty-one in the Ponders End and Green Street quarter, and five in Bulls Cross. The total annual cost was £672. The poor rate for the year ended Easter 1776 had raised £1022 and £850 had been expended on the poor. Such high expenditure gave rise to grave concern. A committee was set up in 1778 to confer on the matter, a sort of parish 'think tank'. After due deliberation it was solemnly declared that the current mode of maintaining the poor was expensive.[91] It was therefore recommended (though it had already been tried) that the vestry should contract with some person to provide for all the poor in the parish who sought relief. Should the vestry however decline this option, then a master and mistress should be appointed and the parish should cease to provide outdoor relief and send all applicants into the workhouse. The committee had again overlooked the fact that the workhouse was not nearly large enough, and that proposal had to be rejected.

As an alternative the parish appointed William Collier of Clay Hill to take charge of the poor. He proved to be yet another contractor apparently unable to to find a profit in his contract, for he wrote to the select vestry in July 1782 complaining that he now had to cope with numbers far greater than he had expected. He had, he claimed, an average of ninety-two paupers in the workhouse,[92] besides pensioners and casual poor. Many of them, he said, came with scarcely a rag to stand up in and he had had to clothe them entirely. Money also had to be found to meet crises which occurred in families belonging to other parishes and their overseers were often grudging and recalcitrant in repaying. Henry Sedgewick the overseer in the Ponders End quarter, in 1784 wrote complaining to an overseer at Buntingford:

'You promest to call on me to pay the money i let John Edwards have when he was sick and his family a-starving, which was as follows
    5 February 4s
    14 February 3s
    24 February 2s
    28 February 2s
His wife came for more and made great complaints, but i did not let her have any more, so pray let me have eleven shillings which i let them have'

About this same time Mr Smart the vestry clerk at Enfield received this warning from an overseer at Ware, concerning another destitute family in Enfield[93]

'Sir . . . in respect to Brooks' family I hope [your] overseer has relieved them cautiously, as the family is very expensive.'

There were twenty-four pauper burials in the parish in the year 1781–2.[94] Some sympathy for the poor survived until this time. The rights on Enfield Chase which had enabled poor men to live through harvest failures and cold winters since the earth had first been cultivated hereabouts, had been lost to them by the enclosure of the Chase in the year 1777. The wood was now energetically protected against the poor by men like William Squire, the high constable, though with less enthusiasm by others like Mr Hughes, his assistant. Squire was proud that he had at last been able to apprehend the 'most notorious' of all the wood stealers, Mrs Burgess. She was taken into custody at Enfield from where she was to be conveyed by Hughes before a magistrate at Edmonton. Even Scott the beadle was reluctant to be involved in the matter and failed to provide a cart. Because of this Mr Squire was kept waiting in Edmonton for two hours and then the magistrate declined to hear the case on the grounds, or the excuse, that he was himself an interested party. Squire was infuriated that his criminal should go free, but his supreme mortification came when, after giving his assistant Hughes a shilling to have a drink, he watched while that dissolute man spent the shilling (his shilling) on the released prisoner and, upon his remonstrance, Hughes had the audacity to declare 'that he thought that it was the poor's right to take their wood from the Chase'. Squire, feeling that the whole world must be mad, offered his resignation; at the same time he solemnly admonished the vestry to choose a proper person to take his place (and on no account should it be Hughes). The man appointed should act as both beadle and constable and, so empowered, he might patrol 'the avenues at the top of Parsons Lane' with his staff of office. 'My small staff' he added, looking back with pride, 'has put to flight upwards of eighty women and children and I have seized their bundles and confiscated their bills.'[95]

The vestry assisted sometimes in the payment of rents for the poor but only to a limited amount, £12 15s for instance, in the year 1776. The parish also owned a very small stock of housing. Usually the houses which came into the possession of the parish were sold; in 1731 after James Burroughs died his house was sold for £30 and the money was set aside for the maintenance of his four orphan children aged between twelve and four. The following year Nicholas Moore resigned to the vestry two houses adjoining Longfield which were sold for £10; presumably the money was to be used by the parish for the care of Nicholas now that he was old.[96] General Mocher (in May 1786) wrote to the churchwarden, Mr Brown, concerning a man who worked for him by the name of Staker who lived in a house belonging to Mr Vaughan for which he paid five guineas a year. The General thought this beyond the man's means as he had three children already and his wife was pregnant. There was a small cottage belonging to the parish standing near the workhouse, he suggested, which would suit the man well; it had been let for forty or fifty shillings a year. Such a rent seems to have been the average for a small cottage in Enfield at this time. For example, old Barker had paid £2 12s 6d; when he died in June 1786 he had left a year's rent unpaid. He had been in receipt of one of the parish charities distributed half-yearly and due at midsummer and his landlord wrote to the vestry clerk asking that he be paid the rent out of the pension now due.[97]

Alderman Sir Robert Clayton, in July 1676, took a lease of a house and orchard in Turkey Street where some time afterwards he erected a brick terrace of four separate houses facing east on a cartway leading from Turkey Street into Dung Field. In these he housed poor people of the parish of Enfield. The houses were sold in 1734, after Sir Robert's death, for £50 to Thomas Crowe of London, a doctor of physic. They came to be known as Crowe's Almshouses because Mrs Ann Crowe by her will provided £500 bank stock, the interest to be employed in repairs to the building and the provision of coal for the tenants.[98]

Further sleeping accommodation had to be added to the workhouse in the 1780s to cater for the increased numbers. The new building contained four rooms, two up and two down, each with five beds. New stump sacking bedsteads with feather beds and bolsters, new blankets and coverlids, replacedthe old oak boarded bedsteads. The rooms were made more comfortable, chairs and stools were found and an additional number of coarse chamber pots were provided at the very reasonable price of 2s a dozen. In each room a bath stove was installed and fires were allowed from the beginning of November until the end of May.[99] New regulations prescribed the food which was to be given to the paupers and rigidly ordered their daily routine. The diet was adequate, though the presentation was hardly designed to entice the more fastidious palate. The food was mostly boiled, and it was served in wooden bowls or on wooden trenchers. Nevertheless it was so plentiful that if the inmates consumed it all they would have been fat and fully fed. The daily routine was tedious rather than harsh. The paupers were roused from their beds on Monday mornings at six in the summer and seven in the winter. Washed and combed, they presented themselves before the master to hear prayers read. Shaving was done once a week when the barber came round. The parish paid him a penny a pauper. Haircuts or heads shaved cost twopence.[100] After prayers they gathered in the dining room for breakfast. This room was furnished with two long deal dining tables and four long forms.[101] There was an oak dresser attached to the wall. A wainscot oval table was set aside for the master and mistress. Among the paraphernalia in a corner was a pair of brass scales with lead and brass weights and a larger beam and plank scale for the weighing-in of bulky provisions. There was a fireplace fitted with a fender and equipped with a small spit and dripping pan. A brass warming pan hung upon the wall. Among the other odds and ends about the room was a sword, a type of short sword called a hangar, and a boot-jack.

Breakfast on Monday mornings consisted of one ounce of butter and thirteen ounces of bread (approximately equal to eight medium-thick slices of a modern cut loaf); it was washed down with a quart of weak beer (table beer). The bread was sometimes bought and at other times was baked on the premises. This same breakfast was also provided on Sundays, Tuesdays and Wednesdays, but on Thursday they had rice pudding, which contained a pint of milk, together with the same vast quantity of bread but with no butter, and again a quart of beer. On Fridays and Saturdays each had a pint of milk pottage with the quart of beer, the same quantity of bread, but again no butter.

Breakfast over the whole family (this euphemism encompassed all the workhouse paupers with their master and mistress) were to be employed in such works as they were capable of doing. The workroom, or spinning room, held eight spinning wheels, a long deal form, two reels and a stand, two stools and cross-reels and a large deal press for the wool. There, or elsewhere about the house or grounds, the paupers worked, or lounged, until noon and then to dinner. Grace was said by one of the children both before and after the meal. Dinners on Mondays, Wednesdays and Fridays always consisted of meat broth, though on Fridays they got a pint of peas pottage with it. On Tuesdays they had boiled beef or mutton with vegetables. On Thursdays it was meat pudding (twelve ounces of suet pudding with eight ounces of meat). Saturday dinner by contrast was a light meal, two ounces of cheese and a quart of beer. An hour was allowed each day for dinner, from twelve until one; then it was back to work until six on winter evenings and seven in the summer. After work they had supper; this was a light meal, either two ounces of cheese or one ounce of butter, though undoubtedly they would have had bread left from breakfast to eat it with. Supper over, there were evening prayers and so to bed with candles out by eight in the winter and nine in the summer. This was mostly for the sake of economy for candles were very expensive at 8d each (in 1790). Since there were only forty-eight beds in the house and up to ninety-two paupers, some must have had to sleep two in a bed. There were strict injunctions against smoking after lights out.[102]

The routine of eating, working, prayers and sleep was varied only on Sundays when the whole 'family' was conducted to St Andrews Church by the master and mistress, both for morning service and service in the afternoon. The long hours of the sabbath not thus occupied had to be employed in reading, or in hearing some portion of the Holy Scriptures, or some part of the '*Whole Duty of Man*' (prescribed reading for paupers), or in singing psalms. Some may have been tempted to claim that they were non-conformists, but this still meant that they would have to go to the appropriate chapel under the direction of proper person and that might have been worse.

These rules were not however consistently adhered to. Jabez Straker, one fine Sunday afternoon in September 1814, feeling the call of religion and there obviously being no organised church visit arranged, asked leave to attend divine service at the parish church. He returned at nine o'clock that night much the worse for drink and, upon Mr Davidson remonstrating with him for staying out late, he seized the workhouse master by the collar and threatened to knock the life out of him. Religion had obviously had an adverse effect upon this pauper.[103]

Looking at the prodigious diet laid down for the inmates, a modern sceptic might think that such quantities could never have been ladled into the pauper's bowl. A glance however at some of the tradesmen's bills for supplies delivered to the house reveals that the sceptic could be wrong. William Feast, for instance, was paid for an average of twelve stone of meat each week in 1727 and there were then between fifty and sixty inmates. This is more than one-and-a-half pound of meat a week to each pauper[104]. All the food was boiled. There were two copper boilers in the kitchen and there was another in the wash-house which served both to boil the washing and to cook the food. Ready to hand by the copper was a pudding stirrer, a large soup ladle, six square tin pudding pans, two large stew pans and three pottage pots.

In 1784 a contract was made with William Rocket[105] who, for £700 a year, was to provide for all the poor in the workhouse and all others who sought relief within the parish, as well as those from Enfield who, with certificates, dwelt in other parishes but were maintained out of the Enfield poor rate. The new master was required to live in the house and was responsible, with the assistance of the beadle, for conveying paupers out of the parish back to their place of settlement; for this he was to be paid a shilling a mile.

Once again however this arrangement proved unsatisfactory. In the very next year after entering into his contract Rocket wrote to the vestry pleading that 'the great number of his "family", being upwards of ninety', and the many outdoor poor made it impossible for him to continue unless the parish would allow him £100 above the sum agreed. Two years later he was accused by the vestry of providing false returns; these showed ninety-three paupers in the house but when the vestry investigated only seventy-one were present. He had not provided good and sufficient meat and drink according to the prescribed diet, nor adequate clothing according to the regulations, nor had he and his wife resided constantly in the workhouse. The children had not been taught to read, nor had the paupers been conducted to church to attend divine service. Mr Rocket offered his resignation and it was accepted.[106]

There were difficulties too concerning the parish charities. It was in the nature of such enterprises that efficiency declined over the years until the decline was halted by some reforming spirit. On the death of the vestry clerk (Mr Hunt) in 1792, it was found that there were arrears of rents from the various properties owned by the charities amounting to £652. The boundaries of parish properties were in many cases not known. Mr Peter Hardy, a conscientious parish reformer, overhauled the system of management. Plans of the various properties were made and lodged with the deeds and muniments in the store-room over the south porch in St Andrews Church. These plans, with information on current leaseholders, were published in a book which was distributed among the trustees and other responsible parishioners to preclude the possibility of future irregularities.[107]

8. Settlement and Removal

While it made sense, with the existing machinery of government, to make each parish responsible for its own poor, the poor were always on the move. They sought employment in one place after another, married partners from other villages, and were apprenticed in London or elsewhere, and so it often became difficult to establish which parish ought to be held responsible for their welfare. Thus when any poor person arrived in a village, the parish officers were faced with a dilemma. They must either expel him immediately, in case he secured a settlement there and subsequently became chargeable on the poor rate, or allow him to remain to fill such employment as was available. Mobility of labour was as important in the eighteenth century as it is in the late twentieth century.

There grew up over the years a body of legislation and case law which sought to provide guidance in establishing the parish to which a man belonged; this was called his settlement. The Act of 1662 specified that those whom the overseers had decided to expel from a parish must be removed within forty days: forty days residence therefore became the basic qualification for acquiring a settlement. It was easy then, with the connivance of an employer who needed hands or a landlord who needed the rent, to escape the vigilance of overseers for forty days. The loophole however was closed by the Act of 1685 which decreed that the forty days should ensue from the day on which written notice was given to the overseers, which notice (by an Act of 1691) had to be read out in church. The attention of the overseer henceforth became more difficult to evade and the poor, as they moved from village to village in search of work, found themselves harassed by beadles and constables and liable to be ignominiously carried out of any parish.

To protect themselves from such treatment men sought certificates from the parish of their settlement by which the authorities there accepted responsibility for them and asserted a readiness to support them or to take them back at any time, should they be forced to seek relief. A hundred and forty-four such certificates, made out in the years 1698 to 1730, survive in the Enfield parish records. They represent (with wives and children) some four hundred souls.[108] One hundred and ten of the certificated men came from villages and towns in the Home Counties. Twenty came out from London and only fourteen from beyond the Home Counties. There were certificates from Carmarthen, Illogan in Cornwall, Portsmouth, Wootton-under-Edge, Crayford in Kent, and Trentham (either Staffs or Worcestershire).

Twenty-five of the certificates give the trade and they are mostly what might be expected in a village like Enfield; bricklayer and carpenter, farrier and wheelwright, as well as four labourers and six shoe-makers, though there was also a rat catcher all the way from Berkshire and, in 1726, a hackney coachman from the City.

These certificates gained acceptance in the most unpropitious circumstances, even for 'Elizabeth Miles and the child, or children, she is now big with, being a bastard', who came from Edmonton; and large families too, like John Bonwick (aged twenty-eight) Lucretia his wife, Robert (aged eleven), John and Isaac (aged six), Mary (five), William (four), and little Lucretia aged one, all the way from St Martins in the Field. Usually certificates were issued to meet an immediate threat of removal.

Overseers became particularly concerned about any stranger who had a large family. They foresaw unemployment, illness or death and their parish being forced to foot the bill; they foresaw their vestry involved in interminable litigation. Therefore they required the man to procure a certificate from his own parish. The overseers there, to whom he applied, may have considered it more humane to grant a certificate than to force the family to return; moreover it might save the parish a great deal of money. A man who was perhaps willing and able to earn his living where he was might face unemployment if he returned. His family would then have to be taken at great parish expense into the workhouse. Thus the overseers of the parish of Barton were faced with an order to remove from Enfield, David Warren, Sarah his wife and their four children. Instead they provided him with a certificate by which they undertook to reimburse the parish of Enfield should David Warren or any of his family ever be forced to seek relief. The family remained in Enfield.

Stephen Dobson[109], a respectable and literate man, well situated among many of his relatives and having employment at Northowran near Halifax, was sent for by the gentlemen of that town at their monthly meeting in October 1783 and told that, though they had nothing to say against him, since he had always endeavoured to do well for his family, yet they would issue an order to carry him out of the town unless he could get a certificate from Enfield guaranteeing that the parishioners of Northowran would incur no expense on account of him and his family. His letter to the Enfield vestry clerk asking for a certificate contains a threat as well as an entreaty . . . 'for my family is very large and small' [young], he writes, 'and likely to increase, for which there will be a great charge to you'. He threatens that if he should be forced to return he would live henceforth at the expense of the parish.

Such men, intelligent and reasonably literate, knew how to exploit the system and wrote to the officers of the parish without the obsequiousness which was to grow by the end of the eighteenth century. Another of the same sort was William Pickton.

'I have received your letter requesting a quarters allowance for the maintenance of my wife and family', he wrote, 'which I am sorry to inform you is out of my power at present to do. Owing to the badness of the weather and short days my wages at present (December 1806) average no more than 16s a week, nor I don't expect they will for a month to come. I hope the overseers will take it into consideration and not put themselves to the trouble and expense of fetching me with a warrant for, if they write to me and require it, I will attend them at the bench of magistrates. I hope the committee will let it remain for a few weeks when I shall be able to send more money. Or if the gentlemen in the parish will find me in work and wish me to come home I am very willing to do so'.[110]

A person could gain a settlement, under the 1662 Act, by renting property worth £10 a year. The Act of 1691 granted settlement by paying taxes and rates, by serving in a parish office or by being bound apprentice in a parish; in 1697 this was extended to include persons hired for a year as servants. Children born out of wedlock took their settlement from the parish where they were born. Henry Clarke, a labourer, achieved a settlement by working two whole years in Enfield as a hired servant. William Blake, a plumber, got his settlement at St Giles in the Field by renting a house there for eight years on which he paid rates and taxes, William Pond by serving apprentice as a cordwainer for five years in Hertford, Elias Bliss by renting a house at Edmonton at £5 a year and land there to the value of £5. James Taylor claimed settlement in County Fife by having served an apprenticeship as a tailor there for three years.

People were often sent back as complete strangers to places they scarcely knew. Poor old Martha Bakewell, a widow, was insane in the Enfield workhouse in 1772 so she could scarcely enlighten anybody on the matter of her settlement, but an overseer recalled that in the previous April, before she went mad, he had given her 2s as casual relief and she had told him that her late husband had served before marriage as a hired servant at Aldbury in Hertfordshire. Thus the Enfield vestry were able to shift the burden of poor Martha all the way to Aldbury.[111]

The parish sometimes found it cheaper to provide relief to those living elsewhere who had fallen temporarily on hard times, usually through illness or unemployment, rather than to order their removal to Enfield where the whole family would have to be taken into the workhouse, at least for a time, and when they emerged there would be the difficulty of finding employment and housing in what might be, to them, a new place. Thus the parish of Ashwell in Hertfordshire paid Thomas Goodchild 4s a week for five weeks when his wife fell sick in 1771 and the parish of Enfield refunded the money. John Hicks held a certificate from the parish of Enfield promising either to succour him when he required help or to take him back. He fell ill in Upminster in 1776. There the vestry provided him with medical attention (which cost a guinea) and 17s relief before he was able to resume work. The money was refunded by the parish of Enfield.

The process worked both ways of course. Thomas and Jonathan Brooks, whose settlement was in Hunsdon in Hertfordshire, were that same year given one guinea in relief when they fell unemployed in Enfield. 'But', wrote John Smart the Enfield parish clerk in February, 'both paupers are now got into work and will want no more relief at present'. Arrangements were made for the overseers of the two parishes to meet at the Cross Keys in Hertford to settle the Brooks account.[112] These agreements between parishes might continue for years. The pension list presented to the vestry in October 1805 shows that 2s 6d was paid to Edward Barnes, destitute and suffering ill-health in Nottingham. He had a wife and three dependent children, Thomas aged six, Ann aged four and the baby William only three months old. Nevertheless the prolonged struggle of the family to survive on parish liberality took its toll and by 1809 the wife had become mentally deranged. The Nottingham magistrates refused to sanction her removal fearing that it would endanger her life. Edward Barnes had by now partially recovered but could no longer work at his own trade. However he had found friends to employ him in attending their horses and doing their errands. The eldest boy, now ten or eleven years old, had been offered an apprenticeship and the Enfield vestry was asked how much they would contribute, the parish in Nottingham suggesting five or six guineas. Taking into consideration the improved condition of Edward Barnes the Enfield vestry cut his allowance from 7s to 5s. The troubles of this poor family were by no means at an end. More than ten years later Ann Barnes, now a widow, wrote (May 1820) to an overseer at Enfield of her endless troubles. Through a severe seizure she had lost the use of her limbs and had 'convulsed in her head'. Since the death of her husband the pension from Enfield had been discontinued and she had been entirely dependent on her children. Now that trade was so bad they were no longer able to support her. She was too ill to be removed, and begged for a small allowance.[113]

Where difficulties looked likely to persist the remedy was usually, but not always, removal and the workhouse. Sarah Hainsworth with her four children, John aged ten, Robert nine, Thomas eight and Sarah only two, had fallen destitute in Southwark. Their father had left them. The authorities provided them with a pass to walk to Enfield; it protected them from molestation by the parish beadles and constables on route, providing they used only the post roads. They were given two days for the journey. Desertion by the husband usually led to the removal of the family back to the parish of settlement where they would be consigned to the workhouse. In 1773 Thomas Renolds left his wife Rebecca alone to care for their three children, Sarah aged five, Fanny aged three and Charles not yet one. They had been married eleven years yet she insisted that she knew nothing of her husband's settlement. Rebecca had been born in Cheshunt and at eighteen had been engaged by Mr Pell who kept a boarding school there, she had worked for him for eighteen months. Thus it was to Cheshunt that the family was removed.[114]

In cases where the parish of settlement was willing to make a reasonable allowance the family was usually allowed to remain. John Bronston, whose settlement was at Islip in Northamptonshire, had been working as a labourer in Enfield for twenty-two years. He died in 1783 and left four children, all born in Enfield. His eldest had gone into service. Three girls remained at home, Sarah aged twelve, Ann aged ten and Mary, a cripple aged six. The widow had been forced to apply to Enfield for relief and therefore faced removal. John Lucas Smart, the vestry clerk, thereupon wrote to Islip; 'Unless you are willing to make a reasonable allowance we must send her and her children to your parish'. Such a proposal must have placed the vestrymen of Islip in a dilemma; it might well prove cheaper to help the family in Enfield than to pay the expense of removal and perhaps to have to maintain them in the workhouse when they were received back.

As in the late twentieth century, the articulate were likely to fare better than those unable to plead their case. Edmund Carter[115] lay very ill in Richmond for a year before he died. During his long illness all he and his wife possessed was spent, and at last Ann his widow was left to shift for herself. It was just before Christmas 1772 that she wrote to John Smart asking whether the gentlemen of Enfield would allow her something. 'Everything being very dear, it is hard for a woman to get her bread without a little help . . . It will be cheaper than taking me home, till I see how things turn out', she writes, and holds out the prospect that she might be able to obtain employment. 'The mistress of the school is very old and, when please God to take her, if I am on the spot I may get that place.' Her eloquent request was at first rejected. The vestry clerk replied 'I am sorry for your misfortunes and must acquaint you that our officers will not grant weekly pensions to any'. She subsisted throughout the rest of the winter by selling off her furniture and belongings, then in June she tried again. She had found employment but had had to take furnished accommodation at £6 a year.'Now if the gentlemen will pay my rent', she pleads, 'I hope I shall be able to get my liven, it is the rent that runs away with what I earn'. The vestry relented.

But parishes were seldom generous unless they were urging some other vestry to pay. Thus the gentlemen of Brinkworth wrote to Enfield much concerned at the deplorable state of Hannah Gardiner, a pauper maintained by Enfield in Brinkworth on a pittance of 1s 6d a week. She was being cared for by her daughter and supported by her brother, but he had a large family of his own. Enfield vestry had proposed that she should be returned. It was felt in Brinkworth that this could not be done without a great deal of expense and some hazard to her life but, if this was insisted upon, the gentlemen of Brinkworth thought it incumbent upon them 'to see it done in as decent a manner as possible (the expense be what it will) as we think a woman in her desperate situation cannot be taken too much care of'. Under this thinly veiled threat the Enfield vestry abandoned the idea of removal, but still refused to increase her pension.[116]

A letter from the Revd Mr Pomfrett at Emberton in Buckinghamshire is illustrative of the generosity which emanated from parishes when calling upon others to pay. He wrote to the Enfield overseers in 1785.

'Gentleman, I have taken the liberty of troubling you on behalf of a family which now and for some time past have been under a state of great affliction and distress'.

Samuel Coleman, his wife and child, had been dependent for some time on his mother; they had now applied for relief. Samuel had been afflicted for two years with ague and fever, and his wife had been 'a poor helpless object for this year past', incapable of moving or feeding herself. Being 'moved by common humanity,' Mr Pomfrett asked what Enfield would grant for their support.

Enfield proved unsympathetic. The overseers thanked the Revd Pomfrett for his letter; for the distresses of Samuel Coleman's family, 'as individuals', they were truly sorry but 'their established rule was to make no allowance to a pauper out of the parish. The family if burdensome was to be sent back to Enfield.

A similar case occurred in Enfield in 1787.[117] Old Sarah Armstrong, who had come to Enfield with her husband almost fifty years before, was now a widow, blind and helpless. Nevertheless she retained the certificate granted to her husband by the parish of Sedburgh (near Darlington) in 1739. The Enfield overseers had given her a little assistance which amounted so far to 12s. They now wrote to claim the money and enclosed a copy of the certificate and with it a warning, signed by the parish apothecary, that no removal should be attempted as so great a journey would inevitably cause the old woman's death. Lest the cost of all this should cause too much nail-biting among the northern overseers the Enfield officers reassured them that, 'She cannot live long, being about eighty years of age and very weak'. After considerable heart searching the overseers of Sedburgh agreed to allow the princely sum of one shilling a week and sought to devise a method of transferring the money free. Perhaps, they said, the Enfield vestry were acquainted with one of the London riders who could be persuaded to carry the money. By July the Enfield vestry had spent £1 15s. This, they suspected, might be difficult to reclaim therefore, to limit any further drain on their resources, they had placed the old woman in the workhouse. The charge there was 2s 6d a week. The Durham overseers expressed themselves satisfied in principle but were deeply shocked by the cost, 'We can have them kept so much cheaper here', they said; nevertheless, having little alternative, they agreed to pay.

Removal of the poor kept the beadle busy. Men, women and children, though they had never asked the parish for a penny in relief, were rounded up and unceremoniously trundled out of town by the beadle. Elizabeth Welchman, a widow, although she had asked for no relief, was removed to Enfield from the parish of St Giles in the Fields in January 1750. That same month Thomas Basson, found wandering and begging at Monken Hadley, and Thomas Eames, his wife and their four-year-old daughter who had asked for relief in Hornsey, were removed to Enfield and consigned to the workhouse. February saw the removal from Enfield to Tottenham of Mary Capp, 'likely to become chargeable', and young Love Matthews was taken from the care of her mother Elizabeth, now the wife of John Sorrell, and removed to Bishops Hatfield. In March, John Bowyer was removed to Corsham in Wiltshire, George Hambleton and his wife to St Michaels, Wood Street, John Hollingworth and his wife to Iver in Buckinghamshire and James Levit to Ashwell in Hertfordshire. The warrants were signed by Pierce Galliard and Merry Teshmaker, justices of peace. None of the victims had asked for relief. During that same year, which was an average one, twenty-four poor souls were removed out of Enfield into the care of overseers and workhouse masters as provided by the system. The same period saw ten people, labelled as paupers, conveyed from various places and deposited in the Enfield workhouse.

Alexander Young the beadle, on 17 October 1773, delivered Ann Hotly to the overseers of the parish of St Luke, Old Street. On 27 October he carried Elias Frennery, his wife Mary and their two-year-old son to St Mary Whitechapel and William Spencer and his family to St Giles Cripplegate. The following day he conveyed Henry Povey, Sarah his wife and their daughter Hannah, aged nine, to Essendon. Alice Broderick with her two children did not wait for the beadle with his order to carry them to Twickenham, but fled.[118]

All poor people were given the status of certificate men by an act of 1795. That is to say they could no longer be removed unless they had in fact sought parish relief. This act, in addition, did something to render removal more humane by forbidding the removal of those unfit to travel.

9. Vagrants

From Elizabethan times onward the intractable problem of vagrancy vexed and worried those with property to protect. Vagrants were liable to arrest either for begging or for wandering and lodging in the open air. Enfield and South Mimms were the parishes to which hundreds of these homeless people, picked up in the neighbourhood of London, were brought before being handed over to the authorities in Hertfordshire in transit to counties further north. The routine of transfer out of Enfield was done by the constable for the Bulls Cross quarter; it was a large-scale operation. In the year 1697, for instance, he moved 496 persons including 135 men, 163 women and 198 children. During the summer months the constable had comparatively few to deal with, but as winter approached the numbers grew and reached a peak in March.[119]

Below are the figures month by month of vagrants moved through Enfield between June 1697 and May 1698

June	40
July	19
August	11
September	26
October	28
November	51
December	47
January	51
February	55
March	92
April	46
May	30

The vagrants were often lodged overnight and then taken on to the next parish out of the county where the constable responsible gave a receipt to acknowledge that yet another parcel of homeless humanity had arrived within his sphere of jurisdiction. The costs of so much journeying at public expense were chargeable, before 1699, on the parish where the vagrant had been arrested, but by an act of that year the county became chargeable and from 1700 the constable for the Bulls Cross quarter was reimbursed by the county treasurer. John Howett, for a long time the constable responsible, was paid £20, for instance, in July 1710 and a further £20 the following September.[120]

Some of these vagrants were so weighed down with children, and with such worldly possessions as they could cling on to, that in twenty-three cases in the year 1697, the constable had to provide a horse and cart and, in a further eighty-two cases, he provided a horse. Among the vagrants moved through Enfield that year there were forty-eight married couples, fifty-nine single women and eighty-two single men. Perhaps the most forlorn among them all were the sixty-two women, without men, and burdened with a hundred and eleven children.

Vagrants who passed through Enfield in the year 1697:

Women with one child	27
Women with two children	25
Women with three children	6
Women with four children	4
Men and women with no children	10
Men and women with one child	12
Men and women with two children	15
Men and women with three children	9
Men and women with five children	2
Men with one child	1
Men with two children	3
Women alone	59
Men alone	82
Seamen	4

Making a total of 496 human souls.

The numbers passing through Enfield remained high into the eighteenth century:

1727	338 persons on 167 passes
1728	425 persons on 210 passes
1729	546 persons on 271 passes
1730	444 persons on 188 passes

The system involved an ever increasing expenditure from the county rate, both in the cost of carrying the vagrants and to pay rewards to those who had apprehended them. There were 1,951 orders to convey vagrants from the north, east and west parts of Middlesex in the year ending July 1757, the cost to the county ratepayers being £678. During that same year rewards had been paid to 498 persons and this added a further £246 to the cost. The extraordinary and growing expense induced the Middlesex sessions to appoint a committee to enquire into ways and means of reducing the expenditure. Vagrant passes, this committee found, had been issued to the casual poor who had committed no act of vagrancy, merely as a means of sending them home on the county rate and avoiding trouble for the parish. More-over the Middlesex magistrates were much perturbed by the attitude of the common people towards begging: they 'have in many instances, by their obstruction, rend-ered it very dangerous for the peace officers to whip sturdy beggars. Your committee think', they went on, 'that the severe whipping of sturdy beggars would be sufficient to drive them out of this county without the expense of a pass . . . if only the objects of real distress were passed . . . it would produce considerable saving.'

The county was able, by eliminating all but legally defined vagrants, to reduce the number of passes issued in the following year from 1,951 to 1,240. Rewards for the apprehension of vagrants had often been paid to beadles though they received wages for this very purpose. Vagrants, it was decided, were to be henceforth moved by the contractor, James Sturgis Adams, at 7s an order. He was to clear the Bridewells and other places of lodgement in London four times each week, twice westward to Colesbrook and Staines and twice northward to South Mimms and Enfield. They were to be lodged in Enfield at threepence per head per day (for not more than three days) and then conveyed in covered carriages across the boundary, towards their places of settlement.[121]

Something of the troubled wanderings of the vagrant population can be seen in the story of Elizabeth Morgan, found lying ill in a barn at Enfield. She was twenty-nine years old and had been born in Billericay. She was illegitimate and her mother had, soon after her birth, been married in Barnet, but not to Elizabeth's father. Four years before her arrest in Enfield, Elizabeth had given birth to an illegitimate daughter fathered by Hugh Suderd of Enfield. The child had been christened, appropriately, Charity Suderd. Their relationship seems to have endured for a number of years which gives it a sad tinge of respectability, for since that time she had had another child by him, baptized Richard and born at Watford. After Elizabeth had been picked up as a vagrant the overseers took action as sanctioned by the law. Richard, aged eight months, was removed in June 1750 to the care of the parish of Watford and his mother was conveyed on a vagrant pass in the opposite direction, to Great Burstead in Essex.

The movement of vagrants was of course not always through or out of the parish; on many occasions they were returned from other places to Enfield. Their stories often reveal a lifetime of poverty. William Miller and Mary his wife were apprehended in January 1752 wandering and begging in South Mimms. He was then twenty-eight years old and claimed to have been born in Highsted in Kent. His family had moved from that parish to Romford where his parents continued to live protected by a certificate from the parish of Enfield. William had inherited his father's settlement and so he was held to be the responsibility of the ratepayers of Enfield and, following their arrest, Miller and his wife were brought home to join the 'family' in the Enfield workhouse.[122]

Bridget Smith, an unmarried woman, was arrested in Whitechapel in 1777 for vagrancy, 'being forced through distress and poverty to lay in the open air not having the wherewithall to pay for any kind of lodging'. Eight years earlier she had been employed by Mr Hughes of Brigadier Hill, boarding and lodging with her master at 30s a year rising by annual increments of 10s while she continued in his employment. She had stayed there for five years; therefore, following her arrest she was sent back to Enfield.

Elizabeth Daniel, apprehended for vagrancy in the parish of St Giles in the Fields in 1780 got her settlement from her grandfather who had once rented a house in Enfield of an annual value of £10 a year. Elizabeth was thirteen years old. The child told the magistrate that she had been without food and shelter and 'forced to wander abroad and lodge in the open air'. Another woman picked up the following year in Hampstead for the crime of being homeless was Dinah Britton, the widow of John Britton. She had been born at Forty Hill and had met her husband while she was serving as a dairymaid for his father there. They had been subsequently married at Reading.[123]

There are many such cases which concern the unfortunate poor, but for the really undeserving poor we have to turn to Mary Ricketts.[124] She was thirty when she was taken into custody. About six years earlier, that would be in 1740, she had worked as a hired hand in Enfield for a gentleman named Moore at South Lodge who paid her £4 a year. She stayed with him for fifteen months but then grew tired and restive and went on to London. She had money and so she took lodgings. There she caught the smallpox, was very ill and for a time blind. When she recovered she went back to Bagshot, her birthplace, but found no work. She lived by begging for three years but, she said proudly, she had never asked for relief (except for small beer). When she could get no lodgings she slept in barns. On 20 January she set off on one of her begging expeditions towards Dorking in company with another young lady called Jane Wells. At this time she was pregnant and had about two weeks to go, time enough, she thought, to get back to Bagshot, though she had made no preparations there or anywhere else. She was passing through the village of Horsel (west of Woking) when her labour began. Seeing an ale-house in the village kept by Widow Causlin she entered and called for a pint of beer and presently gave birth. She had nothing wherewith to pay, either for the beer or for the baby, so the expense fell on the landlady, who was not trying to claim her costs from the parish of Horsel and the parish of Horsel was endeavouring to shift the problem to where it legitimately belonged, the parish of Enfield. Mary, not much concerned with the legal niceties of the problem, left the parishes to settle and once again resumed her trade and travels bearing her latest asset with her.

Notes to Chapter Five

1   GLRO Hearth tax 1665
2   Peter Hardy *Hints for the benefit of the inhabitants of Enfield* 1809
3   GLRO Acc 903. 32A
4   GLRO Acc 903. 21, Vestry order book 1812
5   Vestry order book eg 23D1688, Peter Hardy *Enfield charities* 1834
6   Hardy *Enfield charities*, Vestry order book, Osborne's gift described in GLRO Acc 903. 102
7   Vestry order book Je 1694, Cal. Sess. Books Oct. 1679
8   Vestry order books 1671–1744
9   Vestry order book various entries 1698–1703, GLRO. DRO4. 1. 3, 4, 5
10 Enfield D 1167
11 Vestry order book March 1672
12 GLRO DRO4. 2. 13, Vestry order book 7S 1815
13 GLRO DRO4. 25. 1
14 Vestry order book 1670–1691
15 Vestry order book Ap 1741, Ap 1742
16 GLRO DRO4. 3. 16. 14
17 GLRO DRO4. 8. 47. 76
18 GLRO DRO4. 19. 1
19 Vestry order book *passim*
20 Vestry order book 14 My 1681, 5 Mr 1682
21 Vestry order book
22 Parish register, GLRO OB.SR D 1766
23 Vestry order book 7 Mr 1720
24 GLRO DRO4. 22. 417, 420, 424
25 GLRO DRO4. 3. 16. 71
26 GLRO DRO4. 3. 16. 112
27 Vestry order book Ja 1739
28 GLRO DRO4. 3. 17, DRO4. 3. 16. 23

29 Hardy *Hints* . . .
30 Vestry order book Jl 1800
31 GLRO DRO4. 3. 17. 63, 50, 49
32 GLRO DRO4. 3. 16. 108
33 GLRO DRO4. 1. 2
34 GLRO DRO4. 8. 44
35 GLRO DRO4. 7. 43. 127
36 GLRO DRO4. 7. 43. 64
37 GLRO DRO4. 7. 43
38 GLRO DRO4. 19. 1
39 GLRO DRO4. 19. 1 Au 1772
40 Guildhall OBSP 1785 D 74
41 GLRO DRO4. 8. 44. 65. 1, DRO4. 8. 47. 33
42 GLRO DRO4. 20
43 *ibid.*
44 Vestry order book 1671–1691
45 GLRO DRO4. 20 and Vestry order books
46 GLRO DRO4. 3. 16, 30, 131, 77, 80, 83
47 GLRO DRO4. 20 contains bonds to idemnify churchwardens made by those to
     whom pauper children were apprenticed
48 GLRO DRO4. 3. 17. 36
49 GLRO DRO4. 2. 10. 20
50 GLRO DRO4. 5. 29. 20A
51 GLRO DRO4. 7. 43. 97
52 GLRO DRO4. 12. 62. 7
54 GLRO DRO4. 5. 29. 19
55 GLRO DRO4. 7. 2, 11, 14
56 Vestry order book 2 My 1686, 11 Mr 1688, 7 D 1690 etc
57 Vestry order book 2 S 1688 and passim.
58 GLRO DRO4. 2. 9, Vestry order book, Vestry clerk's accounts
59 GLRO DRO4. 8. 47. 38
60 GLRO DRO4. 12. 62. 91, 19. 2, 25. 2
61 GLRO DRO4. 8. 44. 104
62 Enfield Newspaper cuttings
63 GLRO DRO4. 4. 21
64 GLRO DRO4. 2. 13, 19. 2
65 GLRO DRO4. 4. 21
66 GLRO DRO4. 8. 44 Vestry order book F 1677, S 1682
67 GLRO DRO4. 8. 47. 67
68 Guildhall 9172 134A 58
69 Vestry order book
70 GLRO DRO4. 12. 62. 29A
71 Vestry order book
72 Letter to William Hone 12 Au 1825
73 Vestry order book 21 S 1719, 7 Mr 1720, 3 Mr 1740, parish register
74 GLRO DRO4. 25. 1
75 Vestry order book Je 1739, GLRO DRO4. 1. 2
76 Vestry order book passim and 23 Mr 1743, GLRO DRO4. 25. 1
77 GLRO DRO4. 1. 2
78 E112. 1228. 3141
79 GLRO DRO4. 2. 10
80 GLRO DRO4. 26. 4
81 GLRO DRO4. 4. 21
82 GLRO DRO4. 2. 13
83 F. M. Eden *The State of the Poor* 1797 V. 2 p 419

84 GLRO DRO4. 25. 2
85 GLRO DRO4. 4. 21
86 GLRO DRO4. 26. 4
87 GLRO DRO4. 25. 2
88 GLRO DRO4. 26. 4 (1773)
89 GLRO DRO4. 2. 9, 10. 21
90 Enfield D1167
91 GLRO DRO4. 2. 10. 34, 27, Parl. P 433. 1. 12(2)
92 GLRO DRO4. 3. 17. 38
93 GLRO DRO4. 3. 16. 129, 76
94 Enfield D1115
95 GLRO DRO4. 3. 16. 43
96 Vestry order book
97 GLRO DRO4. 3. 16. 111, 115
98 GLRO DRO4. 3. 16. 118, Acc 305. 5
99 GLRO DRO4. 3. 19
100 GLRO DRO4. 4. 21 (1790)
101 GLRO DRO4. 26. 4
102 GLRO DRO4. 4. 21, 26. 4
103 GLRO DRO4. 9. 49. 20
104 GLRO DRO4. 1. 2
105 GLRO DRO4. 3. 19
106 GLRO DRO4. 3. 16. 76, 17. 24
107 GLRO DRO4. 5. 29, Hardy *Enfield Charities*
108 Settlement certificates in GLRO DRO4. 18. 1, 19. 1, pauper examinations in
     DRO4. 26. 1
109 GLRO DRO4. 3. 16. 59
110 GLRO DRO4. 7. 43
111 GLRO DRO4. 26. 1
112 GLRO DRO4. 2. 10. 45, 32A, 33
113 GLRO DRO4. 7. 43. 126, 8. 47. 1, DRO4. 17
114 GLRO DRO4. 26. 1
115 GLRO DRO4. 19. 2, 24 (N 1778) DRO4. 3. 16, DRO4. 2. 10. 41, 41–45
116 GLRO DRO4. 2. 10. 39
117 GLRO DRO4. 3. 16. 98, 3. 17. 26, 2
118 Removal orders in GLRO DRO4. 1. 2, DRO4. 19. 1, 2
119 Vagrancy in GLRO DRO4. 1. 1, DRO4. 19. 1
120 Cal Mdx Sess Rolls passim. GLRO MJ. SBB 782. 61, 785. 59
121 GLRO MJ. OC 6. 117, MJ.OC 7 Mr 1759
122 GLRO DRO4. 1. 17. 1, 2 DRO4. 19. 1
123 GLRO DRO4. 19. 2
124 GLRO DRO4. 19. 1

Chapter Six
Businessmen, Tradesmen and Farmers

1. Late Seventeenth Century Houses

The 1660s in Enfield saw civilised behaviour extending down the social hierarchy. All the middling sort of people used table cloths and they all had napkins, sometimes several dozen of them, both flaxen and coarse. These were all the more necessary because scarcely anybody seemed to have spoons, not even the schoolmaster, though Helen Deicrowe, despite the disasters which had overtaken her family, still had twelve in 1667.[1] Until later in the century no one apparently had knives or forks. People took their meals in the hall or in the kitchen and ate out of pewter dishes or porringers. The occasional pie plate is mentioned in inventories and the schoolmaster had six pewter platters and four plates. Few of the middling sort ate out of wood. Beer was taken in pewter pots, beakers or cups.

Kitchens were well equipped. Roasting was done on spits turned automatically by lead weights. There were plenty of pots, skillets, brass and copper kettles, frying pans, and almost inevitably there was a mortar and pestle, either of stone or of brass. A flitch of bacon could sometimes be seen hanging among the rafters. They bought their beer by the barrel and stored it in their cellars, which were equipped with beer stands or stalls. Later in the century home breweries became more common.

Most houses belonging to the middling sort contained chairs in plenty. The single hearth house of Thomas James,[2] whose estate amounted to less than £32, had five chairs in the kitchen. Even Richard Betts, a husbandman whose property was valued at only £11, had three chairs in the kitchen and a wicker chair in the bedroom. There were leather chairs, wooden chairs and wicker chairs, and sometimes cushions to relieve the hardness. William Billings, a substantial yeoman, had eight chairs and six stools.

All the middling sort used sheets. Richard Betts,[3] despite his straightened circumstances, had two pairs of flaxen sheets and nine pairs of coarse sheets. Among the goods of Richard Broughton,[4] a yeoman, were eighteen pairs of sheets. One of the best would be used for funerals to cover the body on the way to the churchyard, but it would be brought back. The one used at the burial of Jane Goddard[5] was valued at 7s 6d. Over and above this she had five pairs of flaxen sheets, five pairs of towen sheets, a dozen flaxen napkins, a flaxen table cloth, two flaxen towels, a pair of holland pillowbeers and a cupboard cloth. All the beds, except perhaps those used by servants, were hung around with curtains to keep out the draughts. Window curtains were rare, though John Dunn[6] the blacksmith had a pair in the chamber over the kitchen in 1663. Thomas Bridges,[7] a gardener, had two old window curtains in 1669 and Richard Broughton, a yeoman,[8] had window curtains. Many homes had chamber pots, usually of pewter, and warming pans were not uncommon. The middling sort spent heavily on mourning. Benjamin Venables, an Enfield innkeeper, anxious to ensure that those who attended his funeral were suitably dressed, left £5 each to Ralph Duboys and his wife Mary and to his brother John and his wife Hannah, to buy them mourning.

There were eight-one houses in Enfield in 1665[9] with five hearths or more and of these eighteen were mansions with more than ten hearths. Wood was burned, not coal. Most people had candlesticks of brass or wood. Attention was increasingly paid to personal appearance. Mary Newman[10] had a looking glass, John Billings a smoothing iron, as had Mary Hill. A few owned books; John Dunn,[11] the blacksmith, had a Bible and three other books.[12] Walter Turner had nine books, but he was a Londoner with property in Petticoat Lane. William Holmes[13] the schoolmaster had a parcel of books in his study. Thomas Bridges,[14] a gardener at Bulls Cross, had a Bible.

The reader who may wish to see for himself should accompany Edward Wilford, Thomas Curtis and Francis Neve as they enter on the afternoon of 12 September 1667 into the house where William Hawes, the barber, has recently died.[15] Mr Wilford is a formidable character continually in dispute with either the vicar or the schoolmaster. He lords it at the vestry and resents contradiction. It would be well to remain quiet. Their solemn duty is to take note, list and put a monetary value on the dead man's possessions. Through the door they enter the hall, merely a vestibule furnished with only a table and a pair of andirons in the fireplace. They climb the stairs into the chamber above the parlour. It has a bedstead (a four-poster of course) with green serge curtains and a feather bed, bolster and pillows. This room has a fireplace and there are a table, two cupboards and three chairs. The maids sleep in the room beyond where one bed has striped curtains, a mattress and two pillows and is covered with a rug. There is also a small trundle bedstead and a court cupboard. Each room connects directly with another; there are no corridors. Mr Wilford leads the way into the chamber over the hall. There is a fireplace in this room and before it stand three leather chairs; it has a long table and a striped carpet on the floor. The bedstead is very fine, hung around with striped curtains and roofed over with a wooden panelled tester. It has a feather bed with two blankets, a feather bolster and pillow. The chamber over the shop has a half-headed bedstead, (that is the headboard, usually panelled, rises to about four feet like a modern bedstead and it has no canopy (tester)); on it a flock bed is covered with a rug. The last room upstairs is the chamber over the kitchen which has an old bedstead with green curtains, a feather bed, bolster and pillows, also a trundle bedstead with a flock bed and a blanket.

The party retrace their steps and descend the stairs to enter the parlour. It contains a fireplace with andirons, four leather chairs, a long table and a drawing table. At the back of the hall is the barber's shop, more like a doctor's consulting room for, as well as shaves and haircuts, he probably did minor operations (even ruptures were treated). It contains two chairs and a desk and the dead man's implements. Through another door is the buttery with several tables and wooden ware. The linen is excellent and lavish, twenty pairs of sheets, ten dozen napkins, ten table cloths and other bits and pieces worth £20.

In the kitchen are pewter dishes, porringers and saucers, twenty-one quart, pint and half-pint pots; six plates and three chamber pots and a pair of candlesticks.

There are kettles of copper and brass and three brass skillets. In the fireplace are two tin pots, five spits, a pair of racks, a pair of fire-irons, the fire-shovel and tongs, a frying-pan, a gridiron and a chafing-dish. Below there is a dripping-pan. There are two tables and some wicker chairs. The spit is operated by leaden weights. In the cellar is a powdering tub (in which the meat was salted), beer stands and washing tubs.

The barber had also been a farmer, mainly arable. There is wheat in the barn not yet threshed (half way through September) worth £18, as well as twenty-five bushels of wheat remaining from the previous harvest. Also in the barn are oats worth £9 not yet threshed, peas worth 30s and hay worth £10. There are three cows and two hogs and, in the stable, five working horses and two colts. He has two long carts, a wheelbarrow, a plough and two harrows. There is wood in the barn for fuel and a pile of dung in the yard.

Orledge Cordell who witnessed the will was the local scrivener. He was responsible for writing most of the wills in the parish in the 1670s.

There were a number of professional men among the middling sort. Robert Rowe[16] was described as 'surgeon of Enfield'. His books and his instruments of 'chirurgery' were stored in a desk in the study, which was equipped with two mortars and pestles, an oil press, a rose mill, a still and an alembic (an antique distilling apparatus). The study was adorned with 'old hangings'. His London house was at Covent Garden where the lease was worth £30. When he died in 1670 the outstanding debts owing to him, but thought to be retrievable, amounted to £300; his total estate was valued at £426.

A sad contrast was James Blowes,[17] the Edmonton surgeon, who died early in the year 1707. Everything within his house and surgery was in a deplorable state of dilapidation. His bedroom contained 'an old feather bed, two sorry blankets, seven sorry old chairs . . . and three old pillows'. In the garret were an 'old little feather bed, two old flock bolsters and a pair of sorry curtains'. The state of the surgery must have inspired less than confidence in the minds of his patients. There were a few salves, pottles and pots and glasses . . . and a 'few sorry old razors', but he displayed the surgeon's arms and had his pole outside the premises. His possessions were valued at only £16.

Matthew Patteson was an instrument maker and sufficiently well-off to be able to promise his two daughters £60 each after his death. He died in 1685, but a branch of the family, the Parnells, continued to function as instrument makers in Enfield into the eighteenth century.[18]

2. Late Seventeenth Century Tradesmen

Such industry as existed in post-Restoration Enfield was concerned with the processing of the products of the land; the knacker, the butcher, the fellmonger, the tanner, the cordwainer, the saddler and collar-maker; spinners, weavers, tailors; the miller, the baker, the brewer, the inn-keeper; the sawyer, the carpenter, the wheelwright. Only one step removed were the blacksmith, the brickmaker and the builder.

An examination of the wills made by Enfield men in the late seventeenth century suggests that tanners and other workers in leather had replaced maltmen as the leading traders in the parish. Nine wills have survived which were made by Enfield

Tanners Hall, Green Street, beyond the White Horse.

tanners in the period from 1660 to 1700, also those of a farrier, a glover, a knacker, a horse-collar-maker and three cordwainers.

Leather was a widely used material in the seventeenth century, for boots and shoes, saddles and cart saddles, horse-collars and harness, bellows and buckets, and wearing apparel and gloves for men and women. The industry nationally was second only to the cloth trade. Enfield was well placed for the making of leather. There were ample supplies of hides from the slaughterhouses which supplied meat to London and easy access to three thousand shoe-makers in the City. Adequate supplies of oak bark were available from Enfield Chase and from the coppices in the western half of Edmonton, the area now known as Southgate. Water could be obtained from a number of little streams flowing eastward through the parish towards the River Lea. According to Dr Burnby (J. Burnby *Drovers and Tanners of Enfield and Edmonton* p. 21) two leather searchers were appointed at the Enfield court leit in the late seventeenth and early eighteenth centuries; it was their duty to test the leather and certify its quality.

Examination of the surviving inventories of five local tanners show that two of them engaged in farming but even for these the value of their tanning enterprises amounted to over sixty per cent of their total assets. Among the other three tanners the proportion of assets employed in tanning ranged from eight-two to ninety-six per cent of their total estates.

John Spencer had a small business, probably in Green Street. He was a widower and if he had any children they were dead before 1665. His inventory, taken that year, shows that he had been an unostentatious man. His total household goods were worth only £2 16s, his clothes a mere £2. His money was invested in his work. He had hides to the value of £60 and two loads of bark stored in his barn, worth £5. His little working nag to carry him and his wares, with his tools, made up the remainder of his worldly goods, valued in all at £72 16s. Some of the tanhouses in

Green Street seem to have been small. Elizeus Wiberd the tanner mortgaged five tenements in Green Street in 1671, with their 'tanhouses, barns, stables, outhouses . . .' all for £100. One of these he occupied himself.[19]

In a much bigger way of business was the tanner William Dodd[20] who lived at Bulls Cross. His was a large house of the old type built around the hall. A parlour and a chamber lay at one end, a kitchen and a buttery at the other. There were bedrooms above these and a loft over the hall. The hall was furnished with a long table and 'seven great joined stools'. There was a leaf table covered with a table cloth, a press cupboard and a rush chair for the master before the great fireplace. A wealth of pewter was displayed, a musket and a silver bowl. The fireplace in the kitchen backed onto the one in the hall. The kitchen gleamed with brass, six kettles great and small, a pan, three skillets, a chafing-dish, candlesticks, a scummer, and a pestle and mortar. There was a table and form, a couple of stools and a wicker chair. A warming pan provided some comfort in the unheated bedrooms.

In the warm dry loft over the hall he stored his corn; even at the end of June (1666) he had plenty left to last until the harvest. He was a farmer as well as a tanner which was the old way of managing things. His corn ripening in the fields was worth £18; he also kept four heifers and two cows worth £12; there was a cheese press in the buttery. He had no other livestock except five horses and a pig. More than half his capital was invested in the 240 hides on which he was working which, with the bark and his tools, were worth £140 out of a total estate of £230. Money owing to him amounted to £10.

William Dodd died in 1666 'being well in years and crazy in body' and left a wife, a grown-up son and daughter and two younger children, Henry and Alice. Henry was to receive £100 by his will; Alice was to receive £50 and the interest was to be accumulated with her capital until she came of age. His eldest daughter Susanna was comfortably married to Edward Bridgeman and living in a substantial house with five hearths in Edmonton. She would presumably have received her portion as a dowry. His 'well-beloved wife' Alice was given only £5 and must have been provided for in some other way. William, his eldest son, was to receive the bulk of the property and would carry on his father's business.

The tanner Samuel Sare was a bachelor whose total estate was valued at £83 in 1669. It was made up of a hundred hides valued at £70, four loads of bark at £10 and his gelding at 30s. His clothes were worth a mere 30s. The inventory had been drawn up by the Curtis brothers, Richard and Thomas who were both tanners, and it seems possible that they were engaged in some sort of joint enterprise since Samuel Sare seems to have owned no household goods.[21]

Wills tell us little about the day to day work of the tanners but are further evidence of the prosperity of the trade. William Archer who died in 1662 was burdened with seven children, yet he felt able to provide £40 for his eldest son, £20 each for two other sons, while his four daughters were to receive £10 each.[22] Another prosperous tannery was that of William Saunders[23] which came at his death in 1675 to his son Francis. William also proposed to provide £60 each for two younger sons and his unmarried daughter from the residue of his estate.

Many prosperous Enfield tanners invested their profits in real estate. Richard Mugg had a number of properties; a new cottage and a shop at Tottenham, premises recently purchased at Bounds Green and an alehouse at Edmonton.[24] The tanner William Hunsdon had property in many parts of Enfield in 1690. The house where he lived was in Green Street; he also owned two houses at the Woodside (Chase Side Enfield) in one of which lived John Field the butcher, two houses in

Mill field, a dwelling house at Fresillwater (Freezywater), as well as the Rose and Crown at Enfield Highway where the landlord was Robert Young. The proceeds of the property would provide for his son Thomas and for his grandchildren by his dead son William. James Wyberd, describing himself as being 'in years and something crazy in body', had also invested much money in the purchase of freehold property. Since he had no sons or daughters alive, he left the bulk of it to his wife.[25] The term 'crazy in body' seems to have been in common usage in the latter half of the seventeenth century; the reader will remember that it was also used to describe William Dodd's physical condition.

Much of the leather made by the Enfield tanners must have been sold in London, but there were also shoemakers, collar-makers and harness-makers using leather locally. Four wills survive of shoemakers in the area in the forty years following the Restoration. It takes an effort of imagination to picture Abraham Burnaby's[26] shop in the Market Place with the cows, bullocks and calves, 'being sixteen in number', in the yard behind. The shop was used for work rather than retail and contained his lasts and other working tools. There was a hall, kitchen and a cellar, with bedrooms over the shop and over the hall. Abraham was also a farmer; he had an old dray plough and a pair of harrows in the shed, and a long cart and a dung cart. He held, by lease, arable and meadow elsewhere in the parish and in his barn there, known as Bostock's barn, he had hay and wheat stored to the value of £9. He had two-and-a-half acres of wheat growing, worth £5. There is no mention of barley or oats but the inventory was taken early in February and it would not then have been sown. He died at the end of December 1663 leaving much of his property to his son-in-law who was to find a pension of £8 a year for the widow, to be paid quarterly. His servant, Elizabeth Bettes, was to have his 'youngest red calf'.

Few tradesmen were dependent solely upon their trade. Stephen Goddard[27] called himself a cordwainer (ie shoemaker), but he might more appropriately have distinguished himself as the landlord of the Swan at Ponders End and the owner of orchards, gardens, barns, stables (and silver spoons). Having no sons or daughters he left the property to his wife during her life and then to his nephew, Nicholas Goddard. Nicholas was to receive an immediate legacy of £50. Stephen's other bequests in money amounted to a further £60 and included 40s with which to buy bread for the poor of Ponders End and Green Street. It was to be dispensed by his widow, at the Swan, upon the next St Stephen's day (most appropriately) following his death.

The shoemaker Matthew Billings[28] could not be considered poor for he owned property other than that in which he lived. On his death in 1684 it was to go to his wife and after her death to his eldest daughter Hannah. The younger daughter was to have £30 which would be paid to her at the rate of 40s a year following her mother's death.

Leather was also used for the making of horse collars and harness. George Knevett the collar-maker, who was buried in 1682, was another property owner for as well as his house and shop on Enfield Green, he let a house and orchard at Whitewebbs to Daniel Brittridge a husbandman. He seems to have prospered very well after 1665, for at that time he had been so poor that he had been exempted from payment of the hearth tax.[29]

Cloth exports nearly doubled between 1660 and 1700, yet the overseas trade must have been but a fraction of the home trade. Inventories show that the houses of the middling sort were stored with vast quantities of good quality textiles and linen from the sale of which considerable profits must have arisen, yet some parts of the trade still employed the poor, especially for spinning, and parishes distributed materials as a form of poor relief. Only one will made by an Enfield weaver is recorded in the London Commissary Court, a fact which perhaps indicates the poverty of the trade even before the mechanisation of weaving during the Industrial Revolution. The weaver in question was Roger Addams, and he was certainly not poor.[30] He lived in a large house (eight hearths) at Ponders End and his will of 1674 shows that he had recently purchased land from Edward Wilford, although he had to borrow £18 from his daughter to pay for it; she died at the same time as her father. Roger left two sons, the eldest being an apprentice, and two daughters.

Robert Tapper,[31] an Enfield tailor, made his will in 1658 but did not die until 1682. At the time of writing his will he had purchased two acres of forest land at Woodford where he was building an imposing house with a gatehouse. He owned the dwelling where he lived in Enfield as well as the one next door which had an orchard attached and in which dwelt his youngest daughter. John Joyner, also a tailor, rented his premises on Enfield Green from Joshua Wright the Quaker to whom he left, when he died in 1672, his great Bible and his morning gown; to Joshua's grandchild Sarah Hedger he left a cupboard and £5. His books he gave to Susan the wife of Thomas Flendall. His lands and his goods he bequeathed to a brother-in-law in Mepshall in Hertfordshire, and £30 to a brother-in-law in Shillington in Bedfordshire. He also left 20s to the poor of Enfield. Matthew Smith[32] was a farmer as well as a tailor. It is difficult to determine just how prosperous he was, but he was able to leave £10 which he intended should be used to set his son up in business when he had completed his apprenticeship.

Beer was supplied throughout the parish by brewers like Robert Prentice[33] at the King's Head in the Market Place. His brewery was equipped (in 1678) with a copper, three coolers, a hand-mill and other vessels and utensils, all valued at £7 13s 4d. He also farmed on a small scale, had three acres sown with wheat (it was November) and wheat, oats and hay in his barn worth £15 and five pigs in his pigsty.

Francis Rosse held the George on a twenty-one year lease at an annual rent of £15. His landlord was Edward Heath, a citizen and fishmonger of London though he belonged to an Enfield family long associated with the George. Heath agreed to sell the house in 1666 to Thomas Taylor of Enfield, gentleman, for £174, but before the sale could be completed he received a better offer from a London brewer.[34]

Shambles for twenty-four butchers were set up in Enfield Market Place. Fourteen wills made by Edmonton butchers survive from the years 1660 to 1700 but only three from Enfield. Francis Parker[35] at Bulls Cross combined the trades of butcher and brewer and also kept a public house which is described in an inventory of 1666. There was a parlour, but it was used only as a bedroom, having no fireplace and no chairs. There was a kitchen with a settle bed, a long buttery and a milk-house. There were two bedrooms and a loft over the kitchen. In the slaughterhouse were scales and weights, a cleaver, a block with ropes and a malt mill. He also had a brew-house. Downstairs in the cellar were the barrels and beer-stalls. He kept two little carts and a water cart in the yard, and had a store of wood there and a dunghill, and there he kept his grindstone. He was owed money that seemed unlikely ever to be collected; it amounted to £29 though his total assets were only £76.

A more wealthy butcher at the end of the century was Edward Rookes[36] who made a will on 19 December 1702 and died on 7 January 1703. His appraisers took a somewhat derogatory view of his property; even the livestock they listed as 'three poor old battered horses and an old cow'. He had hopeful and hopeless debts amounting to £100 from a total valuation of £140, but a glance at his will shows that he had already provided for his wife Mary and his son Edward by a deed of settlement. His daughter Mary was to have £100 from what remained.

The knacker Robert Empson[37] lived in Green Street. The house had a parlour, hall and kitchen on the ground floor, three chambers on the first floor and a garret above. He used the skins of slaughtered horses to make horse collars, pannets and saddles which he sold from Green Street and from his little shop on Enfield Green. He carried out all the processes himself, having tan-pits behind the house in Green Street. His home, though large, was poorly furnished, the total value of its contents being only £14, the remainder of his lease was worth £5.

Wills and inventories give evidence of three blacksmiths working throughout this period in Enfield. John Dunn[38] died in January 1663. He worked full-time at his trade, and did no farming. His stock and tools were valued at £22 5s out of a total inventory of £63. His kitchen served as a living room with a long table, a form and a bench and five little chairs. A buttery and his shop were on the ground floor; there were two chambers above and a garret. The shop contained articles ready made, two cart tyres, sprigs (headless or almost headless nails) and horse shoes, also nine hundredweight of new iron and some old iron. He was a literate man for he had two Bibles and three other books.

Thomas Church,[39] another smith, left his house, barn, stable and shop to his wife Anne in 1682, but it had all to be sold to pay his debts. The smith Edward Randall bequeathed his house at Forty Hill to his daughter Hannah, wife of Ephraim Greene. It had a barn, stable, orchard and a close of pasture attached. The hall and the chamber above, with the furnishings therein, were to be reserved for the use of the widow. His son-in-law was to pay her an annuity of £6 a year and to provide her with two loads of firewood every year. Hannah was given the tenement in Parsonage Lane and a close of pasture which had been lately ploughed near the Chase at Phipps Hatch. Because the property was mortgaged he required that his trusted friends Joshua Wright and John Archer of Enfield, a gardener, should sell the two tenements which stood together at Phipps Hatch and use the money to pay Mr Parish the remainder of the mortgage.

Brickmaking had been carried on in Enfield since mediaeval times. A case in Chancery in 1660 shows that Arnold Maynesborowe had had a flourishing business. Evidence concerning a disputed will relates that before 1653 he had purchased two acres of 'brick clamps' from Stephen Barnes. His profits from brickmaking had been invested in houses and land, both in Chingford and in Enfield.[40]

Henry Ducke[41] an Edmonton brickmaker had twenty thousand bricks in stock when he died in 1667 and ten thousand roof tiles. The scale of his operation can be judged from the fact that he had fifteen hundred fagotts ready for use. He had two old carts, four horses and hay worth £5 to keep them fit for the heavy work. He did no farming. His stock and tools were worth £57, his household goods only £13. The workshop must have taken up most of the ground floor, for the only other room was the kitchen. There were two bedrooms upstairs.

Bricks were produced locally in considerable numbers at 12s to 14s a thousand and roof tiles at 18s, plus the cost of the carriage. Bricklayers were paid 2s a day, though a master craftsman like Robert Pratt earned 2s 6d; his man had 20d, his labourer 16d or 18d, though the usual payment for a labourer in the years after

The Hermitage, Forty Hill.

the Restoration was 14d. His boy was paid 10d a day.[42] Thus building wages in Enfield had doubled in a hundred years, but this was not enough to compensate for inflation.

Master carpenters do not appear from their wills to have been among the most prosperous tradesmen in the village until towards the end of the century. Oliver Shepherd, the carpenter (probate 1693), had purchased a large messuage in Chase Side Enfield which he had converted into three dwellings to house his two daughters and his wife. The carpenters employed by such men were paid 15d or 20d a day. Glaziers were kept busy replacing quarries in the windows of the church and even more often at the school. The work proved profitable for John Kirby the casement maker in his little shop in the Market Place.

The end of the seventeenth century saw an increase in building and a consequent enhancement in the fortunes of the master builders. The quality of Edward Helder's work has already been described, and the high standard of Enfield tradesmen can be seen in the local houses which have survived from this period, such as the Hermitage and Worcester Lodge at Forty Hill and in photographs of such houses as Churchbury House, formerly in Baker Street. Giles Knight, a master bricklayer, doing repairs on the house where Roger Piggott lived, paid himself 2s 6d a day, his bricklayer 1s 8d a day, his labourer 1s 4d, and John his boy a shilling.

Some people earned a living by turning their hands to whatever came along. Robert Archer described himself as a carter and ploughman, 'and doth any other country work'. His wife Sarah helped out too, and his son. For a day's work for Mr Dashwood Robert charged 1s 2d and for the use of his horse a shilling a day. His boy was able to plough and for this Mr Dashwood paid 6d a day. Carrying work by cart was charged for according to the load and the distance; for taking five and a half quarters of barley to Mr Hilyards he received 8s 3d, for six and a half quarters 9s 9d, for four bushels of bran 5s, for five bushels of malt 15s. His

Worcester Lodge, Forty Hill.

Churchbury House, formerly in Baker Street.

wife, for the work she did in Mr Dashwood's house, got £2 10s and in addition for brewing for him eight times she received 8s; for knitting stockings for him he paid her 3s. Mr Dashwood paid in kind not cash, letting Archer have two loads of hay worth £2 15s, half a quarter of barley worth 10s, six trusses of hay at 1s 3d a truss, and three weeks grass (ie pasture) for two cows and a colt valued at 9s. Sarah Archer received a gown, a petticoat and a hat. Taking all these transactions into consideration, Robert Archer claimed that Mr Dashwood still owed him £1 14s.[43]

The parish registers from July 1702 until July 1706 set down the trades of the parishioners, and these records must encompass a good proportion of the working population. The textile trades are represented by a woolcomber, seven weavers, two fullers, seven tailors, John Halstid a laceman, and Mr Samuel Spragg and George Greenaway silkmen. Only five tanners are named but ten shoemakers, also John Norton a heel-maker, and two makers of horse collars. Four bakers are listed. Christopher Hill was the only one engaged in the once predominant malt trade and John Hill was the only brewer named. There was a distiller, and Richard Thredder was a cooper, and of course there were a number of victuallers. The registers name eight butchers and John Etherington, a coffee man. Not a single brick-maker is listed, but there are nine bricklayers and two glaziers; no plumbers are mentioned, no thatchers but eight carpenters. Twelve blacksmiths are listed, and John Mackeriss a whitesmith calling himself on occasions an instrument maker, of which trade there were no fewer than six in the parish. Thurston Ford earned his living as a brazier, Robert Batterton as a clockmaker. There was one sword-maker, a tinker and a patternmaker. Transport in the pre-turnpike era provided little employment, only two coachmen, just one badger, an ostler and a wheel-wright. There were two barbers and a periwig maker and most surprisingly there were seven seamen listed. The parish registers in these four years name 123

The George about 1890.

tradesmen, twenty farmers, seven gardeners, two shepherds, 149 labourers and twelve domestic servants.

3. Local Businessmen and London Merchants

Peter Reeve was a Quaker shopkeeper, a man of wide interests and enterprise who died early in the year 1703. His premises were small but well furnished, three chambers on the first floor, the kitchen, parlour and shop below. The parlour boasted two looking-glasses and a chimneypiece, the kitchen a silver tankard and six silver spoons. In the cellar were stored half a barrel of soap, five casks of tobacco, a chaldron and a half (ie 38 cwt) of coal, and two hundredweight of tallow. He also kept his horse there (presumably it had ground level access at the back) and some hay and wood for the fires.

His shop sought to make available everything needed by the more prosperous classes in the village, only excluding those things provided by the bakers, butchers, tailors and blacksmiths. In stock were seventeen dozen candles, a bushel and a half of oatmeal, two dozen black links (a torch of pitch and tow used to light the way, there being no street lighting), thirty mops, six beehives, thirty-three pounds of cheese, twelve pounds of butter, one and a quarter hundredweight of sugar, twenty-eight pounds of currants and raisins, and nutmegs, cloves and mace, French barley, pearl barley, ginger, jamaica pepper, fenegrew, sweet almonds, liquorice powder, carroway seeds, wafers, ellewinpaine, stone and pewter blue, frankincense (used as incense), alum, honey and beeswax, white starch, rice, writing paper, red herrings, dried sprats, corks, Burgundy pitch, bed cords, thread of all kinds and small cord, oil and vinegar, vargess,[44] gartering, caddis (a worsted ribbon), gunpowder, whipcord, curtain rings, brushes and loaf sugar.

Not only was he a shopkeeper but he was a trader, trading to Maryland. He judiciously divided his ventures, holding a thirty-second part in the voyage of the 'William and Jacob', burden 130 tons which was worth £15, and a sixteenth part in the 'Recovery', burden 130 tons worth £25. He had money owing to him in Maryland amounting to £344, and £52 was owed to him in Rotterdam.[45]

The role played by women in early eighteenth century society has sometimes been underrated. The tentacles of Hannah Sells reached into many homes in the neighbourhood. She was the landlady at the George in Enfield Town which she rented from Mrs Wyburd at £30 a year. Apart from running the house, she was both pawnbroker and money-lender to the village and beyond. Many of the goods in her hands at the time of her death in 1725 were undoubtedly the unredeemed pledges of her less fortunate customers. There were seven gold rings, two rings with stones, a diamond rose ring worth £3, a silver watch, a case of instruments, a tortoiseshell snuff box and some old broken silver. She made loans by bond and by book as well as in return for goods pledged.

Larger sums of money had to be secured by a mortgage on property. Such transactions were often registered by collusive suits in Chancery or Exchequer. Bernard Halfpenny of Lincolns Inn, Esq (the family of Halfpenny had lived in Enfield over the previous two centuries) described as a 'gentleman of plentiful fortune and very good character', applied to Mrs Sells in 1717 for the loan of £100 and offered a house in St Clement Danes as security. The money was repayable in one year at five per cent interest. The principal remained unpaid after five years and Mrs Sells took the precaution of ensuring the enrollment of the transaction in the Exchequer Court.[46]

Her executors had collected debts of more than a £1000 in the months following her death and only £67 remained outstanding. The undertaker had to be paid, his bill was £33, there were parish duties at the funeral of 7s 8d and expenses on that occasion for wine, beer and fowl for the mourners, a most modest repast which cost only £1 18s. Her poor rate was due at 18s 9d, which puts the burden of the poor in a proper perspective, and a highway rate at 6s. She owed 15s for window tax and £2 2s for the King's tax.

Many Enfield tradesmen had to await payment for goods supplied or services rendered to Hannah Sells. Money was owed to Mr Smith the baker, Mr Welchman the bricklayer, Mr Sams the carpenter, Mr Williams for tobacco, Mr Crowder the soap-maker, Mr Blackwell the glazier and his brother the carpenter, Mr Freebody the corn chandler, Mr Batson the wine cooper, Curry Comb* for grooming horses, Mrs Hodge and Mr Rider the chandlers, Mr Ibbott, Mr Phillips and Mr Golfe the butchers, Mr Wheeler for gravel, Mr Ganney for oats, Mrs Beele the draper, Mrs Dutton for small wares, Mr Allen the vintner (£16 10s), Mr Mackworth the sawyer, Mr Waller the smith, Mr Pulleston the distiller for strong waters, Mr Champion for arrack (a spirit made in the East from coco or rice), Mr Linney the paviour, Mr Stevens the apothecary (£4 9s), Mrs Flanders at Ponders End Mill, Mr Feast the butcher and Mr Jefferies the glazier. William her son took over at the George. There were ten butts of beer in the cellar worth £45.

The market continued to flourish in the early eighteenth century. It was leased in 1721 to the existing tenant, Robert Simonds, for forty-one years at a rent of £25 a year for the first seventeen years and at £40 annually for the remainder of his term. Robert Simonds obviously anticipated that the market would remain profitable. It was certainly active for a time. In a case among the Old Bailey records we catch a glimpse of Enfield Market Place at eleven o'clock at night on Saturday 10 June 1732. Tom How, one of the market traders, was standing at the door of the King's

*a nickname surely

The market-house, the stocks and the north front of the Manor House ('Palace') about 1790.

The Kings Head in the Market Place.

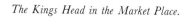

Head strapping his packs onto his horse while the ostler stood by holding a candle. At that moment there rode into the dim circle of candlelight a man on a black horse. He called for a pint of beer, looked full into the face of Tom How who returned the stare, then, without waiting for the beer, he turned his horse around, muttered that he was going to Dr Wilson's (he lived at Redlingtons in Silver Street), and rode off. Tom How and the ostler waited apprehensively and when he failed to return they hastened into the King's Head to warn the market folk. 'There's Will Shelton come' says Tom, 'and if we don't leave our money here we shall be robbed'. He had taken £6 that day which, in fact, belonged to his master and which he now left with the landlord, putting only 3s into his pocket. All the others, being warned, did likewise and Tom How and Ben Johnson, bidding goodnight to the company, set off homeward together. They had reached Forty Hill when Will Shelton appeared out of the shadows. He bade them deliver, and addressed How by name. 'Give's yer bag, Tom,' says he, 'for you have taken money today at the market'. 'Indeed master' Tom replied 'I have got but 3s'. 'No Tom' says he 'you must have made but a bad market'. 'Why to tell you the truth' says Tom 'I left the rest of my money behind me'. 'Well then give's the three shillings'. And so Tom handed over what he had.[47]

Robert Simonds,[48] the landlord at the King's Head, held the lease of the market at this time. He kept fifty pairs of trestles with boards to be set out on Saturdays, also a beam and scales with 114lb of iron weights and 43lb of lead weights to ensure fair trading.

An advertisement for two houses in Chase Side,[49] published in a newspaper in 1765, offers the proximity of Enfield Market as an inducement to would-be buyers, yet Lysons writing in 1791 speaks of an attempt to revive it in 1778 which had met with no success. A committee of the trustees inspected the Market Place in November 1784 and found the whole of the outside to be in need of repair. The lease was due to be renewed but the tenant, Thomas Vaughan, was reluctant to undertake the repairs. No new lease having been agreed, in January 1786 Vaughan wrote to the vestry clerk declining to have anything further to do with the Market Place.[50] He nevertheless finally agreed on terms in 1789 at a reduced rent of £12 a year. He was to spend £50 over the ensuing five years on repairs to the houses and shops. Small temporary stalls were to be set up on fair days and market days. He was to clear and carry away all the dirt and rubbish made by the market 'on the afternoon of the same day'. This suggests that only a morning market was intended. Whether the market did re-establish itself at this time is doubtful. Lysons writing only two years later states that it had long been discontinued.

The Market Place by 1813 was in a sad condition. The old market cross had been removed in about 1810 and despite a threat of legal action from the trustees Thomas Vaughan would do nothing to replace it. Nor would he carry out his contract to repair the houses and shops. Mr Patman was engaged in building the new cross in January 1820[51].

The fairs at Enfield were still held regularly as was the Bush Fair at Southgate on the edge of Enfield Chase. This was a cattle fair. The inspectors of distempered cattle attended there in September 1752, when disease was prevalent, to prevent any horned cattle being exposed for sale.[52]

There were small dilapidated shops on every street like that of James Elsom, a butcher, who figured in an Old Bailey case in 1730 when Richard and Martha Dean were indicted for stealing his meat. The evidence was proffered by Thomas Hancock, Elsom's errand boy aged twelve. Twenty-five pounds of mutton worth

7s, forty-five pounds of beef worth 10s and a cloth coat valued at 15s, were missing. The boy said that Dean had asked him how he could get into Elsom's and he, knowing the ways of the shop, told him that if he shook the door at the bottom it would open. Dean promised him 2d but had no half-pence about him and young Thomas never got the money. The Deans were taken before a magistrate where the boy gave sworn testimony against them. He had gone only a few yards from the magistrate's house, however, when he began to have misgivings. He asked the constable if kissing the book was swearing and when told that it was, he said he thought swearing had been to swear as fast as he could and then he could have out-sworn them all. In consideration of this and of the general ill-character of this witness, the Deans were acquitted.[53]

William Cockett, who was a shoemaker in Enfield, told how he had shut up his shop on the night of 4 December 1796 before going to bed. He was awoken by his neighbours at seven o'clock the following morning. They informed him that he had been burgled. The shop, attached to the house, was built of wood. 'There was a board taken out big enough for a man to put his arm in', he said. He had lost forty yards of Irish cloth worth 2s a yard and ten yards of 'huswife' cloth worth 2s 6d a yard. William Cockett and the constable caught up with the two thieves later that morning; so weighed down were they that they had gone only as far as Tottenham.[54]

The village was also served by pedlars. A poor man, says a newspaper of 1774, 'who sells lemons and oranges about the country' was set upon by two ruffians on his way across Enfield Chase. They knocked him down and robbed him of 13s 8d but because he pleaded that they had left him with nothing to support his wife and family they returned to him the odd eighteenpence.[55]

An ever increasing number of Londoners held property in Enfield which might be used as security for loans required for their business transactions. Enfield property might also be used to make provision for widows and children. Some families had members who chose to move to London to transact business and who subsequently returned to the parish.

John Oneley had a goodly house at Ponders End and seems to have traded in millinery. Illness was the cause of his losses, a lameness of such severity that he 'could neither go nor stand', just at the time when the greatest part of his stock was 'abroad in customers' hands'. Because of this he was forced to seek credit from Mary Hebbe, a milliner on the Royal Exchange with whom he had dealt over many years. He at length ran up a debt of nearly £200 and was forced to use his property at Ponders End for security, but on the understanding that the milliner would be prepared to wait for payment. The property comprised the house, the garden and an orchard of eight acres. Once, however, she had secured the mortgage the milliner required the sale of part of the property so that payment could be made towards the debt. Over the ensuing years the debt increased and by the year 1672 John Oneley was dead and the debt remained. Mary Hebbe had secured possession of his 'great house' and the widow complained in the Court of Chancery that through the cunning machinations of the milliner she and her son would be cast out and become a burden upon the parish.[56]

William Welch, citizen and vintner, but by trade a brewer, used his property in Enfield as security for a loan of £50 in 1676. His premises consisted of a house, a brewhouse, three barns, outhouses and a garden, together with four acres in the common fields, all let to John Archer a gardener at £12 a year. The loan was not repaid and four years later the mortgage was assigned to Archer who now retained the rent to himself. When William Welch died in 1694 his property remained in Archer's hands. William Welch, his only son, had been far away beyond the seas on His Majesty's service for seven years and did not return home until 1699. He at once claimed his property and demanded of Archer an account of his profits over the previous twenty years. At this juncture however he died leaving the premises and the problem to his wife, who brought an action in the Court of Chancery.

Another Londoner with a country house in Enfield was James Angell, citizen and fishmonger. He died in 1638 and left this property to his wife Anne. Anne, apparently not wishing to live in Enfield, came to an agreement with the executor of her husband's will that he should sell the property. It was sold for £350 and the money was put out at interest which was to be paid to the widow. The principle, it was stipulated, should be kept intact for James Angell's four children when they came of age and any loss through bankruptcy should be made good out of the interest.[57]

Many Enfield families moved into the parishes nearer London and carried on business there while they retained their property in Enfield. Such was the Mansborough family which had been in Enfield for centuries. John Mansborough moved to Whitechapel. He was another who became enmeshed in debt. Early in the year 1663 he borrowed £140 at six per cent (and later a further £40) from Christopher Millnes citizen and baker, on the security of two houses in Enfield. Mansborough defaulted on repayment and Millnes in consequence obtained possession of, and proposed to sell, the property in order to secure immediate repayment. Mansborough however thwarted his ambitions by warning all potential purchasers that their title might prove invalid since he intended to redeem the mortgage. He finally managed to clear the debt upon payment of £248.

Borrowing was becoming safer and easier, for interest rates had fallen throughout the seventeenth century. When Robert Tunbridge, an Enfield yeoman, applied in 1609 to Leonard Hodges of Shoreditch, 'a man that did lend money upon interest' to borrow £10, he was charged ten per cent per annum and had to assign over the lease of his house and lands in Enfield with twelve years yet to run. He claimed that this was worth £10 a year after paying rents and charges. Robert was unable to find the £11 at the end of twelve months and had to apply for an extension. This was promised by Hodges and in an endeavour to secure a better return on the land, Robert spent £4 on compost. But soon afterwards Hodges had him arrested and committed to the prison of the Counter in Wood Street. While he was a prisoner his wife and children were turned out of the house, his household goods were taken, and the lease was sold for £60.[58]

The common law had formerly taken a strict view of any infringement of the terms of a mortgage; one day late might result in the loss of the property pledged as security. Chancery however became kinder and by the second half of the seventeenth century the right of the mortgagor to redeem his land was established. Short term mortgages sometimes persisted for generations and where forfeitures did occur, grandchildren might sue to retrieve property lost by their grandparents. Oliver Hodge mortgaged three acres of meadow in Southmarsh to William Curle, in 1597, for £35 10s; the principle with interest was to be repaid within three years. The only income from the meadow was the value of the hay crop, for the meadow lay in the common marsh and once the hay had been gathered in it had to be thrown open to the cattle of all tenants. Nevertheless the original owners claimed that it was of great value. When the loan was not repaid the meadow fell into the hands of William Curle. After his death it was held by his son Henry who died in 1650 and left it to his widow, Ann. She was old and lived ten miles away in London, which circumstances provided a favourable opportunity for William Hodge, the grandson of Oliver, to retrieve the family land. Though the meadow was leased by William Chawkley, a local farmer, Hodge gathered the hay himself and carried it away claiming in the Court of Chancery, probably with some truth, that the profits over all these years far surpassed the original loan and interest.[59]

Lending money on mortgages could have its hazards. A case in February 1678 smacks of sharp practice. William Birkin, a tailor in London, was approached by Elizabeth Morkett, a single woman, seeking a loan. She was a lodger with John Lee, a gardener at Enfield. Birkin was unwilling to lend without security, she therefore invited him to Lee's house where, she said, he would be satisfied on this matter. Lee was apparently away from home when Birkin called but his wife, after whispered discussion with Elizabeth in the garden, produced the deeds and writings of her husband's property in Enfield, three tenements and two acres of arable. She delivered these deeds into the hands of Elizabeth Morkett who handed them to Birkin as her security. On this basis he agreed to lend her £40 considering, he said, that he held a mortgage on Lee's property. John Lee however disowned any knowledge of the transaction and sued in Chancery for the return of his deeds. Birkin found it difficult to justify their retention. He alleged nevertheless that he had since discovered that these same deeds had been used on more than one occasion to obtain money which had never been repaid.[60]

There were various means used to avoid the repayment of debts. John Knight, an Enfield innkeeper, at the time of his death in 1667 owed £30 to Edward Randall a local brewer, and £10 to Edward Butler a local baker, these debts with others amounted to £80. His widow and executor attempted to avoid repayment by giving priority to fictitious debts arranged in conspiracy with William Drinkwater and Henry Rastell. Rastell for some reason undisclosed subsequently admitted the plot and, 'wished his hands might rot off . . . if John Knight did owe him anything.'[61]

Many London merchants came to dwell in Enfield in the eighteenth century. They played little part in parish affairs though no doubt they contributed substantially to the rates and taxes and helped to push up the price of property. Some houses were sold at auctions, some by direct sale, some were advertised in the press, some by handbills written out and distributed. Joseph Fisher was a shoemaker who also grew carnations commercially. He had a brick tenement in Turkey Street by the New River bridge with a chaise-house, stables and a hay loft; there was a piece of pasture and a garden adjoining the house. He met the auctioneer, Mr Jones, in the nearby Angel public house to discuss the auction which was to be held on the 6 August 1764. They arranged that a certain Mr Loomworth Dean should bid on behalf of the vendor in order to ensure a good price. Despite this careful collusion, the auctioneer accepted less than Joseph had stipulated and he refused to complete the transaction.[62]

John MacNamara, described as 'late commander of the "Rhoda", East Indiaman', had no intention of severing his connection with trade when he moved to Enfield around 1760. He at once sought a ship suitable for employment in the government service. Through the ship-broker Samuel Brooks he negotiated the purchase of the 'Hardy', a frigate lying in the Thames at Deptford. The owner claimed that it was a fine ship, 'exceedingly good for the West India trade'. The owner claimed that it could be made ready for sea within a few days. He had an inventory drawn up of the anchors, cables, sails, guns, arms, ammunition and stores, and this was printed and distributed at Lloyds Coffee House where the vessel was advertised to be sold by candle. MacNamara bought the ship for £1005 without even going down to Deptford to examine it. When at last he sent his broker he found to his dismay that the frigate was unseaworthy and totally unfit for government service.[63]

John Edwards a London merchant had his home in Enfield though he continued to trade from his warehouse in the City. His goods were listed in May 1717 following his death. His Enfield house was finely furnished; the parlour contained a Dutch table, six cane chairs, two elbow chairs with cushions, a green couch with pillows, a brass lampstand and two glass sconces (wall lights on brackets holding candles) a tea-kettle and a tea table. There were two family portraits and an escutcheon. The room next to the parlour held two oval tables and a square table, a looking-glass and a weather-glass. He had seven bird cages and two fishing rods, a fowling piece and a blunderbuss, a number of pictures and prints and fifty printed books. There was an iron plate-warmer in the kitchen, a copper chocolate pot, a coffee pot, a tea kettle and knives and forks. In the garden was a frame with a glass cover, a rake, a hoe, a watering pot, a spade and a stone roller. He had a great deal of pewter, fifty-six plates, dishes, a cheese plate, a pie plate, and three chamber pots. There was just a little china but a good quantity of Delft including dishes, plates and basins. All the rooms had window curtains except the garrets, and each bedchamber had hangings of a distinct colour, green, blue or brown. Only the closet at the head of the stairs was papered.

His premises in London consisted of a stable, two rooms and a counting-house, all attached to his warehouse. In it was an odd miscellany of goods, six small boxes of cinnamon weighing 197 lb at 10s a pound, a bale of Sherbassle silk worth £108, Roman vitriol to the value of £108, twenty-six bundles of beaver skins worth £74, fourteen barrels of Carolina rice valued at £24, and fifteen vats of potash of Italy. He had recently shipped to the Barbadoes, on board the 'William and James', 562 half-pieces of ordinary linen which he had purchased in Bremen. He held Bank of England stock to the value of £1330 and South Sea stock worth £855. There were also 116 blank lottery tickets in the 'million and a half lottery' for the year 1710, but his widow had sold them since his death for £40.[64] Why on earth blank lottery tickets for the year 1710 should be worth £40 in 1717 is a mystery to me, perhaps a reader may offer a solution.

The home of Charles Feltham who died in Enfield in 1721 was lavishly furnished, even to the point of ostentation. Had been a partner with Mr Henry Doldene in a brewing busines in London. Servants occupied the top of the house. The maid's garret had a bedstead and curtains, a feather bed, bolster and pillows, a quilt and three blankets, a rug and a counterpane. It also had a table and two chairs. In the back garret was a table bedstead, a feather bed and bolster and a box. In these two rooms Hannah, Mary, Catherine and Sarah the cook-maid slept two in a bed; they were each paid £5 a year. The footman slept in another garret; as well as his bedstead with a feather bed and bolster he had two tables, a chair, and even a chest of drawers.

There were three parlours on the ground floor. The great parlour contained six cane elbow chairs and four stools with a cushion for each. A Delft flower-pot was placed carefully in the middle of the Dutch table. In the evening the calico window curtains were drawn, the candles in the two sconces lit and the lamp upon its stand was drawn out into the middle of the room. Flames flickering in the gleaming brass hearth against the black of the iron fire-back cast light upon the twenty-one prints around the walls; the table with its tea board and eight china cups and saucers would then be brought forth and the servant would make tea in the stone tea-pot and music would be played upon the harpsichord. Perhaps the reality was less delightful, but at least Mr Feltham's great parlour held the ingredients for such a scenario.

Charles Feltham owned both a coach and a chariot. His coachman was resplendent in livery; coat, waistcoat, breeches and hat. He slept over the stables. The other room there belonged to Thomas Buxton the gardener on £6-a-year wages. There was a summer house in the garden furnished with a table and chairs and a turkeywork couch. A number of garden glasses were kept there. Four statues on pedestals and two gilt vases on plinths adorned the walks around the house. The brewer, probably to provide for his household, kept a cow and two calves and some poultry. There was also a plough and a harrow but no crops are mentioned in his inventory.[65]

Samuel Davies, a weaver from Petticoat Lane who died in 1729, was another London trader who made his home in Enfield. His money was invested in property in Petticoat Lane, Montague Court, New Court and Wentworth Street from which he derived rents amounting to £294 a year. He owned three houses in Enfield Wash, two of which he had built at a cost of £200. He occupied two of these houses and lived like a gentleman. The parlour was lit by a glass sconce in a gold frame and was heated by a brass wind stove. The room was furnished with a large oval table, a small table, a tea table and a card table, two elbow chairs and three cane chairs. There was a spice box, two bird cages, six china cups and saucers, two earthenware tea-pots and a coffee pot. The walls were decorated with eight 'India' pictures and there was a head in wax. Twenty-five paintings were hung upon the stairs including another six 'India' pictures. There were tapestry hangings in the dining room and three more paintings. In the best bedroom of his second house he displayed two family portraits and on the stairs there were two paintings and three maps. A clock in a japanned case stood in the parlour; there was also a pier glass in a golden frame.[66]

Such people continued to lavish money on family portraits. 'This year', said J. T. Smith, writing of 1789, 'proved more lucrative to me than any preceding, for at this time I professed portrait painting both in oils and crayons; but alas after using a profusion of carmine, and placing many an eye straight which was misdirected, before another season came my exertions were mildewed by a decline of orders'. Those who sat for him, he complained, 'would neither die nor quit their mansions but kept themselves snug within their King William iron gates and red brick crested piers so that there was no accommodation for newcomers'. He went on; 'I profiled, three quartered, full-faced and buttoned up, the retired embroidered weavers, their crummy wives, and tightly laced daughters'. J. T. Smith had come to live near his patron Sir James Winter Lake in Firs Lane. His walks, ever in search of antiquities, took him to Ponders End to see 'King Ringle's well' behind the Goat, to Durants Arbour, to Green Street and on to Waltham Cross. His drawings, turned into prints, show many a damp tumble-down labourer's cottage romanticised into the picturesque. Matthew Michell, a London banker and collector of fine paintings, lived at Grove House in Turkey Street. He was patron to Thomas Rowlandson the famous caricaturist of English life in the late eighteenth and early nineteenth centuries. Rowlandson did a painting of the art gallery at Grove House. Another one of his pictures shows the White Lion nearby at Enfield Highway.

Many Enfield men crossed the seas to find their fortune and perished in far away places. James Swithin, having left his house in the charge of his mother-in-law, and his daughter in the charge of the mistress of a boarding school, took his young son and set off for Bencolen in the East Indies where he died in 1775. He intended to sell jewelry there and took a consignment of that merchandise, worth £4,100, from a Mr James Cox, to sell in the East Indies. As the goods were on credit, he had to pay Cox twenty-three per cent over twenty months and the loan was secured by seven bonds for £1,200 each. His son, his money and personal effects were brought home to Gravesend in the East Indiaman, the 'Alfred'. There was £541 and a quantity of rupees and 'finams' (fonams, a gold coin from India) which had been sold for £242, also a gold snuff box which sold for £17 and a set of table china which bore his arms. The house at Bulls Cross was rented from Charles Boddam of Capel Manor. Swithin's household goods and furniture were sold by auction. His executor had received £1,725 from Lawrence Sutherland Esq, and from his attorneys at Bencolen 6,774 dollars were due.[67]

Shopkeepers and tradesmen from the end of the seventeenth century had the advantage of a system of banking which allowed payment to be made without resource to cash. The system had its disadvantages, then as now. William Jones had a horse for sale at Waltham market on 3 May 1790. He was riding it back and forth hoping for a buyer when he was approached by George Allet. Jones told him the price of the horse was £25 which Allet thought was too much. Nevertheless about two hours after Jones had arrived back home, Allet called and offered him £24 5s. This being agreed, Allet gave him a note (or cheque) to the value of £25 made out on Prescott, Grote and Co, bankers of Threadneedle Street. Prescott himself lived at Theobalds, and William Jones therefore had no qualms about accepting the note. The following morning however, when he presented it for payment it was not accepted. He had even lent Allet a pair of spurs and a bridle to ride the horse home. Allet was taken some months later and paid for his fraud with his life.[68]

Among the Enfield tradesmen who had dealings with the formidable Hannah Sells was John Blackwell the glazier, who died in 1730. He had a house and shop at Northaw which was full of materials salvaged from former jobs; 56 lb of old pipe lead, 112 lb of old window lead, four old iron casements, and three old sashes with the glass. More old windows were stored in the garret of his house in Enfield; ninety-eight feet of old crown sashes and glass, fifty feet of squares and quarries in lead, eight old casements and 4 lb of old sheet lead. There were four broken lights of old glass in the yard. New glass and old glass was stored everywhere, even in the bedrooms, both glass for sash windows and quarries for the repair of the old leaded casements. In his two shops he kept his glazing irons, hammers, rasps, files, paint brushes, a set of moulds to make lead weights and rain-water head moulds, moulds for pipes and pumps, materials for the making and repair of beer pumps, a squaring board and rule, a plumber's plane, pulley blocks, colour stone and sander stone, red lead and sheet lead. In the evenings when work was done he would sit at his desk in the bedroom at Enfield, dip his pen into his pewter ink pot on its stand and write up his accounts. His stock and his property were valued at only £31 but money was owed to him amounting to £248. Those in his debt included leading landowners, minor gentlemen and tradesmen, eight-eight in all. Jeremiah Sambrook Esq of Gobions near Northaw, the man who built 'Gobions Folly', owed him £40, Mr Sams the builder owed him nearly £70. These debts were considered by his executor to be recoverable, those of which she despaired she did not list.[69]

William Sams died a couple of years later. He was a carpenter and builder, and probably also a timber merchant. He had employed workmen in 1722 to cut down eighty oak trees on Enfield Chase (illegally) for the ranger Major General John Pepper, and undoubtedly he sold the timber on behalf of the ranger. He died prosperous with goods valued at £507. His farmyard served also as a woodyard and there he kept the wagon and tackle. Timber was stored to the value of £58 and wood worth £46. Thirty-two loads and five sacks of charcoal, with five loads and two sacks of charm, were worth £102. That May, in 1732, forty-four acres of grass were growing in his fields worth £55, also thirteen acres of wheat worth £39 and eight acres of oats and tares valued at £8. He had three ploughs and three harrows. His livestock comprised sixty sheep, fifty lambs, two sows, six pigs and seven cows.

Mr Sams's house was on three floors, two garrets above and three bedrooms on the first floor. The bedstead in the first chamber had harateen hangings, and there he kept a tea table. On the ground floor the best parlour was furnished with two mahogany tables, a wainscot table, eight walnut tree chairs, an easy chair with a cushion, a chimney glass and a pier glass. He had brass locks on the doors. On the walls in the little parlour were displayed ten prints. In the counting house was his bookcase, a writing table and a nest of drawers, and in the kitchen a wind-up jack. The cellar held five beer vessels with two stands, a funnel and three pails. He had his own brewery. He dressed plainly – four coats, three waistcoats, five pairs of breeches, stockings, shoes and a hat. He had two perukes and a brass tobacco box. Like so many other Enfield tradesmen, the money owed to him at the time of his death exceeded the value of his goods in hand; £982 was owed to William Sams.[70]

John Ward who died in January 1716 was another builder, also a brickmaker. He had thirty bushels of lime in stock, two hundred bricks and a thousand tiles. His tools consisted of trowels, a brick hammer, a lathing iron and two sieves; there was timber stored, ladders, and three crowding barrows. He owned a piece of brick land in Churchbury field and another piece of land in Turkey Street near the two bridges. From his property he received rents of more than £21 a year and had debts owed to him for work done amounting to £67.[71]

Another local builder, John Crawley, died in 1747. His inventory reveals something of his work and his life-style. He was engaged on building a house at the time of his death. When it was built he would either sell it, let it, or raise a mortgage on it. As yet it stood unfinished, two rooms up and two down. In the front room downstairs his appraisers found four pieces of stone, four oak posts, two scaffold boards, two bins, a pair of steps and an iron porridge pot. In the back room were five twelve-foot pieces of slit deal and three twelve-foot whole deals, one and a half inch thick oak board, a bunch of sap lathes, two casement windows and the glass (the glass was presumably to be re-used, for sash windows were now the fashion). Upstairs was more deal, three pieces of old matting and some lead and, incongruously, a hay-fork and a child's cradle.

His building materials were spread around his premises. In the lime-house were forty bushels of lime, pantiles, sieves, a pair of criples, spades, shovels, a mattock and a tub containing tar. In the long shed were stored sand, ridge-tiles, plain-tiles, hart lathes, twenty-nine scaffold boards, paving tiles, paving bricks, ladders and a wheelbarrow. Even the street outside was used to store the old boards and other old timber and bricks which had once comprised a stable. In the garden were bundles of lathes and oak pales; in the adjoining field were 875 pantiles, six twenty-two foot scaffold poles with the boards and six pairs of window shutters.

He also kept three geese and a gander in the yard and, in the hen house, three ducks and a drake and three hens and a pullet. Debts owed to him amounted to £42, all from gentlemen, including Mr William Salt £16 and Colonel Inwood £20 13s. At the time of his death he held a leasehold house at Forty Hill let at £10 a year, another leasehold house which was mortgaged for £50, and a copyhold house which was mortgaged to Mr Thorpe for £100. This was said to be more than the house was worth and immediately after the death of John Crawley, Mr Thorpe with the consent of the executor, took possession of the property. Luxury was not eschewed; he had a tea table with seven china cups and ten china saucers, a tea-pot and stand, silver teaspoons and tongs, also two chocolate pots and a coffee pot. His clothes were plain and serviceable; a suit of blue-grey cloth, a pair of buckskin breeches, a great duffel coat, three hats and a wig, a leather belt and two leather aprons. His appraisers, who had taken careful note of each item of his property, were paid 21s with 5s for expenses; 2s was paid for the window tax and 2s for the poor rate. Dr Nesbitt's fees for his attendance on the deceased during his last illness amounted to 21s, the bill of Mr Armiger the apothecary was 15s 6d. His funeral had cost £5 4s 6d.[72]

The bricklayer and the brick-maker were often one and the same tradesman. Ralph Phillips, an Enfield bricklayer, occupied an acre of brick ground which in 1772 he leased for twelve years to John Hill an Enfield brick-maker. John Hill also rented William Mellish's land in Southbury field and Fishers field from which he dug, in the last seven years of the eighteenth century, sufficient brick earth to make 4,695,742 bricks. William Mellish was building a hunting establishment on Chingford Green which became the home, from 1798 until 1806, of the Epping Forest stag hunt. Over a hundred thousand stock bricks were delivered to his site there from Ponders End, as well as thirty thousand from Baker Street at a total cost of £245. Much of this cost lay in the carriage, the brick-maker adding 10s to the price of a thousand bricks for the extra distance between Baker Street and Ponders End, about a mile and a half. Thus 66,450 stocks were delivered from Ponders End at 32s a thousand while 21,000 from Baker Street cost 42s 6d. Soon afterwards (October 1800) Mr Mellish purchased bricks to build an ice-house and a garden wall at Bush Hill Park; these cost him £122 10s.

Early in the nineteenth century the presence of brick earth much enhanced the value of land, especially where it lay in what were called 'eligible situations for building'. An auctioneer's catalogue advertising the sale of 118 acres in June 1809, on both sides of the turnpike road at Enfield Highway, described it as ten miles from London and 'presumed to contain brick earth'.[73]

The freehold of the mill at Ponders End was purchased from the Crown in September 1671,[74] and the ancient rent of £6, representing five quarters of bread corn and thirty quarters of wheat, at last became extinct. These mills had always been the most important industrial site in the parish. They came into the hands of James Cowper by his marriage to Ann Wroth. He leased the property in 1671, with some fifteen acres of meadow, for thirty-five years to Joseph Cornish a fellmonger at an annual rent of £100. Higher up the river Mr John Cornish was the owner of an oil mill, the oil from which was probably used at the leather mill at Ponders End. Cornish was taxed in 1671 on £150 stock there.[75] A few years earlier, in 1665,[76] the hearth tax had recorded it as a gunpowder mill. Ponders End mills in 1671 were in the occupation of Charles Whitehead and Nicholas Whare and housed a corn-mill and a leather-mill. The right of the tenant to dry his leather 'as he formerly had' in the line yard on the premises was protected by the lease. The owner in June 1678, Spencer Cowper of London, leased the mill to Thomas Flanders for twenty-one years, but Flanders died that same year and the lease was assumed by his widow Joane.[77]

Ponders End mills were descibed in a marriage settlement of 1739 made in preparation for the marriage of Katherine Flanders to John Clarke of Tottenham, 'wharfinger'. It then comprised 'two water-mills, one leather mill and two tenements.[78] The two houses remain on the site standing one at each end of the mill.' John Clarke probably lived in the one at the south end. An inventory[79] was taken of his possessions in February 1751, after his death. The house comprised on the ground floor the parlour, the room next to it probably used as a dining room, the counting-house, the kitchen, brewhouse, pantry and a back kitchen. The parlour was nicely furnished with three mahogany tables and eight chairs. There was a beaufet displaying china, stoneware, glass and earthenware. He had a tea board and a japan waiter. The room was lit by a glass lantern and warmed by a windstove. A desk with two stools and a corner cupboard stood in the counting-house. In the brew-house and cellar were two coppers with covers fixed with lead and iron work, a leaden pump, four brewing tubs, six brewing vessels, a mashing stick, a water tub, six hogsheads, three barrels, two kilderkins and some earthenware. There was a coffee pot, chocolate pot, tea kettle, a fish kettle with cover and twelve knives and forks in the kitchen.

The two best bedrooms were known as the 'red room' and the 'brown room'. In the 'red room' the bedstead had red mohair hangings and there were seven red shag (shagreen?) chairs and a thirty-hour clock in a case. Everything in the 'brown room' was green. He had a quantity of hops stored there among his elegant furniture. The employees slept in the 'men's room' where there were two bedsteads with feather beds, six blankets, a rug and a coverlid.

The miller had silver to the value of £24 which enabled his guests to take tea in style. It consisted of ten teaspoons, a tea strainer and tongs and a milk jug, also a tankard, a pint mug and a punch ladle, and he had a silver watch. His transactions it would seem had been in cash; no debts are listed, though they may have already been collected for there was £70 in ready money in the house.

John Clarke also farmed. His wheat in the barn, threshed and unthreshed, was worth £73, his five wagons and carts were worth £32, and his eight horses £35. The cows and heifers and the bull were valued at £23. He had a cucumber frame and a quantity of flower pots in the garden. There was a toll-house on the river where he collected payment from bargees passing his lock. His two old barges and his two boats lay at the wharf and coal was stored there; all this was worth £82. The other house with the leather mills was occupied by Dutton Greenwood. The widow Ann Clarke seems to have continued in the business; she is shown as having supplied coal to the landlord at the Nags Head in 1757.[80]

The mills were purchased by Charles Smith in August 1759.[81] Clarke was followed as miller by George Berners. His lease ran out in 1784 and a new lease was issued to Augustine King George, under the terms of which he laid out £2000 'in rebuilding, repairing and improving the mills'. The property included the corn-mill, the two dwelling houses in one of which he lived, an orchard, the lock and the lockhouse, the leather mill, a fishery called Mardykes, and the 'Swan and Salmon', a ferry house leased to Daniel Chase, a brewer. The coal wharf had

The mills at Ponders End, with the two houses.

recently been let to William Naylor. Mr George's lease was to run for sixty-one years at a rent of £280 a year clear of land tax. The two water-wheels operated two pairs of French stones, 4'4" in diameter, and two pairs 4'6" in diameter. They also operated three flour machines, one corn machine, and a boulting mill used to separate bran from flour.[82] Augustine King George was a man of considerable wealth and did not operate the mill himself. The flour mill was rented in the 1830s to the brothers Joseph and William Farmer. Robert Nice was the foreman there. They had a bake-house on the premises. There was only one entrance to the mill, then as now, which was through the lodge gate. Apart from this the mill was entirely surrounded by water. Mr George employed William Pluck as labourer and night watchman. He was an unfortunate choice for he quickly entered into an arrangement with another of the miller's servants to turn a blind eye to his stealing. On Saturday 30 November Robert Nice had taken stock before he left work between six and seven o'clock. On the Monday morning about six o'clock, two sacks of flour were missing. A search revealed one sack buried in Mr George's orchard and another buried in the garden. William Pluck was forty-five. He made an earnest plea for leniency claiming that he had all his lifetime got his living with honesty and sobriety, that he had a wife and seven children under fourteen years of age who would be obliged to commit themselves to the parish if he was convicted. Nevertheless both men were sentenced to seven years transportation.[83]

William Green (1742) seems to have combined the trades of brewer and baker. His house was on two floors with garrets above them and a cellar below. In the bakehouse were five wooden and two iron baker's shovels, a dough knife, two kneading troughs, two scrapers, a wire sieve and a hair sieve, and three hour-glasses. Bran, pollard and corn-flour, fine flour and second flour, and scales to weigh it out, were stored in the two rooms over the bakehouse. There was also a brewery where he kept a water barrow, eleven brewing and washing tubs, a copper and a washtub. In the cellars were eleven barrels, three full of small beer with the beer stands, three eighteen-gallon casks, two of which were full of ale, brass cocks and a dozen bottles of raisin and currant wine. There was a store of bottles in a bottle rack.

His apparel suggests a sporting gent; two greatcoats, a jockey coat, a brown coat, a fustian frock coat, a flannel waistcoat, a cotton waistcoat, a brown Holland waistcoat, an old corduroy waistcoat, two hats, two wigs, ten shirts, five pairs of worsted stockings, three linen and one silk handkerchief, slippers, shoes, boots and pumps, whips and spurs and iron buckles, a silver watch and a snuff box with a silver rim. Since his death, his executors had managed to collect some fourteen of his debts (all of less than one pound) but 120 people still owed him money. They were of all classes. Forty-five were such as could put a 'Mr' before their names or an 'esquire' after it, and Sir Jeremiah Sambrooke also owed him £16 8s 3d. The debts due to him ranged from £20 down to a few shillings.[84]

4. Farming

Enfield fed many sheep, a multipurpose animal which could manure the arable, produce fleeces (though the price of these fell after the Restoration), and provide meat and even milk. The vicars throughout the Interregnum, Walter Bridges first, then Daniel Manning, bewailing their tithes lost over many years up to 1660, listed the parishioners who had not paid and the livestock on which they ought to have paid. The vicars' assessments were of course not disinterested and, despite their profession, their figures may have been a little to their own advantage.[85]

	sheep*	cows*	mares*	pigs born
John Swallow	100	16		
Margaret Taylor	80	8	2	
John Mansborough	80	8	2	
Bennet Wigge	60	6	2	
Richard Fulham	60	9	2	
George Richardson	160	8	2	
Robert Wood	160	9	3	
Widow Collum	80	8	3	
William Hodge	300	12	4	10
William Covell	400	12	6	
William Newman	200	6	3	10
Edward Wilford	300	8	2	

*Sheep were titheable to the vicar on fleeces and lambs, cows on calves and milk (thus bullocks are not listed here) and mares on foals born.

After the re-establishment of the Chase the Duchy of Lancaster revived a long-disputed decree by which the commoners were forbidden to pasture their sheep on the Chase. Those sufficiently powerful, like John Wilford of Hadley, could flout the law at least for a time while he fed over a hundred there.[86] Others, especially from South Mimms where there were no fences to deter them, defied the decree and took what they considered their right. Jonathan Wackett an underkeeper at West Lodge, finding a flock of sheep feeding in his walk, set out to drive them to the pound but the owner appeared, one Robert White of South Mimms. He had with him a large mastiff bitch which seized the underkeeper and dragged him to the ground whereupon Robert White alighted from his horse, beat and kicked the fallen gamekeeper, and so retrieved his sheep.[87] Wackett's deposition against White seems to have led to no prosecution.

The tenants of Enfield continued to claim an unrestricted right to common for their sheep. The vestrymen who met in November 1689 solemnly passed a resolution on behalf of themselves and the rest of the inhabitants declaring that they should endeavour to restore their rights and that the cost of defending any suit brought against any of them should be met from parish funds. The motion was signed by twenty-one leading parishioners.[88]

Samuel Wyburd was a wealthy farmer who died at the beginning of the year 1708 and his total estate was valued at £984. He was engaged in mixed farming, sheep, arable and meadow. He had seventy-seven ewes with lambs and 168 'dry' sheep worth £58, but only six cows and four heifers. There were four horses, a mare and five colts and one pig. Hay to the value of £90 was found stored in the barn that February, three years' wool worth £24, a hundred quarters of wheat worth £125, fourteen quarters of oats £12, and thirty-five quarters of barley valued at £39. Twenty-five more quarters of wheat lay yet unthreshed and were worth £32 10s. He had seventeen and a half acres of wheat growing, valued at £51, and eight and a half acres already prepared for wheat to be sown in the following autumn, the work he had done on this land was appraised at £7. Twenty acres had been set aside to sow winter crops. The dung he had laid there had cost him over £12.

That same year died Matthew Brown the publican at the Star, Ponders End.

He kept ninety-four sheep and fifty-two ewes with lambs, but only nine cows and bullocks.[89] John Ward was a builder and a farmer. Wheat, straw and chaff to the value of £45, hay worth £36, barley £6 and rye £4, were stored in his barn. His wheat in the ground (it was January 1716) was worth £14 12s 6d, and the ploughing done in preparation for winter sowing was valued at £3 5s.[90]

A list of cattle branded on Enfield Chase for the year 1727[91] shows that 169 villagers took advantage of common on the Chase and they owned 842 cattle, an average of only five each. Only five farmers kept twenty or more; William Bosgrave had fifty-eight and John Maycock forty-nine. At the other end of the scale there were forty-six who kept a single beast and thirty-seven who owned two. This shows why the poor were so loathe to see their common rights diminished and why the eventual confiscation of the common resulted in such demoralisation.

The buying and selling of cattle in the eighteenth century often took place in pubs. Of course details of such transactions seldom survive, except occasionally in the Old Bailey and other courts. Such examples tend to mislead a little since they were carried out surreptitiously and well away from any place where the vendor might be recognised whereas more honest dealings would occur in local hostelries. James Macdonald faced trial at the Old Bailey in 1730 for stealing three cows worth £8 out of Thomas Watt's grounds in Enfield. He drove them to the White Horse at Mile End and sought to sell them below their value. This was unwise for it immediately aroused suspicion and led to his arrest and transportation[92] to one of our colonies in the New World.

Sheep were kept now more for the meat than for the fleeces. The meat was sold by the stone. When Samuel Keep a clay-carter stole eleven wethers and a ram from Ann Carter in Enfield in 1745, a butcher at Southwark claimed that he had paid the market price for them, 17d a stone. The transaction was negotiated in a public house over a drink and the sheep were butchered in a common slaughter-house. The skins were sold elsewhere at 18d a piece and the fat (used for candle making) for 15s 9d. Keep was sentenced to death[93] though the execution was not carried out.

The record of an auction can sometimes enable the reader to catch sight of an eighteenth century farm as it stood with each item displayed and awaiting the auctioneer's hammer. Bartholomew Ibbot's death in September 1761 was followed by the death of his widow and his property was put up for sale. His wheat growing on nine plots in the common field called Churchbury field amounted to twenty-two acres. The largest plot was of eight acres, the others were all of less than three acres. His Lent corn in Windmill field lay in eight pieces and added up to forty-three and a half acres. It included seven and a half acres of black oats, twenty-six acres of white oats, and ten acres of peas. All these crops, unreaped, were sold for £187. He had seventy acres of grass which were sold for £231.

Cow cribs, hurdles and hogs' troughs were in the sale, but there were no cattle, pigs or sheep. He had a wheeled plough, a fallow dray plough and two old seed ploughs, three harrows and a grass roller 'with a trough fixed'. There was a wagon with a hair cloth awning and a jack, and two carts with six-inch-wide wheels and a dung drag, a dung fork, four pitching forks and seventeen wooden rakes, also a number of sieves and riddles. His carthorses, 'Brown', 'Sharper' and 'Doctor', were named like faithful servants; they sold at around £16 each.

Margaret, the widow, before she died had collected most of the money due to her late husband. As was usual, almost all of it had been owed by the more well-to-do inhabitants of the parish. Some was for hay, straw, peas and chaff, and some for household effects which had been sold soon after her husband's death. The widow had become involved in two Chancery suits, one of which had originated back in 1748 when Robert Paltock, who had owed Bartholomew £547, had conveyed to him his freehold estate in Enfield and an annuity payable by the government. Paltock had been indebted to several other persons and the estate had been conveyed to Bartholomew in trust. It was his duty to sell it for the benefit of all the creditors. They had belatedly sued the widow for their share but she too was now gone. The appraisers calculated that after deductions there remained £306 to be distributed.

There was another debt due to the estate amounting to £767 owed by George Bourne Esq. A decree in Chancery had recently been made ordering the sale of Bourne's shares in the New River Waterworks. Apart from this debt there remained due to the executor hopeful debts amounting to £45 and hopeless debts, some from as early as 1725, amounting to £487.[94]

By 1800 local farmers did not normally go to market themselves to sell stock. This is seen in a case at the Old Bailey when David Dyer, who stole two heifers, took them to Enfield Highway to Richard Field, a butchers' drover. Field required to know whether his salesman should sell them and bring the money back to Enfield. Dyer answered in the affirmative. The two heifers were sold for ten guineas but Dyer failed to call for the money. When asked whether it was the usual mode for a farmer to send his beasts up by drover Field simply replied 'yes'.[95]

The planting of fruit trees increased the value of the land. Lot 16, in the Breton sale of 1787, was Southbury orchard of nine acres planted with 300 fruit trees. It was let to tenants at will for £27 per annum and it was sold for £680. Five acres of orchard on the east side of Enfield Highway, let to a tenant at will at £10 a year, was disposed of at this sale for £270.

Common field lands were let at 20s an acre per annum. Thus Lot 30, thirty acres in Dungfield, was let to a tenant at will for £30. The common field arable was distributed in thirteen fields. The age-old system of three-year crop rotation remained in operation, its complexity reduced to a routine by use over many hundreds of years. In the year 1787 all the land in Dungfield, Mapledown, Waterhedgefield and Churchburyfield, lay fallow. Longfield, Broadfield, Windmillfield and Hayden were sown with wheat, while Lent corn was growing in Southfield, Eastfield, Birdfield great and small, and in Southburyfield.

Notes to Chapter Six

1   Guildhall 9174. 18.
2   Guildhall 9174. 11
3   Guildhall 9174. 5
4   Guildhall 9174. 25
5   Guildhall 9174. 16
6   Guildhall 9174. 3
7   Guildhall 9174. 23
8   Guildhall 9174. 25
9   C8.355. 173, GLRO Hearth tax 1665
10 Guildhall 9174. 6
11 Guildhall 9174. 3
12 Guildhall 9174. 4
13 Guildhall 9174. 10

14 Guildhall 9174. 23
15 Guildhall 9174. 19
16 PROB 4. 13941
17 Guildhall 9174. 30
18 Guildhall 9171. 39–198, 9172. 134
19 Guildhall 9174. 13, C8. 351. 252
20 Guildhall 9171. 33. 127, 9174. 15
21 Guildhall 9174. 24
22 Guildhall 9171. 31. 186
23 Guildhall 9171. 35. 28
24 Guildhall 9171. 35. 419
25 Guildhall 9171. 42
26 Guildhall 9171. 31. 312, 9174. 5
27 Guildhall 9171. 38. 322
28 Guildhall 9171. 39. 67, 78
29 Guildhall 9171. 38. 219
30 Guildhall 9171. 35. 30
31 Guildhall 9171. 37. 541
32 guildhall 9171. 36. 142, 9171. 31. 197
33 Guildhall 9177. 9, 9171. 36. 367
34 C5. 633. 40
35 Guildhall 9174. 17
36 Guildhall 9174. 28, 9171. 51. 261
37 Guildhall 9174. 15
38 Guildhall 9174. 3
39 Guldhall 9171. 38. 21
40 C5. 594. 211, C8. 144. 5
41 Guildhall 9174. 18
42 DL44. 1217
43 Guildhall 9171. 45. 319, C8. 398. 25
44 verjuice; an acid juice of green grapes, crab apples or other sour fruit, much used for cooking and medicinal purposes.
45 Guildhall 9174. 29, 9185. 3
46 E112. 998. 1284 Thanks to Bert Mason for bringing this document to my attention
47 Guildhall OBSP 6–11 Sept 1732
48 GLRO Acc 903. 37
49 Enfield cuttings file
50 GLRO DRO4. 3. 16. 74, 3. 17
51 GLRO Acc 903. 39a, Vestry order book 3 Je 1813, 6Ja 1820
52 GLRO MJ. OC 5. 249
53 Guildhall OBSP Ja 1730 p. 9
54 Guildhall OBSP 1796–7, p 110
55 Enfield cuttings file
56 C5.532. 23
57 C5. 307. 52, C10. 55. 126
58 C5. 50. 34, C5. 619. 37, C8. 18. 105
59 C8. 136. 77
60 C8. 517. 86
61 C6. 46. 153
62 E112. 1579. 310
63 E112. 1577. 247
64 PROB 32. 61. 37
65 PROB 31. 12. 250
66 Guildhall 9174. 48
67 J. T. Smith *Book for a Rainy Day*, PROB 31. 654. 169

68 Guildhall OBSP 1790/91 p 265–7
69 Guildhall 9174 48
70 PROB 3. 31. 78
71 Guildhall 9174. 36
72 PROB 31. 283. 389
73 GLRO Acc 285. 2, Acc 655. 3A
74 C54. 4323 pt 7
75 E179. 253. 23
76 GLRO Hearth Tax 1665
77 GLRO Acc 262. 1. 11, 12, 13
78 GLRO Acc 801. 38
79 PROB 31. 370. 473
80 PROB 31. 357. 446
81 GLRO Acc 407. 1
82 GLRO Acc 407. 7
83 information from Bert Mason, Guildhall OBSP 1832. 252
84 PROB 3. 41. 81
85 E112. 321. 420, 471
86 David Pam *Story of Enfield Chase.* p. 82
87 DL9. 14
88 Enfield D630
89 GLRO 9174. 31
90 PROB 3. 31. 78
91 Enfield D222
92 Guildhall OBSP Je 1731 p 13
93 Guildhall OBSP Mr 1745 p 108–10
94 PROB 31. 497. 160
95 Guildhall OBSP 1799–1800 128, 396

Chapter Seven
Friends and Neighbours

1. The Public Houses

There were forty-seven licenced public houses in the parish in 1752 and many that were not licenced. They clustered together in the settlements along the Old North Road; Ponders End had the Two Brewers at the corner of South Street, the Falcon in South Street, and along the High Street the Swan, the Star, the Goat and the White Hart. Enfield Highway had the King's Arms, the Black Horse, the Red Lion, the Bell and the Leather Bottle. At Enfield Wash was the White Hart and the Sun and Woolpack. Around Enfield Town stood the Nags Head, on the corner of what is now Southbury Road, the Greyhound and the King's Head on the Market Place, the Rising Sun on the south side of Church Street, the George and the Green Dragon. Each of the outlying hamlets had its pub. There was the Plough on the corner of Cattlegate Road, the Rose and Crown at Clay Hill, the Goat at Forty Hill (the old building still stands at the corner of Goat Lane) the Bull at Whitewebbs, now called the King and Tinker, and William Crew's house, the Chase, opposite where Crews Hill Railway Station now stands. The Pied Bull is not listed but at that time it may have have had another name. Closer to the centre of the village were the Three Butchers, the Five Bells and the Fighting Cocks (Gordon Road was formerly Fighting Cocks Lane) all in Baker Street, the Sergeant in Parsonage Lane, the Holly Bush, Chase Side and the Crown and Chequer (now the Crown and Horseshoes by the New River) and there was the King's Head on the River Lea near Enfield Lock.[1]

Some publicans in Enfield were exceedingly prosperous; they owned property and had land to farm. Mathew Browne styled himself a yeoman, but his style of life was superior to that of most yeomen. In 1708 he owned and lived in a substantial house at Ponders End called the Star. It was built in the old style. There was a great hall furnished with two oaken tables, two leather chairs, nine stools, two forms and an old settle. In the wide fireplace were a pair of grates, two iron dripping pans, three spits, iron racks and a jack worked by weights. The parlour also had a fireplace and a number of old turkeywork and leather chairs. There was a pump in the brewhouse with a wooden gutter and butts, barrels and tubs.

The bedroom over the hall had a closet. There were further bedrooms above the porch, over the entry and over the brewhouse. A shovel-board was provided for the entertainment of the customers. Below was a cellar. An old cider press stood in the cowhouse and there he kept a quantity of timber and a pile of sheep pelts. He had ninety-four sheep worth 3s each as well as a further fifty-two ewes which had lambed and were worth £11 13s. There were nine cows and bullocks with the straw to feed them, forty-eight hurdles and a number of cow cribs.

That February following his death his appraisers took note of his grain growing and in store. The oats had not yet been sown but what he had stored in various barns was worth £36. He had wheat kept in the barns and lofts valued at £8 13s and there were nine and a half acres sown in the preceding autumn which were worth 40s an acre. Also in store was barley valued at £1, hay worth £3 15s, straw £2 8s and chaff worth 13s 4d. He owned freehold properties in South Street, one let to Edward Bridgeman, another to William Waterman, another to Martha Horner, and a barn which he used himself. Besides the Star he owned another place at Ponders End which he had let to Richard How. Much of his land was leased either from Ann, Countess of Suffolk or from Sir John Cooper.[2]

The King's Head in the Market Place seems to have been the meeting place for the better class of people in the parish. An inventory of the house in 1730 reads like the inheritance of Bernard Shaw's 'chocolate cream soldier'; sixteen bedsteads with their furniture, thirty-two tables, 107 chairs, eighteen forms and two stools, twenty-seven pairs of sheets, twenty-three pillow-beers, thirty-one table cloths, sixty-seven napkins, twenty-seven towels and eight caps, presumably worn by the serving maids.

There was a well furnished cellar,[3] thirty-eight barrels of the best beer at 30s a barrel, one and a half barrels of second quality beer at 12s and fourteen gallons of small beer worth 2s 9d, not much more than 2d a gallon (a barrel held eighteen gallons). The best of the stock however was in 'old red port' to the value of £346. There was also white wine worth £25, 'Lisbon' worth £28, and 'Canary' to the value of £8. As for spirits, there was rum, brandy and arrack, but it was worth in all only £2 10s and though the craze for drinking cheap gin was at its height in London, none was stocked at the King's Head.

The lease of the premises was valued at £675 but it was subsequently sold for £800. The landlord also farmed, though on a modest scale, keeping oats, beans, straw and hay in the lofts like any other farmer. Debts owed to him amounted to £125 and his debtors were the best sort of people in the village: there was not one but could claim a 'Mr' before his name and there was even the occasional esquire or baronet. The landlord's total assets amounted to no less than £1793.

The Long Room where the Enfield Assembly was held, was in the building behind the inn. It had been a coffee house, probably in the late seventeenth century, and was later known as the 'Old Coffee House'. It was truly elegant in 1730, brilliantly lit by twenty-seven candles mounted on brackets around the walls, with six glass candelabra and two of brass. The room was furnished with nine tables, thirty-three chairs and ten forms. There were curtains on both doors to exclude the draughts and curtains at the windows. It had a fireplace and three carpets on the floor. Off the Long Room was the Club Room, its two tables had carpets to cover them and there were sixteen chairs; it too had a fireplace. There was also a Bowls Room where players could gather for the bowling green which had been laid out in 1717.

The Coffee House also included four bedchambers, a maid's room, two parlours, a kitchen and a bar room. The Enfield Assembly, as advertised in the press in the 1740s, was held every other Monday during the season, 'No gentlemen or ladies to be admitted without being introduced by a subscriber'. It was so important a part of the social life of the better class of people in the neighbourhood that property advertisements presented it as an inducement to buyers. When two brick houses

The Assembly Rooms at the Kings Head.

The old 'Nags Head' about 1870; the opening into Southbury Road (Nags Head Lane) was very narrow. South of the public house was the 'Railway' coffee house.

in Chase Side were offered for sale in 1765 they were described as 'near the church, market and assembly house where there is dancing in the summer and cards in the winter'. Stagecoaches, it was pointed out, run three times a day. Robinson, in his *History of Enfield* 1823, tells of the death at the Assembly in July 1778 of the Reverend Sir Samuel Bickley adding, alas without detail, that he had dishonoured his family by crimes 'which had involved him in distress and infamy'.[4]

Another flourishing house at Enfield Town was the Nags Head, the name of the landlord was William Wilson. The house stood out in the middle of what is now Southbury Road where it meets the Town, it was the first pub awaiting the dusty traveller arriving on the road from London or along the track from Ponders End. He would pass under the sign swinging on its irons above the door and into the tap room. There were two bar boards where the customers could sit themselves at the bars, there were also four chairs and a settle. Behind each bar was a nest of shelves to hold the pots and glasses; the two half-gallon pewter pots must have posed a challenge even to the most hardened drinker. There were fifteen quart pots, a number of pint pots, and even five half-pints. The wine glasses came in smaller sizes (slightly), quart, pint and half-pint. Four pewter chamber pots were provided in the bar for the immediate relief of over-burdened customers. Apart from the pewter there was much stoneware and Delft, also glasses, six wooden punch ladles and one of pewter, and two shove-ha'penny boards. Outside in the brew-house they kept some old skittle boards and pins, and in the room over the brew-house there was a billiard table.

The back parlour invited the traveller to sit down and rest. A glance in the looking-glass would assure him that the dust or the mud from the roads had not too much marred his appearance. The room contained a good oval table and a claw table and eight rush and leather chairs. He could probably get a meal here for the traveller would observe that there were some two dozen horn-handled knives and forks and another two dozen with ivory handles and also plates in plenty. The windows had crimson 'China' curtains and window blinds of painted canvas. There was a japanned corner cupboard and the tea board was laid out with tea cups and saucers; there were also coffee cups to hand and, of course, an abundance of glasses of all sizes. A painting was hung upon the wall and two prints framed and glazed, and there were two china lions.

Across the yard he could see the brew-house with a room built over it. It had a water trough with a spout from the pump, a mashing tub, a copper pump, a hop net and four square coolers. In the room above there were corn measures, a jack with 'multiplying wheels and pulleys', lead and iron weights and scales. Hay, oats and firewood were stored there. There were twelve dozen candles and five bushels of coal in the cellar where the beer was also stored. There were thirty butts and five casks of twopenny beer, each butt contained about a hundred and sixteen gallons. In stock were two quarts of rum at 8s a gallon, also eleven gallons and two quarts of brandy at 8s 6d a gallon, one gallon two quarts of aniseed at 2s 10d a gallon, six bottles of shrub (a mixture of rum and lemon juice) and only nine bottles of gin which was valued at 5s 4d the lot.

When the publican died in 1757 he had money owed to him amounting to £74. His appraisers also listed the bills which his executors would have to pay; for rum £31, to his brewer £54 14s, James Abbot the butcher £8 14s 8½d, his year's rent at £19 10s and, for the rent of a barn, £1 15s. Mrs Brouaneer who had shaved him through his last illness was paid 15s, Vincent Mauser the apothecary for his services 14s 9d, Mr Bainbridge for the funeral £16 4s 6d and Mr Robert Lockford for the gravestone £3.

Local public houses in the early nineteenth century began to come under the control of brewers. Samuel Odell who took over the George in 1812 had to enter into a bond for £200 to William Christie and George Catherow brewers of Hoddesdon, to buy all his beer, ale and malt liquors from them. They also owned the King's Head at Winchmore Hill which in 1815 they let to John Smith.[5]

2. Sporting Life

To Enfield races haste away
And see the pleasures of the day.
So humoursome I do declare
To see the sport and fun that's there;

Lords and nobles how they drive
Enfield Town is all alive,
Chariots, coaches, chaises run,
For Enfield races is begun.

There's your knowing Hats and city Jews
They've come to either win or lose,
Undertakers all in black,
Mounted on their borrow'd hacks;
Journeymen have left their jobs,
Taylors, barbers and the snobs.
Horse and foot by droves they come,
For Enfield races is begun.

When the horses start, O what a roar,
Of three to one, and five to four,
Horsemen riding in full chase,
Sweat a-pouring down their face;
Some tramp'd over, maim'd and hurt,
Others sprawling in the dirt,
Aye, and some thousand pounds was lost and won
When Enfield races they begun.

At the drinking booth you may regale,
With wine and punch, strong beer and ale,
The hungry gluttons how they cram,
Poultry, veal, and beef, and ham;
The landlords they took care withal,
To mix the strong beer with the small;
A groat a pot was charming fun,
For Enfield races was begun.[6]

The Enfield races, a three-day event in September each year, took place on the marshes at the end of Green Street from about 1750. The big event there was the Fifty Pound Plate. The meeting drew large numbers from all classes out from London. They ranged from the aristocratic racehorse owner like the Duke of Ancaster to the professional gamblers who brought their E O tables* which in 1752 were ordered to be broken to pieces by Mr Justice Galliard, 'to the great satisfaction of all the company'.

Criminals, aristocrats and country fellows intermingled at the races. A number of country fellows at the end of the races in 1762 assembled at Millmarsh bridge armed with stout sticks offering to defend the bridge against all horsemen who wanted to cross. Fighting ensued, many riders were dismounted and the conflict long remained in doubt, but at last the horsemen gained the pass and drove down the foot. (*Enfield Gazette* 9 August 1929 quoting a newspaper of 1762). George Barrington, the notorious pick-pocket, was arrested there in 1789 after robbing Henry Hare Townshend (of Bruce Castle Tottenham) of his gold watch in the subscription booth on the racecourse. At the Old Bailey he was sentenced to transportation for seven years to Botany Bay. On the day before the races in 1795, a lady was robbed near her house in Southgate at four o'clock in the afternoon; a pedlar was stopped by three footpads who took his money; a whiskey (a light gig) was overturned; one of the hangers-on who earned a few shillings by minding horses had his wrists slashed when he asked for something for his trouble and, on the last day, the stand caught fire.[7] *The Gentlemans Magazine* was indignant at these events: 'For these evils . . . government provides no remedy and our representatives and magistrates do not suppress but sanction them by assisting at matches made by the lowest blacklegs and supported only by a few publicans'.

The races however were becoming distasteful to the more moral members of the community. The *Morning Advertiser*, with obvious disapproval, reported (23 September 1801) that 'Enfield races began on Tuesday and attracted a vast concourse of spectators, particularly farmers' daughters, bedizened in white muslins richly ornamented with most costly laces'. Not long afterwards according to Robin-

*a game of chance determined by a ball falling into niches some marked E some marked O.

son, the races ceased to function. Attempts were made to revive them after the war. They were held in 1816, 1817 and in 1821, on the marshes near Mr George's mill at Ponders End and, although Robinson writing in 1823, states that they were no longer held, they were still going strong in 1830. The case of William Webster of Waltham Abbey was recorded in January 1831. He had gone into an eating house at Shoreditch, he told the court, where he got into conversation with two strangers who said they were drovers. He went with them to a public house opposite Shoreditch church and they had a glass or two of wine together. Webster must have been either naive or intoxicated or both, for he took out his money to wrap it up in a piece of paper on the table. One of his new 'friends' picked it up, saying that he would put it into Webster's back pocket for him very securely, but he put in a lot of farthings instead. Webster had recognised the 'friend' at the Enfield races in July but this time he was dressed like a gentleman and was behind a thimble table. He was secured after a violent struggle and handed over to an officer but the case against him was dismissed at the Old Bailey.[8]

The races were still held on the marshes in 1834. Robert Harvey came over from Epping on 17 September that year and while he was there an attempt was made to steal his handkerchief. 'Turned round', he said, 'and saw my handkerchief on the ground'. Joseph Coppin a lad of thirteen had picked it out of his pocket and had passed it to Cornelius Bowen a youth of fifteen. William Servant, police constable A14, was on duty however and was watching; he saw the incident and arrested the miscreants. They were brought to trial at the Old Bailey. Bowen was condemned to transportation for seven years, the lad got away with six days and a whipping. Constable Servant caught two more pick-pockets there that same day, young men of twenty-two and twenty-three. They too were transported for seven years.[9]

To the school of modern social historians for whom only quantified statistical evidence is valid, anecdotal evidence has little or no validity, yet it is only the relation of incident that can capture the spirit of the eighteenth century. The people were ignorant and enterprising, courageous and careless, hard workers and heavy drinkers. When the Lincoln stage stopped at the Black Horse in Enfield Highway one Tuesday afternoon in the summer of 1787, the party drinking outside included Edwin Swain the blacksmith, a remarkably strong man and the best bruiser in the neighbourhood. On the coach was William Ward the prize-fighter and his party. They were on their way to see the encounter between Mendoza and Humphries. Swain immediately challenged Ward to fight and when he refused, the blacksmith pulled him from the box and, throwing down a guinea, swore that he would fight him for it. In the fourth round Swain received a heavy blow to the head from which he never recovered. He left a wife and three children.[10]

Cricket on Chase Green became very popular among the shopkeepers and trades-men of Enfield at the beginning of the nineteenth century. This area of land, formerly part of Enfield Chase, had come to the parish by the 1803 Inclosure Act and it proved to be an asset.

The *Tatler* about 1835 printed a letter from a gentleman who obviously had received his education at the 'Palace' school. He tells of re-visiting Enfield many years later. Looking out of the window of an inn in Enfield Town he could see the old house where he had been at school and could hear the bell, that same bell whose appeal he had answered 'six or seven times a day for an eighth of a century'. He was apparently staying at the Greyhound. 'In the dusk of the evening under my window', he writes, 'a bevy of children were playing at thread and needle'.

Earlier that day he had met up with some of his former cricketing companions though he is too coy to spell out their names. His memories of cricket in Enfield seem to have been of a time early in the century because he could also remember the Chase before it was enclosed; this was probably the enclosure of the parish allotment in 1803. He tells of the great hitters of earlier days, W . . ., R . . ., and T . . ., the butchers, and S . . ., the fishmonger. He remembers L . . . the shoemaker 'with the frailest body and the toughest heart among them'. He recalls a match at Ware park where they played although it rained incessantly from nine in the morning until sunset. All his old friends had now become 'fat and pursy'.[11]

Away fixtures appear to have been a regular feature of local cricket. The 'News' a Sunday paper distributed in the metropolis which boasted that 'No advertisements of any description are ever inserted', carried a report (1 September 1816) of a 'grand cricket match' played at Walthamstow between the Walthamstow Club and the 'Strength of Enfield'. It took place on a Thursday, lasted until darkness fell, and was resumed on the following Monday . . . There was a great concourse of spectators including Lord Viscount Maynard and many others of the neighbouring gentry. A great deal of money was wagered on the result. Walthamstow won by forty-two runs.

The vestry, anxious for the preservation of Chase Green, met in April 1816 to consider the encroachments made upon it. It was declared unanimously that it should remain under the 'exclusive management of the vicar, churchwardens, overseers, freeholders and copyholders in vestry assembled', and they appointed a surveyor to investigate the encroachments. Rents were to be charged for those which had already been made, and it was decreed that no further encroachments were to be allowed without the consent of the vestry.

Cricket was played there regularly in 1819, usually for some small wager. 'Match for 5s each on the losing side and 2s 6d each on the winning side', or 'Match for 1s each on the losing side'. Scores were seldom high and two innings were played on a single day. The 'notches' (runs) were marked up in a score book where the bowler's name was recorded when he hit the wicket but only the fielder's when the batsman was caught. Nevertheless on June 19 T. Lungley took at least eight wickets in one innings for his side and Brown took five wickets for the other side and also scored twenty-one runs out of his side's total of twenty-nine. Cricket obviously gave the name to the Cricketers, a public house on Chase Side, where the spectators and players gathered to celebrate victory or to argue over defeat. A witness identifying a man accused at the Old Bailey of stealing from Enfield church in 1820 described him as having large dark whiskers which came down towards his mouth. He added, 'I have seen him at cricket matches on Chase Green with his child.'

The game was taken seriously; the field was mowed and the pitch well rolled, for which the pay was sixpence an hour or 2s 6d a day plus 1s 1½d beer money. The umpire, only one apparently, was paid 2s 6d for the day. The beadle was in charge of the ground; in May 1827 he received from Mr Gutterson 'for mowing, rolling and cleaning the cricket ground and for the bill at the Cricketers, £3 6s'. A new cricket ball cost 2s 6d. Less officially the beadle was also the bookmaker, and occasionally his transactions remain recorded among the vestry clerk's papers.

'Bet with Mr Cheek 3s to 1s that Ware beats Waltham'. 'A bet with Redlington 1s that Waltham beats Ware'. 'William the hostler lays that no one of Enfield gets twenty'. 'Mr Abbot lays me six to four that Enfield wins'. 'Mr Seaton lays one that he gets five the first innings'. 'I lay Nancy Brown that three to two that Thomas Simons do not get twenty runs in two innings'. 'I lay that Wheeler do not get twenty runs in two innings'.[12]

There was a theatre in Enfield in 1823. A large barn and the remains of a small house in Baker Street behind the chapel were used. A company of players would come regularly on their provincial tour and enact some of the standard plays.[13]

3. Susannah Wells and her Neighbours

The records of the Old Bailey often throw light into obscure corners of village history. One case in particular, the case of Elizabeth Canning, has been most effectively exploited by Pauline Phillips in her delightful paper '*Upon my word I am no scholar*'.

In the year 1754 the attention of all London was concentrated on the fate of this young woman. To tell the story briefly, Elizabeth was the eighteen-year-old daughter of a widow living at Aldermanbury; she was in service with Edward Lyon a carpenter, not far from her mother's home. He gave her the day off on New Year's Day and carrying half a guinea and three shillings, presumably her wages, in a little box, she set off to see her aunt and uncle who lived at Saltpetre Bank. There she spent the whole day and about nine o'clock she left for home. The aunt and uncle went with her as far as Hounsditch where they said goodbye. From that moment her friends neither knew nor heard anything of the girl for a whole month.

It was on 29 January about a quarter past ten, as Mrs Canning's apprentice was about to lock up the house for the night, that the string on the latch was pulled from the outside and in walked Betty, half-clothed and in a most distressed condition. Within minutes the news spread and people, sympathetic or just curious, crowded in. Little by little the girl was drawn to tell what had happened over these four long weeks.

Just after she had left her aunt and uncle, she said, she was passing under the walls of the Bedlam Asylum at Moorfields when she was set upon by two men. They tore off some of her clothing, stole her money, gagged and bound her and dragged her for miles along a road to a house where she had been imprisoned. There she was threatened by an old woman with a knife who had cut off and stolen her stays. She was pushed up a short flight of stairs from the kitchen into a long sparsely furnished room in which she had to survive for four weeks on bread and water. At last she had broken down the boards over one of the windows, jumped down into the lane, and made her way home. She was questioned and cross-questioned by all and sundry until, at last, a consensus was arrived at by which it was concluded that she must have been held at Mother Wells's place at Enfield Wash.

The story was related to a magistrate who found it unconvincing. Nevertheless he issued a warrant and an arresting party, accompanied by an officer from London, made its way to Enfield Wash, eight of them in a coach as well as Elizabeth. Arriving there, they went straight into the Sun and Punchbowl (now the Sun and Woolpack) kept by John Cantrel and, once refreshed, they trooped over and crowded into Mrs Wells's house, herding all the occupants into the parlour. Mary Squires, the gypsy, was sitting quietly by the fire smoking her pipe, and Elizabeth identified her as the woman with a knife who had cut off her stays.

Mother Wells's house where Elizabeth Canning claimed she was held prisoner for four weeks.

The arresting party, urged on no doubt by a love of justice, arrested Mary Squires, Mother Wells and Virtue Hall. A cart was hired, driven by Mr Richardson of Turkey Street, and in it the suspects were paraded along the road through Ponders End and Edmonton on their way to be examined by Mr Alderman Chitty.

Virtue Hall turned king's evidence. At the trial Wells and Squires were found guilty. Wells would be branded but for Squires it was a hanging matter. Sentence was to be solemnly pronounced, and the gypsy was asked whether she had anything to say. Mary Squires had been waiting for the opportunity. She had not even been in Enfield on 1 January she told the court; she was on the road with her son and daughter coming up from Dorset by way of Epping and she listed all the places where she had stopped and all the people who had seen her there. This caused a sensation in court and almost at once Virtue Hall retracted her evidence. The death sentence on Mary Squires was respited and she was subsequently given a free pardon.

Elizabeth Canning now faced trial for perjury. Her guilt or otherwise depended on whether it could be proven that Mary Squires was in Enfield on 1 January. Witnesses were called from all the places along the road from Dorset and from among the people of Enfield Wash. The evidence provides a graphic picture of these commonplace people. They were mostly unprepared to take the centre of the stage in what had become a national controversy.

Mary Larney kept a chandler's shop on the corner of Turkey Street where she sold beer, bread, bacon and tobacco. Her husband was a bricklayer by trade but he turned his hand to almost anything that came along. He had done some plastering for Mrs Wells and came over to lop some elm trees for her behind the house. The proprietors of two other shops in Turkey Street were in court. One was Mrs Waterhouse who sold 'butter and cheese and all manner of things for poor folk'. The third shop was that kept by Jane Dadwell; it provided a similar range of goods, butter, cheese, coffee and tea. That Christmas, she told the court, she had 'dressed a nice piece of meat for her customers' which they had eaten in the shop and she had come in on the Thursday after Christmas to wash up the dishes from Tuesday and Wednesday. She remembered seeing the gypsy who had called

Mary Squires, one of the accused.

in for coffee, tea and butter and had sat there for a while smoking her pipe. Squires had also been to Mary Larney's shop to buy some things. Mary said she had taken the precaution of putting the money straight into a pail of water to prevent the gypsy spiriting it away again.

Mary Squires had also visited Mary Gould's house in Turkey Street; Mr Gould rented a farm nearby. She had no Delft to mend, she somewhat abruptly told the gypsy and by way of retaliation, Mary Gould was informed that she did not have long to live. The gypsy went down as far as Green Street where she called at Mrs Basset's house to get a light for her pipe. Mrs Basset gave her some breakfast perhaps more out of fear than kindness. Mr Smitheram had a boarding school at Enfield Highway; also he ran a shop and, as a third enterprise, he employed women to spin yarn. Anne Hudgel did his book-keeping. This came to light in court when Anne Johnson gave evidence that on a certain day she had seen the gypsy as she was on her way to Mr Smitheram's to take some yarn, but quite another day was recorded in the book.

Next door to Mrs Wells's place in Ordnance Road lived Mr Starr and his wife Sarah. He was called to give evidence. Apparently he was a carter, and had gone to Hertford on 19 January 'for a load of peas for a gentleman in town'. About fifty yards away on the other side of the road lived another witness, William Howard, a man of independent means though he was employed from time to time as a surveyor of the window tax. The Howards had a pump in the garden which they allowed their neighbours to use. If the gypsies came across for water Mr Howard's servants had instructions to keep the doors bolted.

Evidence from farmers shows that even they were willing to turn their hands to odd jobs. William Smith who rented land at £105 a year from the Duke of Portland told the court that he had gone to Turkey Street in December to 'stamp apples' for Mrs Crow who had a cider press. He was asked why they were doing it so late in the year but he assured the judge that it was best to leave the apples a couple of months after gathering. Many of the witnesses were people who went from job to job as the opportunity arose. They were scarcely ever paid immediately but despite their illiteracy they usually had some way to keep account of the work they had done. This came in handy at the trial. William Smith refers to 'keeping a minute' of stamping the apples. Humphrey Holding, who worked from time to time for Dr Harrington, would usually have to wait until the end of the quarter, sometimes to the end of the half-year, for payment. He wisely kept a note in his book of all the work he had done.

The upper classes in the area were represented by 'Squire' Parsons. Parsons, who had lodgings in Grosvenor Square, had his country house in Turkey Street. He employed John Frame as both footman and gardener, and Sarah Vass to do the washing and ironing; Humphrey Holding also helped in the garden and Mary Gould did the housework. He usually came down to Enfield only for a month or six weeks in the summer, but this year he had come down in January.

Widow Wells's house was an old double-fronted building with a kitchen and parlour on the ground floor and three bedrooms upstairs. The loft where Elizabeth said she had been held captive was at the back of the house up a short flight of stairs from the kitchen. It had originally been added to the house by John Howitt, the first of Mrs Wells's husbands, who used it as a carpenter's shop. At the time when Elizabeth Canning was alleged to have been imprisoned there the room had become dilapidated and was used for storing odds and ends. Nevertheless Fortune Natus and his wife Judith paid Mrs Wells ninepence a week to sleep there on a bed of hay and straw with a bolster of wool. It was not very cosy; there was a great hole in the floor through which they could see into the kitchen. Animal feed was stored in it and a couple of inn signs, one of which was used to support the bed. Judith was employed from time to time by neighbours as a general help, at other times she would earn a few coppers picking up stones for local farmers.

The house had a bad reputation, 'there had been a great many broils and troubles', though Fortune Natus who must have known the place as well as anyone, 'never saw any harm in it. It is a very sober honest house', he maintained. He and his wife could not have been very comfortable there; they even had to put their bread and cheese in a drawer or the mice would run off with it and they had no privacy. On one occasion when Ezra Whiffin came in with Mrs Wells, Judith was in bed. Whiffin was the landlord at the White Hart. Someone had told him that there was an inn sign stored there, 'which has been sawed down in the rebellion time', perhaps during the panic as Bonny Prince Charlie approached London in 1745. The sign was used to support Judith's bed, so he couldn't have it, but Mrs Wells sold him the irons for a shilling.

Ezra's evidence was vital in the case for he went into the loft at the time Elizabeth was supposed to have been imprisoned there. He remembered the date 8 January, because he owed his London brewer £11 7s and went to Wormley to try to borrow it. He was unlucky and had to get back to London to pay what he had. Counsel for the defence, trying to catch him out, wanted to know if anyone had asked Ezra the exact time he went into the room. 'I don't remember' answered Ezra stolidly 'but if anyone did it was a silly question'.

But the question of dates was of the greatest importance in the case. Unfortunately the people of Enfield Wash seemed neither to know or care what date it was, or even what month. They might perhaps be forgiven for being a little confused, for in October 1752 England had adopted the Gregorian calendar and eleven days had vanished from their lives. In London people rioted in the streets demanding their eleven days back, but Ezra Whiffin had been unperturbed, 'I went by the new stile' he said 'and I hope all other people did'. Judith Natus seemed not to go much by either style. They asked her when she had come to stay in the Wells' house, obviously a matter of some importance in the trial; she did not know. Was it September, October, November, December? 'I cannot tell'. Was it before the new Christmas? 'It was'. How long ago was it? 'Upon my word' she cried in her bewilderment 'I am no scholar, I cannot tell'.

Elizabeth Sherrard who rented rooms at Ponders End was no better informed. She was unable to tell the court what month Christmas was in. Was it June or July? 'I cannot tell' Was it April? 'No not April, it might be June for whatever I know'. But she knew when it was Christmas because people gave her Christmas boxes; Mrs Wells had given her a penny. The only people who did not give Christmas boxes before Christmas, she told the court, were the Quakers at Bush Hill, and they gave after Christmas.

Thus the obscurity in which these people of Enfield Wash lived out their little lives was illuminated for a short while by the glare of public interest surrounding the case. Literally hundreds of pamphlets, broadsides, prints and ballads were printed and absorbed by a rapacious public. But what of the girl at the centre of it all? Plain and ignorant, she was totally unfitted for the role. She was found guilty and sentenced to be transported to some of His Majesty's colonies or plantations in America for seven years. But where she spent the month of January that year has never been resolved.

Susannah Wells had slipped down the social scale. Her first husband was John Howitt a respectable carpenter. It was he who had added the loft where, thirty years later, Elizabeth claimed that she had been imprisoned. He had built it as a carpenters' shop. At the time of his death in 1727 it was full of wood, timber and the tools of his trade. Forty-one whole deals (pine or fir) five beech planks, a long saw, some iron hoops and some odd pieces of deal and beech were stored there. By the work-bench was a chest where he kept his tools and 'an old pewter piss pot'. Little space was left in the yard where were stored fifteen 'baucks' (unslit timbers from four to ten inches square) twenty-one oak quarters (timber for the uprights of partitions) a little room frame, about a hundred faggots and other firewood and two planks. His grindstone was there and the signpost with its sign. In the lane outside, (later Ordnance Road) he had a load and a quarter of fir timber and eight pieces of hornbeam for firewood, the stable contained five walnut tree planks, very expensive timber; a single tree sold for £14 in 1699. Walnut tree furniture was very popular in well furnished houses in the neighbourhood though imported mahogany was beginning to take its place. There was also a beech plank and two whole deals, a pickaxe and an old ladder.[14] After she married Abraham Wells she ran into a lot of trouble. Old Margaret Richardson who lived in Turkey Street – it was her husband who drove the prisoners to London in a cart – was not sorry when she thought she had seen the back of her, and told her that she had 'done for herself this time'. She also told the court that Wells had been in 'a great many broils and troubles and nobody thought she would have got out of them', but she did. The Wells family had appeared at the Old Bailey before.

Abraham and Susannah had been witnesses for the defence in a case of highway robbery some years earlier. Accused were Edward Bonner and Cocky Wager. A robbery had taken place in Philip Lane, Tottenham. It happened that on 23 July 1736 a certain Mr Samuel Hasswell was travelling home to Southgate from the

City. He came by way of Tottenham High Road in a chariot driven by his coachman. About two o'clock in the afternoon, just before reaching Tottenham High Cross, the vehicle turned off the main road down what is now called Philip Lane. As it did so the coachman heard two men shout to each other and turning round he observed that they were following the coach. As they were not masked he merely thought that like themselves they were travellers going homeward. But about a mile along the lane the two men came up one each side of the coach; their faces were covered and they brandished pistols. The coachman was forced to halt. Mr Hasswell was obliged to surrender his silver watch, worth £3, which went into the pocket of Cocky Wager; a gold ring worth 10s and £3 5s in money were pocketed by Bonner.

The two horsemen then rode on two or three hundred yards ahead towards Green Lanes while the coach slowly followed. It was still following the highwaymen when it reached the turnpike in Green Lanes. There the coachman told the people what had happened. Bonner, looking over his shoulder and seeing a group gathered about the coach, came riding back shouting 'Damn his blood, where is the coachman? Why don't he go about his business?' But the coachman had run into the backyard of a house nearby where he had borrowed a gun and seeing Bonner still looking for him he clapped the gun to his shoulder and shouted, 'Now I have you'. Bonner fell from his horse but jumped up again and escaped.

The people thereabouts knew the two of them and had seen them lurking about the lanes for some days. They alerted the constable who, knowing Bonner and Wager to be 'desperate villains', took two or three men with him and sought them in the Spread Eagle alehouse in Paternoster Row. Bonner was seized there and taken for committal to the house of Alderman Sir Richard Brocas but as the Alderman was unable to deal at once with the matter, they were forced to wait with their prisoner in a public house called the Bull's Head. There they spent an uncomfortable hour in the bar while two or three of Bonner's mates in one corner were audibly discussing where they might procure arms. However they managed to get their prisoner to the magistrate before any rescue could be attempted and he was committed to the Compter to await a hearing at the Old Bailey.

This is where Abraham and Susannah Wells come into the story for they were employed to provide an alibi for the defence. Abraham at first seemed a little uncertain of his lines. 'I live at Enfield Wash' he told the court, under oath of course, 'and I am a butcher. I came to Smithfield in June-July, I mean – aye, July it was – I am no scholar, an't please you my lord. I came to buy a bullock. I bought it, and up comes Mr Bonner. "How do you do" says he, "how do you do Mr Bonner" says I. "What, have you bought a bullock?" says he. "Will you go in and have a drink?" says I, "yes" says he.' After this somewhat over-elaborate attempt at realism, made in an endeavour to redeem his error over the month, Abraham went on; 'I bought a bullock of a customer I deal with. I paid him for it and also paid him £10 I owed him. Mr Bonner was with me and saw me pay the money. It was in July' he reiterated, 'and we were in company together five or six hours'. Another individual by the name of Lyon was then brought forward to swear that he had written the receipt for Abraham and that he had dated it, naturally, the 23 July. His services had been required, he said, because Wells could neither read nor write. Wells, said a witness for the prosecution (who sought to discredit his evidence) kept a butcher's shop and a public house called the Rising Sun at Enfield Wash. It was known locally that he harboured criminals there.

Susannah Wells proved a better witness than her husband but the whole elaborate network of lies fell to pieces under cross-examination. Abraham and Susannah Wells, with Lyon, were committed to Newgate for their perjuries and despite their efforts, Bonner was hanged. Cocky Wager was never taken and with him, went Mr Hasswell's watch.[15]

Abraham Wells with his cousin Simon Wells from Epping found himself again before the court at the Old Bailey, three years later. This time it concerned the theft of a mare off Enfield Chase and that was a hanging matter. The crime had been committed before the perjury discussed above but did not come to trial for a long while afterwards. His accuser in this matter was his brother-in-law, Simon Lewis, an unaimiable character who kept a public house somewhere along the road at Freezywater. Lewis had himself been involved in taking the mare but subsequently he became much troubled in his conscience, it appears, partly because of Wells's perjury, of which he most strongly disapproved, and partly because Wells had promised him ten shillings for his services in catching the mare and this had never been paid to him.

Battling for his life at the trial, Abraham could find no one to say a good word for him. Benjamin Garland had, it is true, said he had 'never heard no ill of him'. It was he who had arrested Lewis, and Lewis, eager to save his own neck, had offered 'to get Wells into Newgate,' which he did.

Benjamin Parnell, another in-law of Wells, divulged that Abraham had 'the character of a very great rogue'. When Wells had formerly been committed to prison Parnell had taken all his household goods, presumably by some arrangement to avoid confiscation. He had paid Wells something to make it appear legal but he had subsequently held on to the goods. This was the source of the enmity between the two.

Abraham's apparently more honest neighbours would say nothing in his favour. Said Christopher Woodham 'His general character is but a very indifferent one'. John Keys, who held a farm at the end of Ordnance Road which was sometimes known as Keys Lane, also dwelt on Abraham's indifferent character. Henry Long described him as 'a very bad neighbour, in respect of stealing (he) . . . gets his bread by it'. Richard Fletcher had never heard 'a man have a worse character . . . except a murderer'. 'No one's worse' said John Slighter. William Green stated; 'I have known Abraham seven or eight years, his general character is base . . . using his neighbours ill'. James Elson had 'never heard any character of him but that of a thief'. And so it went on, every witness driving another nail into Abraham's coffin. Thus the cousins were hanged and Susannah, for the second time in her life, had become a widow.[16]

4. The Labourers

Peter Kalm writing in 1748 tells of a farmer who paid his labourers 8d to 10d a day for twelve hours work and they had to supply their own food. The story of Emanuel Slater shows that a labourer could do better than that hereabouts. He informed the court at the Old Bailey that he was coming from Tottenham High Cross on Whitsunday afternoon 1747 and had bought himself a twelvepenny loaf and eight penny-worth of cheese. 'So I sat myself down to eat some of my bread and cheese' he said, 'when two fellows came up and asked me where I lived. I told them Tottenham. Then they asked me what business I followed and what I got a day. I said I worked at hay making and earned 14d a day. They said that they could help me to a master who would pay me two shillings and then asked me for some bread and cheese. When they had finished my bread and cheese they took me to Marylebone to have a drink. It would cost me nothing they told me but there they robbed me of my coat and gloves'.

Kalm also noticed large numbers of migrant labourers, mostly from Ireland, who descended on the countryside around London in the summer.[17] They had a hard time over here. A case in the Old Bailey in May 1747 discovers seven of them at Kitts End on the outskirts of Barnet. They had come over to look for work and had spent most of their money though, as one of them told the court, 'I would have paid for lodging but they said I was an Irishman and they would not let me have any'. Forced to sleep in the open, they were cold and hungry when daylight came. They had found no work and they decided to make their way to Coventry, 'to get what would carry us home'. Not however having sufficient means to do that, two of them stopped a coach belonging to the Green Man at Barnet on its way from St Albans and robbed the post boy of his peruke, a silk handkerchief and 8s 10d in money. The boy drove on to the Crown at Kitts End where Thomas Nichols and two soldiers were drinking. A party set off in pursuit and found the Irishmen still at the bottom of the hill at Kitts End. They took several of them, one of whom was hanged.[18]

Inflation climbed from the 1760s but its effect locally was softened by the higher wages in this area as compared with those at a greater distance from London. The contrast is apparent in the examination of two labourers in 1771. William Joyce had worked as a yearly hired servant at Hugsden in Bedfordshire; he had then been a single man and had been paid £4 10s a year. William Clark, a yearly hired servant in Enfield before his marriage, had been paid £10 a year. Both had moved on, presumably when they married and each of them was now encumbered with a wife and a small child, which was the reason for the examination to establish their settlements.

Wages for women servants were very low indeed. They received most of their remuneration not in wages but in bed, board, tips and perks. Bridget Smith, who was taken into custody in Whitechapel in January 1777 as a rogue and vagabond, said that she had been forced through distress and poverty to sleep in the open, not having the wherewithall to pay for any kind of lodging. Eight years earlier she had been employed as a yearly servant by Mr Hughes of Brigadier Hill at a yearly wage of 30s for the first year, with annual increments of 10s a year. She had worked and boarded there for more than five years. Ann Harvey a single woman was hired about 1775 by Mr Fletcher, a butcher of Chase Side, on a yearly contract at 50s a year. Three years later she was arrested as a vagabond in the parish of St Giles.[19]

As the century progressed and farmers grew more prosperous and farmhouses more elegant, there was a decline in the number of young labourers who lived in with the family. When labour was wanted it was hired by the day and where labourers had to be on the premises they were lodged away from the house.

If every village in England in any way resembled Enfield then estimates of men's incomes in the late eighteenth century would have to be accepted with an even greater degree of scepticism than they now are. Scarcely anyone depended on a single source of income. Take the case of John Bastick; he was living in East Lodge on Enfield Chase in 1796 with Captain Munro and was hired by the week at 13s to look after the animals. He had to pay the gardener a shilling a week for his lodgings in the Captain's house because the bed belonged to the gardener. He had his own pigs, eight boars, seven sows and two old sows. His master's right of common allowed him to turn them out into the woods where they fed themselves. He paid a boy 4s a week to look after them. The boy rounded them up at night and put them in the Captain's stables. One night in January they were stolen by William Bird from Bush Hill. He took them over to Romford Market and displayed them for sale in the pens. John Baker, a pig-jobber from West Ham, enquired the price. He was asked 8s but would pay no more than 5s. How much would he pay for the sow? They agreed 18s, so Bird let him have the pigs at 5s each. Baker then agreed for the other sows.

They adjourned to the King's Head at Romford to settle the deal, Baker and his neighbour and Bird and a red-haired man he had with him. They had three pots of purl and gin (purl being ale, warmed and spiced) and he was paid the £5 10s. Baker then went back to the pen and there sold the pigs making 1s 6d a head profit and sold two of the sows for 50s to John Biggs a master baker at Tottenham. Subsequently it was revealed the pigs had been stolen. Baker came over to Enfield Highway where he left a description of the thief whose subsequent arrest by George Law I will describe below.[20]

5. Parliamentary Elections

The Enfield electorate was a relatively large one since it included not only the forty shilling freeholders, but also those who held leases for lives, rent charges and other claims. Excluded were tenants who rented land, even substantial farmers like John Keys whose land was assessed at £60 per annum, or Edward Ellis who rented land worth £40 a year. Enfield was part of the Middlesex constituency which returned two members to Parliament. Ninety-two electors voted on the basis of property held in Enfield in the 1749 Parliamentary elections, and fifty-one of these lived in the parish. Two candidates stood, George Cooke and Fraser Honywood Esqs: 1617 votes were cast for Cooke and 1201 for Honywood, a proportion of four to three. The margin in Enfield was greater, seventy-seven voted for Cooke and only fifteen for Honywood.[21]

The Middlesex elections of 1768–9 were fought under the impact of the intervention of John Wilkes. His exile in Paris had become burdensome to him and he yearned to be at the centre of politics. Also his creditors pressed as heavily in Paris as they had done in London. Early in the year 1768 he returned and presented himself as a candidate in the City of London elections for Parliament. The winter that year was exceptionally severe. The Thames was frozen, bread prices soared and there was great distress. Wilkes was the hero of the small City masters and craftsmen who would have elected him with an overwhelming majority, but few of them had votes. When it came to the official election he emerged at the bottom of a list of seven candidates.

Totally undeterred, he announced that he would fight the Middlesex election. His opponents were the two sitting members, George Cooke, a supporter of Lord Chatham, and Sir William Beauchamp Procter, a prosperous barrister. The count gave 1292 votes to Wilkes, 827 to Cooke and 807 to Procter. For two days his supporters, mostly of the poorer sort, celebrated his victory in the streets. The voting in Enfield conformed broadly to the pattern in the county; Wilkes thirty-one, Cooke twenty-seven, Proctor twenty-five. But Wilkes had returned home still under sentence of outlawry. His decision to surrender and his subsequent imprisonment was followed by rioting in London. A number of people were shot by footguards on 10 May and the event came to be known as the Massacre of St Georges Fields. Wilkes was released and in June he was presented with another opportunity to embarrass the government. George Cooke had died and Procter, supported by both the court and the opposition, was presented as candidate. Wilkes's friend and barrister, Sergeant John Glynn, was nominated to oppose him. Despite his powerful backing Procter was defeated though in Enfield he received forty-five votes to Glynn's thirty-nine.

Wilkes was expelled from Parliament in February 1769 following his denunciation of a congratulatory message to the troops who had fired on the crowd at St Georges Fields. More riots followed his expulsion and again Wilkes was adopted as a candidate. The opponent chosen to keep him out was Henry Luttrell, an unfortunate choice, for he was a young colonel in the army with a bad reputation. Wilkes's victory was overwhelming, 1143 against 296. The victory in Enfield was even more decisive, thirty-two voting for Wilkes, only four for Luttrell.[22]

6. The Parish Constable and the Magistrate

Throughout the eighteenth century law enforcement remained the business of the parish constable. Few would welcome election to this humble, unpaid and unwanted office, it was neither much respected by those who governed the parish, nor much feared by the criminal classes. The contempt in which this office was held by the better class of people is revealed by John Sherwen's delightful verses written about 1780. He describes the Enfield manorial court and a trick played there on an over-assertive juryman who obviously held himself in the highest esteem. His volubility and triviality had driven the jury to distraction. He was to be chosen to fill an office of 'importance' and 'renown'; to his dismay it turned out to be that of petty constable.

So t'other day in deep debate
The Lords of Enfield gravely sate;
Doubtless inspired with anxious care,
Some portion of the rates to spare.

When all at once the Court admire,
The obtruding form of noisy squire,
Genius of nonsense quick up sprung
And settles on his silly tongue;
Spluttering responsive to his will,
Unanswerable jargon still,
Six inch incroachment – shameful jobs-
Expensive signpost – dirty dubs,
Turnips and Chase and common fields,
A fund of noise and nonsense yields,
Nor ceased he till a plan was laid
And thus the fool a jest was made.

"The jury sir, with common voice,
On you have fixed their prudent choice.
My duty and my pleasure both-
Administer the usual oath".

The usual oath the noodle took
And grinned content and smacked the book,
Nor question asks, nor fraud suspects,
But office of renown expects-

Laugh loudly dins through all the court,
Dullness itself enjoys the sport,
When Oh! with rueful length of face,
The *petty constable* is told his place. . . . [23]

The high constable was appointed at quarter sessions; three petty constables were
appointed at the court leet together with five headboroughs, three branders, two
aleconners and, in the Green Street, Ponders End quarter, a hayward of the
marshes. Early in the century the manor court met 'in Dr Uvedale's great barn
on Enfield Green.'[24]

The constable's expenses were met by the vestry. Many of the duties of the office
are revealed by typical entries from the accounts of Thomas Brown who was
constable in the Green Street quarter for the year 1710; by trade he was an ale-
house keeper but at which house is not recorded.

'25 Nov 1710.   For keeping a woman all night and carrying her to Bridewell
                the next day by justice's order
                                                                       5s

9 Dec 1710.   A note of the charge a-pressin, laid out
                                                                       6d

25 Dec 1710.   For keeping John Crawley and William Knight part of two days
                and a night and firing and candle and what the aid (a hired
                assistant) had come to
                                                                 £1 12s 4d

                Paid for a coach and laid out at London upon the aid
                                                                       3s

                Paid for a horse to go to London with them
                                                                       6s

                Paid William Curtis for a coach and four horses to carry them
                                                                      16s

6 Jan 1711.   For taking up two boys by justice order and for keeping one four
                days and the other three weeks and for firing, came to
                                                                      12s

20 Jan 1711.   For keeping Richard Blundell and George Turner four days and
                four nights
                                                                       4s

For firing and candle and the aid sitting up with them
                                                                       6s

Paid aid for going out several times with the churchwarden and the overseer[25]
                                                                       3s

Despite the fact that the office of constable was generally unpaid, as can be seen, the
duties involved the parish in considerable costs. Deputies or aids were frequently
employed by the constable and paid for by the parish; they took over a substantial
proportion of the work. A paid constable was occasionally appointed by the parish,
like Robert Turner who was paid £16 a year to act as constable for the Bulls Cross,

Green Street and Ponders End quarters in June 1699,[26] but this may have been because of the extensive duties in the Bulls Cross quarter in moving vagrants by pass into Hertfordshire. (see above p 206–7)

The character of the constable rather than the prestige of the office determined his effectiveness. One Saturday in September 1741 Henry Porter was trudging along the road through Freezywater. He fancied a drink and seeing a lonely alehouse by the roadside he decided to rest awhile. It was the house of Simon Lewis the man who had sent Abraham Wells to the gallows. Porter entered and called for a pint of beer. They sold no liquor they told him curtly, only cherry brandy, so he ordered some small beer and some brandy and, being either naive or already a little drunk, he pulled out his purse to pay for it. It contained two guineas, a quarter moidore (a gold coin of Portugal) and 8s in silver. He was seated in the kitchen where a girl who was frying beef steaks kept her eye on him to observe where he replaced the purse. He drank the liquor and fell asleep.

His money was gone when he awoke and he began loudly to demand its return, whereupon Simon Lewis stormed into the room, threatening and cursing, and threw him out of the house. He made his way disconsolately down the road for half a mile to the next dwelling where they sent him to Rondeau the constable who bravely accompanied him back to Simon Lewis's. Hearing the constable knock Lewis locked the door. The constable, showing a somewhat foolhardy persistence, continued to bang loudly. At last two lusty fellows rushed out 'and gave them black eyes, and knocked them up and down the house' so that the constable was forced to flee for fear of being murdered, leaving his hat behind him.

One of the fellows pursued Henry Porter swearing that if he caught him he would kill him, but fate relented; his pursuer fell into a ditch full of water and Henry Porter escaped. The following morning the constable obtained help and with reinforcements went back to the house and carried all the occupants off to await the attention of a justice. Then, because he had his own private business to attend to, he paid some onlookers to take charge of his prisoners, but Simon Lewis got them drunk and the prisoners escaped. Almost incredibly, the Lewis household were acquitted when they finally came to trial at the Old Bailey.[27]

George Law was a more formidable constable and undertook his duties with obvious enjoyment and an unexpected degree of ingenuity. He gave evidence at the Old Bailey in the case of the robbery perpetrated against Robert Adair Esq, sergeant surgeon to George III. Adair was returning homeward from London to Enfield Highway in his coach, accompanied by two ladies and two children, at about ten o'clock on a night in June 1791. His coach was stopped by three highwaymen armed with pistols and a cutlass. They swore a great deal and with gross and intimidating language forced him to hand over a gold watch worth £40, a gold chain worth £5, a £10 bank note and other valuables. The thieves made off towards London and the coach proceeded to Ponders End where some of the militia were stationed. Mr Adair dispatched the militia in pursuit of the thieves, but they returned without finding any trace of them. He therefore went on to Enfield Highway where he entered the King's Arms and sent for the constable. It was George Law, by trade a barber and hairdresser.

Law, revelling in his temporary authority, sprang into action. He secured a post-chaise and set off at once, ordering the boy to drive in the manner of a return (as though the chaise was for hire). He then instructed Mr Adair's groom to get up on the bar by the post boy while he himself climbed inside with his dog. At the Golden Fleece in Edmonton they were given information about the three thieves and came up with them at last on the hill leading up to Tottenham High Cross. The boy, following the constable's plan, shouted 'London hoy' and drew up alongside the highwaymen. 'Are you hired?', one of them asked.'No' he replied. 'What shall we give you to ride to town?' he was asked. He said '1s 6d apiece'. They offered him 2s for the three of them. He protested that it was not enough but then relented and told them to get up.

They opened the chaise door and the constable, following step by step his ingenious plan, called out 'Young men', says he, 'I will get out'. 'No sir' they protested, 'do not by any means'. 'Yes, I have my dog with me', replied the constable and climbed up with the post boy and groom. The constable fell a-singing and the groom sang likewise. Making light conversation to deceive their new passengers, he said to the groom, 'I shall be home before you'. The groom, taking the cue, replied that his wife would be angry with him. And thus the chaise went gently on as far as the Ship (on the west side of the main road south of Bruce Grove). Then says the constable, 'I will get down, for it is very heavy driving. Here is a shilling for you'. The chaise moved slowly up the hill until it reached the turnpike gate at the top of Stamford Hill. The post boy opened the gate and let the horses just through, then the constable sprang his trap and arrested the three. He ordered them out of the chaise one at a time and searched them. The groom with a stick guarded one door, the post boy the other. Three gentlemen came along and rendered assistance. The watch was discovered inside the coach. The prisoners were found guilty at the Old Bailey but were recommended to mercy by the jury, both on account of their youth and because they had used no violence.

George Law so enjoyed his role as constable that he appears to have been a little reluctant to relinquish it. Four years later and no longer in office, he arrested a pig thief at Enfield Highway. This was William Bird from Winchmore Hill. Law recognised him from a description which had been circulated. Seeing him along the road, the former constable seized him by the collar. Bird demanded to see his authority. 'You are my authority,' said the barber. Bird threatened to knock him down and began to struggle and pull away. Boswell, a tailor living nearby, was urgently called upon to help but seeing so dangerous a conflict in progress he went back indoors. However a soldier, an acquaintance of the barber, came to Law's assistance, and the thief was brought to justice and sentenced to transportation for seven years.[28]

Convicts were transported to America, later Australia, into virtual slavery and few were able to accumulate sufficient money to return after the end of their sentence. Those who returned before their time faced death on the gallows if caught. David Kilpack, a labourer of Tottenham received seven years transportation for stealing two turkeys and two hens worth altogether 4s 6d (22½p) in January 1783. He was back by August, taken 'at large in the parish of Sandhurst' and was hanged.

Francis Geeves, a parish constable in 1804, received the highest accolade awarded by the vestry, five guineas for 'his great exertions', being severely cut and maimed while apprehending Daniel Inch who, with others, had attempted to rob a wagon on the road at Enfield Wash.[29]

The magistrates sat not only in quarter sessions but locally in petty sessions at the office of Henry Sawyer in Silver Street. There they dealt with cases of bastardy, breach of contract of employment, assault, short weight in the sale of bread and other commodities, failure to pay composition in lieu of statute duty on the roads, misbehaviour by paupers in the workhouse and the affairs of friendly societies.

Magistrates were not above the law and any transgressions or high-handed conduct by any one of them could be seized upon by the vestry, especially if the justice was a foreigner, from Edmonton for instance.

A whole series of complaints were made in 1816 against Edward Rowe Mores Esq, a justice of the peace from Edmonton. He had called before him at the Plough in Tottenham, John Knight a butcher, who was a parish constable in Enfield. Mores had indicted Knight for his failure to execute his warrant against Mary Hayden and Catherine Else, wanted for stealing beans. Mores had fined Knight £2 and had handed the money straight over to John Holmes, a Tottenham constable ('who does the principal part of Mores's business'). The money should have gone to the use of the Enfield poor. Subsequently Mores had fined the young women £1 each.

To make matters worse he had then caused the Enfield headborough to be arrested at the Edmonton Statute Fair 'under the pretence of some neglect of duty' and had held him two days. The headborough was then brought before Mores who acquitted him of the charge but said that because he was drunk at the time he would put upon him a small fine, and ordered him to pay £2. It was pointed out in vestry that there should always be two magistrates to fine a constable for neglect of duty, and that the penalty for drunkeness was 5s not £2. The church-wardens ordered the clerk to send depositions to the Treasury and to make a request to the Clerk of the Peace for the county for a copy of returns of convictions made by Edward Rowe Mores. This revealed that no returns for these cases had ever been made by this magistrate. The Enfield churchwardens ordered the matter to be laid before the Attorney General.[30]

Notes to Chapter Seven

1   GLRO MR. LV 7. 29
2   Guildhall 9174. 31 (F 1708)
3   PROB 31. 87. 904
3   Enfield cuttings file, Robinson *Enfield* V2 p 101, GLRO DRO4. 26. 1
5   PROB 31. 357. 446, GLRO DRO4. 9. 50, 35
6   in *Castle of Antiquaries* ed. David Pam 1980
7   Enfield cuttings file
8   Robinson *Enfield* V1 p 23, Guildhall OBSP 1831 (1790)
9   Guildhall OBSP 1833/4. 1577, 1519
10 Enfield cuttings file, Robinson *Enfield* V2 p 155
11 Enfield cuttings file
12 Walthamstow Vestry House Museum, scorebook GLRO DRO4 box 27, Vestry oder book, GLRO DRO4. 25. 6 Guildhall OBSP 1820. 90
13 Enfield *Articles on Enfield* (ms)
14 Pauline Phillips *Upon my word I am no scholar* EHHS 1982, Guildhall 9174. 47
15 Guildhall OBSP 13–15 Oct 1736 p 205–6, 8–13 D 1736 p 176–9
16 Guildhall OBSP 2–5 My 1739 p 78–80
17 Guildhall OBSP 6–9 Jl 1747. 145, Peter Kalm quoted in D. Jarrett *England in the Age of Hogarth* p 86
18 Guildhall OBSP 1747 p 217–8
19 GLRO DRO4. 26. 1, 19.2
20 Guildhall OBSP 1794–5 p 492
21 GLRO MR PP 1749
22 GLRO MR PP 1768–9

23 *Castle of Antiquaries* 1980
24 Guildhall 9171. 55
25 GLRO DRO4. 1. 2
26 Vestry order book 5 Je 1699
27 Guildhall OBSP 1741. 63 p 15
28 Guildhall OBSP 1791. 246 p 359, 1794–5 p 492
29 GLRO OBSR S1783, Vestry order book 30 My 1804
30 GLRO DRO4. 9. 50. 3, 38, 39, 83

Chapter Eight
Education and Religion

1. Schools of Many Kinds

The house of William Holmes the schoolmaster stood next to the Grammar School; it was large but poorly furnished. The total value of all his goods and furnishings there was less than £32. An inventory of his property was taken after his death in 1664. On the ground floor was the parlour, the kitchen, the study and 'two low rooms next to the churchyard'. He had four bedrooms, one with a closet. Only the best bedroom and the kitchen had fireplaces. There were two instruments of music in the parlour and a parcel of books in the study.[1]

The trustees now requested Mr Dearsley, the minister at St Andrews Church, to recommend a suitable successor. He suggested Robert Uvedale. Uvedale had graduated and had been made a fellow at Trinity College, Cambridge, in the preceding year. At the time of his appointment he was informed that there was a school-house at Enfield where the children would be taught, and also a house for the master where he could 'take in and entertain ten or twelve boarders' which was as many as the master's house could accommodate, the garret in the school-house being no longer available for that purpose. It was suggested to him that other children not belonging to the parish might attend the school and be boarded nearby and these would be worth to him yearly 40s a head. Thus it would be possible considerably to augment his salary which still stood at £22 per annum. The trustees also offered to allow him £12 a year to employ an usher, providing that there were as many as sixty to eighty pupils.

Relations between Dr Uvedale and the vestry remained amicable for some ten years but difficulties subsequently arose. As the reputation of the schoolmaster grew, more students were sent to him from outside the parish. Certain of the parishioners were of the opinion that he spent too much of his time and attention on these paying pupils. The Edward Wilfords, both the father and the son, Orledge Cordell, William Hunsdon, William Parnell the elder, with others, visited the school and claimed that they had found only seven Enfield children present. The local people, they said, were sending their offspring elsewhere to be educated, even paying for them as boarders, which they could scarcely afford. Writing and arithmetic were neglected. The usher Nathaniel Bosce who was paid only £12 a year, was unable to keep order among the wealthy students; it was the opinion of the vestrymen that Uvedale encouraged the boarders to be rude to him. The four churchwardens and twenty-three of the inhabitants decided at a vestry that Uvedale should be dismissed with six months notice and, in consequence, the trustees assembled in a body and proceeded to the school-house where they demanded possession. Their demand was firmly rejected. Thereupon they secured a writ, but

The Grammar School and the master's house, about 1800.

when the bailiff came to eject the schoolmaster he produced a protection (a writing which guaranteed him against molestation) and the bailiff did not dare to proceed. Following this a well attended vestry unanimously approved a motion that the parish should contest the matter at law and the costs should be met out of the parish rents.

Robert Uvedale in the meantime had commenced a suit of his own in Chancery against those who sought to turn him out. He had secured the support of three of the trustees and had persuaded them to make a lease to him of the school premises. He defended himself, protesting that he was as mindful of the town boys (he maintained that there were thirty) as of his twenty-five boarders, even though these included the sons of peers of the realm. Nevertheless forty-six of the trustees met on 16 April 1676 and unanimously elected William Nelson, clerk, to be schoolmaster from that day. Uvedale persisted in his adamant refusal to surrender his office and his house, and the mounting costs of the lawsuit burdened the parish and swallowed up rents which could have been used for the relief of the poor.

Uvedale's privatisation of the school had been a financial success for he had attracted a far greater number of boarders and of a higher social class than any of his predecessors, so many that the master's house next to the school proved far too small and too mean and ill-suited to accommodate them. He decided therefore to take a lease of the Manor House on the south side of Enfield Green so that he might invite other persons of quality to place their sons with him. Here he lodged his boarders and lived himself, letting the schoolmaster's house to Rebecca Dawkins. Meanwhile he continued to teach in the school. The Manor House was at that time in a state of dilapidation. The lease from the Crown was owned by Sir Thomas Trevor. He had sub-let the house to Tempest Milner Esq, an alderman of the City of London. It was the largest house in the parish in 1665, taxed on twenty-five hearths. Milner had cut vast quantities of wood, he had ploughed the meadows and had pulled down chimneys and an outhouse in 1662 and had removed pumps,

The Manor House was in a state of dilapidation when Dr Uvedale took it over.

pipes and cisterns.[2] Though Uvedale was obliged to spend great sums of money to restore and beautify the mansion, the move proved successful and the school doubled in size.

Eventually, as a result of a judgement in Chancery, an inquisition was held in July 1676 to enquire into the administration of the Poynetts charity which provided the funds to maintain the Grammar School. It was revealed that Edward Wilford, the chief instigator of the action against Uvedale, had never been elected by the parishioners in vestry but had 'intruded into the trust' in 1649 by pretence of a deed of grant, although election was required by the terms of the trust. He had moreover acted as treasurer (receiver) since 1663, that is for more than ten years and no vote had ever been taken to legalise his appointment, yet this was an office which should have been filled by annual election. Edward Wilford, it was alleged, had received the rents of the Benfleet property and Prounces amounting to £63 a year and had retained the money. The commissioners decided that the Wilfords together with other trustees should be removed and replaced by a number of powerful and influential gentlemen in the parish. These included Henry Coventry, one of His Majesty's principal secretaries of state, Benjamin Young the vicar, Mr Justice Joshua Galliard, Sir Charles Rich, Sir Robert Jason, Nicholas Rainton, William Avery and others, being sixteen of the wealthiest inhabitants of Enfield. The former trustees were to pay £756 into the hands of Henry Coventry which was the amount, it was said, which had been retained in the hands of Edward Wilford and others.

The Wilfords were thrown into considerable difficulties in consequence of this order. Edward Wilford the younger was in 1679 forced to mortgage a house with

Dr Robert Uvedale, the schoolmaster at Enfield.

an orchard, a garden and four closes of pasture attached, eleven acres in all, and seventeen acres of arable dispersed in three common fields. He received £309, repayable in six months. The loan was never repaid and the mortgage was transferred twice, the debt growing all the time till at last he was forced in 1686 to sell the property to James Lambert for £860; £630 of this had to be used to pay off the mortgage and only £230 was left. The family seems not to have recovered from this untimely blow. In 1724 when Charles Wilford died, the goods in the house were valued at £97 but many of them belonged to his lodgers, Mr Willis, Mrs Mary Allen and Mrs Ann Wilford. His old chaise lay in the yard without wheels or harness, and the house, though worth £250, was mortgaged for £150.[3]

Uvedale appears to have achieved total victory; nevertheless he resigned as master of the Grammar School in 1676, probably in order to concentrate his attention on his school in the Manor House. His reputation continued to grow and his pupils began to appear at Trinity College, Cambridge, where by 1721 he had sent twenty-one students including his own three sons. Eighteen months after leaving the Grammar School Robert Uvedale married. He was then thirty-five; Mary Stephens his bride was twenty-two. She was to bear him eleven children over the next twenty years. He received his doctorate of laws in 1682. There is little doubt that he was recognised as an accomplished scholar for he is said to have been asked to collaborate with Dryden, Somers and others in a translation of '*Plutarch's Lives*' from the Greek.

His reputation as a botanist, for which he is mostly remembered, spread throughout this country and into Europe. There is a description of his garden written in 1691 which tells that

'Dr Uvedale of Enfield is a great lover of plants and having an extraordinary art in managing them (he) is become master of the greatest and choicest collection of exotic greens that is perhaps anywhere in this land. His greens take up six

Dr Uvedale's cedar of Lebanon

or seven houses or roomsteads. His orange trees and largest myrtles fill up his biggest house . . . and those nice and curious plants that need closer keeping are in warmer rooms and some of them stoved when he thinks fit. His flowers are choice, his stock numerous and his culture of them very methodical and curious.'

He suffered much from the incompetence of gardeners. In one letter he wrote, 'My bulbs are confused by the roguery of my gardeners . . . so that I am sometimes minded wholly to leave my pleasures'. In another letter he complained, 'I have never yet found any blue-apron man (but one poor Scotchman who was my gardener) that had any relish for that part of gardening, or indeed of any other, in comparison with their wages and perquisites'. He had no high opinion of the Enfield postal service. 'If you send by post, direct for me to be left at the Bull in Bishopsgate without mentioning Enfield . . . for our . . . letters to a post office set up here frequently stay three or four days and sometimes longer before we receive them.'

Uvedale's great cedar looked down upon the roofs of the Town for two hundred and fifty years. Traditionally it is said to have been brought to this country in a portmanteau by one of his former pupils, but it is more likely that Henry Uvedale, his brother, trading to Scanderoon (the present day Iskerderum), the port for Aleppo, brought home the sapling. Doctor Uvedale is given great credit in Enfield as having been the first to introduce the cedar of Lebanon into this country. This however Dr Juanita Burnby and Audrey Robinson, in their excellent biographical study of the Doctor, consider to be false. They do however uphold the claim made on behalf of Uvedale that he was the first to grow the sweet-pea in Britain, probably in 1699.

Robert Uvedale, the Doctor's son, became vicar of Enfield in 1721. By then the schoolmaster was seventy-nine years old and suffering from gout; so for the first

The roof of the Manor House and Dr Uvedale's great cedar can be seen above the buildings on the south side of the Town.

Uvedale House, the Grammar School and the church from the north-west, about 1800.

time in his life, his beloved garden lay neglected. We catch a last glimpse that year of the dignified old gentleman in church, looking very frail. There seemed to be no convenient seat for him at communion and observing this, the East India man Sir Robert Nightingale, more often drunk than sober, who had formerly been one of his pupils, dispatched his servants for an elbow chair but the schoolmaster declined to use it.[4] He died on 17 August 1722 and is buried in the parish church.

Following the resignation of Dr Uvedale, the Grammar School became once again a parish school, commonly referred to as 'the free school', and thus the road was abandoned which might have led to the development of a public school on the lines of Eton, Harrow or Winchester. The offspring of the aristocracy were replaced by the children of farmers, tradesmen and shopkeepers, also the children of the poor recommended for a place by the gentlemen of the parish.

William Nelson who had been appointed by the vestry during the dispute of 1676 remained schoolmaster until 1700 and was succeeded by Thomas Harper, another graduate of Trinity College Cambridge. During his time improvements were carried out on the schoolmaster's house and a house for the parish clerk, Jeremiah Solly, was built on the north end of the school.[5] This house is still there though obviously much changed. Harper was followed by the Revd John Davis, who was schoolmaster until 1732 and then the Revd John Allen (1732–1761) was appointed. He was required to assist the vicar, James Whitehall, by reading prayers in church on weekdays, holy days and twice on Sundays when he was to preach the sermon in the afternoon. His salary was thereby augmented by £20.[6] Allen gave up the old master's house which was let and a new wing was built for his accommodation in 1739–40, on the back of the school-house against the turret. It consisted of a parlour, kitchen, pantry and brewhouse, all on the ground floor, with two rooms over. Doors had to be cut in the spiral staircase to give access to both floors. Behind there was a yard with a pigsty and a stable containing two stalls with racks and mangers.[7]

The vestry at this time relinquished the top floor of the Elizabethan school-house known as the gallery and it was divided into ten small bedrooms to accommodate boarders. Only the room adjoining west on the north end (no longer there) had a fireplace, a brick hearth with four plain ten-inch tiles. Another room, the third from the south end of the gallery, had a 'drawing stove grate'. The first floor was converted into three larger rooms. At the south end was the dining room in which there was a Portland stone hearth with a marble chimneypiece; the room was part plastered, part panelled. The middle room, or study, was wainscotted and warmed by a 'blowing stove'. That at the north end was papered 'with red sprigged paper' and had a chimney set with seventy-two galley tiles under a wooden mantlepiece. This first floor had sash windows apart from one casement in the north room. In the school-room on the ground floor were ten forms and ten writing seats, with twenty-two lead ink-horns. Warmth was provided by a hooped grate with a fender. There were four rows of pins upon which the boys hung their coats. At that time this room had its original casement windows. A door led into the yard behind and the front door opened into the churchyard.[8]

The Revd Allen was succeeded by the Revd Daniel Shipton in 1761 and he by the Revd Samuel Hardy in 1762. Hardy was a theologian of some repute and the author of a number of books and pamphlets. He was paid £50 a year in 1775 as a schoolmaster and lecturer. Benfleet Farm was let at this time at £80 a year and the parish was very profitably selling off the timber on the estate which brought in £603 in 1774 and £446 in 1776. The usher appointed in 1780 was Thomas Lily who was also employed as church clerk at £20 a year. His article in the _Gentlemans Magazine_, May 1789, gave a precise admeasurement of Dr Uvedale's great cedar. This was done 'at the desire of the well-known antiquary of Enfield, Mr Richard Gough'. Lily died in 1794 at the age of fifty-one; an obituary in the _Gentlemans Magazine_ described him as having been the master of a considerable day school at Enfield (although he had never been master), parish clerk and 'agent to the Pheonix Fire Office in that town'.[9]

Samuel Hardy resigned as lecturer in the church and as schoolmaster two years before his death in 1793. That he had been ill for some time is suggested by a letter to the vestry clerk in January 1791 from Major Cooke at the Rectory. The Major offered his apologies for being unable to attend the vestry as he had 'the gout in both feet'; he was especially concerned because the business of the lecturer was to be considered. 'I confess I should be glad to hear', he says, 'that the parish, in consideration of Mr Hardy's age, infirmities and long worn out services, would make his life easy by settling his salary on him during his life which by the course of nature and state of his health cannot continue long . . .'. His salary was continued 'out of regard to his merits and long service'.[10]

The Revd John Milne of Aberdeen University was appointed schoolmaster and lecturer in 1791. After six years the trustees were so pleased by his 'diligence and attention and by (his) engagement of an usher at very great expense (which had) considerably increased the number of poor scholars,' that they raised his salary by £40 a year. Many of the parents were so poor that in the bad years around 1800 they were unable to buy even the few books required for the modest education provided. Mr Richard Barefoot, the usher, had been paying for them out of his own very inadequate salary, which he preferred to do, he said, rather than allow them to remain at school doing nothing or to send them home. He claimed that it had cost him four or five pound every year and the vestry agreed to allow him £5 a year.[11]

To say that Mr Milne was a harsh disciplinarian would be a serious understatement; his methods of chastisement amounted to brutality. The first note of criticism in the vestry occurred in November 1805 when the master was told that he had no right to refuse re-admission to the child of any inhabitant without an order in writing from the trustees. Complaints had also been made about 'the offensive conduct of the assistant' which had descredited the school. He had been appointed by the master. Nevertheless there was so great an increase in the number of scholars that in March 1807 the vestry authorised the appointment of a second usher and allowed £10 a year for his salary. Two months later they voted £30 to be equally divided between the Revd Milne and his assistant.[12]

A serious complaint against the master for the ill-treatment of pupils came in October 1808. Mr Clarke the surgeon examined Mr David Draper's son and found that his collarbone was broken. Isaac Robinson, aged fourteen, said that he had seen Mr Milne strike young Draper on the shoulder with his elbow; he had been sitting only two yards away he claimed. His account was corroborated by Michael Nicholson, aged twelve. The master declared that he had used no other means of chastising the boy than a piece of leather; this he produced for examination by the vestry. The trustees felt that no great violence had been intended, but made it clear that they would listen to any further complaints of improper punishment.

They had not long to wait for in January Mr Fox's boy came home and complained that he had been severely beaten by the Revd Milne. There were several bumps on his head and his ear was much swelled and so bruised as to appear quite black. There were bruises on his arm from the back of his hand upward. The master had offered the boy's mother half-a-crown to give to the boy, but she refused it. Then Mrs Williams complained that her son, who was deformed, had been frequently beaten by Mr Collier the usher for trifling causes, on one occasion so severely about the head as to prevent him from attending school for three days. Collier was dismissed. The master replaced him by appointing Henry Bewley who had formerly been a pupil at the school. The trustees were dubious about his capacity to maintain discipline and recommended that he be put on six months' probation. He was to be paid £40 a year; the master was to have £100 but he was asked to resign his appointment as lecturer from which he had derived £26 a year.[13]

Boys were now admitted to the school at the age of seven and had to leave at fourteen. The accounts committee was much alarmed at the increased cost of books, pens, ink and paper for the poor boys. They recommended that no allowance for this purpose should be made in future but that slates and pencils should be provided for their instruction in arithmetic. The vestry firmly rejected a proposal in November which would have allowed £5 for the purchase of copy-books for those children whose parents could not afford to buy them. Mr Milne pointed out however that the pupils were not all children of the poor; many were sons of tradesmen and farmers.[14] The vestry also rejected a proposal to increase the salary of Henry Bewley to £50.

Hostility against the Revd Milne persisted and continued to grow. He had for many years derived a regular profit from the sale of books, copy-books and other materials to the parents. It was ordered in February 1817 that this must cease; the parents must purchase whatever was necessary from Mr W. Lake's shop in Enfield Town and, if unavailable there, from the vicar the Revd Henry Porter. The trustees refused to compensate the schoolmaster for any loss of income.[15]

A more virulent attack was made on Mr Milne a few months later. 'Though there are in the school, upwards of a hundred scholars', declared the trustees, 'no other attention is paid by him to their instruction than hearing them read and repeat the catechism which occupies less than an hour in the morning and about the same time in the afternoon, leaving the whole remaining business to the care of the usher'. The trustees considered the salary paid to the schoolmaster to be a waste of the funds.

They further asserted that he had been admitting boys who did not belong to the parish for whom he received payment, and that he continued to supply books and stationery at a profit in gross contempt of the vestry. He was threatened with dismissal. The master defended his conduct on each count. Describing his day at school he told the trustees that his morning began at nine o'clock with the reading of prayers. He then heard each class read, which took an hour or more, following which he came out for a few minutes, he said, to assist his own son in his studies. During this time the boys were to prepare for his return. He then instructed them in the catechism, taught them hymns and examined them on Crossman's '*Introduction to the Christian Religion*', which almost all the boys could say by heart. Meanwhile the older boys did English grammar or orthographical exercises.

Mr Milne made a larger claim before the Commissioners on Education of the Poor in 1819 when he stated that he taught reading, writing, arithmetic and the English grammar, and further, 'geography, mathematical learning and classics, for those who stay long enough and have the capacity for it'. None of this was part of his contract but he provided it free, though 'sometimes the parents may make small presents for the higher instruction'. He claimed that all those boys who were now making a livelihood by the learning they had acquired at the school would, 'with a unanimous voice, declare how carefully and diligently they had been instructed', and since he could not for the moment call forth these declarations in his defence, he cited his usher, Henry Bewley, 'who had received the whole of his learning in the school'.[16]

Further serious accusations of brutality were made against the Revd Milne in June 1818. Thomas Abrams was eleven years old. 'I could not learn my catechism', he said, 'Mr Milne struck me three times on the hand with a strap and having turned me back to learn it struck me on both sides of my head. On the following day I went up to Mr Milne to say my catechism but I could not say it. Mr Milne told me to hold out my hand and came towards me in a great passion. I was very much frightened and I fell down in a fit'. The boy was taken home where he remained unconscious for several hours. His parents alleged that this had impaired his intellect; they asserted that the boy had never before been subject to fits.

The catechism seems to have been causing problems. The boy William Taylor described how the pupils ranged themselves in an uneasy circle around the master. Taylor could not say his catechism and was told to kneel down and learn it. While in this posture of prayer the Revd Milne struck his head knocking him against a desk so violently that his head swelled up. He then struck him twelve or fourteen times on the hand with a leather strap, which caused a great swelling and then punched his arm. The vestry was by now of the opinion that the Revd John Milne was unfit to continue any longer as schoolmaster. At a meeting on 9 July 1818, attended by forty-six of the leading parishioners and many other inhabitants, it was ordered that Mr Milne be removed. Mr Milne declined to accept the verdict of the vestry and filed a bill in Chancery disputing the legality of the decision. The trustees in consequence not only withheld his salary but even refused to provide coal to heat the school-room.[17]

The Court of Chancery eventually maintained the schoolmaster's right to retain

The Girls' School of Industry, established by the nonconformists in 1806 and later known as Kingdom Hall.

his office. Relations between the master and the vestry thereafter improved. In December 1828 he consented to relinquish his claim to the rent of the old Coffee House which was now allowed to the usher. The vestry in return, anxious to avoid any further conflict, conceded his claim to the rooms on the top floor of the school-house.

A new scheme of education had been obtained in 1825. It was held at this time that because the boys were mostly from the poorer classes, there being then no other schools in Enfield to provide for their needs, Latin was no longer necessary. The standard of education was thus allowed to fall below what had been required by the founders of the school. The 1825 scheme specified the arts of reading, writing, grammar and arithmetic. The school remained dependent on the rents from the Benfleet Farm given to the parish by Agnes Myddleton in the fifteenth century. The estate was leased in 1817 to George Harrison Wilson for twenty-one years at £270 a year. In 1819 however, in consequence of a depreciation in the value of the land, Wilson applied for a reduction of his rent. The parish would not agree. In the years that followed the Benfleet Farm produced little income.[18]

Bewley continued as usher and was highly thought of, being from time to time granted gratuities of £20 or £30 by an appreciative parish. He died in 1821 and the vestry voted that a head and foot stone be added to his grave, feeling that 'such a memorial is deservedly called for', though the expense was not to exceed £10. The Revd John Milne finally resigned on 25 November 1830[19] after a troubled tenure of some thirty-nine years.

There were three applicants for his office, the Revd Robert Leman Page B.A., Mr John Barker, lieutenant Royal Navy (into whose garden Charles Lamb was nearly deposited on his way home dead drunk from Mr Asbury's in Silver Street), and Mr James Emery. Obviously Robert Page was the most highly qualified candidate but the parish had probably had enough of clerical gentlemen. A crowded vestry, by a show of hands in May 1831, elected James Emery. The defeated contestants refused to accept the vote and demanded a poll. This did not however change the verdict; Emery received 190 votes, Barker 125 and Page only twenty-three. Emery became schoolmaster on 7 July 1831.

Peter Hardy and Thomas Browning, the two auditors appointed by the parish, reported in May 1833 on the sad state of their once well-endowed school. The Poynetts farm had remained for many years untenanted; now at last a tenant had been found and a twenty-one year lease had been issued, but the trustees had been forced to reduce the rent from £270 to £120 a year. The loss of rents, the repairs required to the buildings, together with the suit brought against the parish by John Milne had, notwithstanding the sale of timber on the estate, involved the trust in considerable losses. About £40 in taxes remained unpaid, £190 was due to the schoolmaster and £28 to the attorney.[20]

'The great and prevailing ignorance which appeared among the lower classes of the inhabitants of this extensive parish (said Robinson, v2, p127) had long been the cause of regret to the more opulent.'

A school for the education of the children of the poor was opened in what had been part of the former Fighting Cocks alehouse in Baker Street in January 1787. Boys were taught reading, writing and arithmetic and the girls learned 'to read, sew, mark and knit', older girls received instruction in writing. By the time Robinson wrote in 1823, this school had declined almost to nothing. Turpin's gift in the 1770s provided £7 a year for the education of three poor girls of the Town quarter in reading, writing and needlework. There were two schools for poor girls in the parish in 1818.[21] One in Baker Street had been set up by the nonconformists in 1806 and was maintained entirely by voluntary subscriptions according to Robinson (vol. 2 p129). About £50 was collected at the Baker Street meeting house and at the two chapels in Chase Side, £75 resulted from annual subscriptions and £20 from the sale of the work done by the children. Fifty pupils attended who were all given dinners on school days throughout the winter, and were instructed 'in working and reading' and forty of them were provided with school uniforms.[22]

Another girls' school of industry had been established in 1800, in the Old Coffee House in the churchyard. About forty girls there were clothed, given a practical elementary education and instructed 'in the doctrines of the established Church of England.' (Robinson 2. p130) It remained there until, in September 1874, the trustees of the Grammar School to whom the building belonged, gave notice that they would require the premises from mid-summer following.

There were undoubtedly a number of dame schools where the children of the poor could be taught to read and write for a small payment. Such establishments leave but little trace in the records; one however at Enfield Highway, kept by a mother and daughter, comes to light in the unfortunate story of the daughter, Sarah Biscoe. She was twenty-one years of age when, in September 1813, she married Abel Bingham in Tottenham Church. The marriage was not a success. It was about two months after the wedding that he came home one evening, about ten o'clock, to the house where they lived with her mother. Mother had obviously been discussing the husband's conduct with her daughter and the young woman, thus urged on, gathered all her courage and ventured to express the hope that he had found some employment for, she said, they were somewhat distressed at the expense of boarding and lodging him, besides which there was the money which he had borrowed from her mother.

He met her mild remonstrance by flying into a rage and having locked the door threatened her with a pocket knife, and with dreadful oaths swore that if she ever told a magistrate he would blow her brains out with a pistol. In consequence of this she obtained a warrant and because he could not find bail he was committed to prison. She was however unable to proceed against him because she had no money left and he was released. He at once returned to Enfield Highway where for three months he laid siege to this quiet household, shouting abuse and threatening violence against the two women. On Sunday 3 April, having had a little more than usual to drink, he forced his way in and mother and daughter had to flee to a neighbour's house. There they called the constable who took him into custody. Unfortunately for him it had been discovered by this time that he was a married man at the time of the wedding. The peace and prosperity of this little establishment however seemed gone forever. All the children had been taken away and for nearly three months mother and daughter had not dared to go into the street.[23]

Private boarding schools were the province of the middle class. At their best they turned out students widely read and well educated in the humanities, like young Norton Nichols who wrote home from Enfield to his mother in April 1754;

'The books I desired you to buy me were Shakespeare's plays, the *Tatlers*, the *Adventurers* and the *Universal Traveller* (the second volume is not yet finished) to which I must beg leave to add three more; *Charles Twelfth, King of Sweden, Peter Alexiowitz, Czar of Muscovy* and *Louis the Fourteenth*' (history was obviously included in the curriculum) 'My master says, if you'll give consent, he will get them for me, and save you the trouble.'

The boy's mother was on vacation at Bath. He goes on to tell her that his master had appointed an usher who,

'both writes and cyphers (does arithmetic) very well and in a little while he will have a Frenchman who will teach only French.'.[24]

William Bicknell had a school at Ponders End in 1800. The Gothic Hall School was situated in Baker Street. In 1826 James Rondeau kept the school at the Manor House.

No schools catered for the likes of John Nightingale, Thomas James, William James and John Farraway all aged between eleven and thirteen, nor is it likely that it was any thirst for knowledge which induced them to steal the box of books which belonged to Master Peter Henry Edlin (a very different type of boy) from the Reverend Stephen Freeman's academy at Ponders End. The four of them carried the box with some difficulty, for it contained twenty-eight books, across a field. When they came to the fence two of them procured a stick and with this they pushed the box up to Farraway who was perched on top but he let it fall and it landed on a stone and broke. Until that moment they had no idea what it contained. They eventually managed to get it into John Cracknells' cow shed where they hid it. Thomas James sold one of the books for sixpence. He would have preferred to keep the money but his friends objected and they trooped off to a public house and changed it for sixpennyworth of half pence which they shared out. Three more of the books went to an Irishman, James Ready, who sold oranges and fruit about the district. He met the boys near the Cock at Houndsfield and gave them an orange for each book.

They were arrested by John Mead and put into the cage on the following Sunday. The four of them proceeded to make themselves objectionable to all respectable parishioners passing the place, by creating a great noise, until Mr Mead came by

John Ryland, minister at the Zion Chapel Chase Side, who ran a nonconformist academy at what was later called the Cowden Clarke schoolhouse.

on his way to church. He told them that if they did not behave he would put the cane on them and the threat had a somewhat sobering effect. Brought before the court at the Old Bailey, all four were sentenced to be transported for seven years. If these children had parents their concern is not apparent; perhaps it can be presumed that they were orphans or abandoned.

But to stay the tears which even now must be coursing down the cheeks of my more tender-hearted readers it is only fair to point out that two of the boys had appeared at the Old Bailey not long before this time (at the beginning of May 1832). They must have been eleven at the time. John Chappell, the bailiff to Mr Herman Meyer of Forty Hall, had lost a lamb. John Broxup, one of the servants, had found the remains of it in Contemplation field. It had not been skinned but its forelegs had been tied together and it had been ripped up the belly. The bailiff, after having been informed of this, was going along Forty Hill when he noticed William James. The boy hastily and somewhat conspicuously hid himself behind a tree and immediately aroused the suspicion of the bailiff. Asked why he had killed the lamb, young James replied 'It was not me it was John Nightingale'. John Mead took both lads into custody and in due course they appeared before the court at the Old Bailey. The jury proved tender-hearted and against all the evidence dismissed the charge.

James Lemon's boarding school at Capel House also comes to our attention in 1825 through a case heard at the Old Bailey in which he accused Elizabeth Wiltshire his cook and Robert Bridon his gardener of stealing 8lb of beef worth 4s and 4lb of bread worth 8d. On discovering the beef and bread in the gardener's tool shed, Mr Lemon at once summoned the gardener and asked if it was his. He replied that the cook had given it to him. Mrs Sarah Lemon admitted that she had formerly allowed cook to give away pieces of meat off the plates. The case was dismissed.[25]

John Collett Ryland ran a non-conformist academy in the house which formerly stood in the site of Enfield Town railway station. He was the preacher at the Zion Chapel in Chase Side. He had come to Enfield from Northampton where he had been both minister and schoolmaster. He had resigned the care of the chapel there to his son in 1789, before moving the school to Enfield where he had entered into partnership with John Cowden Clarke who formerly had been his usher. Members of the established church retained a deep hostility to nonconformity. This was given vent in a long poem by John Sherwen attacking John Ryland and deriding his Calvinistic doctrine of predestination by which it was held, according to Sherwen, that only the chosen could hope for heaven, and that neither faith nor good deeds could raise a man into the ranks of the elect unless this had been pre-ordained by God. It was obvious to the members of John Ryland's congregation, he said, that they and no one else had been chosen; by definition no sinners could be admitted into their chapel.

> Though in no licensed house he deals the word,
> The meanest hut will do to serve the Lord
> To the poor cottage on the Chase repair*
> By John, weak instrument, Grace triumphs there.
> These all demure, all orderly, devout,
> The chosen few keep all the wicked out,
> The pre-ordained are all secure within,
> And yet this preacher is to extirpate sin!
> Ope' then your doors, let not the gracious word,
> Meant for the sinner's good, be kept unheard.
> The candle of your zeal should burn in day
> Not skulk in coach loft, nor be scared away . . .
>   *The Zion Chapel in Chase Side[26]

The school was subsequently taken over by John Clarke and many years afterwards was described in some detail by his son Charles Cowden Clarke. The house was airy, roomy and substantial and especially fitted for a school. He talks of the 'eight bedded room' and the 'six bedded room', which gives some idea of the dimensions of the appartments. The schoolroom, which occupied the site where formerly had been the coach house and stabling, was forty feet long. The playground was a spacious courtyard between the schoolroom and the house. Beyond the playground stretched a garden, one hundred yards in length, where in one corner were some small plots set aside for certain boys.

At the far end beyond a pond were meadows 'whence the song of nightingales in May would reach us in the stillness of the night'. There stood a rustic arbour where John Keats and Charles Cowden Clarke used to sit and read Spencer's 'Faery Queen' together. After Keats had left the school he often walked over from Edmonton where he was apprenticed to Thomas Hammond, the surgeon, in Church Street. John Clarke gave up the school in 1810.[27]

Subsequently it became May and Bluck's academy.

'I keep an academy in Enfield', stated John Bluck in court at the Old Bailey.

On the night of 15 October 1818 the premises were broken into by Daniel Short and James Markwell, two young labourers who lived nearby. They stole two legs of mutton, twelve quartern loaves, the schoolmaster's coat and a large number of sixpenny pinafores belonging to the children. The labourers were sentenced to transportation for seven years.[28]

2. Chapels and Meeting Houses

The Act of Uniformity was passed in 1662 though with no great majority in Parliament. All ministers who could not conform to the liturgy of the Church of England by St Bartholomews day (24 August 1662) were to be deprived of their benefices and no provision was made for their subsequent maintenance. St Bartholomews day seemed particularly significant to the Presbyterians as recalling the massacre in Paris ninety years before. About two thousand ministers were ejected, among them Daniel Manning of Enfield. He was replaced briefly by John Hawkins who was followed by Henry Dearsley. Mr Henry Young was presented to the vicarage on 1 September 1672. He was to preach two sermons every Sunday and the vestry agreed to provide him with an assistant. The parish pledged that his tithe would be paid in full and promised to prosecute those who failed to pay. Mr Joseph Gascoign became vicar in October 1681.[29]

Thus those who would not conform were excluded from the Church of England in 1662. Three ejected ministers came to Enfield and gathered about them congregations of Presbyterian dissenters. John Chishull had formerly been the rector at Tiverton in Devon. He was described as 'a very lively florid preacher'. He was one of those who gave evidence in 1666 to persuade the nation that the Roman Catholics had started the Fire of London. After being turned out of his living he opened a school in Enfield and, following the Declaration of Indulgence in 1672, he received a licence to preach at his house, a fairly substantial one assessed at £18 a year. The house of Mr John Hockley was also licenced for Presbyterian worship in 1672. It seems to have been in Baker Street, and the congregation met there in a barn.

Another ejected minister who came to Enfield was Haslefoot Bridges. Calamy spoke of him as 'a reserved but admired and learned gentleman and scholar'. He died about 1677 leaving money to the poor of Enfield. John Sheffield, another Presbyterian, was licenced in 1672 to preach at his own house and two other houses in Enfield. The Toleration Act of 1688 allowed nonconformists freedom of worship though they remained excluded from political life. The Presbyterians took over the former Baptist chapel in Baker Street in 1689 and Obadiah Hughes, an ejected minister from Plymouth, was appointed pastor there. The chapel was rebuilt in 1702 and enlarged and repaired throughout the eighteenth century. Extensive alterations were made in 1771 when the floor and the pews were replaced. This building survived until 1862.[30]

A congregation of Baptist dissenters was well established in Baker Street by 1669. Evidence of this is derived from the will of Susanna Williams who died that year. She left many gifts, not only to her kinsfolk but to members of her church, naming our sister Sarah Freebody, our sister Margaret Clarke, our sister Batham, our sister Plaish, our sister Mary Green, our sister widow Lupton, who each received gifts which ranged from 10s to 40s. The residue of her estate she left in the hands of her executors that the money might be used in loans to the poor of

Obadiah Hughes, an ejected minister from Plymouth, became the Baptist minister at the Baker Street Chapel in 1689.

From an original Picture in the possession of Mr Maundy

her church to meet their needs; repayment should not be demanded of them until they had sufficient to pay. Her will distinguished in particular Mr Joseph Maisters, the preacher, who was to have £10 and a silver tankard. Maisters was also the minister at Theobalds where he had been reported by an informer in 1663 for holding conventicles. He preached at Baker Street and Theobalds on alternate Sundays. In 1692 he became pastor of a Particular Baptist congregation at Joiners Hall in Upper Thames Street. In spite of this new appointment he continued to preach at Theobalds once every month.[31]

William Parnell, related to a family of instrument makers, was another named as a preacher in 1666. He preached in his own house and was prosecuted in 1685 for holding unlawful conventicles there. Also there was Joshua Wright, a Quaker, who preached at Edmonton (probably at Winchmore Hill). The Wrights became prosperous. Joshua, who died in 1699, kept a chandler's shop next to the George on Enfield Green. He also held the Green Dragon at Cheshunt, a tenement at Epping and pasture at Latton in Essex.[32] The first recorded meeting at Winchmore Hill was about the year 1662 when William Brend was the preacher. Between 1662 and 1689 persecution of dissenters was intermittent but often severe. The Quakers in particular were treated badly; many were thrown into prison and innumerable small tradesmen were ruined by the plunder of their property. The movement was still tainted by that political radicalism which had made it feared at the time of James Nayler's famous entry into Bristol in 1656 riding on a donkey while women strewed palms before him as at Christ's triumphal entry into Jerusalem. Certain

Quakers were still given to extravagant gestures and this aroused the antipathy of an increasingly sceptical society.

Solomon Eccles preached at a Quaker meeting at Tanners End in Edmonton on 24 May 1663. The quiet of this small assembly was broken by the constable who stormed in followed by his drunken assistants, cursing and swearing. 'Come' cried the constable, 'you must go along with me.' He produced a warrant but it was old and invalid and it bore none of the names of the Quakers present. They therefore refused to leave, whereupon the constable's men fell violently upon them. They dragged out both men and women by the legs and arms and threw them, one upon another, at the side of the highway. A cart was brought and they were forced into it. Still they would not submit but climbed out and endeavoured to resume their service. They were seized once more and thrown again into the cart, bruised and beaten, their legs tied and fastened, and so they were carried to Durants Arbour near Ponders End, the ancient home of Sir Henry Wroth, a justice of peace. He greeted them at the gate. 'Bring them in, bring them in', he cried, 'I'll tender them the oath of allegiance, I know they will not take it'. This he did with may scoffs and much abuse in which he was imitated by his son and others. The Quakers were committed to Newgate. The names of some of them were Clement Webb, who was a local man (taxed on three hearths in 1665), John Goodwin, William Guppy, Joseph Bryan, Laurence Aplin and David Smith.

Solomon Eccles, an extraordinary character, was arrested again a short time afterwards. On this occasion he walked through Smithfield at the time of the Bartholomew Fair, naked and with a pan of fire and brimstone burning upon his head, calling upon the people to repent and remember Sodom. 'This well meant zeal of his', wrote Joseph Besse, 'met with ill-reception, the common lot of prophetic monitors from the despisers of instruction'. Eccles was committed to Bridewell. His companion who had merely carried his clothes, was imprisoned at Newgate.[33]

The Act to Suppress Seditious Conventicles (i.e. services other than those of the Church of England) was passed in 1664. Any person over the age of sixteen present at an assembly of five or more, for the exercise of religion in any manner other than was allowed by the liturgy of the Church of England, could be convicted by two justices and committed to a house of correction for three months or fined five pounds, which was to be paid to the churchwardens for the use of the poor. Penalties were to be doubled for a second offence and a third offence could be punishable by a sentence of seven years transportation. The Conventicles Act lapsed in 1668 to be renewed in 1670 with diminished penalties. It now allowed, however, conviction by one justice only, prescribing for the first offence a fine of 5s and 10s for a second offence. The money to be paid went one third to the King, one third to the poor, the remainder into the pocket of the informer. Nevertheless the prosecution of nonconformists, even of Quakers, was not pursued with any enthusiasm until it was revived as part of the successful campaign against the Whigs in the years 1682 to 1686.

Dissent was still suspected of republicanism. Many local Quakers were prosecuted in April 1682 by Mr Justice Joshua Galliard of South Lodge. The name of Justice Galliard was feared by all who broke the law, particularly by the shivering cottager who had picked up a few sticks from off the Chase and by the pious Quaker at his prayers. Some thought that Mr Galliard's enthusiasm for the law was not entirely altruistic.

His informers in the year 1682–3 were Thomas Saltmarsh, an innkeeper and one of the constables for Chipping Barnet, South Mimms and Barnet, and Samuel

Stoner, a churchwarden at Barnet. These two had presented evidence upon oath against William Belton, a mealman of South Mimms, who had suffered a Quaker meeting to be held at his house, also against Richard Saunders, a tallow chandler of Chipping Barnet, William Wild of South Mimms a butcher and Judith his wife, Henry Hodge, Henry Nicolls described as a goldsmith of London and Sara his wife, and others who had attended the prayer meeting.

Joshua Galliard seems to have persecuted in particular the leaders of the local Quaker community. These devoted men attended meetings over a wide area. They held a meeting on 1 October 1682 in the house of Richard Clare 'in a certain street called Silver Street* near a certain hill called Winchmore Hill' in Edmonton. They met on 7 October 1683 at the house of Samuel Hodge, a butcher at South Mimms where twenty or more people took part in a service. This meeting had been broken up by two informers, Saltmarsh again and a labourer named John Heele. It was said that the parish constable, David Chappell, by trade a wheelwright, had known that the meeting was in progress and knew the name of the preacher yet had not divulged this information; he was fined £5. Samuel Hodge, for allowing the meeting to be held in his house, was fined £20. The preacher evaded arrest but was fined £20 in his absence. The organisers of the meeting refused to reveal his identity; therefore Joshua Galliard 'in his discretion', adjudged that £4 should be levied on the goods and chattels of William Wyld, Richard Saunders, Henry Nicholls, and John Bowman, all shopkeepers. His victims appealed to quarter sessions, both against this arbitrary action and against the illegal way in which the fines were levied on their goods. As a result of the information which they revealed, Galliard and his informers were themselves subsequently (January 1683) prosecuted by the attorney general on behalf of the poor of South Mimms and Barnet, on the charge that one-third of the fines imposed should have been paid over for the use of the poor. It was alleged that Galliard had distrained and sold goods from which he had derived more than £1000, yet he had failed to make any return to quarter sessions of the names of those convicted, the goods distrained, or the fines levied. The proceeds, it was alleged, had been surreptitiously divided between himself and his informers. Galliard had stated that he had not been able to distrain sufficient goods to meet the fines whereas in truth, it was alleged, Saltmarsh and Stoner had seized far more than would suffice. They had neither sought nor secured any appraisement of the goods by neighbours, as was required on such occasions, nor had they ever returned any overplus to the offenders.

Total goods to the value of £165 had been taken from William Belton. These had been sold and not one farthing had been returned to him although his fines had amounted only to £40. According to Stoner, on the first occasion, to meet a fine of £20, the officers had seized a copper, several brewing vessels, a mill and mill cloths, (said to have been worth £4 17s) thirty sacks of meal (said to have been worth £34) as well as flour, a number of sacks, seven weights, a bushel measure, a table and five chairs, and all the coal and wood about the place. Stoner admitted that he had made no inventory. He told how Mr Hickman of Barnet, a friend of Mr Belton, had intervened and deposited 30s to prevent them from taking the copper, the brewing vessels and the mill. The meal, flour, pollard and sacks, he said, had all been sold to John Joyner for £10. John Joyner the Enfield tailor, was a close friend of Joshua Wright and almost certainly was himself a Quaker. These goods were therefore probably returned to Mr Belton. The table and five

*probably the road which is now called Church Hill, Winchmore Hill was then part of Edmonton.

chairs had gone for £1, the coal and wood, according to Stoner, for 29s. He claimed that he had received 27s for his information against Belton and 3s 6d as informer against Thomas Watson and William Wyld. He believed that Saltmarsh had paid £14 15s 6d to Mr Justice Richardson at Mount Pleasant, Cockfosters. The Quakers of Winchmore Hill were indicted at this same time by Justice Richardson and Justice Galliard. Members of the meeting who refused to pay fines had their property savagely distrained. John Oakley was fined 10s for himself and his wife and £8 for a preacher whose name he refused to divulge. His goods to the value of £12 were distrained. For being at this same meeting, James Lowry of Southgate lost two horses and two quarters of malt worth £14 10s; the constable broke down his doors in his ardour to seize them. Richard Chare of Winchmore Hill had goods taken from his shop to the value of £10, including a tub of flour, a tub of white starch, a bag of hops and a half firkin of butter.[34]

George Fox often called at the home of this Richard Chare when he attended the Winchmore Hill meeting. He also stayed, sometimes for weeks, at Fords Grove, the home of Edward and Elizabeth Man. The house was considered secure for it stood back from the road sheltered behind a high brick wall. At Enfield he would rest in the homes either of Elizabeth Drye, Thomas Hart, formerly a Barbadoes merchant, William Shewen, once a pin-maker in Bermondsey, or George Watts of Aldersgate whose country house was at Chase Side, Enfield.

Thomas Drye had died in 1669. He called himself citizen and goldsmith but he was by trade a confectioner in business at the 'Three Sugar Loaves' in Wapping and prosperous like so many of the Quakers. He had a house in the Enfield Green quarter of the parish. It was small but elegantly furnished. The ground floor comprised a hall, parlour and kitchen. There were three chambers on the first floor and a garret above. The furniture was not of the kind made by local craftsmen. There were six Turkeywork chairs in the parlour and a Spanish table in the hall. His silver was worth £15 and included a tankard, a beaker, two salt-cellars, a dozen spoons and a sugar dish. His linen was valued at £20 and comprised twenty pairs of sheets, twenty dozen napkins and eight table cloths. Debts outstanding to him and thought likely to be paid amounted to £2,093; there were desperate debts of £329.

He took great pains to provide for his wife and children. He left to his wife, Elizabeth, his house and his copyhold land in Enfield, also £300 and the remaining years of the lease of his shop at Wapping. His land in Northamptonshire and £900 went to his son Thomas, his property in Hertfordshire and £600 to his son William, and £600 and the reversion of the Enfield property to Sarah his daughter. The children would have to wait until they reached the age of twenty-three, though the girl, if she married with the consent of her mother, might get her portion earlier. In the meantime, their legacies were to be managed by five of his Quaker friends, Amos Stodart, Gerard Roberts, Samuel Newton, Arthur Cooke and Thomas Yoakley who were to care for the education of the children 'in the fear of the Lord, and among friends of the truth'. These same men were to administer a legacy of £200 which he provided for the use of the poor 'amongst the people of God called Quakers'. He also left £5 for the relief of the poor of Enfield.[35]

Permission was sought in 1687 to move the Winchmore Hill meeting to a house which had formerly belonged to John Oakley and a meeting house was built there following the Toleration Act of 1689. The letter to the Middlesex quarterly meeting seeking permission was signed by Joshua Wright, the shopkeeper on Enfield Green, William Shewen and others. There was a Quaker school at Waltham Abbey run

The Meeting House at Winchmore Hill.

by Christopher Taylor with 'forty or fifty young boys and maidens'. It moved to Edmonton in 1680. Taylor subsequently emigrated to Pennsylvania.

The Enfield monthly meeting, which originally included the Winchmore Hill Quakers, was recorded in 1676 at the house of Samuel Newton. Meetings were later held in the homes of Elizabeth Drye and Thomas Hart. A barn in Baker Street was converted to a meeting house in 1697, the trustees coming mostly from Waltham Abbey and Cheshunt. Thirteen years later the building was found to be unfit for use through the winter and it had to be rebuilt at a cost of £160. During the eighteenth century the Enfield meeting declined as the Tottenham one grew, at least relatively, and though they spent £70 on repairs to the building in 1788 it was given up in 1794 and was finally sold in 1803 for £90.[36] At this time there not more than 20,000 Quakers in the United Kingdom.

No trace remains of any of the chapels built in Enfield before the beginning of the nineteenth century though the delightful Quaker meeting house, set in its graveyard at Church Hill Winchmore Hill, has happily survived. The story of nonconformity in Enfield has been told in an excellent paper by Geoffrey Knight. I intend therefore only to provide a brief outline here. Ponders End lay two miles distant from St Andrews Church in Enfield Town and parish roads were poor. It proved therefore a good situation for the Congregational chapel built there in 1745. The Congregationalists in 1780 again challenged the Established Church but this time in an area much nearer to St Andrews. That year Matthias Dupont took a house in Chase Side where he held a service each Sunday. When the congregation had increased he purchased a freehold site nearby for £30 and the Zion Chapel was erected thereon at a cost of £268. Contributions amounting to £222 were received from 247 supporters, the balance was paid by 'a friend', probably Dupont. It was a plain square building and seated 210. It had high-backed pews and a

The two Independent chapels in Chase Side, the nearer is the Chase Side Chapel, the further the Zion Chapel.

narrow gallery on three sides. It was opened and consecrated, said the '*Gentlemans Magazine*,' with prayers by Mr Woodgate and Mr Medley and an 'extempore sermon lasting an hour and a half, from Mr Brewer'. The company dined copiously at the George and, in the afternoon, Mr Medley preached a sermon of equal duration. One wonders how many kept awake. The congregation stood to pray and sat to sing, led by a bass viol and other instruments; the clerk loudly read each verse before it was sung. This probably indicated a low level of literacy; indeed in the Sunday school, as Geoffrey Knight relates, spelling books were more used than Bibles. The first minister was Mr Whitefoot (1782–86). He was followed by Dr John Ryland, the great preacher and schoolmaster whom I have described above.

A serious crisis occurred in 1791 which split the congregation. It concerned the appointment of a new minister. Some members were insistent that the choice should fall upon the Reverend Chalmers, but the majority were determined to exclude him on moral grounds. Chalmers's supporters thereupon walked out. They purchased a piece of land only a few yards away and built their own chapel which they called the Chase Side Chapel and Chalmers became the first minister. Two years later it was shown that he was not married to the woman with whom he was living and that he had a wife. Chalmers was dismissed and those who had deserted the Zion Chapel because of him now proposed the reunion of the two churches. The two congregations however found it impossible to agree terms and continued their separate existences. A burial ground was opened at the Zion Chapel in 1831 and on the formation of the Enfield Gas Company, (about 1858) it became the first building in the parish to be lit by gas. The second was the parish church. When the Reverend Thomas took over the Chase Side Chapel in 1794 there were only twenty members, eight men and twelve women. Others of course attended at the services but acceptance as a member required a high standard of moral rectitude and applicants were carefully examined before admission. Enfield Highway had a Congregational chapel from 1820.

The Methodists had built themselves a chapel by 1790 and were said to have 'increased of late'. It was inherent in nonconformity that diversification, once commenced, should spread as each new prophet found the right path to heaven. The last decade of the century saw the beginnings of a number of probably short-lived churches. The Independents began worship in an outhouse in the garden of Mr Patrick Drummond in August 1791 and by October that year they had built themselves a chapel of brick and slate. Another group of Independents set up a place of worship at Scotland Green in South Street Ponders End in 1797. The following year the Calvinists began worship in the house of James Dagnel at Enfield Highway, but they moved within twelve months to the house of John Lent and by 1805 Mr Lent's house was used by the Independents.

Harry Porter, the vicar of Enfield in 1810, had the nominal care of 6000 souls but he had to share them with the ministers of the meeting houses, though only four were mentioned that year. Again it was said 'the number of Methodists is increased of late years'.[37]

3. The Rye House Plot

A last remnant of republicanism survived about Theobalds in the years following the Restoration of Charles II. The park and palace had been acquired by officers of Thomas Fairfax's regiment of horse after the sale in 1650 and several of them took up residence there under the leadership of Major William Packer. Here too was the home of Captain William Covell, whose extreme views had resulted in his being cashiered from Cromwell's army. The palace had been demolished; its site, some thirty acres, had been divided into plots, and the materials had been used in the building of houses. The park also was divided and enclosed and was now farmed. Six of the occupants were former army officers, and there were some two dozen civilian families living there. This community was centred around a radical Baptist chapel where Joseph Maisters was the minister. The chapel was the object of unremitting attention from informers:

> 'We have a restless enemy amongst us', wrote Eyton to Francis Manley in 1666, 'I mean the whole fanatic party, the head of which serpent lies in or near London, especially upon the confines of Essex and Hertfordshire . . . taking either side of the Ware river from Edmonton down to Ware and particularly those retired places of Epping Forest and Enfield Chase . . . About the road near Theobalds there is a crew of them lie concealed . . . that should there be the least commotion in London, we should find to our cost that they would be (only) too ready to second it'.

Eyton went on to report that Hugh Courtney and Walter Thimbleton had been seen in the area. Thimbleton, he claimed, had been an emissary between the regicides abroad and their supporters at home. He regarded Courtney as being the leader of the republican faction. Eyton went on to press for action; 'For should it please God that the sickness do continue', (the bubonic plague of 1665) 'this desperate faction, if not weeded out in due time, will attempt to weed us out'. Secret collections, he alleged, were being made among supporters and sent up to London. He proposed that Sir Henry Wroth be approached to keep a vigilant eye on their activities and householders should be warned to be careful to whom they gave lodging. He reported that Daniel Carey, formerly a cornet in Captain Bullard's troop, had often stayed at the home of William Moore, an Enfield labourer, and had gone from there to preachings in Theobalds Park. This Daniel Carey had frequently expressed his antipathy towards the government.[38]

George Knevett, the horse-collar-maker, looking out of the door of his little shop on Enfield Green, had observed a cart pass by, not once but ten or twelve times, bearing barrels covered with pitched cloth which looked very much like gunpowder. On one journey it carried a blunderbuss and two drums. He enquired and was told that the cart belonged to Mr Walker, a brewer of Southwark, who had a house at Theobalds Park. He decided that it was his duty to investigate; full of zeal, upon the Sunday he headed out to Theobalds. His worst fears were confirmed for there were horses tied in Mr Walker's yard, strongly suggesting that an unlawful meeting was in progress. He therefore hastened back to Durants Arbour to lay his discoveries before Sir Henry Wroth, justice of peace[39].

This genius for plot invention was best displayed in the personality of Titus Oates who, aided by the lugubrious ramblings of Israel Tonge, all but brought about the premature collapse of the Stuart Dynasty. Oates was the willing tool of the Whigs among whom there was a strong movement in Parliament to exclude the legitimate heir, James, the Roman Catholic Duke of York, from succession to the throne. Following the dissolution of the first exclusionist Parliament in July 1679, the Duke of Monmouth, Charles II's illegitimate but protestant son, was welcomed in London with bonfires and church bells. The second exclusionist

Parliament was dissolved in January 1681, just in time to prevent the passing of a resolution which asserted that the Great Fire of London had been a papist plot. The King immediately summoned a new Parliament to meet in March 1681, at Oxford, safe from the pressure of the London mob.

Sir William Roberts and Nicholas Rainton of Enfield were the members elected for Middlesex. Both were radicals, perhaps even republicans. Upon election they accepted an address from their supporters in which it was demanded that action be taken to prevent 'the horrid and hellish villanies, plots and designs of that wicked and restless sort of people, the papists'. It went on to require that Parliament should act to prevent the 'misery and ruin which must follow if James, Duke of York should ascend the royal throne of this kingdom'. It further proposed that there should be annual parliaments[40].

The Oxford Parliament proved to be the last of the reign of Charles II. The extravagant behaviour of the radical Whigs had awakened a new sympathy for the King; it even encompassed the Duke of York. A reaction set in and the Tories (the supporters of a legitimate succession) retaliated against the Whigs by uncovering plots of their own which were as genuine, though less ingenious, than those uncovered by Titus Oates. Details were revealed of an alleged attempt by Whigs and former Cromwellian soldiers to murder the King and the Duke of York at Rye House in June 1683, on their way back from the races at Newmarket. Nicholas Rainton and Major Childs of Enfield were among those who were placed under serious suspicion through the machinations of the informer, Samuel Starkey.

Starkey, in an elaborate and long-winded statement[41], told how he had received a letter from a Mr Peter Essington, a member of the Common Council of the City of London, which revealed that the perpetrators of this dastardly attempt at regicide lay in hiding at Forty Hall. The intrepid informer came immediately to London, to the Tavern at Aldgate, where he sent for Essington who related his story, surreptitiously and at great length, sitting in the dining room and apparently unaware that a second informer, Hartshorn, was lurking in the shadows to witness this 'private' conversation. Essington confessed that he himself had been a party to the conspiracy. He offered to go to Windsor to prostrate himself before the King. He had, it seems, been belatedly converted to the view 'that the attempt to murder so good and gracious a king was a horrid piece of iniquity'.

Starkey invited Essington to produce the names of those involved. It was a copious list, eleven or twelve sheets of paper bearing some twelve hundred names. 'They were no King's men', he said, 'but downright Commonwealth men.' He had had a letter only yesterday from Roger Goodenough, one of the principle conspirators and now a fugitive. He, with his companion, ill and exhausted, had stayed two nights with Sir Roger Hill near Uxbridge, but there were so many troops about that the place was unsafe. 'No house was better', the letter went on, 'than that of honest Nicholas at Enfield'. It was private and they had the master's welcome and would be secure.

A warrant was obtained from the Earl of Sunderland and Starkey, eager to follow up the investigation, hastened to Lord Craven who directed Captain Morgan to detail nine men and an officer. They marched out to Forty Hall, found no trace of the fugitives, and Rainton survived. He may be considered fortunate for Algernon Sidney and William Lord Russell were executed on equally flimsy evidence, as were a number of less important Whigs, and the Earl of Essex committed suicide.

On his death in 1696, Nicholas Rainton left his property to his daughter Mary who had married John Wolstenholme in Enfield church in May 1675. King William departed this life in March 1702 'in a unique odour of unpopularity' (Ashley) and a new war, the War of the Spanish Succession, began under an English queen. Yet Anne was not only a Stuart but a Tory and the antipathy of the family at Forty Hall towards both had not diminished. Only one month after her accession Nicholas Wolstenholme of Forty Hall, the eldest son and heir to Sir John, was accused of uttering scandalous words against the Queen. A heated political argument had apparently been in progress in the Bell at Edmonton. Mr Pott had declared with patriotic fervour, yet with some denigration of the dead King William (a foreigner), 'We now have a lawful and rightful Queen of our own country, King James's daughter, and I like her the better and thank God for her'. The allusion to the Roman Catholic James so infuriated Nicholas that he imprudently replied 'If the Queen were King James's daughter, I am sorry she is crowned'[42]. He too may be considered fortunate to have escaped retribution.

4. The Established Church

By the eighteenth century strong feelings concerning religion had become outmoded, fervour was no longer fashionable in the Church of England. Property was now sacrosanct. Each important worshipper held that he should have a pew in church which accorded with his status in the community, but it was becoming increasingly difficult because the church was crowded. This circumstance had its advantages, for money could thereby be extracted from the wealthy who would pay heavily for the prestige of a good position. Even church improvements could be privately financed. The vestry gave permission in 1703 to Richard Fountain, a gentleman of Baker Street, and Thomas Woodcock to build an extension on the front of the old gallery at the west end of the church. They were to make it twenty feet wide and eight feet from west to east, large enough to accommodate four new pews. Stairs were to be constructed ascending from the north door to give access to this gallery.[43] The rents received could subsequently be employed to lighten the burden of the poor rate.

The parish constantly sought thus to secure extra income, and not only from the wealthy. A black cloth was purchased in 1727 to be hired for the burying of the poorer sort and, in order to ensure a reasonable return on the outlay, the parish forbade the use of any other cloth. Economies were made, so ringers were to be paid on only seven state occasions each year; to mark the King's accession, his birthday, his coronation, the Gunpowder Treason, the Queen's birthday, the Nativity of Christ and the Reformation.[44]

The vicar, Dr Gascoign, received fees for all his services except the christening of his own parishioners in church. He charged 5s for the privilege of having a child christened at home and many were prepared to pay; there were three home baptisms for instance in August 1712. Parishioners paid 6d for a churching, 1s 6d for a burial, and a child burial cost 1s 2d. Those who were not parishioners had to pay double. Burial inside the church cost 10s, a child 5s. The burial of the poor was paid for by the parish.[45] The principal source however of the vicar's income was the vicarial tithe which, by the eighteenth century, was commuted for a cash payment. The rate of composition was stated in 1718 by the vicar, Dr Joseph Gascoign;

For each cow fed 2d, in lieu of the tithe of milk
    each calf fallen (ie born) 6d
    each sheep fed 1½d, in lieu of the tithe of wool
    each lamb fallen 2d
    each colt fallen 6d
    each pig fallen 1½d

for each hive of bees kept 1s in lieu of the tithe of wax and honey, for each field sown with turnips 2s in the pound of the annual value of such a field, for every orchard 2s in the pound of the annual value of the crop, for the poultry;

1d for every cock
½d for every hen
1d for every duck
½d for every drake
¾d for every goose
1d for every gander
2d for every turkey

for every garden 1d, for every house 1d in the name of smoke penny; and every inhabitant above the age of sixteen ought to pay the vicar the sum of 2d at Easter for his offerings.[46]

That year Dr Gascoign alleged that twenty-four of his parishioners had neglected to pay tithe for eight years. Tithes were unpopular and the recalcitrant were ingenious in finding excuses to deny payment. The reason these men had devised was that the turnips which they had sown in their fields and the produce of their orchards had been sold in the ground or on the trees and had been gathered by those who had purchased them. It was therefore, they claimed, the purchasers who ought to pay.

Following the death of Joseph Gascoign in July 1721 at the age of seventy-seven, Dr Robert Uvedale the son of the former schoolmaster was inducted, and a curate Mr John Davis was appointed. It was the curate's duty to read prayers 'on the three usual days of the week' and he was expected to preach every Sunday in the afternoon. The vestry allowed the vicar £40 a year for the curate's salary. The five bells had deteriorated so badly by 1724 that they were taken down and recast, with an extra hundredweight of metal added to make six bells. A subscription of £50 was demanded of the congregation towards the cost and a sixpenny rate was levied. The extension made to the old gallery in 1703 proved inadequate and in 1724 it was raised and eight new pews were built in it which were to be let or sold by the churchwardens. The following year one of the front pews was purchased by Major General John Pepper, the ranger on Enfield Chase, another by Mr Cravenburgh who lived at South Lodge, and a third by Mr Foster; they each paid £15. The four pews behind were offered for sale at £8 each.[47]

A sexton was paid 40s a year; he also received casual payments for a wide variety of tasks. From Christmas to March 1731 he was paid 1s 6d for cleaning the leads on the roof, a shilling for whipping the dogs out of the church, another shilling for sweeping down the cobwebs, another for cleaning the church tower (inside I presume), 3s for picking up the stones in the churchyard, 2s 6d for splicing the bell ropes, 2s 6d for cleaning the clock and 10s for keeping it wound and correct. Watchmen must have been employed to guard the church, for the sexton received 2s 6d 'for looking to the watch in the church'.

A print of the church by J. T. Smith. Longitude and latitude were provided by John Adams,
Latymer schoolmaster at Edmonton. The seats around the yew and the elm in the churchyard were
painted in 1731 at a cost of 8s.

St Andrews was decorated with greenery at Christmas and in the spring the seats in the churchyard around the yew tree and around the elm tree were painted at a cost of 8s. There was continual expense in replacing the quarries (the small pieces of glass in leaded windows), twenty-eight were replaced in February 1731 and a further 260 in July. From 1728–1730 glaziers work at the church cost £102 4s 1¼d, though £60 was recovered from the sale of the old lead. James Nicholls, the glazier, did further work between September 1733 and February 1734. His labour and the materials cost £25 2s 11d, but the old materials had been sold for £7[48]. Since similar extensive repairs were required on the windows at the Grammar School, one wonders whether the parish was plagued, then as now, with widespread vandalism.

The church, in May 1751, received a gift of £900 by the will of Mrs Mary Nicholls for the purchase of an organ. Whatever money was left over was to be invested and the interest was to be used towards paying an organist. Her conscientious executor, Phineas Patteshall, made no delay but at once busied himself to carry out the donor's intentions. He was to the fore at the next vestry meeting and there he read aloud the relevant section of the will which met with the approval of the minister, churchwardens and inhabitants present. Armed with their consent, he at once approached Mr Thomas Griffin, an organ builder, who agreed to set up the organ by the summer for £450. Preparatory work in the church and the obtaining of a faculty cost £48 2s. As the work neared completion, Phineas called upon a broker and required him to purchase stock to the value of £399 10s 6d. The remaining £1 18s, after the broker's commission had been paid, he retained, designing therewith to have the donor's name put on the organ.

Phineas next engaged himself in selecting an organist; he chose Mr Philip Markham. On the day on which the new instrument was installed he took his appointee with him, and the key to the organ, and went to church to meet Eliab Breton, one of the churchwardens. Breton expressed no objection to his choice of organist and offered by proxy the assent of his two fellow wardens who, he said, had desired him to act for them as he mostly resided in Enfield and they did not. Nevertheless Phineas also obtained the approval of a second warden, Henry Voght and of the vicar, the Revd James Whitehall, and he felt pleased that the matter had been agreed to the satisfaction of all. Parish business however seldom flowed so smoothly and this equable arrangement lasted only two months. Phineas then discovered to his dismay that an election had been arranged in vestry to choose an organist. He protested bitterly at the meeting, asked the vestry to take the matter to the attorney general, but this was refused and a new organist was elected. Much aggrieved, Phineas refused to hand over the key of the organ, whereupon Mr Howell, the third churchwarden, told him bluntly that if he did not 'it would be worse for him' and, much taken aback, Phineas gave the key to the vicar.[49]

There was an article on the organ in the *Musical Standard* in 1867, at which time considerable improvements had been carried out by Messrs Gray and Davidson, at the expense (£100) of James W. Bosanquet. The article described it as an interesting instrument and claims that it was built by Richard Bridge in 1752. This claim in confirmed by the *Daily Advertiser* (25 October 1753). Eric Pask, for many years the organist at St Andrews, says that Griffin was a financier and not an organ builder, and he liked to have his name associated with organs built under his instructions (*The Organ in Enfield Parish Church* in *The Organ* 68.267). The *Musical Standard* particularly praised the handsome carved mahogany case with three towers, but said that the tone was decidedly thin. The vestry, in January 1880, voted to instal a new instrument, but there was so much opposition to the destruction of the old organ that for once the preservationists triumphed. The original case was handsomely regilded and placed back against the west wall of the west gallery while the organ itself was re-erected in the south chancel chapel.

St Andrews served a very large parish, some twenty-five miles in circumference divided into four quarters; the Town, Bulls Cross (the whole of the northern part of the parish), Green Street and Ponders End. One churchwarden was appointed for each of the first two quarters and one to serve the last two. The vicar in 1766 was Robert Newbon; his living was worth £150 a year. John Tench, his curate, was paid an annual salary of £42. The lecturer was Samuel Hardy. Services were held twice on Sundays and there were about sixty communicants. The children were catechized in Lent. There were 544 houses in the parish on which rates were paid and a number of cottages which were not charged. The church could seat 970 worshippers. Many attended at the meeting houses, the Quaker and Presbyterian in Baker Street and the Congregationalist at Ponders End which had opened in 1745. The Methodists had not yet arrived in Enfield.[50]

The vestry, through its churchwardens, looked after the church. The surplices had to be washed, the plate cleaned, the communion bread purchased, and also a mop and broom. Parish pride was expressed in 1772 by the erection of a board with a frame and entablature whereon were displayed the very generous gifts made by pious parishioners over the centuries towards the relief of the poor. Salaries were paid in 1782 to Peter Levesque the organist, £15 a year, and to William Spenser the organ blower, £3.[51]

St Andrews was robbed of its plate in 1785 and the parish advertised in the press offering a reward for its recovery. Thomas Hobbs, who arranged the matter and had expended thereon a guinea and a half, now had some difficulty in getting his money back from the vestry. 'I have not had any intelligence concerning the plate or any person concerned with the robbery' he wrote, and asked to be paid. 'Tomorrow will be Christmas Day and money will be wanting for Christmas boxes'. He had to write again in January, 'It is only a trifling sum but it would be of service to me at present, having a sick family for a long time past and now a dead wife in my house.'[52]

The church was in such a sad state of disrepair by this time that the vestry in 1787 set up a committee to consider the matter and a survey was ordered from Messrs Wyatt and Holland. Following the report the committee requested James Wyatt, the eminent architect, to carry out the work, but he declined. 'It is out of my line of business' he wrote, and advised the committee to contract with some person on the spot and to employ an active young man as clerk of works to prevent misconduct by the contractor. 'I imagine the business might require his attendance five or six months and his pay might be about one guinea a week'. The committee suggested that the chancel, which was the responsibility of Lord Lisburne as rector, should be repaired at the same time. The chancel arch was in so ruinous a condition that they thought it might be necessary to take it down.

The vestry considered a proposal by Augustus Mitchell in March 1805 to repair the church at a cost of £175, but it was decided that repairs ought to be done in a more permanent fashion. Then they decided that the external parts of the church were not in immediate need of repair and postponed the matter '*sine die*'. A sixpenny rate was levied in January 1810 for the repair of the church. It was proposed that the plaster be removed from the outside where it had perished, and the crevices filled up. The outside should be washed with strong lye consisting of washed sand the best Dorking lime.

Mrs Judith Liberty retired from her duties as sexton in November 1807 on account of her great age and infirm state of health. She was granted a pension of 12s a week and her grand-daughter Mrs Burts was appointed in her place during the lifetime of her grandmother. Judith died in 1813 and Mrs Burts's appointment came to an end. Her husband Samuel, however, was appointed in her place and the duties of the office were set out in the order book. He was to keep the church clean and aired, to open the pews and keep order in the church during divine service, to toll the bells at all accustomed times, to dig graves and open vaults for the burial of the dead and keep the churchyard clean. He was to be paid £35 a year.

The church bells were re-hung in 1808 and two treble bells were added. In August 1809 the 'Cumberland Youths' rang a peal of 5084 changes on the new bells in three hours and eight minutes. Mr Thomas Brown was so impressed that he offered to paint and put up an inscription in the church at no expense to the parish.

Vandalism remained widespread and was aimed at the church. A reward of £10 was offered in May 1809 for information leading to the prosecution of persons who had thrown down and broken headstones in the churchyard. The vestry in 1817 ordered the printing and distribution of handbills offering a reward of £5 for information leading to the conviction of any person found breaking the church windows. The churchwardens in November 1821 were authorised to erect an iron fence next to the Market Place to protect the churchyard and a further warning was issued that any person damaging the church windows or hanging clothes to dry in the churchyard would be prosecuted.

The wealthy who attended the Lord's house parked their coaches ostentatiously in the roads around and, their duty to the Almighty performed, their coachmen raced away from church at high speed obviously competing one against the other for some wager. The churchwardens essayed the usual means of remedy, a hundred handbills were printed and distributed warning the coach drivers against such unseemly behaviour. A notice was put up in January 1824 forbidding children to play in the churchyard. The beadle and the sexton were ordered to apprehend transgressors.

The need to build a gallery in the north aisle of the church was the cause of much concern among the congregation. A subscription was launched in 1819 to meet the costs. This was a matter more likely to move the hearts of the wealthy parishioners than the impoverished condition of the village labourers and they dug deep into their pockets to raise £560. That same year the vestry expressed strong approval of the alterations made to the windows on the north side of the church and to the pulpit.

Mr Lochner in May 1824 was asked to prepare a plan and estimate for raising the walls on the south side of the church to the same height as the walls on the north side, and for a gallery on the south side similar to the one recently erected on the north side. The churchwardens were empowered to raise £1200 on security of the church rate, to be repaid within three years. The work was to be offered for tender but the competitors were to be tradesmen of Enfield parish.

When the work was completed a second pew-opener for the two galleries was appointed at £10 a year. The original pew-opener was to be employed in the body of the church. In 1834 it was ordered that the church was to be cleaned, repaired and painted (except the monuments), the woodwork to be in Portland stone colour. The screen at the east end was to be removed to 'open the eastern window'. It was to be replaced by a Gothic screen.[53]

Notes to Chapter Eight

1 Guildhall 9174. 10
2 J. G. L. Burnby and A E Robinson *And they blew exceeding fine: Robert Uvedale 1642–1722* EHHS 1976, Vestry order book Mr 1672, J1 1675, Mr 1676, DL 5. 37. 401, DL 9. 13, DL5. 38. 71
3 C5. 579. 3, C93. 36. 4–3, C8. 517. 86, PROB 31. 24. 489
4 J. G. L. Burnby *op. cit*, PROB 18. 37. 73
5 GLRO DR04. 26. 1, Vestry order book S 1720
6 GLRO DRO4. 1. 2, Vestry order book 6N1732
7 L. Birkett Marshall *Enfield Grammar School* 1958 p 28
8 GLRO DRO4. 26. 1
9 Vestry clerk's accounts, L. B. Marshall p. 30
10 GLRO DRO4. 5. 29. 15
11 L.B. Marshall p 30, Vestry order book Ja 1800
12 Vestry order book Au 1805, N 1805, My 1807, My 1808
13 Vestry order book N 1808, F 1809, Mr 1809, D 1809, GLRO DRO 4. 7. 43. 125
14 Vestry order book Ap 1810, N 1810, N 1812, *Second report on the education of the poor* PP 1819 p 264
15 GLRO DRO4. 9. 50 . 342
16 Vestry order book 1817, Au 1817, *Second report* XB p 264
17 GLRO DRO4. 9. 50. 69, Vestry order book Je 1818, J1 1818
18 Further report . . . concerning charities PP 1819 XB p 187–9
19 Vestry order book N 1822, D 1828, N 1830
20 Vestry order book My, J1 1831, My 1833
21 PP 1819 XB p 194, PP 1819 IX. 1 p. 536
22 Enfield cuttings file.
23 GLRO DRO4. 9. 49. 29
24 Enfield D 1134
25 Pigots directory 1826, Guildhall OBSP 1834. 336, 1832. 1238, 1825–6. 1275
26 *The Castle of Antiquaries* ed. D. O. Pam
27 Charles and Mary Cowden Clarke *Recollections of writers*
28 Guildhall OBSP 1818. 1540
29 parish register, vestry order book
30 *Calamy revised* ed. Matthews, V C H *Middlesex* 5. 250 G. W. Knight *Nonconformist churches in Enfield* EHHS 1973
31 Guildhall 9171. 50. 260
32 Guildhall 9171. 39. 198, 9171. 49. 459
33 Joseph Besse *Sufferings of the people called Quakers* 393, 451
34 J. Friends Historical Soc. V. 35. 1938, E112. 582. 22, GLRO MR. RO 5. 14–16
35 PROB 4. 13893, PROB 11. 331. 122
36 Enfield D 218, *Enfield Observer* S 1869
37 G. W. Knight *op cit*, Guildhall 9558. 432, 9580. 1. 16, 19, 150, 172, 9580. 2. 154, 176
38 Ian Gentles *The management of Crown lands 1649–60* in *Agricultural History Rev.* 19. 1. 1971, SP 29. 144. 71, SP 29. 85. 84
39 CSPD 10 Je 1667
40 Enfield D 1174
41 SP 29. 431. 42, 68, SP 29. 427. 88

42   parish register, CSPD 11 My 1702, 15 My 1702
43   Vestry order book Je 1703
44   Vestry order book N 1727, Ja 1728
45   parish register
46   E 112. 1013. 2095 S 1712
47   Vestry order book N 1721, D 1723, Jl 1724
48   GLRO DRO4. 1. 3
49   GLRO Acc 727. 41
50   Guildhall 9558. 432, 9557
51   Enfield D 1146, vestry order book
52   GLRO DRO4. 3. 16
53   GLRO DRO4. 3. 17, 27, 38, vestry order book, GLRO DRO4. 22, 9. 50

Chapter Nine

Transport by Road and River

1. The Turnpike Roads

An Act of 1555, in the reign of Queen Mary, made each parish responsible for the roads within its boundaries. Each year the vestry appointed surveyors of the highways, unpaid and usually reluctant, to undertake the responsibility and the work involved. Both Enfield and Edmonton, being large parishes, appointed a surveyor for each ward. The surveyor was empowered to call upon all villagers except servants to do four days (later increased to six days) statute labour on the roads. Those who owned ploughland (defined as fifty acres in Middlesex) or possessed a cart with horses or oxen, had to send a team comprising a cart with two men and three good horses. The team was to work for eight hours each day.

Highway rates approved by the vestry could be raised to meet extraordinary expenditure. John Selby, a carpenter, was paid £7 in 1672 to provide materials and to repair 'the two bridges' near the Enfield Wash end of Turkey Street and a footbridge half way along that road. The two bridges, however, had to be replaced in 1678; this cost £30 and to meet the expense a highway rate was levied. Parish rates and statute labour proved totally inadequate where important and heavily used highways passed through a village. The repair of the Old North Road through Ponders End to Waltham Cross became an insufferable burden on Enfield. The condition of the road deteriorated towards the end of the seventeenth century with the rapid expansion of London and the growth of inland trade. Describing a journey into London in May 1695 Ralph Thoresby wrote in his diary:

'The ways were very bad, the ruts deep and the roads extremely full of water which rendered my circumstances, often meeting loaded wagons in very inconvenient places, not only melancholy but very dangerous'.

Again, in January 1709, he tells how he

'overtook the Scotch posters and got before them to London, though at Enfield had the mischance to be plunged almost belly deep by the breaking in the ice that the water ran in at the pockets and stained my papers, as well as at the boot tops'[1]

A remedy was found in the early eighteenth century by the creation of turnpike trusts with powers to set up gates and to levy tolls for the repair of the roads. In 1713, among the earliest of an interminable sequence of these turnpikes acts which continued throughout the eighteenth century and into the nineteenth, came one for the important stretch of road to be known as the Stamford Hill Green Lanes Turnpike.[2]

The Act was preceded by a petition submitted on 17 April 1713[3] by the justices of peace, gentlemen and principal inhabitants of the parishes of Enfield, Edmonton, Tottenham, Hackney, Newington, Hornsey and Shoreditch. They complained that the highways from Enfield to London were so worn out by frequent travelling . . . that it was very dangerous in the winter season. A second petition was presented to Parliament from farmers, wagoners, pack-carriers, stage coachmen and higlers who complained that their goods were frequently overturned on the road.

Witnesses before a committee of the House of Commons substantiated these complaints. Mr Hexeter, whose business brought him to London three times a week, said that he had 'scarce come once this winter but he had seen some cart or carriage overturned and sometimes several'. Mr Boulton, who knew the road well from Enfield to Shoreditch, described it as

> 'the worst road about London . . . and it has now become almost impassible . . . That from a place called Ponders End . . . for three miles . . . is as bad as any other part of the road. And that a place called Duck Lane (Fore Street Edmonton between the Green and Silver Street) is so very dangerous that . . . ten thousand loads of gravel is not sufficient to repair it'[4]

The Act setting up the Trust appointed forty-six trustees who were to take up their responsibilities from 24 June 1713. It also laid down a schedule of toll charges. The trustees were empowered to employ surveyors and collectors and were granted wide powers to dig gravel and to cut drains on private land. The Act was originally intended to last thirteen years after which time it was apparently expected that the road would be adequately repaired and could be returned to parish supervision. The trustees seemed to have no such expectation for they formed a self-perpetuating body which could appoint new trustees when their numbers had fallen to below twenty.

It soon had to be admitted that thirteen years were inadequate and in 1714[5] the term was extended until 1728. A new Act that year brought the road from the Watch House in Church Street Edmonton to the Market Place in Enfield under the control of the trustees.[6]

This was the route taken by the Enfield stage-coach out of Bishopsgate, along Church Street, up over Bush Hill and down into Enfield Town. It was waylaid in Church Street by four footpads between five and six o'clock one evening in October 1737. They threatened the coachman James Mead with a pistol and forced him to stop, broke open the wooden window of the coach and forced the door. There were two gentlemen inside, Harry Gough and Abraham Adams, both on their way home to Enfield. Mr Gough handed over his purse which contained a guinea but the footpads demanded more and seized his gold watch and the silver in his pocket. They cut Mr Adams's breeches to get at his money and took all he had, over eleven guineas. The thieves then made off towards London on foot stopping about three fields away to share out the money. The watch was sold the following Saturday for six guineas to a Jew named Solomon Moses, 'a fellow with one eye that goes about with a bell harp'. He pawned it for £16 and it finally found its way to the watchmaker who had advertised for it on behalf of Mr Gough. One of the robbers, being traced, turned King's evidence to save his neck; he even sent his brother to arrest two of his accomplices. They were both found guilty at the Old Bailey and were hanged.[7]

Further turnpike acts were found necessary in 1744 and 1768. The 1744 Act[8] gave an increase of toll charges and introduced payment according to the number of horses. It provided a penalty of 20s for taking off a horse in order to avoid payment. The trustees were given power to farm the tolls for periods of three years, but they do not seem to have employed this method until later. The Act of 1768[9] renewed the powers of the Trust for a further twenty-one years and excluded any publican from becoming a trustee.

The maintenance of this road proved difficult and expensive. A report to the Select Committee on Metropolitan Turnpikes in 1763[10] stated that the road was frequently flooded and passengers prevented from travelling, the mail having several times been unable to get through. It was said that the Trust had spent no money on drainage which, if done adequately, would cost between £1500 and £1600. Neither Pymmes brook nor Salmons brook in Edmonton had been bridged for traffic, nor had the Turkey brook at Enfield Wash though there had been a footbridge since before 1675. The flooding of the road caused the Stamford Fly to overturn near the seven milestone at Edmonton (near Edmonton Green) one Saturday morning in 1762 and the passengers had to wade to safety.[11]

Despite these difficulties there were people who commuted to London daily like John Cartwright who told a court in 1746 that he worked at the Custom House and lived at Enfield. The court seemed incredulous demanding 'how can you live at Enfield and have a place in the Custom House?' But Cartwright persisted that this is what he did.[12]

The trustees appointed to administer the road were men of standing locally. They had to have property with an annual value of £50, or be heir to property with an annual value of £100, or have a personal estate valued at £3000. That they had a very real interest in maintaining the road may be seen from the fact that in the first year of operations they lent £3000 to the trust, for a year, without interest. Their numbers included, from the 1760s, a solicitor Robert Winbolt who was constantly employed in a professional capacity by the trustees, also a number of justices of peace, one at least of whom, Pierce Galliard of Bury Hall, had legal training which he place at the disposal of the trustees. Throughout the late eighteenth century they held their meetings and their annual dinner, 'the expense thereof not to exceed ten guineas' at the Oldest Bell (later the Angel Edmonton). They met frequently, twice or even three times a month. When a parish had handed over its responsibilities for any stretch of road to a turnpike trust, the trust became entitled to a proportion of the statute labour. During the period covered by the Stamford Hill Green Lanes Turnpike Trust order book, 1764–1773, the statute labour was performed exclusively by teams. There was a penalty, 10s a day, laid down by an Act of 1670, for failure to carry out statute labour; it still applied a hundred years later though it seems by then to have become a payment in lieu rather than a punishment.

Parishes were often recalcitrant, after a road had been turnpiked, about contributing their statute work. The 1728 Stamford Hill Turnpike Act pointed out that the powers of the Trust had hitherto been insufficient to compel the parishes of Stoke Newington, Tottenham, Edmonton and Enfield either to contribute teams or to compound with the trustees. The Act therefore ordered that surveyors in each parish should submit to the trustees lists of persons chargeable with the repair of highways.

Statute labour in the 1760s seems to have worked effectively. In the year up to April 1768, for example, on the Enfield section of the road 106 teams carried 1473 loads of gravel or about fourteen loads a day. No hired work was required for the carriage of gravel that year. The surveyors of the highways in each parish were called upon by the Trust to attend at the Board and present a list of teams to be employed on the road during the ensuing year.

The trustees were not always eager to have the road under their control extended. The inhabitants of the Town quarter in Enfield petitioned Parliament in 1767 to place Baker Street under the control of the Trust. The trustees, not relishing the additional responsibility which could bring them no additional income, excused the quarter from all future statute work on the turnpike road on condition that the petition should be withdrawn. Wards which were overburdened by the cost of repairs to parish roads within their areas were from time to time excused work on the turnpike road as, in 1772, was the Bulls Cross ward in Enfield and the Fore Street ward in Edmonton.[13] Statute work was not finally abolished until 1835 by which time it had persisted for almost 300 years.

Legislation as to toll charges and the design of vehicles became highly complicated. The charges laid down by the first Act for this road in 1713 were as follows;

Coach, chaise, chariot, one or more horses	3d
Wagon	6d
Wagon carrying hay or straw	2d
Cart	2d
Horse, ass or mule	1d
Cattle per score	10d
Hogs and sheep per score	4d

Charges, by 1744, were varied according to the number of horses drawing at a penny a horse, except for wagons carrying hay or straw. The Stamford Hill Turnpike Act of 1768 increased the charges;

Coach, berlin, landau, hearse, chaise, etc;	
drawn by six horses	1s 6d
three or four horses	1s 0d
two horses	6d
one horse	4d
Wagon loaded with hay or straw	3d
Wagon otherwise loaded	8d
Cart loaded with hay or straw	3d
Cart otherwise loaded;	
drawn by five horses	6d
by four horses	5d
by three horses	4d
by one or two horses	3d
Horse ass or mule laden or unladen, not drawing	1d
Oxen and other cattle	10d a score
Calves, hogs, sheep, lambs	5d a score

There were only two gates on the road in 1765, at Stamford Hill and at Kingsland, though there was a subsidiary gate on Green Lanes to the north of the junction with Hornsey Lane (now Turnpike Lane). This was moved to a site south of the junction in 1767. Further gates were erected, at Kingsland in 1769, at Dalston Lane end in 1770 and at Dirty Lane end in 1771, but there were no gates north of Stamford Hill so that local traffic in Tottenham, Edmonton and Enfield could use the road free.

Collectors were paid 10s a week and hours were long. The collector in Green Lanes was instructed to be on duty at five o'clock at the latest and to remain until half past nine in the evening or until dusk. The gates at Stamford Hill and Kingsland remained closed but attended throughout the night.

With the vast increase of heavy traffic throughout the eighteenth century the turnpike trusts found it ever more difficult to prevent the deterioration of the roads, since it had not been found possible to improve the technique of making roads to render them capable of standing up to the increased use. An attempt was made instead to adapt the heavy vehicles so that they would no longer wear out the roads. Narrow wheels cut deep ruts into the soft road surfaces, and charges were therefore varied according to the width of the fellies (the outer rim of the wheel). A minimum charge was devised for a wagon with nine-inch fellies, the axle-trees varying in length, so that the fore and rear wheels rolled tracks that ran side by side. The law stipulated that the wagon should roll a track at least sixteen inches wide each side. Wagons so designed, laden with hay and straw, were charged 1½d in 1765, otherwise laden 3d and they were exempted from being weighed.

A great weighing machine was built at Stamford Hill following an Act of 1751. It had to be replaced in 1766 at a cost of £130. This contraption, which could accommodate vehicles twelve feet long and eight feet wide, lifted the carts and wagons off the ground. It is not surprising therefore that three years later one end of the engine was found to be sinking and a platform of timber had to be constructed to support it. Savage penalties were enforced for vehicles which were overweight; those with wheels less than nine inches wide were charged 20s for every hundred-weight over six tons. The trustees made representations in 1773 to a committee of the House of Commons concerning the damage done by the great quantities of turnips carried to London. They also complained of the timber carriages which were too long to be weighed, and of the great weight carried on stage-coaches which had narrow wheels and which were not liable to be weighed.

It was not too difficult to evade the weighing engine; all the wagoner had to do was to transfer part of the load into a cart before he reached Stamford Hill. The Leeds wagon was on its way to London about eleven o'clock one morning in May 1791. It should have been manned by two men but the porter 'was behind at the time'. Among the goods on board they carried a truss containing over eighty yards of woollen cloth of various qualities, worth around £26. It was addressed to Read and Co, Inverness and it was undoubtedly intended that it should be sent from London to Scotland by sea.

At Ponders End the truss and other goods were off-loaded into a cart which they towed behind. 'We mostly bring a cart with us', the wagoner later informed the court at the Old Bailey. Soon afterwards he noticed three men in a cart and one on horseback, who overtook the wagon, dropped behind, then overtook it again. The driver became suspicious. He watched and saw the man on horseback ride up behind, cut the cord and pull the truss off his cart onto their own which then drove away fast towards London. The wagoner halted at Tottenham where he engaged a man to watch the wagon and himself followed the thieves to some brickfields at Wood Green where men were working. He saw the cart and the four men in the far distance and headed off after them for about a mile across brickfields but as he caught up they turned and attacked him, dragged him from his horse and threatened to bash out his brains with a brick if he followed any further. One of the thieves was taken later and sentenced at the Old Bailey to transportation for seven years. The truss was recovered from under a hedge.[14]

The Two Brewers at
Ponders End.

From a Drawing by HERBERT RAILTON.

The Two Brewers at the corner of South Street, Ponders End, in 1888.

Horses had to be fed and watered. This provided a precarious living for ostlers who were often unpaid and existed on the coppers given to them by wagoners and coach drivers. 'I was a hostler for a week at the Horse and Groom' (in Edmonton) said William Hooper, 'I watered their horses and gave them hay. When they came out they gave me a penny for my trouble which is my wages.' William Lodge was engaged about 1795 as a postillion by Mrs Bellamy who kept the Rose and Crown at Enfield Highway. He was given board and lodging but no wages. He stayed there for three years until he got married and had to leave. John Hill was another who worked at the Rose and Crown. At first he was employed as a chaise washer and was paid 3s a week by the post lads. Later he was paid by the landlord, Mr Williams, and after him by Mr Cornwall, to look after the cow and the post boys' house. At the end of three years he left the Rose and Crown and went to the Bell at Hertford (later called the Salisbury Arms) where he had his board lodging and tips, but no wages. Despite this he remained in the job when he got married. By the time he died he had four children.

The ostler at the public house was often expected to find his own fodder, like James Roberts ostler at the White Lion, Enfield Highway. 'I have nothing to do with finding hay, corn and straw for the horses,' said the landlord, William Briggs, 'Roberts did that'. He did it after dark, mostly from Mr William Walker's haystack in the farm next door. Suspecting what was going on Walker placed a servant in the summer-house in the garden of the White Lion to watch. About eight o'clock that evening two of Walker's labourers were seen pushing trusses of clover hay through a hole in the hedge where they were picked up by Roberts and carried into his stable. He was transported for fourteen years, the two labourers for seven.

Public houses along the road remained open very late, for traffic was moving

The White Lion in 1822 stood in what later became known as Old Road; at this time it was part of the main road.

throughout the night. The guard of the Leeds wagon was walking beside his great trundling vehicle (it was around the end of May 1806). Just before midnight they passed the Two Brewers at the corner of South Street. A foot traveller wiping his boots on the grass outside the pub invited him to have a drink. He replied that he would not for they were going to stop at the White Hart at Ponders End to water the horses. When they arrived there the stranger was awaiting them again at the door and had bought a glass of ale each for the guard and the wagoner. He was going to Hoddesdon he said. The wagoner was suspicious and warned the guard not to let him ride. But they went into the public house and the stranger joined them to have a mouthful of meat for his supper. It was the guard's turn to drive as they resumed their journey and the wagoner climbed up into the hay bag near the front of the wagon. The stranger was still with them and the wagoner warned his colleague not to sleep. They had gone about a mile down the road when they saw the stranger jump up on the wagon, cut open a sack, pull out the wool and stuff it into a bag which he had borrowed (on 6d deposit) from Mrs Littlechild at the White Hart. They seized him and took him back to the White Hart. The house was still open though it must have been one o'clock in the morning. William Low, the wagoner, sent for Stephen Cressingham the constable. Tried at the Old Bailey the prisoner pleaded inebriety. 'I have had,' he said, 'a character with reputation. I leave myself to the mercy of the court'. He was transported for seven years.[15]

Certain public houses along the road remained open all night. 'I keep the White Lion at Enfield,' said Joseph Turner . . . 'Mine is a night house'. Asked if he could identify several men who had come in about three o'clock in the morning, he replied, 'I was very busy at the time, I can't possibly say,' but he remembered that John Wilson the constable was there and was watching the men through a partition.

Strong criticism of the Turnpike Trust was expressed in the report of the Select

Committee on Metropolitan Turnpikes in 1763. The road had been maintained by what we would now call direct labour, working under the supervision of the surveyor, Benjamin Munday. His salary at £50 a year had been reduced in 1760 to £40, but he had been given an allowance of £5 for a horse. Late in the year 1764, the Trust set up a committee of its own to examine the state of the road and was shocked to discover that labour alone was now costing £1000 a year. Following the fashion of the time it was decided to farm out the road repairs and tenders were invited from those prepared to do the work for three years. Munday was discharged. The road was to be made thirty-three feet wide and convex with a fall of one and a half inches in a foot from the crown. It was to be divided into five sections and the quantity of gravel which was to be laid on each was specified, ranging from fifteen loads to a pole (five and a half yards) at Shoreditch, to less than one load per pole at the northern end of the road.

More primitive methods were used to repair the Green Lanes where brushwood was laid down and covered with gravel or road sand; this created a temporary drainage system. The trustees had power to dig gravel on all private land except orchards and laid out gardens. They were expected to replace the top soil afterwards and to compensate the owner. Mr Galliard was paid £15 an acre and Mr Schrider £10 an acre for the use of their land at Ponders End.

Brick bridges were built in 1766 over Pymmes Brook near the Angel and over Salmons Brook by the Cross Keys in Edmonton, but the trustees showed less eagerness to bridge the stream at Enfield Wash near the northern end of the Turnpike road when in 1769 the Cheshunt Turnpike pressed for this to be done. Finally, in the summer of 1772, a wooden bridge was erected there.

Though the road had been in a sorry state before the improvements in the 1760s, the finances of the Trust had been sound. Income, mostly from tolls over eleven years from 1752 just exceeded expenditure and averaged £1884 a year. The original debt of £3300 was still outstanding but no further money had been borrowed. Good roads however cost money and since the income was rising only slowly, money had to be borrowed. In the year 1765, £4025 was spent although the income was only £2228. The Trust borrowed £1500, almost entirely from among its own members. By December 1767 the cost of improvements on the road had forced the trustees into further borrowing and the debt had risen to £9000, whereupon the Board petitioned Parliament for an increase in the toll.[16]

The Trust in 1774 introduced a system of street lighting and policing along the road but only as far as the Tottenham/Edmonton boundary, though it was extended in 1815 through Edmonton as far as the Green and Church Street.[17] The Green Lanes was widened and improved under the Act of 1789 and the part from Bowes to Bush Hill was taken under the control of the Trust.[18] Some £2000 was borrowed towards these improvements and over the following four years £3470 was spent on transforming the Green Lanes into a road which could be used by wheeled traffic at all times of the year. The New River Company complained that before 1789 one of their timber bridges had lasted for the best part of a century but now, 'from the very great number of heavily laden carriages passing, a much stronger bridge will hardly remain serviceable for twelve or fourteen years.'[19]

Travel by stage-coach became common in the later years of the century. Coaches were improved by the use of more efficient springs and in 1784 the mail coach service began with coaches protected by armed guards. The wooden bridge, built by the Trust at Enfield Wash in 1772, had deteriorated so badly by 1814 that the Post Office threatened to prosecute the parish. The parish petitioned the Trust

The bridge at Enfield Wash.

and a committee was sent down to view the road and the bridge. It declared that the road was in a perfect state of repair and as for the bridge, that must belong to the parish of Enfield. But when the vicar produced proof that the bridge had been built by the Trust, the trustees decided that it must belong to the county.

Eventually the bridge fell down and the county accepted the responsibility. The road at Enfield Wash was rendered impassible for much of each winter because of flooding. The vestry was of the opinion that no bridge would be effectual unless the course of the brook was diverted from the line of the road (it followed the eastern side of the road from Turkey Street to Bell Lane). A contract was signed with George Munday in 1821 to build a new oak carriage bridge for £400. Sixteen oak piles, ten inches square, pointed and shod at one end and capped at the other with 1¼inch cast iron, were to be driven in by a pile-driver using a six hundred-weight weight dropped fourteen feet onto the top of the pile. The driving was to continue until the pile moved less than a quarter of an inch in twenty strokes. Oak beams, ten inches by six, were to be bolted to the top of these piles and joists, ten and a half inches by five, were to be laid on the beams and secured with nuts and bolts. The road planks, three and a half inches thick and eighteen inches wide, were to be of 'African growth, straight grained and free from sap'. The planks were to be caulked and pitched. The rest of the woodwork was to be painted four times in white lead and oil. The surface of the bridge was then to be covered by 'a strong loam', ten inches deep, and on that were to be laid eight inches of sifted gravel. The work was due to be completed in five weeks.

Robinson, writing in 1823, describes London Road where it joined Enfield Town, as very narrow and dangerous to passengers. Plans were then in preparation to make improvements. 'When the cottages in London Lane are taken down' he says, 'and the road widened . . . it will be much improved, the width may be extended to twenty feet'.[20]

Many goods from Enfield to London were carried by John Smith who called himself the 'Enfield errand carrier'. He comes to our attention because in 1823 he had to prosecute a thief. His cart was outside the Bull in Leadenhall Street where he had stopped to deliver a message to the book-keeper. As he was returning to the vehicle he saw a man standing on the footboard lifting a box out of the cart. It contained, he said, 7lb of pork, a large knife, three shifts, a petticoat, two muslin

caps and two pairs of stockings, goods worth altogether just over £1. Seeing the
errand carrier rushing down the steps the thief jumped down and fled with the
box, but thus handicapped he was soon caught and was sentenced at the Old
Bailey to seven years transportation. He was aged twenty-one.[21]

Letters were carried by the Post Office. The penny postman, Gardiner, was shot
by highwaymen in 1753 on his way from Edmonton to Winchmore Hill after he
had refused to give them his watch.[22]

Everybody of importance owned a coach and a coach-making trade flourished
locally. Eleazer Booker had a considerable coach manufactory in Fore Street
Edmonton. He was approached in May 1823 by William Jude who had four or
five hundred coach wheel spokes to sell. The transaction is recorded because the
wood had been stolen off the Chase. Booker purchased 123 spokes for £3 but
returned some as bad. Jude took the rejected spokes to Benjamin Hagger, a
wheelwright at Lower Edmonton, who bought twenty for 6s. Jude was sentenced
to three months in prison.[23] There was another coach manufactory at Ponders End
in 1827, which belonged to Thomas Wood.[24]

The years after the end of the war in 1815 saw rapid technical advances in road
making. Macadam re-made the roads for the Bristol Turnpike Trust both cheaply
and well, using the system to which he gave his name. Thomas Telford's reconstruc-
tion of the road from London to Holyhead provided a model to be followed. There
was a movement afoot to consolidate all the turnpike roads around London under
a single board. The existence of this large semi-urban area with a radius of twelve
miles had been recognised in 1792 when Daniel Lysons wrote his five-volume
historical survey, '*The Environs of London*'. The advantages of consolidation were
obvious but its advocates had to overcome the entrenched opposition of the trustees
of many turnpikes.[25] No fewer than eight petitions against the proposals were
received in June 1820.

An act was passed in 1826 to consolidate the turnpike trusts in the neighbourhood
of the metropolis north of the Thames and the Stamford Hill Turnpike Trust
henceforth ceased to exist.[26] A new body, the Commissioners for the Metropolitan
Turnpike Roads was formed and a uniform toll of 3d a horse at each gate was
collected. Improvements were made in 1832 on Green Lanes and a dangerous bend
at Enfield Highway was straightened, by-passing the old Road (Old Road) and
leaving its inn, the White Lion, isolated from the traffic it had formerly served.
About this time communications with the West End were greatly improved by the
construction of Seven Sisters Road.

Turnpike gates were set up in Edmonton and Enfield early in the year 1830.[27]
Ebenezer Gibbons remembered the one that stood in London Road 'on the corner
of Genotin Terrace passage'. 'I am afraid,' he wrote, 'that we used often to annoy
poor old Williams the pike keeper by tapping at his door'. 'The turnpikes', he said,
'used to make a journey to London pretty expensive in those days. We had to pay
3d to go through the London Road gate even if we only wanted to go to Red Lane
(Lincoln Road), 3d more at Stamford Hill and 3d more to clear Kingsland, and
at Bishopsgate there was another 2d, making 11d altogether'. The London Road
gate so close to Enfield Town was obviously a great inconvenience and it was
subsequently moved further along the road to the junction of Lincoln and Village
Roads where it would interfere less with purely local traffic. The year 1864 saw an
Act passed by which all the turnpike roads in the Metropolitan area were transferred to the parishes. The gate in Enfield continued to exist but from that time
only 2d a horse was charged. At last in July 1872 all surviving turnpikes were

12th district.

Enfield gate

clears Edmonton, Tornsey,
Manor house,
and all bars on this district.

42

Potter Printer, Kingsland.

The turnpike in London Road, with a turnpike ticket.

abolished. Thus the burden of the main through roads, particularly Hertford Road and Green Lanes, was returned to the parish. A motion was passed in the Enfield Local Board of Health urging that the cost of maintenance should be undertaken by the county.

Seventeen short-stage coaches made thirty-nine journeys a day between the City and Edmonton in 1825, Only two coaches, making three journeys, served Enfield Town (the same service as had operated in 1765), but five served Ponders End and they ran eight times a day.[28] Charles Lamb wrote to William Hone (12 August 1825):

'I sent you a note by post today, but this comes sooner by a friend. Put yourself in a coach (Bell, Holborn) tomorrow (Saturday) afternoon, half past four. Come and take a bed at an inn and waste Sunday with us gloriously. We have dainty spots to show you. If you can't come, come Sunday and stay Monday. Coaches to Edmonton go hourly from Bishopsgate . . .'

Many travellers for Enfield Town alighted from the short-stage coach at Edmonton and walked from there by way of Church Lane and across the fields, passing through the little hamlet of Bury Street and coming into the Town behind the old Cowden Clarke school-house which later became the Enfield Town railway station.

Evidence in a case at the Old Bailey in 1826 shows the Enfield stage arriving in the Town. Behind it ran the ragged figure of Stephen Markwell. Just before it stopped he grabbed a bundle (any bundle) out of the back and ran off with it into a yard near the George where the Markwell family lived. Sarah Sells alighted outside the George to discover that her bundle was missing. It was the following day, when she and her husband were out in the field drawing turnips, that she saw her bedgown hanging in the yard where the Markwells lived. She at once marched over. Emma Markwell said she had had it to wash, which wasn't very clever; then she said she had found it on the bridge. John Mead, the constable, was called and found Sarah's towel by the fire with the end burned off. The remainder of the goods that had been in the bundle were retrieved from John King, the pawnbroker. Emma got six months. Stephen was one of those whose life was to be a series of petty thefts until justice finally caught up with him in August 1832 when he was twenty-five. He was arrested by Mead in a public house, accused of stealing 12s out of the ostler's box at the George, and also the ostler's hat which he was wearing at the time of his arrest; none of the Markwells were very subtle. He was sentenced to fourteen years transportation.[29]

Coach operating costs were high for three horses were often used and they had a working life of only four years. Moreover it cost some £20 to replace a horse. Many of the short-stages were owned and operated by the proprietors of London inns, like Mr Eames of the Angel at St Clements. He had a coach station at Enfield Highway in 1826 near the Black Horse, where William Ansell his foreman changed six coaches every day and fed and watered the horses there.[30]

Valuable cargoes were sometimes carried by coach. Stephen Adams, a silversmith, giving evidence, described how he had sent his apprentice to the Saracen's Head in Snowshill in November 1799 with a box containing silver spoons and silver watches worth £18 15s. It was directed to Spalding in Lincolnshire. This was among seven boxes stolen at dusk out of the boot of the coach at Ponders End. The thief merely climbed up behind the coach and handed out the boxes to an accomplice in a one-horse cart. The coach drove on to Royston before the loss was discovered. The proprietors of the coach (but not the coachman) could be held responsible.[31]

The poor travelled long distances on the great wagons which trundled slowly along at about three miles an hour, moving day and night until they reached their destination. One appears in the story of William Cooper, a most naïve groom who met a man and his wife on the road between Enfield and Tottenham. The weather was warm (it was July 1822) and the two men stood in the door of a public house and had a pint of beer and a little conversation. Said the groom, by way of getting to know his new friend, 'I have 15s in my bundle; I will put it in my breeches pocket'. Replied his new friend, 'You had better keep it in your bundle', and so he did. It was very late before they continued on their journey. About half-past three in the morning a wagon came along. They were about to clamber aboard when the groom dropped his bundle and cried 'Damn me if I haven't lost my money'. He accused his new friend who was indicted and found guilty at the Old Bailey. He was sentenced to be publicly whipped and imprisoned for one year.[32] Thus this short-lived friendship ended.

Omnibuses served the Town by 1838. Three were run by the Glover brothers, John and William, who also had two short-stage coaches working between Enfield and Bishopsgate. William was the landlord at the King's Head.[33] Travelling by Glover's omnibus was the stylish method of getting to London; the fare was 2s 6d each way. If you wanted to go for less you would take one of the carriers, Anderson, Moore or Young; the charge was 9d to Bishopsgate, beyond that 3d extra. Edward Anderson left Baker Street every morning at ten, taking parcels to London for 6d or collecting them from any office in London.

2. The Parish Roads

The enclosure of Enfield Chase in 1777 imposed upon the vestry the duty to build new roads across the Enfield allotment. This was the eastern part of Enfield Chase, some thirteen hundred acres, granted to Enfield parish in compensation for its loss of common rights over the whole Chase at the time of the Chase enclosure in 1777. A salaried surveyor was appointed for this purpose. The roads which the parish was to construct were (using their modern names) those parts of Hadley Road, Coopers Lane Road, The Ridgeway and East Lodge Lane which crossed the Enfield allotment. The expenses were high; more than £60 for instance was paid to the gangs of workmen employed in March and April 1783. The surveyor, John Horne, was continually at loggerheads with the vestry until at last he was dismissed. His observations on their proceedings bear quoting:

> 'Gentlemen', he wrote, 'from the confusion that generally attends your vestry, by all speakers and no hearers, which renders it impossible for any man, let his cause be ever so just, to plead for himself. If he attempts, he is sure to be interrupted by a s . . . s,* or some other fool. To avoid such insults I shall lay before you the state of my case . . .'.[34]

The vestry had questioned his bill for a shilling a week expenses when workmen were paid. They demanded to know why it was necessary to pay them in public houses instead of at his home. The surveyor complained that he never had the

---

*The author will discreetly refrain from offering an interpretation of this abbreviation.

cash in his hands for the wages until six or seven o'clock on pay night. On occasions he had even been obliged to ask Mr Benjamin Vaughan to advance the money or the men would have had to go home without their pay. When he did get the money, he had to ride out to Whitewebbs, Clay Hill or Chalkleys, sometimes on a cold winter night, to settle with three companies consisting of thirty to forty men. There were times when he was given a draft on Prescott's (the firm of the banker who lived at Theobalds) and the only way to cash this was in a public house. Landlords naturally welcomed the custom this brought and the opportunity it provided to collect the money the men owed them. They therefore willingly provided accommodation for the surveyor and may perhaps have allowed a little for his good will.

The turn of the century had seen a new interest in the improvement of the parish roads. In October 1802 the vestry ordered plans to be made for a carriage bridge over the brook at Clay Hill, with an estimate showing the difference in cost between brick and wood. The following May £10 was paid for a survey and estimate for a bridge in Turkey Street. Compensation was sought the following year for damage done to Maidens bridge by a carriage belonging to Jacob Bosanquet of Broxbourne.

Transport between the eastern and western parts of Enfield was particularly difficult. The vestry in 1806 urged the Commissioners for Inclosure to build a road to link the Ponders End end of Nags Head Lane (Southbury Road) to the Town end, also to make Hoe Lane into a public carriageway of sufficient width that two carriages could pass, and also to widen parts of Carterhatch Lane. It was reported in June 1807 that the New River Company had rebuilt the bridge at the western end of Church Street, Enfield Town.[35] (over the New River).

The vestryman and reformer, Peter Hardy, always vigilant to uncover waste in parish administration kept an eye on expenditure and intervened with sharp criticism, pointing out that road surveyors should not be allowed to spend more money during their year in office than they had collected from composition unless they had obtained a rate by order of the justices. He attacked the lavish composition dinners provided free on the parish. Nobody would compound, he said, unless it was an advantage to himself. 'Why then should the parish treat them to a dinner for doing it? The table' he added, 'is generally surrounded by those that have nothing to do there but to eat and drink.'[36]

Those who owned horses and carts were liable to be called upon for the carriage of gravel, but the majority in 1814 chose to avoid the duty by paying composition money. There were some who, having secured exemption, failed to pay and these were summoned before petty sessions: John Knight, the butcher, Thomas Jelly, the baker, Isaac Fox, the corn chandler, Thomas Griffiths, a shopkeeper, John Illyot, a labourer, William Cook of Clay Hill gent, William Game the younger, a coachmaker, and William Cobb, a farmer, all had to appear. The system thus endeavoured to ensure that it was the road users who bore the cost of road maintenance and improvement.[37]

Sixty people chose to do their statute work in 1817 while 243 compounded and paid £460. William Mellish, for instance, with a rental assessed at £897, was required to perform thirty-four days work (valued at £23 16s) and to pay £1 5s 5½d, making a total of £25 1s 5½d. He performed (not personally of course)

26½ days work at 14s	£18 11s
Provided land to dig gravel worth	£6 5s
	£24 16s

The balance due from him was therefore 5s 5½d
The parish employed three or four men to dig gravel at 14s a week

King, Coomes, Scott, Staker digging gravel	£2 16s
beer for the gravel men	£1 5s 8d

(the beer money was abolished in 1822)
The Stamford Hill Turnpike Trust was paid £130 in lieu of the provision of labour.[38]

Mr Joseph Bell, who was the surveyor for the Ponders End and Green Street quarters in 1816, was required to put the road over the marshes in temporary repair. A dispute arose in 1821 when the Board of Ordnance demanded that the parish build a bridge over the River Lea to give access to the Royal Ordnance Factory (RSAF). The parish contested the matter in the courts and won. By this time Enfield parish was responsible for nearly twenty miles of roads; from the Ridgeway to Baker Street along what is now Lavender Hill and Lancaster Road, the present Holtwhites Hill and Parsonage Lane to Baker Street, one and a quarter miles of the Ridgeway, the Barnet Road from Enfield Town to South Lodge, Brigadier Hill, Phipps Hatch Lane and Cocker Lane (now the northern end of Browning Road) to Clay Hill, Enfield Town to Bulls Cross along Baker Street and Forty Hill (2½ miles) from Gough's Bridge (Gough Park) along Clay Hill then following the present Theobalds Park Road and Cattlegate Road to Coopers Lane Road (3½ miles), Whitewebbs Lane (1¾ miles), Bullsmoor Lane, Turkey Street, Carterhatch Lane, Green Street, South Street and the road from Ponders End to Enfield Town (the present Lincoln Road).[39]

The appointment of a salaried general surveyor of the highways was first proposed in 1804. The proposal was revived in September 1822 when the name of Henry Young (the younger) was put forward and an allowance of £80 was suggested. The parish surveyors (unpaid) were recommended, in November 1823, to engage him as foreman over the labourers at a weekly wage of 20s and finally, in October 1824, he was appointed general surveyor of the highways. Under his management far more men were employed. They were engaged on a casual basis though there were some who worked fairly regularly, anything from a day or two to a whole week at a time. One week might see seventeen employed, another only seven or eight.[40] The system still failed to work efficiently and the use of the roads in all parts of the parish increased as the century progressed. Mr Augustin King George had reason to complain of the condition of South Street, the road leading to his mill. 'It used to be repaired by the parish' he wrote in 1830, 'until a few years ago . . . It is now more wanted as many of the coals are carted this way in the summer months to the Town' (from the wharf on the Lea near his mill) 'It also leads to two houses in the marsh' (at each end of his mill). 'The foul water from the crape manufactory now flows over the road which makes it unpleasant to pass and unhealthy to live near'. He was speaking of the Grout and Baylis's works where crape was finished and dyed black to meet a growing middle class demand for prolonged and ostentatious mourning.

A highways board was set up in 1830 to handle such problems. The board laid down the duties of its surveyor. He was to attend all meetings, to oversee the work of those employed, to look after the tools which belonged to the parish and to provide a clerk of the board with a weekly account of money spent.[41]

Yet the system still failed to work well. After three years Mr Peter Hardy was asked to investigate. He reported that the accounts were in 'a disreputable state . . . made out in a very inaccurate manner, the sums to be collected had not even been inserted' before the books were passed to the surveyor. This was almost at the end of the year, so that he had to collect composition money without knowing precisely what he should collect. Mr Hardy urged that nobody should pay composition unless the book was produced. He proposed that the surveyor should reduce the duty to one and a half days for a £50 assessment and that 4d in the pound be paid as composition. He attributed the improper state of the accounts to the apathy of the ratepayers. 'In 1831 and 1832 nobody attended the vestries called for the examination of the accounts. It would be lamentable if the management of the roads was thrown back under the old system, for then the highways cost the parish more than double the sum expended by the paid surveyor, including his salary, and the work was not so well done.'[42]

3. The River Lea

The waters of the River Lea served so many conflicting interests that navigation was constantly impeded throughout the seventeenth and eighteenth centuries until John Smeaton's improvements, following the Act of 1767, brought efficiency at last and greatly increased traffic. The most serious conflict of interest lay between the millers and the barge owners. It continued unabated along the whole length of the old River Lea, for water taken to drive the mills lowered the level in the navigable river so that barges could not pass. Thomas Worrill of Tottenham Mills in 1666 was alleged to have held up twenty barges after he had altered his sluice to divert additional water into his mill stream. The barges could not pass unless he released water into the navigable river, and for this he demanded 5s or 10s. It was accused against him that his real motive was to compel the barges to unload at his wharf from where the cargoes would be carried to London by road. He was ordered to accept the accustomed toll which he had formerly received to provide water for the boats to pass.

Navigation on the river was made more difficult by the New River Company which contrived to take as much as a third of the water. The frustrated bargees responded by sabotage. The dispute intensified and the City of London found it difficult to adjudicate, for transport by river provided cheap food in London and the New River provided clean water. Compromise between the two interests was not arrived at until 1738.

In the meantime conflicts continued intermittently both with the New River Company and with the mill owners. A survey of 1694 found that barges were often held up for twelve or sixteen days. The cost of water transport had risen to 19s a ton, only one shilling cheaper than transport by road. Nothing more than minor improvement was carried out in the years 1670 to 1700 and the river remained in a state of mediaeval inefficiency, of more use as a source of power than as a means of transport. For much of its length there was no towpath for horses and the barges were still hauled by men.[43]

The Commission of Sewers in 1719–20 initiated a survey and found that John Flanders, the miller at Ponders End, had, some ten years before, pulled down the old lock called Enfield lock and had built a new one there, contriving in so doing to divert an even greater quantity of water out of the navigable river into his mill stream. When the old lock had been in place, only boats coming fully laden from Ware required water from the miller to navigate the river between the inlet and the mouth of his mill stream. Mr Flanders would open the gate of his old lock, which was four feet wide, so that the water would be of sufficient depth in the navigable river. For this service he had charged 1s a barge on Tuesdays, Thursdays and Saturdays, and 2s on Mondays, Wednesdays and Fridays (presumably when he was grinding). The water had formerly been of a sufficient depth for barges returning from London, either empty or part laden, to pass upstream, without paying Mr Flanders to open his lock gate. Now, since the new lock had been built, the laden barges were sometimes forced to lie for days for want of water and even those returning empty found the river too shallow to pass upstream unless the lock gate had been opened. They were forced to pay the miller 2s a barge. John Flanders was ordered to raise the sill of his new lock gates by twenty inches in order to increase the flow of water into the navigable river.

Thomas Niblett of Sewardstone Mill had also diverted additional water out of the river which he did by enlarging the mouth of his mill stream. Then, taking advantage of the obstruction he himself had thus caused, he had progressively increased his charges for opening the sluices. In the summer of 1719 he had demanded 5s from each barge and many were laid aground for fourteen days together when they refused to pay.[44]

The City pressed for a new cut with locks to ensure that at all times the river had adequate water, and also the construction of a good tow-path which could be used by horses; this would enable barges to carry twice the weight and to do the journey much quicker. Yet even the influence of the City failed to get the Bill through Parliament and the navigation continued to be operated in its old and inefficient way. Barge owners in 1735 were claiming that forty years earlier they had been able to do the return journey in less time and at a lower cost. It was revealed in 1760 that malt from Ware was again being carried by road although this had been discontinued as uneconomic in the seventeenth century.[45]

A survey of the Lea was made in 1766 by John Smeaton the engineer. The navigable river then extended thirty miles from Hertford to Bromley Lock with a fall of 111 feet. Smeaton proposed to make a navigation which would remain three feet deep at all seasons. He would retain the river where it was tolerably straight and of sufficient depth. Locks would be built. His intention was that barges should be able to travel at an average of two miles an hour including the time taken to negotiate the locks. They should thus complete the journey from Bow Bridge to Hertford in thirteen hours. The new cuts were to be six feet wide at the bottom and three feet deep, with four passing places in each mile. There were to be fourteen new cuts. Near Enfield a new cut was to run from the river above Newman's weir to join Enfield mill stream a hundred yards below Enfield Lock. The navigation was to use Enfield mill stream, widening it where necessary, to a point 340 yards above the mill and from there a cut was to be made to run eastward round the mill to rejoin the mill stream two hundred yards below the mill. Another cut was to be made from the tail stream across Enfield, Edmonton and part of Tottenham marshes to join the tail stream of Tottenham mill. (The tail stream is that part of the mill stream below the mill).

At Waltham Abbey special arrangements had to be made to continue water to the corn mill and to the powder mills, and also to the calico grounds where stages had been built for washing the linen. Access had to be provided for barges from the powder mills into the new cut. Also means of access had to be devised to Sewardstone mill, there being no way of reaching it by road, for this purpose a wharf was built on the east side of the new cut within twenty yards of the old river so that materials could be unloaded there and re-laden on a wharf on the west side of the River Lea. The piece of ground between the two watercourses, twenty

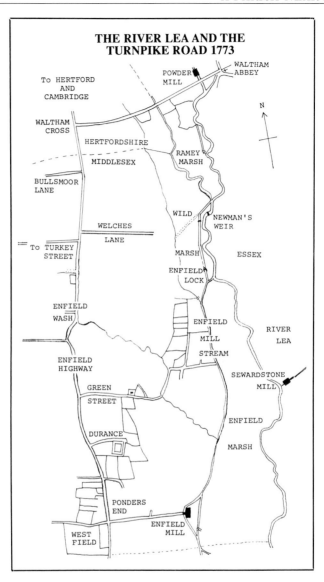

THE RIVER LEA AND THE TURNPIKE ROAD 1773

feet wide, was to be enclosed by a pale fence, ten feet high, with gates each end to give access to the wharfs.

To ensure uninterrupted navigation through the Enfield mill stream it was provided that when the level of the water fell below five feet above the level of the sill of the waste gate, the flow of water to the mill should cease; at such times the mill would have to stop working. The mill owners were to be paid £40 a year compensation.

Tolls were to be collected at King's weir, and Newman's weir by Enfield lock, at a rate of 8d for every chaldron of coal or cinders and 6d for every ton of other goods. The charges through Lea bridge were 4d and 3d and through the new cut from Bromley lock into the Thames 3d and 2d. Pleasure boats were to be charged a shilling. There was no charge for boats carrying oil cakes, malt dust, pidgeon dung or manure.[46]

Income from tolls rose from £3300 a year in 1771 to £4100 in 1777/8, to £7500 in 1780 and continued to rise to between £9000 and £10,000 a year in the years from 1785 to 1804.

I have dwelt at no great length on this subject since there is an excellent paper written by Dr. J. G. L. Burnby and Michael Parker, '*The Navigation of the River Lee (1190–1790)*'.

Notes to Chapter Nine

1 GLRO Middlesex Sessions book 1680 p. 53 *Diary of Ralph Thoresby* ed. J. Hunter 1830.
2 12 Anne c. 19.
3 HCJ 17 Ap 1713.
4 HCJ 4 My 1713.
5 1 Geo I c. 37.
6 2 Geo II c. 14.
7 OBSP 7–12 D 1737 p. 8–10.
8 17 Geo II c. 41.
9 8 Geo III c. 45.
10 HCJ 1763 v. 29 pp. 645–664.
11 Enfield newspaper cutting, VCH Middlesex 5.209.
12 OBSP 16–19 Ja 1747 p. 72.
13 Vestry order book 1764–1773.
14 OBSP Je 1791 230 p. 339.
15 OBSP My 1806, Jl 1795. 346, GLRO DRO4 Box 17, OBSP 1832 633.
16 Vestry order book 1764–1773.
17 HCJ 28F 1774 v. 34 p. 512, 14 Geo III c. 116.
18 29 Geo III c. 96.
19 Enfield. Stamford Hill Turnpike Trust minute book 26 Oct 1807.
20 *ibid* 25 Ap 1814, 25 Jl 1814, GLRO Acc 526. 22, Robinson *Enfield* 1.46.
21 OBSP 1823. 1312.
22 Enfield newspaper cuttings.
23 OBSP 1823. 786.
24 OBSP 1826/7. 751.
25 HCJ My 1825.
26 7 Geo IV c. 142.
27 T. Fairman Ordish. *Metropolis Turnpike Roads* in London Topographical Soc. Trans V8. 1913.
28 T. C. Barker and M. Robbins *A History of London Transport* 1963 V1 App 2 p. 396–7.
29 OBSP 1826/7. 153.
30 OBSP 1826/7. 882.
31 OBSP 1799/1800. 303.
32 OBSP 1822. 1062.
33 *Recollections of Old Enfield* p. 11.
34 GLRO DRO4. 3. 16. 88.
35 Vestry order book.
36 Peter Hardy, *Hints* 1809, p. 36, 37.
37 GLRO DRO4. 9. 49.
38 GLRO DRO4 El. 21, 20.
39 Vestry order book.

40   Vestry order book.
41   GLRO DRO4 Box 14. 70.
42   Vestry order book N1833.
43   J. G. L. Burnby and M. Parker *The Navigation of the River Lee* EHHS 1978.
44   Enfield. River Lee book of sewers 1719–20, GLRO Acc 262. 1, 2, 3.
45   Burnby *op cit.*
46   Enfield. John Smeaton Report on River Lee, 7 Geo III. c 51.

Chapter Ten

The War Years 1793–1815 and the Post-War Depression

1. The Poor and the Possibility of Revolution

The French Revolution cast its shadow over Europe. On 1 February 1793 the National Convention declared war on Britain. That year saw the widespread dissemination of Paine's *Rights of Man*. In August 1794, a mob defied Militia and Guards for three days and attacked and destroyed the houses used for army recruiting in Holborn, the City, Clerkenwell and Shoreditch. The government took action. Constitutional societies throughout the country were suppressed, *Habeas Corpus* was suspended and Jacobins were hunted in every village. The local historian of the late twentieth century is unlikely to do any better than the important parishioners of the late eighteenth in finding the Jacobins in his village, but there certainly is evidence of a reaction to their existence, real or imagined, by the better sort of people in Enfield. These gentlemen met at the Greyhound on 28 June to form an association; similar action had been taken in many towns and parishes throughout the country. At this meeting a declaration was made by those assembled that they would hold themselves 'in readiness to act as special constables for the support of the civil power as occasion might require and be sworn in accordingly when called upon for that purpose'.

The committee earnestly recommended that the declaration be signed by the *respectable* inhabitants of the parish and drew up a list of those gentlemen qualified to serve by the level of their land tax assessment. A book was made out and left in the coffee room at the Greyhound. Thus the Enfield Association was more a measure of self-defence by property owners against the danger, real or imagined, of a revolutionary insurrection among the poor, than a measure towards national defence.[1]

The condition of the poor was desperate. The harvest for the year 1794, nationally, was one-fifth below the average for the previous ten years. The price of corn almost doubled. In the year 1795 there was another harvest failure and food riots occurred throughout the country. Even labourers in employment were forced to seek relief. This situation was the reason for the famous meeting of magistrates at Speenhamland in Berkshire to consider measures to relieve widespread distress among agricultural labourers. They advocated a system of outdoor relief by which the wages of indigent labourers were to be supplemented from the poor rates even when they were in work. There is no indication that this Speenhamland system, as it came to be known, was adopted in Enfield at this time. A pensions list, (that is a list of those regularly receiving outdoor relief) for the Town quarter, April to

October 1796, contains fifty-three names of which, at the most, seven are men. A list of the casual poor for the same period and quarter has twenty-nine names of which only eight could possibly have been working labourers. The weekly pensions, regular and casual, were mostly small, ranging from 1s 6d to 2s 6d.[2]

The Enfield vestry was placed in something of a dilemma, however, when it had to deal with those parishes which had adopted the Speenhamland system. A letter was received in April 1801 from a magistrate at Woodford concerning John White whose settlement was in Enfield. White was married with four children and apparently was working. He was described by the magistrate as sober and industrious. 'Was it not for the very great pressure on the labouring poor he would not have troubled you . . . I can also say', wrote the magistrate, 'that (other) parishes have seen the necessity of allowing, to their non-resident poor with us, temporary relief during the great scarcity of provisions.[3] The Enfield vestry felt obliged to allow the man 4s a week.

Even in 1797, before the further immense rise in the price of bread which occurred in 1800, many labourers could scarcely make ends meet. Eden (1797) provides a sample budget for a labourer's family living in the Home Counties and consisting of a man, his wife, two boys aged eight and six, and two girls aged four and eighteen months.

		£	s	d
Income	Wages at 11s a week	28	12	0
	Extra earnings from the master	6	0	0
	From others	3	0	0
	Wife at hay harvest	1	0	0
		38	12	0
Expenditure	Rent of a cottage and small garden	3	18	0
	A quartern loaf of wheaten bread at 10d a day	15	3	4
	Meat at 1s 9d a week	4	11	0
	Small beer at 6d for 4 quarts a week	1	6	0
	Small quantity of cheese	1	0	0
	2oz tea a week at 4s a pound		19	6
	2lb sugar a week at 9d a pound	3	18	0
	½lb soap a week at 9d a pound		19	6
	Candles		10	0
	Coal, 1 bushel a week at 1s 6d	1	19	0
	2 pairs of shoes a year at 7s 6d, and 1s mending, 3 pairs of stockings at 2s, an old coat 7s, shirts 10s	2	9	0
	Wife's clothes not more than	1	1	0
	The two eldest learn to read at a day school at 3d a week each	1	6	0
		39	0	4

It will be seen that nothing is charged for clothing the children for the wife contrived to provide them from her husband's old clothes. He was allowed potatoes and vegetables from his master's garden and a quart of skimmed milk every morning from the dairy. Thus a very large part of the income of this family was spent on best wheaten bread which was held to be an essential part of the labourer's diet throughout the south-east of England. The well-being of labourers therefore depended on the price of wheat.[4]

Those who boarded with their employers were no better off. William Stallion was hired by Mr Kingston of Belmont House at Cockfosters in October 1804 (that is after the great price rises at the turn of the century) as a cowman at a yearly wage of twelve guineas (less than 5s a week). He was then single and lived and slept in the dairy with the cows. His wages were to rise at the rate of one guinea a year for each year of service. He remained there until he married in November 1812, by which time he was getting nineteen guineas and fourteen for board but, since he could no longer sleep in the dairy and give his undivided attention to the cows, he was discharged.[5]

The surrender of Austria in April 1797 left Britain standing alone against the might of Revolutionary France which controlled the Channel coastline from Brittany to the Frisian Islands and could now command the fleets of Spain and Holland as well as her own. The British Navy no longer thought of an invasion of France but rather of preventing a French invasion of this country. Matters were made more perilous because many British ships lay out of action in harbour at Spithead and the Nore, incapacitated by the mutiny of that year. A French crossing of the Channel seemed imminent. In towns and villages throughout the country, gentlemen came forward to adopt measures for the defence of the realm.

A committee was set up in Enfield in March 1798 headed by General Flower Mocher (he died May 1801 aged seventy-two) to collect voluntary subscriptions. A multitude of local gentry offered their services. Representatives agreed to sit daily in the vestry room from twelve o'clock until two to collect contributions. In April the lord lieutenant of the county invited men willing to be armed and exercised for the public defence within their own neighbourbood, provided they could be vouched for by two householders, to offer their services. They were 'to hold themselves in readiness for the preservation of public tranquility'. Persons were also sought who would be willing to furnish carts and horses, either gratuitously or for hire, in case of emergency.[6] Thus again one must strongly suspect that the measure was aimed as much against the lower orders in this country as against the French.

The winter of the year 1799–1800 saw even greater distress among the poor. Their children were cold and hungry; coal had risen to such a price that they could no longer buy it. By order of the vestry, hornbeams on Enfield Chase were lopped, made into faggots, and sold to the poor at one penny each. Bread became so dear that men in full employment were forced to apply to the overseers for relief. The Enfield vestry ordered that a subscription be raised to purchase bread to be re-sold at a reduced price to the poor, and soup was provided at a penny a quart. A committee was set up to meet the crisis. It comprised all the major landowners, General Mocher, William Mellish, Newell Connop and other important gentry. More than £200 was collected; many of the wealthy parishioners contributed five guineas each to the fund.[7]

Sir Francis Burdett was now the idol of the London crowds with their slogan 'Burdett and no Bastille'. Following his success in the Middlesex election of 1802, his local supporters invited him to dine at the King's Head in the Market Place. There was great expectation and excitement and the crowds began moving out along the London Road to meet him. It had been put about that they would draw his coach in triumph into the Market Place. Sir Francis, however, avoided the intended honour and came another way in a private coach. Some two hundred people had been invited to dine; many of them, said the *Gentlemans Magazine* with some contempt, were not even freeholders. Nevertheless they had paid 7s a head

A labourer's cottage in Green Street 1797, drawn and engraved by J. T. Smith.

and partook of a fine dinner of venison. Meantime the crowd returned disappointed and gathered in the Market Place. Strong beer and wine had to be sent out to keep them happy, so that by the time the meal inside was finished, the mob outside was in a drunken turmoil. They broke into the King's Head, overthrew the tables, smashed the glasses and bowls, all which caused them to become so enthusiastic for Sir Francis and his cause that they needs must draw him in his coach in grand procession around the town. The drunken orgy resulted in only two fatalities; old Edward French a journeyman carpenter, and a young tailor unnamed. Both, unable for some reason to keep their feet, fell; their friends, too drunk to notice, pulled the coach blindly over their bodies.[8] Thus the story is told in the *Gentlemans Magazine* which would have had little love for Burdett and less for his radical supporters.

2. The Parish War Effort

The war had reached a stalemate by 1801 and in March the following year a peace treaty was signed with France though it endured only until May 1803. The government was now much concerned to raise an effective militia to resist the French should they land. An act in 1802 ordered the mobilization of a force of fifty thousand men to be selected by ballot. Those upon whom the lot fell were allowed to pay for a substitute; the vestry would contribute half the price. When the lottery fell upon Joseph Leach in 1803, his place in the Middlesex militia was taken by Joseph Liddell who was paid £10, of which Enfield parish contributed £5 and also 5s a week thereafter to support his wife and two daughters at those times when he was on active service. John Nash, being chosen by lot to serve in the militia, provided William Lewis of Saffron Hill to serve as his substitute. Nash too was paid £5 by the parish of Enfield.[9]

Eleven Enfield men were serving as substitutes and their families at home had to be maintained by the parish of the man they had replaced. Thus Edward Lawrence went as a substitute in February 1803 for William Pettit of Bengeo, near Hertford, as a private in the Hertfordshire Regiment of militia. Mary Ann Lawrence, left in Enfield, being unable to maintain herself and her ten-month-old son George, was thereafter paid three shillings a week (being the usual price of two days labour in husbandry) by the parish of Enfield. The money had to be reclaimed from the county of Hertfordshire and in turn the county would eventually get the money from the parish of Bengeo. In 1807 Edward Lawrence transferred to the regular army and the payment of relief came to an end.[10]

Various motives impelled men to enlist. Henry Newman, a butcher at Barnet, lost a side of mutton on 12 November 1797 from a place he had at the Roebuck (Barnet) where he did the slaughtering. Henry Hughes (aged thirty-one), who purloined it, carried it all the way to Enfield where he called at the shop of Robert Poole the butcher and offered the meat at threepence a pound. The butcher unlocked his door and Hughes staggered in with his burden. Poole however was a conscientious parish constable and, suspecting that the meat had been stolen, he sent Hughes off to a butcher lower down the road and meanwhile sought out a magistrate. Hughes was arrested and secured in the watch-house. On the following day he was brought before the justice of peace who, with his country's interests no doubt at heart, proposed that the prisoner should enlist as a soldier. Aware that the alternative would be prison he volunteered at once but when examined by the doctor he was rejected. Thereupon he was taken into custody once again and sentenced to six months in the House of Correction.[11]

Many of the same sort did enlist and made themselves a nuisance wherever they were billeted. Richard Jackson, who had enlisted in the Fifeshire Fencibles because he was out of work, came to the George with a billet on 21 January 1797. After sitting drinking in the bar for about two hours he arrived at a suitable state of bemused recklessness. He ordered another pint and, taking the opportunity while Letitia Hobkirk, the landlady's daughter, was busy drawing the beer, he slipped out of the door with the nearest objects available, a ham and a mortar. Mr Taylor and Mr Young were riding past on their way home and observed him making a desperate attempt to clamber over a nearby hedge. They stopped to reprimand him for breaking down the fences but then they noticed his bulging pockets and seized him by the collar. His greatcoat was so much too big for him, however, that he slipped out of it and escaped. With some difficulty they secured him again. Taken before a magistrate, he was sentenced to be publicly whipped and given twelve months in the House of Correction.[12]

The troops quartered in various public houses around Enfield caused disquiet among the respectable inhabitants. Mrs Mary Cockett, whose husband kept a shop in Baker Street, was sitting in the little parlour behind the shop one evening in April 1800 between nine and ten o'clock, when a man lifted the latch and entered. In the dark he tripped over the scales and disturbed her. She seized him, but he broke free and fled. Whereupon she rushed out to call her husband. Together they found the culprit in a public house about a hundred yards down the road. He still had in his pockets the eleven pairs of stockings which he had just stolen. Once again he managed to give them the slip, but he was arrested on the following day as he came off parade. Though the publican where he was billeted and his paymaster-sergeant both gave him a good character, he was sentenced to transportation for seven years.[13]

Daniel Rogers of Forty Hill lost a goose in July that same year from off the Enfield common. While searching for it he saw a soldier endeavouring to conceal a bag under his greatcoat; the bag was soaked in blood. His suspicions thus aroused, Rogers sought out Poole the constable and together they went to the soldier's lodgings. In one corner of the room they found the goose hidden under a blanket, but the soldier denied all knowledge of it; there were five of his comrades living in that room, he said, and the bag was the one in which they always fetched the meat. He was, perhaps unaccountably, acquitted by the jury and poor Daniel, because he could not meet the cost of the prosecution, was committed to prison; there's justice![14]

Napoleon, like a colossus, cast his shadow over Europe and the nations trembled. The parish threw itself earnestly into the campaign in 1803, to furnish volunteers. A vestry was called in the parish church on 23 July to consider measures for raising this necessary force for the defence and security of the kingdom and the more vigorous prosecution of the war. Upon a motion of John Legh Esq, seconded by Rawson Hart Boddam Esq of Capel Manor, the church-wardens and overseers were authorised to provide volunteers. The vicar and all the leading gentlemen of the parish, James Meyer of Forty Hall, Thomas Holt White of Chase Lodge, Peter Hardy, Richard Gough, Newell Connop of Durants, William Mellish of Bush Hill Park, and everyone else of consequence in the parish, joined shoulder to shoulder in an all-out effort to raise the quota of men demanded of Enfield. A subscription was set on foot to defray the expenses of the infantry.[15]

Even some of the lower orders were caught up in this wave of patriotic fervour, in a way, and from this obscure corner of Britain came a clarion call for indomitable resistance. It was John Hurran, the bellows blower in Enfield church who, crutches in hand, thus stood forth and hurled defiance in the teeth of the tyrant:

> My worthy masters and mistresses all
> I take the liberty on you to call,
> To welcome you, this next, a happier year
> Than the last, as we have been kept in fear.
>
> That tyrant Bonaparte does threat our land
> To invade with his bloody sword in hand;
> But I, your servant, though but with one leg,
> Will take my crutch and fight till I am dead.
>   (which is a fine sentiment but a bad rhyme)
> Before that tyrant e'er shall stain our land
> I'll perish in the combat, crutch in hand;
> Before he shall come, or venture here to stop,
> I'll lose my blood, e'en to the last drop.
>   (Having thus aroused his readers to a fever pitch of patriotic
>   fervour, his final verse is something of a let down)
> I hope you'll think of me your bellows blower,
> As this is the first year your pittance I implore,
> Times are so altered, and my salary so small,
> A trifle I crave, and do thank you all.[16]

Admirable as it all was, the effort failed and in November 1804 the parish somewhat ignominiously paid a penalty of £20 for each recruit not forthcoming.[17]

The patriotic fervour had evaporated. Mainwaring, the county treasurer wrote repeatedly to the vestry. In February 1805 he exhorted, 'The balance now due from you amounts to £137 11s 4d, I cannot omit this opportunity to urge payment.' In June he mourned, 'Mr Mainwaring has made frequent application to the overseers of Enfield for the payment of the balance due on the militia accounts of which not the least notice has been taken.' He now informed the overseers that if the whole balance, viz £142 1s, be not paid within fourteen days 'he will be under the unavoidable necessity of pursuing legal measures'. Again in September he wrote urging payment. 'The sums owing to the several counties of England from the county of Middlesex are so large.'

The government built 'a cannon and other foundaries' in the parish in 1812 (the Royal Small Arms Factory). The vestry was much concerned and instructed the clerk to write to Deptford and Woolwich to discover whether similar government works had resulted in the burdening of those parishes with poor.[18]

3. Peter Hardy and Parish Reform

The maintenance of the poor had become an insupportable or at least an unwelcome, burden on the parish; the system was not working well, inefficiency and waste were causing the ratepayers great concern. A poor rate of 1s 6d had to be levied in February 1800 with a supplementary rate of 6d in May, a further rate of 2s in September and 2s 3d the following February.[19] Poverty and sickness prevailed in the village. The parish register from January to December 1800 shows 132 baptisms and 191 burials including thirty-five strangers. Many of these were travellers who died on their way to or from London along the Old North Road. Fifty-one pauper burials are noted, but this number is swollen by twenty-three because various London parishes housed their poor in Enfield. If we strip these figures of the paupers who did not belong and of all the strangers, 133 Enfield people were buried and among them were twenty-eight paupers. There had been an outbreak of smallpox in the autumn which left twelve dead; but far worse was an unspecified epidemic which coincided with the smallpox and which killed sixty-five infants of less than one year old. Nine died in July, twenty-six in August, eighteen in September and ten in October. Thereafter the number of infants dying returns to what was then considered normal.

The price of bread in 1801 rose higher than ever. Expenditure on the poor from Easter 1800 to Easter 1801 amounted to £3980. The population was 5881, but the ratepayers numbered only 460. They were becoming ever more reluctant to pay and £580 remained that year uncollected.[20] The average number of inmates in the workhouse had grown to eighty-nine, and they cost the parish £1862 in that year, more than 8s a week to maintain each pauper.[21]

Certain parish officers had been accused of graft. Mr Henry Young, formerly churchwarden for the Town quarter, had supplied large quantities of goods to the workhouse. Since, as churchwarden, he had been in a position to pass his own bills, there had been no check on what he had delivered. Moreover he had allowed no discount to the parish as was customarily done by tradesmen. Mistakes were found in his bills and they were almost invariably in his own favour. Nathaniel Gundry (of South Lodge) went so far as to propose that he should be prosecuted for the embezzlement of parish funds but this was negatived by a majority in the vestry. Mr Thomas Wood, another churchwarden, had supplied breeches to the workhouse and had deducted payment out of the church rate. He had also claimed money which he said he had paid out to paupers, though that duty was entirely the responsibility of the overseer.

Between £50 and £60 of parish money had been spent each year, during the transaction of parish business, on refreshment in various public houses. It was considered that this could in no way be justified in view of the difficulties encountered by industrious tradesmen and poor labourers with families of their own to support, who yet were obliged to contribute to the rates.[22]

The reforming and economising element among the rulers of the parish was led and directed by Mr Peter Hardy, with Major John Cartwright of Chase Hill and Nathaniel Gundry of South Lodge. They were supported by such excellent and co-operative overseers as Thomas Browning and Daniel Beck. John Cartwright, the great reformer, moved to Enfield towards the end of the year 1804, his name first appearing in the vestry order book in December of that year. He played a major role, with Peter Hardy, in an attempt to impose honesty and fair dealing in the administration of the parish. He remained in Enfield for five years.

Peter Hardy began his campaign to reduce the rates by the imposition of strict control over parish expenditure in 1801. Upon his proposal it was ordered that all bills for provisions should be examined by the workhouse committee. Accurate lists were required to be made of people in receipt of relief both those living in Enfield and those maintained in other parishes. It was required that these lists should state the reason why relief had been thought necessary, give the pauper's age, the number of his children and the cause of his distress. There were at that time two hundred names on the parish pension list.[23]

The reformers became members of a committee in 1805 appointed by the vestry, to prepare an improved system for the management of the poor. The impoverished and ever shifting population of paupers in the workhouse provided their most intractable problem. Between January and October in the year 1802 no fewer than fifty-five persons left the house,[24] their places taken by others. Hardy and the reformers showed little sympathy for them. The rags and idleness of these people, they said, were deplorable, their existence a discouragement to those who had to work for their bread. The very substantial menu to which these paupers were treated when in the house was the object of their most unfavourable comparisons. The workhouse diet was contrasted with the quantity of food which a working labourer would be able to afford, a man who had a family to support on his wages. The advantage they found was in every respect with the pauper in the house. This workhouse food moreover could be purchased in bulk, cheaply, while the labourer must buy his from week to week at the high prices charged by small retailers. It was urged that paupers ought never to do better than the families of labouring men in full health, full work, and full wages. The top wage that they could find in Enfield was that of an agricultural labourer (unnamed) who earned 17s a week, on average, over twelve months. This man had a wife and seven children and, in addition to food, he had to buy clothing, fuel, furniture and pay for occasional medical attention. Beyond this he faced a yearly rent of five guineas. Yet it would have cost the parish 16s a week just to maintain the man and his wife in the workhouse. Fortified by the moral justification derived from this labourer's predicament, the committee formulated a new table of diet to substantially reduce the food given to the paupers in the workhouse. It took no immediate measures however to ensure a living wage for the labourer.

Table of Diet for the Paupers in Enfield Workhouse 6 February 1806

	Men and Women	Boys and girls
Sundays, Tuesdays and Thursdays		
Breakfast	Water gruel	Water gruel
Dinner	8oz meat 12oz potatoes	4oz meat (Sundays 6oz) 8oz potatoes
Supper	1oz cheese or ½oz butter	12oz rice (Sundays 1oz cheese or ½oz butter)
	6oz bread and one quart beer for the day	7oz bread for the day, on Sunday 11oz, and half pint beer
Wednesdays and Fridays		
Breakfast	Water gruel	Water gruel
Dinner	One quart pea soup	One pint pea soup
Supper	One oz cheese or half oz butter	One oz cheese or half oz butter
	12oz bread and one pint of beer for the day	8 oz bread for the day
Mondays		
Breakfast	One pint pea soup	three quarter pint pea soup
Dinner	16oz suet dumpling	12oz rice pudding
Supper	One pint of pea soup	three quarter pint pea soup
	One pint of beer for the day	half pint beer for the day
Saturdays		
Breakfast	Water gruel	Water gruel
Dinner	16oz suet dumpling	12oz rice pudding
Supper	1oz cheese or half oz butter	1oz cheese or half oz butter
	12oz bread and quart of beer for the day	half pint of beer and 8oz bread for the day

The new menu could hardly have been greeted with enthusiasm by the paupers but it saved the parish £200 a year.

Attitudes towards the able-bodied poor who sought relief had hardened; it was felt that they must either be reformed or punished. The committee expressed this view forcibly. 'It cannot be thought right,' it declared in its report of 1806, 'so to feed and maintain the poor at the expense of the parish as to hold out a perpetual premium and reward to the idleness and improvidence of the labouring class. (It would) be a constant source of indignant mortification to all who have the honest pride of independence to see those who have become paupers, by your (the vestry's) temptations and their own vices, living in luxury compared with their own fare earned with the sweat of their brows. Neither', went on the report, 'can the committee imagine, with regard to the boys and girls in the workhouse, that it can be thought right that they should be so fed as to make them dread the thoughts of that mode of living to which they must submit when sent away.'[25] And with that the vestry gave its approval to the placing out of all suitable boys and girls from the workhouse with Mr Morley, silk throwster, of the Sewardstone Silk Mill. He was to be paid 1s 6d a week for each child.[26] The aged and infirm in the house continued to be treated with relative consideration. Many of them were in rags and the overseer was authorised to lay out sufficient money to clothe them and to provide rugs to cover their beds to keep them warm at night. He was told to get essential repair work done on the outside of the building to shelter them from the wind and the rain and to stop-up and lime-white the interior. They further recommended the installation of cast iron stove-grates in the dormitories, such as those made by Mr Moser of Dean Street, Soho.[27]

The financial methods of the parish were carefully examined. No new poor rate was to be levied unless the previous one had been collected in full. Nobody was to be exempted from payment of poor rate on the grounds of a debt owed to him by the parish; any such creditor must seek payment from the overseer who contracted the debt. Every overseer must settle his accounts before leaving office. The local magistrates had taken exception to these resolutions but, on Mr Hardy seeking legal opinion, their opposition had been withdrawn. All parish debts were discharged by Easter 1806.

The reformers had achieved many of their objectives. The pension list for October 1805 includes very few men who were not incapacitated in some way. Few pensions were paid on account of large families and low wages, only seven in fact and three of these lived in other parishes. William Scales of Chase Side had been getting 4s a week and a loaf; it was now reduced to one loaf of bread only. William Staker had received his 1s 6d a week rent and this too was now discontinued. John Trundle of Enfield Town, with a wife and four children all between two and six, had his pension of 4s continued, but he may have been incapacitated in some way because a couple of years later he was provided with a pension from a parish charity. He died in 1811. Daniel Camp and his family still continued to receive rent at 1s 6d a week.

The policy of filling the workhouse with the old, the infirm and widows with young children, was pursued. Widow Libertey and her son James were ordered into the house. They had been living in a cottage in the churchyard, supported by the parish on 1s 3d a week and two loaves. Widow Oakley of Chase Side had three children aged between ten and fifteen. Their rent, at 1s 9d a week, had been paid by the parish and they had been in receipt of a pension of 6s a week. The children were now taken into the house but the parish continued to pay the mother's rent.[28]

A curious side-effect of the removal of the young and able-bodied from the house was that in August 1807 the parish had to order a platform on four wheels because the old men remaining in the workhouse were not strong enough to carry the dead to the graveyard. The inmates were now encouraged to produce all their own vegetables and a rule was enforced that all provisions purchased must be paid for in cash.[29]

'In few parishes' wrote Peter Hardy, looking back on the work of reform up to 1808, 'could parochial evils have been carried to a greater extent than in Enfield. Our poor were numerous, insolent and miserable, our rates oppressive and unjust. But now parish expenditure has been reduced by nearly one half. Our workhouse, which used to be a receptacle for vice, has now become a refuge for the aged and helpless. Waste and improvidence have given way to comfort and economy.' All persons capable of earning their own living had been removed, and this, with the new diet, had saved the parish £1000 a year on the workhouse alone.

Mr Hardy went on to deplore the pauperisation (degeneracy he called it) of the poor. 'It has been the means of nearly annihilating that provident care, that pride and independent spirit . . . which used to distinguish the virtuous and industrious from the idle and the dissolute. Parochial relief, which used to be thought disgraceful, is now sought after as a right . . . so little attention is paid to these evils that children are actually trained to the trade of parish relief at the workhouse door by the parish officers themselves (in Enfield the weekly outdoor payments had amounted to nearly £30 a week) . . . 'Every means' he went on, 'should be resorted to which could in any way enable the labourer to keep himself above seeking relief at the workhouse'. He proposed that benefit societies should be set up 'to assist the industrious and helpless. Tables might be spread at which the children of the *industrious* poor might fare sumptuously.' Farmers ought to allow their labourers to buy food at cost. Parochial stores should be established at which labourers might be supplied with fuel and food at reduced prices. 'It would be better to teach our poor the comforts of a milch-cow and a potato garden than to train up their children at the workhouse door.' Thus Hardy reaches almost to the dream world of William Covell. Not one of these munificent reforms was imposed, but the vestry did insist that children be no longer permitted to receive the weekly dole for their parents at the workhouse.[30]

Nevertheless the new paternalism sought to encourage self-help among the poor by the provision of materials so that they could make their own clothes. This system must have created a great deal of work and trouble for the overseers, but the improvident pauper found that calico was more difficult than cash to fritter away in the nearest beer-house. From June to September 1810 the parish laid out £26 in the purchase of materials, stockings, shoes, jackets, trousers, leather caps, flannel waistcoats, and one handkerchief. Throughout September the overseers were kept busy distributing the stock among the poor; Ann Williams had a pair of shoes, Mrs Blake 9½ yards of calico, a smock-frock and a leather cap; Mrs Dodson had one yard of nail check and Mr Haydon a man's kersey jacket, that cost 8s. Innumerable others had stockings and shoes, Mrs Markwell had three pairs at from 3s 3d to 3s 9d. The most common material and the cheapest was calico at little over a shilling a yard, then flannel at 1s 2½d. Also a great deal of coarse linen cloths were dispensed, holland at 1s 4d, dowlas at 1s 8d. Printed cottons cost 1s 4d or 1s 6d.[31]

The workhouse was now run directly by the vestry. Mrs King, the mistress retired in January 1814 on account of her age and infirmities and was provided with a pension of £30 a year. Andrew Davidson and his wife were appointed. The numbers in the house now varied between fifty and seventy. The vestry thought so well of the Davidsons that in April 1815 they were given £10 'in recognition of their assiduity' and further gifts of £10 followed in each of the next two years.[32]

4. The Loss of Common Rights

The pauperisation of the poor which Peter Hardy so eloquently denounced, the annihilation of their pride and independent spirit, had begun long before his time. The first great blow to the independence of the poor had been the enclosure of Enfield Chase in 1777. It was this that had robbed them of 'the comfort of a milch-cow' which Hardy had so strongly advocated thirty years too late. The Chase had stood for centuries as a barrier between poverty and disaster. Thence the cottager had taken timber to keep a roof over his head, wood for his fire, pasture among the trees to feed his cow and acorns and beech mast to fatten his pig. The Act, it is true, had transferred common rights to 1532 acres of land but the poor were largely excluded, for these rights were now reserved to the owners of property assessed at £10 a year (only 156 proprietors). The new allotment was protected against the poor who were arrested and prosecuted for taking fuel, while the timber was sold to relieve their more wealthy neighbours of a proportion of the poor rate. The pasture, now denied to them, was overcharged with the cattle of the farmers.

The rents from the Two Hundred Acres, granted to the vestry in compensation for rates and taxes lost when considerable areas of the parish had been transferred to Edmonton, South Mimms and Monken Hadley in 1777, were also employed to relieve the ratepayers of a proportion of the poor rate and when, in 1800, half this land was sold, the proceeds were used to redeem their land tax.[33]

There yet remained to the poor their right to pasture on the common arable and the common marsh after the crops had been gathered in, but the interruption of trade caused by the outbreak of war with France had increased the potential profits from farming and an avalanche of enclosure acts was now pouring through Parliament. Inevitably, the wealthy landowners in Enfield felt compelled to jump upon the band-wagon. A petition was submitted in February 1801 by Sir George Prescott, William Mellish, Newell Connop and other proprietors of estates in Enfield, setting forth that the common fields, meadows and marshes within the parish could be greatly improved by being enclosed and divided among them. Nor did the surviving common on Enfield Chase escape their notice. Their petition, and one against enclosure which was not thought worthy of a summary in the Journals of the House of Commons, were submitted to a committee. The committee report, in June, argued that since the property of those who supported the Bill was valued at £1338 while its opponents had property assessed at a mere £112, the majority concerned had given its consent and the Bill could proceed. It received royal assent on 2 July 1801.[34]

There were those who felt that the Bill might not be conducive to the well-being of the majority (in numbers, not property) and one gentleman even set out his objections which were printed and distributed among the landowners, their tenants and under-tenants. 'If the enclosures take place', he warned, 'where are hundreds of poor cottagers and their children to find bread to eat or employment for their hands two or three years hence? Surely these are a very important part of the subjects of this kingdom from whose labour and loins spring our soldiers, sailors, husbandmen and servants. Let me beg you to ask your neighbouring parishes, Cheshunt and Edmonton,' he goes on, 'if they do not already repent of their petition? I fear this is only the morning of their troubles and you have in prospect much greater.'[35]

His warning passed unheard, or unheeded, for there were too many with too much to gain from enclosure.

The Inclosure Act for Enfield was to abolish common rights over 3540 acres of common field arable and common marsh and on the 1532 acres of the Enfield allotment. All this land was to be redistributed among persons who had held common field land, according to the quantity of land they had held. The land they were to be given was to lie as close as possible to the proprietor's homestead or to any enclosed land he already held. Thus compact and more viable holdings would be created. Compensation would have to be paid to former occupiers for crops growing on land thus acquired. Those who had been entitled to common rights by tenure of cottages could also lay claim to land in compensation. Claimants were required to set out their claims, stating the number of houses and cottages and the quantity of land in respect to which they claimed.

Tithes were abolished by the Act and the vicar received 383 acres in compensation. The rector, Trinity College Cambridge, received 1407 acres, this land and the vicar's, were to be fenced and the fences maintained for seven years at the expense of the community. Manorial rights were abolished and the lords of the manors were compensated with land.

A map and a schedule showing the proposed allotments was laid open for inspection and each man received a copy of the schedule as far as it related to himself. The costs of the commissioners in making the survey and in fencing the glebe and other tithe allotments were met by the sale of common land by auction. The sale of 100 acres raised over £10,000, that is about £100 an acre. It was declared lawful for claimants to sell their common land before they had enclosed it, or to sell a right to land based upon an entitlement to common rights. Many fences around the new enclosures had been put up by June 1804 and notices had to be displayed around the parish to warn those who had damaged them, but whether the damage was due to resentment against enclosure, or a shortage of fuel, or both, is not clear. It is certain however that the poor had lost a safeguard against disaster; they had nothing now to fall back on but parish relief.[36]

Another remedy urged by Peter Hardy had been to set up benefit societies 'to assist the industrious and helpless.' The industrious , however, were not so helpless that they must wait upon the initiative of their betters. They formed friendly societies themselves in their usual places of resort, the public houses. These societies aimed to provide their members with help in sickness and in old age. We hear of them because they were carefully watched by the magistrates in petty sessions. One such benefit club was held at the King's Arms at Green Street, the house of James Hare. The stewards, George Dearman and Thomas Thorogood (a labourer) were summoned to appear before the magistrate, the Reverend W. A. Armstrong, in May 1814, because Samuel Brace, lately a member of the club, had complained that his name had been unjustly erased from the list of members and that he had been deprived of his benefits. All parties were heard and it was adjudged that Brace had violated no clause in the rules sufficient to justify the stewards' action. The stewards refused to reinstate Samuel Brace and a further peremptory order was issued. Soon afterwards the publican was deprived of his licence, but whether this was connected with the friendly society dispute I don't know.[37] There were 535 men enrolled in friendly societies in Enfield by 1818; in Tottenham, a few miles nearer to London, over a thousand were enrolled.[38]

5. Peter Hardy the Ale-Conner

The industrious labourer earned little enough on which to live. With no land to produce food of his own he was forced to buy from local shopkeepers who cheated him with impunity. It was this evil to which Peter Hardy next turned his attention, courting thereby the hostility of the trading fraternity of the town. He revived for his purpose the ancient manorial office of ale-conner whereof the duties had lain neglected for centuries. He secured for himself appointment to this office for the Town and Chase quarter in 1813. First he obtained authorisation to purchase weights and scales, both for himself and for use in the Highway division; with these he could now check the honesty of the local traders.[39]

During his first year of office he seized and destroyed seven hundred deficient weights and measures, some of which had been in use in that same state for fifty years. Most shopkeepers caught cheating showed no shame or remorse but repeated the offence and were detected again and again, although printed notices had been issued warning them of prosecution.

Not only were the weights scandalously deficient but the scales were biased, and when this was pointed out to them they expressed not regret but indignation at such interference with trade. Many claimed that it was their right because they made losses in weighing out small quantities, ignoring the fact that they already charged extra in such trading. Peter Hardy found flour scales with two or three ounces of flour sticking to them, butter scales with an ounce or two of butter and water hanging about them. Half a dozen pieces of lead as makeweights were not uncommon. One pair of scales was balanced by a potato, another by a bed screw. Another, which was taken from one of the smallest shops in Enfield, had been used to cheat the poor over many years out of one and a half ounces in every quarter-pound.

Seven-pound weights had been seized up to 1½ lbs short, and smaller weights that were scarcely more than half the weight claimed. There were measures which contained not much more than half the quantity inscribed on the outside. Thirty weights and three deficient scales were confiscated on three visits to a single shop. The good magistrate had subsequently turned his attention to the traders from the neighbourhood of London who were making their fortunes bringing their carts, laden with produce, down to Enfield where they robbed their customers with short measure, on average one peck in a bushel (ie twenty-five per cent short). He had waged such a vigorous campaign against these people that many had discontinued their visits. Others galloped away at the sight of the ale-conner. With patriotic fervour he described how he had intervened when one of these carts, standing in Enfield Town loaded with potatoes, was selling short weight to a soldier from the Dragoons just returned from France.

Bread was seized from bakers' shops and from the general shops to which they delivered it. Many bakers were brought before petty sessions and fined 5s for each ounce deficient from a loaf. On 24 August Peter Hardy visited Benjamin Cann's shop at Cockfosters and took away two half-quartern loaves. Then he inspected Susan Nash's shop in the same hamlet where he found five quartern loaves deficient in weight. Both shops had been supplied by Ann Smith a baker of Chipping Barnet. A hundred and seventy loaves were seized during the year, twopenny loaves as much as 2½ ounces deficient (two and a half medium-thick slices of a modern cut loaf).

Upward of two hundred and fifty beer measures had been seized and destroyed, many of them nearly half a pint short in a quart measure. Wine and spirit measures had also been found to be deficient in proportion. Coal measures, which had been used for years, were found to give fifteen or sixteen per cent short measure.

Mr Hardy was shocked and angry. Bread in the previous winter had cost 20d a quartern loaf, coal had cost 4s a bushel. A labourer, he said, might well work one day's labour in six to put money into the pockets of dishonest tradesmen. At the end of his year in office the ale-conner surrendered to the Enfield court leet 356 false weights, six false corn and coal measures, fourteen false wine and spirit measures, forty-two false ale measures and eight incorrect pairs of scales.[40]

Itinerant traders on Windmill Hill from a painting by George Forster.

6. Law Enforcement

By the beginning of the nineteenth century the petty constable was no longer alone in his fight against crime. Cases could now be referred to the police at Hatton Garden. The level of violence used or threatened sometimes made this necessary, as in an incident which occurred just before Christmas 1806 when four armed men raided the house of Mr John Spencer in South Street. About an hour and a half after sunset they banged on the door; it was opened by the maid Sarah Taylor. She was so roughly thrust aside that in a panic she ran upstairs, threw open the sash and jumped out of the window. Unhurt she climbed the fence and ran to the Falcon for help. A number of the customers ventured down to the house but, seeing four men armed and masked emerge, they decided upon caution and the thieves escaped down the lane towards the mills. The age of detection had however dawned. The matter was put into the hands of the police at Hatton Garden. Pawnbrokers were visited and some of the stolen goods were traced. This led directly to one of the thieves. The threat of execution induced him to turn evidence against his fellows who were arrested, tried and hanged.[41]

The first beadle who appeared in the records of the parish was William Billington, appointed on 26 December 1730 at wages of 4s a week. He was provided with a greatcoat, hat and a staff proper to his office. Four years later he was replaced by William Sackford, still at only 4s a week and in July 1738 Richard Dennis was chosen. These men were no more than paupers selected to control other paupers.[42] The office grew slowly in prestige. When Alexander Young was appointed beadle of Enfield in January 1773 his duties as defined were to search out paupers newly come into the parish and to assist the workhouse master to remove them.[43] He remained beadle until about 1778 when John Scott was appointed at a salary (in 1782) of 10s 6d a week. His authority was enhanced by the provision of a coat, waistcoat and breeches of a superfine plain blue cloth at a cost of £4 10s. His uniform by 1791 cost £5 9s but it was made far more impressive, perhaps oppressive, by a vast quantity of gold braid to the value of £3 12s 6d.[44] He retired as a consequence of his increasing infirmities in February 1807 and the parish continued his salary as a pension. His place was taken by Joseph Scott, probably his son. Joseph was not liked by the vestrymen. A statement of his duties and his salary, as a reminder, was stuck up in the committee room at the workhouse in June 1813 and a warning was issued that any demand he might make to the overseer, beyond what was warranted, would be considered fraudulent. Two months later he was reprimanded for lack of diligence in passing a pauper to his place of settlement. The pauper had died and the parish found itself 'likely to have to maintain the family'. He was discharged in March 1814 for 'great misconduct in the execution of his office.'[45]

Richard Matthews took his place even more magnificently arrayed than his predecessors. He wore olive velveteen breeches, a blue waistcoat of fine cloth with sleeves, and a blue milled greatcoat, lined with shaloon, with gilt buttons. Five yards of gold lace were provided for the two coats at 16s 6d a yard, with lace loops. All this magnificence was surmounted by a laced cocked hat, at a total cost of £17 10s 6d.[46]

During the years which followed the end of the war in 1815 the beadle took over many responsibilities from the parish constable. The Enfield beadle was William Cuffley, a man to be treated with respect. 'I am beadle of Enfield,' he pronounced before the court at the Old Bailey, and went on to present his evidence with authority.

> 'On 13 September, about three o'clock in the morning, I stopped the prisoner with a sack nearly full of beans and bran mixed. I said "Halloo". He immediately threw the sack down and attempted to run away. I asked what was in it. He said he did not know. He said "I hope you will let me go, and I will leave the country quite".'

Well, the poor young man did leave the country, for he was condemned to transportation for seven years.[47]

During this same period a Bow Street patrol was stationed at Enfield. The patrolman was John Mead, another formidable character. Thereafter Mead consistently described himself in court with the words, 'I am constable of Enfield.' He was involved in the prosecution of many criminals and unfortunates within the parish. The church was ransacked in June 1820. This followed the funeral service there of John Vaughan, Earl of Lisburne, and the pulpit, the desk, the communion table and the Earl's pew remained draped in black cloth, sixty yards of it and valued at £1 a yard. The robbery was discovered by William Cuffley who found the church door unlocked at two o'clock in the morning. The three thieves had reached the Two Brewers at Ponders End by twenty past two. There they hailed the driver of a passing wagon, offering him a shilling to take their bundles as far as Shoreditch church. He agreed to let them be carried on the shafts. The three men accompanied the wagon on foot. One offered to drive and the wagoner, grateful for the break, settled down to sleep. When he awoke they had reached Tottenham High Cross and it was getting light. He resumed the whip and the man who had been driving rejoined his friends on foot. Near Kingsland, John Mead appeared; riding up briskly he spoke a word in the wagoner's ear and then fell behind. The thieves were suspicious. 'Do you know him?' they asked, but the driver told them that Mead had only enquired whether he had brought a letter from his mother. And so the wagon reached the Mail Coach public house where Mead signalled the driver to stop so that the men could take off their bundles. As they did so Mead intervened, secured one of the thieves and handed him over to bystanders, then went after the others. They had made off, however, and Mead had a long and arduous search before he was able to arrest a second. This man appeared in the dock at the Old Bailey;[48] he was found guilty and was condemned to death.

Bow Street constantly intervened in dealing with crime in Enfield. Thomas Reeves of the Bow Street patrol was responsible for the arrest of Henry Millard whom he confined in the Enfield watch-house in 1823, accused of some petty theft at the house of Mr Milner at Bush Hill Park. Millard was sentenced to transportation for seven years.[49]

The Town was not a safe place at night. Edward Law, a bricklayer, had spent the evening at the Rose and Crown at Clay Hill. About eleven o'clock he set off home. It was October 1824 and a moonlight night, he was quite sober. When he got to Enfield, he said, he saw three men standing against 'the new buildings' (probably 79, 81, and 83 Chase Side). As he passed by, one of them named Thomas Roberts, whom he knew by sight, seized him and dragged him against the poles (presumably these were scaffold poles). Then he was kicked and hit over the head. His assailant grabbed his watch and the glass was broken in the scuffle. Edward Law demanded to know what his attacker wanted. 'I want to rob you, what do you think?' Roberts replied, still trying to get hold of the watch. Law struggled

The Vestry House, built 1830. The beadle was to live there, paying £6 6s a year rent.

free and ran with the drunken Roberts in pursuit, but when he reached his lodgings and rapped on the door, his pursuer cleared off. John Mead arrested him the following day in the Rising Sun, about two o'clock in the afternoon, still drinking. 'I have known him since a boy', said Mead regretfully. Roberts, aged twenty-six, was transported for seven years.[50]

Richard Watkins, who took over from Mead as the Bow Street patrolman in 1827, was stationed at London Road in Enfield. He was a Waterloo man and he remained in Enfield for a long time. Charles Plume remembered him as he was thirty years later, still living in his little wooden cottage in London Road. He had been appointed after John Mead had taken over as assistant beadle with a salary of £15 a year and a hat and a suit of clothes annually. William Cuffley died during the following summer and his widow was granted a pension of £25 a year. John Mead then became the beadle and in November he was also made assistant overseer of the poor, to recover money owed to the parish by the fathers of illegitimate pauper children, and money due from officers of other parishes.

That same year it was reported that the watch-house in London Road was in a state of ruin. It was first proposed to rebuild it on the same site, but Edward Harman suggested to the vestry the exchange of two cottages and a small piece of land at Clay Hill which belonged to Cocks Charity, for his two dwellings next to the Greyhound. Demolition there began in April 1829 and was completed the following month, but more than a year passed before the new building was begun. In July 1830, £50 was voted towards furnishing the watch-house. The beadle was to live there at an annual rent of £6 6s. Cells were constructed on each side of the house in 1832 and an iron fence was put up in front. From that time, declared the

Bowes Farm in Green Lanes near the present junction with Bowes Road, crowded and insanitary and the refuge of thieves, 1848.

vestry, it was to be known as 'the cage'. A plan to replace the watch-house at the Highway was abandoned.

Among the last prisoners to be incarcerated in the old London Road watch-house was William Green, the gingerbread man. 'I am a hawker of gingerbread', he began his complaint before the court. 'I was in a public house at Enfield and had a few words with the landlord and he sent me to the watch-house at half past nine at night'. He had nearly £1 worth of silver when he went to sleep but in the morning when they came to let him out, it was missing. He went back to search the bed and John Wilson the constable asked what he was looking for. Being told, Wilson ordered the other prisoners to strip and found the money, 17s, on John Lawson. Lawson protested his innocence. He had saved up that money by industry, working for the parish at 9s a week, he claimed; it was to see him through the winter. He was not believed and was sentenced to transportation for fourteen years.[51]

Some of those tried were habitual criminals. Usually they lived in the worst of the slum dwellings and spent what time and money they had in the public houses. Bowes Farm, on the Green Lanes, sheltered a number of thieves and receivers. Two men who had robbed the laundry at Pymmes House in Edmonton in 1822 of several bags of wet washing made their way the first thing the following morning to Bowes Farm to see Deakin, on whom they relied to dispose of the goods. He lived there with Elizabeth Bonner. 'I am not his wife, I lived with him for seven years,' she told the court at the Old Bailey. 'On the morning of the Wednesday . . . between six and seven o'clock, some persons came to our house. I and Deakin were in bed.' The thieves were James Tufnell and Thomas Wilson. The bundles had to be picked up. Thomas Balaam, who also lived at Bowes Farm, had a cart. He sent his boy down with Deakin to a field in White Hart Lane to pick up the washing. The whole shabby affair was crudely done and the law soon caught up with them. Wilson and Tufnell were sentenced to death.[52]

Tufnell was only twenty-four but he had been in trouble not long before. He had been in the Bell at Enfield Highway one night with a couple of his mates, Isaac Johnson and Tom Godfrey. Jim Dalton, who worked for Mr Green the baker

Myddelton House, the home of the Bowles family, 1821.

at Enfield Wash, was sitting having a drink and had hung his coat over the screen behind him. There was a £1 note in the pocket. Tufnell and his mates took the coat and left without paying for their drinks. Fortunately someone saw the coat slide off the screen and called out to Dalton, 'Your coat is gone.' Dalton went after them and caught them in about twenty yards. He grabbed his coat, the £1 note was still in the pocket, but it was so dark that he could not identify the thieves. Later the three of them went back into the Bell but the landlord, Richard Morris, refused to serve them. Dalton accused them of taking his coat but there was no constable nearby to send for. They hung about in the bar until eleven o'clock without money, hoping that something would turn up. They were arrested the following morning by John Mead. They got six months and were publicly whipped.[53]

Another of the residents of Bowes Farm was Thomas Denton. On the morning of 22 March 1824 Mr William Gladwin, who lived at Southgate, was surprised to find that his alarm bell had been stolen during the night – surprised because the bell weighed nearly two hundredweight. On hearing of this, Samuel Fitch, the patrolman stationed at Southgate, recalled that between twelve and one o'clock the previous night he had observed Thomas Denton wheeling an empty barrow. Despite the very early hour he had affably greeted the constable with 'Good morning Mr Fitch'. Denton was arrested at Bowes Farm where the bell was found covered with sacks. His story, not altogether convincing, was that he had left the Cherry Tree at about eleven o'clock and had found the bell in the street and he announced confidently that if he found anything, he thought he had a right to it. The jury thought otherwise and he was sentenced to transportation for seven years.[54]

The more elaborately planned criminal enterprises in the area were organised, if that word is not allowed to imply too much efficiency, from London. The thieves who perpetrated a robbery at Myddelton House, the home of Mr Henry Carrington

The Crown and Horseshoes.

Bowles, in October 1830, came out some in a gig and some on the stage coach, from the Flower Pot in Bishopsgate Street. 'The stage came up with Tottenham and Edmonton written on it,' one of them told the court at the Old Bailey. The gig followed the stage to the Ship in Tottenham where they stopped for a drink. They described the pub as having 'a round bar with a very handsome machine in it' (presumably the beer pump). Some of the party had brandy and water, the others had a pint of porter, with biscuit and cheese. They then went outside together and drank a quartern and a half of gin. All this time the stage had waited. It was about ten o'clock when they arrived at the Rose and Crown in Church Street Edmonton, which was the terminus for the stage coach. There they had another pint of porter, then set off in the chaise for Enfield, some riding, some running behind. They arrived at Mr Bowles's house (about five miles) at half past eleven. They had brought liver and poison to put the dog out of action. The liver had to be tied up. 'I got a piece of string out of my shoe' one of them told the court, 'the dog barked very much at first, but it was soon quiet.' They had come equipped with a dark lantern, a centre bit, a crowbar and a chisel and spent about two and a half hours ransacking the house, emerging at length with an odd collection of clothes, silver and paintings. Some of them rode off in the chaise, the others walked, stopping for refreshment at the White Lion (on the main road, now called Old Road) where they had beer, bread, cheese and onions sometime after three o'clock in the morning. They finally reached Shoreditch about six o'clock.[55]

In December 1832 the parish was shocked by the murder of Benjamin Danby. It was widely reported in the national press and was commemorated by a crude piece of doggerel verse.

'Give ear ye tender Christians all and listen unto me
While I relate a deed of blood and great barbarity
A murder of the blackest dye I now repeat in rhyme
Committed on Benjamin Danby, a young man in his prime

This young man was a sailor and just returned from sea
And down to Enfield Chase he went his cousin for to see
With money in his pocket so jolly and so free
But little did he dream of such dismal destiny'.

There are numerous verses but I won't afflict my readers with any more of it.

This man Danby came down to Enfield on 12 December 1832 to stay with his cousin who had married Peter Addington a baker in Chase Side, not a hundred yards from the Crown and Horseshoes. He had recently been to the East Indies and had returned loaded with money and, as the versifier says, he was of a free and easy disposition.

The Crown and Horseshoes stood on the banks of the New River looking very much then as it does now, though it has been perhaps a little improved. On the opposite bank was the brewery, known later as Sutton's Warehouse and demolished in 1971. Things were very quiet in the tap room on the night of 19 December. Danby, Richard Wagstaff and a couple of others were playing dominoes for pints of beer throughout most of the evening. William Johnson, the man subsequently hanged for the murder of Danby, was invited to play. He was a gardener by trade, aged twenty-nine and married. He probably lived in what later became known as Loves Row, now Chapel Street. Johnson replied that he had no money. 'Never mind about money,' says the good-hearted Danby, 'If you lose, I will pay', and he pulled out some halfpence and gave them to Johnson.

Joe Matthews the pot boy was serving in the bar. He went out about eight o'clock as usual to take beer around to various households in the neighbourhood and returned around nine o'clock. John Cooper who worked at the brewery, came in soon afterwards. He was eighteen and spent most of his time, when he was not working, in the bar. He was deeply implicated in this murder. The landlord, Joseph Perry, looked in about ten o'clock. At that time Sam Fare (otherwise known as Sleith) was lying along a bench, apparently asleep. He was twenty-two and seldom worked; for his part in the crime he was to be transported for seven years. William Johnson was laid across two chairs with his head on a bench. A character called Wager was asleep on another two chairs. The landlord roused them and told them that he would not have them sleeping in his house. Fare became aggressive and threatening. 'Damn your eyes,' he said 'You would not serve me so but you think I cannot pay for a pot but I have money that will pay for a gallon.' He put his hand in his pocket and pulled out two shillings and sixpence. He was known to be out of work at the time and receiving parish relief.

The landlord went to bed soon afterwards telling his wife not to serve them with any more beer, but they stayed on. Then Danby said, 'We will have half a pint of gin before we go.' By the time they had finished that it was ten past eleven. Wagstaffe, Johnson, Cooper and Fare left the house together. Danby came out last and was staggering drunk. The landlady, seeing his condition, told the pot boy to see him across the New River in case he fell in and Joe Matthews led him over the bridge and then called Fare to see the gentleman safely home. Fare took one arm and Cooper the other. Johnson was with them; Richard Wagstaff stood up against the corner of the house by the bridge making water.

Wagstaff, a journeyman baker, went indoors when he reached his house which probably stood near the site of the Cricketers, between the Horseshoes and Addington's where Danby was staying. He had told Cooper not to go with Fare and Johnson because he had an idea, he said, that they were going to rob Danby, but Cooper followed on behind them. Johnson and Fare, with the drunken seamen supported between them, were pushing each other about and falling on the ground as they went along what is now Chase Side Place, undoubtedly so that they could get their hands into Danby's pockets. There were no street lamps until they reached Chase Side. They went right past Addington's house as far as the corner of Holt Whites Lane. There Fare left them and continued towards the Holly Bush, near to which he lived. Johnson then said, 'Let's get a pint of beer', and the three of them turned up Holt Whites Lane towards Pinnock's beer shop, but before they got as far as that Johnson turned around (according to Cooper) and started back, saying 'I will be damned if Sam (Sam Fare) hasn't robbed him'. And with that he put out his foot and tripped Danby up and they all fell into the ditch, Cooper underneath and Johnson on top. There was a foot of icy water in the bottom. When Cooper managed to clamber out his cap was missing. He groped around for it and found it under Danby's face. The cap was soaked with blood. According to Cooper (and for some reason the court seemed to believe him) he pleaded with Johnson not to harm Danby. Johnson, he said, had his knees on Danby's chest, and the seaman was groaning. Johnson came up to Cooper and said, 'You take this knife and go and finish him', but Cooper refused. Johnson then went back to Danby and said, 'What will you give?' Danby raised his head and begged that he would not hurt him. 'What will you give?' again demanded Johnson. 'Anything,' said Danby, but Johnson cut his throat. Cooper heard the gurgle as he stood in the road. They left the body there, the feet in the road, the head in the ditch and made their way back down Holt Whites Lane into Chase Side. From there they turned off across Corneys fields* to the bridge over the New River (the one about fifty or sixty yards north of the Crown and Horseshoes) and Johnson washed his hands and the knife in the New River. The two of them then continued on without speaking, crossing again by the Horseshoes bridge where they turned left towards the next bridge (the one that leads to Gentleman's Row). There they parted company. Johnson went over the bridge and Cooper turned right down the little alley towards Chase Side where he lived.

The body was found the following morning about half past five by William Wheeler, a labourer. He was on his way to work in Parsonage Lane. Danby was lying on his face in the ditch on the south side of the road about three hundred yards below Pinnock's. Wheeler, thinking it was a drunken man, called two or three times, pulled and kicked the body, but getting no response, he turned back up the hill and met James Ashby with a cart load of straw coming down. They secured a light and a shutter on which they carried the body down the lane past the gates of Mr Holt White's house to the Sergeant in Parsonage Lane. John Cuffley, the landlord, sent for Mr Asbury, the surgeon, and for John Mead, the beadle.

Mead arrested Johnson first. 'Bill, I want you,' he said, 'you must go with me'. Then he took Fare, put him in the Watch House, (now known as the Vestry House in Enfield Town), searched him, and found some of Danby's property. After that he went after Cooper; Richard Watkins the patrol man was with him. They picked

*The track followed the line now Parsonage Gardens.

up the suspect near Potters Bar. 'You've heard about the murder?' said Watkins. Cooper denied all knowledge. Mead questioned him about the blood inside his cap. He said he had been carrying horse flesh for his master's dog. 'When was that?' said Mead. 'One day last week'. This was Thursday and the blood was still wet. 'That gammon won't do for us,' said Watkins. 'You must get up in the cart and come with us.' They locked him up in a private room at the George; there he offered to turn evidence against the others. He was taken before Dr Cresswell, vicar and magistrate, and made the sworn statement which sent Johnson to the gallows, Fare to Australia, and allowed Cooper to go free.[56]

Thus the Crown and Horseshoes was a house best avoided by respectable people. Even Richard Wagstaff previously mentioned as a journeyman baker who had been drinking in the Crown and Horseshoes on the night of the Danby murder, could consider himself fortunate that he was not in prison. He had appeared at the Old Bailey the previous year charged by his master, Thomas Jelly, with stealing flour. Jelly had employed Wagstaff since 1826, (about five years) and trusted him, but on searching his bakehouse as a result of information received, he had found a bag of flour concealed. 'I wrote my name on an old Post Office bill,' he said, 'put it in the bag and tied it up again.' He then sent a message to Richard Watkins, the Bow Street patrolman. Wagstaff was stopped the following morning about ten o'clock as he left the baker's premises in a cart and the bag was found hidden under some straw. Despite the weight of evidence, the case against Wagstaff was dismissed.[57]

John Mead frequented the Crown and Horseshoes to pick up information on this and that. He was there on the evening of 4 August 1834, on the bowling green outside. John Clay and John Henry Stanley were playing bowls; it was nearly seven o'clock in the evening. Mead noticed that they were very respectably dressed; they looked too respectable, he thought, so he got into conversation with them. They told him that they had just returned from the Cape (South Africa). Stanley had on a drab jacket and waistcoat. He proudly showed it to Mead saying, 'I never saw a better bit of cloth'. He said it had been made for him at the Cape. He and his mate had gone there, one as a baker, the other as a cook.

The following evening Mead received information about a robbery at a baker's shop in Wapping where a considerable quantity of clothes had been stolen. Once again he walked round to the Crown and Horseshoes. Stanley was there but not Clay. Stanley had a complaint to make to the beadle; 'John', he says, on intimate terms already, 'I am glad you have come; Clay has taken my jacket and I won't leave the house till I get it'. The beadle responded as one friend to another. 'As you are shipmates, go with me and I will find it for you'. He took him to the cage and searched him. The following morning he took him to the Thames Police Office. That same evening he found Clay at his grandmother's, very tipsy. Clay tried to jump out of the window, which was about twelve feet from the ground, but the beadle restrained him.[58]

Another of the public houses where labourers drank was the Holly Bush. The landlord there was Thomas Brewer. He gave evidence at the Old Bailey during the trial of three labourers. 'The three prisoners were all at my house in company on the Saturday night,' (18 May 1833) he stated. They had come in about nine and had stayed until eleven. The landlord had then gone into the tap-room and called 'Gentlemen, it is shutting-up time', and they had all left. The three labourers were back in the bar on the Sunday morning at half past seven, on their way home, having spent the night carrying out a robbery at Beech Hill Park some four or five miles away. Thus they appeared so completely indifferent to their fate that they neglected to take the most elementary precaution to ensure the secrecy of their venture. All three were found guilty.

Pubs did a great deal of their business by sending drinks out to houses in the neighbourhood. Mary Warner, eighteen years old, was employed by William Walpole, a publican at Enfield Highway. She would be sent out with beer at noon and at night time, and the customers would either give her the money, or a bill would be made out. She went to Dr Smart's on 21 June 1825 with beer, and Elizabeth Jeaps his servant paid her the 5½d. She also took a bill to Mr Hobbs's house and the servant there paid her 4s 2d, all in halfpence. She failed to return with the money. When arrested she claimed that she was owed for wages, but she was transported for seven years.[59]

The Metropolitan Police was set up in 1829 but it covered only the area later controlled by the London County Council, i.e. no further north than Stamford Hill. Its jurisdiction was extended to Enfield in 1839.

7. Labourers

Poverty in the countryside in the bad years after the defeat of Napoleon drove many people towards London, seeking a living wage. In consequence, parishes like Enfield saw their population increase in the ten years from 1811. There was a twenty-five per cent growth in Enfield, despite the fact that employment prospects were diminished by the temporary closure of the Small Arms Factory at the end of the war. In these same ten years the population of Edmonton increased by sixteen per cent and that of Tottenham by twenty-seven per cent. This rapid expansion slowed down in the ten years 1821–1831, even in Tottenham, though the growth rate there was nineteen per cent. This was attributed in the census report to vaccination and also to 'the encouragement afforded to improvident marriages by the present provision of the poor laws'. The growth of population in Enfield was seven per cent, in Edmonton only 3.7 per cent.

Enfield had a population of 8812 in 1831, an increase of thirty-four per cent since the beginning of the century. The years of prosperity for landowners and farmers came inevitably to an end with the return of peace in 1815. Prices fell, profits declined, and labourers found it still harder to find work throughout the winter. The Corn Laws passed in 1815 to protect the agricultural interest worsened the condition of the labourers by raising the price of bread. Wheat bread was still the principal ingredient of a labourer's diet. The number of families employed chiefly in agriculture in Enfield declined in real terms in the years 1811 to 1821, from 604 to 482. The decline in percentage terms is more dramatic, from forty-six per cent to thirty per cent. The number of families employed in trade, manufactures or handicraft increased in real terms from 339 to 410 but remained at twenty-six per cent. The greatest increase was in the number of families whose source of income is unspecified in the census reports of 1811 and 1821, this number increased from 358 to 681.

Families employed in:	Agriculture	Trade	Other	Total
1811	604(46%)	339(26%)	358	1301
1821	482(30%)	410(26%)	681	1573
1831	599(30%)	578(30%)	708	1885

Agriculture had revived a little by 1831 to employ almost as many families as it had in 1811. There had been an increase of 168 in the number of families employed in trade which, in percentage terms, rose from twenty-six to thirty. There were, in Enfield in 1831, 2061 males of twenty years of age or more, 987 of them described as labourers, that is forty-eight per cent. 641 of these were employed in agriculture, an average of nearly fifteen labourers employed by each farmer. There were also six small proprietors who employed no labour. The remaining 346 labourers were employed in other trades. The rest of the adult male population comprised 199 'capitalists, bankers, professional and other educated men', 101 employed in manufacture, (this would have been mostly at the Royal Small Arms Factory and in Grout and Baylis crape manufactory in South Street, 539 in retail trade and handicrafts, either as masters or workmen, and eighty-five as servants.

	Upperclass	Manufacture	Retail & Handicraft	servants	labourers	others
1831	199	101	539	84	987	101

There were also 382 females employed as servants in Enfield.[60]

The parish register for the period around the end of the Napoleonic war gives the father's trade when infants were baptised; forty-six per cent were labourers. Farmers at this time employed labour by contract, either to do certain specified work, or over a period. William Hornet hired himself for the winter and summer of 1813/14 but, having received his wages through the winter at 3s a day, he left in May giving no reason or notice. He was summoned by William Cobb his employer to appear at petty sessions. William Cobb also summoned three other Enfield labourers who had contracts with him. These had been paid to complete certain work but they had walked out and left their tasks unfinished. Another labourer summoned to appear before the magistrates, the Revd Armstrong and Mr Mellish, at Henry Sawyer's office in Silver Street, was Samuel Lawrence who had been hired by William Nash, a farmer, on a contract for one year but he had left before his time had expired. With the end of the war short term hiring became more common. John Sibley was hired by the farmer and baker, Thomas Young, by the week at 18s. When he was discharged his master owed him 10s. This too was brought before petty sessions.[61] The difference was that labourers in breach of contract could be imprisoned; their masters could only be fined.

Labourers worked long hours for low wages. They lived only on the fringes of society. Many spent what they earned in the public houses and some stole (without subtlety) to supplement their earnings. Punishment was harsh but juries were reluctant to convict. John Game was employed by this same Thomas Young in February 1821. He had been sent to the mill with the wagon to pick up nine sacks of flour and on his return to the bakery at eleven o'clock that night the wagon was stopped and searched. Six of the sacks had been opened and left open. Young discovered a bin containing fourteen pounds of flour concealed under the man's greatcoat. The six sacks were weighed and found to be deficient but, because no one had been called into court to witness to their weight on leaving the mill, the prisoner was acquitted.[62]

The conduct of the poor too often speaks of degradation beyond measure. They seemed ever willing to inform against each other in order to reap a reward and promptly turned evidence to save their necks; yet they were ready to risk dire punishment for dubious profit. There can be no denying the connection at this time between crime and poverty. Many local men were among those who stood in the dock at the Old Bailey and almost without exception they were labourers. A man named Starr (of a family which habitually sought parish relief) waited upon John Barnard, his mistress's son, on their farm at Enfield Highway to offer information against two of his fellow labourers. William Hornet and Thomas Dimmock. It was on Sunday morning 26 January 1809. He reported that they had stolen four bushels of oats and two sacks worth a pound altogether. Hornet had owed him half-a-crown, said Starr, and when he had asked for it that morning he had been offered oats in payment. He at once told Mr Barnard and between them they set a trap and were able to take the two labourers red-handed. They were publicly whipped at the cart's tail through Enfield in front of their neighbours and this was followed by a month in Newgate. Such humiliation was thought necessary for the protection of property.[63]

Labourers were so poor that if they were seen with money any respectable person would become suspicious. In 1820 three labourers, John Head, William Lawrence and William Clayton, broke into the house of William Bate, an employee of the Trustees of the River Lea. His house was near Ponders End Mill. They stole three guineas in gold, two five-pound notes, five one-pound notes and a quantity of silver. The labourers made their way straight to William King's shop in Silver Street, Edmonton and bought themselves a pair of breeches each offering the shopkeeper a five-pound note. He immediately became suspicious and asked where they worked. They said that they had been working at a tanyard in Enfield and had been given the note as wages for the three of them.

Undeterred by the suspicion they had aroused in the first shop, they then went to another nearby and each bought two pairs of stockings which cost 4s 6d. Each proffered a one-pound note. The shopkeeper took note of the numbers. These labourers seem to have had a death wish. An hour or so later, while the Edmonton constable was in a nearby public house with a prisoner, who should come in but Lawrence in his new clothes, with a woman. He had a drink with the prisoner to whom he related the success of the afternoons venture. Lawrence was picked up that evening in the King's Head Edmonton, much of the money still in his pockets. He also had with him a new casting net which he said he had bought for 36s. Clayton was there too, but he ran. He was arrested a few days later at Rickford (Surrey) and turned evidence against his mates. Head and Lawrence were sentenced to death but escaped because they were recommended for mercy by the prosecutrix;[64] Clayton escaped punishment because he had turned evidence.

Meanwhile property owners, seeing the deterioration in the condition of the labouring class, became alarmed and set up associations for the protection of their property in parishes throughout the country. The Enfield Association was established in November 1815. It comprised all the important people and sought to protect its members by the offer of handsome rewards for information leading to the arrest and conviction of those guilty of housebreaking and arson (£20), highway robbery and the theft of lead and other materials from houses (£15), the killing, maiming or stealing of farm animals (£10), the destruction of wood, timber, hedgerows and farm implements (£5) and the theft of corn, turnips, potatoes or peas (£1 to £5).[65] Punishment upon conviction was brutal and many local labourers faced trial at the Old Bailey without the help of counsel, groping alone in their ignorance to devise an adequate defence.

There were rumblings of discontent. Handbills were printed in March 1816 offering a reward of £50 for information leading to the arrest of the writer of a

The Fallow Buck, June 1902, decked out for the coronation of Edward VII.

threatening letter sent to an Enfield churchwarden.[66] Food riots broke out in East Anglia that May.

The drab poverty-stricken life of a labourer whose endless toil could earn no better reward in old age than the parish workhouse drove many of them to drink and in their stupor their befuddled minds turned to crime. Daniel Wilson and Richard March had spent most of the day together in the Fallow Buck. It was a Monday in September 1827. During the afternoon March sold his cow for £12 14s to two people in a chaise who called at the pub. He was paid in guineas and silver. Later that night both labourers left the Fallow Buck and made their way down the hill to the Rose and Crown. It was kept at this time by William Williamson. In his evidence the publican described how Richard March came in that night with Daniel Wilson. They sat down on a bench about two yards apart and drank rum and water. After about five minutes March got up to fight, and Wilson, not wanting to be involved, moved away. They remained in the house for about an hour and went out together. March was back soon afterwards saying his wife had gone to bed and wouldn't let him in; so they gave him a bed at the pub.

The following day he sought out John Mead the beadle and reported that Daniel Wilson had robbed him of a £10 note. Mead was not a man to be easily duped. He warned March not to be in a hurry and demanded to know where he got a £10 note. March said that he had been given it by the auctioneer at Mr Cook's sale. Mead suggested that he had lost the money, but March insisted and said he had felt Wilson's hand in his back pocket. 'I asked him what he was about, and he said I'll give it to you presently.' Mead went out and arrested Wilson. On the Thursday morning, as he was on his way with the prisoner to see the magistrate, Mr Peter Hardy, March sidled up to the beadle, said he did not want to hurt Wilson, and if the prisoner would pay some down and so much a week he would be willing to spend half a sovereign of his own money to meet any expenses. Mead did not stop, 'It's nothing to do with me', he said, 'the prisoner must go before the magistrate'. Mr Hardy examined Wilson and discharged him at once, then issued a warrant for the arrest of March. He was charged that he had accused Wilson of a felony with the intent to extort money. March absconded.[67]

Many labourers were so sodden with alcohol that they scarcely knew what they were doing. John Brown and John Alligan spent the evening drinking in the Three Tuns at Edmonton and about ten o'clock they decided that they would break into the house of the Misses Susanah and Ann Walker at Ponders End. They forced the outside shutter of the kitchen window, broke the glass and unfastened the catch. Once in they lit a fire in the parlour and cooked some eggs which they ate with bread and butter taken out of the pantry. Alligan broke the lock of the cupboard in the hall and took out several sorts of liquor and wine. And thus they drank and feasted and then fell asleep in the parlour.

The servant girl came down first at about half past seven. She saw that the window was open and screamed. At this Brown came staggering out of the parlour with a lighted candle stuck in a bottle in one hand and the carving knife in the other. The girl took one look at him and fled. Brown was found by a labourer later that morning staggering aimlessly across a ploughed field with a bundle under his arm. The labourer went across to help him out of the ditch, couldn't manage it and left him there while he went to breakfast. That was when he was told about the robbery. Alligan was picked up later that day, blind drunk, in the Angel Edmonton, and Brown, in a similar condition, in the Jolly Farmers in Church Street. Both were sentenced to death but were recommended to mercy by the two Miss Walkers, bless their hearts.[68]

Drink was indeed the downfall of many. John Rapley was involved, just before Christmas 1822, in breaking into the brewery belonging to Richard and Robert Brailsford, the main brewers in the Town. His two mates, William Drage and Sam Rainberd, got seven years transportation but he escaped. The following June he broke in again, between three and four o'clock in the morning and drank a great deal of beer. John Mead found him in the morning asleep in the cooperage.[69]

Some of the pubs along the main road remained open all night. 'I keep the White Lion at Enfield' said Joseph Turner . . . 'Mine is a night house'. Asked if he could identify certain men who came in about three o'clock in the morning, he replied, 'I was very busy at the time, I cannot possibly say'. He remembered that John Wilson the constable was there at the time and was watching the men through a partition.[70]

Drink for the men may have been a release from endless drudgery, may have provided light, comfort and company, leaving to their wives the care of their half-starved children in the cold discomfort of their homes. Drink added to the misery of many women. 'We had been married seven weeks' said Sophia Richardson. Richard her husband had gone out that morning at a quarter past six telling her to find him at the Greyhound which was about a mile and a quarter from the house where they lived with her parents. He would be there, he said, by half past six in the evening. She left home at six and arrived on time but he was not there yet. At seven when she returned he was in the bar drinking. She opened the door and beckoned to him to come out. Three quarters of an hour later he came and told her to come in; she declined the invitation. He asked if she wanted to go home. She said she did as soon as she could, but he said he wasn't going yet and went back inside. A few minutes later he came out with 5s hoping to get rid of her. She asked if that was all he had got because she had only had 3s 6d the week before, but getting no more she went off to a shop to buy some things and then came back to wait for him again. It was after ten o'clock when he came out. Again she asked if he had any more money; he said he only had 1½d. She continued to complain so loudly of his spending everything in the public house that at last he gave her another shilling. Nevertheless she assailed him with her many grievances all the way through Enfield Town until they reached Mr Fox's the cornchandler. There he gave her a further shilling and she went in and bought a quartern loaf and a peck of coals which she thrust on him to carry. They pursued their acrimonious way along Silver Street, Baker Street, Forty Hill until, at Maidens Bridge, he struck her with his hoe knocking her to the ground where covered with blood, she began to scream violently. John Cranston who kept the post office at Forty Hill was awakened by the noise. He had no clothes on and so was unable to sally forth to the rescue but, seeing a woman approaching with a lantern, he sent her to enquire. They got Sophia home and sent for Mr Asbury, the surgeon. Her husband was arrested the following morning in the Rummer. He was sentenced to death but escaped, being strongly recommended to mercy by the jury (which contained no women), 'on account of the great provocation he had received and their having continually quarrelled since their marriage.[71]

Common law marriages were common among labourers. Charles Pratt and Sarah Creek lived together. They were accused of stealing forty-eight pounds of mutton from a butcher in Edmonton, after he had shut up shop at eleven o'clock on the Saturday night. Enquiries were made immediately at bakers' shops, since labourers seldom had anything on which to roast meat, even if they had meat to roast. It was established that Sarah had taken mutton to Mr Wood's but Pratt maintained adamantly that he had purchased it in London at 4d a pound and he was believed or at least he received a verdict of not guilty.[72]

The gap between labourers and their better-off neighbours had widened; they were scarcely considered to be a part of the community. Any employer could complain to a justice of their misbehaviour. Mr Williams, a farmer, in 1831 complained of John Collier 'his servant in husbandry for one year,' that he had been guilty of misdemeanours and had neglected his work and service. He also reported Thomas Wilkinson, his cowman, that he had neglected his work and had left his service before his contract had ended.[73]

A case at the Old Bailey shows labourers mowing clover in Mr Paris's meadows at Beech Hill (now the Hadley Golf Club club house) in June 1821. There were seven of them. They stopped about one o'clock for dinner, which they took together in the field with a pint of strong beer each. Everyone was in a good humour. Before two o'clock they picked up their scythes and returned across the swath of clover to their work. But on the way a quarrel broke out between Charles Johnson and James Richardson as to which of them had cut the wider swath. The argument became heated. Richardson threatened to strike Johnson and Johnson, who was the smaller, threatened Richardson with his scythe. The more they argued the more their anger grew. At last Johnson struck Richardson with his scythe which went right through one thigh and into the other. He fell backward crying 'O Lord you have killed me'. Someone ran for a horse and cart but it was half an hour before it came. Richardson was still alive and Johnson had fled. They lifted the wounded man onto the cart and took him home where they sent for Mr Walter Morrison, the surgeon, but the labourer died after a few hours. Johnson was hanged.[74]

Many labourers had only the crudest accommodation. James West lodged with his master, Mr Cracknold of Enfield. 'I had a box of clothes in a shed in his orchard,' he said. He had left his brand new breeches locked in the box on the Thursday (9 February 1828). He had worn them only once, the previous Sunday, and had told his master that he would not put them on again until Easter, but somebody stole them. They were recovered later from John King, the pawnbroker.[75] Another example of primitive living quarters is that of Edward Drayton who was

Beech Hill, where the labourers were working in Mr Paris's meadow, now the Hadley Golf Club House.

employed by Mr Palmer, a farmer at Enfield Wash, regularly for three or four months and slept in his hayloft.[76]

It is small wonder that labourers spent so much of their free time in the public houses, for their homes offered little comfort. 'I remember the night this robbery is said to have been committed' said Sarah Smith. 'My father came home at half past eleven.' He was one of three labourers accused of a robbery at Beech Hill Park. He had been at the Holly Bush which was about a hundred yards from Smith's cottage. She continued: 'He did not go out again until seven o'clock the next morning'. He was back in the Holly Bush soon after seven. 'We all sleep in one room,' she went on. 'It is impossible that he could have got up and dressed himself and gone out without my knowing. I and my two sisters sleep in the room.' She was aged eighteen but away in service during the week, the two sisters were aged eight and eleven. There was also a married sister, Ann Boreham, aged twenty-one. 'Have you a mother alive?' Sarah was asked. 'Yes,' she replied, 'she slept there too,' They had had supper that night at about a quarter to twelve; it being Saturday they had bread, cheese and porter.

Smith was unfortunate, for as Mead, the beadle, was taking him and the other prisoners to Newgate, Mead noticed the shirt he was wearing which was made of a particularly coarse kind of cloth. Mr Edwin Walker, the brewer, had lost a cloth of just such material which he had laid over his tulip bed at the beginning of May; it had been stolen during the night. Once again Smith's daughters were prepared to swear anything in an endeavour to protect their father. It was the married one this time, but it was to no avail; he was found guilty on both the charges.

Thomas Brewer, the landlord at the Holly Bush, giving evidence in the same case, described the circumstances of another of the three accused labourers. 'Young,' he said, 'has left his father and lives anywhere.' This was Frederick Young, aged twenty. Another witness had seen him wheeling a barrow through the streets about four o'clock that morning. 'He had on a dirty fustian jacket, a pair of breeches, a gaiter on one leg and a white stocking on the other,' he said.[77]

Labourers could not even be sure that they would be paid. 'I worked over hours,' said William Adams, a twenty-one year old labourer, in August 1822, 'and my master gave me ale instead of money'. He had been working for Mr Poyser until about half past ten that night.[78] Daniel Poyser treated his workmen with contempt. 'He was my labourer,' he told the court at the Old Bailey. 'I had some suspicion and I searched his house'. He had lost a beetle (a heavy wooden mallet) about six weeks before and had discovered it during the search. The labourer however claimed that he had picked it up in the brook and the jury dismissed the charge.[79]

Stark poverty drove many labourers into petty crime who might otherwise have been honest men. It was sometimes the only way to get enough to eat. A labourer living near Whitewebbs Lane was hanged in 1821 for stealing a sheep. The owners found the head and skin under a hedge. The man, John Chiles, married and forty-six years old, was so inept a thief that the owners were able to follow his footsteps imprinted in the mud all the way down Whitewebbs Lane and across three or four fields to the back of some cottages in one of which he lived. They found half the sheep in a closet under the stairs.[80]

James Withers, a man of thirty-seven with a wife and four children, worked for Henry Walker, the farmer. He was in the habit of selling his master's chaff to the ostler at the Weaver's Arms at Newington for a shilling a sack. Walker was suspicious and set his son-in-law to watch. That morning Withers had to take a load of potatoes to market. He set off at four o'clock, but had gone only about thirty yards from the premises when he was stopped. A sack of chaff was found concealed under his greatcoat. The chaff was taken and he was allowed to go on to market. When he returned that night he was brought before the master. 'He begged me to forgive him,' said Walker. 'I said I would not as I suspected he had robbed me many times before'. He ran away but was brought back from Wandsworth and given in charge. He was recommended for mercy and got two months in prison.[81]

Having caught and got rid of this carter Walker so intensified his vigilance that, two years later, he managed to trap a second. He set John Palmer to watch his farmyard on the night of 22 November. There were several tons of potatoes in his barn. At twelve o'clock as usual the carter, James Dearman, came into the stable to harness the horses. This took about fifteen minutes and he then came out and went over to the barn. Palmer had to wait three quarters of an hour but at last saw him take out two sacks of potatoes and put them on his cart which was already loaded with twelve sacks ready to go to Covent Garden Market. As Dearman drove out, Palmer sprang the trap and the carter got six months.[82]

Labourers were constantly watched by their employers and were prosecuted for the most trivial theft. George Perry, a man of fifty years of age, was stopped by Richard Watkins, the horse patrol on the Enfield station, on information provided by his employer the wealthy William Mellish of Bush Hill Park. He had been working at threshing, which was particularly exhausting work and was on his way home between five and six o'clock on a January evening in 1831. 'I took off his hat,' said Watkins 'and found in it a bag of wheat undressed,' It was the sort of bag in which labourers usually carried their food. Perry was arrested and taken to the watch-house. His home was searched and there they found three pecks of wheat and a small hand mill. Perry had worked for Mr Mellish for more than three years, had threshed many hundreds of quarters of corn, all of which, he said, had been measured out to the last bushel. He was sentenced to a year in prison.[83]

The theft of crops kept the beadle busy through the winter of 1825. He picked up Allen and Brace for stealing Mr Vaughan's potatoes; Vaughan also had his turnip tops purloined. The beadle also arrested R. Bredon and E. Wilshire for stealing bread and meat worth 4s. Crops were so vulnerable that night patrols were instituted costing 6s a night.[84] Potatoes were much sought after when times were hard. The crop was harrowed up at the end of October, more than a ton to an acre, and left on the ground to be picked up by the women. John Walpole had a field at Holwhites Hill opposite Pinnock's beer house. 'I have missed a great many,' he said, even though he employed a man to guard them. About half past eight in the morning on 1 November 1831 William Pinnock saw William Fairbrother, a young man of twenty-two, in the field with his sister. They were picking up potatoes and putting them in a bag. Fairbrother pleaded poverty and got three months. The following day William Jude, aged twenty, was caught in the same field with a bushel of potatoes in a bag; he got twelve months. Charles Russell, who lived at Winchmore Hill, lost so many potatoes out of his potato-house that November, that he sat up all night to watch. At twenty past five he caught two labourers, one of whom was his carter, carrying away a sack of potatoes. The carter, George Spikesley, got twelve months. The following month Edward Drayton aged twenty-five and on parish relief was arrested for stealing two loaves of bread off the counter in Amos Butt's baker shop. He pleaded poverty and got three months.[85]

The age-old custom which had allowed a labourer to poach a few rabbits to feed his family was now punished with severity. Joseph Peach and William Walton who used a 'lurcher to take and kill conies' were fined £10 each. Since their total possessions were worth much less than this, they were delivered to the keeper of the House of Correction.[86] For an easier option, though a potentially more dangerous one, the labourer might take sheep. Thomas Henry White of Chase Lodge lost two small Welsh ewes on the night of 19 April 1828. The following day, at dinner time, his servant with John Mead the constable, armed with a warrant, visited the house of Richard March, the prime suspect. He lived up a little lane ten or fifteen yards off Chase Side. They found him and his wife at dinner. His wife was eating breast of mutton and he had part of the breast and the neck on his plate. They were asked where it had been bought. He claimed that he had paid half a crown for it at Mr Taylor's. The constable took him to the shop. Mr Taylor declared that he had not sold him any mutton. A further search ensued. In the wash-house the constable found more incriminating evidence, a mutton pie and, in a large pot, a quantity of stewed mutton. The remainder of the carcase, with the feet, he found crammed down in the privy. Convicted, the labourer would have hanged. Despite overwhelming evidence the jury would not find him guilty.[87]

David Taylor a labourer told how he was in the George during the afternoon of 1 December 1830 and was approached by Joseph Markwell who asked him whether he wanted to buy a couple of ducks; he could let him have them for 3s. 'Were they alive or dead?' he asked. They were dead and at Markwell's lodgings in Baker Street; Markwell offered to fetch them and Taylor bought them, paying 2s with the promise of another shilling later. The ducks turned out to have been stolen from Benjamin Williams in Silver Street and Markwell, for a total profit of 2s, was sentenced to seven years transportation.[88]

It was in 1830 that the labouring poor began at last to retaliate, blindly, against the impoverishment and degradation imposed from above. The destruction of threshing machines and the burning of haystacks and barns first took hold in Kent whence it spread into Sussex and Hants and thence across the counties of southern England, then north into East Anglia. It was nearly Christmas before it approached Enfield. There was a fire on 15 December at Wrotham Park, followed by one in Enfield on the 19th. 'A great fire was blazing last night in the barns and haystacks of a farmer about half a mile from us', wrote Charles Lamb, then living at Chase Side, Enfield. That farmer was Daniel Poyser. 'Seven goodly stacks of hay with corn barns proportional lie smoking ashes and chaff . . . It was never good times in England,' continued the "gentle Elia", 'since the poor began to speculate upon their condition. Formerly they jogged on with as little reflection as horses. The whistling ploughman went cheek by jowl with his brother that neighed. Now the biped carries a box of phosphorous in his leather breeches and in the dead of night the half-illuminated beast steals the magic potion into a cleft in a barn and half the country is grinning with new fires . . . What a power to intoxicate his crude brains, just muddlingly awake to perceive that something is wrong in the social system . . . Now the rich and poor are fairly pitted. We shall see who can hang or burn the fastest . . . Fortunately for the likes of Charles Lamb it was the rich who prevailed, and though few were hanged, many were transported.[89]

8. Parish Relief

'Mrs Corney' said the beadle, smiling as men smile who are conscious of superior information, 'out-of-door relief properly managed; properly managed ma'am, is a parochial safeguard. The great principle of out-door relief is to give the paupers exactly what they don't want and then they get tired of coming'. (Oliver Twist)

The cost of the poor to the ratepayers of Enfield by 1813, was £3842, out of a total parish expenditure of £4488. The number in the workhouse was now only forty-two compared with eighty-two in the neighbouring parish of Edmonton, but 212 persons collected regular out-door relief for themselves and dependents, compared with 167 in Edmonton.[90] The population was 6636, the number of ratepayers 590. The lack of full-time employment increased the demand for casual relief and the cost of maintaining the poor inevitably rose. The heaviest parish expenditure remained the provision of regular pensions to the impotent poor. These were difficult to reduce because the amounts paid were already minimal. Nevertheless the vestry undertook a thorough examination of the pension list in May 1815.

The only real economy they could find was in the support given to children; it was decided that henceforth they must work to maintain themselves. All those chargeable to the parish who were of sufficient age were to be sent to the silk mills at Sewardstone. Thus Ann Eastwick had her pension reduced from 5s to 2s 6d and William, Elizabeth and Hector, her children, were sent to the mills. With them went Ann Lynes who had been in receipt of 3s 6d a week, Mary and Sarah March who had received 3s, James Simmonds who had had 3s 6d, and the Crick orphans, Sarah aged thirteen, Ann nine, William seven and Thomas only five. They were joined by Ann Shepstone an orphan aged six, and two of widow Rainberd's three children, Sarah and Joseph. The remains of the silk mills, the water wheel and the ruins of the house, were in existence in 1909 on the Sewardstone bank of the River Lea, due east from Brimsdown station. The site is now submerged beneath the

King George reservoir. Other children on the pension list were found to be already gainfully employed; thus Jane Brinkley had her pension reduced because her two children, Eleanor aged thirteen and Charles aged eleven, were employed at the pin manufactory were the girl earned 2s 9d and the boy 4s a week.[91]

Things had deteriorated further by December 1816 and a meeting of the inhabitants was called 'to take into consideration the most effectual means for relieving the distress of the industrious and necessitous poor'. The vicar took the chair and the meeting was attended by all the leading landowners, farmers, businessmen, clergy, proprietors of schools, and many others named and unnamed. Whether this was a first abortive attempt to institute a select vestry I do not know, for the list of those attending is followed in the vestry order book by two blank pages.

A select vestry was appointed in May 1819. Its sole function was to be the management of the poor and although it was called a select vestry it had no control whatever over other affairs of the parish. All its accounts and decisions had to be submitted to a general vestry where each year the select vestry was nominated by the inhabitants assembled and subsequently appointed by a justice of peace. Usually this was Peter Hardy, a member himself. Thus in April 1823, Peter Hardy, James Meyer, also a magistrate, Thomas Gutterson, William Augustus Mitchell, Thomas Westwood (later Charles Lamb's landlord), Samuel Langley, John Whaley, Joshua Tolputt, John Strange, Robert Thompson, Thomas Browning, Charles Wright, Matthew Long, William Hobbs, George Coell, Charles Elmore, William Walker, Joseph Vale, Robert Joyning and Richard Browning, all substantial householders, were appointed.[92] The usual chairman was James Meyer of Forty Hall or, in his absence, Peter Hardy. Thus poor relief came to be administered exclusively by landlords, great farmers and other substantial men of business.

The select vestry faced great difficulty in keeping parish expenditure within limits. They sat at the workhouse every two weeks to consider the claims of the old, the sick, the lame, the injured, the unemployed, deserted wives, widows with children, women in childbirth, and those who did not want to work. They had to assess the needs of the poor for shoes, shirts and breeches, and assistance in the burial of their dead.

Abraham Anderson was given calico for two shirts for himself and a shift for his wife, also a pair of shoes and stockings for himself. Thomas Boreham's wife was given 5s and a pair of shoes because her husband had deserted her and their two children; an order was issued for his apprehension. Thomas Lee, taken into the workhouse with bad legs, was sent to the London Hospital. George Robertson with a broken leg, was given 5s. William Peck's wife and four children, left unsupported when her husband was imprisoned in Aylesbury gaol, were allowed 5s a week during his absence. It was ordered that Henry Guest's wife was to have 5s a week during her lying-in, Joshua Staker's wife 3s a week for four weeks for the same purpose. James Hocket's wife got 5s a week and during the sickness which followed the birth of a child, the 5s was continued for a further four weeks. Thereafter she was paid 2s 6d weekly over several months. Thomas Spencer's pregnant wife also got 5s a week for a month. Louisa Ricketts twenty-four year of age, who suffered from fits, was put on the parish pension list at 3s a week. James Camp was given two shirts, a jacket and a pair of breeches at a cost of 15s. John Head's wife, whose husband had deserted her and their three small children, was given 6s to keep her for two weeks. John Ward with a broken rib was given 15s, George Robinson with a broken leg 10s. Sophia Scott and Elizabeth Jauncy had £1 to clothe them on going into service. Abraham Cox received 10s for two weeks' relief, also 10s for a water tub.

An order was issued in August 1819 that all persons who wished to apply for casual relief must appear before ten o'clock in the morning. Many were turned away but returned time and again to face refusal. Others voiced their resentment like James Jarman's wife who, when refused, 'rudely thanked the committee'. In an endeavour to deter those considered capable of work the select vestry rented a field called Osbornes (or Birdsfield) behind the workhouse in September 1819. There they proposed to employ all able-bodied men who applied for casual relief. The land was used to grow potatoes. The crop was sold in 1827 to Mr Henry Young for £25. The wages paid were minimal, ranging from a shilling a day up to 1s 8d. On 20 December 1820, for instance, £12 11s 6d was handed out in casual relief to forty-one applicants and eleven were refused assistance. Ten men were given work in Osbornes field; to many this was a repeated and unwelcome response to their applications for money. John Brace and his wife were refused relief on 20 December 1820, refused again on 3 January. On 17 January he was given six days work at a shilling a day, another six days work on 31 January and again on 14 February and on 28 February. He had three days work on 14 March, six days again on 28 March at 1s 8d a day but, on 11 April, being ordered to do three days work for his 5s, he refused. Soon afterwards he found work with Daniel Poyser, an Enfield farmer. Suspected with two others of stealing from his master he was sacked, but he begged to be taken back and swore that he would never again take anything, for he had suffered enough from being transported before. But soon afterwards (February 1822), he was stopped by John Wilson the patrolman at midnight, a mile and a half from his employer's place. He had a bag on his shoulder containing a bushel of wheat worth 4s. Brace begged the patrolman; 'For God's sake don't take me before a magistrate', offering him his coat and all the money he had. He was transported for a second term of seven years.

John Bye also resented being made to work for his meagre relief. His resentment at last boiled over and on 5 December 1821, when he was given an order for six days work, he threw it down on the workhouse floor and walked out. Sam Rainberd was another who was regularly forced to work for his relief until at Christmas 1822, wishing to celebrate in style, he and a couple of his mates broke into Brailsford's brewery; they were caught and he was transported for seven years. Thereafter his wife called for the relief money but within a short time she came to be known, in the parish register wherein were recorded the baptisms of her children, as Sarah Hankin (alias Rainberd). Joseph Whitebread was another reduced to enforced labour in Osbornes field, until he was sent to prison and his wife was able to get the relief without the labour.

Bread was dispensed either in lieu of or in addition to money, from January until the end of March 1823. On 15 January 242 loaves were distributed, and 218 on 29 January; thereafter the numbers diminished.[93] An order was made in 1834 to Mr Young the surveyor to employ the poor to dig gravel in the parish pits on piecework, 'so that no person shall earn more than 10s.[94]

The report of the select vestry, submitted on 1 June 1820, shows that regular pensions paid to the poor had amounted to £3000; £547 had been distributed in casual relief and the workhouse had cost £1052. The salary paid to the beadle was £40 and his expenses had amounted to £66. The master of the workhouse was paid £40 a year and had been given a £10 gratuity. The salary of the apothecary was £80 and that of the vestry clerk £105. Presenting its accounts again in 1825 the select vestry lamented the increased charge of the casual poor, 'being double the sum for the same period last year . . .' This had arisen solely from 'the extent of disease among the labouring poor.'[95]

The attitude of vestrymen and parish officers to those who begged assistance from the rates had become increasingly hostile. Sympathy was no longer aroused by suffering. William Abrahams with his wife Sarah arrived at his mother's home in Cheshunt around the middle of April 1822, both very ill. The parish of Enfield was responsible for their welfare but it was some time before any help was sought. At last the mother, driven to desperation by the long continuing sickness of the young couple, made her way to the Enfield workhouse to seek help. It was not the day on which casual relief was handed out, but she was sent to an overseer who told her that he had no power to give her money and that she must attend the select vestry which would sit on this same day the following week. Accordingly, seven days later, she again trudged all the way to Enfield and was given three shillings with which to provide food, warmth, medicines and medical attention. Seeing no improvement in the health of her son and his wife she again made the journey to Enfield the following week where the overseer, Mr Joyning, dispensed a further three shillings. Throughout all this time the condition of the household deteriorated until in desperation she sought the help of Dr Saunders a local physician. He questioned her as to what relief she had had and advised that she should not go to Enfield again but should seek relief for herself from the overseers at Cheshunt. This would be the means of getting her son and his wife removed to Enfield. The condition of the poor young couple however had gravely worsened by the time the removal order was issued. Dr Saunders, concerned for their condition (and aware that the parish of Enfield would have to pay his account), attended them assiduously over a number of weeks. The resulting bill so shocked and distressed the Enfield select vestry that they refused to pay.

The poor couple were visited at this time by the Reverend W. A. Armstrong, justice of the peace and lecturer at Enfield church. He was most shocked at the awful state in which he found this family and most scathing concerning the conduct of the select vestry. He suspended the removal order and fully justified Dr Saunders's claim. 'Such was the wretched condition of disease and poverty in which I found these poor creatures that I am less surprised at the magnitude of the account than I should have been had it been less. The poor parents were absolutely obliged to tear up their last sheets. I heartily lament the cruelty shown to these people by the parish of Enfield.' He went on to express a hope that Enfield would avoid litigation over the matter and would 'for the future show a kindlier charity to the poor and less disposition to throw the burden on neighbours.' The select vestry remained unmoved and continued in its refusal to pay the physician's bill for so long that at length a warrant was issued to distrain goods belonging to the overseer Joyning in order to recover the money. A mahogany table was seized from his house, a chimney glass, a carpet, six chairs, a mahogany sideboard, a druggett, a pier glass, and a set of fire irons, all of which were required to meet the physician's bill.[96]

A greater concern for suffering was however expressed by the Enfield select vestry in November 1824 when it passed a strongly worded resolution concerning William Smith and his wife, a poor couple who had arrived in Edmonton on their way home to Huntingdonshire. The man was desperately ill and the Edmonton beadle, with the constable, foreseeing the possibility of the expense and trouble of a pauper funeral, refused to allow them to rest in Edmonton. Despite the entreaties of the family they carried them north across the boundary. The man died the following day in the Enfield workhouse. The indignation of the Enfield vestrymen on this occasion, the cruelty being perpetrated by another parish and at Enfield's expense, knew no bounds.[97]

Even the parishioner who sought only medical help from the parish doctor could find himself summarily removed as a pauper, if he had no right of settlement. This is what happened to a man named White who applied to Mr Asbury in 1825 asking him to come to see his wife who lay ill. Mr Asbury, a kindly soul, pointed out to him that this would render him chargeable to the parish, reason enough for the select vestry to remove him and his family. White suggested hopefully that Mrs Paris (of Beech Hill Park) would be willing to pay rather than see this happen. Mr Asbury duly attended; Mrs Paris however refused to pay and the doctor's visits had to be continued at parish expense. The family was eventually removed and Asbury received no payment for that first visit; he was told by Enfield vestry to apply to White's parish for recompense.

The extent to which overseers would, on occasions, bully, browbeat and even break the law to prevent bastards being born in the parish, is demonstrated in the story of Sarah Godfrey. This somewhat gullible young person was removed from Hoddesdon to Enfield while pregnant with a bastard child; that was in the year 1825. She was brought to bed in the Enfield workhouse where the baby died. She then went into service at Ware and remained there about ten months before obtaining a situation in London. Her new misfortunes began when she was courted by a man who told her that his name was John Davis. She married him at Holborn on 27 August 1827 and three days after the wedding she received a visit from a woman who claimed that she was Davis's wife but that his real name was Boulton. At this Boulton (alias Davis) absconded and poor Sarah returned to her mother and father at Hoddesdon; unfortunately she had already become pregnant. She lived quietly at home maintaining herself by going out to do needlework at which she earned three shillings a week and her board. She also did further needlework at home. Late in February, however, her condition became apparent to the eagle eye of Gocher, the overseer. On Monday 25 February he came, with Crosby the churchwarden, to shatter the fragile peace of this little household. 'You are the lady we want to see,' said Gocher. Fearfully she asked him why. 'Because you are pregnant and I must remove you.' In vain she pleaded that she was lawfully married but the overseer refused to listen. 'I know', he said 'it is a bad job for you but you must go and I will give you a week . . . to get ready'. Crosby, the churchwarden, seeing the mother and daughter much agitated and crying at being parted at such a time, when the mother's help was so particularly needed, said, 'Don't frighten yourselves, we did not come here to frighten you.' They then went away but within half an hour Gocher was back by himself to say that Sarah must be off the following morning for another young woman had been brought to bed. She begged for time, pleading that it was impossible for her to be ready so soon but he replied that if she was not ready to go she must be removed by force.

Then, forseeing that the parish of Enfield might contest his too precipitate action, he offered the young woman a shilling relief. This she refused a number of times until her mother, trying to indicate to her that she should again refuse, touched her foot. The young woman misinterpreted the sign and took the shilling. Gocher was triumphant; now he pronounced she must go and the very next morning. That same evening she was sent for to Gocher's house to see the Reverend Mr Pickthall, the magistrate, who examined her as to her settlement. Although she told him repeatedly that she was married, he refused to listen and ordered her to sign the examination in the name of Sarah Godfrey. Again she protested that she was Mrs Sarah Davis but the magistrate insisted and at last she signed.

The following morning Gocher took her to Enfield, calling in on the way on the Reverend Mr Cullick, another magistrate, to secure a second signature on the removal order. The document was sent in to Cullick by his servant and returned by the same hand, so that this second magistrate did not even see the young woman. This order was therefore rendered void and the Enfield overseer, quick to perceive this, sent her back to Hoddesdon on the following Friday. Inevitably Gocher was round that same day; Sarah was from home but he laid wait for her that evening and greeted her with, 'So you have come back, have you, then,' said he, 'you must go back tomorrow.' Tearfully she replied that she would not, where-upon he said 'If you do not and I see you in the town tomorrow I will take you to Hertford' (meaning that he would imprison her in Hertford gaol). The following day she went to the Reverend Mr Pickthall, begging to be allowed to stay in Hoddesdon. He told her he had no power to give her permission, as he was not a parish officer, but that she might remain a day or two and he would see Gocher about it. But on the Monday following, the parish beadle knocked upon the door and demanded that she should accompany him. In vain she offered to go by herself but he replied 'You must go with me to Cheshunt Churchgate' (the place where the magistrates met). Dreading the public disgrace she begged that she should not be forced to walk through the town with the beadle but he would not leave her. At length a horse and cart were procured and in it the poor young woman was carried to Cheshunt church to appear before the magistrates who issued a new removal order by which she was conveyed to the Enfield workhouse.[98]

The Davidsons remained in charge of the workhouse until September 1821. The parish then placed an advertisement in the *Morning Advertiser* for a man and his wife (with no children) to superintend the poor at the parish house in Enfield. One interesting but unsuccessful application was that received from Robert Scotcher, foreman rope-maker at Samuel Jackson's manufactory at West Green in Tottenham who had also been master of the workhouse at St Georges in the East for the past twenty years. His proposal was to employ the Enfield poor in the rope, twine and doormat business, presumably bringing the materials down from Tottenham so that the work could be done in the house.

Mr Tisley and his wife were appointed but they lasted only a few months. Their places were taken by the Morgans in January 1822. Many of the workhouse buildings were in a state of dilapidation, particularly the 'miserable old building used for the men'. Rebuilding had been postponed for some years owing to the depressed state of agriculture but things had now so far improved that the select vestry asked the parish to sanction the expenditure of a sixpenny rate and work was begun.[99] An inspection in October revealed that the lead on hips and ridges of the new building was deficient in weight and the carpenters' work was not up to specification. The clerk of works was dismissed and the builder was ordered to replace the materials. The following May (1826) tenders were invited for the completion of a new south wing and the old buildings at the workhouse were sold by auction. Twenty-five new iron bedsteads were purchased. The report of the select vestry in November 1827 declared that the new building was finished and the select vestry felt able to congratulate itself 'on the completion of the new workhouse which, for cleanliness and convenience, does credit to the parish.'

The days of the parish poor law were numbered. In 1834 came a Parliamentary investigation. Questionnaires were distributed, not so much to find out what the parishes were doing as to prove the need for a change. The age-old problem of profitably employing the paupers in the workhouse had never been resolved. When asked whether all or any of the paupers were employed the vicar could only relate what the parish ought to have done. 'Greater pains ought to have been taken for the finding of employment for the poor . . . Various kinds of task-work, and especially the picking of feathers by the aged and infirm, and the knitting of stockings might be tried. The robust might be employed in grinding corn, in picking oakum and in beating hemp. They might easily be taught to make coarse mats.' But in reality they had never been employed to any financial advantage.

Many of the children from the workhouse were now working at the silk mills at Sewardstone where the parish still paid 1s 6d a head towards their maintenance. A few worked at a manufactory, presumably the crape works in South Street, and some on mat or rope making.

No regular relief, said the vicar Daniel Cresswell, was given to able-bodied labourers outside the house. Many had been put to work on the roads but they could not all be employed there and the parish had rented ground on which they had been paid to dig. This had cost the parish money but it was felt that it was better than giving out unconditional relief. Most of the distress in the parish existed among the agricultural labourers whose average earnings for day work was 2s, though they might earn more on piecework. There were many small houses and cottages in the parish.

The price charged for wheaten bread was so high in comparison with the price of wheat and flour (and with what the labourers earned) that a resolution critical of the bakers was passed in vestry and pasted up throughout the parish in January 1835. It effected an immediate reduction in the price. The vestry was languishing; it had been found impossible to secure the regular attendance of a sufficient number of respectable and independent men, either at the vestry or at the select vestry. Business there, said Dr Cresswell, had been managed by a small number of persons, often men of strong prejudices who felt excessive animosity against those of the poor who applied for relief. A ladies committee however had recently been set up to visit the poor in their houses.[100]

The year 1834 saw the culmination of Peter Hardy's last battle for the honest and economical administration of his parish. This time he campaigned alone to break up what he described as 'a nest of the greatest scoundrels that were ever congregated together, drunken decayed gentlemen, German Jews, Polish counts, swindlers and blacklegs and', he went on more dramatically than ever, 'if I am rightly informed, returned transports'. All these had settled and were comfortably established in the Enfield workhouse. They were the friends and guests of the master Thomas Barker. For years they had fed at parish expense. 'Fed', cried the irascible old justice, 'I ought to have said feasted, for while they were eating roast duck many of the people who paid them went to bed supperless'.

When Barker was finally forced to leave many of the workhouse furnishings went with him. The new master reported the following missing; three feather beds, a mattress and a pair of blankets, the window rods, the hearth rug and fire irons from the committee room, plates, basins, pails, a hand broom, a scrubbing brush, the old committee room table, several parish poes, an easy chair with a pan which had been used in the lying-in-room, and also the large prayer book'. Several ancient female paupers laid hands upon the Bible and swore that the former mistress had taken their belongings. A search warrant was issued and Jonathan Docker with

Sanders the constable entered Thomas Barker's house and seized many items of parish property.

Thomas Barker (probably one of the decayed gentlemen referred to by Mr Hardy) protested his innocence in words as magniloquent as ever were used by Mr Micawber himself. 'I have neither error to gloss over nor crime to vindicate. I am the offended not the offender, the target to which the shafts of malice, envy and cowardice direct their mark. I have reason to dread the effects of their malicious purpose unless (he was writing to the select vestry) I possess myself of the ear of an impartial portion of your respectable board . . . The individual to whom the worthy magistrate (Peter Hardy) gave credence, and upon whose oath granted a warrant to ransack my dwelling, was once a respectable, respected friend. Pity for his degraded state induced us (even in humbler station than now we revolve in) to succour him. At the workhouse he was ever received kindly – yet, to two or three such friends we are indebted for the onus under which we now labour . . . Suffice it to say to this drunken assassin, his counterpart the deputy-master of the workhouse, my successor, and the ungrateful girl at the Holly Bush (no reflection upon her father) I am indebted for the chance of ruin and disgrace. But No! It cannot be! You would not allow me to be crushed by sanctioning such base conduct. No!'

Mr Barker then proceeded most ingeniously to explain away every item of parish property found upon his premises. After some three pages he concluded, 'But I am trespassing upon your patience and will only make one request, namely that if not sanctioned by your respectable vestry you will stop the further propogation of calumny by the drunken cowardly fellow (misnamed master of the workhouse) who publicly states in the tap room of the public that he has not done with us yet. The exultation of the disreputable female paupers touches me not,' he added with some dignity, 'still it is very galling to hear a little bad girl exult and exclaim in the open road that she has at last "done the old girl" – meaning my wife . . . Conscious of integrity I invite the gentleman to any investigation. My avocation will not allow me to attend you on Wednesday but I shall be ready at all times to obey your commands.[101] No criminal proceedings appear to have been undertaken against Thomas Barker and no doubt he continued to 'revolve' a little longer in some suitably elevated station.

Mr Peter Hardy, for many years a presiding magistrate, died in 1835. He had striven long and hard for the good of his parish as he saw it. He honestly shared the prejudices and patriotic aspirations of his class. He had, he said, 'carried arms in defence of my King, and have drawn my sword in defence of the laws'. He had considered it an honour to have received at the head of the Enfield Volunteer Corps on Enfield marshes the thanks of the magistrates of the county. 'So great was the respect entertained for this gentleman', wrote John Tuff in 1850, 'that it was seriously contemplated raising a public monument to his memory'. 'His untiring efforts to secure the honest administration of the parish, to enforce fair dealing upon the Enfield tradesmen, to oblige the trustees of parish charities to adhere to the objects of pious benefactors long dead, and generally to maintain the rights and privileges of the parish of Enfield, has rendered his name', said Tuff 'as familiar in the mouths of the older inhabitants . . . as a household word'. He was buried at Tottenham.[102]

Notes for Chapter Ten

 1 GLRO DRO4. 5. 30
 2 GLRO DRO4. 5. 32
 3 GLRO DRO4. 7. 43. 8
 4 F. M. Eden *The State of the Poor* V2 p 418
 5 GLRO DRO4. 9. 50
 6 Vestry order book 5 Mr 1798, 30 Ap 1798
 7 Vestry order book 7 F 1799, 9D1799
 8 *Gentlemans Magazine*
 9 GLRO DRO4. 7. 43
10 GLRO DRO4. 22
11 OBSP 1797/8 16 p 28
12 OBSP 1797/8 428 p 449
13 OBSP 1799/1800 440 p 392
14 OBSP 1799/1800 665 p 553, vestry order book 7 Au 1801
15 Vestry order book 21 J1 1803
16 David Pam ed. *Castle of Antiquaries* 1980
17 Vestry order book 1N1804
18 GLRO DRO4. 32. 10, 12, 13, 14, Vestry order book 4 Mr 1813
19 Vestry order book
20 Vestry order book 6 Ja 1803
21 Vestry order book 15 N 1802
22 Vestry order book Ja 1803
23 GLRO DRO4. 7. 43
24 GLRO DRO4. 6. 35, DRO4. 7. 43. 64
25 Vestry order book 20 Ja 1806, GLRO DRO4. 7. 43
26 GLRO DRO4. 8. 44 50–51, Vestry order book 5 D 1806
27 Vestry order book 22 My 1806, GLRO DRO4. 7. 43. 54a, DRO4. 14. 70
28 GLRO DRO4. 7. 43. 64
29 Vestry order book
30 Peter Hardy *Hints for the Benefit of the Inhabitants of Enfield* 1809
31 GLRO DRO4. 8. 44. 9, 11, 12, 13, 14, 34 etc
32 Vestry order book 14 Mr 1814
33 David Pam *The Story of Enfield Chase* EPS 1984
34 HCJ
35 Enfield D1155
36 Enfield. Inclosure Act, award and map, vestry order book Je 1804
37 GLRO DRO4. 49. 57, 12
38 PP 1818 v 19
39 Vestry order book S1813
40 Peter Hardy *The Ale-conner* 1814, GLRO DRO4. 9. 49. 26, DRO4. 9. 50. 24, 25
41 OBSP 1807. 73
42 Vestry order book 26 D1730, 26 D1734, 3 J1 1738
43 GLRO DRO4. 2. 10
44 GLRO DRO4. 2. 13
45 Vestry order book Mr 1807, Je 1813, Mr 1814
46 Enfield D 1107
47 OBSP 1818. 1235
48 OBSP 1820. 90
49 OBSP 1823 1365
50 OBSP 1824 1380
51 Vestry order book 6N1828, 4D1828, 5 F1829, 9 Ap 1829, 29 J1 1829, OBSP 1829/30. 1939
52 OBSP 1822. 222

53 OBSP 1821. 309
54 OBSP 1824. 708
55 OBSP 1830. 503
56 David Pam ed. *Castle of Antiquaries* 1980, OBSP 1833. 333
57 OBSP 1830/31 773
58 OBSP 1834. 1123
59 OBSP 1833. 1118, 1825/6. 1590
60 Census reports 1801, 1811, 1821, 1831
61 GLRO DRO4. 9. 49. 30, 60, 39. 40
62 GLRO DRO4 Box 14. 70
63 OBSP 1809. 194
64 OBSP 1820. 19
65 GLRO DRO4. 9. 51
66 Vestry order book 7 Mr 1816
67 OBSP 1827. 647
68 OBSP 1825. 413
69 OBSP 1825. 1199
70 OBSP. 1830. 503
71 OBSP. 1827. 36
72 OBSP 1821/2. 187
73 GLRO DRO4. 9. 50. 16a
74 OBSP 1824. 479
75 OBSP 1827/8. 728
76 OBSP 1832. 7
77 OBSP 1833. 1118, 1119
78 OBSP 1822. 1189
79 OBSP 1825. 1194
80 OBSP 1821. 530
81 OBSP 1824. 712
82 OBSP 1826/7. 203
83 OBSP 1830/31. 463
84 GLRO DRO4. 25. 6, OBSP 1825/6. 1275
85 OBSP 1831/2. 163, 501, 484
86 GLRO DRO4. 25. 6
87 OBSP 1828. 1115
88 OBSP 1830/31. 29
89 E. J. Hobsbawm and Geo. Rude *Captain Swing*, Charles Lamb *Letters*, HO41. 9. 138
90 PP 1818 V.19
91 GLRO DRO4. 9. 50. 16a, 18a, 18b *Enfield Gazette* 18D1931
92 GLRO DRO4. 9. 50. 70, Vestry order book
93 GLRO DRO4. 22, Vestry order book S 1819, OBSP 1822 p. 224
94 GLRO DRO4. 14. 70
95 Vestry order book Je 1820
96 GLRO DRO4 Box 17
97 GLRO DRO4. 12. 62. 84
98 GLRO DRO4 Box 17
99 GLRO DRO4. 12. 62. 20, 128
100 GLRO DRO4. 12. 64, PP 1834 V36, Vestry order book
101 GLRO DRO4. 14. 70
102 John Tuff. *History of Enfield*

Subscribers' List.

London Borough of Enfield.
The Worshipful The Mayor of Enfield,
   Cllr. Duncan Lewis.
McAndrew, Brian, Chief Executive LBE.

Bowes Primary School.
Brimsdown Junior School.
Capel Manor Primary School.
Carterhatch Junior School.
De Bohun Junior School.
Eastfield Primary School.
Edmonton School.
Enfield Grammar School.
Galliard Primary School.
Hazelbury Junior School.
The Latymer School.
Lavender Primary School.
Merryhills Primary School.
Oakthorpe Junior School.
St. Andrew's C.E. School, Enfield.
St. Ignatius College.
St. John's C.E. Primary School
St. Michael's C.E. Primary School.
St. Paul's School.
Suffolks Primary School.
Worcesters Primary School.

Adam, David M., Esq.
Addington, Mr. & Mrs, E.W.
Amos, Denis W.
Andrews, Mrs. E.
Andrews, Geoffrey L.
Andrews, Mrs. Vera.
Angus, Mr. W.R.
Arbuthnot Lane, Carinthia.
Archer, E.M.
Artiss, Mr. E.F. & Mrs. I.J.

Ashton, Mr. Ernest E.
Ashton, Mr. W.W.
Authers, Mr. Ellis W.
Bagley, Mrs. K.A.
Baker, Mrs. June Mavis.
Baldock, Philip J.
Ball, Anne Elizabeth.
Ball, H.F.A.
Barker, Mr. J.D.
Barnard, Mr. C.R.J.
Barnard, Richard A.C.
Barnes, Mr. & Mrs. L.T.
Barton, Timothy H.
Bayford, Mr. Frank.
Bayliss, Rev. Maurice.
Beadle, Mr. S.M.
Beagles, Mrs. Mary C.
Beale, Edwin Terry.
Beale, T.Edward, C.B.E.
Bennett, B.
Bennett, Herbert F.
Bennett, Mr. T.R.
Berkeley, Mrs. Sonja.
Berry, Irene M.
Berry, Miss Margaret.
Bevan, S.H. & G.B.
Biggs, Mr. A.J.A.
Bignell, Victor & Janet.
Blake, Helen.
Blaskett, S.R.J.
Boardman, Mr. F.T.
Bolden, Keith F.
Bone, Mrs. J.M.
Booker, S.
Bostock, Mr. J.D.
Bouchard, D.
Bouffler, Mr. D.V.

Bougnague, Mr. Peter.
Boulton, Gordon.
Bourne, Mr. E.C.W.
Boxer, Mr. C.R.
Boyes, Mr. & Mrs. B.
Brewer, R.J.
Briggs, Mr. P.L.
Brown, T.E.
Browning, Miss Sheila.
Bruce, Ms. Janice.
Buckle, Allan T.
Bull, G.A. & L.M.
Bull, J.H. & D.
Bull, L.H. & D.M.
Bullock, Alan.
Burgess, D.V.
Burke, Mrs Doreen M.
Burnby, Dr. J.
Burrell, Mr. & Mrs. R.S.
Burton, Merle & George.
Butler, Mr. Frank.
Butler. Miss I.G.
Byron, Pat.
Campbell, James.
Capp Alan.
Carnaby, Miss L.G.
Carr, Mr. Ronald F.
Carroll, Wynne
Carter, B.F.
Carter, Henry & Valerie.
Carter, Mr. T.
Chaplin, Edgar.
Chapman, Mr. E.G.
Chapman, Eric S.
Chapman, Norma.
Charge, Stephen, B.A.
Chase, Roland F.
Cherry, Mr & Mrs. J.
Christen, Mrs. Leta Christina.
Churchill, Mrs. Ruth.
Clark, Miss B.D.
Clark, Miss D.
Clarke, Geoffrey T.
Clarke, L.C.
Clarke, Mr. R.P.
Clifton, D.J.
Clifton, James.
Close, David M.
Coleman, Mr. & Mrs. K.L.
Collie, Mrs. Rita.

Combe, Andrew & Christine.
Connolly, Mr. & Mrs. A.
Conrich, Gilda.
Cook, Miss E. Barbara.
Cooper, Mr. F.J.
Cooper, Marion & David.
Cooper-Bland, Mrs. Alma.
Coote, Major Alan Dudley.
Coote, Stephen.
Coote, William Raymond.
Corbett, Robin B.
Cordell, Mr. J.R.
Cornock, Maureen.
Cotton, Shirley and Albert.
Cox, Helen May.
Critchlow, Mr. F.P.M.
Crofts, J.W.
Cross, Mrs. V.E.B., I.S.O.
Crouch, Mr. & Mrs. John R.
Crutchley, G. & J. & M.
Dane, Peter D.L.
Daniels, H.W.
Darling, M.
Davies, J.E.
Dawe, Richard.
Day. Erik.
Deacon, M. John.
de Warrenne, Anna.
Deamer, Mr. J.R.
Deer, Mr. L.E.
Deering, P.H., J.P.
Delvin, Stuart.
Dixon, Mr. David A.
Dixon, John George.
Dormer, R.J.
Dorrington, Albert & Beryl.
Douglas, John.
Doust, Mr. P.
Draper, Mrs. G.M.
Draper, R.P. & K.J.
Drinkwater, Mr. John.
Dugdale Sykes, R.H.
Dumayne, Alan.
Duvergier, Ted.
Eccleston, Matthew.
Eddington, Roger.
Edwards, Mr. & Mrs. D.W.
Edwards, John E.
Egan, Jean M.
Eldon, Simon.

Elkin, Mr. Roger.
Elliott, Mr. G.K.
Ellis, Mrs. J.M.
Elmes, Miss S.D.
Eustance, Margaret.
Evans, H.H.
Fairhurst, David.
Farquharson, Carole.
Farthing, Mr. & Mrs. M.G.
Featherstone, Laurence.
Fenn, Mr. S.R.
Ferguson, Mr. R.J.
Finch, Leonard W.
Finkel, Mrs. J.
Fish, Mrs. Eileen.
Fisher, Mr. Brian.
Fisher, David and Paula.
Fishpool C.E.
Fleming, Mrs Hazel.
Flether, Mrs. Alice L.
Fletcher, Mr. & Mrs. K.E.
Fletcher, L.J.
Flitter, Joyce.
Flitter, Miss J.R.
Foret, Raymond M.
Foster, Miss E.L.
Fowler, Mr. Stanley.
Freakes, Mr. Harold L.
Frear, Brian.
Freer, Mrs. P.
French, Mr. Sidney W.
Fretten, Les.
Frost, Mr. Lionel John.
Fry, Mr. S.R.
Gale, Paul.
Ganderton, Mr. Colin.
Ganderton, Mrs. Margaret C.
Garey, Mrs. E.W.
Garrett, Mrs. Olive.
Gay, Mr. Ken.
George, Leslie J.
Gibbs, Mr. J.G.
Gibbs, Mr. & Mrs. R.A.
Gilburt, Stephen.
Gillam, Geoffrey.
Gillan, Marjorie.
Gitter, Mr. Alfred.
Goulding, Mr. T.G.
Gowers, Mr. R.
Grant, Mr. Russell.

Gravell, Mr. & Mrs. T.J.
Green, Mrs. B.K.
Greenhill, Mr. & Mrs. J.E.
Greening, Alan.
Gregory, Mrs. V.M.
Groen, Mr. & Mrs. D.F.
Groom, Mrs. Audrey E.
Guest, B.L.
Haffenden, Mr. G.R.
Haigh, Douglas R.S.
Hall, Mr. C.E.
Halstead, Miss Margaret B.
Hamer, Miss Doris.
Hamilton, Mr. W.Y.M.
Hammond, Mr. David H.
Hampton, Janet.
Handley, Dr. Graham.
Hardwick, Mrs. A.M.
Harris, Harold.
Harris, Susan.
Hart, Mr. D.J.
Hart, Mrs. Joan.
Hartridge, R.J., M.A., M.Sc. (Econ.).
Harvey, Laurence C.F.
Hatton, Robert V.
Hawkes, Mr. Bert.
Hawkins, Mr. & Mrs. G.
Hayes, Miss Joan.
Healey, John & Lilian.
Hersant, Mr. & Mrs. T.
Hicks, Elizabeth.
Hicks, Mr. & Mrs. R.A.
Hillsdon, D.J.
Hobbs, Mrs. M.J.
Hodge, Mr. P.R.
Holland, Mrs. B.A.
Hollings, David.
Holmested, Dr. S.A.
Holtam, Sydney.
Hope, Mrs. Sheila.
Hornby, Bryan F.
Hoult, Constance.
House, M.N.
Hoy, Mr. & Mrs. D.L.
Hudson, Norman.
Hughes, Mr. Kenneth J.
Hulley, J.R.
Hurry, Mr. Alex.
Hutchings, Mr. W.N.
Huxley-Robinson, Kenneth Esq.

Jachim, Mrs. J.M.
James, Barry T.
Jaques, Kay.
Jenkins, Mrs. P.A.
Jerwood, Arthur S.
Johnson, John C.
Johnstone, Miss Kirsty.
Jones, Mrs. Catherine.
Jones, Mr. E.E.
Jones, Mr. Ian K.
Jordan, Leslie J.
Kearney, John.
Keeble, L.
Kelly, Kay.
Keyte, Christopher & June.
Knight, Arthur.
Knowles, Dr. W.A.
Lambe, Mrs. C.A.
Lambert, Joyce & Prue.
Lambourn, E.H.
Lancaster, M.T.
Lancucki, Mrs. J.M.
Lancucki. T.S.J.
Lane, Mrs. Elsie.
Larrett, Mary.
Law, Mr. & Mrs. C.
Lawrence, Wm.
Leftwich, Mr. Darren, B.A.
Leighton, M.B.E.
Lewis, Ewan.
Lindsay, Cllr. John L.
Lipert, Mrs. J.
Lister, Miss Doreen.
Lister, Mr. P.
Little, Mrs. D.
Love, Philip.
Lowe, Bob.
Lowen, Mr. & Mrs. S.J.
Lowen, Miss S.M.
Luck, J.E.
Lunn, Colin A.
Luxton, Richard.
Macdonald, Mr. B.E. & Mrs. S.M.
Malone, Mr. C.N.
Manning, E.S.
Mantell, G.A. and A.C.
Marks, Miss L.
Martin, Bob.
Martin, Mr. R.W.
Mason, H.S.

Matthews, Derek C.
Matthews, June Rose.
Matthews, Mr. Paul R.
May, Mrs. Margaret I.
McDonald, Sheila.
McEleney, J.
McKean, Douglas and Anne.
McKenna, Caroline.
McLellan, Mr. Kevin.
Meekings, June.
Middleton, Mrs. B.C.
Miller, Mrs. V.G.
Molony, Mr. M.P.
Money, Patrick.
Mooney, David, B.A.
Moore, Mr. & Mrs. Fred.
Morris, M.A.
Mortimer, Anthony.
Mortimer, Owen.
Morton, B.D. & L.M.W.
Moulden, Jack L.
Mowbray, Mr. Warwick.
Muffett, Tim.
Mungall, P.W.
Mussett, Mrs. Frances.
Nafzger, Alan.
Needham, D.P.
Negus, Eileen.
Newens, Mr. A.S.
Newton, Mr. & Mrs. Brian.
Nicholls, Mr. & Mrs. J.
Niehorster, Mrs. Audrey Jean.
Noble, Harold & Sheila.
Oakden, Mrs. G.M.
Oliver, Barry.
Parker, M.A.
Pask, Brian J.
Pavey, David.
Payne, Debby.
Peach, John Christopher.
Peacock, Sylvia F.
Pearce, Kathleen M.
Pearl, Mr. & Mrs. C.J.
Pepper, Mrs. L.S.
Perry, Mrs. Frances, M.B.E. V.M.H.
Perryman, Cllr. Peter.
Pethers, P.E.
Pile, Mrs. Pat.
Pinkham, Miss M.J.
Pope, Dennis.

Potter, Daphne E.L.
Prentice, Mr. & Mrs. R.
Prescott, Mrs. M.L.
Price, Lawrence.
Price, Maryrose W. & John Rea.
Pritchard, Mr. & Mrs. Peter.
Prudames, Anne.
Ramsbotham, Leonard.
Raphael, Cdr. & Mrs. R.F.
Read, Mrs. Mary G.
Read, Mrs. Norah.
Reeve, Harry.
Reeve, Mr. & Mrs. J.E.
Rehahn, Anne.
Reid, A.G. & J.A.
Richards, Mr. & Mrs. James.
Richardson, Brian & Margot.
Richardson, David.
Richardson, Jamie.
Richardson, Mr. Stanley I.
Richardson, Dr. W.W.
Ricketts, Betty.
Ridgewell, Mr. W.L.C.
Rippingale, M.E.
Roberts, Mr. P.H.
Roberts, Dr. Philip G.
Robinson, Mr. A.L.
Robinson, Audrey.
Robinson, Miss J.O.
Robinson, Sid.
Rolfe, Eric.
Ross, Dr. Elaine C.
Rowley, Mrs. Joy.
Rubenstein, Dr. I.D.
Rudall, Rev. M.E.
Rugman, Miss E.H.
Rumsey, Marian.
Ruskin, Douglas.
Rye, Mr. Michael J.
Sargent, A.E.
Sargent, Irene.
Saunders, Mr. S.C.
Say, P.I.
Schartau, Mr. & Mrs. D.A.
Schutte, James W.
Seaborne, Mrs. F.D.
Seaman, John.
Sedgwick, Mrs. Dilys.
Seeley, Mrs. O.M.
Seeley, Mr. & Mrs. R.H.

Sellers, Mrs. M.S.
Sellick, Olive.
Sewell, Miss Carol Ann.
Sewell-Alger, Philip.
Shallcross, Mr. C.J.
Sharkey, Mrs. Joseph.
Sharman, Betty.
Sheppard, Mr. A.G.
Shotter, Mrs. D.
Simmons, Stan & Amy.
Simons, Sally & Christopher.
Singleton, Mrs. Jean S.
Skilton, Alan J.
Slatford, Mr. Kenneth.
Sluter, Mr. F.A.
Smart, Philip J.
Smee, Mr. & Mrs. F.H.
Smith, Alan K.
Smith, Mrs. B.M.
Smith, Mr. D.M.
Smith, Donald, C.Eng.
Smith, Mr. E.A.H.
Smith, Irene & Stanley.
Smith, Mr. M.R.P.
Smith, Mr. P.B.M.
Smith, Mr. Philip Francis.
Smith, Mr. & Mrs. R.L.
Somerville, Stephen.
Soutar, Mrs. B.
Southan, David.
Southan, Mrs I.E.
Spiegel, Mrs. M.M.
Spray, Zygmunt.
Stamp, Doreen.
Standbrook, Mr. S.W.
Stanford, D.W.
Stanford, Mr. E.F.C.
Stevens, Miss A.J.
Stevens, Mrs. D.M.
Summerfield, Arthur and Angela.
Sutton, William Arthur.
Symons, Ivan P.
Tait, W.J.
Talbot, Margaret.
Taplin, Mrs. J.B.
Taylor, Dr. Alan.
Taylor, Miss Barbara.
Taylor, Jenny & Michael.
Temerlies, Mrs. Esther.
Tether, Pam.

Thompson, Mr. & Mrs. E.G.A.
Thompson, Mr. P.A.
Tibbatts, Mr. Kenneth L.
Tillbrook, Mr. C.J.C.
Toms, Alan E.J.
Trayhorn, John.
Triggs, Miss S.E.
Trussell, Mr. D.G.
Turnbull, Peter.
Tuson, Jean & John.
Tyler, Elizabeth.
Tyrrell, Mr. T.G.
Upton, Iris.
Vacher, Robert & Alison.
Valentine, Graham.
Vaughan A.J.
Vick, Rex D.
Vickers, Mr. D.T.
Voisey, Mr. Roger J.
Wade, Mr. Dennis A.
Walby, Janet.
Ward, Trevor.
Warren, Audrey.
Warren, Mr. B.
Washbourne, John F.
Waters, Mr. T.H.
Watkins, Ronald W.
Watson, G.W.
Watson, Mrs. Vera.
Wayland, Mr. T.M.
Webb, Patrick A.
Welsh, Sylvia B.

West, Mr. E.G.C.
West, Mrs. M.C.B.
West, Peter D., B.A.(Hons),
    L.R.A.M., F.Coll.P.
Whatmore, Mr. Rhys D.
Whitaker, Mr. J.
White, Mr. David J.
White, Miss J.L.
Wibberley, Mrs. R.A.
Williams, Mr. C.D.
Williams, Edith A.
Williams, Dr. M.
Williamson, Dr. J.
Willmott, Rosemary.
W, A.E.
Wilson, Alan G.
Wincott, Mr. N.T.E.
Wittenbach, Mrs. Gertrude.
Wolton, Joan & John.
Wood, Gladys E.
Wood, Mr. S.H.
Woodfield, Mr. & Mrs. W.T.
Woodroffe, Mr. & Mrs. S.E.
Woods, Brian & Gillian.
Woods, H.G.
Woollett, Peter.
Woolveridge, H.T.
Worrall, Mr. Edward S.
Wright, Mr. & Mrs. John H.
Wright, L. & A.L.
Yarrow, John H.
Young, N.B.

Index to Volume One